Residential Real Estate Transactions

Fifth Edition

MSBA
MARYLAND STATE BAR ASSOCIATION

The Maryland State Bar Association, Inc.
520 West Fayette St.
Baltimore, Maryland 21201
(410) 685-7878

Cataloging-in-Publication Data

Title: Residential real estate transactions.
Description: Fifth edition. | Baltimore, Md. : MSBA, 2024.
Subjects: Vendors and purchasers—Maryland. | Residential Real Estate—Maryland.
Other name: Maryland State Bar Association.

LCC KFM1326 .R47 2024
ISBN: 978-1-960444-19-6

TABLE OF CONTENTS

VOLUME I

CHAPTER ONE

BEGINNING THE SALE OF RESIDENTIAL REAL ESTATE

CHAPTER TWO

CONTRACTS OF SALE—RESALE OF EXISTING RESIDENCES

CHAPTER THREE

RESIDENTIAL CONSTRUCTION CONTRACT

CHAPTER FOUR

TITLE INSURANCE IN THE RESIDENTIAL TRANSACTION

CHAPTER FIVE

THE LENDER'S ROLE

CHAPTER SIX

PRE-CLOSING PROBLEMS

CHAPTER SEVEN

SETTLEMENT OF TITLE OF RESIDENTIAL REAL ESTATE

VOLUME II

CHAPTER EIGHT

FEDERAL TAX ASPECTS OF THE ACQUISITION, OWNERSHIP, AND SALE OF A TAXPAYER'S PERSONAL RESIDENCE

PART 2: THE LAW FOR SALES OR EXCHANGES PRIOR TO MAY 7, 1997

CHAPTER ONE

BEGINNING THE SALE OF RESIDENTIAL REAL ESTATE*

W. Scott Tinney, Esq.
Cohen & Forman, LLC

* This Chapter is an excerpt of Chapter 12, Real Estate Transactions in Maryland, which originally appeared in the Practice Manual for the Maryland Lawyer, 6th Edition (MSBA 2023). The MSBA gratefully acknowledges past contributions to this chapter from the original and updating authors, Jeffrey H. Scherr and the late Herbert Burgunder III.

ABOUT THE AUTHOR

W. Scott Tinney

Scott Tinney is a 1999 graduate of the University of Baltimore School of Law. Scott has been with Cohen and Forman, LLC since graduating, handling a wide variety of legal issues with a heavy concentration on real estate related matters.

TABLE OF CONTENTS

I. INTRODUCTION

This chapter identifies and discusses the early issues in the purchase and sale of residential real property, and explores the relationship between the average homeowner or home buyer and licensed real estate brokers.

II. THE MARKETING PERIOD

A. Generally

Recent advances in technology are altering the process of buying and selling residential real estate. Through the use of GPS, smartphone applications can now identify properties for sale in specific neighborhoods. Information on websites easily shows recent sales and prices. You no longer need access to the Multiple Listing Service (MLS) to find comparable sales. The use of photographs and video now permit an interested buyer to "preview" homes more easily so that the process of finding a new home is shorter. Many buyers are narrowing their search for a new home without engaging a real estate agent. All of these changes present opportunities for the real estate lawyer to be more involved in residential real estate transactions.

In the traditional scenario, most sellers incur legal obligations by executing a listing agreement with a real estate broker. The terms of this listing agreement may be negotiable, especially during periods when the housing market is brisk and brokers are competing for listings and the opportunity to earn commissions or when the housing market is slow and brokers are willing to lower their commissions to gain a listing. Among other things, the listing agreement will specify the commission rate, the duration of the listing period, and whether the property may be listed only by a single broker or will be subject to "multiple listing." A careful practitioner will review a listing agreement to determine when a commission will be paid. Some broker agreements require a payment to be made upon the execution of a contract of sale while others make settlement on the property a precondition to payment.

Lawyers should make sure that their clients understand the type of commitment that the client is undertaking. For example, often sellers will sign a listing agreement that will cover a period of time, such as six months, with a commission being paid even if the broker is not the procuring cause. Clients should understand that the broker will receive a commission even if the seller finds the buyer. The other type of listing agreement is the "procuring cause" agreement. With a procuring cause listing agreement, the agent will only be paid if the agent brings the buyer. The procuring cause listing agreement is used less frequently because, in a residential transaction, it is much more difficult to identify the reason that a buyer comes to submit a contract. The procuring cause listing agreement is better suited to situations where the seller will do their own marketing.

In addition to preparing a listing agreement, an agent acting on behalf of either a buyer or a seller in a residential transaction must prepare a disclosure statement specifying their specific role in the transaction.[2]

The Real Estate Licensing Reform Act (the "Act"), passed by the Maryland General Assembly on April 10, 1998, became effective on Jan. 1, 1999.[3] The law altered the standard duties of a real estate agent in a brokerage relationship. The Act changed the presumption that an agent represents the seller to the presumption that an agent represents the buyer as long as the agent is not acting as the listing real estate broker.[4]

The Act also changed the point when brokerage agency begins and provided for a new written disclosure.[5] The Act also set out what must be included in a brokerage agreement.[6] The disclosure statement replaced the former statement that unless a licensee agrees to assist the buyer as the buyer's agent or as a dual agent, the licensee represents the seller. The disclosure section included language that stated:

> [A] licensee who assists a buyer . . . in locating residential real estate for purchase . . . and is neither affiliated with nor acting as the listing real estate broker for any real estate shown or located, is presumed to be acting as a buyer's agent on behalf of the prospective buyer . . . unless either the licensee or the prospective buyer . . . expressly declines to have the licensee act as a buyer's agent.[7]

On April 26, 2016, the Governor signed into law Senate Bill 1469, which made several revisions to the Act. The 2016 revisions repealed the Act's presumption created by § 17-533 that an agent represents the prospective buyer as long as the agent is not acting as the listing real estate broker. Under the 2016 revisions, for a real estate broker or salesperson to be a "buyer's agent," they must be representing a prospective buyer or lessee in accordance with a written brokerage agreement.[8] The

---

2 Md. Code Ann., Business Occupations & Professions § 17-530 (2018 & Supp. 2022) (hereinafter Bus. Occ. & Prof. § ___).

3 *See* Bus. Occ. & Prof. §§ 17-528–17-535; 1998 Md. Laws, Ch. 628 § 1.

4 *See* Bus. Occ. & Prof. § 17-533 (repealed by 2016 Md. Laws, Ch. 311 § 1 (Md. S.B. 1469)); *see also* Bus. Occ. & Prof. § 17-528(f).

5 Bus. Occ. & Prof. § 17-534.

6 Bus. Occ. & Prof. § 17-534(b).

7 Bus. Occ. & Prof. § 17-530(b)(5)(iii).

8 Bus. Occ. & Prof. § 17-528(f); *see also* Bus. Occ. & Prof. § 17-528(m) ("'Seller's agent' means a licensed real estate broker who, in accordance with a written brokerage agreement, acts as the listing broker for real estate, or a licensed associate real estate broker or licensed real estate salesperson who is affiliated with the listing broker.").

Act continues to require a written disclosure for licensees involved in a transaction as a seller's agent, buyer's agent, or cooperating agent.[9]

The 2016 revisions to the Act also changed the disclosure requiring it to explain:

(1) The differences between a seller's agent, buyer's agent, subagent, dual agent, and intra-company agent;

(2) The duties of a licensee to exercise reasonable care and diligence and maintain confidentiality;

(3) That regardless of whom a licensee represents in a real estate transaction, the licensee has a duty to treat each party fairly and honestly, promptly present each written offer and counteroffer, respond truthfully to each question, disclose all material facts that are known or should be known relating to a property, and offer each property without discrimination;

(4) That a licensee is qualified to advise only on real estate matters and that legal or tax advice should be obtained from a licensed attorney or accountant;

(5) The need for an agreement with a seller's agent, buyer's agent, or dual agent to be in writing and to include the duties and obligations of the agent, how and by whom the agent will be compensated, and any fee-sharing arrangements with other agents;

(6) The duty of a buyer's agent to assist in the:

  (i) Evaluation of a property, including the provision of a market analysis of the property; and

  (ii) Preparation of an offer on a property and to negotiate in the best interests of the buyer;

(7) The possibility that a dual agency may arise in a real estate transaction and the options that would become available to the buyer and seller or lessee and lessor; and

(8) That any complaints concerning a licensee may be filed with the Commission.[10]

The duties of a real estate broker to a client are set forth in the Act. The real estate broker must do the following:

  (i) act in accordance with the terms of the brokerage agreement;

  (ii) promote the interests of the client by:

---

9 Bus. Occ. & Prof. § 17-530(b)(1).

10 Bus. Occ. & Prof. § 17-530(f).

1. seeking a sale . . . at a price . . . acceptable to the client;
2. seeking a sale . . . on terms specified in the brokerage agreement or on terms acceptable to the client;
3. unless otherwise specified in the brokerage agreement, presenting in a timely manner all written offers or counteroffers . . . ;

(iii) disclose . . . all material facts as required . . . ;

(iv) treat all parties . . . honestly and fairly and answer all questions truthfully;

(v) in a timely manner account for all trust money received;

(vi) exercise reasonable care and diligence; and

(vii) comply with all

1. requirements of [the law];
2. applicable federal, State, and local fair housing laws and regulations; and
3. other applicable laws and regulations.[11]

The state Real Estate Commission developed a standardized disclosure form that agents must use in residential real estate transactions.[12]

In addition to the statutory requirements for real estate brokers, the Code of Maryland Regulations (COMAR) provides a Code of Ethics for brokers and real estate agents. COMAR 09.11.02.01–09.11.02.03. The Code of Ethics covers a licensee's relations to the public, to the client, and to other licensees.

While the actions of real estate professionals are not as closely monitored as those of other professionals such as lawyers or accountants, relatively recent changes bring more scrutiny to real estate agents. In 2004, the Maryland legislature changed the continuing education requirements for real estate professionals. A licensee must complete at least one three-hour ethics course, which includes Maryland Code of Ethics and a discussion of the practices of flipping and predatory lending, every two years.

The focus on ethics for real estate professionals does not alter the basic fiduciary duty of a Realtor to their client.[13] The Maryland legislature regulates the field of real

---

[11] Bus. Occ. & Prof. § 17-532(b)(1).

[12] See Form 12-1.

[13] *Silverman v. Kogok*, 239 Md. 71, 76, 210 A.2d 375, 378 (1965); *Sellner v. Moore*, 251 Md. 391, 398, 247 A.2d 523, 527 (1968) (a client who hires a broker bargains for the disinterested skill, diligence, and zeal of the agent for the client's exclusive benefit).

estate sales by statute and regulation.[14] As a regulated profession, much like physicians, attorneys, or certified public accountants, real estate brokers have a responsibility to the public to conduct themselves in a reputable manner.[15] The statutes and regulations set minimum guidelines for professional conduct, their purpose being to safeguard the public.[16] A real estate broker's license is subject to suspension or revocation if the broker "intentionally or negligently fails to disclose to any person with whom the applicant or licensee deals a material fact that the licensee knows or should know that relates to the property with which the licensee or applicant deals."[17] The statute governing real estate brokers protects the public in its dealings with real estate brokers, and places a duty of good faith and fair dealing on real estate brokers.[18]

Real estate agents and brokers should be careful to avoid liability for promising too much. A real estate agent's or broker's liability is founded on the law of agency, and, unless there are special circumstances, there is no duty for agents or brokers to investigate or to ascertain if any defects exist in the property.[19] While a real estate broker or agent has no duty to investigate the zoning of a property, if the real estate agent or broker affirmatively undertakes this task, they must use reasonable care and present accurate information.[20] In other words, if the real estate agent or broker undertakes a task, then the real estate agent or broker has a fiduciary duty to complete the task.

If the parties do not use a real estate broker during the marketing period, the lawyer representing the seller should discuss with the seller the need to exercise extreme caution in the representation and marketing of the real property, to avoid violations of the Consumer Protection Act.[21] Violations of the Consumer Protection Act can subject an individual to civil penalties.[22] Furthermore, violations under the Consumer Protection Act may subject an individual to criminal penalties.[23]

---

14 *Lewis v. Long & Foster Real Estate, Inc.*, 85 Md. App. 754, 760, 584 A.2d 1325 (1991).

15 *Id.*

16 *Id.*

17 *Gross v. Sussex Inc.*, 332 Md. 247, 274, 630 A.2d 1156, 1169–70 (1993).

18 *Id.* at 274, 630 A.2d at 1170.

19 *Dyer v. Criegler*, 142 Md. App. 109, 119, 788 A.2d 227, 233, *aff'd sub nom. Dyer v. Otis Warren Real Estate Co.*, 371 Md. 576, 810 A.2d 938 (2002) (a real estate agent is not an "owner" for purposes of the lead paint laws).

20 *Lewis v. Long & Foster Real Estate, Inc.*, 85 Md. App. 754, 763, 584 A.2d 1325, 1330 (1991).

21 Md. Code Ann., Commercial Law §§ 13-101–13-501 (2013 & Supp. 2022) (hereinafter Com. Law § ___).

22 *See* Com. Law § 13-408; *see also Hartford Accident & Indem. Co. v. Scarlett Harbor Assocs.*, 109 Md. App. 217, 674 A.2d 106 (1996), *aff'd on other grounds*, 346 Md. 122, 695 A.2d 153 (1997).

23 *Long v. Am. Legion, Potomac Post 202, Inc.*, 117 Md. App. 18, 28–29, 699 A.2d 456, 461 (1997) (finding that Maryland has expressly imposed both criminal and civil remedies in remedial

B. Advice to Give Client

During the marketing period, the attorney should provide their client with advice on the following:

- seller's right to negotiate a sale on their own behalf;
- seller's ability to exclude certain buyers from the effect of the listing agreement (for example, a buyer found by the seller before entering into the listing agreement);
- the effect of multiple listing;
- duration of multiple listing;
- disposition of earnest money in event of buyer's default;
- the effect of a default and the requirement to mediate disputes prior to filing a lawsuit;
- the effect of a buyer's failure to obtain financing and the buyer's obligation to get financing;
- disclosures required to be made by seller;
- broker's rights if seller is unable to deliver marketable title; and
- the point at which the brokerage fee is earned (the standard contract of sale does not require closing for a commission to be earned).

III. PROBLEMS ARISING FROM NEGOTIATION AND DRAFTING OF CONTRACT

A. Introduction

Because it is the subject of Chapter 2, only very brief mention will be made of perhaps the most important part of the initial stages of the buying and selling process: the negotiation and drafting of the contract. Often the attorney is not involved in the marketing period and is consulted only after a potential buyer has been found and an initial offer made. While the seller is trying to sell the house and doing their best to market the house, the actual "offer" in a contractual sense is made by the potential buyer. The broker (or brokers, as the case may be) usually steers the parties through the offer and counter-offer stage. The process typically begins with the buyer submitting a signed contract offer together with a deposit of "earnest money" to the broker. Earnest money in residential transactions is usually a relatively small amount ($1,000 to $2,000) with a promise to pay an additional sum to bring the total deposit up to 10 percent of the offered purchase price upon acceptance of the buyer's

---

legislation such as the Consumer Protection Act); *McGraw v. Loyola Ford, Inc.*, 124 Md. App. 560, 575–76, 723 A.2d 502, 509–10 (1999) (imposing both civil and criminal penalties).

offer by the seller. Customarily, the broker will hold all sums deposited until the sale is consummated, or until the offer is refused, or a contract contingency fails.

In the great majority of cases, the parties execute a binding legal contract of sale without having consulted a lawyer. If, however, the parties merely sign a letter of intent indicating their willingness to negotiate a contract of sale, the parties should be aware that the letter of intent is not enforceable.[24]

In some cases, if one or the other of the parties has sought legal advice prior to execution of the contract, then the attorney may be requested to draft the contract of sale. To assure that all essential terms are included in the contract of sale, the attorney should consider using a standardized, widely accepted form as the basis for drafting. An example of such a form is the Standard Contract of Sale published by the Maryland Association of Realtors or the Greater Baltimore Board of Realtors for use by its members.[25] Such a standard form must, however, be tailored to the particular transaction. Because the form contract is intended to be used in a wide array of transactions, much of the form can be eliminated when a custom contract is written. A rider or addendum to the form may be used for this purpose.

IV. THE PERIOD AFTER THE SIGNING OF THE SALES CONTRACT BUT BEFORE THE CLOSING

A. Generally

Frequently, the buyer's attorney is presented with an executed contract to review prior to closing. Some common situations that might require amendments include the following: conveyance of personal property as well as realty, a warranty for appliances, a move-out or move-in date. The parties can draft a simple addendum to make sure that the contract reflects their agreement and understanding. Counsel should be aware that the filing of bankruptcy by either the seller or the buyer could have an impact on the conduct of settlement. Also, during this period, buyer's counsel might recommend an environmental survey of the property, if that is a concern. Environmental concerns, including hazardous waste, underground storage tanks, lead paint, etc., and bankruptcy issues are not specifically addressed in this chapter.

---

24 *Paramount Brokers, Inc. v. Digital River, Inc.*, 126 F. Supp. 2d 939 (D. Md. 2000) (an agreement to negotiate a contract is unenforceable); *see also Phoenix Mut. Life Ins. Co. v. Shady Grove Plaza L.P.*, 734 F. Supp. 1181 (D. Md. 1990), *aff'd*, 937 F.2d 603 (4th Cir. 1991); *ABT Assoc., v. JHPIEGO Corp.*, 104 F. Supp. 2d 523 (D. Md. 2000), *aff'd*, 9 Fed. App'x 172 (4th Cir. 2001).

25 See Form 12-4.

B. Role of Buyer's Attorney

Buyer's attorney may play one of two roles. They may act as closing attorney in the transaction, or simply as the buyer's legal advisor for review of documents relevant to closing.

If acting as the closing attorney, they may be required to:

1. Provide title insurance if a lender is involved; in which event the attorney must be approved by the title insurance company;
2. Obtain for lender an insured closing letter; and
3. Be responsible for all functions of closing attorney, including:
   - Title Search and Examination
   - Title Binder or Opinion
   - Preparation of Closing Documents
   - Obtaining Survey
   - Preparation of Settlement Sheet
   - Recording of Papers
   - Disbursement of Funds
   - Obtaining Final Insurance Policy

It is usually required that all documents prepared by buyer's attorney be reviewed by the lender's attorney, for which a fee will be charged to buyer. Most buyers' attorneys will not serve as closing attorneys. Title is usually placed with a title insurance company for closing, and the buyer's attorney represents buyer prior to and at settlement.

A checklist for buyer's attorney includes:

1. Obtain title insurance binder and all supporting documents; review and explain to client;
2. Contact closing officer to arrange a mutually agreeable closing date;
3. Review closing documents (Deed, Deed of Trust, Note) and explain to client;
4. Review survey to look for encroachments;
5. Verify that termite inspection has been performed and obtain copy of report;
6. Obtain estimated settlement sheet and explain items to buyers;
7. Verify that buyer has obtained all insurance policies required under lender's commitment;
8. Arrange a final inspection as close to the settlement date as possible to ensure that the property is in the same condition that it was in on the date of contract; and

9. Be sensitive to issues of hazardous waste or other hazardous substances on the property (e.g., underground storage tanks). If necessary, an environmental survey should be performed.

C. Role of Seller's Attorney

The seller's attorney is normally not extensively involved in the preparation for settlement. A checklist for seller's attorney includes:

1. Obtain copy of title binder and seller's Deed and verify the description, parties, and spelling;
2. Examine any covenants or restrictions applicable to the property as well as ingress and egress, rights of way, or easements across the property;
3. Have seller request a "payoff" statement from seller's lender and review seller's records (review the title commitment to see if any satisfied mortgages or deeds of trust are still listed as encumbrances on the property);
4. Verify termite certification and determine if report satisfies contract;
5. Obtain estimated settlement sheet and verify figures;
6. Make sure seller gathers all water bills, tax bills, and ground rent bills before settlement; and
7. Arrange for a transfer of the utilities and telephone (usually a joint call to the provider is sufficient to arrange the transfer).

Real Property § 3-105.2 creates a process by which a settlement agent, an officer of a title company, or a lawyer may send notice to a lien holder, mortgage holder, or holder of a deed of trust that has failed to release a satisfied mortgage and release the mortgage by means of an affidavit that is recorded in the Land Records. The process of filing a Statutory Release Affidavit requires 60 days' notice.[26]

V. FORMS

These sample forms are illustrative of proper format and content. However, no form should be relied upon as a substitute for independent research, knowledge of the applicable laws, and consideration of the context in which the form is to be used.

Forms begin on next page.

---

26 *See* Real Prop. § 3-105.2(d)(1).

Form 1-1. Agency Relationship Disclosure

STATE OF MARYLAND REAL ESTATE COMMISSION

Understanding Whom Real Estate Agents Represent

THIS NOTICE IS NOT A CONTRACT

In this form "seller" includes "landlord"; "buyer" includes "tenant"; and "purchase" or "sale" includes "lease"

Agents Who Represent the Seller

Seller's Agent: A seller's agent works for the real estate company that lists and markets the property for the sellers and exclusively represents the sellers. A seller's agent may assist the buyer in purchasing the property, but his or her duty of loyalty is only to the seller.
Subagent: A Subagent means a licensed real estate broker, licensed associate real estate broker, or licensed real estate salesperson who is not affiliated with or acting as the listing real estate broker for a property, is not a buyer's agent, has a brokerage relationship with the seller, and assists a prospective buyer in the acquisition of real estate for sale in a non-brokerage relationship capacity. The subagent works for a real estate company different from the company for which the seller's agent works. The subagent can assist a buyer in purchasing a property, but his or her duty of loyalty is only to the seller.
If you are viewing a property and you have not signed a Brokerage Agreement, that agent represents the seller

Agents Who Represent the Buyer

Buyer's Agent: A buyer may enter into a written contract with a real estate broker which provides that the broker will represent the buyer in locating a property to buy. The agent from that broker's company is then known as the buyer's agent. The buyer's agent assists the buyer in evaluating properties and preparing offers and developing negotiation strategies and works in the best interest of the buyer. The agent's fee is paid according to the written agreement between the broker and the buyer. If you as a buyer wish to have an agent represent you, you must enter into a written brokerage agreement.

Dual Agents
The possibility of **dual agency** arises when the buyer's agent and the seller's agent both work for the same real estate company, and the buyer is interested in property listed by that company. The real estate broker or the broker's designee, is called the "dual agent." Dual agents do not act exclusively in the interests of either the seller or buyer, and therefore cannot give undivided loyalty to either party. There may be a conflict of interest because the interests of the seller and buyer may be different or adverse.
If both seller and buyer agree to dual agency by signing a Consent For Dual Agency form, the "dual agent" (the broker or the broker's designee) shall assign one agent to represent the seller (the seller's "intra-company agent") and another agent to represent the buyer (the buyer's "intra-company agent"). Intra-company agents are required to provide the same services to their clients that agents provide in transactions not involving dual agency, including advising their clients as to price and negotiation strategies.

P 1 of 2

If either party does not agree to dual agency, the real estate company must withdraw the brokerage agreement for that particular property with either the buyer or seller, or both. If the seller's agreement is terminated, the seller must then either represent him or herself or arrange to be represented by an agent from another real estate broker/company. If the brokerage agreement is terminated, the buyer may choose to enter into a written brokerage agreement with a different broker/company. Alternatively, the buyer may choose not to be represented but simply to receive assistance from the seller's agent, from another agent in that company, or from a subagent from another company.

No matter what type of agent you choose to work with, you have the following rights and responsibilities in selling or buying property:

>Real estate agents are obligated by law to treat all parties to a real estate transaction honestly and fairly. They must exercise reasonable care and diligence and maintain the confidentiality of clients. They must not discriminate in the offering of properties; they must promptly present each written offer or counteroffer to the other party; and they must answer questions truthfully.

>Real estate agents must disclose all material facts that they know or should know relating to a property. An agent's duty to maintain confidentiality does not apply to the disclosure of material facts about a property.

>All agreements with real estate brokers and agents must be in writing and explain the duties and obligations of both the broker and the agent. The agreement must explain how the broker and agent will be paid and any fee-sharing agreements with other brokers.

>You have the responsibility to protect your own interests. **You should carefully read all agreements** to make sure they accurately reflect your understanding. A real estate licensee is qualified to advise you on real estate matters only. If you need legal or tax advice, it is your responsibility to consult a licensed attorney or accountant.

Any complaints about a real estate licensee may be filed with the Real Estate Commission at 1100 North Eutaw Street, Baltimore, MD 21201. (410) 230-6200.

We, the □ Sellers/Landlord □ Buyers/Tenants acknowledge receipt of a copy of this disclosure

and that ______________________________ (firm name)

and ______________________________ (salesperson) are working as:

(You may check more than one box but not more than two)
□ seller/landlord's agent
□ subagent of the Seller
□ buyer's /tenant's agent

______________________________ ______________________________
Signature (Date) Signature (Date)

* *

I certify that on this date I made the required agency disclosure to the individuals identified below and they were **unable or unwilling** to acknowledge receipt of a copy of this disclosure statement.

______________________________ ______________________________
Name of Individual to whom disclosure made Name of Individual to whom disclosure made

______________________________ ______________________________
Agent's Signature (Date)

Rev. 10/1/2019

P 2 of 2

Form 1-2. Consent for Dual Agency

STATE OF MARYLAND
REAL ESTATE COMMISSION

Consent for Dual Agency

(In this form, the word "seller" includes "landlord"; "buyer" includes "tenant"; and "purchase" or "sale" includes "lease")

When Dual Agency May Occur

The possibility of Dual Agency arises when:

1) The buyer is interested in a property listed by a real estate broker; and
2) The seller's agent and the buyer's agent are affiliated with the same real estate broker.

Important Considerations Before Making a Decision About Dual Agency

A broker or the broker's designee, acting as a dual agent does not exclusively represent either the seller or buyer; there may be a conflict of interest because the interests of the seller and buyer may be different or adverse. As a dual agent, the real estate broker does not owe undivided loyalty to either the seller or buyer.

Before the buyer and seller can proceed to be represented by a broker acting as a dual agent, they must both sign Consent for Dual Agency. If the buyer has previously signed this Consent for Dual Agency, the buyer must **affirm** the buyer's consent for the purchase of a particular property before an offer to purchase is presented to the seller. If the seller has previously signed Consent for Dual Agency, the seller must **affirm** the seller's consent for the sale of the property to a particular buyer before accepting an offer to purchase the property. The **affirmation** is contained on Page 2 of this form.

Your Choices Concerning Dual Agency

In a possible dual agency situation, the buyer and seller have the following options:

1. **Consent in writing to dual agency.** If all parties consent in writing, the real estate broker or the broker's designee (the "dual agent") shall assign one real estate agent affiliated with the broker to represent the seller (the seller's "intra-company agent") and another agent affiliated with the broker to represent the buyer (the buyer's "intra-company agent"). Intra-company agents are required to provide the same services to their clients that agents provide in transactions not involving dual agency, including advising their clients as to price and negotiation strategy.
2. **Refuse to consent to dual agency. If either party refuses to consent in writing to dual agency**, the real estate broker must terminate the brokerage relationship for that particular property with the buyer, the seller, or both. If the seller terminates the brokerage agreement, the seller must then either represent him or herself or arrange to be represented by another real estate company. If the buyer terminates the brokerage agreement the buyer may choose not to be represented but simply receive assistance from the seller's agent, from another agent in that company, or from a subagent from another company. Alternatively, the buyer may choose to enter into a written brokerage agreement with a different company.

1 of 2

Duties of a Dual Agent and Intra-Company Agent

Like other agents, unless the client gives consent to disclose the information, dual agents and intra-company agents must keep confidential information about a client's bargaining position or motivations. For example, without written consent of the client, a dual agent or intra-company agent may not disclose to the other party, or the other party's agent:

1) Anything the client asks to be kept confidential; *
2) That the seller would accept a lower price or other terms;
3) That the buyer would accept a higher price or other terms;
4) The reasons why a party wants to sell or buy, or that a party needs to sell or buy quickly; or
5) Anything that relates to the negotiating strategy of a party.

* **Dual agents and intra-company agents must disclose material facts about a property to all parties.**

How Dual Agents Are Paid

Only the broker receives compensation on the sale of a property listed by that broker.

If a financial bonus is offered to an agent who sells property that is listed with his/her broker, this fact must be disclosed in writing to both the buyer and seller.

Consent for Dual Agency

I have read the above information, and I understand the terms of the dual agency. I understand that I do not have to consent to a dual agency and that if I **refuse** to consent, there will not be a dual agency; and that I may withdraw the consent at any time upon notice to the dual agent. I hereby **consent** to have

____ act as a Dual Agent for me as the
(Firm Name)

_____ **Seller** in the sale of the property at:

____

_____ **Buyer** in the purchase of a property listed for sale with the above-referenced broker.

______________________________ ______________________________
Signature Date Signature Date

AFFIRMATION OF PRIOR CONSENT TO DUAL AGENCY

- The undersigned **Buyer(s)** hereby affirm(s) consent to dual agency for the following property:

____
Property Address

______________________________ ______________________________
Signature Date Signature Date

- The undersigned **Seller(s)** hereby affirm(s) consent to dual agency for the Buyer(s) identified below:

____
Name(s) of Buyer(s)

______________________________ ______________________________
Signature Date Signature Date

2 of 2

eff. (10/1/19)

Form 1-3. Buyer's Exclusive Agency Agreement

Maryland REALTORS®

EXCLUSIVE BUYER/TENANT RESIDENTIAL BROKERAGE AGREEMENT

DATE: ____________________

1. BUYER (List all):____

Mailing Address:____

Office Telephones:____________________ **Office/Home Fax:**____________________

Home Telephones:____________________ **Cell Phones:** __________/__________

Email Addresses: ____________________ / ____________________

2. BROKER:____

Office Address:____

Office Telephone: ____________________ **Office Fax:**____________________

Buyer Agent:____________________ **Direct Line:**____________________

Home Phone:____________________ **Cell Phone:**____________________

Email Address:____

3. BUYER AUTHORIZATION: ("Broker") is hereby authorized by the undersigned Buyer(s) or by the authorized representative of Buyer(s) ("Buyer") to represent Buyer as the exclusive real estate broker in the acquisition of real property, which shall include cooperatives. **As used in this Agreement, "acquisition of real property" shall include any purchase or lease of property. The term "Seller" shall include landlord. The term "Buyer" shall include tenant.** The Buyer seeks the following type of property:____________________

____

____

____

____

4. BUYER AGENCY TERM/RIGHTS OF PARTIES FOLLOWING EXPIRATION OR TERMINATION OF AGREEMENT: This agreement shall be effective on ____________________ (mm/dd/yyyy) and shall continue until midnight on ____________________ (mm/dd/yyyy), (the "Term") unless terminated in accordance with the provisions of this section. Pursuant to Maryland Code, Real Property, Section 14-903, the Buyer Agency Term may not be longer than a year in duration.

As required under Section 17-534(b)(5) of the Maryland Real Estate Brokers Act, the parties agree to the following provision for the termination of this Agreement ***(Broker to insert terms of termination)*:**

____

____

____

____

____

An expiration or termination of this Agreement by Buyer or Broker shall be subject to the provisions of Paragraph 8 of this Agreement, and Paragraph 8 of this Agreement shall survive the expiration or termination of this Agreement. Notwithstanding the rights of the parties to terminate this Agreement as provided herein, Broker, in Broker's sole and absolute discretion, may terminate this Agreement at any time and effective immediately in the event Buyer provides any false information or misrepresents any fact to Broker or other third-party. If a Contract of Sale is entered into by Buyer during the Buyer Agency Term, which provides for settlement to occur after the expiration of the Buyer Agency Term, this Agreement shall be automatically extended until settlement, as provided for in the Contract Sale, has occurred, including any extension of the settlement by mutual written agreement between Seller and Buyer, but in no event shall the Buyer Agency Term, including any extension, extend beyond one year in duration.

5. FAIR HOUSING: Federal, State, and Local Fair Housing laws grant broad protections from discrimination in housing. **It is unlawful to discriminate based upon certain protected characteristics, which include, but are not limited to, race, color, religion, sex, national origin, disability, familial status, marital status, sexual orientation, gender identity, and source of income.** Buyer agrees to comply with all such Federal, State, and Local Fair Housing laws. Some buyers attempt to stand out to a seller by submitting a letter, photo, or video to describe why the seller should select their offer. Such tactics raise fair housing concerns, and could expose Buyer and Broker to possible violation of Fair Housing laws. To avoid seller consideration of such characteristics when selecting an offer, Buyer agrees not to prepare or submit a letter, photo, video, or any other similar items and instructs and directs Broker to remove from any offer, counter-offer, or any other communication exchanged during the transaction, any letters, photographs, videos or any other similar items other than the contract documents.

6. BUYER RESPONSIBILITIES AND NOTICE REGARDING "COMING SOON" LISTINGS:

A. Exclusive Relationship with Broker: Buyer will work exclusively with Broker during the term of this relationship.
B. Financial Information: Buyer will furnish Broker with necessary financial and personal information to reasonably establish Buyer's ability to purchase or lease property.
C. Signs or Advertisements for Property: If Buyer sees any signs or advertisements for properties being offered for sale or lease, Buyer will not contact the Seller or agent of the Seller but will first contact Broker named herein, who will provide information about the properties and then make arrangements to see them.
D. New Home Builders and Open Houses: In order to avoid the possibility of confusion over the agency relationship and misunderstandings about liability for compensation, Buyer agrees not to make a first visit to any new home builder's model nor contact any other agents representing sellers of new homes without being accompanied by Broker. Buyer agrees not to enter "Open House" properties unless accompanied by Broker or after having had Broker make arrangements with the listing broker.
E. Notice Regarding "Coming Soon" Status in the MLS: The "Coming Soon" listing status is an option for properties listed in the MLS that are not available but will be soon. MLS subscribers may view listings under this status. **However, properties listed under the "Coming Soon" status may not be shown *and* are not syndicated to public real estate websites.** The "Coming Soon" status is automatically updated to "active" on the expected on-market date if not made "active" sooner.

7. BROKER RESPONSIBILITIES: The Agent and Broker agree to:
A. Locate Real Property: Use professional knowledge and skills to locate and present real property, which is available for purchase or lease and suitable for the Buyer's needs.
B. Assist the Buyer: Assist Buyer through the process of property acquisition.
C. Represent Buyer's Interests: Represent the interests of the Buyer in all negotiations and transactions regarding the acquisition of real property.

8. BROKER'S COMPENSATION: The amount of Broker compensation is not prescribed by law or established by any membership organization with which Broker is affiliated.

A. Compensation to be Paid by Buyer: In the event of a sale or lease, the Compensation to be paid by Buyer to Broker shall be: ____
____

The Compensation shall be deemed to have been earned by Broker and shall be due and payable to Broker if:

1. During the term of this Agreement or any extension thereof (i) Buyer or any person or entity acting on Buyer's behalf executes a written agreement to purchase or lease any Property, through the efforts of anyone including Buyer, in which event Buyer, within seventy-two (72) hours thereof, shall furnish Broker a copy of such written agreement; or (ii) if during the period of ______________ days following the expiration or termination of this Agreement, Buyer executes a lease or written agreement to purchase any Property that Buyer inspected, made inquiry about, or negotiated to purchase or lease during the term of this Agreement or any extension thereof, in which event Buyer, within seventy-two (72) hours thereof, shall furnish Broker a copy of such written agreement;

2. Buyer defaults or voluntarily agrees to terminate a sale or lease; or

3. Buyer breaches this Agreement.

In the event a lease is executed, the Compensation due Broker shall be paid as follows:__________________
____.

In the event of a sale, the Compensation due Broker shall be paid at settlement as a convenience to Buyer. Buyer acknowledges and agrees that settlement on the Property shall not be a condition precedent to Buyer's obligation to Broker as herein provided. If Broker prevails in any action brought to obtain payment of the Compensation, Broker shall also be entitled to recover in such action Broker's reasonable attorney's fees and court costs. Buyer shall have no obligation to pay the Compensation to Broker if Buyer enters into a Buyer Agency Agreement with any other licensed real estate broker following the expiration of this Agreement, or any extension thereof, or following the termination of this Agreement as herein provided, unless such termination by Buyer shall have been made for the purpose of avoiding the obligation of Buyer to pay the Compensation to Broker.

B. **Fee Paid By Seller:** Broker is authorized to receive compensation from the listing broker/seller. Compensation may be offered from the listing broker to Broker through the multiple listing service or from seller as negotiated by Broker and seller for real property which is not listed with another broker. The amount of compensation received by Broker from a listing broker or from a seller shall be credited against the Compensation agreed upon in Paragraph 8.A. Buyer shall be obligated to pay any difference between the amount owed and the amount paid by the listing broker/seller. In the event the amount of compensation offered by the listing broker/seller is greater than that specified in Paragraph 8.A., Buyer authorizes Broker to receive such compensation and to retain any such additional compensation without pro ration or rebate to Buyer. The amount of any such payment made by listing broker/seller shall be with the seller's and Buyer's prior knowledge and consent and shall in no way affect the obligation of the Broker to act on behalf of the Buyer in the transaction.

9. DISCLAIMER AND LIMITATIONS:
A. Limitations of Broker's Ability: Buyer acknowledges that Broker is being retained solely as a real estate agent and not as an attorney, tax advisor, lender, appraiser, surveyor, structural engineer, certified home inspector or other professional service provider. Buyer has been advised to seek professional advice for legal, tax and other matters.
B. Representation of Other Buyers: Buyer acknowledges that Broker may represent other Buyers and that other potential Buyers may consider, make offers on, lease or purchase properties through Broker. Buyer consents to Broker's representation of other Buyers before, during, and after the expiration of this Agreement.
C. Subsequent Offers: Upon entering into a Contract of Sale or Lease pursuant to this Buyer Agency Agreement, Broker shall have no further obligation hereunder to procure any subsequent properties for Buyer.
D. Ministerial Acts: Buyer hereby consents to and authorizes Broker and Broker's agents to provide ministerial acts as defined by law on behalf of Buyer to third persons in connection with the purchase or lease of the Property.
E. Confidentiality of Offers: Buyer acknowledges the possibility that sellers or seller's representatives may not treat the existence, terms or conditions of the Buyer's offer as confidential information.

10. INTRA-COMPANY AGENT REPRESENTATION: When the Buyer and seller are each represented by sales associates of the Broker, the Broker is a dual agent. Dual agency is permitted only when disclosed and with the knowledge and written consent of both parties. However, the sales associate assigned by the Broker as an intra-company agent may continue to provide the same services that a buyer's agent can provide on a property listed with another broker.

In the event Buyer elects to consent to dual agency, buyer agrees to sign the required Consent For Dual Agency form as published by the Maryland Real Estate Commission. In the event Buyer elects not to consent to dual agency, Buyer acknowledges and agrees that Buyer will not be advised or shown properties listed by Broker and will only be shown properties listed by other real estate brokers.

11. FLOOD DISCLOSURE NOTICE:
A. FLOOD INSURANCE PREMIUMS: The Property or part of the Property may be located in an area established by the government as a "flood plain" or otherwise in an area where flood insurance could be required. In addition, construction on the Property could be prohibited or restricted.

The National Flood Insurance Program ("NFIP") provides for the availability of flood insurance but also establishes flood insurance policy premiums based on the risk of flooding in the area where properties are located. Due to amendments to federal law governing the NFIP those premiums are increasing, and in some cases will rise by a substantial amount over the premiums previously charged for flood insurance. As a result, premiums paid for flood insurance on the Property may not be indicative of premiums that will apply after the Property is purchased. Detailed information regarding flood insurance coverage, the premiums that are likely to be required to purchase such insurance and any available information about how those premiums may increase in the future may be obtained at: https://www.fema.gov/national-flood-insurance-program.

B. FLOOD INSURANCE RATE MAPS: The State of Maryland in conjunction with the Federal Emergency Management Agency has been systematically updating flood insurance rate maps. The Property may be affected.

Buyer is advised to contact the Maryland Department of the Environment and consult a flood insurance carrier to inquire about the status of the Property. Detailed information regarding updated maps may be obtained at: http://www.mdfloodmaps.net.

12. REPAIRS OF PROPERTY: Buyer is hereby notified that repairs of the Property may require that the individuals engaged to perform such repairs must be duly licensed.

13. LEGAL CONSTRUCTION: This Agreement is binding upon the parties hereto, and their personal representatives, successors, heirs and assigns. If this Agreement is signed by more than one person, it shall constitute the joint and several obligations of each. This Agreement contains the entire Agreement of the parties and cannot be changed except by the written agreement of the parties hereto. Buyer warrants that there are no other existing agreements

or conditions other than as set forth herein. This is a legally binding Agreement; if not understood, seek competent legal, tax or other professional advice. Buyer has not relied upon any statement or representation of Broker except as set forth in this Agreement. This Agreement shall be interpreted and construed in accordance with the laws of the State of Maryland.

14. ADDENDA: The Addenda marked below, which are hereby attached, are made a part of this Agreement:
- □ Consent for Dual Agency
- □ Notification of Dual Agency within a Team
- □ Disclosure of Licensee Status Addendum

Other Addenda/Special Conditions:

____

____

RECEIPT OF COPY: Buyer/Tenant acknowledges receipt of a copy of this Agreement at time of signing hereof.

Buyer/Tenant	Date	Broker (Company Name)
Buyer/Tenant	Date	Broker or Authorized Representative Date

Form 1-4. Maryland Residential Property Disclosure and Disclaimer Statement

MARYLAND RESIDENTIAL PROPERTY DISCLOSURE AND DISCLAIMER STATEMENT

Property Address: ____

Legal Description: ____

NOTICE TO SELLER AND PURCHASER

Section 10-702 of the Real Property Article, *Annotated Code of Maryland*, requires the seller of certain residential real property to furnish to the purchaser either (a) a RESIDENTIAL PROPERTY DISCLAIMER STATEMENT stating that the seller is selling the property "as is" and makes no representations or warranties as to the condition of the property or any improvements on the real property, except as otherwise provided in the contract of sale, or in a listing of latent defects; or (b) a RESIDENTIAL PROPERTY DISCLOSURE STATEMENT disclosing defects or other information about the condition of the real property actually known by the seller. Certain transfers of residential property are excluded from this requirement (see the exemptions listed below).

10-702. EXEMPTIONS. The following are specifically excluded from the provisions of §10-702:

1. The initial sale of single family residential real property:
   A. that has never been occupied; or
   B. for which a certificate of occupancy has been issued within 1 year before the seller and buyer enter into a contract of sale;
2. A transfer that is exempt from the transfer tax under §13-207 of the Tax-Property Article, except land installment contracts of sales under §13-207(a) (11) of the Tax-Property Article and options to purchase real property under §13-207(a)(12) of the Tax-Property Article;
3. A sale by a lender or an affiliate or subsidiary of a lender that acquired the real property by foreclosure or deed in lieu of foreclosure;
4. A sheriff's sale, tax sale, or sale by foreclosure, partition, or by court appointed trustee;
5. A transfer by a fiduciary in the course of the administration of a decedent's estate, guardianship, conservatorship, or trust;
6. A transfer of single family residential real property to be converted by the buyer into use other than residential use or to be demolished; or
7. A sale of unimproved real property.

Section 10-702 also requires the seller to disclose information about latent defects in the property that the seller has actual knowledge of. The seller must provide this information even if selling the property "as is." "Latent defects" are defined as: Material defects in real property or an improvement to real property that:

(1) A purchaser would not reasonably be expected to ascertain or observe by a careful visual inspection of the real property; and
(2) Would pose a direct threat to the health or safety of:
  (i) the purchaser; or
  (ii) an occupant of the real property, including a tenant or invitee of the purchaser.

MARYLAND RESIDENTIAL PROPERTY DISCLOSURE STATEMENT

NOTICE TO SELLERS: Complete and sign this statement only if you elect to disclose defects, including latent defects, or other information about the condition of the property actually known by you; otherwise, sign the Residential Property Disclaimer Statement. You may wish to obtain professional advice or inspections of the property; however, you are not required to undertake or provide any independent investigation or inspection of the property in order to make the disclosure set forth below. The disclosure is based on your personal knowledge of the condition of the property at the time of the signing of this statement.

NOTICE TO PURCHASERS: The information provided is the representation of the Sellers and is based upon the actual knowledge of Sellers as of the date noted. Disclosure by the Sellers is not a substitute for an inspection by an independent home inspection company, and you may wish to obtain such an inspection. The information contained in this statement is not a warranty by the Sellers as to the condition of the property of which the Sellers have no knowledge or other conditions of which the Sellers have no actual knowledge.

How long have you owned the property? __________________

Property System: Water, Sewage, Heating & Air Conditioning (Answer all that apply)

Water Supply ☐ Public ☐ Well ☐ Other ___________
Sewage Disposal ☐ Public ☐ Septic System approved for ________(# bedrooms) **Other Type**
____
Garbage Disposal ☐ Yes ☐ No
Dishwasher ☐ Yes ☐No
Heating ☐ Oil ☐ Natural Gas ☐ Electric ☐ Heat Pump Age ____ ☐ Other ________________
Air Conditioning ☐ Oil ☐ Natural Gas ☐Electric ☐ Heat Pump Age ____ ☐ Other ________________
Hot Water ☐ Oil ☐ Natural Gas ☐Electric Capacity __________ Age_____☐ Other ________________

Please indicate your actual knowledge with respect to the following:

1. Foundation: Any settlement or other problems? ☐ Yes ☐ No ☐ Unknown
Comments:____
2. Basement: Any leaks or evidence of moisture? ☐ Yes ☐ No ☐ Unknown ☐ Does Not Apply
Comments:____
3. Roof: Any leaks or evidence of moisture? ☐ Yes ☐ No ☐ Unknown
Type of Roof:__________________Age________
Comments:____
Is there any existing fire retardant treated plywood? ☐ Yes ☐ No ☐ Unknown
Comments:____

4. Other Structural Systems, including exterior walls and floors:
Comments:____
Any defects (structural or otherwise)? ☐ Yes ☐ No ☐ Unknown
Comments:____
5. Plumbing system: Is the system in operating condition? ☐ Yes ☐ No ☐ Unknown
Comments:____

6. Heating Systems: Is heat supplied to all finished rooms? ☐ Yes ☐ No ☐ Unknown
Comments:____
Is the system in operating condition? ☐ Yes ☐ No ☐ Unknown
Comments:____
7. Air Conditioning System: Is cooling supplied to all finished rooms? ☐Yes ☐ No ☐ Unknown ☐ Does Not Apply
Comments:____
Is the system in operating condition? ☐ Yes ☐ No ☐ Unknown ☐ Does Not Apply
Comments:____

8. Electric Systems: Are there any problems with electrical fuses, circuit breakers, outlets or wiring?
☐ Yes ☐ No. ☐ Unknown
Comments:____
8A. Will the smoke alarms provide an alarm in the event of a power outage? ○ Yes ○ No
Are the smoke alarms over 10 years old? ○ Yes ○ No
If the smoke alarms are battery operated, are they sealed, tamper resistant units incorporating a silence/hush button, which use long-life batteries as required in all Maryland Homes by 2018? ○Yes ○ No
Comments:__________________________________
9. Septic Systems: Is the septic system functioning properly? ☐ Yes ☐ No ☐ Unknown ☐ Does Not Apply
When was the system last pumped? Date__________ ☐ Unknown
Comments:____
10. Water Supply: Any problem with water supply? ☐ Yes ☐ No ☐ Unknown
Comments:____
Home water treatment system: ☐ Yes ☐ No ☐ Unknown
Comments:____
Fire sprinkler system: ☐ Yes ☐ No ☐ Unknown ☐ Does Not Apply
Comments:____
Are the systems in operating condition? ☐ Yes ☐ No ☐ Unknown
Comments:____
11. Insulation:
In exterior walls? ☐ Yes ☐ No ☐Unknown
In ceiling/attic? ☐ Yes ☐ No ☐ Unknown
In any other areas? ☐ Yes ☐ No Where? __________________
Comments:____
12. Exterior Drainage: Does water stand on the property for more than 24 hours after a heavy rain?
☐ Yes ☐ No ☐ Unknown
Comments____
Are gutters and downspouts in good repair? ☐ Yes ☐ No ☐ Unknown
Comments:____

Page 2 of 4

13. Wood-destroying insects: Any infestation and/or prior damage? ☐ Yes ☐ No ☐ Unknown
Comments:____
Any treatments or repairs? ☐ Yes ☐ No ☐ Unknown
Any warranties? ☐ Yes ☐ No ☐ Unknown
Comments:____

14. Are there any hazardous or regulated materials (including, but not limited to, licensed landfills, asbestos, radon gas, lead-based paint, underground storage tanks, or other contamination) on the property?
☐ Yes ☐ No ☐ Unknown
If yes, specify below
Comments:____

15. If the property relies on the combustion of a fossil fuel for heat, ventilation, hot water, or clothes dryer operation, is a carbon monoxide alarm installed in the property?
o Yes o No 0 Unknown
Comments:____

16. Are there any zoning violations, nonconforming uses, violation of building restrictions or setback requirements or any recorded or unrecorded easement, except for utilities, on or affecting the property?
☐ Yes ☐ No ☐ Unknown
If yes, specify below
Comments:____
16A. If you or a contractor have made improvements to the property, were the required permits pulled from the county or local permitting office? ○ Yes ○ No ○ Does Not Apply ○ Unknown
Comments:____

17. Is the property located in a flood zone, conservation area, wetland area, Chesapeake Bay critical area or Designated Historic District?
☐ Yes ☐ No ☐ Unknown If yes, specify below
Comments:____

18.Is the property subject to any restriction imposed by a Home Owners Association or any other type of community association?
☐ Yes ☐ No ☐ Unknown If yes, specify below
Comments:____

19. Are there any other material defects, including latent defects, affecting the physical condition of the property?
☐ Yes ☐ No ☐ Unknown
Comments:____

NOTE: Seller(s) may wish to disclose the condition of other buildings on the property on a separate RESIDENTIAL PROPERTY DISCLOSURE STATEMENT.

The seller(s) acknowledge having carefully examined this statement, including any comments, and verify that it is complete and accurate as of the date signed. The seller(s) further acknowledge that they have been informed of their rights and obligations under §10-702 of the Maryland Real Property Article.
Seller(s) ______________________________ Date ____________

Seller(s) ______________________________ Date____________

The purchaser(s) acknowledge receipt of a copy of this disclosure statement and further acknowledge that they have been informed of their rights and obligations under §10-702 of the Maryland Real Property Article.

Purchaser ______________________________ Date____________

Purchaser______________________________ Date____________

Page 3 of 4

MARYLAND RESIDENTIAL PROPERTY DISCLAIMER STATEMENT

NOTICE TO SELLER(S): Sign this statement only if you elect to sell the property without representations and warranties as to its condition, except as otherwise provided in the contract of sale and in the listing of latent defects set forth below; otherwise, complete and sign the RESIDENTIAL PROPERTY DISCLOSURE STATEMENT.

Except for the latent defects listed below, the undersigned seller(s) of the real property make no representations or warranties as to the condition of the real property or any improvements thereon, and the purchaser will be receiving the real property "as is" with all defects, including latent defects, which may exist, except as otherwise provided in the real estate contract of sale. The seller(s) acknowledge having carefully examined this statement and further acknowledge that they have been informed of their rights and obligations under §10-702 of the Maryland Real Property Article.

Section 10-702 also requires the seller to disclose information about latent defects in the property that the seller has actual knowledge of. The seller must provide this information even if selling the property "as is." "Latent defects" are defined as: Material defects in real property or an improvement to real property that:

(1) A purchaser would not reasonably be expected to ascertain or observe by a careful visual inspection of the real property; and
(2) Would pose a direct threat to the health or safety of:
  (i) the purchaser; or
  (ii) an occupant of the real property, including a tenant or invitee of the purchaser.

Does the seller(s) have actual knowledge of any latent defects? □ Yes □ No If yes, specify:

____
____
____
____
____
____
____
____
____

Seller ____ Date____________________

Seller____ Date____________________

The purchaser(s) acknowledge receipt of a copy of this disclaimer statement and further acknowledge that they have been informed of their rights and obligations under §10-702 of the Maryland Real Property Article.

Purchaser ____ Date____________________

Purchaser ____ Date____________________

Page 4 of 4

FORM: MREC/DLLR: Rev 07/31/2018

CHAPTER TWO

CONTRACTS OF SALE—RESALE OF EXISTING RESIDENCES*

Erika A. Mason Madden, Esq.

Universal Title, LLC
The Mason Law Firm, PLC

* MSBA gratefully acknowledges the contributors to previous editions of this chapter, Bruce L. Benshoof, Esq., Krista M. North, Esq., and Gregory Reed, Esq.

ABOUT THE AUTHOR

Erika A. Mason Madden, Esq.

Erika A. Mason Madden, Esq., is the Director of Business Development at Universal Title, Howard County and an associate with the Mason Law Firm. She received a Bachelor of Arts degree from Texas A&M University in the year 2000 and a Juris Doctorate degree from The Catholic University of American, Columbus School of Law in 2003. Prior to her current position, she has worked for a variety of different title companies in Maryland holding positions ranging from Managing Attorney to General Counsel and was a Partner and Yungmann and Madden, LLP. She built her career educating Realtors and consumers on the MR and GCAAR contract forms and assisting them with their legal questions.

TABLE OF CONTENTS

I. INTRODUCTION

A. [§ 2.1] Generally

After mortgage financings and refinancings, the resale of a residential lot, parcel, or condominium unit is by far the most common kind of real estate transaction. Most families own their homes and move several times during each generation. With rare exceptions, dwellings are sold and resold numerous times during their lifetime. The attorney whose practice includes residential real property matters will have frequent occasion to become involved in such resales and should therefore be familiar with the law and practice surrounding them.

In many ways, residential resale transactions are more "traditional" in nature than are builder sales of new homes. Buyer and seller usually are on a more equal footing than are builder and new homebuyer, and thus are more willing (or able) to make the sales contract reflect both parties' needs. While a homebuilder frequently has arranged, in advance, mortgage financing for its buyers, a resale purchaser typically is responsible for obtaining its own purchase money financing (sometimes with the broker's help). Buyers of existing homes are not offered a menu of optional fixtures, appliances, and improvements from which to select for incorporation into the dwelling. Resales are generally "as is," with little or no warranty protection, except for occasional negotiation over whether the washer, dryer, or other appliances are to be included in the sale. In these respects, residential resales have more in common with many commercial property sale transactions than with sales of newly-constructed homes.

B. Formal Requisites of Purchase and Sale Contract

1. [§ 2.2] Generally

Little discussion is needed of the formal legal requirements of a binding contract for the sale and purchase of residential real property. Under the Maryland version of the Statute of Frauds,[1] a fee simple, leasehold, freehold, or other corporeal or incorporeal estate or interest in land may not be created other than by a deed, contract, or other writing signed by or on behalf of the party creating it. Thus, a contract for the sale or disposition of real property is not enforceable unless in writing and signed by or on behalf of the party against whom it is to be enforced.[2] Surprisingly,

---

1 Md. Code Ann., Real Property §§ 5-101–5-108 (hereinafter Real Prop. §). Unless otherwise indicated, all citations to the Annotated Code of Maryland are to the Code as amended through the Maryland General Assembly's 2022 legislative session.

2 *Id.* Technically, § 5-101 states that any such interest in land not created by such a contract "has the force and effect of an estate or interest at will only. . . ." Real Prop. § 5-102 creates an exception to this rule for leasehold estates not exceeding a term of one year.

if the requirement of the Statute of Frauds is met, a contract need not be signed by *all* parties to be enforceable against the signing party, unless it provides otherwise or the parties manifest their intent that it not be enforceable until fully signed.[3] The same rules apply to offers to sell or purchase, and to amendments of contracts or offers. In theory, "part performance" of an *oral* agreement to sell or dispose of real property may, under narrow circumstances, suffice to remove the bar of the Statute of Frauds to enforcement of such contract; however, as a practical matter, oral real property contracts are quite difficult to establish under Maryland law, and hence rarely are recognized.[4]

Aside from Statute of Frauds concerns, the contract law principles applicable to residential real property contracts are the same as those for contracts generally,[5] and are largely derived from common law rather than statute.[6] The usual requirements of offer, acceptance,[7] and valid consideration[8] apply. For a real property sale contract to be valid, it must identify the parties,[9] set forth their agreement to buy and sell the property,[10] and contain the essential terms of their agreement.[11] The contract must identify the property in question with reasonable certainty,[12] and state the purchase price or other consideration.[13] Moreover, even a signed contract for the sale of real property is legally ineffective unless delivered.[14] Where one party submits an offer and the other responds by altering its terms and returning the modified offer to the first party, the latter is not an acceptance of the original offer but is instead a counteroffer. Its effect at law rejects the original offer (except when first party states in the offer, or second party states in the counteroffer, that the original offer is not terminated by the counteroffer).[15] Maryland Realtors, in their 2022 update of their contract of sale, redefined "acceptance," for purposes of their contract, to be when the final signature/initial is placed and there is a meeting of the minds regarding all material facts.

Due to the way in which many residential sales contracts are created—through an offer-counteroffer process involving numerous interlineations and addenda to an

---

3 *Huse v. Reed,* 157 Md. 504, 146 A. 579 (1929).

4 *Beall v. Beall,* 291 Md. 224, 434 A.2d 1015 (1981).

5 *Born v. Hammond,* 218 Md.184, 146 A.2d 44 (1958).

6 An exception to this generality exists in the case of land installment contracts (discussed in § **2.5** of this chapter), which are largely governed by statute.

7 *Post v. Gillespie,* 219 Md. 378, 149 A.2d 391 (1959).

8 *Nagengast v. Alz,* 93 Md. 522, 49 A. 333 (1901).

9 *London v. Riebel,* 189 Md. 376, 56 A.2d 34 (1947).

10 *Born v. Hammond,* 218 Md. 184, 146 A.2d 44 (1958).

11 *Quillen v. Kelley,* 216 Md. 396, 140 A.2d 517 (1958).

12 *Sears v. Polan's 5¢ to $1.00 Store, Inc.*, 250 Md. 525, 243 A.2d 602 (1968).

13 *Moran v. Hammersla,* 188 Md. 378, 52 A.2d 727 (1947).

14 *Huse v. Reed,* 157 Md. 504, 146 A. 579 (1929).

15 *Ebline v. Campbell,* 209 Md. 584, 121 A.2d 828 (1956).

original draft—these principles are overlooked. Most frequently forgotten is ensuring that the "final," signed contract versions which come to rest in the hands of buyer and seller are in fact identical counterparts of each other, and that each party has initialed or otherwise evidenced its agreement to all interim modifications and addenda; in other words, the buyer and seller must sign the same document.

2. [§ 2.3] Equitable conversion

Maryland has long recognized the common law doctrine of equitable conversion in real property sale transactions. In essence, this means that a contract purchaser becomes the *beneficial owner* of the property the instant the contract of sale becomes legally effective. While the contract is still executory, seller is deemed to hold only *bare legal title* to the property, in trust for buyer and as security for seller's contract right to be paid the purchase money.[16] Once closing occurs and the deed of conveyance or other instrument transferring the record title to buyer is recorded among the Land Records, buyer becomes the legal title holder as well. Of course, if the contract terminates without settlement having occurred, seller once again becomes the beneficial owner.

While the doctrine of equitable conversion can have various consequences for any given real estate transaction, one significant effect is that someone becoming a judgment creditor of seller after a sales contract becomes effective obtains a lien only on seller's rights under the contract—essentially, the right to be paid the purchase price—but not against buyer's beneficial title.[17] However, a subsequent third-party purchaser of the same property for good and valuable consideration, who has no actual or constructive notice of the existence of the prior contract, and to whom seller delivers a deed which is recorded before recordation of a deed to the prior purchaser, takes title free and clear of the prior contract.[18] Thus, a buyer concerned about the possibility that seller will grant rights to the property to a third-party bona fide purchaser should consider recording the contract of sale or a memorandum of it, to prevent any such third-party from being a bona fide purchaser.[19]

---

16 *Stebbins-Anderson Co. v. Bolton*, 208 Md. 183, 117 A.2d 908 (1955); *DeShields v. Broadwater*, 338 Md. 422, 659 A.2d 300, 307–08 (1995). Seller is deemed to hold bare legal title as a vendor's lien for payment of the purchase price.

17 *See* Real Prop. § 3-201, which provides in part that a deed, when recorded, "takes effect from its effective date as against the grantor, his personal representatives, every purchaser with notice of the deed, *and every creditor of the grantor with or without notice*" (emphasis added). Under the same section, the effective date of a deed is its date of delivery, which is presumed to be the later of its stated date or the date of its last acknowledgment. *See also Frederick Ward Assocs. v. Venture, Inc.*, 99 Md. App. 251, 636 A.2d 496 (1994).

18 Real Prop. § 3-203.

19 *S. Halt. Harbor & Improv. Co. v. Smith*, 85 Md. 537, 37 A. 27 (1897).

C. Other Varieties of Contract

1. [§ 2.4] Option agreements

Occasionally, a residential transaction will involve not a contract of sale, but an option agreement under which the owner grants to the "buyer" an option to purchase the dwelling, exercisable during and only during a prescribed period after the contract is signed. The contents of such agreements differ from those of contracts of sale in only one significant respect: they contain additional terms which grant the option and provide that, until the option is exercised, the buyer holds the right, *but not the obligation,* to complete settlement and purchase the house in accordance with the agreement. Once the option is exercised, the parties' positions are essentially the same (and require the same contractual protections) as those of buyer and seller under a regular contract of sale. Hence, the points concerning contracts of sale discussed in this chapter are generally applicable to option agreements as well.

If the parties desire to use the option agreement format, it is important that the agreement contains several provisions in addition to those required for contracts of sale generally:

(a) First, the agreement must set forth a date (either a stated date or a date which is a stated number of days after the date of the agreement) within which the option must be exercised, if at all. Otherwise, as discussed in **§ 2.56** of this chapter, the agreement will be void under the Rule Against Perpetuities. Of course, the date must fall within the perpetuities period.

(b) Second, the agreement should require that the option be exercised, if at all, only by a *written* notice given by buyer to seller. To avoid any misunderstanding about casual written communications between the parties which express an interest in exercising the option but, read literally, fall short of actually doing so, the parties should consider attaching a prescribed form of exercise notice letter as an exhibit to the agreement.

REAL PROP. § 3-101(f) permits the recording of a memorandum of an option agreement, which is an abridged version of the option agreement designed to give notice to the world of the existence of an option agreement, its duration, a description of the property under the option, and the identity of the parties.

2. [§ 2.5] Land installment contracts

Although not commonly used, sometimes a residential sale is accomplished using a land installment contract—a device which combines the characteristics of a contract of sale, deed, and purchase money mortgage. In a land installment contract, seller contracts to sell the property to buyer under terms calling for buyer to pay the purchase price to seller in installments, usually over a period of years. Buyer takes possession of the property when the contract is signed, and typically pays all real property taxes and other operating expenses for the property accruing thereafter, just as if buyer had acquired record title to the property. Once the purchase price is paid in full, seller delivers a deed to the property to buyer.

In Maryland, land installment contracts are highly regulated by statute.[20] Whenever a contract falls within the statutory definition of a land installment contract—essentially, a contract for the sale of real property under which the price is to be paid in five or more installments, exclusive of any down payment, and seller retains the title as security for buyer's payment obligation—it is subject to the statutory rules. These include requirements that (a) seller record the contract within 15 days after it is signed (failing which, buyer may cancel the contract at any time and receive a full refund of all money paid); (b) the contract contain various terms and notices; and (c) once at least 40% of the price has been paid, seller must, on demand by buyer, tender a deed of conveyance to buyer in exchange for a purchase money mortgage for the unpaid balance, with payment terms of the mortgage being no less favorable to buyer than those of the land installment contract.

Aside from these statutory requirements, land installment contracts should be viewed by the parties and their attorneys as simply another variety of contract of sale, in which all of the same issues must be addressed as those dealt with in regular sales contracts, discussed later in this chapter.

While a land installment contract is in effect, a seller is prohibited from encumbering the property with a mortgage whose principal amount or installment payment amounts are greater than those of the land installment contract. However, even a mortgage meeting these standards, but senior in priority to the land installment contract, may be foreclosed if seller defaults, regardless of whether buyer has honored buyer's own payment obligations under the contract.

II. SELECTING A FORM

A. [§ 2.6] Use of Forms Generally

Residential resale transactions are form intensive. Attorneys, brokers, and other professionals involved in such transactions rely heavily on pre-prepared, printed forms, in drafting contracts and related documents. There are important reasons for such reliance.

1. [§ 2.7] Forms are efficient

Residential transactions can (surprisingly) be legally complicated, due largely to the multitude of financing, inspection, and other options typically given buyer, and the ever-lengthening list of disclosure obligations imposed by law on seller. Despite

---

20 REAL PROP. §§ 10-101–10-108.

this complexity, in most cases such documents must be prepared quickly—typically within hours—so that an offer can be submitted promptly when buyer is of a mind to buy. Their preparation often occurs outside of a traditional office environment and work hours, such as at buyer's kitchen table after an evening strategy session. Notwithstanding these facts, the relatively small amounts of money involved in most residential transactions—when compared to commercial sales—usually do not justify the expense or effort required to have an attorney or other professional custom draft the contract. Thus, it is essential for the professional to have readily available a well-drafted, legally current set of forms which, for a given residential sale transaction, can be adapted quickly and with a minimum of effort.

2. [§ 2.8] Some forms have broad acceptance in the marketplace

Residential transactions depend heavily not just on pre-prepared forms generally, but on particular sets of forms having familiarity and acceptance in the marketplace. Many forms—especially those printed forms developed and used by local associations of realtors—have acquired through popular use such acceptance in their locales that they are viewed with trust as being "standard" and, therefore, as not requiring the degree of scrutiny by buyer, seller, attorney, broker, or lender which would be warranted by a document based on an unfamiliar, "nonstandard" form, even one of equal or higher quality. Trust in such standardized forms tends to reduce the elapsed time, negotiating time, expense, effort, confusion, misunderstanding, and emotional turmoil needed to arrive at an agreement which the parties and their professional advisors can accept and sign. Awareness of these benefits in turn significantly enhances the perceived and, to a somewhat lesser extent, actual desirability of published, "standard" forms as forms of choice to those anxious to "tie up" a sale by getting it "under contract."

To some extent, the notion that standard printed forms—or *any* pre-prepared forms, for that matter—require less scrutiny is justified. Professionals who use them repeatedly become familiar with their terms, and therefore need not spend time getting up to speed when called upon to use them. However, familiarity alone does not justify an assumption that, without substantive modification, a form will *necessarily* prove adequate to protect the parties' respective positions under the peculiar facts of a given sale transaction. This distinction is sometimes overlooked by professionals and their clients who, having seen such forms occasionally, allow their quality of "standardness" to persuade them that they may safely pay reduced attention to their contents. For this reason, the attorney who handles a residential resale transaction must be fully sensitive to the benefits and pitfalls of using either a standardized form or one of their own. They should not be lulled by a form's familiarity and quality of "standardness" into failing to give real consideration to the appropriateness all of its language to the transaction at hand when viewed from the client's position, or to modify that language where needed.

On the other hand, the attorney must be ever mindful of the client's desire to "do the deal," and that, precisely because the preprinted contract form is the norm for most residential transactions, both the client and the other party are more likely than in other kinds of transactions to become wary, impatient, or both if, in protecting the client's legal position, the attorney demands changes to the printed form which are perceived—correctly or not—as overkill or overlawyering. The attorney's judgment as to where the point of compromise lies on this issue must reflect the attorney's view of the parties' respective bargaining positions, and their own experience.

3. [§ 2.9] Forms serve as the medium of negotiation

The very process by which residential contracts are negotiated and signed tends to inhibit significant deviations from the standard printed form contract. An attorney often is brought into a transaction too late to be afforded any real opportunity to participate in either the selection or the negotiation of the form contract. This phenomenon reflects the realities of the process by which houses are bought and sold.

The delivery to seller of a formal draft contract, prepared by a real estate broker on a printed form, and already signed by a would-be buyer, frequently represents the very first contact between the parties to the sale and purchase of an existing residence. Occasionally, the purchase offer which this represents is accepted by seller "as is." More often, seller will counteroffer by making and initialing interlineated and other changes to buyer's document, signing it, and returning it to buyer. Buyer may in turn accept this counteroffer by initialing seller's changes and redelivering the well-traveled form to seller; may instead reject seller's changes and do nothing; or may reject seller's counteroffer by making further changes and, after initialing these revisions, return the document to seller for further consideration.

Note that all of this activity takes place on the original printed form or its duplicate. While firing these salvos back and forth, the parties usually are not in direct contact. While each is represented by a real estate agent, the agents themselves seldom spend much, if any, time discussing anything but the most essential sale terms.

Although either party is free at any time to rewrite, add to, or eliminate *any* of the terms of buyer's initial form, or indeed to substitute an entirely new form, experience shows that most changes made by parties or brokers to the initial form involve merely adding or deleting a few words here or there, and that even these slight efforts are confined to a few key areas of the contract.[21] Because the parties focus on these few terms, most other areas of the original form—including some

---

[21] Clauses in the contract that are commonly modified include those stating the price, the fixtures and personalty included in or excluded from the sale, and financing and other key conditions to buyer's closing obligation.

important ones—are soon perceived as "not at issue" and therefore effectively are no longer negotiable. They emerge from this process untouched and, for the most part, unconsidered. In many instances, the parties do not really understand the import of the more "legal" terms of the contract they have signed, and often believe their rights to be other than what they actually are.

Thus, by serving as the basis for negotiation between parties who may be reluctant to tamper with any but its most essential and easily modified terms (unless one or both parties are represented by an attorney at this stage), the language of the original contract form tends by default to become, virtually unmodified, that of the final contract. In this respect, the residential sales contracting process differs fundamentally from the practices followed in buying and selling commercial real property. There, the formal contract usually is drafted by a lawyer and tailored to the transaction, but only after buyer and seller have had direct contact and have arrived at a non-binding understanding of the material terms of the sale, through an exchange of memoranda or a letter of intent.

Although most buyers and sellers would benefit from a lawyer's advice when buying or selling a house, many do not consult an attorney, allowing a broker to draft the contract and trusting in their own judgment as to the appropriateness of its contents. Those who do consult a lawyer often wait to do so until the offer-counteroffer process described above is well underway or even completed, and then present the lawyer with a broker-prepared contract form which they hope they will bless without suggesting changes. In many instances, this form already has been signed and delivered by both parties or, if not signed, its basic business terms—price, deposit amount, closing date, and principal conditions—have been agreed upon, and the essential choice of form has already been made. At this stage, the attorney is left with little latitude to make changes without endangering the sale for the client.

The lawyer consulted by buyer or seller *before* a contract is prepared or before the negotiation process begins can help their client by advising as to the rights and benefits the client should receive in the transaction, and the burdens which they should expect to assume, by ensuring that the contract accurately and completely reflects the terms negotiated, using language as favorable to the client as is permitted by the form-selection and drafting process. Thus, the lawyer asked to advise a client concerning the sale of an existing residence must first ascertain the stage to which the offer-counteroffer process has progressed.

B. [§ 2.10] Real Estate Board Forms

Maryland Realtors, the Greater Baltimore Board of Realtors, the Carroll, Harford, and Howard County Associations of Realtors, the Greater Capital Area Association of Realtors, and some realtors' boards in other Maryland counties have for many years published forms that are in prevalent use and have been adopted, often with minor variations, by many brokerage firms. These forms (Board Forms) consist of a series of form contracts, each designed for use with a particular type of property or transaction. For example, most Board Form series contain separate contract forms for the sale of houses and of unimproved lots. In addition to the basic contract forms, they include various forms of addenda, some of which are used in nearly all transactions and others of which are not. Such addenda forms include those providing for various financing conditions, inspection rights, and statutorily required disclosure provisions.

As noted, Board Forms have gained such a degree of acceptance by brokers, attorneys, and parties who have previously bought and sold houses that there is much to be said for using them or their variations. They may appear to be neutral documents usable by both sellers and buyers without favoring either. However, many practitioners believe that their orientation is to ensure a transaction that closes. Thus, such forms may be more advantageous to one party over the other. The forms are revised and supplemented regularly by their issuing bodies to reflect legislative or other changes in the law, and thus serve as helpful checklists to such developments. Maryland courts have frequently been called upon to construe their more important provisions, thus lending a degree of predictability to the outcome of contract disputes involving their terms.

This is not to say that Board Forms are in all respects legally acceptable documents. Indeed, there is much room for improvement in most of them. However, for the reasons discussed above, both attorney and client should weigh the benefit to be derived from a given improvement against the risk of losing the benefit in ease of negotiation to be derived from the Board Forms' known quality. They should consider whether asking for the modification may delay or prevent entry into the contract, and/or prompt the other side to request "improvements" to other form provisions which, from the first party's standpoint, are better left unimproved.

Many experienced lawyers are able to take advantage of the Board Forms' familiarity to and general acceptance by brokers, other attorneys, and clients, using them as the basis of a contract while attaching a specially prepared rider which, by its terms, gives greater protection to the client by replacing or supplementing some of the printed form's key provisions. A sample form for such a rider is included in § **2.85** of this chapter.

A word of caution: *The Board Forms are copyrighted and may not be used or copied without specific authorization from the preparing Realtor organization.*

C. [§ 2.11] Broker Forms

In addition to the Board Forms, countless other forms have been prepared by individual brokerage firms and their attorneys. These forms differ depending upon the geographic area involved, the individual broker, the expertise of the broker's attorney, and even the type of sale with which the broker is most experienced. Because of their variety, little can be said that is generally applicable to such forms, except that they must be scrutinized with great care for errors of commission and, even worse, errors of omission. Many bear a great resemblance to the area's corresponding Board Form, but may differ from the latter in subtle but important ways. Moreover, to the extent that a given broker form differs significantly from the corresponding Board Form in the property's locale, it will tend to lose the benefits of familiarity and acceptance among principals and professionals which the Board Forms possess. Thus, in dealing with broker-prepared forms, the attorney must proceed with particular caution.

D. [§ 2.12] Attorney Forms

Many attorneys and law firms have developed their own residential forms, often reflecting the attorney's own experience. Such forms are easily produced and adaptable with word-processing computer software or document assembly programs. They offer the prospect of a freshly typed or printed document in each individual case, which may be preferable to the attorney and the client. On the other hand, by not being "standard"—that is, by differing in appearance and, to a greater or lesser extent, content from the printed Board Form—such tailored documents lose much of the advantages in ease of negotiation and lack of scrutiny by the "other side" which the Board Forms possess.

In any case, other than in those infrequent circumstances in which the attorney is requested to prepare the initial draft of a contract, it is often difficult for an attorney to introduce their own form into a sale transaction, due to the late stage at which they are usually brought in. The attorney's insistence at this stage on using their own form, rather than amending the form presented by the broker, may jeopardize the sale. The broker will balk, the other party and that party's attorney will object, and the client will wonder whether they paid to "re-invent the wheel," only to lose the sale. The principal question is whether demanding use of the attorney's own form is worth the risk to the success of the transaction. Where the transaction is not complicated by special problems, such as those associated with non-subdivision properties, the attorney may be better advised to amend the Board Form presented to them, than to attempt to substitute their own form.

III. ANALYSIS OF THE CONTRACT OF SALE

A. [§ 2.13] Scope

The discussion which follows in this section deals with the terms of residential resale contracts generally. It addresses issues and concerns which must be dealt with in all such contracts, regardless of the form on which they are based. Due to its importance in residential sale transactions in Maryland, we will frequently focus on the manner in which these matters are dealt with in the Maryland Realtors Residential Contract of Sale.[22] and the Greater Capital Area Association of Realtors (hereinafter GCAAR) contract of sale. Since the same issues usually are raised by the forms published by boards of realtors in other areas, as well as other broker and attorney forms, the discussion will be relevant to other jurisdictional forms as well.

B. Names of Parties

1. [§ 2.14] Generally

Although seemingly too obvious to require comment, the names of the requisite parties are so often omitted or inaccurately recited in a residential sale contract as to warrant a reminder that they must be correctly set forth. Each person holding an interest in the property should be named as a party and, accordingly, should be a signator.

Particular attention should be given to naming the seller in precisely the same manner as their name is reflected in the Land Records as owner of the property. If the property is titled in the names of both spouses, each should be named, and each should execute the contract. Where a seller's full, current name differs from that reflected in the Land Records, both names should be recited and the difference explained. For example, if due to marriage or divorce, a seller's name has changed since they acquired title to the property, their current name should be recited, followed by the words "formerly known as" and the record name. If a current owner holds title by virtue of an event not reflected in the Land Records—such as inheritance on the death of the last owner recited in the record title chain—this fact should be recited.

While a failure to include such recitals will have no legal effect—adverse or otherwise—on the transaction, including them will at least help to avoid confusion for someone reviewing the property's title, and may prevent an evidentiary dispute over whether a necessary party has signed the contract.

Similarly, all purchasers, regardless of whether they will be borrowers on a note should be recited on the contract of sale as a buyer.

The MR form calls for an identification of all parties involved in the sale transaction (including the listing broker, the listing broker's salespersons, the selling broker, and the selling broker's salespersons). Telephone numbers for each broker and agent and the license number of each and addresses of the parties, are included for ease in communication for giving notices and as a requirement of the TILA-RESPA Integrated Disclosures Law.

---

[22] Revision, dated October 2023 (hereinafter MR). This form is set forth in §2.76 of this chapter.

2. [§ 2.15] Individuals

Where individuals are parties, their precise names should be used wherever possible, including their full first names and either middle names or initials and their names should match their government issued identification (no nicknames or abbreviations unless a middle initial).

Where the buyer consists of more than one person or entity, it is recommended but not required that the contract state the tenancy by which they will own the property when they acquire it. Ordinarily, spouses hold title as tenants by the entirety; indeed, under Maryland law, a conveyance a married couple is presumed to be as tenants by the entirety unless the deed or other conveyancing documents provides that they are to hold as tenants in common, joint tenants, or in another manner.[23] In the case of conveyances to multiple persons or entities who are not spouses, the tenancy defaults to tenants in common unless the deed or other conveyancing document expressly provides that they will hold as joint tenants.[24] Thus, if the persons or entities constituting the buyer plan to hold title other than in accordance with the legal presumption, they should insure that the contract and resulting deed so provide.

To avoid confusion as to the respective interests, when married persons intend to create a joint tenancy with other persons, any references to marital status should be omitted from the contract of sale and the deed in order to leave no doubt as to the unity of interests among all of the parties creating the joint tenancy with a right of survivorship (unities of time, title, interest, and possession).

3. [§ 2.16] Decedent's estates

Decedent's estates are frequently sellers under contracts for the resale of existing residences, as the result of their former owners' death. Where an estate or a trust is a party, regardless of whether it is the buyer or seller, it should be correctly identified by reference to the decedent's name or the instrument by which the trust was created, plus the name(s) of the incumbent fiduciary. However, REAL PROP. § 2-122 validates a conveyance when real property is conveyed to a trust or to a decedent's estate without naming the trustee or the personal representative. The attorney should be sure that the requisite power exists for the estate or trust to enter into and perform its obligations under the contract, that the person signing is the personal representative of the estate or a trustee of the trust, or otherwise has the legal power to bind the estate or trust to the contract without third-party approval. If a trust is a party, the attorney should ascertain whether it still exists,

---

23 *See Columbian Carbon Co. v. Kight*, 207 Md. 203, 208, 114 A.2d 28 (1955).

24 REAL PROP. § 2-117.

and whether all required Orphans' Court or other approvals, if any, have been granted.

4. [§ 2.17] Corporations

Although it is less common for a corporation to be a party to a contract for the resale of an existing residence, where a corporation is a party, its state of organization should be inserted, and its continued existence and current good standing in that state should be verified. If the corporation was formed outside of Maryland, its qualification to do business in Maryland should be verified. Since the contract must be signed on the corporation's behalf by an individual, that person's authority to bind the corporation by their signature should be established. Where the signator is the corporation's president, such authority ordinarily may be presumed. Where the signator is another officer or not an officer at all, the source of their authority to bind the corporation should be recited in the contract, and confirmed by, for example, a corporate secretary's certificate reciting the adoption of directors' resolutions authorizing the person signing to bind the corporation by entering into the contract. If this technique is used, the resolutions should be set forth at length in the certificate, and be reviewed to ensure that they confer the authority to execute either this specific contract, or a range of documents broad enough to include this specific contract. If the resolutions do not identify the signator by name but merely by office or position, the secretary's certificate should include a recitation that the individual holds the office or position in question.

It is advised that the deed from the corporation, if not the contract of sale, contain a declaration that the conveyance is not a sale, lease, or transfer of all or substantially all of the assets of the corporation, in order to take advantage of the protective provisions of Real Prop. § 14-113.

5. [§ 2.18] Partnership

Similarly, although it is less common for a partnership to be a party to a contract for resale of an existing residence, where a general partnership or a limited partnership is a party, its state of organization should be inserted, and its continued existence and current good standing in that state should be verified.

(a) Limited partnerships

Where the partnership is a limited partnership, its certificate of limited partnership, with all amendments, should be obtained from the filing office where it was organized—the State Department of Assessments and Taxation (SDAT) for Maryland limited partnerships; usually the office of the secretary of state of the organizing jurisdiction for foreign limited partnerships—and its general partners identified *by reference to the certificate*. While under the Revised Uniform Limited Partnership Act, in force in Maryland, *any* general partner has the power to bind a limited partnership to a contract with a bona fide purchaser,[25] prudence suggests that, wherever possible, all general partners be required to sign on the partnership's behalf. It is not necessary that limited partners sign, except in those narrow cases where the Act requires their joinder in order to make effective any provisions which the Act requires to be consented to by the limited partners including for example, a confessed judgment clause where the general partners have not already been given the internal authority to confess judgment against the partnership.

(b) General partnerships

Unlike a limited partnership, a general partnership's existence does not depend on the filing of a certificate or other document with a public filing office, such as SDAT.[26]

However, under Corps. & Ass'ns § 9A-303(a), a general partnership may file a "statement of partnership authority," which "(m)ay state the authority, or limitations on the authority, of some or all of the partners to enter into other transactions on behalf of the partnership and any other matter." Section 9A-303(c) further provides that, unless cancelled, "a grant of authority contained in a filed statement of partnership authority is conclusive in favor of a person who gives value without knowledge to the contrary, so long as and to the extent that a limitation on that authority is not then contained in another filed statement." Thus, it is important when dealing with a general partnership to determine whether the partnership has filed any statements at SDAT, either evidencing or limiting the authority of some or all of the partners to bind the partnership to a real estate contract or conveyance. If the general partnership has not filed a statement of partnership authority, its partners may be ascertained only by reference to its (unfiled) partnership agreement or other organizing document, *if any* (keeping in mind that a *general* partnership may be created by either an oral or a written agreement). While, as with a limited partnership, any partner in a general partnership that holds title in the partnership name ordinarily has the power to bind the partnership to a contract,[27] prudence again dictates that, wherever possible, all partners be required to sign on the partnership's behalf. This is particularly important in the case of an *oral* general partnership since, if a contract dispute arises, it may be difficult to establish in the absence of a written agreement whether a partnership even exists or, if so, whether the purported

25 Md. Code Ann., Corporations and Associations §§ 9A-302, 10-108, and 10-403(a) (hereinafter Corps. & Ass'ns §).

26 This is true even for limited liability partnerships, which are merely general partnerships (created by oral or written agreement) which have elected limited liability partnership status by filing a certificate of limited liability partnership with SDAT pursuant to Corps. & Ass'ns § 9A-1001`.

27 Corps. & Ass'ns § 9A-302.

signatory "partner" is in fact a partner. Thus, where a general partnership is a party, its partners must be carefully identified and, if fewer than all are signatories, a statement or representation as to the signing partners' authority to bind the partnership should be included and verified for accuracy.

6. *[§ 2.19] Limited liability companies*

Where a limited liability company (LLC) is a party, its state of organization should be inserted, and its continued existence and current good standing in that state should be verified. Since the contract must be signed on the LLC's behalf by an individual, that person's authority to bind the LLC by their signature should be established. In Maryland, an LLC is formed by filing articles of organization with SDAT.[28] Unless such agency relationship is expressly disclaimed in its articles of organization, by statute each member of an LLC is the LLC's agent for the purpose of its business,[29] including signing contracts to buy and sell real property for the LLC. However, even where such disclaimer has not been made, prudence again dictates that, wherever possible, all members be required to sign on the LLC's behalf.

7. *[§ 2.20] Powers of attorney; agencies*

Occasionally, a party's joinder in a contract will be effected by another person using a power of attorney. In such cases, not only must the contract contain the information concerning the party itself which is discussed in §§ 2.**14**–2.**19** of this chapter, but the power of attorney should be reviewed to determine:

- that it meets all statutory requirements as dictated in Md. Code Ann., Estates and Trusts §17-1-101 through §17-204;
- that it authorizes the attorney-in-fact to join in and perform under the contract;
- that it is still in effect and has not been revoked;
- that the person granting the power is alive when the power is exercised; and
- that, in the event of such person's disability, the requisite provisions allowing the power to survive the disability have been included either expressly, or pursuant to Md. Code Ann., Estates and Trusts § 13-601 (2022), for Maryland powers of attorney executed on or after Jan. 1, 2000.

If the deed conveying the property pursuant to the contract is to be signed (by grantor or grantee) using a power of attorney, the power of attorney must be signed

---

28 Corps. & Ass'ns § 4A-202(b)*; see also* Corps. & Ass'ns §§ 4A-101–4A-1103.

29 Corps. & Ass'ns § 4A-401(a).

and acknowledged in the same manner as the deed and recorded with or before recordation of the deed.[30]

Similarly, where a party's joinder in or performance under a contract is to be effected by an agent, the attorney must review the agency agreement before execution to verify that the relationship continues to exist, and that it is broad enough to include entry into the contract.

Where the attorney-in-fact or agent is an entity rather than an individual, the information discussed in §§ 2.**14**–2.**19** of this chapter must be obtained for the entity and the individual(s) signing on its behalf.

8. [§ 2.21] All signators

All of the above presumes an absence of fraud or mistaken identity. When in doubt as to whether the person signing is whom they are supposed to be, the attorney should require verification and, if appropriate, notarization. Keep in mind that, in the absence of an overriding equitable principle such as estoppel or apparent authority, neither seller nor buyer will be bound by a forged signature or, in the case of an entity, by even the genuine signature of a person lacking statutory, contractual, or organizational authority to bind the entity.

The above also presumes the legal competence of the signator. Where the signator is a minor or is legally incompetent, the contract will be void or voidable as a matter of law.[31]

C. Date of Contract

1. [§ 2.22] Generally

The contract should bear a date. The date is evidence (although not *conclusive* evidence) of when the contract became effective, a fact which would be important for, among other reasons, establishing the relative priority of buyer's rights as against judgment creditors of seller and other persons having competing claims to the property.

One or both parties' obligations under a contract of sale often are expressly conditioned on the satisfaction of certain conditions precedent (e.g., financing, home inspection, or the sale of buyer's own residence) within a stated number of days

---

30 Real Prop. § 4-107(a). However, Real Prop. § 4-107(b) permits a power of attorney to be recorded after the deed executed by the purported attorney-in-fact. While this section has been amended to permit the recording of an effective power of attorney after the recording of the deed executed under the authority of a post-recorded power of attorney, the circumstances permitting this are limited. Reliance on this procedure is not recommended.

31 *Potter v. Musick*, 247 Md. 39, 230 A.2d 91 (1967).

after the date of the contract. For this reason, it is important not only that the contract be dated, but that the date be the *correct* date. If the party signing the contract first (typically the buyer) is required to take some action within a period beginning on the contract date, it will want the contract to be dated, not as of the date on which the first party signs it, but as of the date on which the other party signs *and delivers* it back to the first party. This is so that the first party will not lose the benefit of the time elapsing before it receives the fully signed contract. For example, the contract may give buyer the right to terminate the contract if not satisfied with the results of an inspection of the residence to be made within seven days after the contract date. If the contract is dated when buyer signs and delivers it to seller and is not ultimately signed and returned by seller to buyer for another five days, buyer is left with a two-day period—and not the bargained-for seven-day period—within which to accomplish the inspection. Please beware, the MR contract does not require delivery to be a component of acceptance.

2. [§ 2.23] MR form

Paragraph 1 of the MR form,[32] entitled "Date of Offer," contains a blank space into which the date of the initiating party's (usually the buyer's) offer to sell or purchase is to be inserted. At the end of the form, next to the spaces for each party's signature, is a line designated "Date" in which the date of that party's execution of the contract is to be inserted. The last line of the contract is entitled "Date of Acceptance," into which is inserted (presumably) the date on which the final version of the contract, including all modifications made to the initial offer, is signed by both parties. Other provisions of the MR form and the REB forms refer, variously, to either "the date of this Contract" or "the date of execution of this Contract by all parties. In MR's 2022 MR contract update they removed the delivery component from the "acceptance" definition. Therefore, the "date of this contract," date of execution" and "date of contract acceptance" are all the same date. It is imperative that communication is made that the contract has been executed and that the timeline began upon execution for all contingencies

D. [§ 2.24] Description of Property—Generally

Often the most difficult clause to prepare is that describing the property. A proper description includes several elements, including (a) a physical description of the land and improvements being sold, (b) an identification of the legal estate being sold, and (c) a recitation of the appurtenances, fixtures, and personal property included in the sale.

---

32 *See* § 2.**76**

Property descriptions are frequently the subject of litigation. Thus, every effort should be made to include the fullest and most accurate description possible.[33] To do this, the attorney drafting or reviewing the contract must first ascertain from the client precisely what is being bought and sold. This task may not be as easily accomplished as it would seem at first blush, particularly if the client is the buyer (who at this stage typically is uncertain about the property's physical and legal details).

E. Description of Property—Land

1. [§ 2.25] Generally

(a) Descriptive techniques

It is crucial that the contract accurately describe the land being sold. To begin with, and as already noted, the contract will not be enforceable if it does not identify the land "with reasonable certainty."[34] However, it is self-evident that in describing the land, the draftsman should satisfy a stricter standard than mere enforceability. The description should be accurate enough to avoid *any* misunderstanding about what land *is* being sold, and what is *not*. If the property in question is an assemblage of more than one parcel (i.e., an additional side or rear yard is acquired after the purchase of the dwelling and original lot), it should be expressly stated that the property to be conveyed consists of more than one tract. Such information will help to ensure that proper orders can be placed for the necessary title abstracts.

Land may be described using any one of several different devices.

(i) Metes-and-Bounds description

The contract may employ a metes-and-bounds description physically attached as an exhibit. Often, such a description may be obtained from the recorded deed to the seller, or from the seller's own title policy, if available. If such a description is used, care must be taken that the described boundaries of the land are (and remain) accurate.

If, as is sometimes the case, a metes-and-bounds description is legally accurate (that is, it is consistent with the record chain of title), but outdated (in that, for example, it recites natural features or other monuments which are difficult to locate or no longer exist), the parties should consider providing in the contract for replacement of the old description with a new one prepared by a registered professional engineer or land surveyor based on a modern boundary survey. If this approach is

---

33 *See, e.g., Lucas v. Wagner*, 269 Md. 188, 192, 304 A.2d 828, 830 (1973); *Boyd v. Mercantile Safe Deposit & Trust Co.*, 28 Md. App. 18, 23, 344 A.2d 148, 152 (1975).

34 *See* § 2.**2** of this chapter.

chosen, the contract should set forth a mechanism for obtaining approval or verification of the accuracy of the new description, so that the parties can be satisfied that it describes the same property as that set forth in the old description appended to the contract. The contract also should specify which party bears the expense of obtaining the new boundary survey. Buyer should have the right to require that the new description be satisfactory to its title insurer, whose policy will incorporate the new description.

An inherent potential problem with a metes-and-bound description is that it may have been prepared independently of the descriptions of adjoining properties, and hence may be (or at least *appear* to be) inconsistent with them. Such inconsistencies may result in real or apparent *overlaps* between adjoining descriptions (calling into question the ownership of the land lying within both descriptions), or real or apparent *strips* or *gores*, i.e., land lying between the two descriptions but not included in either (calling into question the ownership of the strip or gore).

(ii) Plat

The contract may identify the land by coloring, hatching, or other special marking on an attached plat, or by reference to a label for the land shown on an attached plat. The plat may be one of several types, having differing legal effects: it may be a formal, recorded subdivision plat (which, as a matter of law, actually *creates* the boundaries of the lots or parcels shown on it), or a *de facto* subdivision plat which, having been used for descriptive purposes in a deed or other document conveying part of a larger tract, similarly creates as a matter of law some or all of the boundaries of the parcels conveyed by reference to the plat. Alternately, the plat may be merely a descriptive plat, such as a tax map, which purports to show the existing boundaries of the parcels shown on it but does not itself create those boundaries (they having already been created in some other manner, such as a prior conveyance).

As with a metes-and-bounds description, care must be taken that the boundaries of the land as shown on the plat are accurate. Where a plat is used to create the boundaries between two or more adjacent parcels (even using metes and bounds set forth on the plat), the problem of overlaps, strips, or gores discussed above will not arise, since by definition the adjacent parcels will have consistent boundaries. Where the plat merely sets forth the boundaries of parcels created in another manner, it is possible for such descriptions to be inconsistent with each other. The lawyer preparing or reviewing a contract using a plat description should take care to ascertain which type of plat it is.

Although sometimes used as an expedient, real property tax plats, purporting to show the land being sold as a particular tax parcel, are a poor basis for descriptions. They are not prepared using the degree of detail called for by a modern legal description. Moreover, they are updated only periodically, and therefore may not even represent the current boundaries. If a tax plat must be used, the attorney should be certain to couple the reference to the plat with a provision reciting that the contract covers all property owned by seller within the area in question (or, if that is not the case, describing in as much detail as is possible what portion of the tax parcel is being sold, and what is not). As with outdated metes-and-bounds descriptions, provision should be made for replacement of the tax plat with a more precise description, which will be needed in any event for use in the actual deed of conveyance.

(iii) Incorporation by reference

The contract may identify the land by incorporating by reference a description found in *another* document or plat. When this technique is used, the document or plat referred to *must* either be physically attached to the contract as an exhibit or recorded among the Land Records or in another public record, and its correct record reference recited in the contract description. For example, a contract may identify the land as "all of that land which, by a deed dated Oct. 20, 1945, and recorded among the Land Records of Baltimore County, Maryland in Liber 1234 at folios 567 *et seq*., was conveyed by Cranston Snord to Ellwood Bloat," the present seller. Descriptions found in documents and plats which are *neither* attached as exhibits, *nor* recorded, should not be incorporated by reference, since later they may be difficult or impossible to locate or identify with certainty. Of course, where a description is incorporated by reference, the same care must be taken to verify its accuracy as when it is physically attached.

(iv) Recital (Being Clause)

Many deeds contain a description that essentially is a recital of a prior deed. There may be a number of deeds in a chain of title that merely recite a prior deed as a legal description. It may be necessary to go back a substantial period of time in the chain of title to find a usable metes-and-bounds description to bring forward.

(b) What is being described

While there usually is little confusion about which house is involved in a sale, misunderstandings frequently arise over the boundaries of the land being sold with it. For example, where seller owns other land adjacent to or in the vicinity of the land which it intends to sell, such disputes occasionally concern whether this other land is also included in the contract.[35] Thus, it is important that the would-be seller and buyer together walk the boundaries of the land being sold in order to identify them, and (where only part of seller's land is being sold) to agree on any new boundaries to be created in the transaction.

---

[35] *See Boyd v. Mercantile Safe Deposit & Trust Co.*, 28 Md. App. 18, 344 A.2d 148 (1975).

These perceived or agreed-upon boundaries should be consistent with the contract description. A *caveat* is warranted here: even where there is no question about whether all of seller's land is included in the sale, and the true legal boundaries of the land to which seller has record title, as set forth in the chain of title found in the Land Records and other public records, are effectively incontrovertible (such as where the land consists of a lot defined by a modern recorded subdivision plat), such legal boundaries may differ materially from what, to the prospective purchaser, they *appear* to be when viewed "in the field." Often, this occurs because the *apparent* boundaries are demarked by fences, hedges, and other physical barriers, which on closer scrutiny turn out to be located not on the actual boundary but somewhere either inside or even outside the actual boundary. Since the attorney or other reviewer of the record title rarely has occasion to compare the property's record description with its apparent boundaries, such discrepancies often go undiscovered until after closing. If ignored long enough, occasionally such discrepancies give rise to a claim of title by a neighboring landowner based upon adverse possession.

Thus, regardless of the device used to describe the property, the careful attorney will make certain that the contract description of the underlying land is consistent with what the client believes is being sold from having visited the property. Where significant inconsistencies appear, the attorney should consider requiring a title survey to be prepared by a licensed engineer or surveyor, which will locate the "record" boundaries in relation to survey monuments, fences, plantings, and other improvements on the ground.

2. *[§ 2.26] Property in established subdivision*

In describing a residence located in a subdivision for which a subdivision plat is recorded, it is always prudent to use the lot and block number, if any, for each lot being sold, as shown on the recorded subdivision plat. The plat should in turn be identified by its record reference among the Land Records. A reference to the lot number often is included on the listing agreement between the broker and seller, although this should be verified.

It is common for property in an established residential subdivision to be described in a contract by its street address. Although this may be the only description readily available when the contract is being prepared, it may be deficient. For example, if the house in question is located on a so-called "double lot" (i.e., two or more contiguous lots owned by the same person, improved by a single house, and used as a single residence), each lot typically will have been assigned its own, individual street address. Unless all such addresses are listed in the description, a question may arise as to whether all of these lots are included in the sale.

Age of a recorded subdivision plat is no bar to its legality or usefulness. Various towns, cities, and villages were laid out in lots on plats recorded in colonial times or shortly thereafter, and the references to the lots shown on those plats are used today.

3. [§ 2.27] Property not in established subdivision

Where the property is not in an established subdivision, a subdivision plat description will not be available, and therefore one of the other methods discussed above must be used to describe the property. MARYLAND ANN. CODE, LAND USE § 5-301 makes it illegal, with some exceptions, to even negotiate to sell real property that is subdivided from a larger tract of land prior to the recording of a properly approved subdivision plat, even if metes and bounds are used to describe the subdivided parcel. Where the land is not being sold in gross, so that its precise acreage is material to the sale, the contract should recite such acreage (to the nearest hundredth or thousandth acre, if necessary), and should provide for its verification by a survey conducted by a civil engineer or surveyor. This is particularly important where the purchase price is a function of the property's area.

A note of caution is warranted in dealing with residences outside of established subdivisions. The City of Baltimore and the metropolitan counties each prohibit the sale of less than all of an entire tract or parcel of land owned by the same person without first complying with that jurisdiction's subdivision regulations. Unless such sale falls within an exemption allowed by the regulations, compliance normally will entail obtaining approval (by the county itself and, sometimes, by state agencies) of a subdivision plat establishing the land being sold as a separate, entire subdivision lot or parcel for purposes of the regulations. In many cases, obtaining such approval will necessitate the landowner's entry into public works agreements for the installation of public roads, water mains, and sanitary sewer lines, setting aside of open space areas, and compliance with wetlands, reforestation, and other governmental regulations.

Since compliance with subdivision regulations—whatever that may entail—is mandatory in these jurisdictions and will usually prove to be expensive and time-consuming, a seller contemplating the sale of a *portion* of its parcel should satisfy itself in this regard before becoming obligated to make the conveyance. Similarly, a prospective buyer of part of a parcel should assure itself that the subdivision regulations will have been complied with before the title is conveyed at settlement, not only to protect the buyer itself, but because lenders and future purchasers may balk at accepting title to an illegally subdivided lot.

While seller will typically take the lead in obtaining plat approval (and must, as the landowner, in any case sign the proposed plat and approval application for them to be effective), sometimes buyer will undertake this responsibility. Where subdivision compliance is required, it is common for a contract to be signed under which *both* seller's and buyer's obligations to close are conditioned on compliance.

The contract purchaser may be required to sign the prospective subdivision plat in order to reflect all interests in the property to be subdivided.

Once a subdivision lot is created, the subdivision regulations will restrict how it can be improved. In particular, setback requirements under the regulations typically prohibit the construction of a house closer than a specified distance from the lot's boundaries.

Thus, if the real property being sold under a contract consists of part of a larger tract which must, therefore, be legally subdivided, (a) recordation of the approved subdivision plat should be a condition precedent to both buyer's and seller's obligations to close, and (b) the parties should ensure that the boundaries and configuration of the proposed subdivision lot are such that any house existing or intended to be placed thereon will be located outside of the setback areas. Each party should have the right to approve any covenants or other restrictions imposed on the use of the lot through the subdivision process.

F. [§ 2.28] Description of Property—Seller's Estate

In addition to physically describing the property, the contract should identify the nature of the seller's estate.[36] If the property is owned in fee simple, the contract should include the words "fee simple."

If the property is subject to a ground rent, the contract should recite that a *leasehold* estate is being sold, identify the ground lease by date and record reference, and recite the amount of the rent. A failure to indicate clearly that the property is subject to a ground rent may force seller to redeem the ground rent (assuming it is redeemable) in order to convey the quality of the title called for by the contract, and thereby avoid defaulting. Even if the rent is nominal, a leasehold title does not satisfy a requirement of good and merchantable fee simple title. In any event, as noted in § 2.**49** of this chapter, the Real Property Article requires that a contract for the sale of ground leased property make certain disclosures to buyer concerning the existence of the ground lease and the fee owner's rights under it and that the property may be redeemed

The MR form contains blank spaces to be checked, to indicate whether a fee simple or a leasehold is being sold, and also sets forth the required statutory language concerning leaseholds on a separate Ground Rent Addendum.

G. [§ 2.29] Description of Property—Improvements

Most resale contracts devote little, if any, effort toward describing the improvements being sold, instead referring to them only generically as "the improvements

---

[36] Issues concerning the *quality* of seller's title to their estate are discussed in §§ 2.**35**–2.**38** of this chapter.

thereon," after describing the underlying land. This approach is taken by the MR form. In most cases, this will be sufficient, since—absent any agreement to the contrary by the parties—a sale of land will automatically include any improvements on the land. For this reason, if the parties agree that any improvements—such as a storage shed or "built in" play equipment—are *not* to be included in the sale, they should so state in the contract, describing the excluded improvements in enough detail to prevent any confusion about what is being excluded.

As discussed in § 2.**46** of this chapter, there are generally no implied warranties in the sale of residences (except for builder sales of new homes) and, as a result, such improvements are sold "as is" unless the parties otherwise agree. For this reason, it would seem that the parties could only risk controversy by attempting to describe, in any meaningful detail, the improvements being sold. However, the opposite approach should be taken in dealing with fixtures, as is discussed below.

H. [§ 2.30] Description of Property—Fixtures and Personal Property

The word "fixture" is a term of art referring only to those items physically attached to land or improvements and falling within the legal definition of a "fixture."[37] Thus, anything which is legally a fixture is—unless the contract provides otherwise—automatically *included* in the sale and, therefore, may not be retained by seller. Items not part of the improvements or fixtures are mere personal property, and therefore are automatically *excluded* from a sale of real property unless identified and specifically included.

Unfortunately, in many cases the draftsman cannot be certain that an item is legally a fixture.[38] Where such uncertainty exists, the contract should make clear whether or not the item is included in the sale. The lists of included and excluded items should be as comprehensive as is necessary to eliminate misunderstanding.

In recognition of the need for certainty in dealing with these questions, MR has created the Inclusions/Exclusions, Leased Items & Utilities addendum which includes a helpful "laundry list" of items that may be included. However, buyers and sellers should be advised to inspect the property carefully, and to compile their own lists of that personal property which they desire to be included or excluded. Among the items commonly found in the lists of included or excluded items are screens, storm windows and doors, security systems, TV mounts, cabinet doors, rugs, carpets, drapes, curtains, curtain rods, built-in bookshelves, appliances,

---

[37] *See* Shale D. Stiller, *The Maryland Law of Fixtures*, 25 MD. L. REV. 21 (1965); *see also Anderson v. Perpetual Bldg. & Loan Ass'n*, 172 Md. 94, 97, 190 A. 747, 749 (1937); *Chambco v. Urban Masonry Corp.*, 101 Md. App. 664, 647 A.2d 1284 (1994), *vacated, remanded*, 338 Md. 417, 659 A.2d 297 (1995); *In re Reese*, 194 B.R. 782, 789 n.2 (Bankr. D. Md. 1996).

[38] For example, many kitchen appliances technically are not fixtures.

lighting fixtures, ovens, refrigerators, washers, dryers, window air-conditioners, fireplace equipment, and outdoor sheds and shrubbery.

Buyer will want to require seller (1) to remove from the real property at or before closing all personal property not included in the sale, (2) to leave the dwelling "broom clean," vacant and (3) as a condition to removal, to repair any damage to the dwelling caused by the removal of fixtures or personal property. Many disputes have developed at (or shortly after) closing over the existence of holes and unpainted areas left as a result of removal of bookshelves, built-ins and carpets, or seller's failure to remove unwanted furniture or appliances when vacating the house.

I. Description of Property—Appurtenances

1. [§ 2.31] Generally

A standard contract description of the land should be followed by the words "together with all appurtenances and fixtures belonging thereto." Although the term "appurtenances" will generally include seller's rights to alleys, land within the beds of adjacent public roads,[39] and the benefit of any easements or other rights encumbering adjacent properties, specific reference thereto is advisable.

2. [§ 2.32] Private rights-of-way and other easements

Special care must be taken in describing a property to which pedestrian or vehicular access is by a private right-of-way or other easement. Buyer's attorney should confirm the adequacy of the legal document creating such easement, and of the state of seller's title to the easement. The latter, done correctly, requires that the title to the easement area (that is, the land—owned by a third party in most cases—on which the private roadway is located) be examined in the same manner as is the title to the residence itself, and that buyer's title policy insure buyer's rights in and to the easement. The same degree of care should be used in reviewing the legal description of the easement area as is used for the description of the land being sold in fee simple.

Some subdivisions contain one or more "flag lots," which include a narrow strip of land running between the main part of the lot and a public street. While in some cases this strip is wide enough to contain the lot's driveway, in other cases it is by itself too narrow for this purpose, and must be combined with contiguous, parallel strips owned by one or more adjacent lot owners to form a single, shared private driveway. Unless, for each such lot, a satisfactory easement for access is established by a recorded instrument over those strips within the shared driveway which are part of the other lots, the first lot owner's right to use the *full* width of the private

---

[39] A statutory presumption concerning the conveyance of title to adjoining public roadbeds is created by REAL PROP. § 2-114.

roadway may be subject to challenge, a fact which, among other problems, could cause the lot to be unfinanceable. The buyer of such a lot should make sure that satisfactory arrangements have been made for common maintenance of these private roads. The contract of sale should specifically provide, as a part of the property description, that access will be available over a private roadway of specified width, with provisions for joint maintenance.

Occasionally, a new easement for access must be created as part of the sale transaction. This occurs frequently when the land being sold is only part of a larger tract owned by seller, the balance of which seller is retaining. Regardless of whether the new easement is to benefit the land being *sold* to buyer (and, thus, will cross seller's remaining land), or is to benefit the land being *retained* by seller (and, thus, will cross the land being sold to buyer), the parties should agree in detail on the boundaries of the easement area, and on the form and substance of the document which is to create and govern such easement and any accompanying maintenance and repair obligations. The owner of the land to be burdened by the easement should consider retaining the right to relocate the easement, if necessary to accommodate future building on the burdened land. The parties should take the same degree of care in dealing with the title to the land to be burdened by a new easement as is described above with respect to pre-existing easements. In particular, the party to be benefited by the new easement will want to require that all mortgagees and other lienholders on the burdened land subordinate their liens to the easement, to avoid having it extinguished if the mortgage or other lien is subsequently foreclosed upon.

Where the property depends on an easement over adjoining property for a private septic system, private water line, or other nonpublic utility service, the same degree of care should be used in reviewing the documents creating such easement as is used in reviewing those creating an access easement.

J. Purchase Price

1. [§ 2.33] Amount

The contract must accurately state the purchase price. Indeed, as noted in § **2.2** of this chapter, a contract in which the price cannot be ascertained is unenforceable. In most residential sale transactions this is easily accomplished, since the price is a set, fixed amount. However, occasionally it is not a set amount, but is a function of a stated formula. For example, the parties may agree that the purchase price for an unsurveyed parcel is in an amount "per acre." In such cases, the contract should state the formula accurately and precisely, and require that (a) the acreage be determined and certified, to a stated fraction of an acre (usually the nearest 100th or 1,000th), by an agreed-upon surveyor or civil engineer, and within a specified period after the contract is entered into, and (b) once the acreage is calculated, the parties confirm the exact price by a written supplemental agreement. Although not required by law, to avoid any error the purchase price should be stated both in words and numerically.

Occasionally, the parties will agree that the purchase price will be increased by an "interest" factor applied to some or all of the period between contract signing and closing. Such agreements frequently are made after the contract is signed, when buyer discovers that it will not be prepared to settle within the closing period specified in the contract, and the parties agree on an extension. In other cases, the parties anticipate when signing the contract that an extension may be needed for various reasons and agree that buyer and/or seller may have this election. In such cases, the wise seller will ask for the price to be increased during the extension period, to compensate for the loss of use of the purchase money which seller would have received had closing been held as scheduled, and for the additional interest (but not principal), real property taxes, and other expenses which seller is required to pay on its own financing during the extension period. If the parties agree on such an increase, the contract or contract amendment setting this forth should specify the rate at which interest is calculated, whether it is to compound and, if so, the frequency of compounding.

Sometimes, the parties agree that furniture, appliances, and other items of personal property are to be included in the sale. If these have significant value or otherwise materially increase the purchase price, they should consider assigning a separate purchase price to them, rather than including the consideration for them in the purchase price for the real property. Not only will this reduce the transfer and documentary stamp taxes to be paid on recordation of the deed (since these taxes are based only on the price paid for the *real property*), but it will tend to prevent the amount paid for the personalty from being considered by the real property tax assessor, who may be counted on to give significant weight to the real property purchase price when next assessing the property.[40]

2. [§ 2.34] Manner of payment

The contract must specify the time and manner in which the purchase price is to be paid. Typically, this will involve providing for an initial deposit made contemporaneously with contract signing, with the balance to be paid "in cash" at settlement.

---

[40] On the other hand, the Maryland sales tax probably applies to the sale of the personalty. *See* MD. CODE ANN., TAX-GENERAL §§ 11-101–11-108 (2022) (hereinafter TAX-GEN. §).

(a) Deposit

(i) Generally

As with the amount of the purchase price, whether there is to be a deposit and, if so, its amount, who is to hold it, the terms under which it is to be held, and whether it will be forfeited as liquidated damages on a buyer default, are fully negotiable. As between buyer and seller in residential resale transactions, occasional broker assertions to the contrary notwithstanding, the parties are free to negotiate whatever terms will satisfy them.[41]

There is no such thing as a "standard" deposit amount or percentage, although deposits generally are larger where purchase prices are larger. As houses have become more expensive, the former custom of a requiring a deposit of 10% of the purchase price has generally been abandoned. The broker usually will seek a deposit large enough to cover the broker's commission, since in *most* cases the broker is entitled (under its separate listing agreement with seller, by which buyer is not bound) to retain one-half of any forfeited deposit.[42] Seller will want a deposit large enough that the prospect of its forfeiture will tend to deter buyer from failing to honor the contract.

If buyer is to deliver a deposit or a series of deposits before closing, the contract should specify the amount, time, and manner of payment of each deposit installment, and should make clear that the deposit is to be delivered to or retained by seller at closing in partial payment of the purchase price.

(ii) Who holds the deposit?

The broker is a convenient party to act as the escrow agent, and the broker's actions with regard to the deposit are governed by statute.[43] However, contrary to popular belief, the law does not require that the broker hold the deposit, and the parties are free to agree that it may be held by any person, including occasionally seller itself (although a buyer should consent to this only reluctantly). Current practice dictates the title company as a neutral party hold the earnest money deposit and a separate escrow agreement is executed.[44]

(iii) In Escrow

Regardless of who holds the deposit, the contract should require it to be held in escrow. Both parties will wish to require that the funds be placed in an escrow

---

41 However, if the parties follow the usual practice of allowing the selling broker to hold the deposit, the broker itself will be subject to statutory restrictions on dealing with deposit monies.

42 *But see* **§ 2.62** of this chapter.

43 MD. CODE ANN., BUSINESS OCCUPATIONS AND PROFESSIONS §§ 17-501–17-540 (2018 & Supp. 2022)

44 MD. CODE ANN, REAL PROPERTY § 10-802

account separate from the escrow holder's own funds, in order to insulate the deposit from the holder's creditors, and to assure prompt payment to one party or the other, if a stated condition is not satisfied or the other party defaults.

Occasionally, an escrow holder does not promptly deposit buyer's check representing payment of the deposit, thereby delaying the accrual of deposit interest (if any) and enabling buyer to gain leverage by stopping payment on its check if a subsequent dispute arises under the contract. Although this failure may render the escrow holder liable for the amount of the deposit and any lost deposit interest, seller should avoid the problem by making sure that the check is promptly negotiated.

The contract should also provide for those circumstances under which the deposit is to be returned to buyer (such as failure of a stated condition to be satisfied, or a default by seller) or delivered to seller (such as a default by buyer).[45] Paragraph 9 of the MR form provides that the disbursement of deposit monies is to be made in accordance with a "release of deposit agreement" to be signed by buyer and seller. The MR form contemplates that in the event the release is not signed, the broker may utilize the provisions of BUS. OCC. & PROF. § 17-505(b)(1). In addition, if the deposit is not held by a Maryland licensed real estate broker, then the MR form dictates that the parties will execute a separate written Escrow Agreement that complies with REAL PROP. § 10-802.

(iv) Interest on deposit

If the deposit is large enough or will be held for a long enough period, the parties should consider requiring that the escrow account bear interest. In such event, the contract should indicate which party receives the interest (or a credit therefor) and when the deposit is paid to seller or buyer—either at closing or on termination of the agreement before closing due to failure of satisfaction of a condition to closing, or a default by seller or buyer, or for any other reason.

Keep in mind that, when interest rates are low, deposits small, and pre-closing periods short, the amount of interest ultimately derived will typically be too small to justify investing any significant time or effort in negotiating these deposit interest terms.

(b) Balance

The contract should also set forth the manner of payment of the balance of the purchase price. Except if and to the extent that seller agrees to defer its receipt of some or all of the purchase money until after closing (by accepting a secured or unsecured promissory note from buyer), the contract should require this entire balance to be paid in cash or other current funds—i.e., wired funds or a certified

---

45 In that regard, see the discussion concerning defaults, in §§ **2.62** and **2.63** of this chapter.

check—at closing. This is true regardless of whether buyer's *source* of some or all of such cash is buyer's own bank account, or a bank or other third-party lender.

Some contract forms state that at closing a specified portion of the purchase money will be paid "out of mortgage proceeds." Such a clause may have the effect of making the financing condition applicable until closing rather than merely until buyer has received and accepted a loan commitment, and thereby cause a serious problem for seller, who may believe that the financing condition has long since been satisfied or waived by buyer.

The practice in Maryland is for the title company to disburse at the settlement table or wire the proceeds after closing and once funding authorization is provided by the lender if there is one. In doing so, these companies take the statistically slight risk that, when the deed is to be recorded, seller's title will turn out to have been subjected to a new lien or encumbrance after the title company's most recent search was completed.

(c) Seller financing

Where seller agrees to take back financing for all or part of the purchase money, the contract should set forth the financing terms. In particular, the parties should agree on the amount being financed, the rate or rates of interest to be earned, whether interest compounds and, if so, how often, the dates and amounts on which principal and interest payments are to be made, whether (as is typical) the debt is to be secured by a purchase money mortgage or deed of trust covering the property being sold and, if so, whether it is to be a first, or a subordinate, mortgage or deed of trust. In a residential deal, if a lender desires to preclude the borrower from prepaying the debt in whole or in part, the documents must so provide, since in Maryland a borrower has the right to prepay unless the note or other loan documents expressly provide to the contrary.[46] If buyer intends to borrow additional money from a bank to finance any of the purchase money to be paid in cash at closing, or (by a loan made either at closing or at some point thereafter) to construct new or additional improvements on the property before the purchase money debt is repaid, the contract and resulting loan documents should require seller to subordinate the lien of its purchase money mortgage to that of the new lender's mortgage or deed of trust, since the new lender can be expected to insist on a *first* lien as a condition to making its loan. If possible, the forms of purchase money note and deed of trust, or mortgage, covering buyer's debt to seller should be negotiated with the contract and attached as exhibits. MR has an addendum that effectuates the above suggestions.

---

46 Md. Code Ann., Commercial Law II § 12-126 (2013 & Supp. 2022).

K. Title

1. [§ 2.35] Generally

The title clause is one of the most important in the contract. Its importance follows from the simple but often overlooked fact that, technically, what is being bought and sold is not land, improvements, fixtures, and appurtenances themselves, but the *title* to a specified *estate* in them. The title clause defines the *quality* of such title to be conveyed by buyer to seller pursuant to the contract. If seller conveys to buyer title having the prescribed quality, seller will have satisfied their principal obligation under the contract. If seller does not or cannot, seller will be in default.

Most contracts require, at the least, that the title be "marketable" or (a synonym) "merchantable."[47] The Supreme Court of Maryland, formerly the Court of Appeals of Maryland, has held that a "marketable title" is "one which a reasonable purchaser, who is well informed as to the facts and their legal bearings, and ready and willing to perform their contract, would be willing to accept in the exercise of that prudence which businessmen ordinarily use in such transactions."[48]

The concept of marketability really addresses two distinct but related issues: First, does seller actually own (is seller *seized* of) title to the fee simple or other estate in the property which is being sold? That is, does seller in fact hold a valid position in the chain of title to the property and, if so, is that position complete and free of defects which would justify reasonable doubt that third parties hold rights inconsistent with and paramount to those which the contract purports to sell to buyer? In this regard, the Supreme Court of Maryland has held that, as long as seller's position is free of reasonable doubt, a marketable title need not be free from all conceivable technical criticism.[49]

Second, even if seller's ownership of the estate being sold is not questionable, is such title free of liens, covenants, or other encumbrances? In Maryland, a title which is not free of encumbrances is, as a matter of law, not a "marketable" title.[50]

Most buyers would, reasonably enough, insist that their sellers be the unequivocal owners of the titles which they have contracted to sell. Not unexpectedly, the typical contract title clause is no exception in this regard.

---

[47] In many states there is a distinction between "merchantable title" and "marketable title," but in Maryland the terms are synonymous. *Garner v. Union Trust Co.*, 185 Md. 386, 389, 45 A.2d 106, 108 (1945).

[48] *Schlosser v. Creamer*, 263 Md. 583, 588–89, 284 A.2d 220, 223 (1971).

[49] *New Freedom Corp. v. Brown*, 260 Md. 383, 272 A.2d 401 (1971); *Garner v. Union Trust Co.*, 185 Md. 386 (1945).

[50] *Suburban Garden Farm Homes Corp. v. Adams*, 171 Md. 212, 188 A. 808 (1937); *Fraidin v. State*, 85 Md. App. 231, 583 A.2d 1065 (1991).

On the other hand, few titles are absolutely free of encumbrances; most—and especially those to properties in residential subdivisions—are encumbered at the least by one or more utility easements, and perhaps by architectural or use covenants as well. For this reason, a title clause covering Maryland real property which merely requires the title to be "marketable" without recognizing the likelihood that such encumbrances exist would, in most cases, obligate seller to do the impossible—to deliver title in a state which seller cannot deliver.

The well-drafted title clause attempts to accommodate this reality by taking one of several approaches. The contract may permit seller to convey an otherwise marketable title which is subject to and only to a prescribed list of actual, identified encumbrances which buyer has accepted before signing the contract. More commonly, when such a list is not known when the contract is being signed, the contract will allow seller to convey subject to certain described *types* of encumbrances which, in a generic sense, are acceptable to buyer.[51] Sometimes these approaches are combined, by permitting seller to convey subject both to a specific list of encumbrances, and to other, unspecified encumbrances falling within the permitted generic types; obviously, the best of both worlds for a seller.

(a) "Specific list" approach

Where the "specific list" approach is used, buyer and buyer's attorney should review in advance a title insurance commitment covering the property, to satisfy themselves that seller in fact has otherwise marketable title and will have the ability at closing to convey it in the state required by the contract. They also should review the actual documents listed as encumbrances in the commitment before agreeing to include them on the contract list. This ensures that the encumbrances to be included are acceptable, and that seller will have the ability at or before closing to obtain the release or termination of those which are not. The reviewed documents should include any subdivision plat covering the property, to enable buyer to ensure that the contract description of the property is accurate, and to become familiar with any setback requirements, floodplain use restrictions, easements, or other restrictions noted on the plat itself.

Seller should make sure that the contract list of encumbrances is complete. In doing so, seller should be cautious in relying for such list on the list of "exceptions" contained in *buyer's* title insurance commitment. Instead, in preparing such list, seller should carefully review seller's own title policy and other records to see whether any encumbrance exists which buyer's title insurer overlooked. If buyer's

---

[51] In either case, seller should satisfy itself before signing the contract that seller can deliver title in the prescribed state.

title company erroneously failed to list an existing encumbrance as an exception to coverage in its title commitment or policy, it will be liable to its insureds—buyer and buyer's mortgagee, if any—for any damage sustained from this omission. However, not only is seller not protected by buyer's title insurance, but the insurer, after paying any such damages to buyer or its lender, will become subrogated to any claim which either may have against seller if the existence of such overlooked encumbrance also violates seller's contractual and deed warranty obligations to buyer concerning title. An assertion by seller that it relied on the accuracy of buyer's title search in compiling the list of title encumbrances in the contract or deed will not suffice as a defense to such a claim.

(b) "Generic type" approach

Where the "generic type" approach is used in drafting the title clause, the obvious problem is one of definition: precisely what kinds of encumbrances are to be acceptable, and what kinds are not? It normally will be unarguable that *impermissible* encumbrances will include existing mortgages, deeds of trust, judgment and other liens, leases, contracts of sale, options agreements, and other oral or written agreements under which any third party has a right to acquire, lease, or possess the property. Underground utility easements located within a lot's "setback" areas (within which improvements are prohibited by subdivision and zoning regulations) are usually acceptable, while access easements usually are not, at least on a "generic" basis. When definitional problems arise, they usually concern the kinds of covenants which will or will not be permitted to encumber the title.

(c) "Take-It-or-Leave-It" approach

There is a third approach to the problem of defining the state of title required by the contract, one preferred where time permits and seller is willing to allow buyer the effective power to terminate the contract for a period after contract signing. Here, the contract permits seller to convey marketable title subject to *all* instruments and matters existing of record or in fact as of the signing of the contract, other than existing mortgages, deeds of trust, judgment and other liens, leases, contracts of sale, options agreements, and other oral or written agreements under which any third party has a right to acquire, lease, or possess the property (all of which seller is required to have released at or before closing). By itself these terms would obligate buyer to accept title in a condition largely unknown when the contract is signed so such a title clause goes on to give buyer the absolute right to terminate the contract during a specified period after the contract is signed, if on examining title buyer discovers any encumbrance, condition, or defect which is not acceptable to buyer in its sole judgment. If buyer does not terminate during this period, buyer is deemed to have accepted the state of title existing when the contract was signed (subject, of course, to seller's obligation to terminate encumbrances of the types listed above). In effect, this approach shifts to buyer the burden of satisfying itself as to the *existing* state of title, rather than attempting to define by contract what the state of title *ought to be*.

In drafting or reviewing a title clause, the careful attorney should never forget that, regardless of what the contract requires the state of title to be, as a practical matter its *actual* state as a matter of law or equity is not directly affected by the title clause. A seller normally does not have the unilateral power to remove or modify existing encumbrances to make them conform to the requirements of a contract's title clause. This fact is especially significant where defined "generic types" of encumbrances are permitted or prohibited, since the actual state of title may or may not comport with these definitions. Thus, the legal effect of the title clause in any given contract may be to require seller to convey title in a state which seller does not have the power to convey. While this may entitle buyer to damages, or even to rescind the contract, it will not change the actual state of title—an unsatisfactory result for most buyers, who are less interested in a right to damages or rescission than in simply acquiring title in the state promised by the contract.

Regardless of which approach is used, the title clause should prohibit seller from adding new encumbrances to the title while the contract is in effect, unless buyer gives their express, written consent.

2. [§ 2.36] Title defects

It follows from the above that, regardless of which approach is used in drafting the title clause, if seller fails to convey in accordance with its terms, seller will be in default under the contract. Often, the contract will use as a litmus test the "insurability" of the title by a title insurance company authorized to issue policies in Maryland. Since such companies sometimes can be induced to insure over possible title defects on payment of an additional premium, such clauses usually require that title be insurable by such companies "at regular rates." The contract should make clear that buyer's remedies for seller's failure to convey title in accordance with the title clause include rescission of the contract and/or exercise of its other legal and equitable remedies for such default.

3. [§ 2.37] MR form

Paragraph 48 of the MR form describes the state of title required to be conveyed by the contract in the following manner:

> Title to the Property, including all chattels included in the purchase, shall be good and merchantable, free of liens and encumbrances except as specified herein; except use and occupancy restrictions of public record which are

> generally applicable to properties in the immediate neighborhood or the subdivision in which the Property is located and publicly recorded easements for public utilities and any other easements which may be observed by an inspection of the Property. Buyer expressly assumes the risk that restrictive covenants, zoning laws or other recorded documents may restrict or prohibit the use of the Property for the purpose(s) intended by Buyer.

Thus, the MR form follows the "generic type" approach in identifying permissible encumbrances. As with many terms in the MR form, this language seems intended to enunciate a "standard" compromise between buyer's ideal position (that seller be required to convey an absolutely free and unencumbered title) and seller's (that seller be permitted to convey title subject to whatever instruments and matters actually encumber it), in the hope that further discussion of this issue or modification of the title clause will be avoided in a great number of sales transactions. Indeed, this is often the result. However, several problems are posed by the MR form clause.

(a) Exception for certain "Use and Occupancy Restrictions"

The MR form title clause language permitting title to be encumbered by "use and occupancy restrictions of public record which are generally applicable to properties in the immediate neighborhood or the subdivision in which the Property is located" may cause substantial difficulties for some buyers. The vagueness of this standard often makes it difficult to determine whether a given title encumbrance violates it.[52] Moreover, even where a set of occupancy restrictions clearly falls within this exception, the restrictions themselves may not be satisfactory for a given buyer. For example, a doctor or a dentist may intend to use part of the residence for an office, but the restrictions prohibit non-residential uses. Or a buyer may wish to create a separate living unit in the basement area for parents or in-laws, but the restrictions permit only one residence on the property.

Even where the restrictions themselves are satisfactory to buyer, they may require that further steps be taken before they will be permitted to use the property in the desired manner. A common example is that of the buyer who desires to make substantial (or even insubstantial) architectural changes to the residence, build a fence or pool, or paint the exterior walls, where architectural restrictions either prohibit such actions or require prior approval by an architectural committee. In such cases, buyer's attorney should consider whether it is possible to obtain such approval before closing, and if so, should condition buyer's obligation to close on obtaining it.

---

52 For example, what is meant by the "immediate neighborhood"?

The potential problems are as great as imagination will permit. The attorney should recognize that this exception for publicly recorded use and occupancy restrictions may leave the client faced with the prospect of either being forced to close on a property encumbered by an unpalatable restriction or defaulting under the contract. Thus, the prudent attorney will attempt to tailor the clause to the client's particular needs.

From a seller's standpoint, the vagueness of the MR form title clause standard occasionally leaves in doubt whether seller's actual state of title (which seller is in all likelihood powerless to change) will satisfy it. Seller should be sure to add to the listed generic exceptions any actual title encumbrances known to exist.

(b) Exception for certain easements

The MR form's blanket exception for publicly recorded easements, even when limited to public utilities and easements that may be observed by an inspection of the property, raises similar problems. Easements for public utilities have, on more than one occasion, been found to run through the living room of the residence. More frequently, such easements may be broad enough to cause the property not to qualify for federal Housing and Urban Development (HUD) or Department of Veterans' Affairs (VA) financing. As to those easements that are excepted under the MR form title clause by virtue of being discoverable on an inspection of the property, one need not speculate about the number of purchasers who make no such inspection. The careful attorney will remind a buyer client to make a thorough inspection of the property for this purpose (including asking seller whether any such unrecorded easements exist, and whether seller has or is aware of any existing title survey plats for the property), and to follow up to obtain further information where warranted. This is particularly important where the property includes a larger parcel of land not part of an established subdivision.

(c) Buyer assumption of risk

The sentence by which buyer "assumes the risk that restrictive covenants, zoning laws or other recorded documents may restrict or prohibit the use of the Property for the purpose(s) intended" by buyer may be considered extraordinary. Presumably, it was intended by the draftsman to address the risk that "special" intended uses of the property, beyond its use as a mere residence, might be prohibited. However, read literally, it would require buyer to "assume the risk" (i.e., by agreeing to accept title) that the property might be prohibited even from being used as a residence.

A buyer would be well advised to take advantage of any provision in the contract of sale permitting the examination of pertinent recorded covenants. Presumably, an examination of the neighborhood surrounding the property in question would yield an indication of permitted uses.

(d) Modifications of MR form

Although the need for changes to the MR form title clause will depend on the particular circumstances, where a party's interest is not properly served by the standard title clause, appropriate revision is in order. With regard to encumbrances, one alternative for buyer is to add a proviso that no such restriction shall prohibit buyer from carrying out an identified purpose or intention, such as building an addition or carrying on a professional practice. As for utility easements, an alternative is to provide that the exception shall apply only to easements within a specified number of feet from the property lines. The sentence under which buyer "assumes the risk" that intended uses will be restricted or prohibited should be modified so as to apply only to uses above and beyond the basic use of the property as a dwelling.

The MR form provides that, where seller is unable to deliver title in the state required by the contract, seller has the option of curing such defect, with an accompanying extension of the closing date by up to 14 days.[53] The parties will want to consider whether such an extension is appropriate, given that buyer will normally have sold its present home by this time and will be required to vacate it by a fixed date, and in any case will want to set forth an absolute outside date, beyond which such extensions will not be permitted. The MR form goes on to provide that, if seller is unable to cure the title defect and provide buyer with title insurance against it, buyer has the option (presumably, although not expressly stated to be, in addition to its other rights at law or in equity) of terminating the contract and being reimbursed by seller for costs incurred by buyer in examining the title to the property, not exceeding 0.5% of the purchase price.

Buyer's counsel should anticipate substantial resistance to altering the REB form title clause, especially from the brokers (including, not infrequently, the broker working with buyer). The brokers will typically argue that "everyone" accepts this clause and will portray counsel as unduly complicating the transaction. Given the buyer's potential exposure to an unmodified clause, buyer's attorney should insist that appropriate changes be made, notwithstanding any pressure to the contrary.

4. *[§ 2.38] Deed form*

Most form contracts (including the MR form) provide that a deed for the property containing a covenant of special warranty will be executed at buyer's expense, reflecting the custom in most parts of Maryland. However, general warranty deeds are occasionally used in some areas of the state.

---

53 In addition, the form confirms that buyer has the right to waive title defects and proceed to closing.

The effects of the terms "general warranty," "special warranty," and "further assurances" are set forth in §§ 2-105, 2-106, and 2-112, respectively, of the Real Property Article. In a general warranty deed, grantor (seller) warrants that the title is free of claims by any person whatsoever, whether or not the claim is derived through an act of grantor itself; in other words, it warrants against claims arising from documents or act existing or occurring either before or during grantor's period of ownership. In a special warranty deed, grantor warrants only against claims arising from documents or act existing or occurring while grantor owns the property. Since most sellers will be comfortable in the knowledge that no such claims may be derived through themselves but will not feel the same way about possible claims derived through their predecessors in title, a seller generally will be unwilling to convey by a general warranty deed, particularly in the absence of a full title search and title insurance protection for itself.

Even a special warranty deed renders seller liable for any liens or encumbrances created during seller's ownership of the property so the cautious seller's attorney will inquire as to any easements or other property interests during seller's period of ownership and will make express provisions in the contract (*and in the deed delivered at closing*) for the exception of any such matters from the special warranty.

A fiduciary grantor often will refuse to give either a general or a special warranty deed and will agree only to convey by quitclaim deed whatever interest it holds in the property. The best solution is to use a deed with no warranty. Using a designated quitclaim deed may give rise to unnecessary speculation as to the quality of the title.

Although uncommon in cases involving the sale of a residence, if the property constitutes all or substantially all of a seller corporation's assets, the transfer must be effected by filing articles of transfer in accordance with the Corporations and Associations Article,[54] and the contract should so provide. Articles of transfer should contain the same warranties of title as would have been set forth in a deed.

L. Conditions Precedent

1. [§ 2.39] Generally

Most contracts of sale contain one or more provisions creating conditions precedent (or "contingencies") to the obligation of buyer, seller, or both to complete closing. That is, one or both parties are not required to settle (and will not be deemed to be in default for not settling) unless some prescribed event occurs, or (alternately) does not occur. Although the parties are free to tailor the list of conditions to meet their particular needs certain types of conditions are common.

---

54 *See* CORPS. & ASS'NS §§ 3-107–3-117.

The draftsman should remember that, whenever dealing with a condition precedent, the contract should address several issues. First, it should make clear that the language in question in fact describes a condition precedent, and not an affirmative duty which a party is obligated to perform. Second, it should specify which party has the *benefit* of the condition; that is, which party has the right to refuse to settle unless the condition is met, or alternately to waive it and proceed to closing.[55] In the case of some conditions (such as one for resubdivision of the property or for obtaining an existing lender's approval of buyer's assumption of seller's mortgage), *both* parties are benefited and, therefore, the contract should not permit the condition to be waived by only one. Third, it should make clear which party, if any, has the *burden* of seeking to satisfy the condition. Fourth, it should deal with the timing and mechanics of seeking to satisfy the condition and should require one party or the other to give written notice whenever the condition is satisfied or waived. Finally, although this seems implicit, the contract should provide that, by completing closing, each party is deemed to have waived any unsatisfied condition precedent to its closing obligation.

In Maryland, as in most other jurisdictions, the party charged with the burden of seeking satisfaction of a condition has a common law duty to use reasonable efforts in good faith to try to satisfy it.[56]

Drafting considerations aside, the parties and their attorneys should always keep in mind two practical points concerning conditions precedent:

(a) Be realistic about the practical effect of including or demanding a condition

It is axiomatic that, everything else being equal, the fewer conditions demanded by one or the other party to a contract negotiation, the easier it will be for the parties to reach an agreement. It is always more desirable to one party that the other have fewer unilateral rights to avoid settlement. Thus, each negotiating party should consider carefully whether, in view of their goal of reaching a satisfactory agreement to buy or sell the house, it is tactically wise to insist that the contract contain a clause creating any given condition precedent.

The obvious legal effect of conditioning a party's closing obligation on the occurrence of some event is simply to render that party not in default for refusing to close if the event does not occur, where (absent such condition) the refusal would otherwise constitute a default. Thus, when negotiating whether the contract should include a particular condition precedent, the parties are really negotiating whether,

---

55 Reciting simply that "this Contract is conditioned" on the occurrence of some event is sloppy drafting; it is one or both parties' *closing obligations* which are so conditioned.

56 *Foodmaker, Inc. v. Denny*, 32 Md. App. 350, 360 A.2d 446 (1976).

if the benefited party refuses to settle due to nonoccurrence of the event, the other party should have a *remedy* (other than merely terminating the contract and trying again elsewhere). That is, should the refusal to settle entitle the other party to forfeit the deposit and/or seek damages or specific performance?

The relative importance of such a condition to the benefited party (or, put another way, the degree of risk involved in not including it in the contract) is a function of three considerations: the relative importance of the event, the perceived degree of likelihood that it will occur, and the relative desirability of avoiding the penalties—the other party's legal and equitable remedies—which the benefited party would incur in the absence of the condition, for refusing to settle because the event did not occur. The less important the event, or the greater the perceived likelihood that it will occur, the less need for insisting that the condition precedent be included. Similarly, and considerations of the injured party's theoretical legal rights aside, the less onerous and more limited the injured party's *effective* remedies—the lower the likely penalties—for a default are perceived to be, the less important including the condition precedent will be to the benefited party.

Regardless of how broadly or narrowly the terms governing a condition precedent are drawn, or how onerous the stated remedies for a default, most buyers, attorneys, and brokers are aware of a simple fact: in most cases, the only effective remedy realistically available to a seller for a buyer default in refusing to settle is to forfeit the deposit and terminate the contract. Most sellers are reluctant to pursue other remedies—all of which involve litigation—against a defaulting buyer, due both to the legal and other costs associated with doing so (costs which seller is unlikely to recover even if victorious), and to the possibility that such pending litigation could produce a defensive counterclaim by buyer, which could cloud the title to the property and thereby prevent resale to a third party during the long period while the litigation is pending.

Thus, for many contracts the only likely practical effect of including or not including a condition precedent benefiting buyer is to establish whether they will lose the deposit by refusing to settle if the event in question—issuance of a financing commitment, having a satisfactory home inspection, selling buyer's own residence—does not occur. It follows that the strength of buyer's demand that a given condition—an "out"—be included in the contract will tend to be influenced by the amount of the deposit which otherwise would be at risk. Conversely, the amount with which a seller is "comfortable" accepting as a deposit will be smaller if the contract contains conditions making it realistically unlikely that seller will have a legal right to forfeit the deposit if settlement fails to occur.

(b) Remember de facto conditions precedent

The parties should never view their debate over whether to include a given condition precedent as taking place in a vacuum. The reality is that, in most cases, and utterly regardless of what the contract states or does not state, buyer will be unable or unwilling to pay the purchase money and complete settlement unless buyer obtains financing—in the form of actual funding, not merely a commitment. In many cases, the source of buyer's equity is dependent upon selling *and settling* on buyer's present home. Such a buyer's ability to settle will effectively be conditioned on satisfaction of each and every condition precedent in their lender's purchase money loan commitment (or buyer's own house sale contract), regardless of whether such conditions are also found in the contract itself. Where buyer's practical ability to settle is known to depend on satisfaction of these or other *de facto* conditions, the parties should be realistic by not ignoring them when negotiating the contract. Too often, buyer, seller, and their attorneys invest great amounts of time, legal fees, and mental and emotional energy haggling over contract terms, pretending that these realities do not exist independently of the contract, only to discover that, when reality strikes, the contract is ineffective to prevent it in any meaningful way.

2. [§ 2.40] Buyer financing

The most prevalent condition appearing in the form contract is the financing clause. Cash sales are so rare that form financing clauses are included as a matter of course in most printed form contracts. The MR and REB Forms include a variety of financing clauses to meet the situation at hand, including one for a conventional loan, which contains blank spaces in which the loan amount, the term of the loan, and the amortization and interest rates are to be set forth. Corresponding provisions for payment of points are also included. Other MR and REB Form addenda address HUD, VA, and other kinds of financing. Paragraph 19 of the MR form provides a list of such addenda, which should be checked off if any of them is to be used.

Buyers should think carefully before insisting that a financing condition be included in the contract. So-called "cash contracts"—those containing no financing condition—are naturally popular with sellers, since (once all other buyer conditions are satisfied) buyer and its deposit will go "at risk," and the deposit may be forfeited if buyer fails to settle, regardless of whether buyer obtains financing. A buyer confident of its ability to obtain financing—or to terminate the contract on other grounds if it does not—is frequently willing to agree to a cash contract as an inducement to a seller's acceptance of its offer.

A seller presented with a cash contract should be wary of blithely assuming that because it contains no financing condition, the settlement will necessarily occur (just because it is legally required to occur) if all other conditions are satisfied. In reality, the settlement will only occur if the buyer has the funds with which to settle, regardless of whether the contract is conditioned on this. While a buyer default may ultimately yield for seller a portion of buyer's forfeited deposit, this result may give little solace to the seller whose own plans must be changed, and who, due to declining market conditions, may have "missed the market" for sale of the house at the same price to a more financially qualified buyer. For these reasons, most listing brokers attempt to "pre-qualify" buyers by informally confirming their ability (i.e., income, financial strength, and creditworthiness) to obtain the requisite financing, before allowing a seller to enter into a sales contract, regardless of whether it includes a financing condition. Seller should make sure that this has been done before signing a contract.

Under most Board Forms, including the MR form, the financing condition is for buyer's receipt, within a prescribed number of days after the contract date, of a "written commitment" for a mortgage loan in an amount, and on the other basic terms, outlined in the contract. Thus, once a commitment meeting these criteria is issued to the buyer, the contractual condition is met, even though the funding itself will not have occurred, and even though the commitment itself will invariably set forth a number of conditions precedent to the lender's own funding obligation. As a result (and assuming that all other conditions benefiting buyer are satisfied or waived), under the Board Form buyer will be in default if thereafter it is unable to complete closing because the lender either fails to honor the commitment, or does not fund the loan because the commitment expires or a condition precedent to the funding obligation, set forth in the commitment itself, is not met.

Wherever possible, buyer's attorney should attempt to modify the Board Form contract to condition buyer's closing obligation on *both* the receipt of such commitment, *and* the actual funding of the loan. Sellers can be expected to resist this demand, at least to the extent that the failure could be due to buyer's default under the commitment or a failure to make a good faith effort to satisfy the lender's requirements for funding. Keep in mind that a seller normally has no remedy against a lender which fails to honor its financing commitment to a buyer.

Many Board Forms, including the MR form, suggest that the financing condition is one benefiting both parties, and not (as might be expected) merely buyer, by providing in effect for *automatic* termination of the contract if the financing commitment is not received within the prescribed period. The rationale for this seems to be that, in most cases, the transaction will effectively be impossible to complete if buyer cannot or does not obtain a financing commitment, and that giving a die-hard buyer the unilateral power to keep the contract in effect by waiving the financing condition in the face of this reality would only hurt the seller and the broker, who are anxious at this point to remarket the house. While this approach seems sensible for most transactions, a buyer with demonstrated, adequate financial resources who would like to have financing, but does not require it in order to settle, should consider either eliminating the financing condition altogether, or modifying it to give themselves the unilateral right to waive it and proceed to closing without financing.

In any event, in preparing the financing condition clause, the attorney should make sure that the loan terms which it specifies—loan amount, interest rate, period of amortization, and monthly payment amount—are satisfactory to the buyer. At the same time, and in subsequently reviewing buyer's loan commitment, the attorney must make certain that the commitment does not expire before the date of contract closing. Otherwise, buyer may be legally required to close but will lack the necessary financing.

3. [§ 2.41] Home inspection

(a) Generally

As discussed in § 2.**46** of this chapter, at common law the rule of *caveat emptor* applies to the sale and purchase of residential real property. That is, absent any applicable express or implied warranty or contractual undertaking to the contrary, a buyer is deemed to purchase both land and improvements "as is." Moreover, a buyer has no statutory or common law right to inspect or even enter the property before closing.

Traditionally, a buyer's "inspection" of the dwelling which they contemplate buying has been limited to visiting it (often accompanied only by a real estate agent) before submitting an offer to purchase. Such visits usually occur while the buyer wrestles with the emotional, financial, family, and lifestyle issues underlying the basic question of whether to buy the house. It is of little wonder that the buyer pays little real attention on these occasions to any but the most superficial aspects of the dwelling's physical condition. It is even less remarkable that such buyers often discover unpleasant truths about their new purchases only after leaving the closing table, when they have lost any effective ability to negotiate over them with the former owner. The result has often been a residue of bad feeling between parties who, in the earlier glow of contract signing, may have toasted each other as new-found friends.

Perhaps in recognition of these realities, it is a common practice for a contract to condition buyer's obligation to settle on the completion of a "satisfactory" inspection of the house, by a professional home inspector, for the purpose of identifying "defects" in the residence and/or determining whether environmentally hazardous conditions exist on the property. Such clauses, and the inspection reports which result, are more frequently the source of controversy between buyer and seller than any other term of the contract, so an in-depth discussion of the inspection clause concept seems warranted.

Home inspection clauses tend to differ widely in their details. The typical clause not only creates a condition precedent to buyer's closing obligation, but of necessity gives buyer and its professional home inspector the affirmative right to enter the dwelling and the rest of the property to make the inspection. It states a period within which this may be done, and normally provides that buyer will be deemed to have waived any right to terminate under the inspection clause due to a less-than-satisfactory inspection report, except as to defects, discovered by the inspection, as to which buyer gives seller notice during the inspection period (the length of which tends to vary from clause to clause). Usually, buyer pays for the inspection.

Some inspection clauses impose an affirmative *obligation* on seller to correct the discovered defects, or at least to spend up to a designated maximum amount in doing so. More often, seller is given the discretionary right to elect whether to correct the conditions noted by buyer. In this type of clause, buyer's right to terminate the contract is conditioned on seller's having failed within some prescribed period to notify buyer that seller elects to undertake the corrections, at seller's expense. Where seller elects to do this, the contract then affirmatively obligates seller to complete the correction. Buyer usually is given the right to inspect the results to confirm seller's performance before being obligated to close.

(b) Seller's perspective

From a seller's perspective, a properly drafted home inspection clause is actually desirable in most cases, even though the condition is not, strictly speaking, for seller's benefit (since only buyer, and not seller, may refuse to settle if the condition is not met, or waive the condition). There are several reasons for this:

(i) By giving buyer a full-blown right to have a professional inspect the dwelling, and to terminate the contract if not satisfied with the results, the "moral" burden of pointing out problematic conditions within the dwelling tends to shift from seller to buyer (although such burden would seem to remain on seller as to any significant hidden defects known to seller but which seller knows were not discovered by the home inspector).

(ii) Buyers and sellers can be expected to differ greatly in their view of what constitutes a defect. Since home inspectors naturally tend to err, if at all, on the side of a more detailed and exacting disclosure of even marginally problematic conditions, the early home inspection tends to minimize unpleasant and occasionally controversial "surprises" which might otherwise occur when buyer belatedly discovers a condition before (or after) closing. Buyer is given a list of virtually all of the house's "warts," and thus cannot reasonably complain of their existence if they elect to go forward with the purchase.

(iii) Finally, the home inspector's written report can provide a seller with valuable information, obtained usually at buyer's expense. Not only may the report disclose problems of which seller is unaware (and whose prompt correction may avoid more significant expense), but knowledge of a professional inspector's view of the dwelling can be an important factor in realistically valuing the dwelling if the results of the inspection lead to a repricing negotiation with buyer, or if the contract is not settled and the house is remarketed.

For a seller, the most obvious negative aspect of an inspection clause is that, by allowing buyer to terminate the contract due to any (or at least any significant) defective condition unless repaired by seller, it gives buyer some degree of leverage in demanding a price reduction or other credit to "compensate" for any discovered conditions, unless seller agrees to repair them. This leverage will be greater or lesser, depending on the parties' respective bargaining positions in the transaction.

A more subtle, but hardly less important, problem for a seller with the entire home inspection process is its tendency to change the buyer's expectations about what they are buying. The purchaser of a *new* home from a builder traditionally feels entitled to demand that the dwelling adhere to a standard of "perfection" in design, materials, and workmanship. Significantly, this buyer's notion of what constitutes "perfection" is not derived from the dwelling which they are buying (since it is under construction), but from something else to which the dwelling is compared—often the builder's model home—but overlaid by the buyer's own subjective notions of minimally acceptable quality in a brand-new, expensive purchase, to which in reality even the model may not conform. While the new home rarely meets or even approaches this standard of perfection, buyer's belief that it should do so often gives rise to a fractious process, in which buyer compiles and submits to the builder a series of comprehensive punch-lists of real or imagined "defects" in the new dwelling, over which the parties then haggle before, at, and often after closing.

The dwellings discussed in this chapter are, by definition, not new. Since their original construction, they have been lived in and subjected to ordinary wear and tear. While from a bricks-and-mortar standpoint their quality often exceeds that of newer homes, their kitchens, HVAC systems, and other operating components are frequently outmoded. Alterations (some homemade) may have been made to them over the years, which vary in quality or design from the original construction. They have long since lost any pretense of conforming to any real or imaginary ideal of "perfection" by which they may have been measured when they were new (and which in any event usually would differ greatly from that applied to a new house today). Nor are these homes marketed as anything other than what they are; puffing by owner and broker aside, their knowledge of the house's physical condition is factored in when setting a listing price or accepting a contract price. In short, a used house is unique, and while its condition of repair or degree of obsolescence inevitably are important in determining its desirability to a buyer, it is not something to which a standard of "perfection" can, or reasonably should be, applied.

Unfortunately, one result of the inspection clause phenomenon frequently has been to cause buyers, brokers, and occasionally even sellers, to forget that the sale transaction is not premised on a standard of perfection. Too often the buyer or the broker, presented with a thorough and detailed professional inspection report, treats it as a punch-list by making an unwarranted logical leap to the conclusion that, because a list of "defective" conditions has now been identified, the house is somehow less than what buyer bargained for, and that seller therefore is under some moral or even legal duty to "make it right" by correcting the entire list of defects; in other words, to make the house "perfect." Brokers have been known to press this position on seller, as a way of eliminating a possible obstacle to settlement (and commission).

Sellers and their attorneys should be wary of falling into this trap. The purpose of an inspection clause is to give buyer information so that buyer can decide whether it wants the house as it exists, and not to create a punch-list which seller is supposed to correct. While the language of the inspection clause, or the parties' respective bargaining positions, may in any case compel seller to agree to correct some or all of the listed "defects" in order to preserve the sale, a decision to accept this burden should not ordinarily be premised on a mistaken belief that, regardless of legalities or bargaining positions, it is somehow "only the right thing to do," or that seller would be behaving "unreasonably" in refusing to make the corrections. Seller should remember that what was sold was never intended to be a perfect house, but rather *this* house.

A seller who consents in principle to the inclusion of an inspection clause in the contract should be careful about its precise language. Given what is ordinarily a strong desire of both parties to minimize haggling over "legal" terms, a seller would be well-advised in most cases to view the inspection clause as creating essentially an option. The option would allow buyer to terminate if *any* defect or condition mentioned in the report is unsatisfactory, regardless of how insignificant or easily remedied, unless seller agrees in its *sole* (i.e., not merely its *reasonable*) discretion to correct the problem at seller's expense. In other words, seller forgoes the effort and delay in attempting to narrowly circumscribe the kinds of defects or conditions which will entitle buyer to exercise its termination right and receives as a *quid pro quo* exoneration from any obligation whatsoever to correct any discovered problem. Essentially, this is a "here-it-is-take-it-or-leave-it" approach, coupled with a requirement that the entire process be completed quickly, say, within 10-to-15 days after contract signing. Seller should also make sure that the clause does not obligate seller, as part of the inspection process, to sign certificates or other documents making representations to buyer or the home inspector about the condition of the house, which could make seller liable if they prove to be inaccurate or incomplete.

(c) Buyer's perspective

From buyer's standpoint, the inspection clause enables buyer to obtain a thorough, detailed, and objective evaluation of the dwelling's physical condition—important information when determining whether to consummate a transaction of major financial and lifestyle significance. The very factors which make it unreasonable to expect that the house will be in "perfect" condition warrant a professional inspection to determine its actual condition, since this may not be apparent to a casual or non-disinterested observer.

Buyer will want to consider carefully whether to accept the drafting approach suggested above which, while giving buyer an unfettered right to terminate if any discovered defect or condition is not remedied by seller, imposes no affirmative duty on seller to do so. In particular, if in the negotiations seller has given buyer informal assurances that the house is "problem free," etc., buyer should consider asking seller to back up these statements by agreeing to bear the cost of the first, say, $500 or $1,000 in repairs.

(d) Drafting considerations

The essence of a well-drafted inspection clause is precision since, among virtually all of the typical contract's terms, it has the most potential for dispute, misunderstanding, and litigation. The drafting attorney should be careful to think through in detail the mechanics of the inspection process—dates, notice periods, etc.—and to make clear in the draft exactly what happens to the respective parties' rights if a particular notice or election is given or made within the prescribed period, and (just as importantly) what happens if it is not. Notices should, of course, be required to be given in writing. The notice by which buyer advises seller of the existence of defects, *the failure to correct which will entitle buyer to terminate*, should be required to list these defects with specificity. That is, the clause should not embody an inadvertent presumption that each and every defect or condition noted on the inspector's report necessarily is significant enough for buyer to include it in buyer's formal notice to seller, which seller must agree to repair or risk termination of the contract. If seller is to have the right to elect to repair the noted defects and thereby prevent buyer from terminating, the contract should call for this election to be made by notice to buyer or some other affirmative action, and not by silence coupled by the passage of time, to prevent the repair obligation from being undertaken inadvertently.

Where the parties elect to follow a more restrictive approach than the *de facto* option approach suggested under *Seller's perspective* above, the primary drafting problem will be to establish the basis for buyer's right to terminate. That is, if not *all* "defects" will entitle buyer to terminate, which ones will? Similarly, if seller is to be under *any* obligation to repair defects, which defects does this obligation encompass? Any inspection clause which attempts to limit the types of defects which entitle buyer to terminate, or to impose on seller an affirmative obligation to pay for repairs of defects, must define the kinds of defects which give rise to these rights and duties. The alternative to such definition—vagueness—merely sets the stage for disagreement or even litigation.

Such definitions are not easily agreed upon. Indeed, the parties frequently would disagree (were they to consider the issue) on what is even meant by a defect, as opposed to simply a quirk of construction or design.[57] Seller will wish to limit the right to terminate to defects of a "substantial" nature (presumably measured by the cost of correction), so as not, in effect, to give buyer an outright option. Buyer will want the condition to apply to less substantial defects, as well.

For the same reason, where the parties agree that seller will be obligated to bear the cost of the repairs (whether or not subject to a dollar limitation), seller will be concerned to ensure that the "defects" covered by this obligation will be of a significant nature, to avoid being required to repair every scratch and dent in the house. Where seller is not to be obligated to repair these defects, seller nevertheless will want to retain the *option* to do so and thereby hold buyer to the contract. Buyer will want the right to inspect and approve the results.

(e) MR form

Paragraph 26 of the MR form contract provides that buyer may elect to request a home inspection of the property. If buyer so chooses, an addendum must be signed.[58]

The MR form addendum provides that the inspection of the particular item (structural and mechanical, environmental, radon, and chimney) must be made within a specified number of days (to be agreed upon by the parties) after the date of the contract. The buyer may notify the seller in writing, within the time period specified, that the contract is null and void. If the buyer does not void the contract, the parties will embark upon a course designed to allow the seller the right to review and possibly cure the defects raised by buyer. In such event, buyer must give seller notice of the defects within a period to be specified in the addendum, failing which buyer is deemed to have waived the inspection condition. If buyer gives the requisite notice within the specified period, seller is allowed five days within which to elect, at seller's expense and option, to cure some or all of the defects. If the seller remains silent and does not respond, their silence is considered rejection of the buyer's request. If seller elects to cure none, or some but fewer than all, of the noted defects, buyer is given two days within which to elect to terminate the contract by giving notice to seller, they may accept the seller's counteroffer or they may in turn counteroffer to the seller. Buyer's failure to respond will constitute acceptance of the seller's counteroffer/response. If buyer counteroffers then the seller then has two days to terminate, counteroffer or accept buyer's counteroffer. This time, seller's failure to respond constitutes acceptance. This two-day period of counteroffering,

---

57 For example, most sellers would not consider an outmoded kitchen or an unpainted wall to be a "defect."

58 *See, e.g.*, MR Property Inspections Addendum, § 2.79 of this chapter.

terminating or accepting (with silence equaling acceptance) can then continue until an agreement is formalized between the parties or the contract is terminated. If the contract is terminated by either party during this negotiation, the deposit is disbursed pursuant to the deposit paragraph. If seller elects to remedy any of the noted defects, seller must do so in a good and workmanlike manner, before closing.

4. [§ 2.42] Pest inspection

(a) Generally

Residential contracts commonly contain a clause conditioning buyer's obligation to settle on buyer's receipt of a certificate from a recognized pest control company that, based on the company's visual inspection, there is no evidence that the dwelling is infested by termites or other wood-destroying insects, and that damage from any prior infestation has been repaired. It is essential that buyer be protected by a pest inspection clause (which functionally is but a subspecies of the home inspection clause), and prudence suggests that it cover not only termites but all wood-infesting insects.

Some contract forms provide for seller to bear the cost of this inspection, while others impose this cost on buyer. Likewise, some forms affirmatively obligate seller, at their expense, to treat any infestation and, occasionally, to repair damage from prior infestations. Others give seller the option of doing this or allowing buyer to elect between bearing the expense or terminating the contract. Still others require seller to bear an initial portion of the cost of the repair but not any excess cost.

It probably is a waste of time for a seller to resist including some form of pest inspection clause in the contract. Not only is it hard to justify not allowing buyer to test for infestations, but buyer's lender will in all likelihood require such an inspection as a condition to its financing. Moreover, where the contract already contains a home inspection clause, seller has already effectively committed to allowing a pest inspection, as merely another aspect of the overall inspection of the dwelling.[59] Finally, for obvious reasons it will be important for seller to be aware of any infestation which is discovered, regardless of its effect on the sale, and it is only to seller's benefit that the inspection will be performed at buyer' expense.

A seller should instead be concerned to ensure that the principles embodied in the particular pest inspection clause used in the contract are consistent with those in any home inspection clause found in the contract. For example, seller will want the timing of the pest inspection, the issuance of the inspector's report, and any elections to be made by seller or buyer to be as close as possible to that of the corresponding events under the home inspection clause, so that all issues related to

---

[59] Discussed in § 2.**41** of this chapter.

the physical condition of the house can be disposed of simultaneously. If the home inspection clause imposes no affirmative duty on seller to make repairs, it is not logical to impose such an obligation on seller in the pest inspection clause. If seller is to be obligated to repair damage from a prior pest inspection, the cost of doing so should "count" toward any cost which seller is required to incur in making repairs under the home inspection clause. Moreover, seller will want to condition this obligation on satisfaction or waiver of as many other conditions as is possible, since unless seller is confident that the sale has become "firm," seller may not want to undertake this expense.

(b) MR form

In the 2022 revision of the MR form, Maryland Realtors in an effort to create a more "as is" contract, removed any reference to a pest/wood destroying insect inspection in the body of the contract. If a buyer would like a pest inspection performed, they must negotiate for it in the property inspection addendum.[60] Pest inspections are also addressed in the VA Financing Addendum, FHA Financing Addendum, and the USDA Financing Addendum, and state that "Should Lender require a wood destroying insect inspection as a condition of financing, the parties agree that Buyer may conduct such inspection at Buyer's expense. Lender Required Repairs in connection with a lender required wood destroying insect inspection shall be performed in accordance with the Lender Required Repairs paragraph of this Addendum. Seller shall have no obligation to consider any other request for repairs and/or Seller Credit in connection with a lender required wood destroying insect inspection unless a wood destroying insect inspection was negotiated by the parties as part of a Property Inspections Addendum."

5. [§ 2.43] Environmental inspections

(a) Radon

A relatively recent phenomenon has been the discovery that many dwellings are traps for the accumulation of radon gas, a naturally occurring substance produced underground. It has been reported that extended exposure to high levels of radon can be unhealthy. Radon seems to accumulate in the basements and other semi-closed areas of certain dwellings. Both the Maryland Department of the Environment and the U.S. Environmental Protection Agency have recommended that, once radon concentrations (measured in picoCuries per liter of air) exceed certain levels, remedial action be taken to reduce the concentration.[61]

---

60 *See, e.g.* MR Property Inspections Addendum §2.79 of this chapter.

61 See CONSUMER'S GUIDE TO RADON REDUCTION, published by the U.S. Environmental Protection Agency (EPA document number EPA 402-K-06-094), available from the EPA's National Service Center for Environmental Publications. *See also www. epa.gov/radon/pubs/consguid.html.*

In response to this development, residential resale contracts now routinely condition buyer's closing obligation on the dwelling's passing a radon inspection test, performed over several days by a qualified radon testing firm. Many contracts provide that, if unacceptably high concentrations are found, seller must, at its expense, take appropriate remedial action to reduce them to acceptable levels. Montgomery County requires that an inspection be performed and that the buyer is provided with the results.

As still another subspecies of inspection clause, most of the same issues are inherent in radon inspection clauses as are found in inspection clauses generally, and discussed above in this subsection: What standard must be met for the condition to be satisfied? What are the mechanics of testing/notification of results/buyer election? Is seller to be affirmatively obligated to take any action to remediate and, if so, is there to be a limit on the cost seller must incur in doing so? What is the relationship between this inspection clause and any other inspection clauses found in the contract?

From a seller's perspective, it makes little sense to oppose the inclusion of a radon inspection clause in the contract. Although the passage of a radon inspection test has not yet become a universal condition to a lender's funding requirement, all other arguments for seller's consent to a pest inspection clause[62] are equally applicable here, as are the issues which should concern seller about the clause's details. They need not be repeated here.

(b) Lead-Based Paint

Because of ongoing public health concerns over exposure to lead in the environment and, specifically, the health risks to children from the ingestion of lead paint chips or exposure to lead-contaminated surfaces, Congress enacted Title X, the "Residential Lead-Based Paint Hazard Reduction Act" in 1992. The Act and subsequent regulations calls for inspection and abatement for pre-1960 target housing and inspection and risk assessment for 1960–1978 target housing. "Target housing" is defined as any housing constructed prior to 1978, with certain exceptions for "zero bedroom" dwellings and housing for the elderly and disabled, unless such housing is occupied by a child under the age of six years.

The Act requires that a seller allow the purchaser a 10-day period in which to conduct a risk assessment or inspection for lead paint. Although the Act does not, by its terms, allow a purchaser to rescind the contract in the event the assessment or inspection discloses an unacceptable level of lead contamination, the right to test must be honored. A prudent purchaser will require a contract addendum, conditioning the sale on receipt of a satisfactory report or inspection. The Act also

---

62 *See* **§ 2.42** of this chapter.

requires that the contract of sale contain certain provisions and disclosures, as summarized:

- A "Lead Warning Statement";
- A statement disclosing the presence of known lead-based paint and/or lead-based paint hazards, the basis for same, and any available records or reports pertaining to same;
- A statement by purchaser acknowledging receipt of seller's disclosure statements, records and reports and an approved lead hazard information pamphlet;
- A statement by purchaser that an opportunity to conduct the risk assessment or inspection has been received; and
- Signatures of seller and purchaser certifying the accuracy of their statements.

Besides federal law, Maryland's Reduction of Lead Risk in Housing law (found in §§ 6-801–6-852 of the Environment Article of the Maryland Code) applies to residential rental property. The Reduction of Lead Risk in Housing law provides limited immunity from liability for landlords who comply with the law, in the event that lead poisoning occurs at a participating "affected property." Participation is mandatory for rental properties built before 1978. The landlord must register the "affected property" with the Maryland Department of the Environment and, at each change in occupancy, satisfy the risk reduction standard by testing for lead contaminated dust or performing certain lead hazard reduction treatments such as removing peeling or chipped paint and repainting surfaces. At or prior to the time a contract of sale for the rental unit is executed, the owner must disclose to the prospective buyer, any obligation to perform any required risk reduction treatment. With certain exceptions, a landlord seeking to repossess an "affected property" for nonpayment of rent must include in the complaint a statement that the landlord has registered the property with the Maryland Department of the Environment along with the inspection certificate number. Additional information is available from the Maryland Department of the Environment at: *http://www.mde.state.md.us/programs /Land/LeadPoisoningPrevention/Pages/index.aspx.*

(c) MR form

MR does not address radon in the body of the contract, if a buyer would like a radon test and subsequent remediation, they would negotiate for it in the Property Inspection Addendum.[63]

With respect to lead-based paint, Paragraph 35 of the MR form contains the terms and disclosures required under federal law and provides a place for the seller to make a representation as to whether the dwelling was, or was not, constructed prior to 1978,

---

[63] See, e.g. MR Property Inspection Addendum, §2.79 of this chapter.

or that the date of construction is uncertain. In the event that the dwelling is represented as having been constructed prior to 1978 and/or that the date is uncertain, the parties mutually agree that the provisions of the Residential Lead-based Paint Hazard Reduction Act apply. The Form also includes spaces for buyer and seller to initial to acknowledge reading and understanding the provisions of Paragraph 35. Paragraph 35 also contains appropriate terms and disclosures applicable to Maryland's Reduction of Lead Risk in Housing law. In addition, Paragraph 25 addresses the Lead Renovation, Repair and Painting Rule as adopted by the Environmental Protection Agency and asks the buyer to acknowledge reading and understanding the law.

6. [§ 2.44] Water and septic system inspection

Where the property is served by a water well alone or by a well and septic system, buyer's obligation to settle should be conditioned on the existence of an adequate and sanitary water supply, and on the wells and any private septic systems being in good working order as of closing. There is perhaps no other condition more essential to buyer; accordingly, it is important that the contract set forth clearly the parties' rights if this condition is not met. This kind of clause is really another subspecies of the home inspection clause and should be drafted in a manner consistent with the latter.

Keep in mind that, regardless of what the parties agree upon concerning these matters, buyer's lender will typically include a similar condition in its loan commitment. An even more fundamental fact to remember is that, regardless of what the contract or loan commitment provides, a dwelling's private well and septic system must perform to certain minimum standards for the dwelling to be legally habitable under state and local health regulations.

Since a technical determination of the adequacy of private well and septic systems is generally outside the scope of an attorney's services to their client, this chapter will not discuss from a technical standpoint the minimum and optimum standards which such systems should meet. We note only that, in the case of water wells, the key issues are those of potability (i.e., water quality, measured in terms of both chemical composition and bacteriological content) and yield (i.e., quantity, measured in terms of well recovery rate in gallons per minute, constancy of flow, and adequacy of the underlying aquifer). In the case of septic tanks, the main question is whether they percolate satisfactorily; that is, is the inflow absorbed quickly enough by the surrounding ground.

For purposes of the contract, and absent any special buyer needs for larger than normal quantities of water (a need which, if met, usually will dictate a need for a correspondingly larger septic system capacity), it usually will be sufficient to provide that buyer's closing obligation is conditioned on buyer's receipt, from a qualified testing consultant, of a written report stating that the well and septic system meet the minimum standards required by applicable state and local health and other laws and regulations. In areas having a history of problems with dry wells or insufficient well recovery rates, buyer should give serious consideration to broadening the condition to entitle buyer to refuse to close if buyer (or buyer's hydrological consultant) is not satisfied that a future problem of that nature is unlikely, based on a more detailed expert analysis than is used to determine mere compliance with minimum legal standards.

The REB Forms include separate addenda dealing with private water wells and private septic systems.[64] Conditioning buyer's obligation to settle on receipt of a satisfactory inspection certificate obtained at buyer's expense, they provide for an inspection and generally function in a manner similar to the pest inspection clause discussed above, while possessing many of the same drafting weaknesses.

As with the other inspection clauses discussed above, seller will want to ensure that the inspection/notice/rescission periods provided in the contract's well and septic inspection clauses are essentially co-extensive with those of any other inspection clauses included in the contract, and that their provisions are otherwise consistent with the theory underlying the other inspection clauses.

For Baltimore County properties, a special water well addendum[65] is included as part of the REB Forms to satisfy notice requirements concerning the testing of private water wells set forth in §§ 34-2-103 *et seq.* of the Baltimore County Code. Under this statute, unless the well is tested before closing, buyer must file before closing a written waiver of the testing condition (using a prescribed waiver form) with the County's Bureau of Environmental Services.

7. [§ 2.45] Sale of buyer's residence

(a) Generally

A buyer may insist that a residential sale contract contain provisions conditioning their closing obligation on the sale of buyer's own home. Such clauses are popular with buyers as the housing and mortgage markets have become more volatile and less predictable, and as buyers trading up to more expensive housing are no longer able to pull from their savings accounts (if any) the equity required to complete the purchase, given the larger purchase prices and equity amounts involved.

Sellers are naturally quite wary of such clauses, despite the fact that, in many cases, the sale of buyer's house will amount to a *de facto* condition to completing the sale of seller's house. Such clauses, as customarily drafted, result in the title to seller's home being "tied up" by the contract with buyer, while buyer has nothing at

---

64 *See* §§ **2.91** of this chapter.

65 Entitled "Notice of Baltimore County Well Water Law for Improved Property and Well Water Test Addendum," and set forth in § 2.**84** of this chapter.

risk if buyer is unable to sell theirhome; in effect, seller takes the risk of selling both seller's home and buyer's home, with no deposit to forfeit as a consolation if settlement does not occur. This in turn tends to remove much of what would otherwise be an incentive for buyer to accept a less-than-optimum offer for buyer's own house, in order to be in a position to honor buyer's contract with seller.

As with most clauses creating conditions precedent, the parties have unlimited latitude in agreeing on the details of a buyer sale clause. The details are important, as is precise drafting, because the typical clause involves a series of elections by one or the other party.

A buyer sale clause is often to the following effect: buyer's obligation to close is conditioned on buyer's having entered into a separate contract to sell buyer's own house and, under some versions, on the completion of settlement of that sale. Buyer is required, within a brief period after signing the contract with seller, to list buyer's own home for sale with a licensed broker who is a member of a multiple listing service, in order to maximize the home's exposure to the market. Occasionally, the clause will set a maximum asking or "listing" price for buyer's house, and may prescribe other standard terms as minimums or maximums which buyer must accept in negotiating a contract to sell buyer's home: maximum deposit amount; maximum period within which closing must occur, if at all; minimum "points" which buyer must be willing to pay in connection with the third-party purchaser's financing; even a restriction on the kinds of conditions precedent which buyer may accept in buyer's contract with the third-party purchaser.

Frequently, a buyer sale clause contains "kick-out" provisions. These entitle seller to continue marketing seller's house as if seller and buyer had not signed the contract, as long as buyer's home remains unsold (or, under some versions, unsettled). If seller receives another offer which seller is willing to accept, seller may give notice of this fact to buyer, in which event buyer is afforded a very brief period—24 or 48 hours is the norm—within which to elect to waive the buyer sale condition (in effect, agreeing that buyer's obligation to close on its purchase of seller's house is no longer conditioned on the sale of buyer's home), in which event seller is prohibited from accepting the new offer. If buyer fails to make such election within such period, seller is free to accept the new offer, in which event seller's contract with buyer terminates and (usually) any deposit is refunded to buyer. Seller may, however, elect not to accept the new offer, in which event seller's contract with buyer—including the buyer sale clause—remains in effect.

In negotiating buyer sale clauses, sellers should strive to limit the condition to entry into a *contract* for the sale of buyer's home, but not the *settlement* of such sale (which would entail not only that all financing, home inspection, and other conditions precedent in the contract covering the sale of buyer's house have been satisfied or waived, but also that the third-party buyer and its lender have performed their closing and funding obligations). Excluding the latter requirement from the condition will mean that, all else being equal, seller can forfeit buyer's deposit on a buyer default, if a contract to sell buyer's house is entered into but not settled. Sellers should also insist on the inclusion of "kick-out" language of the type described above. Since the ultimate result of seller's invocation of the kick-out clause may be to terminate the contract, the notice and termination provisions must be ironclad; otherwise, seller could become embroiled in a dispute with buyer over whether the contract was terminated. Sellers should try to control buyer's own asking terms as much as is realistically possible, to prevent buyer from unrealistically (or intentionally) listing buyer's house at too high a price or otherwise demanding terms which make it difficult or impossible to sell buyer's house.

From buyer's standpoint, the ideal clause will allow buyer the greatest latitude in setting the price and other terms for the sale of buyer's house. Buyer will want to be allowed to include in the buyer sale contract the kinds of conditions which the purchaser of buyer's home can be expected to demand: those for financing, home inspection, etc., since having this latitude will make it more likely that buyer will sell its house. Moreover, buyer will want buyer's own obligation to settle with seller conditioned on the satisfaction of these and all other conditions in the buyer sale contract or, even more ideally, on the completion of settlement under the buyer sale contract.[66] While resisting inclusion of any "kick-out" language probably is unrealistic, buyer should try to have the kick-out provisions become effective only if buyer's house has not been sold within a prescribed period of time—say, 30 or 45 days—after the contract with seller is signed.

(b) MR form

Paragraph 22 of the MR form contract declares that, unless a buyer sale clause is set forth in an addendum to the contract, neither the contract "nor the granting of Buyer's loan referred to herein is to be conditioned or contingent in any manner upon the sale, settlement, and/or lease of any other real estate," and then prohibits buyer from applying for or accepting a mortgage loan commitment which is contingent upon the sale, settlement or lease of any other real estate.

The MR Sale, Financing, Settlement or Lease of Other Real Estate Addendum allows the buyer to make the contract contingent upon either the buyer entering into a written contract of sale for the sale of their property, receiving written financing on the sale of their property, upon settlement for the sale of their property or upon the execution of a lease agreement for their property. If buyer elects to remove the

---

66 For obvious reasons, if this approach is followed, a buyer sale condition probably should be prohibited from the *buyer* contract, since otherwise seller's sale will effectively become conditioned on the completion of a *series* of other house sales.

contingency, buyer must also provide a financial statement or similar information to seller, evidencing buyer's ability to complete settlement.[67]

M. Representations, Warranties and Required Disclosures

1. [§ 2.46] Generally

Traditionally, the rule of *caveat emptor* has applied to the sale of residential and commercial real property in Maryland. That is, a seller traditionally has not been deemed by law to have made any *implied* representations or warranties to a buyer concerning either the title to or the physical or legal characteristics or condition of the real property, so that such representations or warranties could be made, if at all, only expressly.[68] Given the "merger" clause found in most contracts, and discussed in § 2.**65** of this chapter, this meant that any express representations and warranties usually had to be made in writing and set forth either in the contract itself or a subsequently signed document for which there was independent consideration.

The effect of this doctrine has been to place on buyer the burden of satisfying themselves as to these matters, except where seller is willing to make a representation or warranty. In most cases, sellers are willing to provide certain title warranties, as discussed in §§ 2.**35**–2.**38** of this chapter but are reluctant to make other representations or warranties concerning the property.

2. [§ 2.47] Disclosures required by law

In recent years a trend has developed in which state and local legislative bodies have enacted a series of statutory exceptions to the common law rule, by requiring sellers of existing homes to make written disclosures of certain facts to their buyers. Initially, these requirements dealt primarily with specific legal aspects of the residence: for example, its location in a special taxing district; the applicability of certain subdivision or other land-planning requirements; the applicability of transfer tax statutes; or, for condominium units and dwellings subject to homeowners' association covenants, the disclosure of certain facts concerning the condominium or homeowners' association regimes. More recently, sellers have been required to make disclosures concerning the physical condition of the residence (or to declare that they are making none).

Some of these required disclosures are, by nature, susceptible to being dealt with using relatively simple form contract clauses. Others call for responses which

---

67 The addendum is set forth in **§ 2.78** of this chapter.

68 Although by statute certain warranties are implied in the sale of "newly constructed" dwelling units, and certain actions by the sellers of such dwelling units are raised to the level of express warranties, these rules have not been extended to the typical residential resale by homeowner to homebuyer. *See* Real Prop. §§ 10-201–10-205.

necessarily will vary from sale to sale, and hence demand individual attention by the contract draftsman. Some disclosures must be made in the contract itself or another document given to buyer simultaneously with delivery of the contract. Others may be made after the contract is signed but before closing.

Some disclosure statutes confer on buyer remedies for a failure by seller either to provide the required information, or to provide it accurately. Other statutes are silent on the subject of remedies or make clear that seller's noncompliance will not constitute grounds for invalidation or rescission of the contract. However, even where no remedy for violation is provided, in most instances it should be assumed that seller's provision of inaccurate or misleading information (as distinguished from a failure to provide any information) in response to a disclosure requirement could, if material, be viewed by a court of law as common law fraud, or as otherwise justifying rescission of the contract and, perhaps, an award of damages to buyer. Of course, the same is true for misrepresentations made independently of any statute.

What follows in the rest of this paragraph is a discussion of some of the more important or broad-reaching statutory disclosure requirements. The list of requirements discussed is not, and is not intended to be, exhaustive. Attorneys and brokers are urged to become and stay familiar with the particular disclosure requirements governing sales in their bailiwicks, many of which are enacted by county or local governing bodies and therefore are only county- or city-wide in their application.[69]

3. *[§ 2.48] Physical condition*

(a) Generally

Easily the most significant and controversial statutory disclosure requirement applicable to residential resale transactions is that which requires that a seller provide to a buyer one of two standardized documents: *either* a written "disclosure statement" setting forth the "latent defects" known to the seller concerning a prescribed list of physical components or other aspects of the residence, *or* a written "disclaimer statement" disclaiming any seller representations or warranties as to the condition of the land or improvements except as may otherwise be provided in the contract.[70]

(b) Applicability

The statute applies to all "single family residential real property improved by four or fewer single family units," except for, essentially, builder sales,[71] and with certain

---

69 See **Chapter 9, Part D** of this book for a listing of disclosure requirements.

70 *See* Real Prop. § 10-702.

71 More precisely, the exclusion is for the initial sale of such property either before any occupancy, or within one year after a certificate of occupancy is issued. *See* Real Prop. § 10-702(b)(2). This means that a house built by a seller on its own lot is covered by § 10-702, once the one-year period has elapsed.

other, narrow exceptions.[72] Although the terms "transfer" and "sale" are not defined, both the enacting Act and, by implication, several provisions of the statute itself make clear that, in addition to transactions encompassed by the common law meaning of those terms, the statute applies to "contracts of sale of real property, land installment contracts, option to purchase agreements, and lease agreements containing an option to purchase provision entered into on or after Jan. 1, 1994."[73] While also not defined, the term "vendor" clearly refers to the seller or (in the case of an option agreement) optionor.

What is meant by "single family" residential real property is not entirely certain, since the statute does not define this term. In the real estate industry, the term "single family" commonly is used to refer to *physically detached* dwellings (that is, free-standing houses), as distinguished from townhouses or condominium or cooperative apartment dwellings. However, it seems clear that the statute applies to both attached and detached dwellings, since it is rare indeed for a single parcel of land to be improved by as many as four detached houses.

The contract is required to contain a notice advising buyer of rights under this statute.[74]

(c) Contents of statements

As required by the statute, the Maryland Real Estate Commission has by regulation adopted mandatory forms for the disclosure statement and the disclaimer statement.[75] They are readily available from real estate brokers and other sources. The 1995 amendments require the Commission to consolidate them into a single form.[76]

The disclosure form contains several notices to seller and buyer mandated by the statute, and begins with a short list of questions about the property which call for objective facts over which there can be little debate: For example, is the property served by public water and sewer service? Does it contain a garbage disposal unit or a dishwasher? Is it heated by gas, oil, or electricity? The form then instructs seller to "Please indicate your actual knowledge with respect to the following." What follows is a lengthy series of topics and related questions concerning various components and operating systems of the dwelling, which require seller to exercise judgment in providing answers. As to these, seller is given three choices of response to be checked: "yes," "no" or "unknown" (or, occasionally, "does not

---

72 REAL PROP. § 10-702(b)(2).

73 1993 Md. Laws, ch. 640, § 2.

74 REAL PROP. § 10-702(l).

75 The form is referenced in Code of Maryland Regulations (hereinafter COMAR) 09.11.07.

76 *See* form at **§ 1.49**.

apply"). The last part of each entry is a line beginning with the word "Comments," clearly asking seller to elaborate on the checked response.

Some of these questions call for legal or technical conclusions.[77] The statute makes clear that the vendor is not required, in preparing a disclosure statement, to undertake or provide an independent investigation or inspection of the property to obtain these answers; in other words, seller may make the disclosures based on seller's actual knowledge alone.[78]

The *disclaimer* statement recites that, except as otherwise provided in the contract, seller makes no representation or warranty as to the condition of the land or improvements, and that they are being sold "as is." But for the consequences provided by the statute for its timely or untimely delivery, the disclaimer statement, once given to buyer, has no legal effect as a document, since it merely reiterates the existing common law rule of *caveat emptor*. Its sole practical effect is to call buyer's attention to this doctrine. However, even when selling the property "as is," §10-7029(d)(2) of the Maryland Real Property Article does require the seller "Disclose any latent defects of which the vendor has actual knowledge that a purchaser would not reasonably be expected to ascertain by a careful visual inspection and that would pose a direct threat to the health or safety of the purchaser or an occupant."

(d) Procedure, consequences of violation

The statute prescribes a procedure to be followed by seller in delivering a disclosure statement or a disclaimer statement, failing which certain consequences attach.[79] In general, seller is required to deliver either a disclosure statement or a disclaimer statement to buyer on or before entering into the contract; i.e., when it has been signed and delivered by both parties. However, for land installment contracts, purchase option agreements, and leases containing purchase options, the vendor must deliver one or the other statement before the instrument in question is signed by the *purchaser*, even if the vendor does not sign until later.[80]

The consequences of a vendor's failure to meet these delivery requirements are significant. If neither statement is delivered to buyer before entry into the contract, buyer has the "unconditional right," by written notice to seller *or seller's agent* (e.g.,

---

77 For example, does the property violate zoning laws, building restrictions, or setback requirements? Is it located in the Chesapeake Bay Critical Area or a designated historic district?

78 Real Prop. § 10-702(e)(4).

79 Seemingly through a drafting oversight, the statute as originally enacted only dealt with the consequences of the late delivery of a *disclosure* statement. The Attorney General of Maryland subsequently construed the statute as providing that such consequences arise only if *neither* a disclosure statement nor a disclaimer statement is delivered on time. 79 Op. Att'y Gen. 402 (March 11, 1994). The 1995 amendments corrected this defect.

80 Real Prop. § 10-702(f).

the broker or agent), to rescind the contract and receive an immediate refund of its deposit, at any time before or within five days after buyer receives the statement.[81] To protect lenders, the statute provides that buyer's rescission right terminates in any case if not exercised either (1) before making a written application for a mortgage loan, if prior thereto the lender gives buyer written notice to that effect, or (2) if the lender did not give such notice before buyer's application was submitted, within five days after buyer's subsequent receipt from the lender of a written notice that the rescission right terminates at the end of the five-day period.[82]

The obvious purpose of this clause—indeed, of the entire statute—is to enable a buyer to withdraw from a contract entered into without the benefit of either the information afforded by a disclosure statement, or the awareness that this is a *caveat emptor* sale which is provided by a disclaimer statement. Given this purpose, it may seem odd that the statute expressly deprives buyer of this benefit, not only when buyer is given one or the other statement *before* they sign the contract (when buyer will have had the opportunity to review the statement), but also where one or the other statement is given to buyer *simultaneously with* "entering" into the contract (clearly, the moment at which the contract is legally created, in most cases when buyer's signed offer, having been countersigned by seller, is delivered to buyer), when buyer may not have had such an opportunity.[83]

This anomaly seems to reflect the reality that many residential contracts are created quickly, by seller's acceptance of buyer's initial offer. In such cases, seller often is unaware of buyer's existence until seller receives buyer's already-signed offer, and thus could not have been in a position to provide either statement to buyer before the offer was submitted. To permit buyer to rescind such a contract because buyer had not received a statement before submitting its offer would force seller to

---

81 Real Prop. § 10-702(h)(1). Oddly enough, as originally enacted subsection 10-702(h) also provided that, if the statement were delivered more than three days after seller entered into a contract of sale with buyer, the contract would be void (and not merely voidable by buyer). This produced an unintended, absurd result, by conferring on a seller the unilateral power to terminate the contract, *even against buyer's wishes*, simply by withholding delivery of one or the other statements until the three-day period had elapsed, a useful tool for a seller having second thoughts about a sale. Regardless of the length of delay in delivering a statement, the statutory goal—that of informing buyers—was already adequately served by the rescissionary right discussed above. Hence, the "remedy" of automatically voiding the contract was eliminated by the 1995 corrective amendments. Note *Romm v. Flax,* 340 Md. 690, 668 A.2d 1 (1995), decided under the statute before amended. The court said the word "void" was not intended to be interpreted literally because there was no clear evidence of legislative intent to alter the common law. The court went on to hold that the term void ". . . was intended to mean 'voidable at the option of the purchaser,' and thus does not render a residential real estate contract void where the seller fails to deliver a disclosure or disclaimer statement as required by statute."

82 Real Prop. § 10-702(h)(2).

83 Real Prop. § 10-702(g).

delay accepting it until a statement had been provided and buyer had been afforded an opportunity to rescind the offer, an unnecessary complication in the marketplace.

Subsection 10-702(k) provides that a buyer's rights under the statute may not effectively be waived in the contract (which presumably would be construed to include any other writing signed before or contemporaneously with entry into the contract), and that "any attempted waiver is void," a statement which could be construed to apply to post-contracting waivers as well. The subsection goes on to provide for an automatic waiver of *any unexercised rescission rights* on the earlier of closing or "occupancy by the purchaser" (or occupancy by the tenant, where a lease with purchase option is involved). Note that this waiver is limited to rescission rights; nothing in the statute suggests that, by going to settlement, buyer waives any rights which it has against seller on account of any misrepresentations in the disclosure statement, and it seems safe to assume that any such rights will survive closing. Subject to the statutory prohibition against waivers made in the contract itself, after the contract is entered into a buyer presumably could waive these rights as well, under the usual common law principles applicable to such waivers that buyer has received consideration for such waiver independent of the original contract consideration or has induced seller into taking some action by agreeing to the waiver.

(e) Seller liability; Buyer remedies

The statute makes clear that a seller's statements made in a disclosure statement constitute "representations,"[84] albeit ones based on seller's actual knowledge. A buyer should keep in mind that there are significant differences between such representations and the warranties typically provided by the builder of a new home. The latter, however limited in scope, are warranties as to the house's *actual* physical condition, under which the builder's state of mind is generally irrelevant. On the other hand, the representations made under Real Prop. § 10-702 are as to seller's state of actual knowledge of certain aspects of the house's physical condition.

Subsection 10-702(i) reiterates this idea. First, it states that a disclosure statement does not constitute a vendor warranty as to the "condition of the property" or "other conditions," in each case if the vendor had no actual knowledge thereof. Second, it provides that seller is not liable for an "error, inaccuracy, or omission" in a disclosure statement, where based on information "not within the actual knowledge of the vendor" (when read literally, an astonishing carveout from vendor liability, given that the contents of the disclosure statement are supposed to reflect seller's actual knowledge, and that buyer may not know otherwise), or on information provided to seller by a governmental body or by a report provided to the vendor, at the vendor's request, by a "licensed engineer, land surveyor, geologist, wood-destroying insect

[84] Real Prop. § 10-702(e)(3)(iii).

control expert, contractor, or other home inspection expert, dealing with matters within the scope of the professional's license or expertise."[85] The statute does not purport to impose liability on sellers even for misrepresentations as to facts of which they do not, but reasonably *should*, have knowledge; however, a court could nevertheless construe the statute as implying such liability, and in any case it often is difficult from an evidentiary standpoint to establish a true lack of actual knowledge in such circumstances.

As might be expected, REAL PROP. § 10-702 does not attempt to elaborate on what is meant by a seller's "actual knowledge," nor could it realistically do so. Unfortunately, this leaves a seller in a quandary if they fear or even suspects that a problematic condition exists but do not actually know that it does. Is a seller required to disclose such fears or suspicions (which may prove groundless), or risk liability for misrepresentation if their existence and accuracy are later proven, or at least alleged?

Similarly, REAL PROP. § 10-702 offers no guidance as to any minimum degree of detail required of the seller in giving "comments" as to its actual knowledge about the conditions listed in the disclosure statement, or as to whether a seller can safely ignore "insignificant" defects when providing a response.

The statute does not provide any remedies to a buyer if such representation as to the state of seller's actual knowledge proves inaccurate. However, a seller presumably will be subject to all common law remedies available to buyer in such circumstances.

(f) Commentary

There are several reasons why an attorney advising a seller should urge the client to provide a disclaimer statement, and not a disclosure statement, to the buyer. To begin with, preparation of a disclosure statement may be time consuming, and may (because it must be delivered *before* entry into the contract) delay the contract signing. Unless prepared by an attorney and treated as what it is—a legal document—it is likely to be legally deficient from seller's standpoint. Having a lawyer prepare it can be expensive.

Second, given the increasingly common practice of buyers[86] to insist on conditioning their closing obligations on a satisfactory professional home inspection, in most transactions seller will be aware that buyer would place minimal reliance on seller's own representations concerning the house's condition, and therefore seller's agreement to provide a disclosure statement will be less important from a bargaining standpoint.

---

85 REAL PROP. § 10-702(h), (i).

86 Discussed in § 2.**41** of this chapter.

Third and perhaps most importantly, for the reasons noted above, the possibility is great that, no matter how careful and diligent the seller, the disclosure statement will contain, or can be alleged by buyer to contain, real or perceived inaccuracies in the form of misstatements or omissions. The meaning of even those statements which it does make could be subject to debate. Even where no such inaccuracies are present, maintenance or repair problems invariably arise after—even long after—closing, and it is the unusual buyer who is not at least tempted to blame them on conditions predating closing. A certain percentage of buyers can be counted upon to seek recovery for these problems against their sellers, where the existence of a disclosure statement arguably gives them a legal basis for doing so.

Thus, the delivery of a disclosure statement could lead to a suit by buyer for fraud or misrepresentation, possibly brought long after closing.[87] In such cases, it will be difficult, from an evidentiary standpoint, to differentiate what was seller's actual knowledge of the physical condition of the house, both from the dwelling's actual physical condition when the representation was made, and from changes in its physical condition occurring since then, even after closing.

That the expense and inconvenience of defending such a suit could be significant, and that as long as such a suit is even theoretically possible seller cannot mentally "close the door" on this chapter in their life, are reasons enough to avoid such exposure. However, a more common scenario arises when, before closing, a buyer believes (or at least alleges) that the disclosure statement contains inaccuracies, and as a result demands concessions from seller, such as a reduction in the purchase price, in exchange for buyer's release of any claim which it might otherwise have for misrepresentation. A seller should avoid giving a buyer such a weapon wherever possible.

4. [§ 2.49] Existence of Ground Lease

Section 7 and 8 of the Real Property Article discuss the requirements for leasehold properties, the registration requirements, disclosure requirements, redemption requirements and collection requirements. §8-811 of the Real Property Article mandates statutory language that must be cited in the contract of sale. Such language is enumerated in the MR Ground Rent Addendum. In addition, contracts in Maryland should designate whether the property is being conveyed in fee simple or subject to an annual ground rent, the MR contract addresses this in Paragraph 6. It is imperative that a seller list the properly accurately, improperly listing the property as fee

---

87 Such suits must be brought, if at all, within three years after the fraud or misrepresentation was discovered or reasonably should have been discovered by buyer through the exercise of due diligence. *See* MD. CODE ANN., COURTS AND JUDICIAL PROCEEDINGS II § 5-101 (2006 & Supp. 2008); *James v. Weisheit*, 279 Md. 41, 367 A.2d 482 (1977); *Merchants Mortgage Co. v. Lubow*, 275 Md. 208, 339 A.2d 664 (1975).

simple when it is in fact leasehold would not render the contract voidable but would expose the seller to the redemption cost of the ground rent.

5. [§ 2.50] Cost of recordation and transfer taxes

Subsections 14-117(c) of the Real Property Article require each contract for the sale of one or two "single-family" dwelling units to contain, in conspicuous type or handwritten in the contract or an addendum, a notice reciting that § 14-104 of the Real Property Article provides that, unless otherwise negotiated in the contract or provided by local law, the cost of state and local transfer or recordation taxes must be shared equally by buyer and seller. Paragraph 51 of the MR form contains the required notice.[88]

6. [§ 2.51] Condominium units

Under § 11-135 of the Maryland Condominium Act,[89] a contract for the resale of a condominium unit by a unit owner other than a developer is not enforceable by seller unless certain conditions are met. These consist of (a) the inclusion of certain notice provisions in the contract itself, and (b) buyer's having been given, at least 15 days before closing, certain disclosure information specified by subsection 11-135(a) (or, where the condominium contains fewer than seven units, subsection 11-135(b)) of the Act. Seller is entitled to obtain this information from the condominium's council of unit owners, which must give seller a certificate containing the requisite information within 20 days after seller requests it. Under subsection 11-135(c), seller is permitted to rely for its accuracy on the information in the certificate, in giving that information to buyer, and will not be liable to buyer for any inaccuracy in such information. However, in the case of the remaining required disclosure information (i.e., that which is not the subject of the council's certificate), a seller who makes an untrue statement of a material fact, or omits to state a material fact needed to make the statements made not misleading, is liable for damages "proximately caused" by the untrue statement or omission unless, when providing the information to buyer, seller had, after reasonable investigation, reasonable grounds to believe (and did believe) that it was true and complete.

The Act provides that buyer may, at any time within seven days after receiving all of the required information, rescind in writing the contract of sale without stating any reason or incurring any liability to seller, and is entitled to the return of any deposit. Although such rescission rights may not be waived by buyer in the contract, by completing closing buyer is deemed to have waived them.[90]

---

88 A discussion of such taxes is found in § 2.**58** of this chapter.

89 REAL PROP. §§ 11-101–11-139.2.

90 REAL PROP. § 11-135(e).

A seller planning the resale of a condominium unit should obtain copies of the condominium declaration, articles of incorporation, bylaws, and rules of the council of unit owners (including any amendments), along with any other information required to be disclosed by seller. The materials and accompanying certificate required to be provided by the council should be obtained as early in the process as is reasonably possible, and seller should remember to include any new or amendatory information as it is received.

The REB Condominium Resale Addendum[91] contains the disclosures required by seller to buyer under the Act.

In addition to mandating these contractual disclosures, subsection 11-135(h) of the Act requires each buyer to notify the council that the transfer occurred, and to provide in such notice certain information, including the names and addresses of buyer and any mortgagee, and seller's forwarding address.

7. [§ 2.52] Dwellings in Homeowners' Association subdivisions

Under the Maryland Homeowners Association Act,[92] a contract for the sale of an improved or unimproved lot within a subdivision which is subject to a "declaration" (defined, generally, as an instrument recorded among the Land Records which gives a homeowners' association the right to impose a "mandatory fee" on the lots or their owners which are subject to the declaration) is not enforceable by seller unless certain conditions are met. For resale transactions, these consist of (a) the inclusion of certain notice provisions in the contract itself, (b) buyer's having been given, before or within 20 days after entering into the contract, certain disclosure information specified by section 11B-106(b) of the Act, and (c) buyer's having been given, "after they become known" to seller, information concerning certain types of material changes to the information previously provided to buyer. Seller is required by the statute to furnish this information, but is permitted to rely for its accuracy on the information concerning the association which is contained in the county's homeowners association depository, maintained pursuant to the Act.

The Act provides that, unless buyer has received all required disclosure information at least five days before entering into the contract, buyer may rescind the contract at any time within five days after receiving such information. Where, after entering into the contract, buyer is given information concerning material changes to the information previously furnished, and such changes "adversely affect" buyer, buyer may rescind the contract within three days after receiving the new information. If buyer rescinds the contract, it is entitled to the return of its deposit, less the

---

91 This addendum can be found in § 2.**83** of this chapter.

92 Real Prop. §§ 11B-101–11B-117.

cost to seller (not exceeding $100) of reproducing the materials furnished to buyer. Although such rescission rights may not be waived by buyer in the contract, by completing closing buyer is deemed to have waived them.[93]

Under § 11B-109 of the Act, a seller who makes an untrue statement of a material fact, or omits to state a material fact needed to make the statements made not misleading, is liable for damages "proximately caused" by the untrue statement or omission, unless, when providing the required information to buyer, seller had, after reasonable investigation, reasonable grounds to believe (and did believe) that it was true and complete. Any suit claiming seller liability under this section must be brought, if at all, within one year after the facts constituting the cause of action are or should have been discovered.

A seller planning the sale of a residence covered by the Act should obtain copies of the declaration of covenants, articles of incorporation, bylaws, and rules of the homeowner's association (including any amendments), along with any other information required to be disclosed by seller. To ensure that the information is accurate and complete, the materials should be obtained from the homeowners' association depository maintained by the clerk of the circuit court for the county, and any additional required information should be obtained, *in writing*, from the homeowners association's management company.

The REB Maryland Homeowners Association Act Disclosure and Notice Addenda[94] contain the disclosures required by seller to buyer under the Act.

In addition to requiring these contractual disclosures, subsection 11B-106(c) of the Act requires each seller, within 30 days after closing, to notify the homeowners' association that the transfer occurred, and to provide in such notice certain information, including the names and addresses of buyer and any mortgagee, and seller's forwarding address.

8. [§ 2.53] Cooperative apartments

Although cooperative housing projects are not numerous in Maryland, the Maryland Cooperative Housing Corporation Act[95] imposes a number of disclosure obligations on the developer of such a project when selling a "cooperative interest" (i.e., a membership in a cooperative housing corporation coupled with a possessory interest in a dwelling unit, usually under a proprietary lease) to a member of the public. However, at present the statute imposes no disclosure obligations in connection with the resale of such cooperative interests.

---

[93] REAL PROP. § 11B-108.

[94] This addenda can be found in §§ 2.**86–2.91** of this chapter.

[95] CORPS. & ASS'NS §§ 5-6B-01–5-6B-20.

9. [§ 2.54] Land installment contracts

REAL PROP. §§ 10-101–10-110, which regulate land installment contracts, require sellers to make certain disclosures in such contracts, although the statute attaches no penalty to a failure to include them.

10. [§ 2.55] Miscellaneous disclosure requirements

REAL PROP. § 14-117 lists a number of other required disclosures, some of which apply to residential resales in particular counties. The MR form includes some, but not all, possible disclosures. For a useful listing of known local requirements, see Chapter 9.

N. Closing

1. [§ 2.56] Date, time, and place

(a) Generally

It is important that the contract specify either a firm date and time of closing, or a procedure for establishing them which is detailed and precise enough to permit them to be determined.

At common law, a contract for the sale and purchase of real property which does not specify a precise settlement date, or from which such a date cannot be determined, is not legally defective, and will be presumed to require that closing occur within a reasonable time after its execution and delivery (except where settlement is conditioned on the occurrence of an event "beyond the control of the parties," in which case the contract will be void under the Rule Against Perpetuities).[96] Nevertheless, little discussion is needed of the practical problems which can arise where a precise closing date cannot be determined by reference to the contract, especially where the parties do not subsequently agree on a date. For the same reasons, it is important that the contract specify where settlement will occur. The parties are always free to agree later to change these terms (by, for example, setting an earlier date), and indeed often do so; as with all contract amendments, such agreements should be written.

---

96 *See Dorado Ltd. P'ship v. Broadneck Dev. Corp.*, 317 Md. 148, 562 A.2d 757 (1989). Under Maryland's version of the Rule Against Perpetuities, a contract or other document conveying or granting the title to any estate in real property is void (and not merely voidable) *ab initio* unless such title must vest in the buyer or other grantee, if at all, within a period after entry into the contract which is not longer than 21 years plus the remaining lifetime of an identified person alive when the contract is signed. In *Dorado*, the Court of Appeals of Maryland held that the Rule applies to contracts for the sale of real property which are enforceable by specific performance, notwithstanding that (as noted in § 2.3) beneficial title to the property passes instantaneously to buyer on creation of the contract, under the doctrine of equitable conversion. The court held that unless the contract requires seller's bare legal title to vest in buyer, if at all, within the perpetuities period, the contract will be void.

The simplest approach is for the contract to recite that closing will occur on a specified date, at a specified time and place. However, in many cases this will not be possible. Frequently, one or the other party is not required to settle until some condition precedent is satisfied or waived, or a party performs some pre-closing duty, and the date or dates on which these events will occur, if at all, are not known in advance. In these cases, the parties generally will agree to settle within a prescribed period (say, 10 days) after the events in question have occurred. Often, they will agree that, if the closing date established by the contract is a Saturday, Sunday, or legal holiday, closing will occur on the next business day.

Occasionally, one result of using this approach is, in effect, to give one party an option to elect whether to settle at all—and, if so, when—by making the closing date depend on that party's subjective judgment that the event in question has occurred (as, for example, where closing depends on satisfaction of a condition precedent, and the party has the right to determine whether it has been satisfied). Even in these cases, it is possible to place some parameters around the party's exercise of its judgment, and hence around its license in setting a closing date, by requiring that the party's "reasonable," and not "sole," judgment be used in determining whether the condition has been met.

Where setting the closing date depends on the occurrence of an event which may not occur, the contract should contain a "drop dead" date, a fixed date on which the contract will automatically terminate if settlement has not occurred. Not only will this satisfy the requirement of the Rule Against Perpetuities (as long as the outside date is within the perpetuities period), but as a practical matter, absent such a date, it will be difficult for the parties to determine whether the contract remains in effect as time passes and no closing occurs. While such difficulty may be hard on a buyer, it usually is much harder on a seller, who is effectively prevented from reselling the house to a third party unless buyer signs a written release of the prior contract, or seller can demonstrate that the title is not still encumbered by the prior contract. In response to the objection occasionally made to a demand that a drop dead date be set—"but what if buyer/seller can't be ready by that date"—the reply should be that the parties should select a drop dead date with which they are comfortable, and not that the contract should omit such a date.

In any case, the contract should expressly state that time is of the essence of the agreement. Otherwise, a party who fails to perform a contractual obligation—for example, payment of the purchase price or delivery of a deed—by the date set for settlement or other date by which performance is stated as being required, will not be deemed in default, as long as performance is tendered within a reasonable time after the prescribed date.[97]

---

97 *Stefanowicz Corp. v. Harris*, 36 Md. App. 136, 373 A.2d 54 (1977).

Finally, where one or the other party is aware that the settlement will have beneficial or adverse income tax consequences, they should consider whether the contract should require closing to occur, or prohibit it from occurring, in a particular tax year. This can be especially important where the date of closing, as established independently of tax considerations, falls at or near the beginning or end of a tax year. Here, an advance or delay of even a few days in having closing can significantly affect the size of the resulting tax benefits or burdens, and the timing of payment of any resulting income taxes.

(b) MR form

Paragraph 10 of the MR form states that settlement is to be on a specified date, "or sooner if agreed to in writing by both parties."

2. *[§ 2.57] Adjustments*

(a) Generally

The contract should provide for the apportionment between seller and buyer of expenses of an ongoing nature which either encumber the title to the property or arise out of its maintenance if liability for such charges will pass to buyer at closing. Such expenses include those for ground rent, water charges, real estate taxes, homeowners' association or condominium assessments, and all other public or governmental charges or assessments payable on an annual basis. They normally do *not* include charges for telephone, gas, electricity, cable television service, oil and gas tanks or other services, where seller's nonpayment of charges incurred before closing cannot result in buyer liability or a post-closing lien on the property. Such charges are merely seller's personal obligations.

Such adjustment clauses usually call for the adjustment to be made as of a particular date. Typically, it is the date of closing, although there may be cases where the logic of the transaction suggests that the adjustment be made as of another date, such as the date of the contract or, where closing has been postponed from an earlier established closing date, such earlier date.

In drafting expense adjustment clauses, the attorney should ascertain whether the expense in question is billed, due and payable *in advance* or *in arrears* (that is, at the beginning or at the end of the tax year or other expense period for which the payment is made). If payable in advance, the contract should provide (and in some cases the law will require) that the expense in fact be paid at or before closing. This is so that buyer will be *debited* at settlement for their allocated share of the amount paid; in effect, a reimbursement to seller of that part of the paid expense allocable to the part of the tax year or expense period which falls after closing.

If, however, the expense is billed, due and payable in arrears, it is often the case that, when closing occurs, the bill for the expense in question has not been rendered and, indeed, that its amount is not even known. Since seller, nevertheless, should bear the cost of that part of the expense which is allocable to the pre-closing period, the contract should provide that if the bill is rendered before closing, it will be adjusted between the parties and paid at closing. It should also provide that if the bill is not rendered before closing, the parties will at closing adjust the expense in question based on either a good faith estimate of its ultimate amount or the expense amount for the immediately preceding expense period. Occasionally, the contract may require the parties to make a corrective adjustment after closing, when the bill for the actual amount has been rendered. In such cases, the parties sometimes provide for a portion of seller's closing proceeds to be retained in escrow until seller's share of any additional payment is known. Since (in the absence of a bill) the adjusted amount cannot actually be paid at closing, buyer will be *credited* at settlement for their allocated share of the expense, and the contract should then require buyer to pay the entire bill when ultimately it is received.

(b) Real property taxes

(i) Generally

In Maryland, state, county, and (if applicable) municipal or special tax district property taxes are levied against individual parcels of land and the improvements on them (commonly known as "tax parcels").[98] Such taxes are levied annually, for a tax year beginning on July 1 and ending on June 30. They are levied in advance and become due and payable on July 1 of the tax year for which they are levied. If payment is made in July or (in most counties) August, a discount is allowed. If paid after September, the amount due is increased by an interest factor.

Although the real property tax is a *state* tax imposed pursuant to state law, the assessment and taxation process is administered by the counties and the City of Baltimore for the properties within their respective boundaries. A separate tax account is maintained for each tax parcel by the local jurisdiction's assessment office. Where property has been subdivided by an approved, recorded subdivision plat, normally each subdivision lot shown on the plat is a separate tax parcel. Thus, where a residence is comprised of two or more (usually contiguous) subdivision lots, separate tax accounts will be established, and separate tax bills issued, for each lot. The same is often true for larger tracts comprised of separate parcels under common ownership.

The state holds a first, super lien on the tax parcel against which the real property taxes are levied, securing payment of taxes then due but unpaid.[99] Such lien has

---

98 MD. CODE ANN., TAX-PROPERTY §§ 6-201–6-204 (2007 & Supp. 2008) (hereinafter TAX-PROP. § ___).

99 TAX-PROP. §§ 14-804 and 14-805.

priority over contracts of sale, deeds, mortgages, deeds of trust, contracts of sale and other liens and encumbrances on the title to the tax parcel, even those created and recorded before the taxes became due. However, a deed conveying the title to any or all of a tax parcel will not be accepted for recordation until all real property taxes levied against it are paid, including those for the current tax year.[100] Thus, after July 1, no deed may be recorded while the taxes which became due on that date remain unpaid.

For these reasons, it is quite important that the contract require seller to pay all unpaid real property taxes accrued before closing or authorize the settlement officer to pay them using all or part of seller's settlement proceeds, after seller receives credit for that part of the current year's taxes which is apportioned to buyer. In theory, seller should retain both the benefit of the discount derived from payment before Sept. 1, and the burden of interest and penalties arising from payment after Sept. 30, although in practice these seldom are considered when the real property tax adjustment is computed.

(ii) Mandatory semiannual payment schedule for owner-occupied residential property

Under TAX-PROP. § 10-204.3, effective July 1, 2000, each county and municipal corporation is required to provide a semiannual payment schedule, applicable to all owner-occupied residential property. The first installment of a semiannual payment is due on July 1 of the tax year and is required to be paid (and may be paid without interest) on or before Sept. 30 of the tax year. The second installment is due on Dec. 1 of the tax year, and except for the service charge, may be paid without interest on or before Dec. 31 of the tax year. The second installment may also be prepaid without the service charge (or interest) on or before Sept. 30 of the tax year.

The service charge consists of (1) an amount reasonably equivalent to the anticipated lost interest income associated with the three-month delay in payment of the second installment, by multiplying the amount of the second installment by a rate not exceeding 1.5%, plus (2) an amount covering administrative expenses, not exceeding the lesser of actual expenses, or 10% of the lost interest component. The service charge does not apply if both installments are paid on or before Sept. 30 of the taxable year.

A lender holding an escrow account for the payment of taxes is required to pay the tax in semiannual installments unless the lender or escrow account servicer has received written direction from the property owner or borrower to pay the property tax in annual payments. The taxpayer must provide written direction to the escrow account servicer at least 60 days prior to the beginning of the tax year if the taxpayer

---

[100] REAL PROP. § 3-104(b).

elects to pay the taxes on an annual basis. If the taxpayer provides the written direction less than 60 days prior to the beginning of the tax year, the escrow account servicer may begin payment of the taxes on an annual basis in the tax year that begins immediately following the year in which the written direction was received.

Only those semiannual payments that are due for the current taxable year are required to be paid prior to the transfer of the property.

The principal intended effect of this section is to reduce the amounts which homebuyers are required to pay at closing into a tax escrow account maintained by buyer's mortgagee. Such lenders typically require buyer to deposit with the lender, at closing, an amount equaling $^{1}/12$ of the anticipated real property taxes for the next tax year, multiplied by the number of months in the current tax year which will have elapsed before the first mortgage payment is due, plus a "cushion" of one or two additional months. Such payment (which is *in addition* to the amount paid by buyer to seller at closing as an adjustment of the *current* year's property taxes) is made to ensure that the lender will hold in the escrow account a full year's taxes (plus the one- or two-month cushion) on the next July 1, when such taxes fall due. The semiannual payment method results in the lender escrowing at closing an amount equaling $^{1}/12$ of the anticipated real property taxes for the next tax year, multiplied by the number of months in the current *half* tax year which will have elapsed before the first mortgage payment is due, plus the same one- or two-month cushion.

This alternate payment method should not affect the manner in which real property taxes for the tax year of settlement are adjusted between the parties, since buyer will still bear the expense of the taxes allocated to the period after closing. The amount adjusted should be the "flat" amount levied for the entire tax year, regardless of when paid by seller. Buyer should consider whether seller should bear the entire cost of any service charge or penalty for late payment associated with the second tax installment.

(c) Special assessments and front-foot benefit charges

Often a residence is encumbered by an obligation to pay what is commonly referred to as a "special assessment" or a "front-foot benefit charge," essentially a governmental or quasi-governmental charge in the nature of a special tax, levied against properties perceived as benefiting from a particular public improvement such as a road or sewer line extension. In these cases, the special charge (representing the property's share of the cost of the public improvement) usually is levied as a lump-sum lien against the property when the public improvement is installed. It is then paid in annual installments over a period of, for example, 20 years, after which the obligation (and lien) are extinguished.

Special assessments typically are administered by the county (or occasionally by a special taxing district or other quasi-governmental authority) in a manner similar to that used for the real property tax. The annual installment frequently is listed as a separate item on the real property tax bill itself and is payable at the same time and in the same manner as the latter. The same lien and other enforcement rights exist for collection of the installments as they become due.

Adjustment clauses normally are uncontroversial. However, sometimes a buyer will raise the economic issue of whether the *entire* unpaid balance of the multi-year front-foot benefit charge—often a substantial sum—should be paid by seller before closing, instead of treating the annual installments as being in the nature of real property taxes, so that the installment for the year of closing is adjusted between the parties as of the closing date or other adjustment date, seller pays all installments for prior years, and buyer pays those for subsequent years. Buyer argues that seller, having gotten the benefit (in the form of a presumably higher purchase price for the house) of the public improvement, should logically bear the full burden of paying for it. Seller counters that, in pricing the house for sale, seller assumed that the special assessment would be adjusted on the basis of annual installments, as if it were another real property tax. Where factually appropriate, seller also argues that (i) seller was not the original owner of the house; (ii) the purchase price which seller paid for the house reflected both the added value conferred by the public improvement and the economic burden of making installment payments for them after the house was bought; and (iii) unless the same approach is used in selling the house, seller will be injured economically (and unfairly). Given that most contracts provide for such charges to be adjusted on an annual basis, seller's argument reflects the prevailing custom. Buyer's demand for a lump-sum payment by seller normally will fly in the face of the unwritten assumptions used in setting market housing prices, and therefore may safely be rejected as unreasonable.

However, from a purely legal standpoint, a contract silent on this point, but containing the customary requirement that title be conveyed free and clear of liens and encumbrances, will often mandate an opposite result. Such assessments usually are not, technically, real property taxes, and thus are not *per se* encompassed by the contract's real property tax adjustment clause. The obligation to pay the full unpaid balance of the special charge (and not merely the current installment amount) is a lien on the property having priority over mortgages and other private encumbrances. Thus, absent anything to the contrary in the contract, seller must deliver title free and clear of this lien, in turn necessitating seller's payment of the full charge.[101] The careful draftsman will make sure that the contract calls for adjustment in the manner discussed above.

---

[101] *Manor Real Estate Co. v. Jos. M. Zamoiski Co.,* 251 Md. 120, 132–33, 246 A.2d 240, 247 (1968). *See also Strass v. District-Realty Title Ins. Corp.,* 31 Md. App. 690, 703–04, 358 A.2d 251, 256 (1976).

Paragraph 49 of the MR form addresses these issues by requiring, among other things, that all "taxes, general or special, and all other public or governmental charges or assessments against the Property which are or may be payable on a periodic basis, including Metropolitan District Sanitary Commission or other benefit charges, assessments, liens or encumbrances for sewer, water, drainage, paving, or other public improvements completed or commenced on or prior to the date hereof, or subsequent thereto, are to be adjusted and apportioned as of the date of settlement and are to be assumed and paid thereafter by Buyer, whether assessments have been levied or not as of date of settlement if applicable by local law."

Many times, the front foot fee or deferred water and sewer charge is not charged by a government entity but by a private company. In this event, Section 14-117(a)(5) of the Real Property Article of the Annotated Code of Maryland requires that "A contract for the resale of residential real property that is served by public water or wastewater facilities for which deferred water and sewer charges have been established by a recorded covenant or declaration shall contain a notice in substantially the following form:

'NOTICE REQUIRED BY MARYLAND LAW REGARDING

DEFERRED WATER AND SEWER CHARGES

This property is subject to a fee or assessment that purports to cover or defray the cost of installing or maintaining during construction all or part of the public water or wastewater facilities constructed by the developer. This fee or assessment is $____, payable annually in (__month__) until (__date__) to (__name and address__) (hereafter called "lienholder").' "

If Buyer is not provided the above disclosure prior to entering into the contract they are entitled to rescind the contract of sale and retain the earnest money deposit. If the aforementioned disclosure, is not provided to the buyer prior to closing and there is a deferred water and sewer fee then the seller shall be liable to the buyer for the full amount of any fee or assessment not disclosed, unless the seller was never charged a fee or assessment to defray the cost of public water or wastewater facilities by the developer, a successor of the developer, or a subsequent assignee.

Paragraph 28 of the MR form and Notice and Disclosure of Deferred Water and Sewer Charges provide the required legal disclosures.[102]

(d) Condominium and homeowners' association assessment*s*

Where a dwelling is a condominium unit or is subject to a homeowners' association (HOA) regime, the contract should provide for an adjustment of any

---

[102] § 2.91 of this chapter

assessments and other charges levied against the unit or dwelling by the condominium's council of unit owners or the homeowners' association, pursuant to the declaration and other constituent documents establishing the condominium or HOA regime.

In Maryland (as in most states), a condominium's council of unit owners has the power, by virtue of both the Maryland Condominium Act[103] and the recorded condominium documents, to levy various assessments against the respective units within the condominium, much like a private tax. If the assessment is not paid when due, the council has the power under the Condominium Act and the Maryland Contract Lien Act[104] to obtain a private lien against the title to the unit in question, by recording a statement of lien among the Land Records. Such lien takes priority as of the date and time of its recordation over subsequent bona fide contract purchasers and others whose priorities are established by recordation or notice,[105] and may be enforced in much the same manner as a mortgage or deed of trust is enforced—through a foreclosure proceeding. Moreover, under subsection 11-110(c) of the Condominium Act, a buyer who accepts title to a unit encumbered by a statement of lien becomes jointly and severally liable with seller for payment of the assessment in question.

Maryland has no statute comparable to the Condominium Act creating a statutory lien and assessment right for HOAs. Such assessment rights are instead created by the private, recorded HOA declaration and other HOA documents, and thus are *contractual*, and not statutory, in nature. Typically, these documents grant the association the power to levy assessments against the respective subdivision lots or parcels whose titles they encumber, under terms substantively identical in function to those of a condominium declaration. However, once such contractual lien rights are created by the HOA documents, their enforcement is empowered and regulated by the Maryland Contract Lien Act. As with a condominium assessment lien, such lien takes priority as of the date and time of its recordation, over subsequent bona fide contract purchasers and others whose priorities are established by recordation or notice and may be enforced through a foreclosure proceeding.

Contracts for the sale of condominium units and dwellings subject to HOA regimes should, for these reasons, provide for the adjustment between the parties of all assessments levied by the council of unit owners or homeowners' association, regardless of whether a statement of lien has been recorded therefor. Obtaining the information needed to make this adjustment is not always easy. Unlike real property tax records, there is no public repository for condominium and HOA assessment

---

103 REAL PROP. §§ 11-101–11-139.2.

104 REAL PROP. §§ 14-201–14-206.

105 REAL PROP. § 14-203(h)(4).

records, which are in a legal sense private records. Parties desiring to make an adjustment must first locate the place in which these records are maintained. Often (but not always), this will prove to be the office of a professional real property management company under contract to manage the council's or HOA's business affairs, and the condominium's or HOA's common property. The parties must then obtain a written statement from the council or HOA as to the needed assessment status information and satisfy themselves that the person giving it has the power to speak for, and bind by estoppel, the council or homeowners' association.

(e) Public water and sanitary sewer service

In the City of Baltimore and most other urban or suburban areas, residences receive public water and sanitary sewer service for which their owners are billed, usually quarterly. Since the amount billed is normally a function of the actual consumption of water, measured by the residence's water meter, water bills must be rendered in arrears. Contracts for the sale of homes in areas served by public water service should recognize this when providing for the adjustment of water charges, in the manner discussed above.

(f) Fuel oil

Where the house is oil-heated, the contract should require buyer to reimburse seller at closing for the cost of any fuel oil left in the storage tank, specifying where possible a dollar amount per gallon. The MR form Paragraph 49 specifically states in bold font "any heating or cooking fuels remaining in supply tank(s)at time of settlement shall become the property of Buyer."

(g) Other utility charges

Even though utility charges (other than those for public water and sanitary sewer service) normally are not adjusted between the parties as part of the closing process, to avoid liability for buyer's post-closing use of such utility services, seller should make sure that the utility provider is notified of the closing date, and that the utility meters are given a final reading immediately before or after closing, so that seller's account with the provider can be closed out and a new account opened with buyer.

(h) Tax and insurance escrow accounts under assumed mortgages

Where buyer is assuming seller's mortgage, and seller has, under the mortgage, paid money into an escrow account maintained by the mortgagee for payment of real property taxes and/or insurance premiums on the property, seller should make sure either that the funds in the account are refunded to seller at closing (which normally would necessitate buyer's replacing them with the mortgagee), or that buyer reimburses seller at closing for the amount in the account, which should then be assigned to buyer.

3. *[§ 2.58] Transfer and recordation taxes; agricultural transfer taxes; forest conservation programs*

(a) Generally

Under both state and (in most counties) local law, various taxes are levied on the recordation of a deed or other "instrument of writing" conveying title to a fee simple or other estate or interest in real property. Such taxes are a function of the purchase money and other consideration paid for the estate or other interest being conveyed, including the unpaid balance of any mortgage or deed of trust debt being assumed by buyer. Currently, the state levies both a *transfer* tax and a *recordation* tax (sometimes called a "documentary stamp" tax) on such instruments. With certain exceptions, the state transfer tax rate is 0.5% of the consideration, while the recordation tax rate varies from county to county and is expressed as a dollar amount per each $500 of consideration.[106] In addition to these state taxes, various counties and the City of Baltimore levy local transfer taxes on the recordation of documents conveying real property within their jurisdictions, generally equaling a percentage of the consideration for the conveyance.[107] In most jurisdictions, the aggregate amount of these state and local taxes is in the neighborhood of two percent of the purchase price, a substantial cost.

While the state and (except in Prince George's County) local *transfer* taxes are not levied on the recordation of a "mortgage, deed of trust, or other contract that creates an encumbrance on real property," such documents are subject to the *recordation* tax.[108] However, an exemption is allowed for a mortgage or deed of trust securing (and so reciting) purchase money payable for the real property which it encumbers, provided that it is "delivered as part of the same transaction" as the

---

106 The state transfer tax is levied pursuant to TAX-PROP. §§ 13-201–13-209, while the state recordation tax is levied pursuant to TAX-PROP. §§ 12-101–12-118. As of October 1, 2023, the recordation tax rates per $500 of consideration varied from a high of $11.35 (if over a Million, sliding scale if price is between $500,000.00 and $1,000,000.00) in Montgomery County to a low of $2.50 in Baltimore and Howard Counties respectively. See generally *Abington Ctr. Assocs. Ltd. P'ship v. Baltimore County*, 115 Md. App. 580, 694 A.2d 165 (1997), stating that Title 13 applies to state and county transfer taxes and noting that § 13-402.1 permits counties with home rule powers to impose transfer taxes.

107 In the metropolitan counties, the local transfer tax rates as of October 1, 2023, are as follows: City of Baltimore, 1.5%; Anne Arundel County, 1.0%; Baltimore County, 1.5%; Harford County, 1.0%; Howard County, 1.25%; Montgomery County, 1.0% (with narrow, but significant, variations); and Prince George's County, 1.4% (with minor variations). As of October 1, 2023, Calvert, Carroll, Frederick, Somerset and Wicomico Counties do not levy a county transfer tax.

108 See the differing definitions of "instrument of writing" found in TAX-PROP. §§ 13-101(e) and 12-101(j).

deed of conveyance, that the deed itself is subject to the recordation tax, and that the mortgage or deed of trust is signed and recorded within 30 days after the deed is signed and recorded. This exemption is required to avoid double taxation, since the recordation tax will already have been paid on the purchase money when the deed itself is recorded.[109]

In addition to these taxes, generally applicable to *all* real estate sale transactions, a state Agricultural Land Transfer Tax is levied on the recordation of a deed or other "instrument of writing" conveying title to or an interest in land which, at the time of conveyance or at any time during the immediately preceding four full *tax* years, has been assessed on the basis of farm or agricultural use for real property taxation purposes, unless the property will continue to be used (and assessed) as farmland.[110] The tax is levied *in addition* to the regular state and local transfer taxes, but is not assessed on the consideration paid for any improvements. The base rate of the Agricultural Land Transfer Tax varies from 3% to 5%, but declines by 25% of this base for each full, consecutive tax year which elapses before the deed is recorded, during which the land is no longer assessed as farm or agricultural land.

In negotiating a contract of sale, careful attention should be paid to the provisions allocating between seller and buyer the burden of these taxes levied on recordation of the deed. With the narrow exceptions discussed below, the following principles will apply:

(i) Buyer and seller are under no legal constraints in agreeing to allocate such taxes entirely to one party or the other, or to divide them equally or in some other manner.

(ii) The general—although not universal—custom observed in residential resales (as distinguished from builder sales) is for these taxes to be divided equally between seller and buyer.

---

109 TAX-PROP. § 12-108(k). Note that chapter 165, Acts 1997, effective July 1, 1997, added (k)(2) regarding the date an instrument is fully executed. Where a mortgage or deed of trust is being assumed by buyer when purchasing seller's *principal* residence, and the recordation tax is paid on the deed of conveyance, a subsequent grant by buyer of a new mortgage or deed of trust encumbering the property, and securing a new debt incurred to *refinance* (and not exceeding) the then-unpaid principal balance of the assumed debt, is also exempt from the recordation tax, provided that the property is also buyer's principal residence. With the same qualifications, a buyer may refinance its own purchase money mortgage debt without payment of the recordation tax. *See* TAX-PROP. § 12-108(e).

110 TAX-PROP. § 13-301–13-308. Assessment as farm or agricultural land normally results in substantially lower real property taxes for the land in question. Note that, for purposes of the Agricultural Land Transfer Tax, the status of the land for *zoning* purposes is irrelevant.

(iii) By statute, if the contract is *silent* on this issue, seller and buyer are deemed to have agreed to divide such taxes equally between them.[111]

Most contracts require that each party's share of these taxes be paid at closing, so that the title company or other person responsible for recording the deed of conveyance will have the funds with which to do so.

If buyer is granting a non-purchase money mortgage or deed of trust to secure, for example, a construction loan, the recordation tax on this document should be paid by buyer.

(b) Exceptions

As noted, there are several exceptions to these general principles:

(i) First-time homebuyer

Chapter 123 of the Laws of Maryland 1995 replaced the former state transfer tax exemption for the first $30,000 of consideration payable for "residentially improved owner-occupied real property" provided by TAX-PROP. § 13-203(b), with a reduction of from 0.5% to 0.25% in the state transfer tax applicable to the sale of "improved residential real property to a first-time Maryland home buyer who will occupy the property as a principal residence." The new statute requires this tax to be paid entirely by seller and does not permit the parties to allocate it in any other manner. This requirement will have no adverse impact on the economics of the typical residential resale transaction (in which, as noted, seller usually bears one-half of the regular 0.5% state transfer) and may in fact be advantageous for such a seller, who can argue that buyer's reduced closing costs allow buyer to afford a higher price. However, a seller whose "bargain" is based on buyer's payment of *all* of the state transfer tax must ascertain whether buyer qualifies for this exemption before signing a contract, since any agreement shifting the tax back to buyer presumably is unenforceable.

Subsection 13-203(b) defines a "first-time Maryland home buyer" as an individual who has *never* owned Maryland residential real property that has been such person's principal residence. If there is more than one grantee, to qualify for the exemption *each* of them must be either (1) a first-time Maryland home buyer who will occupy the residence as their principal residence, or (2) a co-maker or guarantor of a purchase money mortgage or deed of trust covering the property who will *not* occupy the residence as their principal residence (for example, a non-occupying parent who takes title as co-grantee with a first-time Maryland home buyer son or daughter, and who is obligated as co-maker or guarantor of the purchase money mortgage debt). To qualify, each grantee must certify under oath as to their status

[111] See REAL PROP. §§ 14-104(b), which applies to the recordation tax, and to both state and local transfer taxes.

as a first-time Maryland home buyer.[112] A recent declaration by the Attorney General's office has stated that if grantees qualify as first-time Maryland homeowners for different reasons, grantees must execute separate affidavits in accordance with their respective statuses. In response to a ruling by the Attorney General's office, effective July 1, 2001, TAX-PROP. §§ 13-203 and 13-409 were amended to allow the necessary affidavits to be executed by an agent of a grantee. The agent is charged with making a diligent inquiry into the facts averred in the affidavit.

The same enacting Act created another exception to the general principles concerning transfer and recordation tax allocations discussed above. New subsection 14-104(b) imposes the *entire* burden of the state recordation tax, and of any county or City transfer tax, on the seller of "improved, residential real property that is sold to a first-time Maryland home buyer who will occupy the property as a principal residence," unless the parties expressly agree otherwise.[113] This will have no effect on the typical residential sale contract in which the parties agree to divide these taxes between them. However, where a contract selling a residence to a person falling within the above definition is silent on this issue, the usual statutory presumption—that they are divided equally between seller and buyer—will no longer apply. Thus, to avoid this extra burden, a seller should make sure that the contract expressly allocates the burden of these taxes in the manner agreed upon by the parties.[114]

(ii) Agricultural land transfer tax

Under TAX-PROP. § 13-308, unless a seller of land subject to the Agricultural Land Transfer Tax notifies the buyer *in writing* that the transfer may be subject to the tax, the seller is liable to the buyer for the full amount of the tax paid by the buyer.

---

[112] Chapter 123 of Acts of Maryland 1995 also authorizes each county and the City of Baltimore to enact an exemption from the state recordation tax, and/or any county or City transfer tax, for "instruments of writing" for residentially improved owner-occupied real property, where the grantee is a person meeting the same requirements as those for qualification for the reduction in the state transfer tax. *See* TAX-PROP. §§ 12-103(b)(3) and 13-409. In the case of the recordation tax, this authorization substantially overlaps existing subsection 12-103(b)(2), which authorizes these governing bodies to exempt a *specified amount* of the consideration from the recordation tax where the buyer intends to actually occupy the residence for at least seven months of a 12-month period. Under the latter subsection, buyer need not be a first-time Maryland homebuyer, and if buyer is not, the normal principles governing the allocation of such tax, discussed above, apply.

[113] As noted above, the parties are not free to "agree otherwise" as to the imposition of the reduced *state* transfer tax on seller under these circumstances.

[114] Baltimore County has enacted an exemption from the county transfer tax for the first $22,000 of consideration for an instrument of writing for residentially improved owner-occupied property, regardless of whether the buyer is a first-time Maryland homebuyer; the statute makes clear that the savings is divided equally between the parties unless they otherwise agree. *See* County Council Bill 66-95, enacted April 17, 1995.

Thus, absent the required notice (usually set forth in the contract itself), the statute will override any agreement by the parties to allocate this tax in any other manner.

Paragraph 39 of the MR form contains the required statutory notice concerning the possible applicability of the Agricultural Land Transfer Tax, and allows the parties to allocate the cost by designating buyer or seller in the blank space.

(iii) Forest conservation programs

An owner of five or more contiguous acres of woodlands, desiring to preserve the forested state of the land in return for receiving a "frozen" real property tax assessment, may participate in a Forest Conservation Program with the Maryland Department of Natural Resources as described in TAX-PROP. § 8-211. The program requires that the owner enter into a "Forest Conservation and Management Agreement," which must run for a term of at least 15 years. A memorandum of the agreement must be recorded in the local land records. The owner of land that is subject to an agreement must notify a prospective buyer promptly before a sale that the land is subject to an agreement. The buyer may elect to continue the agreement under certain conditions. If the property is transferred to the buyer without the buyer continuing the agreement, the land loses its favorable "frozen" assessment and penalty taxes for prior years would become due. Paragraph 45 of the MAR form includes the required disclosure to the buyer and provides for the allocation of the penalty taxes to the party named.

(c) MR form

Paragraph 51 of the MR form deals with Transfer charges and provides, in part, that the costs of transfer and recordation taxes, other than the Agricultural Land Transfer Tax, will be divided equally between buyer and seller, unless the parties agree otherwise on the blank space. It also provides that the buyer will receive any owner occupancy reduction offered by a jurisdiction. Paragraph 51 also addresses the first-time home buyer regulation and states that other than the state transfer tax which will be reduced from .5% to .25% and paid entirely by the seller, the recordation and county transfer tax shall be split equally between the buyer and seller.

4. [§ 2.59] Recording fees; title insurance charges

In addition to transfer and recordation taxes, a nominal fee is charged for the recordation of any deed, mortgage, deed of trust, release, or other document among the Land Records. Essentially, the fee is $20 for any document solely involving a principal residence, plus a $20 statewide surcharge.[115] By custom, the fee charged for recording a deed is paid by buyer, who of course also pays the fee for recording

---

[115] REAL PROP. § 3-601(a), which sets forth the list of recording fees for these and other documents.

any purchase money mortgage loan documents. Seller typically pays the fee for recording a release of seller's own mortgage, which in most cases is being repaid at closing pursuant to the contract.

The prevailing practice in Maryland (although not in some other parts of the United States) is for buyer to pay all premiums charged by the buyer's title insurer and all title abstracting and title examination charges.

O. Possession and Condition of Property

1. [§ 2.60] Delivery of possession

Unless otherwise agreed by the parties, seller is obligated to surrender possession of the property to buyer at the time of settlement, a legal act usually accomplished by seller's moving from the dwelling. In accordance with the usual practice,[116] the contract should require seller to cause the dwelling to be broom clean and in the same condition as it was in when the contract was signed, except for changes resulting from ordinary wear and tear. Seller should be required to remove all of their personal property from the residence before closing. As discussed in § 2.**29** of this chapter, seller will otherwise want the right to deliver the improvements "as is" as of the time of sale.

In the absence of an agreement to this effect, buyer has no right at law to inspect the property before completing settlement. Since most buyers desire this right in order to be satisfied that no material change has been made since the contract was signed, buyer should make sure that the contract so provides.[117] Paragraph 25 of the MR form grants buyer a right to inspect the dwelling within five days before closing.

Occasionally, a seller may desire to retain possession after settlement or a buyer may desire to take possession before settlement. No such right exists unless included in the contract. An example of such an agreement in letter form is set forth in **§ 2.77** of this chapter.

2. [§ 2.61] Risk of loss

(a) Generally

Most residential sale contracts (including Paragraph 15 of the MR form) provide that the property is to be held "at the risk" of seller (or that seller holds the "risk of loss") until settlement or delivery of possession to buyer, whichever occurs first. The "risk" in question is that of destruction or damage to the improvements.

---

[116] As discussed in § 2.**61** of this chapter, this practice actually is contrary to the classic theory of equitable conversion.

[117] Note that this inspection—commonly referred to as a "walk-through"—is a later, more cursory, inspection than that done for purposes of a home inspection clause.

Despite their frequent use, these phrases have no precise meaning by themselves. Were the contract silent on the issue of risk of loss, the theory of equitable conversion would hold that buyer, as beneficial owner of the property, assumes the risk that the improvements are damaged or destroyed after the contract is signed and before closing.[118] Therefore, this result will be altered only if the contract so provides.

The contract language imposing the "risk of loss" on seller is meaningful only if and to the extent that the contract also imposes on seller the duty to deliver the improvements to buyer at closing in substantially their same condition as on the date of the contract. While most contracts do this, many fall short of requiring seller to restore any casualty damage or imposing liability on seller for damages if the improvements are destroyed by a casualty.[119] Instead, they require seller to maintain at least its present casualty insurance coverage on the improvements. Most contracts also provide that if, before closing or delivery of possession, the improvements are destroyed or substantially damaged other than due to buyer's fault, buyer may terminate the agreement and have its deposit returned.

A variation on this theme permits seller to avoid termination by restoring the improvements if seller elects to do so, in its sole discretion. Most clauses provide that if buyer does not terminate the contract but seller does not elect to restore, the parties will consummate closing if all other conditions are satisfied or waived, without any reduction in the purchase price, and that at closing seller will assign to buyer all proceeds of casualty insurance payable on account of the casualty to the real property.

As noted above, where the contract requires seller to deliver the improvements to buyer at closing in substantially the same condition as on the date of the contract, seller runs the additional risk that, if unable to perform this obligation due to a casualty, seller may be liable to buyer for damages. Since such a result is seldom contemplated when the parties strike their bargain, seller should protect itself by including in the contract a provision limiting buyer's remedies in such event to those discussed above.

It is important that the contract require seller to maintain at least the amount of casualty insurance on the improvements that seller maintained at the time of sale, and that buyer be named as an additional insured in the policy, but only while the contract is in effect.[120] Buyer should satisfy itself that seller's coverage is adequate and, if not, should consider increasing it by purchasing additional insurance in buyer's own name, especially if the purchase price exceeds the amount of seller's insurance.

---

118 *Brewer v. Herbert*, 30 Md. 301 (1869).

119 Of course, seller will always be liable to buyer if seller commits waste as to the improvements, but under a tort, not a contract, theory.

120 Although most contracts include this requirement, it is often ignored by both parties.

(b) MR *form*

Paragraph 15 of the MR form provides that if "all or a substantial part" of the property is destroyed or damaged before settlement, buyer may elect to void the contract and have the deposit refunded. Although the MR form is silent on this point, if buyer does not elect to terminate, the purchase price will not be reduced. Nothing in the MR form purports to entitle buyer to any of seller's casualty insurance proceeds, or to require seller to name buyer as an additional insured in seller's policies.

P. Remedies on Default

1. [§ 2.62] Generally

Most buyers are not aware that if they default, they could be liable for more than forfeiture of the deposit, or that in Maryland both seller and buyer may sue for specific performance. For this reason, the attorney should advise their client of the potential liability that the client will incur if they default.

Strictly speaking, it is not legally necessary for a resale contract to address the remedies which the parties are to have if either of them defaults. If the contract is silent on this point, the usual common law remedies for breach of contract—essentially, rescission, damages, and/or specific performance—will be available. Only if the parties desire to *add* remedies which ordinarily would not be available as a matter of law, or to *limit* those otherwise available as a matter of law, will they need to deal with the subject of default remedies in the contract itself.

In most cases, however, seller or buyer desires to modify the common law rules by enhancing or limiting the remedies otherwise available for default. Typically, these changes center around the contract terms dealing with disposition of the deposit on default. In drafting such provisions, the parties should make sure that they are consistent with those contract provisions dealing generally with the deposit.

(a) Buyer defaults

Sellers of real property almost always want the right, on a buyer default, to elect to declare the deposit forfeited as *liquidated damages* (that is, as damages not dependent on proof of seller's actual loss, if any), and most residential resale contracts so provide. For the deposit amount to be treated in this manner, the contract should specify that seller has the right to declare it "forfeited as liquidated damages." If seller elects to declare a forfeiture of the deposit, the contract is terminated and seller has no further rights against buyer on account of the buyer default.

Most Board form contracts give this right to seller as an *optional* alternative to simply declaring the default and suing buyer for damages or specific performance. If seller wants to have all of these alternate remedies, the contract should make clear that a decision to declare the deposit forfeited is at seller's option; that is, that such election does not automatically flow from a mere declaration that buyer is in default, and unless seller elects to forfeit the deposit, seller is free to pursue all other available remedies against a defaulting buyer.[121]

Buyers occasionally ask that seller's remedies for a buyer default be *limited* to a forfeiture of the deposit, following the common practice in commercial sales. Where the deposit is large enough, this is not unreasonable, especially since, as discussed in § 2.**39** of this chapter, in most cases it is unlikely that a seller, having the remedy of forfeiture available, will want to pursue other remedies. However, from seller's standpoint, merely having the *right* to pursue other remedies often makes it less likely that a defaulting buyer will contest forfeiture of the deposit, since in any legal proceeding concerning the latter seller can be counted on to plead its other remedies in the alternative.[122]

If seller agrees to this request, the contract should make clear that seller's *sole* remedy for a buyer default is forfeiture of the deposit (and any interest accrued on it while being held in escrow), and that seller expressly waives its right to seek specific performance of buyer's contractual obligations. Indeed, if the parties intend to waive *any* remedies, they should make certain that the waiver is clear and explicit.[123]

(b) Seller defaults

Most residential resale contracts impose no limits on buyer's remedies for seller defaults, so that buyer will have all breach of contract remedies available at law or in equity. Occasionally, however, a seller will insist that buyer's only remedy should be to seek specific performance (and not damages) if a seller default occurs. Sellers ask for this both to avoid liability for possible consequential damages, and because even the direct damages flowing from the breach (as measured by the "value" of buyer's bargain) could, in a rapidly rising market, exceed seller's equity.

Buyers should resist this for two reasons. First, obtaining a court-ordered right to specific performance after a costly and lengthy lawsuit may no longer be desirable for buyer, who may have been forced to make other living arrangements due to the seller default, and no longer wants (or is in a financial position) to purchase seller's house. Second, there are circumstances—for example, if the seller's default results from a seller misrepresentation, or from seller's having already sold and conveyed the house to a third-party, bona fide purchaser—in which the remedy of specific performance will not be available.

---

121 *Miller v. U.S. Naval Inst.*, 47 Md. App. 426, 434–35, 423 A.2d 283, 287–88 (1980). Note that, as discussed in *Miller*, a seller's mere *retention* of the deposit pending the outcome of a suit against buyer for *actual* damages is not the same as a forfeiture.

122 Of course, where the deposit is small, such a request is not reasonable.

123 *See id.*

Where seller makes representations to buyer in the contract, seller should consider imposing a shorter limitations period—say, one year—on buyer actions for fraud or misrepresentation than the three years provided by law (and discussed in § 2.**41** of this chapter). Buyer should make sure, before agreeing to this, that the period is measured from discovery of the misrepresentation, and not from closing.

Finally, it is almost too obvious to mention that a contract which purports to limit buyer's remedies on a seller default to the right to have the deposit returned to buyer effectively gives buyer no remedy at all.

(c) Escrowee's position

As noted in § 2.**34** of this chapter, in most cases the deposit is held by a broker or other escrow holder, namely a title company. Although in negotiating the contract the parties sometimes spend a great deal of time haggling over the rules under which the escrow agent is required to return the deposit to buyer or, alternately, deliver it to seller, in nearly every case this will prove to be a waste of time. No matter what the contract or any related escrow agreement provides in this regard, if when the time arrives for disposition of the deposit there is even a suggestion of a dispute between the parties over who receives it, the escrowee can be counted upon not to disburse it to either party and, if necessary, to pay it into court under an interpleader action. Indeed, many escrowees refuse to disburse the deposit—other than at a successful closing—even where there is no apparent dispute between the parties, unless the escrowee has received signed, joint instructions from the parties concerning its disposition. This is not the case however, if the buyer terminates the contract pursuant to a contingency.[124]

The contract should require the losing party to pay all court costs and legal fees incurred by the escrowee or either party if there is a dispute over disposition of the deposit, since absent such a provision these expenses could negate the value to the victorious party of ultimately "winning" the deposit.

A seller should remember that most listing agreements between seller and broker entitle the broker to withhold one-half of the deposit as a commission, if a contract is signed but buyer defaults, resulting in a forfeiture of the deposit. It is not unusual for a seller to insist, when negotiating the listing agreement, that this provision be deleted, on the theory that the broker should not be paid if the settlement does not occur due to no fault of seller. Where seller and broker agree to this change, the listing agreement should be modified to make clear that no commission will be due if settlement does not occur for any reason other than a seller default. In addition, seller should make sure that the contract of sale itself does not contain boilerplate language restoring to the broker the right to a share of the commission if the deposit is forfeited.

---

[124] Real Prop. §10-803 sets forth the definition of contingency and the requirements for seller and escrow holder regarding releasing the earnest money deposit.

2. [§ 2.63] MR form

Paragraph 9 of the MR form follows the customary approach described above, to the extent that it imposes no limits on the remedies available to either party for a default by the other.

Notwithstanding, Paragraph 9 of the MR form also recognizes that a broker holding a deposit may distribute the funds in accordance with the provisions of Bus. Occ. & Prof. § 17-505(b)(1). That section provides a procedural framework whereby the broker may be able to disburse the deposit to the party who in the good faith opinion of the broker, is entitled to receive the deposit.[125]

In the event that the parties' differences cannot be resolved through disposition of the deposit, Paragraph 60 of the MR form provides a compulsory mediation provision, requiring buyer and seller to submit to mediation "any claim arising out of or from this Contract or the transaction which is the subject of this Contract." The mediation clause is applicable to all such "disputes and claims arising whether prior to, during or within one (1) year following settlement." Further, Paragraph 60 precludes the parties from filing suit on the matter, without first submitting the dispute or claim to mediation. A party who does not submit the matter to mediation prior to filing suit will be liable to the other party for all costs, expenses, and reasonable attorneys' fees incurred by such party in enforcing the mediation provision.

Attorneys tend to look unfavorably upon "standard" mediation and arbitration clauses in contract forms. Counsel for otherwise adverse parties often agree to delete such provisions. However, the attorney counseling the client in the context of a residential sale should not dismiss the mediation provisions out of hand. Mediation may be a cost-effective means of getting two otherwise recalcitrant parties back on the right track following occurrence of a problem perceived as "serious," but, perhaps, capable of a reasonable resolution. The parties, themselves, ultimately find, or do not find, their own resolution; the mediator acts only as a neutral and constructive middle person.

Paragraph 61 of the MR form states that in any action or proceeding involving a dispute between the parties and/or the brokers, the losing party must pay the winning party's "reasonable attorney's fees to be determined by the court or arbitrator."

Q. Miscellaneous Clauses

1. [§ 2.64] Entire agreement

Usually, a contract is preceded by a series of oral or written discussions or other communications between the parties or their representatives, some of which could be held by a court to rise to the level of representations, or to modify or add to the

---

125 See the full discussion in **§ 1.37** of this chapter.

terms of the business agreement expressed in the contract itself. Seldom was this the result intended by either party when the contract was signed. To eliminate this possibility, the contract should state that it represents the final and entire agreement between the parties concerning the subject matter of the contract, and that neither they nor their agents shall be bound by any communication or other statement, written or oral, not contained in the contract.

Consequently, if in entering into the contract either party is relying on specific representations or other undertakings made by the other party or its agents, the first party should make sure that they are included in the contract itself, either expressly or by express reference to an identified document in which they are contained, which should be incorporated by reference into the contract.

2. [§ 2.65] Merger

The reverse of the problem discussed in the immediately preceding section could occur at closing. In the absence of a provision to the contrary, buyer's acceptance of the deed creates a presumption that all representations, warranties, and covenants made in the contract of sale are merged in the deed.[126] As a result, at settlement, the provisions of the contract will cease to be enforceable unless they are restated in the deed itself, or unless the parties expressly agree (in the contract or otherwise) that they will survive settlement and not be merged in the deed.[127] Where representations, warranties, or other undertakings are made in the contract as to the condition of the premises or otherwise, buyer should make sure that the contract includes appropriate survival provisions.

3. [§ 2.66] Time of essence

As noted in § 2.**56** of this chapter, unless time is stated to be of the essence of the parties' agreement, a party will not be deemed at law to be in default for failing to perform by a prescribed date, as long as performance is tendered within "a reasonable time." In Maryland, the courts have construed 30 days to be reasonable depending on the circumstances.[128] While normally both parties will want time to be of the essence of their agreement, there may be circumstances where one or the other party should consider removing this provision.

Paragraph 2 of the MR form specifically states, that time is of the essence.

---

126 *Kandalis v. Paul Pet Constr. Co.*, 210 Md. 319, 322, 123 A.2d 345, 347 (1956).

127 *See Randolph Hills, Inc. v. Shoreham Developers, Inc.*, 266 Md. 182, 292 A.2d 662, 667–68 (1972). *See also Dillow v. Magraw*, 102 Md. App. 343, 649 A.2d 1157 (1994), *aff'd*, 341 Md. 492, 671 A.2d 485 (1996) (once contract is executed and deed accepted, under merger doctrine there is *prima facie* presumption that rights of parties are governed by deed; presumption may be negated by contract provision stating terms of contract survive settlement).

128 *See String v. Steven Dev. Corp.*, 269 Md. 569, 577–78, 307 A.2d 713, 718 (1973).

4. [§ 2.67] Assignment

In Maryland, as in most other states, a contract for the sale and purchase of real property normally is freely assignable by both parties, unless it expressly provides otherwise. An assigning party remains liable for performance of all of its obligations under the contract, notwithstanding the assignment.

Seller assignments are naturally rare, except where assignment of seller's rights (usually the right to proceeds) is made as collateral for a loan or other seller obligation. An assignee from seller is, of course, subject to all of buyer's rights under the contract.

On the other hand, it is quite common for buyers to assign their contract rights. Sometimes this is done for marital or estate-planning reasons, as where a contracting spouse assigns the contract to themselves and the other spouse. Often, however, it is done because a third party offers to buy the purchaser's rights and obligations under the contract, either for no profit (where the original buyer no longer wants to complete the transaction) or for a real profit (where the purchase price is below the perceived fair market value of the dwelling, as often happens in a rising market). For these reasons, having the right to assign is usually important to a buyer.

Normally, a seller has few, if any, reasonable grounds for insisting that the contract prohibit all buyer assignments. As long as buyer's only real duty under the contract is to pay the purchase price, buyer cannot be said to be providing services to seller which only the original buyer can adequately perform. However, a seller should be concerned that the assignment be made to someone who will qualify for the financing needed to complete the purchase and should ask that buyer's right to assign be restricted to such persons. For the same reason, a seller who has agreed to take back a purchase money mortgage from the original buyer will want the right to approve the creditworthiness of any proposed assignee.

If buyer does decide to assign the contract, the assignment should be in writing and should contain the assignor's and assignee's agreement concerning the terms of the assignment. The assignee should agree to perform all of the assignor's obligations under the contract. The assignor should represent and warrant to the assignee that assignor owns (and has not encumbered) the rights being assigned, that the copies of the contract provided to the assignee are true and complete, as to whether it has been amended, and as to the status of monetary payments, satisfaction, or waiver of conditions, and other pre-closing events which are required to occur pursuant to the contract.

Paragraph 17 of the MR form provides that the contract may not be assigned without both parties' written consent, and that in the event of an assignment, the original parties remain obligated until closing.

5. *[§ 2.68] Condemnation*

Some residential resale contracts contain clauses prescribing the effect on the parties' rights of a condemnation of any or all of the property by a governmental or other entity possessing the power of eminent domain (a provision which is universal in commercial real property contracts). Many do not. If the property is located in a recorded, modern subdivision, it is unlikely that the clause will ever have to be invoked, and therefore does not warrant any degree of negotiation. In such cases, it will suffice simply to give buyer the right to elect, if *any* of the property is condemned (or threatened to be condemned) before closing, either to terminate the agreement, or to complete closing with no reduction in the purchase price, but with a full assignment by seller of all condemnation proceeds.

Occasionally farmland or other property outside of modern subdivisions is the subject of condemnation in connection with a public road widening or utility right-of-way taking. Frequently, such takings are only of portions of the property. Depending on the nature of the property and the likelihood that this will happen while the contract is in effect (and on the amount and location of the land likely to be taken), the parties may desire to negotiate a more elaborate condemnation clause which recognizes these possibilities and allows for an adjustment in the purchase price, rather than an outright termination, if the taking occurs as anticipated. In that regard, a would-be seller fearing a threatened condemnation would do well to remember that, if they enter into a contract of sale, the contract price could become evidence of the property's fair market value in the condemnation proceeding, a possibility which may or may not work to seller's advantage, depending on the amount of the contract price *vis a vis* the proposed taking price.

The MR form contains no condemnation clause. In the absence of a specific provision to the contrary, the doctrine of equitable conversion would suggest that the risk of condemnation falls on buyer who, if a taking occurs, must pay seller the contract purchase price but will be entitled to receive the proceeds of the taking.[129]

6. *[§ 2.69] Internal Revenue Service filing*

Section 6045 of the Internal Revenue Code of 1986 (hereinafter I.R.C. §6045) requires the person responsible for settlement, customarily the title company, if applicable, to file a return with the IRS setting forth the names and addresses of buyer and seller, and the purchase price paid for the property.[130] Paragraph 54 of the

---

129 See Annotation, *Right and Liabilities of Parties to Executory Contract for Sale of Land Taken by Eminent Domain*, 27 A.L.R. 3D 572 (1969); *see also Record Bldg. & Loan Ass'n v. Safe Deposit & Trust Co.*, 166 Md. 348, 352, 171 A. 43, 44–45 (1934); *Pyles v. Callis* 269 Md. 686, 695–96, 309 A.2d 624, 628 (1973).

130 See **§ 7.30** of this book for detailed information.

MR form obligates buyer and seller to provide this information to the person charged with the duty to file this return, and imposes on seller the costs of the IRS filing.

7. *[§ 2.70] Income tax withholding on sales by non-residents*

(a) FIRPTA—Federal income tax withholding

Where purchase price exceeds $300,000, I.R.C. § 1445 requires a purchaser of real property from a "foreign person" (essentially, a person who is not a U.S. citizen or a resident alien, or an entity which is not organized under the laws of a state, commonwealth, or the United States) to withhold from the purchase money paid for the property an amount (calculated pursuant to the accompanying Treasury Regulations) sufficient to pay the seller's federal income tax liability. A failure to do so subjects the purchaser to liability for some or all of the amount which should have been withheld. In determining whether seller is or is not a foreign person, buyer is entitled to rely on seller's representation in that regard in certain circumstances. For this reason, most contracts require seller to sign and deliver to buyer at closing a so-called "FIRPTA affidavit"[131] to the effect that the "transferor" (i.e., seller) is or is not a foreign person. Paragraph 53 of the MR form contains such a provision. A sample FIRPTA affidavit is set forth in § 2.**92** of this chapter.

(b) Tax-General § 10-912—Maryland income tax withholding

A non-resident of Maryland who transfers property that is not the transferor's principal residence is subject to income tax withholding upon the sale or transfer of the property. The purpose of this law is to improve compliance in collection of income tax on capital gains generated by the sale of Maryland real property by nonresidents. The amount of withholding is based on the "total payment" received by the non-resident transferor. "Total payment" is, essentially, the net proceeds of the sale; however, the transferor cannot deduct a "debt incurred in contemplation of a sale" which is defined as a debt secured by the property and "incurred by the transferor within 90 days of the sale of the property." The amount required to be withheld is 8% of the "total payment" for nonresident individuals and 8.25% of the "total payment" for nonresident entities.

Maryland residents and transferors selling a principal residence in Maryland are exempt from withholding. To qualify for an exemption, an individual transferor must meet the definition of resident found in Tax-Gen. § 10-101(k). Alternatively, the transferor will qualify for an exemption if the property is the transferor's "principal residence" having "the same meaning as when used in § 121 of the Internal Revenue Code," provided that the property is also "listed as an owner-occupied

---

[131] FIRPTA is the unfortunate acronym for the Foreign Investment in Real Property Tax Act of 1980, by which I.R.C. § 1445 was adopted.

residence" with the Department of Assessments and Taxation. The transferor must also sign a certification that the transferor is a Maryland resident or the property being transferred is the transferor's principal residence. As for entities, if the entity is either formed in Maryland, or if not, is qualified or registered to do business in Maryland, it is considered a resident of Maryland for the purposes of the law. Resident entities must also sign an affidavit of residency. The certifications, which are required to be made under penalty of perjury, must be included in the deed, as a recital, in the acknowledgment in the deed, or via an affidavit signed by the transferor or agent of the transferor.

Additionally, certain transfers are exempt, including a transfer "by foreclosure," meaning the transfer from foreclosure trustees to the lender or third party and transfers of REO property from a lender to a third party. Other exempted transfers are those for zero consideration and those from the United States and its instrumentalities and from the State and its units and political subdivisions. The law and regulations found in COMAR 03.04.12, also provide for exemptions from withholding (or partial exemptions) in cases where the transferor has filed for, and received, a certificate of full or partial exemption from the Comptroller. Under the regulations, there are 14 possible grounds for obtaining a certificate for full or partial exemption from withholding. The transferor is required to file the application with the Comptroller at least 21 days prior to the settlement date.

In cases where withholding is collected, the funds and withholding return are collected and processed by the Clerk of the Circuit Court.

The withholding return, exemption certificate applications, and sample affidavit forms can be found at the Maryland Comptroller's web page at *https://www.marylandtaxes.gov/forms/current_forms/withholding_requirement.pdf.*.

8. [§ 2.71] *Tenant right of first refusal in City of Baltimore*

(a) Generally

Under the Baltimore City Code,[132] any person who, at any time within the period of six months before the time in question, has been a tenant or subtenant of any residence in the City of Baltimore, entitled to "possession, occupancy or the benefits thereof," has a "right of first refusal" to purchase the residence before it can be sold to any third party. The statute requires seller, before conveying title to a third-party buyer, to offer to sell it instead to tenant, and provide tenant with a copy of any third-party contract (from which buyer's name may be deleted). Tenant is given a 30-day period within which to accept the offer.

[132] Baltimore City Code, art. 13, §§ 6-1–6-10.

Although tenant's right is styled as a "right of first refusal," it differs in certain important respects from the classic right of first refusal, under which the holder of the right may buy the property on and only on precisely the same terms as those which seller has offered, or intends to offer, to the third-party buyer. Under the statute, seller must offer to sell to tenant on the same terms as seller either has included in a signed contract of sale, or which seller proposes to include in such a contract not yet signed, *in each case except where the statute prescribes limitations on such terms* (which limitations are generally in tenant's favor).

If tenant fails to exercise its right of refusal, and seller subsequently contracts with a third party on terms which either result in "net proceeds" to seller which are less than those embodied in the offer of sale made to tenant, or which are otherwise "materially more favorable" to the third-party buyer than those of the offer to tenant, seller must notify tenant of this fact, and tenant is given an additional 15-day period within which to elect to purchase the property on the same terms. However, if the net proceeds are less than 80% of those embodied in the original offer to tenant, or more than six months has elapsed since the original offer was made to tenant, the 15-day period becomes one of 30 days.

Although tenant may not effectively waive its right to receive an offer and notice of a proposed third-party sale, once these requirements are met, tenant may waive or release its right of first refusal with respect to the sale, by signing a document complying with the statute.

The statute creates exemptions for a list of transactions, including mortgage grants and foreclosures, transfers by will or inheritance, transfers to certain relatives or spouses, and charitable gifts.

One of the most important exemptions is set forth in Article 13, § 6-7(ii) of the Baltimore City Code. That section provides that if the property is listed with a licensed real estate broker and the tenant is provided, within 48 hours of the listing, written notice (along with additional, required information) that the tenant may negotiate for the purchase of the property on the same basis as other members of the general public; the right of first refusal will not apply. Because many single-family residential real estate transactions in Baltimore City are handled through licensed real estate brokers, the exemption has had the effect of greatly reducing the delays and difficulties experienced in otherwise complying with the law's requirements.

A transfer in violation of the statute is a misdemeanor. Moreover, the statute recites that the "validity" of a contract between seller and the third party is "contingent" on compliance with its requirements, and requires that the contract so recite.

The statute requires that the seller transferring (other than to a tenant) title to a residence to which the statute applies file among the Land Records, with the deed, an affidavit in a form prescribed by the statute, certifying that the statutory requirements have been met.[133] The language of the affidavit clearly contemplates that it must be filed even where the residence has not been leased to anyone during the previous six months, if ever. The affidavit functions as a "safe harbor" for buyers, since under the statute, once the affidavit is filed, "the rights and title of a third party transferee, his heirs, successors or assigns shall be free of any restriction or claim" arising in favor of a tenant under the statute. Of course, seller remains subject to liability for violation of such rights if the transfer is in violation of the statute.

A buyer of real property in the City of Baltimore should insist that seller deliver at closing the signed affidavit discussed above, certifying that the requirements of the statute have been met, or, in the case of the exemption for a listed property, sufficient proof of compliance with the requirements of the exemption. Otherwise, buyer runs the risk that a tenant having rights under the statute may assert them against buyer's rights to the residence, even after closing. A seller of a residence which has been leased during the prior six months should make sure that they take the steps necessary to observe these requirements, and that the contract contains the specified language conditioning its enforceability on compliance. Otherwise, seller may find themselves liable for claims by both tenant and buyer.

(b) MR form

The MR form does *not* contain the specified provision conditioning the contract's effectiveness on compliance with the statute, where the residence is in the City of Baltimore. Hence, seller should insist that the following sentence be added to the contract: "If the Property is or has been, within six months of the date hereof, a single-family residential rental dwelling, the validity of this contract is contingent upon compliance with the provisions of BALTIMORE CITY CODE, art. 13, §§ 46–55."

9. [§ 2.72] Inspection right

Buyer should consider asking seller to agree that, from time to time during the pre-closing period, buyer may visit the house to take measurements, and allow its inspection by buyer and any interior designers, remodelers, or other contractors whom buyer expects to employ after closing in making alterations to the dwelling. This will prove to be important if buyer does not plan to move into the dwelling until the alterations are completed.

10. [§ 2.73] House plans

Buyer should also consider including a clause requiring seller to provide buyer with any existing plans and specifications for the residence, if available. This is particularly important in the case of a custom-built home.

---

133 Statutory statements for the affidavits are attached at § 2.**93** of this chapter.

R. [§ 2.74] Execution; Ensealing

It is crucial that all named parties execute the contract. Where this does not occur, it usually is because more than one signator is required for seller or buyer, and fewer than all required signators sign. Thus, the execution lines should be checked carefully against the names of the parties found at the beginning of the agreement, as well as any additional required signators identified as discussed in §§ 2.**14**–2.**21** of this chapter.

Although many contracts routinely recite that they have been signed under seal, or ensealed, or are intended to be sealed instruments, in most cases this is not important. Under Maryland law, the principal effect of signing a document under seal is to extend from three to 12 years the limitations period within which suits for breach of contract may be brought. Most contracts for the sale of residential property do not create obligations for which contract actions are likely to be brought more than three years after a default occurs. Of course, for the same reason, including a seal is not likely to work to the detriment of a defaulting party.

Where the parties want the contract to be a sealed instrument, it will suffice for them to recite that it is being executed under seal or as a sealed instrument, and to write or type the word "(SEAL)" next to each signature. It has long since ceased to be necessary that a seal be embossed or separately affixed by wax or glue on an instrument for it to be effective.

S. [§ 2.75] Recordation of Contract

Although it is unusual for a resale contract to be recorded among the Land Records, occasionally a buyer will want to do so to give constructive notice of the existence of the contract.[134] REAL PROP. § 3-102 specifically permits contracts of sale to be recorded. Moreover, contrary to widespread belief, a contract of sale—unlike a deed, mortgage, or certain other instruments—need not be acknowledged (that is, notarized) to be recordable.[135]

Since the contract is an "instrument of writing" granting an interest (i.e., beneficial title) in real property, the state and any county transfer taxes, and the state

---

134 It is difficult to conceive of a reason for a *seller* to want to record the contract.

135 REAL PROP. § 4-101(a) provides that a deed "is sufficient" if, among other requirements, it is acknowledged. A deed lacking an acknowledgment is, therefore, not "sufficient," and will not be accepted for recordation. Although, as used in the Real Property Article, the term "deed" is defined by subsection 1-101(c) to include "any deed, grant, mortgage, deed of trust, lease, assignment, and release, pertaining to land or property or any interest therein or appurtenant thereto," it does not include a contract of sale. Hence, subsection 4-101(a) does not apply to such contracts. However, as a practical matter, having documents notarized as a prerequisite to recording is so ingrained, if the parties agreed to recording the contract of sale, it would seem that the realistic course of action would be to have the contract of sale executed before a notary public and eliminate any chance of resistance to its being recorded.

recordation tax, will be levied on its recordation.[136] The tax will be based on the purchase price set forth in the contract. However, unless the price is increased thereafter, no additional tax will be assessed on recordation of the deed after closing. On the other hand, if settlement does not occur so that no deed is recorded, the tax will not be refunded.

Unless the contract provides for its own recordation, it will be difficult for buyer effectively to assert a claim that seller should contribute to the cost of such recordation. However, where the contract calls for seller to bear part of the cost of such taxes levied on recordation of the deed, fairness suggests that seller should reimburse buyer at closing for seller's share of the taxes assessed on recordation of the contract, since none will be charged for recording the deed. Most contracts, being silent on the very question of contract recordation itself, do not impose such a reimbursement obligation on seller.

Where a contract is recorded, but later terminates without closing having occurred, it will be important for seller to obtain and record a termination agreement or release of the contract, signed by buyer. Since a seller often will not know in advance (or even afterward) that the contract is being recorded, a prudent seller will insist that the contract itself require buyer to sign a release in recordable form (that is, notarized) whenever the contract terminates before closing, as a condition to any return of buyer's deposit.

A seller who wishes to prevent recordation of the contract should include a provision, occasionally found in commercial land sale contracts, to the effect that if buyer or anyone acting for buyer causes the contract to be recorded, such action will constitute a buyer default, the contract will immediately become void, and seller may declare a forfeiture of buyer's deposit.

IV. APPENDIX

The Appendix begins on the next page.

---

[136] *See* § **2.58** of this chapter.

A. [§ 2.76] Contract of Sale—Maryland Realtors

Maryland REALTORS®

RESIDENTIAL CONTRACT OF SALE

This is a Legally Binding Contract; If Not Understood, Seek Competent Legal Advice.

THIS FORM IS DESIGNED AND INTENDED FOR THE SALE AND PURCHASE OF IMPROVED SINGLE FAMILY RESIDENTIAL REAL ESTATE LOCATED IN MARYLAND ONLY.

SECTION ONE: GENERAL CONTRACT PROVISIONS

1. DATE OF OFFER: ______________________________.

2. TIME IS OF THE ESSENCE. Time is of the essence of this Contract. The failure of Seller or Buyer to perform any act as provided in this Contract by a prescribed date or within a prescribed time period shall be a default under this Contract and the non-defaulting party, upon written notice to the defaulting party, may declare this Contract null and void and of no further legal force and effect. In such event, all Deposit(s) shall be disbursed in accordance with the Deposit paragraph of this Contract.

3. SELLER: ____

4. BUYER: ____

5. PROPERTY: Seller does sell to Buyer and Buyer does purchase from Seller, all of the following described Property (hereinafter "Property") known as ____ located in ______________________________City/County, Maryland, Zip Code ____________________, together with the improvements thereon, and all rights and appurtenances thereto belonging.

6. ESTATE: The Property is being conveyed: _______ in fee simple or _________ subject to an annual ground rent, now existing, in the amount of ____________________ Dollars ($____________) payable semi-annually, as now or to be recorded among the Land Records of ______________City/County, Maryland.

7. PURCHASE PRICE: The Purchase Price is ____ Dollars ($____________________________).

8. PAYMENT TERMS: The payment of the purchase price shall be made by Buyer as follows:
(a) Buyer □ has delivered OR □ will deliver within ________________ Days of the Date of Contract Acceptance an initial Deposit by way of ___________________ in the amount of _______________________ Dollars ($_______________).
(b) An additional Deposit by way of ___________________________ in the amount of ____________ Dollars ($______________________) to be paid ____________________________________ ____.
(c) All Deposits will be held in escrow by: ____.
If Deposit will not be held by a Maryland licensed real estate broker, the parties shall execute a separate written Escrow Agreement that complies with Section 10-802 of the Real Property Article, Annotated Code of Maryland.
(d) The purchase price less any and all Deposits shall be paid in full by Buyer in cash, wired funds, bank check, certified check or other payment acceptable to the settlement officer at settlement.
(e) Buyer and Seller instruct broker named in subparagraph (c) above to place the Deposits in: **(Check One)**
□ A non interest bearing account; **OR**
□ An interest-bearing account, the interest on which, in absence of default by Buyer, shall accrue to the benefit of Buyer. Broker may charge a fee for establishing an interest bearing account.

9. DEPOSIT: If the Deposit is held by a Broker as specified in Paragraph 8(c) of this Contract, Buyer hereby authorizes and directs Broker to hold the Deposit instrument without negotiation or deposit until the parties have executed and accepted this Contract. Upon acceptance, the initial Deposit and additional Deposits (the "Deposit"), if any, shall be placed in escrow as provided in Paragraph 8(e) of this Contract and in accordance with the requirements of Section 17-502(b)(1) of the Business Occupations and Professions Article, Annotated Code of Maryland. If Seller does not execute and accept this Contract, the initial Deposit instrument shall be promptly returned to Buyer. The Deposit shall be disbursed at settlement. In the event this Contract shall be terminated or settlement does not occur, Buyer and Seller agree that the Deposit shall be disbursed by Broker only in accordance with a Release of Deposit agreement executed by Buyer and Seller. In the event Buyer and/or Seller fail to complete the real estate transaction in accordance with the terms and conditions of this Contract, and either Buyer or Seller shall be unable or unwilling to execute a Release of Deposit agreement, Buyer and Seller hereby acknowledge and agree that Broker may distribute the Deposit in accordance with the provisions of Section

17-505(b) of the Business Occupations and Professions Article, Annotated Code of Maryland and Section 10-803 of the Real Property Article, Annotated Code of Maryland.

10. SETTLEMENT: Date of Settlement ______________________________ or sooner if agreed to in writing by the parties.

11. ADDENDA/DISCLOSURES: The Addenda checked below, which are hereby attached, are made a part of this Contract:

□ Affiliated Business Disclosure Notice
□ Additional As Is Provisions
□ ATU/BAT On-Site Sewage Disposal
□ Back-Up Contract
□ Cash Appraisal Contingency
□ Condominium Resale Notice
□ Conservation Easement
□ Disclosure of Licensee Status
□ Disclosure of Information on Lead-Based Paint and/or Lead-Based Paint Hazards
□ FIRPTA
□ Forest Conservation Act
□ Homeowners Association Notice
□ Inclusions/Exclusions, Leased Items, & Utilities
□ Kickout
□ Local City/County Certifications/Registrations
□ Local City/County Notices/Disclosure
□ Maryland Lead Poisoning Prevention Program
□ Other Addenda/Special Conditions:
□ MD Non-Resident Seller Transfer Withholding Tax
□ Notice to Buyer and Seller – Maryland Residential Property Condition Disclosure Law
□ Notice & Discl. of Deferred Water & Sewer Charges
□ On-Site Sewage Disposal System Inspection
□ Property Inspections
□ Property Subject to Ground Rent
□ Purchase Price Escalation
□ Buyer's Sale, Fin., Settlement/Lease of Other Real Estate
□ Seller Contribution
□ Seller's Home of Choice
□ Solar Panel
□ Short Sale
□ Tenant Occupied
□ Third Party Approval
□ Water Quality Test
□ Water Yield Test

____

____

12. BUYER AND SELLER MAY EXECUTE THIS CONTRACT ELECTRONICALLY USING ELECTRONIC SIGNATURES: Buyer and Seller hereby acknowledge that pursuant to Section 21-101 et seq. of the Commercial Law Article, Annotated Code of Maryland, Buyer and Seller may execute this contract electronically using electronic signatures. If a mortgage or settlement company requires wet signatures, all parties agree to promptly re-sign all the documents. The parties agree that this Contract offer shall be deemed validly executed and delivered by a party if a party executes this Contract and delivers a copy of the executed Contract to the other party by facsimile transmittal or delivers a digital image of the executed document by electronic transmittal.

13. ENTIRE AGREEMENT: This Contract and any addenda thereto contain the final and entire agreement between the parties, and neither they nor their agents shall be bound by any terms, conditions, statements, warranties or representations, oral or written, not herein contained. The parties to this Contract mutually agree that it is binding upon them, their heirs, executors, administrators, personal representatives, successors and, if permitted as herein provided, assigns. Once signed, the terms of this Contract can only be changed by a document executed by all parties. This Contract shall be interpreted and construed in accordance with the laws of the State of Maryland. It is further agreed that this Contract may be executed in counterparts, each of which when considered together shall constitute the original Contract.

14. COMPUTATION OF DAYS: As used in this Contract, and in any addendum or addenda to this Contract, the term "days" shall mean consecutive calendar days, including Saturdays, Sundays, and holidays, whether federal, state, local or religious. A day shall be measured from 12:00:00 a.m. to and including 11:59:59 p.m. in the Eastern Time Zone. For the purposes of calculating days, the count of "days" shall begin on the day following the day upon which any act or notice as provided in this Contract, or any addendum or addenda to this Contract, was required to be performed or made.

15. SELLER RESPONSIBILITY: Seller agrees to keep existing mortgages free of default until settlement. All violation notices or requirements noted or issued by any governmental authority (including without limitation, any permit violation notices), or actions in any court on account thereof, against or affecting the Property at the date of settlement of this Contract, shall be complied with by Seller and the Property conveyed free thereof. The Property is to be held at the risk of Seller until legal title has passed or possession has been given to Buyer. If, prior to the time legal title has passed or possession has been given to Buyer, whichever shall occur first, all or a substantial part of the Property is destroyed or damaged, without fault of Buyer, then this Contract, at the option of Buyer, upon written notice to Seller, shall be null and void and of no further effect, and the deposits shall be disbursed in accordance with the Deposit paragraph of this Contract.

16. LEASES: Seller may neither negotiate new leases nor renew existing leases for the Property which extend beyond settlement or possession date without Buyer's written consent. Seller warrants that the Property is not tenant-occupied nor subject to any leases, unless otherwise stated in an attached Tenant Occupied Addendum.

17. NON-ASSIGNABILITY: This Contract may not be assigned without the written consent of Buyer and Seller. If Buyer and Seller agree in writing to an assignment of this Contract, the original parties to this Contract remain obligated hereunder until settlement.

18. SECTION AND PARAGRAPH HEADINGS: The Section and Paragraph headings of this Contract are for convenience and reference only, and in no way define or limit the intent, rights, or obligations of the parties.

SECTION TWO: PAYMENT OF THE PURCHASE PRICE

19. FINANCING: Buyer's obligation to purchase the Property is contingent upon Buyer obtaining a written commitment for a loan secured by the Property as follows:

□ Conventional Financing Addendum	□ USDA Financing Addendum	□ Owner Financing Contingency
□ FHA Financing Addendum	□ Assumption Addendum	□ No Financing Contingency
□ VA Financing Addendum	□ Gift of Funds Contingency Addendum	□ OTHER: ________________

20. FINANCING APPLICATION AND COMMITMENT: Buyer agrees to make a written application for the financing as herein described within ________________ (______) days from the Date of Contract Acceptance. If a written financing commitment is not obtained by Buyer within ____________________ (_______) days from the Date of Contract Acceptance: (1) Seller, at Seller's election and upon written notice to Buyer, may declare this Contract null and void and of no further legal effect; or (2) Buyer, upon written notice to Seller, which shall include written evidence from the lender of Buyer's inability to obtain financing as provided in the Financing paragraph of this Contract, may declare this Contract null and void and of no further legal effect. In either case, the deposit shall be disbursed in accordance with the Deposit paragraph of this Contract. If Buyer has complied with all of Buyer's obligations under this Contract, including those with respect to applying for financing and seeking to obtain financing, then the Release of Deposit agreement shall provide that the deposit shall be returned to Buyer.

21. BUYER RESPONSIBILITY: If Buyer has misrepresented Buyer's financial ability to consummate the purchase of the Property, or if this Contract is contingent upon Buyer securing a written commitment for financing and Buyer fails to apply for such financing within the time period herein specified, or fails to pursue financing diligently and in good faith, or if Buyer makes any misrepresentations in any document relating to financing, or takes (or fails to take) any action which causes Buyer's disqualification for financing, then Buyer shall be in default; and Seller may elect by written notice to Buyer, to terminate this Contract and/or pursue the remedies set forth under the Default paragraph of this Contract.

22. SALE/SETTLEMENT OR LEASE OF OTHER REAL ESTATE: Neither this Contract nor the granting of Buyer's loan referred to herein is to be conditioned or contingent in any manner upon the sale, settlement and/or lease of any other real estate unless a contingency for the sale, settlement and/or lease of other real estate is contained in an addendum to this Contract. Unless this Contract is expressly contingent upon the sale, settlement and/or lease of any other real estate, Buyer shall neither apply for nor accept a financing loan commitment which is contingent upon or requires as a pre-condition to funding that any other real estate be sold, settled and/or leased.

23. ALTERNATE FINANCING: Provided Buyer timely and diligently pursues the financing described in the **Financing** paragraph, the **Financing Application and Commitment** paragraph, and the **Buyer Responsibility** paragraph, Buyer, at Buyer's election, may also apply for alternate financing. If Buyer, at Buyer's sole option, obtains a written commitment for financing in which the loan amount, term of note, amortization period, interest rate, down payment or loan program differ from the financing as described in the Financing paragraph, or any addendum to this Contract, the Financing Application and Commitment paragraph or any addendum to this Contract shall be deemed to have been fully satisfied. Such alternate financing may not increase costs to Seller or exceed the time allowed to secure the financing commitment as provided in the Financing Application and Commitment paragraph, or any addendum to this Contract.

SECTION THREE: PROPERTY CONDITION AND INSPECTIONS

24. INCLUSIONS/EXCLUSIONS: Included in the purchase price are all permanently attached fixtures, including all smoke detectors. Certain other **now existing items** which may be considered personal property, whether installed or stored upon the property, are included if identified on a Disclosure of Inclusions/Exclusions, Leased Items, and Utilities Addendum attached hereto.

25. CONDITION OF PROPERTY AND POSSESSION: EXCEPT AS OTHERWISE SPECIFIED IN THIS CONTRACT INCLUDING THIS PARAGRAPH, THE PROPERTY IS SOLD "AS IS." At settlement, Seller shall deliver possession of the Property vacant, clear of trash and debris, broom clean and in substantially the same condition as existed on the Date of Contract Acceptance. Buyer reserves the right to inspect the Property within five (5) days prior to settlement to confirm the condition of the property.

26. INSPECTION CONTINGENCY: If Buyer and Seller agree, Buyer will be afforded the opportunity, at Buyer's sole cost and expense, to condition Buyer's purchase of the Property upon inspections to ascertain any unsatisfactory conditions. Buyer and Seller acknowledge that Brokers, agents or subagents are not responsible for the existence or discovery of property defects. **Any Buyer Inspection Contingency must be established through Addenda to this Contract.**

Inspection Addenda Attached ______/______
Buyer Buyer

Inspections Declined ______/______
Buyer Buyer

SECTION FOUR: PROPERTY-SPECIFIC DISCLOSURES

27. HOMEOWNER'S ASSOCIATION / CONDOMINIUM REGIME: The Property is not part of development subject to the imposition of mandatory fees as defined by the Maryland Homeowner's Association Act or a condominium regime as defined by the Maryland Condominium Act, unless acknowledged by an attached addendum.

28. NOTICE REGARDING DISCLOSURE OF DEFERRED WATER AND SEWER ASSESSMENTS: Pursuant to Section 14-117(a)(5) of the Real Property Article of the Annotated Code of Maryland, a contract for the resale of residential real property that is served by public water or wastewater facilities for which deferred water and sewer charges have been established by a recorded covenant or declaration shall contain a notice disclosing information about the deferred water and sewer charges. **If a Seller subject to this law fails to comply:**

(a) **Prior to settlement, Buyer is entitled to rescind in writing the sales contract without penalty or liability. On rescission, Buyer is also entitled to the full return of any deposits made on account of the sales contract. If any deposits are held in trust by a licensed real estate broker, the return of the deposits to a Buyer under this law shall comply with the procedures under § 17-505 of the Business Occupations and Professions Article of the Annotated Code of Maryland. Buyer's right of rescission shall terminate five days after Seller provides to Buyer written notice in accordance with this requirement; and**

(b) **After settlement, Seller shall be liable to Buyer for the full amount of any fee or assessment not disclosed, unless Seller was never charged a fee or assessment to defray the costs of public water or wastewater facilities by the developer, a successor of the developer, or a subsequent assignee.**

This law does *not* apply in a county that has adopted a disclosure requirement that is substantially similar to this law. (If the Property is served by public water or wastewater facilities for which deferred water and sewer charges have been established by a recorded covenant or declaration: See Notice Regarding Deferred Water and Sewer Charges.)

29. AGRICULTURALLY ASSESSED PROPERTY: The *Agricultural Use Assessment* (Assessment) is a reduced property tax assessment for agricultural land. To be eligible for the Assessment, the land must be actively used for agricultural purposes. The *Agricultural Land Transfer Tax* (Tax) is a tax imposed under Section 13-301 et seq. of the Tax-Property Article, Annotated Code of Maryland. **If the Property is assessed in the agricultural use category and the Buyer does not intend to use the Property for agricultural purposes, the Tax may become due and could be substantial.** The Tax is imposed on the deed itself and must be paid before the deed can be recorded. At the time of sale, Seller shall notify Buyer in writing that the transfer may be subject to the Tax. Buyer will be responsible to pay the Tax unless the parties negotiate a different agreement. To avoid paying the Tax, Buyer must continue to use the Property for agricultural purposes and comply with the other requirements of the law. **The Property, or any portion thereof, may be subject to an Agricultural Land Transfer Tax as imposed by Section 13-301 et seq. of the Tax-Property Article, Annotated Code of Maryland, by reason of the Property's having been assessed on the basis of agricultural use. The Tax assessed as a result of this transfer shall be paid by** ______________________.

30. NOTICE CONCERNING CONSERVATION EASEMENTS: If the Property is encumbered by a Conservation Easement as defined in Section 10-705 of the Real Property Article, Annotated Code of Maryland, the contract must contain a notice concerning the easement, which is contained in an attached addendum. This Paragraph does not apply to the sale of property in an action to foreclose a mortgage or deed of trust. (If the Property is encumbered by a Conservation Easement: See Conservation Easement Addendum.)

31. FOREST CONSERVATION AND MANAGEMENT PROGRAM:
Buyer is hereby notified that this transfer may be subject to the Forest Conservation and Management Program imposed by Section 8-211 of the Tax-Property Article, Annotated Code of Maryland. Forest Conservation and Management program taxes assessed as a result of this transfer shall be paid by ______________________.

32. FOREST CONSERVATION ACT NOTICE: If the Property is a tract of land 40,000 square feet or more in size, Buyer is notified that, unless exempted by applicable law, as a prerequisite to any subdivision plan or grading or sediment control permit for the Property, Buyer will be required to comply with the provisions of the Maryland Forest Conservation Act imposed by Section 5-1601, et seq. of the Natural Resources Article, Annotated Code of Maryland, including, among other things, the submission and acceptance of a Forest Stand Delineation and a Forest Conservation Plan for the Property in accordance with applicable laws and regulations. Unless otherwise expressly set forth in an addendum to this Contract, Seller represents and warrants that the Property is not currently subject to a Forest Conservation Plan, Management Agreement or any other pending obligation binding the owner of the Property under said Act; further, Seller represents and warrants that no activities have been undertaken on the Property by Seller in violation of the Forest Conservation Act.

SECTION FIVE: GENERAL DISCLOSURES

33. SINGLE FAMILY RESIDENTIAL REAL PROPERTY DISCLOSURE NOTICE: Buyer is advised of the right to receive a "Disclosure and Disclaimer Statement" from Seller (Section 10-702 Real Property Article, Annotated Code of Maryland).

34. GROUND RENT: If the Property is subject to ground rent and the ground rent is not timely paid, the ground lease holder (i.e., the person to whom the ground rent is payable) may bring an action under Section 8-402.3 of the Real Property Article, Annotated Code of Maryland. As a result of this action, a lien may be placed upon the property. If the Property is subject to ground rent, Sections 14-116 and 14-116.1 of the Real Property Article provide the purchaser, upon obtaining ownership of the Property, with certain rights and responsibilities relative to the ground rent. (If the Property is subject to ground rent: See Property Subject to Ground Rent Addendum.)

35. LEAD-BASED PAINT:

A. FEDERAL LEAD-BASED PAINT LAW: Title X, Section 1018, the Residential Lead-Based Paint Hazard Reduction Act of 1992 (the "Act"), requires the disclosure by Seller of information regarding lead-based paint and lead-based paint hazards in connection with the sale of any **residential** real property on which a residential dwelling was constructed prior to 1978. Unless otherwise exempt by the Act, the disclosure shall be made on the required federal Disclosure of Information on Lead-Based Paint and/or Lead-Based Paint Hazards form. **Seller and any agent involved in the transaction are required to retain a copy of the completed Lead-Based Paint Disclosure form for a period of three (3) years following the date of settlement. A Seller who fails to give the required Lead-Based Paint Disclosure form and EPA pamphlet may be liable under the Act for three times the amount of damages and may be subject to both civil and criminal penalties.**

Buyer acknowledges by Buyer's initials below that Buyer has read and understands the provisions of Paragraph 35.A.
________/_______ **(BUYER)**

B. RENOVATION, REPAIR AND PAINTING OF PROPERTY: In accordance with the Lead Renovation, Repair and Painting Rule ("RRP") as adopted by the Environmental Protection Agency ("the EPA"), effective April 22, 2010, if the improvements on the Property were built before 1978, contractor(s) engaged by Seller to renovate, repair or paint the Property must be certified by the EPA where such work will disturb more than six square feet of paint per room for interior projects; more than 20 square feet of paint for any exterior project; or includes window replacement or demolition ("Covered Work"). Before and during any Covered Work project, contractor(s) must comply with all requirements of the RRP.

A Seller who personally performs any Covered Work on a rental property is required to be certified by the EPA prior to performing such Covered Work. No certification is required for a Seller who personally performs Covered Work on the Seller's principal residence. However, Seller has the ultimate responsibility for the safety of Seller's family or children while performing such Covered Work. For detailed information regarding the RRP, Seller should visit http://www2.epa.gov/lead/renovation-repair-and-painting-program.

Buyer acknowledges by Buyer's initials below that Buyer has read and understands Paragraph 35.B.
________/_______ **(BUYER)**

C. MARYLAND LEAD POISONING PREVENTION PROGRAM: Under the Maryland Lead Poisoning Prevention Program (the "Maryland Program"), any residential dwelling constructed prior to 1978 that is leased for residential purposes is required to be registered with the Maryland Department of the Environment (MDE). If the Property was built prior to 1978 and is now or has been a rental property or may become a rental property in the future, a separate Maryland Lead-Based Paint Disclosure form is attached. Detailed information regarding compliance requirements may be obtained at: http://www.mde.state.md.us/programs/Land/LeadPoisoningPrevention/Pages/index.aspx.

Buyer acknowledges by Buyer's initials below that Buyer has read and understands Paragraph 35.C.
________/_______ **(BUYER)**

36. LIMITED WARRANTY: NOTICE TO BUYER: IF A WARRANTY PLAN IS BEING OFFERED WITH THE PURCHASE OF THE PROPERTY, IT MAY BE A LIMITED WARRANTY. SINCE SUCH WARRANTY PLANS DO NOT COVER STRUCTURAL DEFECTS AND MAY NOT COVER PRE-EXISTING DEFECTS, BUYER SHOULD REQUEST THE REAL ESTATE AGENT TO PROVIDE BUYER WITH ANY BROCHURE WHICH DESCRIBES THE PLAN IN ORDER TO DETERMINE THE EXTENT OF COVERAGE PROVIDED BY THE WARRANTY.

37. PROPERTY INSURANCE BROCHURE: An informational brochure published by Maryland REALTORS® titled "Property Insurance Basics – What You Should Know" is available to explain current issues relative to obtaining insurance coverage for the Property to be purchased and may be obtained on Maryland REALTORS® website: http://www.mdrealtor.org/Portals/0/adam/Content/gejh4dXTAEWPU3vfLrkJ1A/Link/FINAL-Property-Insurance-Basics-Flyer-Web.pdf.

38. FLOOD DISCLOSURE NOTICE:

A. FLOOD INSURANCE PREMIUMS: The Property or part of the Property may be located in an area established by the government as a "flood plain" or otherwise in an area where flood insurance could be required by Buyer's mortgage lender as a condition of granting a mortgage. In addition, construction on the Property could be prohibited or restricted. The National Flood Insurance Program ("NFIP") provides for the availability of flood insurance but also establishes flood insurance policy premiums based on the risk of flooding in the area where properties are located. Due to amendments to federal law governing the NFIP those premiums are increasing, and in some cases will rise by a substantial amount over the premiums previously charged for flood insurance. As a result, Buyer should not rely on the premiums paid for flood insurance on the Property as an indication of the premiums that will apply after Buyer completes the purchase. In considering the purchase of this Property, Buyer should consult with one or more carriers of flood insurance for better understanding of flood insurance coverage, the premiums that are likely to be required to purchase such insurance and any available information about how those premiums may increase in the future. The only requirement for purchasing flood insurance from the NFIP is that you live in a community that participates (via floodplain regulations) in the NFIP. The same requirement applies to the mandatory purchase of flood insurance. Detailed information regarding flood insurance coverage may be obtained at: https://www.fema.gov/national-flood-insurance-program.

B. FLOOD INSURANCE RATE MAPS: The State of Maryland in conjunction with the Federal Emergency Management Agency has been systematically updating flood insurance rate maps. The Property may be affected. Buyer is advised to contact the Maryland Department of the Environment and consult a flood insurance carrier to inquire about the status of the Property. Detailed information regarding updated maps may be obtained at: http://www.mdfloodmaps.net.

39. GUARANTY FUND: NOTICE TO BUYER: BUYER IS PROTECTED BY THE REAL ESTATE GUARANTY FUND OF THE MARYLAND REAL ESTATE COMMISSION, UNDER SECTION 17-404 OF THE BUSINESS OCCUPATIONS AND PROFESSIONS ARTICLE OF THE ANNOTATED CODE OF MARYLAND, FOR LOSSES IN AN AMOUNT NOT EXCEEDING $50,000 FOR ANY CLAIM.

40. NOTICE TO BUYER CONCERNING THE CHESAPEAKE AND ATLANTIC COASTAL BAYS CRITICAL AREA: Buyer is advised that all or a portion of the property may be located in the "Critical Area" of the Chesapeake and Atlantic Coastal Bays, and that additional zoning, land use, and resource protection regulations apply in this area. The "Critical Area" generally consists of all land and water areas within 1,000 feet beyond the landward boundaries of state or private wetlands, the Chesapeake Bay, the Atlantic Coastal Bays, and all of their tidal tributaries. The "Critical Area" also includes the waters of and lands under the Chesapeake Bay, the Atlantic Coastal Bays and all of their tidal tributaries to the head of tide. For information as to whether the property is located within the Critical Area, Buyer may contact the local Department of Planning and Zoning, which maintains maps showing the extent of the Critical Area in the jurisdiction. Allegany, Carroll, Frederick, Garrett, Howard, Montgomery, and Washington Counties do not include land located in the Critical Area.

41. WETLANDS NOTICE: Buyer is advised that if the Property being purchased contains waters of the United States, or if the Property contains land and/or waters regulated by the State, including, but not limited to, wetlands, approval from the U.S. Army Corps of Engineers (Corps) and/or the Maryland Department of the Environment (MDE) will be necessary before starting any work, including construction, if the work includes the discharge of dredged or fill material into a regulated area, or certain other activities conducted in a regulated area. The Corps has adopted a broad definition of waters of the United States, which occur throughout the Chesapeake Bay Region, as well as other portions of the State. The land and waters regulated by the State include tidal wetlands, nontidal wetlands and their buffers, and streams and their 100-year nontidal floodplain. For information as to whether the Property includes waters of the United States or land and/or waters regulated by the State, Buyer may contact the Baltimore District of the Corps and/or MDE. Buyer may also elect, at Buyer's expense, to engage the services of a qualified specialist to inspect the Property for the presence of Corps- or MDE-regulated areas, including wetlands, prior to submitting a written offer to purchase the Property; or Buyer may include in Buyer's written offer a clause making Buyer's purchase of the Property contingent upon a satisfactory wetlands inspection.

42. CRIMINAL ACTIVITY AND SEXUAL OFFENDERS. Buyer may contact the state, county or municipal police departments in which the Property is located or check the "Sex Offender Registry" at the Maryland Department of Public Safety and Correctional Services website in order to ascertain criminal activity in the vicinity of the Property or the presence of registered sexual offenders who live or work within the vicinity of the Property. Buyer acknowledges that Buyer is solely responsible to inquire of such matters before signing this Contract. Buyer shall have no right to cancel this Contract based upon criminal activity or the presence of registered sexual offenders in the vicinity of the Property. Buyer further acknowledges that no real estate licensee involved in the sale or purchase of the Property, whether acting as the agent for Seller or Buyer, has any duty nor assumes any duty or responsibility to ascertain criminal activity or the presence of registered sexual offenders in the vicinity of the Property.

43. MILITARY INSTALLATIONS: This Section does not apply in Allegany, Carroll, Frederick, Garrett, Howard, Montgomery, and Washington Counties. Buyer is advised that the Property may be located near a military installation that conducts flight operations, munitions testing, or military operations that may result in high noise levels.

44. NOTICE TO THE PARTIES:

A. NO REPRESENTATIONS: Brokers, their agents, subagents and employees, make no representations with respect to: (1) Water quantity, quality, color, or taste or operating conditions of public and/or private water systems;

(2) Location, size or operating condition of on-site sewage disposal systems;

(3) The extensions of public utilities by local municipal authorities, existence or availability of public utilities, and any assessments, fees or costs for public utilities which might be imposed by local municipal authorities or private entities, should public utilities be extended or available to the subject Property. (Buyer should consult the Department of Public Works to determine the availability of proposed future extensions of utilities.);

(4) Lot size, exact location. If the subject Property is part of a recorded subdivision, Buyer can review the plat upon request at the Record Office. If the subject Property is not part of a recorded subdivision, Buyer may verify exact size, location and through a survey by a licensed engineer or land surveyor, at Buyer's expense;

(5) Existing zoning or permitted uses of the Property, including, without limitation, whether any improvements to the Property required permit(s) and, if so, whether such improvements, were completed pursuant to permit(s) issued and/or whether any permit(s) issued were complied with. Buyer should contact the appropriate local government agency and/or a licensed engineer to verify zoning, permit issuance/status, and permitted uses;

(6) Whether properly licensed contractors have been used to make repairs, renovations and improvements to the Property.

B. NO ADVISING: Brokers/agents are not advising the parties as to certain other issues, including without limitation: soil conditions; flood hazard areas; possible restrictions of the use of property due to restrictive covenants, leases, subdivision, environmental laws, easements or other documents; airport or aircraft noise; planned land use, roads or highways; and construction materials and/or hazardous materials, including without limitation flame retardant treated plywood (FRT), radon, radium, mold spores, urea formaldehyde foam insulation (UFFI), synthetic stucco (EIFS), asbestos, polybutylene piping and lead-based paint. Information relating to these issues may be available from appropriate governmental authorities. This disclosure is not intended to provide an inspection contingency.

C. COMPENSATION OF VENDORS: Buyer and Seller each assume full responsibility for selecting and compensating their respective vendors.

D. PROTECTION OF HOMEOWNERS IN FORECLOSURE ACT NOTICE: BUYER AND SELLER ACKNOWLEDGE THAT, UNDER SECTION 7-310 OF THE REAL PROPERTY ARTICLE OF THE ANNOTATED CODE OF MARYLAND, IF THE MORTGAGE ON THE PROPERTY IS AT LEAST 60 DAYS IN DEFAULT ON THE DATE OF CONTRACT ACCEPTANCE, SELLER HAS THE RIGHT TO RESCIND THE CONTRACT WITHIN 5 DAYS AFTER THE DATE OF CONTRACT ACCEPTANCE. ANY PROVISION IN THIS CONTRACT OR OTHER AGREEMENT THAT ATTEMPTS OR PURPORTS TO WAIVE ANY OF THE SELLER'S RIGHTS UNDER SECTION 7-310 IS VOID.

45. HOMESTEAD PROPERTY TAX CREDIT NOTICE TO BUYER: IF YOU PLAN TO LIVE IN THIS HOME AS YOUR PRINCIPAL RESIDENCE, YOU MAY QUALIFY FOR THE HOMESTEAD PROPERTY TAX CREDIT. THE HOMESTEAD PROPERTY TAX CREDIT MAY SIGNIFICANTLY REDUCE THE AMOUNT OF PROPERTY TAXES YOU OWE. Additional information may be obtained at: https://dat.maryland.gov/realproperty/pages/maryland-homestead-tax-credit.aspx.

46. PROPERTY TAX NOTICE – 60 DAY APPEAL: If any real property is transferred after January 1 and before the beginning of the next taxable year to a new owner, the new owner may submit a written appeal as to a value or classification on or before 60 days after the date of the transfer.

SECTION SIX: TRANSFER OF TITLE AND CLOSING

47. NOTICE OF BUYER'S RIGHT TO SELECT SETTLEMENT SERVICE PROVIDERS: Buyer has the right to select Buyer's own title insurance company, title lawyer, settlement company, escrow company, mortgage lender or financial institution as defined in the Financial Institutions Article, Annotated Code of Maryland. Buyer acknowledges that Seller may not be prohibited from offering owner financing as a condition of settlement.

48. DEED AND TITLE: Upon payment of the purchase price, a deed for the Property containing covenants of special warranty and further assurances (except in the case of transfer by personal representative of an estate), shall be executed by Seller and shall convey the Property to Buyer. Title to the Property, including all chattels included in the purchase, shall be good and merchantable, free of liens and encumbrances except as specified herein; except for use and occupancy restrictions of public record which are generally applicable to properties in the immediate neighborhood or the subdivision in which the Property is located and publicly recorded easements for public utilities and any other easements which may be observed by an inspection of the Property. Buyer expressly assumes the risk that restrictive covenants, zoning laws or other recorded documents may restrict or prohibit the use of the Property for the purpose(s) intended by Buyer. In the event Seller is unable to give good and merchantable title or such as can be insured by a Maryland licensed title insurer, with Buyer paying not more than the standard rate as filed with the Maryland Insurance Commissioner, Seller, at Seller's expense, shall have the option of curing any defect so as to enable Seller to give good and merchantable title or, if Buyer is willing to accept title without said defect being cured, paying any special premium on behalf of Buyer to obtain title insurance on the Property to the benefit of Buyer. In the event Seller elects to cure any defects in title, this Contract shall continue to remain in full force and effect; and the date of settlement shall be extended for a period not to exceed fourteen (14) additional days. If Seller is unable to cure such title defect(s) and is unable to obtain a policy of title insurance on the Property to the benefit of Buyer from a Maryland licensed title insurer, Buyer shall have the option of taking such title as Seller can give, or terminating this Contract and being reimbursed by Seller for cost of searching title as may have been incurred not to exceed 1/2 of 1% of the purchase price. In the latter event, there shall be no further liability or obligation on either of the parties hereto; and this Contract shall become null and void; and all Deposit(s) shall be disbursed in accordance with the Deposit paragraph of this Contract. In no event shall Broker(s) or their agent(s) have any liability for any defect in Seller's title.

49. ADJUSTMENTS: Ground rent, homeowner's association fees, rent and water rent shall be adjusted and apportioned as of date of settlement; and all taxes, general or special, and all other public or governmental charges or assessments against the Property which are or may be payable on a periodic basis, including the Metropolitan District Sanitary Commission and the Washington Suburban Sanitary Commission, or other benefit charges, assessments, liens or encumbrances for sewer, water, drainage, paving, or other public improvements completed or commenced on or prior to the date hereof, or subsequent thereto, are to be adjusted and apportioned as of the date of settlement and are to be assumed and paid thereafter by Buyer, whether assessments have been levied or not as of date of settlement if applicable by local law. **Any heating or cooking fuels remaining in supply tank(s) at time of settlement shall become the property of Buyer.**

50. SETTLEMENT COSTS: Buyer agrees to pay all settlement costs and charges including, but not limited to, all Lender's fees in connection herewith, including title examination and title insurance fees, loan insurance premiums, all document preparation and recording fees, notary fees, survey fees where required, and all recording charges, except those incident to clearing existing encumbrances or title defects, except if Buyer is a Veteran obtaining VA financing, those prohibited to be paid by a Veteran obtaining VA financing, which prohibited charges shall be paid by Seller. If Buyer is a Veteran obtaining VA financing, Buyer's Broker may not charge a flat fee to Buyer nor to Seller per VA Reg. Part 38 CFR 36.4313(b). Seller is advised that should Seller not be able to attend Settlement as scheduled, Seller may be subject to additional charges from the settlement company to cover the reasonable additional costs of accommodating Seller's request. In such event, Seller is advised to contact the title company to determine what charges may apply.

51. TRANSFER CHARGES:

A. IN GENERAL. If Buyer is NOT a first-time Maryland homebuyer, payment of Recordation Taxes and State and local Transfer Taxes will be divided equally between Buyer and Seller unless otherwise stated here:____. Buyer shall be entitled to receive the benefit of any local owner-occupancy reduction offered by the jurisdiction where the property is located.

B. FIRST-TIME MARYLAND HOMEBUYER. Maryland law provides that the amount of state transfer tax due on the sale of property to a first-time Maryland homebuyer is reduced from 0.50% to 0.25% <u>and shall be paid entirely by the Seller</u>. Payment of Recordation Taxes and local Transfer Taxes will be divided equally between Buyer and Seller unless otherwise stated here:____ __________. Buyer shall be entitled to receive the benefit of any local owner-occupancy reduction offered by the jurisdiction where the property is located. Buyer is hereby notified that to ensure receipt of the above reduction, Buyer should check the box on Page 10 of this Contract, indicating that Buyer is a first-time Maryland homebuyer, and complete the required affidavit at settlement indicating that the Buyer is a first-time Maryland homebuyer.

52. MARYLAND NON-RESIDENT SELLER: If the Property is not the Seller's principal residence and the Seller is a non-resident individual of the State of Maryland or is a non-resident entity which is not formed under the laws of the State of Maryland or qualified to do business in the State of Maryland, a withholding tax from the proceeds of sale ***shall*** be withheld at the time of settlement except as otherwise provided by Maryland law. ***Seller may request the Maryland Comptroller to issue a Certificate of Full or Partial Exemption from the withholding requirements, provided that such request is filed not later than 21 days prior to the date of closing. For detailed information, seller should call 1-800-MDTAXES or visit: <u>https://www.marylandtaxes.gov/forms/current_forms/withholding_requirement.pdf</u>.***

53. FOREIGN INVESTMENT TAXES-FIRPTA: Section 1445 of the United States Internal Revenue Code of 1986 provides that a Buyer of residential real property located in the United States must withhold federal income taxes from the payment of the purchase price if (a) the purchase price exceeds Three Hundred Thousand Dollars ($300,000.00) and (b) the seller is a foreign person. Unless otherwise stated in an addendum attached hereto, if the purchase price is in excess of Three

Hundred Thousand Dollars ($300,000.00), Seller represents that Seller is not a non-resident alien, foreign corporation, foreign partnership, foreign trust or foreign estate (as those terms are defined by the Internal Revenue Code and applicable regulations) and agrees to execute an affidavit to this effect at the time of settlement.

54. INTERNAL REVENUE SERVICE FILING: Buyer and Seller each agree to cooperate with the settlement officer by providing all necessary information so that a report can be filed with the Internal Revenue Service, as required by Section 6045 of the IRS Code. To the extent permitted by law, any fees incurred as a result of such filing will be paid by the Seller.

55. AUTHORIZATION TO PROVIDE TILA-RESPA INTEGRATED DISCLOSURES: Buyer and Seller hereby authorize the lender, title company, escrow agent, and/or their representatives to disclose and provide copies of the closing disclosure(s) and/or other settlement statement to the real estate licensees involved in the transaction at the time these documents are provided to Buyer and Seller.

56. BROKER'S FEE: All parties irrevocably instruct the settlement officer to collect the fee or compensation and disburse same according to the terms and conditions provided in the listing agreement and/or agency representation agreement. Settlement shall not be a condition precedent to payment of compensation.

57. BROKER LIABILITY: Brokers, their agents, subagents and employees do not assume any responsibility for the condition of the Property or for the performance of this Contract by any or all parties hereto. By signing this Contract, Buyer and Seller acknowledge that they have not relied on any representations made by Brokers, or any agents, subagents or employees of Brokers, except those representations expressly set forth in this Contract.

58. PROPERTY OWNER'S TITLE INSURANCE: Buyer is encouraged to purchase owner's title insurance at either "standard" or "enhanced" coverage and rates. The coverage afforded by such title insurance would be governed by the terms and conditions thereof, and the premium for obtaining such title insurance coverage would be determined by the extent of its coverage. For purposes of owner's title insurance policy premium rate disclosures by Buyer's lender, Buyer and Seller agree that enhanced rates (if available) shall be quoted by Buyer's lender. Buyer understands that a policy issued to the Lender will not protect the Buyer from losses caused by title defect. Nothing herein obligates Buyer to obtain any owner's title insurance coverage at any time, including at settlement, and that the availability of owner's title insurance coverage is subject to the underwriting criteria of the title insurer. Buyer understands that the Broker does not warrant the condition of title, and Buyer agrees to hold harmless Broker from any damages sustained by Buyer that may result from a defect in title.

SECTION SEVEN: BREACH OF CONTRACT AND DISPUTE RESOLUTION

59. DEFAULT: Buyer and Seller are required and agree to make full settlement in accordance with the terms of this Contract and acknowledge that failure to do so constitutes a breach hereof. If Buyer fails to make full settlement or is in default due to Buyer's failure to comply with the terms, covenants and conditions of this Contract, the initial Deposit and additional Deposits (the "Deposit") may be retained by Seller as long as a Release of Deposit Agreement is signed and executed by all parties, expressing that said Deposit may be retained by Seller. In the event the parties do not agree to execute a Release of Deposit Agreement, subject to the Deposit paragraph of this Contract, Buyer and Seller shall have all legal and equitable remedies. If Seller fails to make full settlement or is in default due to Seller's failure to comply with the terms, covenants and conditions of this Contract, Buyer shall be entitled to pursue such rights and remedies as may be available, at law or in equity, including, without limitation, an action for specific performance of this Contract and/or monetary damages. In the event of any litigation or dispute between Buyer and Seller concerning the release of the Deposit, Broker's sole responsibility may be met, at Broker's option, by paying the Deposit into the court in which such litigation is pending, or by paying the Deposit into the court of proper jurisdiction by an action of interpleader. Buyer and Seller agree that, upon Broker's payment of the Deposit into the court, neither Buyer nor Seller shall have any further right, claim, demand or action against Broker regarding the release of the Deposit; and Buyer and Seller, jointly and severally, shall indemnify and hold Broker harmless from any and all such rights, claims, demands or actions. In the event of such dispute and election by Broker to file an action of interpleader as herein provided, Buyer and Seller further agree and hereby expressly and irrevocably authorize Broker to deduct from the Deposit all costs incurred by Broker in the filing and maintenance of such action of interpleader including but not limited to filing fees, court costs, service of process fees and attorneys' fees, provided that the amount deducted shall not exceed the lesser of $500 or the amount of the Deposit held by Broker. All such fees and costs authorized herein to be deducted may be deducted by Broker from the Deposit prior to paying the balance of the Deposit to the court. Buyer and Seller further agree and expressly declare that all such fees and costs so deducted shall be the exclusive property of Broker. If the amount deducted by Broker is less than the total of all of the costs incurred by Broker in filing and maintaining the interpleader action, then Buyer and Seller jointly, and severally, agree to reimburse Broker for all such excess costs upon the conclusion of the interpleader action.

60. MEDIATION OF DISPUTES: Mediation is a process by which the parties attempt to resolve a dispute or claim with the assistance of a neutral mediator who is authorized to facilitate the resolution of the dispute. The mediator has no authority to make an award, to impose a resolution of the dispute or claim upon the parties or to require the parties to continue mediation if the parties do not desire to do so. Buyer and Seller agree that any dispute or claim arising out of or from this Contract or the transaction which is the subject of this Contract shall be mediated through Maryland REALTORS® or its member local boards/associations in accordance with the established Mediation Rules and Guidelines of Maryland REALTORS® or through such other mediator or mediation service as mutually agreed upon by Buyer and Seller, in writing. Unless otherwise agreed in writing by the parties, mediation fees, costs and expenses shall be divided and paid equally by the parties to the mediation. If either party elects to have an attorney present that party shall pay his or her own attorney's fees.

Buyer and Seller further agree that the obligation of Buyer and Seller to mediate as herein provided shall apply to all disputes or claims arising whether prior to, during, or within one (1) year following the actual contract settlement date or when settlement should have occurred. Buyer and Seller agree that neither party shall commence any action in any court regarding a dispute or claim arising out of or from this Contract or the transaction which is the subject of this Contract, without first mediating the dispute or claim, unless the right to pursue such action or the ability to protect an interest or pursue a remedy as provided in this Contract, would be precluded by the delay of the mediation. In the event the right to pursue such action, or the ability to protect an interest or pursue a remedy would be precluded by the delay, Buyer or Seller may commence the action only if the initial pleading or document commencing such action is accompanied by a request to stay the proceeding pending the conclusion of the mediation. If a party initiates or commences an action in violation of this provision, the party agrees to pay all costs and expenses, including reasonable attorneys' fees, incurred by the other party to enforce the obligation as provided herein. The provisions of this paragraph shall survive closing and shall not be deemed to have been extinguished by merger with the deed.

61. ATTORNEY'S FEES: In any action or proceeding between Buyer and Seller based, in whole or in part, upon the performance or non-performance of the terms and conditions of this Contract, including, but not limited to, breach of contract, negligence, misrepresentation or fraud, the prevailing party in such action or proceeding shall be entitled to receive reasonable attorney's fees from the other party as determined by the court or arbitrator. In any action or proceeding between Buyer and Seller and/or between Buyer and Broker(s) and/or Seller and Broker(s) resulting in Broker(s) being made a party to such action or proceeding, including, but not limited to, any litigation, arbitration, or complaint and claim before the Maryland Real Estate Commission, whether as defendant, cross-defendant, third-party defendant or respondent, Buyer and Seller jointly and severally, agree to indemnify and hold Broker(s) harmless from and against any and all liability, loss, cost, damages or expenses (including filing fees, court costs, service of process fees, transcript fees and attorneys' fees) incurred by Broker(s) in such action or proceeding, providing that such action or proceeding does not result in a judgment against Broker(s). As used in this Contract, the term "Broker(s)" shall mean: (a) the Brokers as identified on Page 11 of this Contract; (b) the named Sales Associates identified on Page 11 of the Contract; and (c) any agent, subagent, salesperson, independent contractor and/or employees of Broker(s). The term "Broker(s)" shall also mean, in the singular, any or either of the named Broker(s) and/or Sales Associate(s) as identified or, in the plural, both of the named Brokers and/or Sales Associates as identified. This Paragraph shall apply to any and all such action(s) or proceeding(s) against Broker(s) including those action(s) or proceeding(s) based, in whole or in part, upon any alleged act(s) or omission(s) by Broker(s), including, but not limited to, any alleged act of misrepresentation, fraud, non-disclosure, negligence, violation of any statutory or common law duty, or breach of fiduciary duty by Broker(s). The provisions of this Paragraph shall survive closing and shall not be deemed to have been extinguished by merger with the deed.

______________________		______________________	
Buyer Signature	**Date**	**Seller Signature**	**Date**
Buyer Signature	**Date**	**Seller Signature**	**Date**

DATE OF CONTRACT ACCEPTANCE: ______________________
(Insert the date on which all final initials and signatures of all parties have been affixed to this Contract.)

□ **Check if First-Time Maryland Homebuyer**

Contact Information:

BUYER / NAME(S): ______________________________
MAILING ADDRESS: ______________________________
____

SELLER / NAME(S): ______________________________
MAILING ADDRESS: ______________________________
____

Information provided for reference only:

LISTING BROKERAGE COMPANY NAME: ______________________________
BROKER OF RECORD NAME: ______________ LICENSE NUMBER: ______________
SALES ASSOCIATE NAME: ______________ LICENSE NUMBER: ______________
OFFICE ADDRESS: ______________________________
OFFICE PHONE: ______________ BROKER/SALES ASSOCIATE MLS ID: ______________
SALES ASSOCIATE PHONE: ______________ SALES ASSOCIATE E-MAIL: ______________

ACTING AS: □ LISTING BROKER AND SELLER AGENT; OR
□ INTRA - COMPANY AGENT WITH BROKER AS DUAL AGENT

SELLING BROKERAGE COMPANY NAME: ______________________________
BROKER OF RECORD NAME: ______________ LICENSE NUMBER: ______________
SALES ASSOCIATE NAME: ______________ LICENSE NUMBER: ______________
OFFICE ADDRESS: ______________________________
OFFICE PHONE: ______________ BROKER/SALES ASSOCIATE MLS ID: ______________
SALES ASSOCIATE PHONE: ______________ SALES ASSOCIATE E-MAIL: ______________

ACTING AS: □ SELLER AGENT; OR
□ SUBAGENT; OR
□ BUYER AGENT; OR
□ INTRA - COMPANY AGENT WITH BROKER AS DUAL AGENT

B. [§ 2.77] Letter Agreement Permitting Seller to Remain in Possession After Closing

____________, 20__

Dear_____________

On this date, you have sold to us and we have purchased from you the fee simple property and improvements known as [property description]. You have asked that you be allowed to remain in the house and lease it from us for a short period of time, and we are agreeable. This letter confirms the understanding which we have made with you in that regard.

We agree to allow you to remain in occupancy of the house for a period commencing on closing and terminating on _____________, 20__. In consideration, you agree to pay us rent in the sum of $____ per month, prorated at the rate of $____ per day for any period less than a full month. Rent shall be due and payable monthly, in advance, commencing at closing, and on the first day of each calendar month thereafter. This rental agreement will terminate on the termination date set forth above without further notice from either party, but you may terminate it at any time prior thereto by giving us at least one week's prior written notice.

Effective from closing, you agree that you will pay all utility expenses; perform all interior, exterior and groundscaping maintenance of the house and its contents; keep the house, its contents and the lawn in good and sanitary condition and repair; and commit or permit no waste. At the termination of this agreement, you will deliver the house and all of its contents sold by you to us in the same condition as when received at closing, normal wear and tear excepted.

During the period of your occupancy, you will continue to maintain in full force and effect liability and extended coverage insurance insuring the house and all of its contents, and naming us as a named insured as may appear.

We or our agent may enter the house at all reasonable times to examine it or do such things as we deem necessary. In that regard, you agree that we may retain a key to the house to enable convenient access.

If this letter accurately sets forth our understanding, please sign the additional copy enclosed herein in coeirmation of our rental agreement.

Very truly yours,

______________________________	______________________________
______________________________	______________________________
Seller	Buyer

C. [§ 2.78] Kickout Addendum

Maryland REALTORS®

KICKOUT ADDENDUM

ADDENDUM dated ______________________________ to Contract of Sale
between Buyer ______________________________
and Seller ______________________________
for Property known as ______________________________.

Seller reserves the right to continue to offer the property for sale in order to obtain other offers. In the event Seller receives another written offer which Seller desires to accept, Seller shall immediately notify Buyer, in writing, that Buyer shall have 72 hours to remove the contingency regarding sale, settlement or lease of other property. Seller shall not be obligated to provide Buyer with evidence of receipt of another offer. The 72 hours shall commence when the written notice is delivered in person or by facsimile transmittal, or a digital image is delivered by electronic transmittal to Buyer or Buyer's agent. If Buyer fails to remove the contingency in writing, or fails to respond within the 72-hour period, the Contract shall be null and void and of no further force and effect and the deposit shall be disbursed in accordance with the Deposit Paragraph of the Contract. If Buyer elects to remove the contingency, Buyer shall do so in a written addendum delivered to Seller or Seller's agent within the 72-hour period together with a financial statement or other financial information, satisfactory to Seller, to demonstrate Buyer's financial ability to complete settlement without the sale, settlement or lease of any other property owned by Buyer. Seller, at Seller's sole discretion, shall determine whether the financial statement or information provided by Buyer is satisfactory evidence of the Buyer's financial ability to complete settlement on the Property and notify Buyer of Seller's decision within 72 hours from delivery. If Seller fails to notify Buyer of Seller's decision within 72 hours from delivery, Seller shall be deemed to have accepted, as satisfactory, Buyer's financial statement or information and the Contract shall remain in full force and effect.

All other terms and conditions of the Contract of Sale remain in full force and effect.

Buyer Signature	**Date**	**Seller Signature**	**Date**
Buyer Signature	**Date**	**Seller Signature**	**Date**

10/18

D. [§ 2.79] Inspection Addendum

Maryland REALTORS®

PROPERTY INSPECTIONS ADDENDUM

ADDENDUM dated ______________________________ to Contract of Sale between

Buyer ____

and Seller ____

for Property known as____.

The following provisions are included in and supersede any conflicting language in the Contract of Sale.

1. **INSPECTION CONTINGENCY:** Buyer and Seller agree that Buyer, at Buyer's expense, shall have the right within __________days from the Date of Contract Acceptance (hereinafter referred to as the "Deadline") to have qualified experts conduct those inspections listed below in subparagraph A **that are initialed by both BUYER and SELLER:**

   A. **INSPECTIONS; SCOPE AND LIMITATIONS:** The purpose of the inspection(s) selected below is to discover unsatisfactory conditions, if any, of the components and systems of the Property. The future condition and performance of the above systems and components are not warranted by Seller and are not to be considered subject to this Addendum. The inspection(s) are NOT for the purpose of making items of a routine maintenance and/or cosmetic nature the subject of further negotiations between Buyer and Seller.

	Buyer's Initials	Seller's Initials	
1)	_____/_____	_____/_____	**Structural and Mechanical**
2)	_____/_____	_____/_____	**Mold**
3)	_____/_____	_____/_____	**Environmental**
4)	_____/_____	_____/_____	**Radon**
5)	_____/_____	_____/_____	**Chimney Inspection**
6)	_____/_____	_____/_____	**Lead-Based Paint Hazard Inspection**
7)	_____/_____	_____/_____	**Wood Destroying Insect**
8)	_____/_____	_____/_____	**Additional Inspection(s)** ______________________

____.

NOTES: Buyer's right to inspect and/or test well and/or septic systems, water quality and water yield shall be reserved through separate addenda. If Buyer intends to obtain financing through the Veterans Administration (VA), Buyer retains the right to conduct an inspection for wood destroying insects at their expense pursuant to VA regulations, notwithstanding the agreement of the parties stated herein.

B. INSPECTION PROCESS:

(i) **RIGHT TO TERMINATE:** If the results of an inspection are unsatisfactory to the Buyer, Buyer may terminate the Contract of Sale by delivering a Unilateral Notice of Termination Under Contract of Sale to Seller by the Deadline. Buyer is not required to specify the basis of Buyer's dissatisfaction. Buyer's right to terminate the Contract of Sale as stated in this subsection expires at the Deadline.

(ii) **RIGHT TO NEGOTIATE:** Instead of exercising the Right to Terminate the Contract of Sale in accordance with subparagraph 1.B(i), Buyer may make a single, written request for repairs and/or a Seller Credit based upon Buyer's dissatisfaction with the results of the agreed-upon inspection(s). This right will expire at the Deadline unless the Buyer delivers to Seller a copy of the inspection report(s) together with a written request that Seller make certain repairs, and/or agree to provide a Seller Credit. The parties acknowledge that Buyer's lender may need to approve any agreed-upon Seller Credit. Should Buyer attempt to deliver multiple written requests for repairs and/or Seller Credit to Seller prior to the Deadline, Seller shall only be obligated to consider the first such request received.

(iii) **SELLER'S RESPONSE:** Within five (5) days after Buyer delivers the written request for repairs and/or a Seller Credit, Seller shall notify Buyer in writing whether Seller agrees to all, some, or none of the Buyer's requests. If Seller agrees to all of the requested repairs and/or a Seller Credit, the Contract of Sale shall remain in full force and effect, as amended. If Seller agrees to only some of the requested repairs and/or Seller Credit, or fails to respond within the five (5) day period, Buyer, by written notice to Seller given within two (2) days of receipt of Seller's notice, or from the date that such written notice was to have been provided by Seller, may elect to: 1) terminate the Contract of Sale; 2) waive the requested repairs and/or Seller Credit to which Seller will not agree, in which case the Contract of Sale shall remain in full force and effect, or; 3) provided that Seller has responded to Buyer, continue negotiations by delivering a counteroffer to Seller in accordance with Section 1.B(iv) of this Addendum. If Buyer fails to timely notify Seller of Buyer's election to terminate the Contract, to waive the right to repair or correct any unsatisfactory conditions which Seller will not repair or correct, or submit a counteroffer, the Contract shall remain in full force and effect; and Seller shall repair or correct, in a good and workmanlike manner and prior to settlement all of the unsatisfactory conditions which Seller agreed to repair or correct, and/or credit Buyer the amount of any credit Seller offered at settlement, subject to lender approval. Buyer shall confirm with lender that the entire credit provided for herein may be utilized. If lender prohibits Seller from payment of any portion of such credit, said credit shall be reduced to the maximum amount allowed by lender.

(iv) **ADDITIONAL NEGOTIATIONS:** Thereafter, within two (2) days after delivery of a counteroffer regarding the requested repairs and/or Seller Credit, the receiving party must:

a. Deliver Notice accepting the terms contained in the immediately preceding counteroffer; OR

b. Deliver Notice continuing negotiations by making a further counteroffer; OR

c. Deliver Notice of termination of the Contract of Sale to the other party.

The failure of the receiving party to timely respond to any counteroffer shall constitute their automatic acceptance of that counteroffer, with all other terms of the Contract of Sale remaining in full force and effect.

(v) **CONTRACT TERMINATION AND DEPOSIT(S):** If either party elects to terminate the Contract of Sale in accordance with the terms of this Addendum, the Contract shall become null and void, and all Deposit(s) shall be disbursed in accordance with the Deposit paragraph of the Contract.

2. **RIGHTS AND OBLIGATIONS OF BUYER AND SELLER:** Seller shall make the Property accessible for agreed-upon inspections and shall have utilities in service at the time of the inspection(s). Neither Buyer, nor any agent or contractor of Buyer, shall in any way excavate, penetrate, or otherwise damage any part of the Property without the prior written consent of Seller, nor shall any furnishings, boxes, or personal property belonging to Seller be moved or relocated unless absolutely necessary in connection with the inspection(s). If the Property is part of a condominium, Buyer shall be given access to the common areas to perform the inspection(s). Buyer and Seller shall have the right to be present during the inspection(s), and Buyer shall give Seller reasonable advance notice of the date and time of the inspection(s). If Buyer or Buyer's agents or contractors damage the Property during the exercise of Buyer's rights under this Addendum, except for damage caused by Seller's negligence, Buyer shall promptly reimburse Seller for all costs incurred in correcting such damage.

3. **REPAIRS, CORRECTION, RE-INSPECTION:** Seller agrees to complete repairs and provide receipts in sufficient time for Buyer to re-inspect prior to settlement. Buyer shall have the right to re-inspect the Property upon the completion of repairs or corrective action by Seller to confirm that Seller has performed, in a good and workmanlike manner, all of the repairs and corrective action which Seller agreed to perform.

All other terms and conditions of the Contract of Sale remain in full force and effect.

Buyer Signature	**Date**	**Seller Signature**	**Date**
Buyer Signature	**Date**	**Seller Signature**	**Date**

E. [§ 2.80] FHA Financing Addendum

Maryland REALTORS®

FHA FINANCING ADDENDUM

ADDENDUM dated ______________________________ to Contract of Sale

between Buyer ______________________________

and Seller ______________________________

for Property known as ______________________________.

The Contract is contingent upon Buyer obtaining a mortgage insured by the Federal Housing Administration (FHA) and secured by the Property as follows:

1. LOAN DETAILS:

Mortgage Insurance Premium (MIP)	$__________	Loan Program	__________
Base Loan Amount	$__________	TERM OF LOAN	______ Years
		INITIAL INTEREST RATE	______%
TOTAL LOAN AMOUNT	$__________		

Buyer agrees to pay to Lender loan origination/loan discount fees of ☐ $__________ / ☐ ______% of the loan amount and Seller agrees to pay loan origination/loan discount fees ☐ $__________ / ☐ ______% of the loan amount. Buyer shall receive the benefit of any reduction in said fees. All loan insurance premiums as required by Lender shall be paid by Buyer.

BY ACCEPTING A LOAN AGREEMENT WHEREBY THE INTEREST RATE AND LOAN DISCOUNT FEES ARE NOT BEING LOCKED IN, BUYER AGREES TO ACCEPT THE RATE AS CHARGED BY LENDER AT THE TIME OF LOCK-IN AND THE RESPONSIBILITY FOR ANY ADDITIONAL FEES CHARGED. BUYER SHALL REMAIN BOUND TO PERFORM UNDER THE CONTRACT, NOTWITHSTANDING ANY SUCH CHANGES IN THE RATE AND/OR FEES.

2. MONTHLY PAYMENT: Payments to Lender shall include monthly principal and interest, plus one-twelfth of the annual real estate taxes, ground rent, special assessments or charges, if any, hazard (fire) insurance premium, flood insurance, private mortgage insurance where required, and FHA MIP payment.

3. LOAN UNDERWRITING: Buyer and Seller understand that the Lender will have to resubmit the loan to underwriting if, from the time Buyer's loan application was approved to the time of settlement, there are any increases to the interest rate and/or the loan origination/discount fees. To the extent such changes do not conflict with the conditions of the Contract, Buyer agrees to comply with Lender's request for additional or updated information as required to approve the loan.

4. FHA AMENDATORY CLAUSE: It is expressly agreed that notwithstanding any other provisions of the Contract, Buyer shall not be obligated to complete the purchase of the Property described herein or to incur any penalty by forfeiture of deposit or otherwise unless Buyer has been given in accordance with HUD/FHA or VA requirements a written statement by the Federal Housing Commissioner, Department of Veterans Affairs, or a Direct Endorsement Lender setting forth the appraised value of the Property of not less than $ ______________. Buyer shall have the privilege and option to proceed with consummation of the Contract without regard to the amount of the appraised value. **The appraised value is arrived at to determine the maximum mortgage the Department of Housing and Urban Development will insure. HUD does not warrant the value or the condition of the Property. Buyer should satisfy himself/herself that the price and condition of the Property are acceptable. NOTICE:** The dollar amount to be inserted in the amendatory clause is the purchase price as stated in the Contract. If Buyer and Seller agree to adjust the purchase price in response to an appraised value that is less than the purchase price, a new amendatory clause is **not** required. However, the loan application package must include the original Contract with the same purchase price as shown in the amendatory clause, along with the revised or amended Contract.

5. **MORTGAGE INSURANCE:** Buyer agrees to pay mortgage insurance premiums (MIP) as required by FHA regulations. MIP must be paid at the time of settlement in cash or included in the loan amount; **AND IN ADDITION**, a mortgage insurance premium equal to a percentage of the loan amount must be paid monthly thereafter.

6. **WOOD DESTROYING INSECT INSPECTION:** Should Lender require a wood destroying insect inspection as a condition of financing, the parties agree that Buyer may conduct such inspection at Buyer's expense. Lender Required Repairs in connection with a lender required wood destroying insect inspection shall be performed in accordance with the Lender Required Repairs paragraph of this Addendum. Seller shall have no obligation to consider any other request for repairs and/or Seller Credit in connection with a lender required wood destroying insect inspection unless a wood destroying insect inspection was negotiated by the parties as part of a Property Inspections Addendum. In all transactions involving FHA financing, all fences and outbuildings shall be included in the inspection and certification.

7. **LENDER REQUIRED REPAIRS:** In the event the FHA and/or Lender require any repairs or improvements ("Required Repairs") be made to the Property, Seller agrees to perform the Required Repairs and pay the cost thereof at or prior to settlement, provided the total cost of the Required Repairs does not exceed $______________, ("Repair Amount"). **This cost shall be in addition to Seller's other obligations under the terms of the Contract.** Should the cost of Required Repairs exceed the Repair Amount:

A. Seller may elect to pay the total cost of the Required Repairs, in which event the Contract shall remain in full force and effect.
B. Seller may terminate the Contract by written notice to Buyer, which must include a written estimate of the cost of the Required Repairs. Said written notice shall be provided to Buyer within five (5) days of Seller's receipt of written estimate(s).
C. The Contract shall remain in full force and effect if, within five (5) days of Buyer's receipt of Seller's notice of termination, Buyer elects, in writing, to pay the difference between the cost of the Required Repairs and the Repair Amount listed above.
D. If neither Buyer nor Seller elects to pay the excess cost of any Required Repairs, the Contract shall become null and void; and all Deposit(s) shall be disbursed in accordance with the Deposit paragraph of the Contract.

8. **CERTIFICATION:** Seller, Buyer and Broker(s) hereby certify that the terms of the Contract to which this Addendum is attached are true to the best of their knowledge and belief. Any other agreement(s) entered into between the parties with respect to the purchase and sale of the Property has been fully disclosed and is attached to the Contract.

9. **FHA REQUIRED NOTICE:** Buyer acknowledges receipt of HUD form #92564-CN entitled: ***For Your Protection: Get A Home Inspection.*** __________/__________

Buyer's Initials

All other terms and conditions of the Contract of Sale remain in full force and effect.

Buyer Signature	**Date**	**Seller Signature**	**Date**
Buyer Signature	**Date**	**Seller Signature**	**Date**

The real estate agent(s)/broker(s) hereby certify as to Paragraph 8:

Listing Agent or Listing Broker	**Date**
Buyer Agent or Buyer Broker	**Date**
Cooperating Agent or Cooperating Broker	**Date**

Page 2 of 2 1/23

F. [§ 2.81] VA Financing Addendum

Maryland REALTORS®

VA FINANCING ADDENDUM

ADDENDUM dated ______________________________ to Contract of Sale
between Buyer ______________________________
and Seller ______________________________
for Property known as ______________________________.

The Contract is contingent upon Buyer obtaining a mortgage guaranteed by the Veterans Administration and secured by the Property as follows:

1. LOAN DETAILS:

VA Funding Fee	$__________	Loan Program	__________
Base Loan Amount	$__________	TERM OF LOAN	__________ Years
TOTAL LOAN AMOUNT	$__________	INITIAL INTEREST RATE	__________%

Buyer agrees to pay to Lender loan origination/discount fees of □ $__________ / □ ______% of the loan amount, and Seller agrees to pay loan origination/discount fees of □ $__________ / □ ______% of the loan amount. Buyer shall receive the benefit of any reduction in said fees. Under the "Settlement Costs" Paragraph of the Contract, Buyer obtaining VA financing is prohibited from paying certain charges, and Seller hereby agrees to pay such charges not to exceed $ __________.

BY ACCEPTING A LOAN AGREEMENT WHEREBY THE INTEREST RATE AND LOAN DISCOUNT FEES ARE NOT BEING LOCKED IN, BUYER AGREES TO ACCEPT THE RATE AS CHARGED BY LENDER AT THE TIME OF LOCK-IN AND THE RESPONSIBILITY FOR ANY ADDITIONAL LOAN DISCOUNT FEES CHARGED, AND BUYER SHALL REMAIN BOUND BY THE TERMS OF THE CONTRACT, NOTWITHSTANDING ANY SUCH CHANGES IN THE RATE AND/OR FEES.

2. MONTHLY PAYMENT: Payments to Lender shall include monthly principal and interest, plus one-twelfth of the annual real property taxes, ground rent, special assessments or charges, if any, hazard insurance premium, flood insurance premium, and private mortgage insurance where required.

3. LOAN UNDERWRITING: Buyer and Seller understand that Lender will have to resubmit the loan to underwriting if, from the time Buyer's loan application was approved to the time of settlement, there are any increases to the interest rate and/or the loan origination/discount fees. To the extent such changes do not conflict with the conditions of the Contract, Buyer agrees to comply with Lender's request for additional or updated information as required to approve the loan.

4. VETERANS ADMINISTRATION GUARANTEED LOAN:

A. VA LOAN: Buyer's deposit shall be placed in an escrow account as required by Title 38, US Code, Section 3706. It is expressly agreed that, notwithstanding any other provisions of this Contract, Buyer shall not incur any penalty by forfeiture of earnest money or otherwise be obligated to complete the purchase of the property described herein, if the Contract purchase price or cost exceeds the reasonable value of the property established by the Veterans Administration or Buyer is not approved by the Veterans Administration and the lending institution. In the event Certificate of Reasonable Value is less than the amount of the Contract price, Buyer shall have the privilege and option for five (5) days after receipt of the VA appraisal to proceed with the consummation of this Contract without regard to the amount of reasonable value established by the Veterans Administration by giving the Seller notice of his intention to do so in writing. If Seller elects to reduce the Contract price to the appraised valuation, Buyer covenants and agrees to be bound to proceed with consummation hereof at the appraised valuation price. If Seller does not elect to reduce the price after Buyer's refusal to consummate this Contract at its full price, then this Contract shall be null and void. This Contract is contingent on the approval of the house and Buyer by the Veterans Administration and the lending institution. If the aforesaid approval is not obtained, it is expressly agreed that Buyer shall be refunded the Deposit and the Contract shall be null and void.

B. VA FEES: Buyer agrees to pay at settlement a VA funding fee equal to _____% of the principal sum of the loan, unless Buyer is eligible for and obtains exemption from the VA or elects to add the funding fee to the principal sum of the loan amount. Buyer hereby (_____ agrees to **pay the funding fee** at settlement) OR (_____ elects to **add the funding fee to the principal** sum of the loan amount). Lender's fees to Seller, if any, shall be paid by Seller at settlement, along with the excess amount of any of Buyer's fees which are limited by the Veterans Administration.

5. WOOD DESTROYING INSECT INSPECTION: Should Lender require a wood destroying insect inspection as a condition of financing, the parties agree that Buyer may conduct such inspection at Buyer's expense. Lender Required Repairs in connection with a lender required wood destroying insect inspection shall be performed in accordance with the Lender Required Repairs paragraph of this Addendum. Seller shall have no obligation to consider any other request for repairs and/or Seller Credit in connection with a lender required wood destroying insect inspection unless a wood destroying insect inspection was negotiated by the parties as part of a Property Inspections Addendum. In all transactions involving VA financing, all fences and outbuildings shall be included in the inspection and certification. Pursuant to VA regulations dated June 15, 2022, VA buyers may be charged for wood destroying insect inspection fees and pay for repairs: https://www.benefits.va.gov/HOMELOANS/documents/circulars/26-22-11.pdf.

6. LENDER REQUIRED REPAIRS: In the event VA and/or Lender require any repairs or improvements ("Required Repairs") be made to the Property, Seller agrees to perform the Required Repairs and to pay the cost thereof at or prior to settlement, provided the total cost of the Required Repairs does not exceed $______________________ ("Repair Amount"). **Seller's obligation to perform and pay for the Required Repairs shall be in addition to Seller's other obligations under the terms of the Contract.** Should the cost of Required Repairs exceed the Repair Amount:

A. Seller may elect to pay the total cost of the Required Repairs, in which event the Contract shall remain in full force and effect.

B. Seller may terminate the Contract by written notice to Buyer, which must include a written estimate of the cost of the Required Repairs. Said written notice shall be provided to Buyer within five (5) days of Seller's receipt of written estimate(s).

C. The Contract shall remain in full force and effect if, within five (5) days of Buyer's receipt of Seller's notice of termination, Buyer elects, in writing, to pay the difference between the cost of the Required Repairs and the Repair Amount listed above.

D. If neither Buyer nor Seller elects to pay the excess cost of any Required Repairs, the Contract shall be null and void; and the Deposit(s) shall be disbursed in accordance with the Deposit(s) paragraph of the Contract.

All other terms and conditions of the Contract of Sale remain in full force and effect.

Buyer Signature	Date	Seller Signature	Date
Buyer Signature	Date	Seller Signature	Date

Page 2 of 2 1/23

G. [§ 2.82] Owner Financing Addendum

Maryland REALTORS®

OWNER FINANCING CONTINGENCY ADDENDUM

ADDENDUM dated ______________________________ to Contract of Sale
between Buyer ______________________________
and Seller ______________________________
for Property known as ______________________________.

Owner financing is a complex transaction governed by many State and Federal laws. Real estate brokers are not qualified, nor licensed, to ensure that the terms of this Owner Financing Contingency Addendum comply with these laws. Buyer and Seller are strongly advised to consult with a competent legal professional.

1. **CREDIT TERMS.** The terms of the Credit Documents referred to in this Owner Financing Contingency Addendum are as follows:

- Principal. $______________ principal amount of the note (the "Note");
- Interest. Interest at _____% per ☐ month or ☐ other ____________.
- Remaining principal balance due in __________ years.
- First payment due on ______________________. Additional principal payments, balloon payments or other terms as follows:

____

______________________________.

2. **CREDIT INFORMATION.** Within ___________ (____) days after the execution of the Owner Financing Contingency Addendum, Buyer shall furnish all credit, employment, and financial information reasonably required by Seller ("Credit Information"). Buyer ☐ **SHALL** or ☐ **SHALL NOT** provide Seller with copies of IRS tax returns for the two preceding tax years.
Buyer shall provide to Seller, at Buyer's expense, a current credit report on Buyer from a consumer credit reporting agency. Buyer acknowledges that Seller may contact Buyer's current employer for verification of employment.

3. **SELLER'S RIGHT TO CANCEL.** If Seller determines, in Seller's sole discretion, that the Credit Information is unacceptable, Seller, within _______ (____) days of receiving the Credit Information, may either: (i) cancel the Contract of Sale by delivering a Unilateral Notice of Termination Under Contract of Sale to Buyer and all Deposit(s) shall be disbursed in accordance with the Deposit paragraph of the Contract or (ii) resolve in writing with Buyer any objections Seller has with the Credit Information.

3.1 **Failure To Cancel Or Resolve Objections.** If Seller fails to cancel the Contract of Sale or attempt to resolve in writing any objections Seller has with the Credit Information, as provided in Section 3 of this Addendum, Seller shall be deemed to have waived Seller's right to cancel the Contract of Sale pursuant to Section 3 of this Addendum.

4. **CREDIT DOCUMENTS.** Seller's extension of credit to Buyer shall be evidenced by : **Note and Deed of Trust;**
or Other ______________________________ **(hereinafter "Credit Documents")** and shall be recorded against the Property at settlement.

4.1 **Creation of Documents.** The Seller shall pay for and be responsible for the creation of the Credit Documents.

4.2 **Deadline for the Delivery of the Credit Documents.** The Seller shall provide the Credit Documents to the Buyer within ___________ (_____) days from the execution of the Owner Financing Contingency Addendum.

Page 1 of 2 10/23

4.3 **Right to Cancel or Resolve Objections**. If the Buyer determines, in the Buyer's sole discretion, that the Credit Documents are unacceptable, the Buyer, within ______________________(_______) days following receipt of the Credit Documents, may either (i) cancel the Contract of Sale by delivering a Unilateral Notice of Termination Under the Contract of Sale to the Seller and all Deposit(s) shall be disbursed in accordance with the Dep o sit paragraph of the Contract or (ii) resolve in writing with the Seller any objections the Buyer has with the Credit Documents.

4.4 **Failure to Cancel or Resolve Objections.** If the Buyer fails to cancel the Contract of Sale or fails to resolve in writing with the Seller any objections the Buyer has arising from the Credit Documents, as provided in Section 4.3 of this Addendum, the Buyer shall waive any right to cancel the Contract of Sale based on the Credit Documents.

5. **TITLE INSURANCE.** Buyer ☐ **SHALL** or ☐ **SHALL NOT** provide to Seller a lender's policy of title insurance in the amount of the indebtedness to the Seller, and, if applicable, shall pay for such policy at settlement.

6. **DISCLOSURE OF TAX IDENTIFICATION NUMBERS.** By no later than settlement, Buyer and Seller shall disclose to each other their respective Social Security Numbers or other applicable tax identification numbers so that they may comply with federal laws on reporting mortgage interest in filings with the Internal Revenue Service.

7. **ADDITIONAL TERMS.**

____

____

____

____

____.

All other terms and conditions of the Contract of Sale remain in full force and effect.

Buyer	**Date**	**Seller**	**Date**
Buyer	**Date**	**Seller**	**Date**

H. [§ 2.83] Condominium Resale Certificate

Maryland REALTORS®

CONDOMINIUM RESALE NOTICE

ADDENDUM/AMENDMENT dated________________________________ to Contract of Sale
between Buyer(s):________________________________
and Seller(s):________________________________
for Property known as:________________________________
Condominium Unit # __________ Building #________________, Section/Regime #______________,in
________________________________ Condominium Association.

PART ONE

NOTICE: This notice applies where the condominium project contains seven (7) units or more. Seller ("unit owner") is required by law to furnish to buyer(s) not later than fifteen (15) days prior to closing certain information concerning the condominium, which is described in Section 11-135 of the Maryland Condominium Act (Real Property Article, Annotated Code of Maryland, Section 11-101 et. seq.). This information must include the following:

1. A copy of the Declaration (condominium plat not required).
2. A copy of the Bylaws.
3. A copy of the Rules or Regulations of the Condominium.
4. A certificate from the Council of Unit Owners which includes:
   a) A statement disclosing the effect on the proposed conveyance of any right of first refusal or other restraint on the free alienability of the unit, other than any restraint created by the unit owner;
   b) A statement of the amount of the common expense assessment and any unpaid common expense or special assessment adopted by the Council of Unit Owners that is due and payable from the selling unit owner;
   c) A statement of any other fees payable by unit owners to the Council of Unit Owners;
   d) A statement of any capital expenditures approved by the Council of Unit Owners or its authorized designee planned at the time of the conveyance which are not reflected in the current operating budget included in the certificate;
   e) The most recent regularly prepared balance sheet and income expense statement, if any, of the condominium;
   f) The current operating budget of the condominium, including the current reserve study report or a summary of the report, a statement of the status and amount of any reserve or replacement fund, or a statement that there is no reserve fund;
   g) A statement of any unsatisfied judgments and the status of any pending lawsuits to which the Council of Unit Owners is a party, excluding assessment collection suits;
   h) A statement generally describing any insurance policies provided for the benefit of unit owners, a notice that the policies are available for inspection stating the location at which they are available, and a notice that the terms of the policy prevail over the general description;
   i) A statement as to whether the Council of Unit Owners has actual knowledge of any violation of the health or building codes with respect to the common elements of the condominium; and
   j) A description of any recreational or other facilities which are to be used by the unit owners or maintained by them or the Council of Unit Owners, and a statement as to whether or not they are to be part of the common elements.

Page 1 of 2 1/23

5. A statement by the unit owner as to whether the unit owner has knowledge:
    a) That any alteration to the unit or to the limited common elements assigned to the unit violates any provision of the Declaration, Bylaws, or Rules and Regulations;
    b) Of any violation of the health or building codes with respect to the unit or to the limited common elements assigned to the unit; and
    c) The unit is subject to an extended lease under Section 11-137 of the Maryland Condominium Act or under local law and, if so, a copy of the lease must be provided.
6. A written notice of the unit owner's responsibility for the Council of Unit Owners' property insurance deductible and the amount of the deductible.

PART TWO

NOTICE: This notice applies where the condominium project contains six (6) units or less. Seller is required by law to furnish to buyer(s) not later than fifteen (15) days prior to closing certain information concerning the condominium, which is described in Section 11-135 of the Maryland Condominium Act. This information must include the following:

1. A copy of the Declaration (other than the plats);
2. A copy of the Bylaws;
3. A copy of the Rules or Regulations of the Condominium; and
4. A statement by Seller of his expenses relating to the common elements during the preceding twelve (12) months.
5. A written notice of the unit owner's responsibility for the Council of Unit Owners' property insurance deductible and the amount of the deductible.

The brokers and agents negotiating this sale assume and accept no responsibility for any representations made in any resale certificate provided in accordance with the Maryland Condominium Act, and by the execution of this Contract of Sale, both Buyer and Seller agree to indemnify, defend, protect and hold harmless the brokers and agents negotiating this contract from any claim demand, suit, cause of action or matter or thing whatsoever arising out of the issuance of any resale certificate.

This Addendum/Amendment is considered part of Contract of Sale and of equal force and effect as all other terms and conditions which otherwise remain the same. This is a legally binding document. If not understood, seek competent legal advice.

BUYER MAY, AT ANY TIME WITHIN 7 DAYS FOLLOWING RECEIPT OF ALL THIS INFORMATION, RESCIND IN WRITING THE CONTRACT OF SALE, WITHOUT STATING A REASON AND WITHOUT ANY LIABILITY ON BUYERS' PART. UPON RECISSION, BUYER IS ENTITLED TO THE RETURN OF ANY DEPOSIT MADE ON ACCOUNT OF THE CONTRACT. THE RETURN OF ANY DEPOSITS HELD IN TRUST BY A LICENSED REAL ESTATE BROKER TO BUYER SHALL COMPLY WITH THE PROCEDURES SET FORTH SECTION 17-505 OF THE BUSINESS OCCUPATIONS AND PROFESSIONS ARTICLE OF THE MARYLAND CODE. ONCE THE SALE IS CLOSED, BUYER'S RIGHT TO CANCEL THIS CONTRACT IS TERMINATED.

Buyer	**Date**	**Seller**	**Date**
Buyer	**Date**	**Seller**	**Date**

Page 2 of 2 1/23

I. [§ 2.84] Notice of Baltimore County Well Water Law for Improved Property and Well Water Test Addendum

NOTICE OF BALTIMORE COUNTY WELL WATER LAW FOR IMPROVED PROPERTY AND WELL WATER TEST ADDENDUM

ADDENDUM NUMBER____________________ to CONTRACT OF SALE dated____________________

BUYER(S):____

SELLER(S):____

PROPERTY:____

NOTICE OF WELL WATER LAW

Since the Property to be purchased by Buyer(s) will be served by a private water supply system as the source of domestic water, the law of Baltimore County requires that, prior to conveyance of such property to any buyer(s), Seller(s) must provide a well with a supply of water meeting the minimum water yield requirements and bacteriological and chemical quality standards of Section 34-2-104 of the Baltimore County Code (2004 edition). Buyer(s) is further advised that the quantity and quality of water is important and that, unless Buyer(s) specifically executes a waiver of testing for minimum water yield and chemical quality standards, such tests must be made on the well existing on the Property to be purchased by Buyer(s) on the form prescribed by the Baltimore County Code and filed with the Baltimore County Department of Environmental Protection and Resource Management at least six (6) days prior to settlement and/or the date of conveyance to Buyer(s), whichever shall first occur. Any such waiver may be revoked by Buyer(s) upon written notice of such revocation delivered or mailed by certified mail, postage prepaid, return receipt requested, to Seller(s) or Seller's(s) agent at Seller's(s) home or business address or the business address of Seller's(s) agent, within five (5) days of the date of the aforesaid filing with the Department of Environmental Protection and Resource Management. Date of delivery includes the date of mailing as aforesaid.

CONTRACT CONTINGENT ON TEST ON WELL

The Buyer, at Buyer's expense, within ________________ (______) days from the date hereof, shall order and cause yield, chemical and bacteriological tests meeting the applicable requirements of the Baltimore County Code to be conducted on the existing well serving the Property. This Contract is hereby expressly made contingent upon the satisfaction of both of the following conditions:

(1) the receipt of water yield test results for the well on the Property performed in accordance with the applicable requirements of Baltimore County stating that the well yield is at least a recovery rate of one (1) gallon per minute measured in accordance with the applicable requirements of the Baltimore County Code, and

(2) the receipt of the results of bacteriological and chemical quality tests for the well performed in accordance with the applicable requirements of Baltimore County stating that the chemical and bacteriological content of the water in the well meets the applicable requirements of the Baltimore County Code and is otherwise safe for human consumption.

Upon receipt of the results of all of the required well tests, Buyer shall promptly provide copies to Seller and Broker(s). Should the results of these tests establish that any of the applicable contingencies are not met, then the Contract shall terminate and be null and void and all deposit money shall be returned to Buyer upon execution of a disposition of deposit agreement by Buyer and Seller, unless, within ten (10) days of the receipt by Buyer and Seller of the results of these tests, either (a) in the case of failure to meet the yield or chemical quality requirements (but not bacteriological test requirements which may not be waived) Buyer waives in writing such contingencies by executing a waiver meeting the applicable requirements of the Baltimore County Code and files an effective waiver with the appropriate agency of Baltimore County; or (b) Buyer and Seller execute an addendum to the Contract under which Seller is given a specified period of time within which to attempt to cure the deficiencies and deliver to Buyer, at Seller's expense, the results of new well tests performed in accordance with the applicable requirements of Baltimore County which establish that the deficiency noted in the original well tests has been corrected.

If Buyer and Seller agree to permit Seller to attempt to cure the deficiencies in the well, Seller shall attempt to cure the deficiencies and deliver to Buyer a report of a new well test performed in accordance with the applicable requirements of Baltimore County which establishes that the deficiencies noted in the original well tests have been corrected. If, at the expiration of the specified time period, Seller has not delivered to buyer the results of a new well test establishing that the deficiencies noted in the original well tests have been corrected, then the Contract shall terminate and be null and void and all deposit money shall be returned to Buyer upon execution of a disposition of deposit agreement by Buyer and Seller.

If Buyer or its agents or contractors damage the Property, the well, any pumps serving the well or any other property of Seller during the exercise of its rights under this Addendum, Buyer shall immediately reimburse Seller for all costs incurred in correcting such damage. If the Contract has been terminated, then the deposit monies may be retained pending payment to Seller of all such costs.

If Buyer proceeds to settlement, Buyer shall be deemed to have waived and relinquished any and all claims of causes of action against Seller or the Brokers arising from the quality or quantity of the water provided by the private water supply system. Buyer further warrants and represents to Seller and the Brokers that buyer understands that the only reliable and available means to ascertain the true quantity and quality of water provided by the existing water supply system is by means of professional testing and the Buyer has not and will not rely upon any representation regarding the quantity or quality of this water, whether made by Seller or the Brokers, except those facts disclosed as a result of such professional testing.

____________________________ ________________
SELLER DATE

____________________________ ________________
SELLER DATE

____________________________ ________________
BUYER DATE

____________________________ ________________
BUYER DATE

J. [§ 2.85] Maryland Homeowners' Association Act Disclosure to Buyer

Maryland REALTORS®

MARYLAND HOMEOWNERS ASSOCIATION ACT
DISCLOSURES TO BUYER AND TRANSMITTAL OF DOCUMENTS
For initial sale of a lot within a development consisting of more than 12 lots to a person who intends to occupy or rent the lot for residential purposes.

ADDENDUM DATED ______________________________ TO CONTRACT OF SALE
BUYER(S): ______________________________
SELLER(S): ______________________________
PROPERTY: ______________________________

The following disclosures are provided by Vendor ("Seller") to Buyer who intends to occupy or rent the lot for residential purposes pursuant to 11B-105 of the Maryland Homeowners Association Act ("the Act"):

(1). The name, principal address, and telephone number of the Seller and of the declarant, if the declarant is not the Seller; or, if the Seller is a corporation or partnership, the names and addresses of the principal officers of the corporation, or general partners of the partnership are:

SELLER
NAME: ______________________________
ADDRESS: ______________________________
TELEPHONE: ______________________________

DECLARANT (IF NOT SELLER)
NAME: ______________________________
ADDRESS: ______________________________
TELEPHONE: ______________________________

If Seller is a corporation or partnership, the name, title and addresses of the officers of the corporation or general partners of the partnership are: ______________________________
____
____

(2). (i). The name, if any, of the homeowner's association is: ______________________________
____

(ii). If incorporated:

A. The state incorporated in is:
____

B. The name of the Maryland resident agent is:
____

(3). (i). The lot which is the subject of the contract of sale is located within the development known as:
____

(ii). A description of the location and size of the development, including the minimum and maximum number of lots currently planned or permitted, if applicable, which may be contained within the development: ______________________________

(iii). A description of any property owned by the declarant or the vendor contiguous to the development which is to be dedicated to public use: ______________________________
____

(4). If the development is or will be within or a part of another development, a general description of the other development: ____________________

(5). If the declarant has reserved in the declaration the right to annex additional property to the development, a description of the size and location of the additional property and the approximate number of lots currently planned to be contained in the development, as well as any time limits within which the declarant may annex such property: ____________________

(6). (i). Attached are copies of the following documents relating to the development and the homeowners association to which the purchaser shall become obligated upon becoming the owner of the lot: (Seller to initial all applicable provisions.)

_______ A. Articles of Incorporation
_______ B. The Declaration (as defined in the Act)
_______ C. All recorded covenants and restrictions of the primary development and of other related developments to the extent reasonably available.
_______ D. The bylaws and rules of the primary development, and of other related developments to the extent reasonably available.

(ii). Obligations contained in the attached copies of documents: (Seller to initial applicable provision.)

A. Are_______ or Are Not _______ enforceable against an owner

B. Are_______ or Are Not _______ enforceable against the owner's tenants

(7). A description or statement of any property currently planned to be owned, leased, or maintained by the homeowners association: ____________________

____

(8). A copy of the estimated proposed or actual budget for the homeowner's association for the current fiscal year, including a description of the replacement reserves for common area improvements, if any, and a copy of the current projected budget for the homeowners association based upon the development fully expanded in accordance with expansion rights contained in the declaration: ____________________

____

(9). A statement of current or anticipated mandatory fees or assessments to be paid by owners of lots within the development for the use, maintenance, and operation of common areas and for other purposes related to the homeowners association and whether the declarant or vendor will be obligated to pay the fees in whole or part:

____

____

(10). A brief description of zoning and other land use requirements affecting the development; or a written disclosure of where the information is available for inspection: ____________________

____

(11). (i). A statement regarding when mandatory homeowners association fees or assessments will first be levied against owners of lots, the procedure for increasing or decreasing fees or assessments, and how fees or assessments and delinquent charges will be collected: ____________________

____

(ii). The seller is to initial "YES" or "NO" for the following:

A. Are unpaid fees or assessments a personal obligation of owners of lots?

_________YES _________NO

If "NO", explain:

____

B. Do unpaid fees or assessments bear interest?

_________YES _________NO

If "YES", what is the rate of interest? _______________

C. Will unpaid fees or assessments be enforced by imposing a lien on a lot under the terms of the Maryland Contract Lien Act?

_________YES _________NO

D. Will lot owners be assessed late charges or attorneys fees for collecting unpaid fees or assessments or face other consequences for the nonpayment of the fees or assessments?

_________YES _________NO

(12). Will sums of money other than prorated fees or assessments be collected at settlement for contribution to the homeowners association?

_________YES _________NO

If "YES" describe the amount to be collected and the intended use of such funds:

____

(13). If applicable, describe any special rights or exemptions reserved for the benefit of the declarant or the vendor, including:

A. The right to conduct construction activities within the development;
B. The right to pay a reduced homeowners association fee or assessment; and
C. Exemptions from use restrictions or architectural control provisions contained in the declaration or provisions by which the declarant or the Seller intends to maintain control over the homeowners association:

____

____

____

Seller hereby acknowledges that Seller has provided all information necessary to complete this Addendum, in compliance with the Act, and that Seller has reasonable grounds to believe and does believe, after reasonable investigation, that the information and statements herein provided to Buyer are true and that there is no omission to state a material fact necessary to make the statements not misleading.

Seller	**Date**	**Seller**	**Date**

Buyer hereby acknowledges that Buyer, on the date indicated below, has received all of the disclosures contained herein, including attachments as indicated, and that Seller has fully complied with the disclosure requirements of the Act.

Buyer	**Date**	**Buyer**	**Date**

Page 3 of 3 1/23

K. [§ 2.86] Maryland Homeowners Association Act Notice to Buyer

Maryland REALTORS®

MARYLAND HOMEOWNERS ASSOCIATION ACT
NOTICE TO BUYER

For initial sale of a lot within a development consisting of more than 12 lots to a person who intends to occupy or rent the lot for residential purposes.

ADDENDUM DATED ______________________________ TO CONTRACT OF SALE
BUYER(S): ______________________________
SELLER(S): ______________________________
PROPERTY: ______________________________

The following notice applies to members of the public who intend to occupy or rent a lot for residential purposes. Under the Maryland Homeowners Association Act ("the Act"), "lot" means any plot or parcel of land on which a dwelling is located or will be located within a development.

This sale is subject to the requirements of the Maryland Homeowners Association Act ("the Act"). For the purposes of the Act, "lot" means any plot or parcel of land on which a dwelling is located or will be located within a development. The Act requires that the seller disclose to you, at or before the time the contract is entered into, or within 7 calendar days of entering into the contract, certain information concerning the development in which the lot you are purchasing is located. The content of the information to be disclosed is set forth in section 11B-105(b) of the Act ("the MHAA" information) as follows:

(1) The name, principal address, and telephone number of the vendor and of the declarant. If the declarant is not the vendor; or, if the vendor is a corporation or partnership, the names and addresses of the principal officers of the corporation, or general partners of the partnership;

(2) The name, if any, of the homeowners association and, if incorporated, the state in which the homeowners association is incorporated, the name of the Maryland resident agent;

(3) A description of:

(i) The location and size of the development, including the minimum and maximum number of lots currently planned or permitted, if applicable, which may be contained within the development; and
(ii) Any property owned by the declarant or the vendor contiguous to the development which is to be dedicated to public use;

(4) If the development is or will be within or a part of another development, a general description of the other development;

(5) If the declarant has reserved in the declaration the right to annex additional property to the development, a description of the size and location of the additional property and the approximate number of lots currently planned to be contained in the development, as well as any time limits within which the declarant may annex such property;

(6) A copy of:

(i) The articles of incorporation, the declaration, and all recorded covenants and restrictions of the primary development and of other related developments to the extent reasonably available, to which the purchaser shall become obligated on becoming an owner of the lot, including a statement that these obligations are enforceable against an owner and the owner's tenants, if applicable; and
(ii) The bylaws and rules of the primary development and of other related developments to the extent reasonably available, to which the purchaser shall become obligated on becoming an owner of the lot, including a statement that these obligations are enforceable against an owner and the owner's tenants, if applicable;

(7) A description or statement of any property which is currently planned to be owned, leased, or maintained by the homeowners association;

Page 1 of 3 10/17

Maryland Homeowners Association Act Notice To Buyer

(8) A copy of the estimated proposed or actual budget for the homeowner's association for the current fiscal year, including a description of the replacement reserves for common area improvements, if any, and a description of the current projected budget for the homeowners association based upon the development fully expanded in accordance with expansion rights contained in the declaration;

(9) A statement of current or anticipated mandatory fees or assessments to be paid by owners of lots within the development for the use, maintenance, and operation of common areas and for other purposes related to the homeowners association and whether the declarant or vendor will be obligated to pay the fees in whole or in part;

(10) A brief description of zoning and other land use requirements affecting the development; or a written disclosure of where the information is available for inspection.

(11) A statement regarding:

(i) When mandatory homeowners association fees or assessments will first be levied against owners of lots;
(ii) The procedure for increasing or decreasing such fees or assessments;
(iii) How fees or assessments and delinquent charges will be collected;
(iv) Whether unpaid fees or assessments are a personal obligation of owners of lots;
(v) Whether unpaid fees or assessments bear interest and, if so, the rate of interest;
(vi) Whether unpaid fees or assessments may be enforced by imposing a lien on a lot under the terms of the Maryland Contract Lien Act; and
(vii) Whether lot owners will be assessed late charges or attorney's fees for collecting unpaid fees or assessments and any other consequences for the nonpayment of the fees or assessments;

(12) If any sums of money are to be collected at settlement for contribution to the homeowners association other than prorated fees or assessments, a statement of the amount to be collected and the intended use of such funds; and

(13) A description of special rights or exemptions reserved by or for the benefit of the declarant or the vendor, including:

(i) The right to conduct construction activities within the development;
(ii) The right to pay a reduced homeowners association fee or assessment; and
(iii) Exemptions from use restrictions or architectural control provisions contained in the declaration or provisions by which the declarant or the vendor intends to maintain control over the homeowners association.

If you have not received all of the MHAA information 5 calendar days or more before entering into the contract, you have 5 calendar days to cancel the Contract after receiving all of the MHAA information. You must cancel the contract in writing, but you do not have to state a reason.

The seller must also provide you with notice of any changes in mandatory fees exceeding 10 percent of the amount previously stated to exist and copies of any other substantial and material amendment to the information provided to you. You have 3 calendar days to cancel this contract after receiving notice of any changes in mandatory fees, or copies of any other substantial and material amendment to the MHAA information which adversely affect you.

If you do cancel the contract, you will be entitled to a refund of any deposit you made on account of the contract. However, unless you return the MHAA information to the seller when you cancel the contract, the seller may keep out of your deposit the cost of reproducing the MHAA information, or $100, whichever amount is less. If the deposit is held in trust by a licensed real estate broker, the return of the deposit to you shall comply with the procedures set forth in Section 17-505 of the Business Occupations and Professions Article of the Maryland Code.

By purchasing a lot within this development, you will automatically be subject to various rights, responsibilities, and obligations, including the obligation to pay certain assessments to the homeowners association within the development. The lot you are purchasing may have restrictions on:

Maryland Homeowners Association Act Notice To Buyer

(1) Architectural changes, design, color, landscaping, or appearance;
(2) Occupancy density;
(3) Kind, number, or use of vehicles;
(4) Renting, leasing, mortgaging or conveying property;
(5) Commercial activity; or
(6) Other matters.

You should review the MHAA information carefully to ascertain your rights, responsibilities, and obligations within the development.

Buyer	Date	Seller	Date
Buyer	Date	Seller	Date

L. [§ 2.87] Maryland Homeowners Association Act Disclosures to Buyer

Maryland REALTORS®

MARYLAND HOMEOWNERS ASSOCIATION ACT
NOTICE OF CHANGES IN MANDATORY FEES AND DISCLOSURE OF SUBSTANTIAL AND MATERIAL AMENDMENTS

ADDENDUM DATED ______________________________ TO CONTRACT OF SALE
BUYER(S): ______________________________
SELLER(S): ______________________________
PROPERTY: ______________________________

The following disclosures and/or attached documents are being provided to Buyer by Seller and constitute substantial and material amendments to information already provided to Buyer by Seller pursuant to the Maryland Homeowners Association Act ("the Act"):

A. The mandatory fees of the HOA have increased by more than ten percent (10%) of the amount previously stated to exist. The new HOA fees are ______________________________ dollars ($______________________) per______________________

B. Description of other amendments to information previously supplied are as follows:
____
____
____
____
____
____

C. The following documents, which have been amended, are attached hereto and incorporated herein by reference
____
____
____

Buyer may cancel the Contract, in writing, within three (3) calendar days following receipt by the Buyer of a change in mandatory fees exceeding ten percent (10%) of the amount previously stated to exist, or copies of any other substantial and material amendment to the information that adversely affects the Buyer. Buyer need not state a reason for canceling the Contract and the Buyer shall be entitled to the return of the deposit made on account of the Contract. If the deposit is held in trust by a licensed real estate broker, the return of the deposit to Buyer shall comply with the procedures set forth in Section 17-505 of the Business Occupations and Professions Article of the Maryland Code.

______________________________ ______________________________
Seller Date Seller Date

Buyer hereby acknowledges that Buyer, on the date indicated below, has received all of the disclosures contained herein, including attachments as indicated, and the Seller has fully complied with the disclosure requirements of the Act.

______________________________ ______________________________
Buyer Date Buyer Date

10/17

M. [§ 2.88] Maryland Homeowners Association Act Notice of Changes in Mandatory Fees and Disclosure of Substantial and Material Amendments

Maryland REALTORS®

MARYLAND HOMEOWNERS ASSOCIATION ACT
NOTICE OF CHANGES IN MANDATORY FEES AND DISCLOSURE
OF SUBSTANTIAL AND MATERIAL AMENDMENTS

ADDENDUM DATED ______________________________ TO CONTRACT OF SALE
BUYER(S): ______________________________
SELLER(S): ______________________________
PROPERTY: ______________________________

The following disclosures and/or attached documents are being provided to Buyer by Seller and constitute substantial and material amendments to information already provided to Buyer by Seller pursuant to the Maryland Homeowners Association Act ("the Act"):

A. The mandatory fees of the HOA have increased by more than ten percent (10%) of the amount previously stated to exist. The new HOA fees are ______________________________ dollars ($______________) per______________

B. Description of other amendments to information previously supplied are as follows:

____
____
____
____
____
____

C. The following documents, which have been amended, are attached hereto and incorporated herein by reference

____
____
____

Buyer may cancel the Contract, in writing, within three (3) calendar days following receipt by the Buyer of a change in mandatory fees exceeding ten percent (10%) of the amount previously stated to exist, or copies of any other substantial and material amendment to the information that adversely affects the Buyer. Buyer need not state a reason for canceling the Contract and the Buyer shall be entitled to the return of the deposit made on account of the Contract. If the deposit is held in trust by a licensed real estate broker, the return of the deposit to Buyer shall comply with the procedures set forth in Section 17-505 of the Business Occupations and Professions Article of the Maryland Code.

______________________________ ______________________________
Seller Date Seller Date

Buyer hereby acknowledges that Buyer, on the date indicated below, has received all of the disclosures contained herein, including attachments as indicated, and the Seller has fully complied with the disclosure requirements of the Act.

______________________________ ______________________________
Buyer Date Buyer Date

10/17

N. [§ 2.89] FIRPTA Affidavit

CERTIFICATE OF NONFOREIGN STATUS OF TRANSFEROR

Section 1445 of the Internal Revenue Code provides that a Transferee of a U.S. real property interest must withhold tax if the Transferor is a foreign person or entity. For U.S. tax purposes (including Section 1445), the owner of a disregarded entity (which has legal title to a U.S. real property interest under local law) will be the Transferor of the property and not the disregarded entity.

To inform the Transferee that withholding of tax is not required upon the disposition by the undersigned Transferor of the U.S. real property interest described on Exhibit "A" attached hereto, the undersigned Transferor hereby certifies as follows:

1. The undersigned Transferor is not a non-resident alien, foreign corporation, foreign partnership, foreign trust, or foreign estate (as those terms are defined in the Internal Revenue Code and Income Tax Regulations);
2. The undersigned Transferor is not a disregarded entity as defined in § 1.1445-2(b)(2)(iii);
3. The taxpayer identification number (Social Security number) of the undersigned is ________________________ or, the undersigned's U.S. employer identification number is ________________________; and
4. Address of the undersigned is ________________________________.

The undersigned understands that this certification may be disclosed to the Internal Revenue Service by the Transferee and that any false statement contained herein could be punished by fine, imprisonment, or both.

Under penalties of perjury, I declare that I have examined this certification and to the best of my knowledge and belief, it is true, correct and complete and in the case of a corporation, partnership, trust or business entity, I further declare that I have authority to sign this document on behalf of the Transferor.

WITNESS OR ATTEST:	[NAME OF TRANSFEROR]
______________________	BY:________________________
	Name:
	Title:
	DATE:______________________

O. [§ 2.90] City of Baltimore Right of First Refusal Affidavit Language

(1) Property not occupied by tenant within 6 months of transfer:

"The property known as (street address) in Baltimore City has not been occupied by a tenant since (date)."

(2) Property occupied within last 6 months but tenant cannot be contacted or has not responded to offer of sale:

"The property known as (street address) in Baltimore City, had been let to (name of last tenant), as a single-family residence, and an offer of sale as required by § 6-4(a) of Article 13 of the Baltimore City Code was sent on (date of mailing) to (last known address), being the last address known to me (us) of the aforenamed tenant and I (we) have received no response to said offer of sale."

(3) Tenant has responded to notice:

"(Name of tenant), being the tenant of the property known as (street address) in Baltimore City, following an offer of sale as required by § 6-4(a) of Article 13 of the Baltimore City Code, sent (date of mailing), has failed to enter into a contract to purchase said property in the manner and time provided by Subtitle 6 of Article 13 of the Baltimore City Code."

(Add if applicable)

"Notice pursuant to § 6-4(b) of Article 13 of the Baltimore City Code was subsequently sent to said tenant on (date of mailing), and tenant subsequently failed to contract to purchase said property in lieu of (name of third party) within the period of time provided by said § 6-4(b), that period being days."

(4) Tenant has waived right of first refusal:

"(Name of tenant), being the tenant of the property known as (street address) in Baltimore City, following an offer of sale as required by § 6-4(a) of Article 13 of the Baltimore City Code, sent (date of mailing), has executed a waiver of the right of first refusal in a manner consistent with § 6-6(c) of Article 13 of the Baltimore City Code."

P. [§ 2.91] Notice and Disclosure of Deferred Water and Sewer Charges

Maryland REALTORS®

NOTICE AND DISCLOSURE OF DEFERRED WATER AND SEWER CHARGES

Contract of Sale between Buyer ______________________________
and Seller ______________________________
for Property known as ______________________________.

Pursuant to Section 14-117(a)(5) of the Real Property Article of the Annotated Code of Maryland, the following Notice applies to the resale of residential real property that is served by public water or wastewater facilities for which deferred water and sewer charges have been established by a recorded covenant or declaration. **This law does *not* apply in a county that has adopted a disclosure requirement that is substantially similar to the disclosure requirements under this law.**

NOTICE REQUIRED BY MARYLAND LAW REGARDING DEFERRED WATER AND SEWER CHARGES

THIS PROPERTY IS SUBJECT TO A FEE OR ASSESSMENT THAT PURPORTS TO COVER OR DEFRAY THE COST OF INSTALLING OR MAINTAINING DURING CONSTRUCTION ALL OR PART OF THE PUBLIC WATER OR WASTEWATER FACILITIES CONSTRUCTED BY THE DEVELOPER. THE FEE OR ASSESSMENT IS $__________,
PAYABLE (annually, quarterly, monthly, etc.) ______________________________
UNTIL (DATE) ______________________________
TO (NAME & ADDRESS) ______________________________
____
(HEREAFTER CALLED "LIENHOLDER").

THERE MAY BE A RIGHT OF PREPAYMENT OR A DISCOUNT FOR EARLY PREPAYMENT, WHICH MAY BE ASCERTAINED BY CONTACTING THE LIENHOLDER. THIS FEE OR ASSESSMENT IS A CONTRACTUAL OBLIGATION BETWEEN THE LIENHOLDER AND EACH OWNER OF THIS PROPERTY, AND IS NOT IN ANY WAY A FEE OR ASSESSMENT IMPOSED BY THE COUNTY IN WHICH THE PROPERTY IS LOCATED.

If a Seller subject to this law fails to comply:

(a) Prior to settlement, Buyer is entitled to rescind in writing the sales contract without penalty or liability. On rescission, Buyer is also entitled to the full return of any deposits made on account of the sales contract. If any deposits are held in trust by a licensed real estate broker, the return of the deposits to a Buyer under this law shall comply with the procedures under § 17-505 of the Business Occupations and Professions Article of the Annotated Code of Maryland. Buyer's right of rescission shall terminate five days after Seller provides to Buyer written notice in accordance with this requirement; and

(b) After settlement, Seller shall be liable to Buyer for the full amount of any fee or assessment not disclosed, unless Seller was never charged a fee or assessment to defray the costs of public water or wastewater facilities by the developer, a successor of the developer, or a subsequent assignee.

All other terms and conditions of the Contract of Sale remain in full force and effect.

Buyer Signature	Date	Seller Signature	Date
Buyer Signature	Date	Seller Signature	Date

10/17

CHAPTER THREE

RESIDENTIAL CONSTRUCTION CONTRACT*

* This chapter was updated by MSBA staff attorneys. MSBA gratefully acknowledges the contributions to this chapter from previous authors Mark D. Dopkin, Esq., James Dorsey Wright, Esq., and Christine J. Warren, Esq.

TABLE OF CONTENTS

I. INTRODUCTION

A. [§ 3.1] Overview

The lawyer's task in regard to a residential construction contract is an unenviable one, since the lawyer must protect the client from the then unseen and unknown problems associated with the construction of a home in the future. Furthermore, unless the client has employed an architect to design and/or supervise the construction of the house, the lawyer is often asked to provide advice on whether the plans and specifications are sufficiently detailed to ensure that the client will be receiving the house they expect to receive—advice that the lawyer is unqualified to give.

B. [§ 3.2] Scope of Chapter

This chapter discusses the role of the lawyer in advising a client about the terms that should be included in a contract for the purchase of real property and for the construction of a residential home thereon. This discussion will not cover situations in which the client has employed an architect to prepare the plans and specifications of the house, or to supervise the construction of the house. While this chapter's focus is on the purchase of a parcel of land and improvements, many similar issues arise if the client has already purchased the unimproved real property and is concerned only with the construction of a custom built house on that property.

II. RESIDENTIAL CONSTRUCTION CONTRACT VS. STANDARD CONTRACT OF SALE

A. [§ 3.3] Similarities

If the client is purchasing an unimproved lot on which a house is to be constructed, the attorney should realize that most of the matters covered by a Standard Contract of Sale should be addressed, including the quality of title, a financing contingency, real estate tax adjustments, risk of loss, and settlement procedure.[1] An attorney should always prepare or review the contract for the initial purpose of ensuring that the client will be protected in the purchase of real property.

Many builders have standard contracts that they submit to the purchaser for execution. These contracts may range from form contracts for the sale of real property, with insertions relating to the construction of the house, to contracts specifically prepared for the builder. See § 3.40 of this chapter for an example of the latter type of contract. In preparing or reviewing a contract, an examination of this example may be helpful. However, please note that the example does not incorporate the disclosures required under the Maryland Home Builder Registration Act discussed in §§ **3.6** and **3.11** of this chapter.

---

1 *See* Chapter 2, Contracts of Sale: Resale of Existing Residences.

B. [§ 3.4] Differences—Generally

In advising a client, attorneys may feel comfortable in providing full and adequate advice concerning the legal details of purchasing the unimproved real property. However, the other portion of the attorney's role, that of providing advice concerning the construction of a house that is to conform to the picture in the purchaser's mind's eye, is much more difficult. The initial problem encountered is how to describe that dream house.

Unless an architect for the client is involved, it is rare that actual plans and specifications for the house will be made available to the attorney or the client. However, so that an attorney can realize how detailed and voluminous plans and specifications may be, plans and specifications for just a portion of the roofing of a residential townhouse project are set forth in **§ 3.41** of this chapter. The plans and specifications for a complete house often are more than 100 pages in length and are written in a manner as difficult for an attorney to understand as a detailed will is for an architect to understand. If an attorney is ever presented with a client who seeks advice on the adequacy of such plans and specifications, the attorney would be wise to immediately acknowledge the limitations of their expertise.

III. THE PARTIES

A. [§ 3.5] Title Holder

Care should be taken to determine the holder of title to the land. If it is not the same entity as the seller in the contract, determine if the seller has the legal ability to acquire title. Consider including the title-holder as a party to the contract.

B. [§ 3.6] The Maryland Home Builder Registration Act

All "home builders" must register with the Consumer Protection Division of the Office of the Attorney General pursuant to the Maryland Home Builder Registration Act.[2]

The Maryland Home Builder Registration Act was enacted to combat consumer complaints about construction problems and irresponsible conduct on the part of certain builders. Except for builders who construct new homes solely in Montgomery County (which has its own home builder licensing and new home warranty laws),[3] the Act applies to all builders building homes in Maryland, including those who sell the land together with the newly built home and those who build a "custom" home on the consumer's land.[4] The Act requires that home builders register with the

---

2 Md. Code Ann., Business Regulation, Title 4.5 (2015 & Supp. 2022) (hereinafter Bus. Reg. §).

3 Montgomery County Code § 31C.

4 Bus. Reg. § 4.5-101(g).

Consumer Protection Division of the Office of the Attorney General.[5] Registration can be denied, suspended, or revoked on many grounds including: fraudulent use of a registration; repeated violations of the Act; a determination that the builder has engaged in a pattern of unfair or deceptive trade practices; and engaging in a pattern of poor workmanship, evidenced by repeated, unresolved building code violations or repeated instances of unsatisfied judgments and/or arbitration awards.[6] A home builder without a valid registration number cannot obtain appropriate building permits from the local government.[7] A contract for the performance of any act for which a home builder registration number is required is not enforceable unless the home builder was registered at the time that the contract was signed by the owner.[8] Unregistered builders are also subject to criminal and civil penalties.[9]

In accordance with the Act, the Consumer Protection Division of the Office of the Attorney General has created *Buying a New Home: Consumer Rights and Remedies Under Maryland Law*, a pamphlet which provides helpful information about the purchase of both newly built and "custom" homes and describes the rights and remedies of the consumer in dealing with a home builder.[10] The pamphlet can be downloaded from the Maryland Attorney General's web page.[11] The home builder is required to provide each potential contract purchaser with the pamphlet, prior to entering into the contract.[12] However, failure to provide the pamphlet cannot be used as a basis for invalidating the contract.[13] Each contract must also contain certain disclosures as described in § 3.**11** of this chapter.[14]

Under the Act, the home builder is required to adopt performance standards or guidelines in the contract, at least as stringent as those adopted by the National Association of Home Builders (NAHB) at the time of the contract.[15] In the event that the local government has adopted performance standards or guidelines equal to, or more stringent than, those adopted by the NAHB, the local government's standards shall apply. Also, the home builder is not precluded from adopting performance standards for the contract that exceed those of the NAHB or the local

---

5 Bus. Reg. § 4.5-301.

6 Bus. Reg. § 4.5-308.

7 Bus. Reg. § 4.5-601.

8 Bus. Reg. § 4.5-605.

9 Bus. Reg. §§ 4.5-501, 502 and 504.

10 Bus. Reg. § 4.5-202(c)(1).

11 *https://www.marylandattorneygeneral.gov/CPD%20Documents/Home%20Builder/booklet.pdf* (last visited Jan. 29, 2024).

12 Bus. Reg. § 4.5-202(c)(3).

13 Bus. Reg. § 4.5-202(c)(5).

14 Bus. Reg. § 4.5-603.

15 Md. Code Ann., Real Property § 14-117(i)(2)(iii) (2015 & Supp. 2022) (hereinafter Real Prop. §).

government.[16] Additional laws affecting home builders were enacted by the Maryland General Assembly during the 2023 session.[17]

IV. THE DESCRIPTION

A. [§ 3.7] Model House

Often the house to be constructed is described as a facsimile of either:

1. an existing model house of the builder, or
2. a model house as shown on certain drawings provided by the builder, both with certain specified additions or deletions, such as air conditioning, type of roofing, fireplaces, patios, special appliances, light fixtures, wall coverings, types of flooring, and floor coverings. In such situations, the client is virtually at the mercy of the builder in many respects because the details of the type of materials to be used are rarely specified and hence are left to the discretion of the builder (subject to the terms of the implied warranties, as discussed in §§ **3.27–3.31** of this chapter). In such situations, the best protection an attorney can provide their client is to insist that the model home be described as fully as possible, either by designating the existing model house or by attaching the drawings of the model; that the contract specifically provide that the construction will be done in a "good and workmanlike manner"; and that all materials will be at least equal in quality to the materials used in the model home.

B. [§ 3.8] Decorating Details

If the model home is designated in the contract, the specific decorating details are usually left to the purchaser's discretion. The contract should provide both for a procedure for the client to convey the client's decorating choices to the builder and for a procedure by which any extra costs of those details can be ascertained. The selection and pricing of such details is often a problem unless the builder has a standard "Specification List-Customer Decorating and Selection Sheet."[18] Such a sheet usually gives a wide variety of decorating choices to the client with an accompanying indication as to the cost of each choice. In the event the builder does not have a sheet, an attorney should advise their client either to negotiate the decorating choices before executing the contract or to specify in the contract that all decorating choices of a quality at least equal to those in the model home shall be provided to the client at no extra cost.

---

16 REAL PROP. § 14-117(i)(3)(iii).

17 *https://www.marylandattorneygeneral.gov/CPD%20Documents/Home%20Builder/NEW_LAWS_AFFECTING_HOME_BUILDERS_2023.pdf* (last visited Jan. 29, 2024).

18 *See* **§ 3.42** of this chapter.

C. [§ 3.9] Landscaping

The attorney should also ensure that the extent and nature of landscaping to be provided by the builder is set forth in the contract. The contract should address the issues of whether particular trees are to be cut down or saved, what type of trees are to be planted, the type of lawn seed to be used, and the type of driveway and walkway to be installed. Often the model house will be of no help in this matter. The attorney should also realize that the weather may affect the ability of the builder to complete the landscaping at the same time the construction of the house is completed. Consequently, an attorney may wish to anticipate this problem, especially if the construction is to be completed during the winter months, and provide in the contract that if the landscaping is not completed at the same time as construction of the house, then settlement will occur only on the condition that an escrow account will be established for the future landscaping work.

V. CONTRACT MODIFICATION AND DISCLOSURES

A. [§ 3.10] Contract Modifications

The attorney should also make sure that the contract provides a procedure for the client to request changes in the construction. Typically, most contracts prepared by the builder provide that all changes or modifications must be made in writing but may be rejected by the builder. Although this right of rejection may appear unfair, it is the protection to which a builder is entitled against a client who requests changes that are beyond the capacity of that particular builder to perform. Moreover, in most contracts prepared by the builder, the builder reserves the right to substitute "materials of similar pattern and design and equivalent quality." Although the right to substitute may not conform to your client's desire for a particular dream house (i.e., not a house just of "similar" pattern and "equivalent" quality), builders usually insist upon such a right, and it can rarely be deleted from the contract. Nonetheless, a purchaser is entitled to receive notice from the builder prior to such substitution. Hopefully, by receiving prior notice, the purchaser may be able to object strenuously if the "equivalent quality" of the material is not acceptable to them.

B. [§ 3.11] Maryland Home Builder Registration Act Disclosure

Under the Maryland Home Builder Registration Act, specific disclosures must be included in every contract for the initial sale of a new home in Maryland (except for a new home in Montgomery County).[19] The contract is required to contain, in conspicuous type: the builder registration number of the seller; a provision stating that the new home shall be constructed in accordance with all applicable building

---

[19] Bus. Reg. § 4.5-603.

codes in effect at the time of the construction of the new home; a provision referencing all performance standards or guidelines that the seller shall comply with in the construction of the new home and that shall prevail in the performance of the contract and any arbitration or adjudication of a claim arising from the contract; and a provision detailing the purchaser's right to receive a consumer information pamphlet as provided under the Act.[20]

C. [§ 3.12] Federal Disclosure Regulations

The Federal government has adopted regulations concerning disclosures to be made in contracts for the sale of newly constructed homes. The Federal Trade Commission (FTC) has established a regulation[21] requiring home builders to disclose, in such a contract, certain information concerning the insulation materials to be installed in the house. Consequently, the attorney for the purchaser should insist upon compliance with this disclosure requirement in each contract.

Particular attention should be given to the notice requirements of § 460.16 of the 16th Volume of the Code of Federal Regulations (hereinafter C.F.R. §). An example of a "Section 460.16 Notice" to the purchaser regarding the type, thickness, and R-value of insulation is set forth in **§ 3.43** of this chapter. This notice is only an example. The specific contents of any notice must be modified to reflect the facts of the particular case.

The reader is advised to consult the Federal Register for information concerning partial exemptions and temporary stays of the provisions of 16 C.F.R. Part 460, which are periodically granted by the FTC. For example, the FTC has exempted new home sellers from specific disclosure requirements concerning insulation when promoting or advertising new homes on television.[22]

VI. PURCHASE PRICE

A. [§ 3.13] Payment Schedule

Almost all residential construction contracts provide for payment to be made much as in the manner of a typical real estate purchase, i.e., an earnest money deposit to be made at the time the contract is signed, with the balance of the payment to be made at settlement.

Only in instances when the client already owns the real property will the builder typically request a "staged" payment schedule, whereby the builder will receive a certain percentage of the total contract price as the work progresses. In those

---

20 Real Prop. § 14-117(i)(l), (2) and (4).

21 16 C.F.R. Part 460.

22 16 C.F.R. §§ 460.18(e) and 460.19(g) (1995).

situations where the builder does require a staged payment schedule, a purchaser's interest is best protected by making certain that the payments do not exceed the value of the work done and by providing for a monetary holdback from the builder of some percentage of the total purchase price (usually 10%) until the house and all punch list items have been completed. The amount of holdback is often determined by the amount which the mortgagee is willing to advance, and the payments established in the contract must conform to the payment schedule established in the building loan agreement of the client's lending institution.

B. [§ 3.14] The Attorney's Role

As an attorney, one should remember the limitations of one's expertise and avoid suggesting the percentages to be paid at each stage, just as an attorney should avoid suggesting the appropriate purchase price of a house. Nonetheless, it is appropriate for an attorney to advise their client of examples of schedules used by other clients in order to give the client a proper framework in which to consider the problem.

C. [§ 3.15] The Down Payment

Regardless of what type of payment schedule is used, an initial down payment is usually made. It is best to require that the down payment be placed in an escrow account of the builder. Maryland law requires that this deposit be placed in an escrow account or that a corporate surety bond or an irrevocable letter of credit be obtained.[23]

D. [§ 3.16] Payment for "Extras"

As discussed in § 3.**10** of this chapter, the purchaser may often request the builder to install "extras" as the house is being constructed. Payment for these extras is made either by an immediate cash payment to the builder at the time of the request, by cash payment at the time the extras are installed, or by cash payment at the completion of all the construction.

Although builders would naturally desire the payment to be made immediately, payment at the time of the installation of the extras is usually considered the appropriate method.

VII. SETTLEMENT CONSIDERATIONS

A. [§ 3.17] Establishing a Settlement Date

Unlike establishing a settlement date for the purchase of a house already constructed, the establishment of a settlement date for the purchase of a house to be constructed is difficult and cannot be done with any precision or certainty. The

---

[23] REAL PROP. §§ 10-301–10-306.

settlement can only occur once the house is completed. Hence, any specific date can only be considered as a guideline. The usual procedure is for the parties to agree on the number of months in which the builder can complete the house (taking into consideration the possible adverse weather conditions) and using that time period as a guideline for the establishment of the settlement date. Because builders usually complete the construction in a longer period than originally estimated, clients are often well advised not to rely on the established settlement date to the extent of canceling their apartment lease or arranging the settlement on the sale of their existing house to be on that exact date. Delays are the rule, not the exception, in new home construction.

It is recommended that all contracts contain some outside date (six months is often an acceptable one) after the settlement date provided in the contract, on which the purchaser can declare the contract to be in default and receive its deposit back. Many form contracts of builders provide that extensions of the settlement date must be granted by the purchasers and hence "lock in" the purchasers for an indefinite time. This may have disastrous effects on the purchasers.

B. [§ 3.18] Completion Criteria—Generally

An attorney's role in helping the client select a realistic settlement date is limited, but the attorney's role in establishing the criteria for determining the "completion" of the house is often significant. There are four criteria often used in this matter:

1. "Substantially Complete";
2. "Complete" (including all punch list items);
3. Issuance of a Certificate of Occupancy (if available in the jurisdiction); and
4. Approval of an inspecting architect.

The purchaser naturally desires to have the house completely finished before making the final payment and taking title, whereas the builder does not want to be denied the final payment (be it the one-time lump-sum payment or the final, staged payment) merely because of the builder's failure to install or complete several items that are minor in terms of cost, but which may take several weeks to install due to the necessity to order certain materials.

C. [§ 3.19] Completion Criteria—Substantially Complete and the Escrow Agreement

An often-used compromise in establishing a settlement date is to provide in the contract for settlement to be held when the house is "substantially complete," with an amount, which is in excess (by as much as 50%) of the amount the parties mutually agree is necessary to complete the house and all punch list items, to be put in escrow at the settlement. Often the attorneys or the real estate agents for the parties are called upon to be the escrow agent. A form of escrow is set forth in § **3.44** of this chapter. For the purchaser, the escrow agreement should allocate the total amount among the items to be completed and should provide that if each item is not completed within a specific time, the amount allocated to the item shall be paid to the purchaser from the escrow account. As a general rule, the attorneys do not want to become the escrow agent. However, they may be the only persons available at the settlement table who can be named the escrow agent. Among the disadvantages of the attorneys being the escrow agent is that if there is a dispute concerning the escrow agreement, the attorneys may not be able to continue their legal representation of the parties because they, as the escrow agent, may be named as a necessary party in the ensuing litigation.

D. [§ 3.20] Completion Criteria—Certificate of Occupancy

Usually neither party desires to have the completion evidenced by a Certificate of Occupancy. From a purchaser's perspective, the Certificate may be issued without regard to the quality of work or the installation or completion of many of the decorating items. From a builder's perspective, the issuance of the Certificate may be delayed by governmental inactivity or bureaucratic delay. However, even if the Certificate is not to be used as evidence of completion, in most jurisdictions in the state issuance of a Certificate is required prior to the occupancy of the house. The approval of an inspecting architect is rarely used except in situations where an architect participated in the preparation of the plans and specifications. Hence the subject of architect approval is not within the scope of this chapter.

E. [§ 3.21] Completion Criteria—Mortgage Commitment

An attorney representing a purchaser must keep in mind the fact that their client's mortgage commitment may specify the criteria for determining the "completion" of the house. Because the commitment is usually received after the execution of the contract of sale, the attorney should either:

(1) provide in the contract that notwithstanding any other terms of the contract, "completion" should be determined by the date on which the mortgagee will advance the funds or, more practically,

(2) make sure that the language of the commitment is compatible with that of the contract.

VIII. DEFAULT BY BUILDER AND MECHANICS' LIENS

A. [§ 3.22] Consequences of Default by Builder

Just as in a situation involving default by the seller pursuant to a typical real estate contract, default by a builder pursuant to the terms of a construction contract has disastrous consequences to the purchaser, consequences from which they cannot be adequately protected by legal remedies. Legal remedies are almost always time consuming and expensive and do not provide the purchaser a house in which to live during the litigation.

Often a default by the builder that delays settlement will result in the loss of the mortgage commitment to the purchaser and consequently may require the purchaser to obtain a new mortgage commitment. The best safeguard an attorney can provide their client against this consequence is to attempt to have the mortgage commitment issued for a term substantially longer than the anticipated period of construction.

B. [§ 3.23] Liquidated Damages

Purchasers often desire to impose a penalty or liquidated damage claim against the builder in the event of a delay and/or default by the builder. Although theoretically such a penalty is desirable, builders will seldom agree to the inclusion of such a provision in the contract. Also, the amount of such a penalty, usually calculated on a per diem basis, is a difficult figure to agree upon. Perhaps the only advice on this matter that an attorney can reasonably give to their client is to ask for such a damage clause, in a reasonable amount, but the attorney should not expect the builder to agree to it.

C. [§ 3.24] Mechanics' Liens

Until the revision of the Maryland mechanics' lien law in 1976, the possibility of the filing of a mechanics' lien after the date of settlement was also a danger for which the purchaser's attorney had to provide. However, the law now provides that real property "may not be subjected to a lien" if, prior to the establishment of a lien (by the filing of a petition in the appropriate court), legal title has been granted to a bona fide purchaser for value.[24] This law now effectively removes the danger to the purchaser of a mechanics' lien filed after the date of settlement. The Supreme Court of Maryland extended the effect of this statute by protecting from mechanics' liens the interest of purchasers who have acquired equitable title prior to the institution of a mechanics' lien suit, even though the petition to establish a mechanics' lien is filed prior to the conveyance of legal title.[25] The builder generally agrees in the contract to deliver the property free of all liens at settlement, and to this end the purchaser may want to require lien waivers from the builder and its subcontractors at settlement.

---

[24] Real Prop. § 9-102(d).

[25] *Himmighoefer v. Medallion Indus., Inc.*, 302 Md. 270, 487 A.2d 282 (1985).

D. [§ 3.25] Completion Bond

Purchasers also often desire the builder to post a completion bond, insuring the timely performance of the contract by the builder. Unless the builder has significant financial backing, it is often impossible or financially impractical to obtain such a bond. If obtainable, the cost of the bond is customarily passed through to the purchaser as an increase in the purchase price. If the builder can obtain such a bond, it is usually in the form set forth in § **3.45** of this chapter. An attorney for the purchaser should review the provisions of Real Prop. §§ 10-301–10-306 whenever a discussion of a bond is held. Although those sections refer to a surety bond, that bond is designed only to protect the initial deposit of the purchaser if it is not placed in an escrow account and does not secure the performance of the contract by the builder.

The standard contract form will likely provide that the purchaser's sole remedy in the event of a default by the builder is to terminate the contract and receive a refund of the deposit. In this event, the purchaser may be substantially harmed by the builder's nonperformance without having any suitable recourse. The purchaser should attempt to negotiate the right to exercise any rights he or she may have at law or equity.

E. [§ 3.26] Settlement Adjustments

Most adjustments to be made at the settlement of the purchase of a newly constructed house are similar to the adjustments made at settlement of a routine real estate purchase. However, there are a few differences to be considered, the most notable one being that in settlements for purchases of newly constructed homes the purchaser usually pays all of the transfer taxes and recording costs, whereas in other settlements, the parties usually split those costs. Nonetheless, if the contract does not specifically provide to the contrary, Real Prop. § 14-104(b) provides that the costs "shall be shared equally between the grantor and grantee." If, at the time of negotiating the terms of the contract, the builder requests the purchaser to pay all of the costs, there is little that the purchaser's attorney can do other than to advise their client that such a practice is normal in Maryland unless the purchaser is a "first-time Maryland homebuyer."[26] The Maryland Code requires the seller to pay the State transfer tax if the buyer is a first-time Maryland homebuyer, whereas the recordation tax and the local transfer tax can be negotiated in the contract.[27] However, if the contract between the first-time Maryland homebuyer does not specifically provide to the contrary, the recordation and local transfer taxes shall be paid by the seller/builder.[28]

---

26 Real Prop. § 14-104(c).

27 Real Prop. § 14-104(c)(1) and (2).

28 Real Prop. § 14-104(c)(1).

An item which should be considered not only at settlement but also at the time of the preparation of the contract is a possible adjustment for the imposition of an "agricultural land transfer tax" on the real property pursuant to the provisions of the Maryland Code.[29] These sections, replacing the former provisions establishing a "development tax," provide that if the real property being conveyed is assessed as agricultural property, a transfer tax of up to 5% of "the consideration payable for the instrument of writing less: (1) the total value of any improvements on the property; and (2) the total value of any land not subject to the agricultural land transfer tax" may be imposed, unless the conveyance is of a type specifically exempted by the provisions of TAX-PROP. § 13-305. The tax is to be paid at the time of the recordation of the deed evidencing the conveyance. The Maryland Code provides that the seller is liable to the purchaser for the amount of the tax unless the seller gives the purchaser written notice that the property being transferred may be subject to the transfer tax in the contract of sale.[30] As a practical matter, the net effect of this section is that if the contract of sale is silent, the seller/builder will be responsible for the payment of this tax.

At the time of settlement, the attorney for the purchaser may wish to advise their client that the real property taxes reflected on the settlement sheet may be significantly increased by a reassessment in the near future to reflect the increase in value to the property caused by the new construction. The attorney should also advise the client of their right to protest that reassessment.

Attorneys should also be aware of a law providing that a contract of sale of improved residential real estate should disclose to the initial purchaser the estimated cost (as established by the appropriate water and sewer authority) of any deferred water and sewer charges for which the purchaser may become liable. Failure to comply with this requirement entitles the purchaser to recover from the seller two times the amount of the deferred charges it is required to pay.[31]

IX. WARRANTIES AND INSURANCE

A. [§ 3.27] Generally

In Maryland, absent specific contractual warranties, the only warranties protecting the purchaser of real property are those "implied warranties" set forth in the Maryland Code.[32] Three significant issues should be considered by the purchaser's attorney concerning implied warranties: inspection, wells, and radon. Although technically not within the scope of this chapter, an attorney should be aware of the

---

29 MD. CODE ANN., TAX-PROPERTY §§ 13-301–13-308 (2019 & Supp. 2023) (hereinafter referred to as TAX-PROP. §).

30 TAX-PROP. § 13-308.

31 REAL PROP. § 14-117.

32 REAL PROP. §§ 10-201–10-205.

case law involving the applicability of the statutory implied warranties to a situation where the client owns the land and has employed a builder to construct a house on that land. The statute has been interpreted by the courts in dicta to apply to that situation as well as the more typical case of a purchaser contracting to buy real property with a house to be constructed on it by the owner-builder.[33]

B. [§ 3.28] Inspection

REAL PROPERTY § 10-203(b) provides that the implied warranties "do not apply to any condition that an inspection of the premises would reveal to a reasonably diligent purchaser *at the time the contract is signed*" (emphasis added). Contrary to the argument of many builders, a pre-settlement inspection, which is customary, is not an inspection "at the time the contract is signed." Consequently, a good pre-settlement inspection does not adversely affect any rights of the purchaser, and the opportunity for such an inspection should never be waived. Without a right to inspect the premises before settlement expressly set forth in the contract, a purchaser may be forced to consummate settlement and then inspect for breaches of the implied warranties after taking possession of the premises.

C. [§ 3.29] Wells

Builders occasionally experience difficulty in drilling wells with a capacity sufficient to serve the house to be constructed. Fortunately for the home purchaser, Maryland courts have held that a sufficient water capacity is an element of "habitability" and therefore is included in the implied warranties.[34]

The Supreme Court of Maryland has upheld the *Krol* finding that a sufficient water capacity is a condition of habitability under REAL PROP. § 10-203, and has provided a method for calculating a proper water supply.[35]

The Supreme Court of Maryland has also implied that potable water is a condition of habitability.[36]

D. [§ 3.30] Radon

If the building site is located in an area where a potential radon gas problem exists, the purchaser should insist that the construction contract provide for radon testing prior to settlement. The home builder should correct any radon gas problem as a condition to the home purchase. If hazardous levels of radon gas are detected in a newly constructed home, a purchaser may be able to sue the builder for breach of an implied warranty of habitability.

---

33 *See Bay State Ins. Co. v. Hill,* 34 Md. App. 593, 368 A.2d 1024 (1977).

34 *See Krol v. York Terrace Bldg., Inc.,* 35 Md. App. 321, 370 A.2d 589 (1977).

35 *Loch Hill Constr. Co. v. Fricke,* 284 Md. 708, 399 A.2d 883 (1979).

36 *See Bosse v. Koehler,* 262 Md. 593, 278 A.2d 602 (1971).

E. [§ 3.31] Consumer Protection

An attorney should be aware that certain provisions of the State's Consumer Protection Act relate to the sale of realty, and that any misleading statement by the builder may give rise to enforcement proceedings by the Consumer Protection Division of the Office of the Attorney General. The relevant provisions of that Act are set forth in MD. CODE ANN., COMMERCIAL LAW II §§ 13-301–13-308 (2013 & Supp. 2022).

X. [§ 3.32] CUSTOM HOME PROTECTION ACT

If the buyer plans to build his or her residence on land currently or previously owned by the buyer, the contract is subject to the Custom Home Protection Act.[37] This Act requires payments to be held in trust[38] and the escrow of monies received by the builder.[39] It also requires disclosures to be included in the Contract.[40]

XI. HOMEOWNERS ASSOCIATION ACT

A. [§ 3.33] Generally

With the passage of the Homeowners Association Act,[41] builders who contract to sell lots which are subject to mandatory assessments must provide the purchaser of such lots with extensive disclosures. If the seller fails to make such disclosures simultaneously with or prior to the execution of the contract of sale, the purchaser may rescind the contract prior to closing and recover all deposits paid by the purchaser.

The purpose of the Homeowners Association Act is to avoid problems commonly caused by the nondisclosure of mandatory fees and restrictions which may have been placed upon the subject lot prior to the purchaser's acquisition of such lot. Specifically, the builder's failure to disclose any mandatory fees and restrictions has often made the assessments difficult to collect or has resulted in the unknowing violation by the purchaser of various restrictions imposed on the lots. The disclosure obligations imposed by the Act vary depending upon whether the sale is the first sale of the lot or a resale and depending upon the size of the development and the percentage of unsold lots in the development.

B. [§ 3.34] Applicability

The Act applies to any situation in which the lot identified in the contract of sale is subject to a mandatory assessment or fee imposed under the authority of a

---

37 REAL PROP. § 10-501–10-509.

38 REAL PROP. § 10-502.

39 REAL PROP. § 10-504.

40 REAL PROP. § 10-506.

41 REAL PROP. § 11B-101–11B-117.

publicly recorded document, whether the document is a deed, covenant, or other type of declaration. Therefore, notwithstanding the name of the Act, the presence or absence of a homeowners association within the development does not govern the application of the Act.

C. [§ 3.35] Disclosure Must Be Before Contract

Because of the technical nature of the disclosure provisions, several pitfalls exist that may flaw the disclosures and provide the purchaser with an absolute right of rescission. For example, for the initial sale of a lot in a development containing more than 12 lots, the disclosure information must be provided to the purchaser *at or before* the time the contract is signed or within seven calendar days of entering into the contract.[42] If the builder does not provide the extensive disclosure information five calendar days or more before the contract is signed, the purchaser will have an absolute right to rescind the contract within five calendar days following receipt of the disclosures.[43]

D. [§ 3.36] Amendment of Disclosure

A second example which may trigger the purchaser's right of rescission would result from the builder's affirmative obligation to amend the disclosures to correct any substantial or material change in the information previously disclosed. If the builder amends the disclosures, the purchaser will have three days following receipt of notice of such an amendment to rescind the contract. Problems may also arise if the development is part of a larger development which has its own assessments and restrictions. If this is the case, the required disclosures must include all restrictions placed on the lot, whether such restrictions are imposed as part of the plan of the smaller development or as part of the plan of the larger development. This will also apply to the budget information which must be disclosed.

E. [§ 3.37] Receipt

Because failure to make the disclosure can result in an unenforceable contract, it is important, though not legally required, that the builder obtain a signed receipt from the purchaser which acknowledges the purchaser's receipt of the disclosures at or prior to the execution of the contract of sale and which specifically sets forth those documents that were delivered to the purchaser. This receipt may prove helpful in an action by the builder to enforce the contract of sale should the purchaser claim that the property disclosures were not made.

---

42 Real Prop. § 11B-105.

43 Real Prop. § 11B-108.

F. [§ 3.38] Improvements to Common Areas

Separate and apart from its disclosure requirements, the Homeowners Association Act also imposes, as a matter of law, limited warranties concerning improvements to those common areas which are to be conveyed to the homeowners association or other party with authority to enforce the restrictions and obligations placed on lots in the development. The warranties are to be made by one of two parties, depending upon whether the improvements to the common areas were constructed before or after the common area was conveyed to the homeowners association. If the improvements were constructed prior to the conveyance, the grantor of the common area is to make the warranty, regardless of who actually built the improvements. Otherwise, the seller of the lots in the development is to make the warranty if such seller or his or her agents, employees, or subcontractors constructed the improvements. Specifically, the appropriate party warrants that such improvements are:

1. free from faulty materials,
2. constructed in accordance with sound engineering standards, and
3. constructed in a workmanlike manner.

The warranty extends for one year from the time the first lot is transferred or when the improvement is completed, whichever is later. Either the homeowners association or individual lot owner can bring suit to enforce the warranty within one year of the expiration of the warranty period.

XII. [§ 3.39] CONCLUSION

In advising a potential purchaser of a house to be constructed by an owner-builder of the various problems and pitfalls discussed in this chapter, an attorney should always keep in mind that his or her goal is to provide a binding contract for the delivery of a house built substantially in the form the purchaser has envisioned, and for the price and on the date established in the contract. If the attorney can provide such a service, the attorney has accomplished his or her task to the best of his or her ability.

XIII. APPENDIX

The Appendix begins on the next page.

A. [§ 3.40] Sample Standard Contract of Sale

THIS AGREEMENT OF SALE, made this _________ day of _________ 20__, between _______________, whose business address is ____________________ (the "Seller") and ____________________ now residing at ____________________ (the "Buyer"):

1. The Property.

The Seller agrees to sell and convey to the Buyer, and the Buyer agrees to purchase from the Seller, the following described property in Howard County, State of Maryland: Lot No. _____, in Section No. _____ of Area No. _____ as shown on the sub-division plat of __________ recorded among the Land Records of Howard County, Maryland, in Plat Book _____, Page No. _____, also known as __________ (the "Lot"), together with the dwelling house described in Paragraph 4 hereof to be built thereon by the Seller (the "Dwelling") and the landscaping, grading, and related outside work described in Paragraph 5 hereof (the "Landscaping") (the Lot, Dwelling, and Landscaping being collectively, the "Property").

2. The Price.

The total purchase price for the Property will be __________ Dollars ($_____). A deposit of __________ Dollars ($_____) has been paid prior to the signing of this Agreement. The Buyer agrees to pay to the Seller the remainder of the purchase price as follows:

a. An additional __________ Dollars ($_____) will be paid in cash on or before __________ 20__.

b. The entire balance will be paid in cash at settlement.

3. Financing.

a. The Buyer will promptly and diligently apply for, and procure from a lender approved by the Seller, a ____________________ purchase money mortgage loan in the principal amount of __________ Dollars ($_____) (the "mortgage loan"). The Buyer will sign such papers and furnish such information as may be required by any lender in connection with the mortgage loan. The Seller will not bear any cost in connection with the mortgage loan.

b. If the Buyer, although acting promptly and diligently, nonetheless is unable, within forty-five (45) days from the date of this Agreement, to obtain from a lender approved by the Seller, a written commitment to make the mortgage loan, then, in that event, either party may cancel this Agreement within ten (10) days thereafter, by giving written notice to the other party, and the Seller will promptly refund to the Buyer the deposit and all other monies theretofore paid by the Buyer.

c. In no event will the Seller have any obligation or liability to the Buyer if the mortgage loan is committed but the lender thereafter refuses, for any reason whatsoever, to make the mortgage loan, as originally committed or otherwise.

4. The Dwelling.

a. Except as otherwise described in this Paragraph 4, the Dwelling to be constructed on the Lot by the Seller will be substantially similar, in workmanship, materials, plan, type of construction and finish, to the Seller's model home known as ______________, which the Buyer has Inspected.

b. Unless either subparagraph c of this Paragraph 4 or Paragraph 5 hereof provides to the contrary, the Dwelling will not include any of the following items shown in the model home or model home area: any air conditioning, wood shake roofing (asphalt shingles will be provided instead), fireplace, patio, landscaping, refrigerator, clothes washer, dryer, shelving (other than closet shelves), light fixtures, wall coverings, mirrowed walls (other than in bathrooms), flooring, floor coverings, painted basement walls and floors, music speakers, curtains or drapes, furniture, furnishings, decorations, or accessories.

c. The Dwelling will include the following:

(1) Flooring and floor coverings selected from those offered by the Seller.

(2) Light fixtures selected by the Seller.

d. The Buyer will have the right to make decorating choices from the selections offered by the Seller. The Buyer must give the Seller written notice of these choices within fifteen (15) days from the date of this Agreement, using the Seller's Customer Decorating and Selection Sheet.

If the Buyer fails to give written notice within that time or if materials chosen by the Buyer are not approved by any controlling architectural committee or are not readily available at the time they are needed for completion of the Dwelling, the Seller may make the choices in its sole discretion, and the Buyer will be bound thereby.

5. The Landscaping.

a. The Landscaping to be provided by the Seller will include three (3) trees (including trees already on the Lot that are not removed prior to settlement), seeding of lawns, a post lamp, a driveway and a walkway from the driveway to the main entrance of the Dwelling. The Seller may remove any trees now on the Lot which, in the Seller's sole discretion, should be removed to permit construction of the Dwelling or the Landscaping or any grading of the Lot. Although the Seller intends to use its best efforts to preserve any trees now on the Lot which it does not remove, the Seller nonetheless will not be responsible for damage or loss of any tree that it does not plant.

b. The grading of the Lot and the location and ground elevation on the Lot of the Dwelling, driveway, walkway, any tree planted by the Seller, and the post lamp may be determined by the Seller, in its sole discretion; however, the location, elevation, and grading will not violate any applicable set-back requirement or any applicable requirement of any governmental authority or controlling architectural committee.

6. *Modifications.*

a. Any change in the Dwelling or the Landscaping desired by the Buyer must be requested by the Buyer in writing on the Seller's Change Order Sheet within fifteen (15) days of the date of this Agreement. No requested change will be effective unless approved in writing by the Seller, who may refuse to give approval in its sole discretion. The Buyer will pay the full cost of any changes in cash at the time the Change Order Sheet is submitted for the Seller's approval.

b. In any event, the Seller will have the right to substitute materials of similar pattern and design and equivalent quality.

7. *Construction.*

a. The Seller will begin construction of the Dwelling and the Landscaping within one hundred twenty (120) days from the date of this Agreement. In no event, however, will the Seller be required to commence construction until after the Seller has received from the Buyer any cash payment required by Paragraph 2.a of this Agreement and a copy of a binding written commitment of a lender approved by the Seller to make the mortgage loan. The Seller will use reasonable efforts to complete construction of the Dwelling and the Landscaping within two hundred seventy (270) days after commencement of construction.

b. The Seller will not be liable for any delay in commencing, prosecuting or completing construction of the Dwelling or the Landscaping caused by any adverse weather conditions, any fire, storm, earthquake or other casualty, any strike, lockout or other labor dispute, any material shortage, any dispute with or act or omission of any lender, governmental authority or controlling architectural committee (including the failure or refusal to issue or give any necessary permit or other approval), any dispute with or act or omission of any subcontractor or other supplier of labor or materials, or any Act of God or other cause beyond the Seller's control. The time for completion of the Dwelling and the Landscaping may be extended, at the Seller's option and in its sole discretion, by the length of any delay of the nature described in this subparagraph b.

8. *Warranty.*

a. The Seller agrees that, from and after settlement, it will be bound by the warranties and all of the other terms and conditions contained in the Registered Builder's Home Owner's Service Policy of the National Association of Home Builders, a copy of which has been delivered to and read by the Buyer prior to the execution of this Agreement.

b. The Buyer will have no cause of action against the Seller for or on account of the Seller's alleged breach of any warranty provided for by this Agreement or by law, unless the Buyer, before bringing the alleged breach to the attention of any governmental agency or controlling architectural committee and before instituting any court action, gives the Seller written notice of the alleged breach and not less than ninety (90) days from the date the Seller receives said notice within which to cure the alleged breach.

c. No written materials other than the Seller's Customer Decorating and Selection Sheet, any Change Order Sheet approved by the Seller, the Registered Builders Home Owner's Service Policy and this Agreement are a part of the basis of the bargain between the Seller and the Buyer.

9. Remedies.

a. If, for any reason whatsoever other than the interference or default of the Buyer, the Seller (i) is unable or fails to commence construction of the Dwelling within the time provided in Paragraph 7.a hereof (as that time may be extended by the Seller pursuant to Paragraph 7.b hereof), (ii) is unable or fails to complete construction of the Dwelling and the Landscaping (to the extent required for settlement to occur pursuant to Paragraph 12 hereof) within the time provided in Paragraph 7.a hereof (as that time may be extended by the Seller pursuant to Paragraph 7.b hereof), or (iii) is unable to deliver at settlement title to the Property satisfying the requirements of Paragraph 12.b hereof, then, either party may terminate this Agreement by giving the other party written notice to that effect (before commencement of construction, if the ground for termination is failure to commence construction on time), in which event the Seller will promptly refund to the Buyer the deposit and any other monies paid under this Agreement and the Seller and Buyer will be relieved from further liability hereunder. The remedy provided for in this Paragraph 9.a will be the Buyer's only remedy in the event the Seller is unable or fails to commence or complete construction of the Dwelling and the Landscaping on time or is unable to deliver satisfactory title to the Property, all as more fully described above in this subparagraph a.

b. Notwithstanding anything in subparagraph a of this Paragraph 9 or in Paragraph 12.a hereof, neither party may terminate this Agreement or delay settlement on account of the Seller's failure to make any change in the Dwelling or the Landscaping covered by any Change Order Sheet approved by the Seller. The Buyer's only remedy in the event of such a failure to make such a change will be a refund from the Seller of any monies paid by the Buyer for such change. The Seller will promptly make the refund upon the Buyer's request.

c. If, for any reason whatsoever, the Buyer (i) fails to make any cash payment required by this Agreement in full on or before its due date, (ii) fails to make full settlement in accordance with the terms of this Agreement, (iii) interferes with the performance by the Seller, or (iv) otherwise defaults in any of the Buyer's obligations under this Agreement, then, at the option of the Seller, this Agreement may be terminated, in which event the Seller will retain as liquidated damages the deposit and any and all other monies paid under this Agreement and the Seller and the Buyer will be relieved from further liability hereunder, or the Seller may avail itself of any legal or equitable remedies and rights which it may have under this Agreement or otherwise.

10. Risk of Loss.

The Seller assumes the risk of loss or damage to the Property by fire or other insured casualty until the date of settlement.

11. Possession.

Possession of the Property will be given to the Buyer at settlement, provided the Buyer complies with all of the requirements of Paragraph 12 of this Agreement. Prior to that time, the Buyer will have no right to enter upon or occupy the Property without the written approval of the Seller. However, the Buyer will have the right to inspect the Property in the company of a representative of the Seller not more than ten (10) days prior to settlement.

12. Settlement.

a. Settlement under this Agreement will take place at any time within sixty (60) days after completion of construction of the Dwelling and the Landscaping, on a date and at a time and place selected by the Seller. The Seller will give the Buyer not less than fourteen (14) days prior written notice of the date, time, and place of settlement. In the event that, on the scheduled settlement date, the Dwelling is habitable but the Landscaping and any exterior painting cannot be completed because of seasonal or other weather conditions, settlement nonetheless will be held as scheduled, in which event the Seller will complete the Landscaping and exterior painting as soon as conditions permit. In any event, the Dwelling and the Landscaping will be deemed to be complete for purposes of settlement on the date the Building Official of Howard County issues a Certificate of Use and Occupancy or Temporary Certificate of Occupancy with respect to the Property.

b. Upon payment by the Buyer of the entire balance due hereunder, all expenses of settlement and all proper fees and charges in connection therewith, the Seller will execute and deliver to the Buyer a deed containing covenants of special warranty and further assurance and conveying the Property to the Buyer by good and merchantable title, free of liens and encumbrances except as specified herein and except use and occupancy restrictions of public record which are generally applicable to properties in the immediate neighborhood in which the Property is located, publicly recorded easements for public utilities and any other easements which may be observed by an inspection of the Property and all the covenants, liens, and other restrictions imposed upon the Property by "______________" a copy of which the Buyer has received prior to signing this Agreement.

c. All settlement costs; including all transfer taxes, recording fees, documentary stamps, insurance premiums, prepaid expenses and title search, surveying, conveyancing and mortgage fees and charges, will be paid at settlement by the Buyer. Rent and all taxes and charges of every kind against the Property which are or may be payable on an annual basis, including Metropolitan District, Sanitary District and other benefit charges, assessments, liens or encumbrances for water, sewer, drainage or other public improvements (commenced or completed on or prior to the date hereof or subsequent thereto) or services or the use thereof and any dues, assessments or other charges of CPRA and _______________ Community Association, Inc., will be apportioned between the Seller and the Buyer as of the date of settlement, whether or not assessments have been levied as of that date, and will be assumed and paid thereafter by the Buyer.

13. Miscellaneous Provisions.

a. The Buyer will not assign this Agreement or any of the Buyer's interest herein without the Seller's prior written consent.

b. Any notice required or permitted by this Agreement will be considered sufficient if sent by certified mail to the party entitled to receive notice at the address for that party set forth above.

c. Time is of the essence of this Agreement.

d. This Agreement contains the complete and final agreement between the parties and may not be modified except by a written document signed by all of the parties.

e. None of the terms of this Agreement will survive the Seller's delivery and the Buyer's acceptance of the deed, except Paragraph 8 hereof, the Buyer's obligation pursuant to Paragraph 12.c hereof to assume and pay certain taxes and other charges and this subparagraph f.

f. This Agreement will be jointly and severally binding on the parties hereto and on their respective heirs, legal representatives, successors and assigns.

IN WITNESS WHEREOF, the parties have executed and delivered this Agreement on the date first written above.

WITNESS:

__________________________ __________________________(SEAL)

Buyer's Signature

__________________________ __________________________(SEAL)

Buyer's Signature

BUYER

[ENTITY NAME]

By ________________________________

SELLER

B. [§ 3.41] Sample Roofing Plans and Specifications Excerpt

ROOFING

1.01 GENERAL INSTRUCTIONS

.1 Attention is directed to ____________________ include all subdivisions thereof, as listed is the TABLE OF CONTENTS, which are hereby made a part of this SECTION.

1.02 WORK TO BE PERFORMED

.1 The work of this Section includes all flashing, sheet metal work, asphalt shingles, gutters and downspouts and all related items necessary to complete the work shown on the drawings and herein specified.

1.03 INSTALLATION OF MATERIALS FURNISHED BY OTHER SECTIONS

.1 Install the following materials as furnished by the designated SECTIONS:
Vent pipe flashing: SECTION, ____ PLUMBING

1.04 RELATED TO OTHER SECTIONS

.1 The following work is not included in this SECTION and is to be performed under the designated SECTIONS

(a) Roof trusses and plywood sheathing: SECTION, ____ CARPENTRY.

(b) Anchorage fir in-wall flashing work: SECTION ____, UNIT MASONRY.

1.05 SHOP DRAWINGS AND TECHNICAL INFORMATION

.1 Shop drawings shall be submitted for sheet metal work in connection with roofing.

.2 Submit names of manufacturers and technical information on all products proposed for use in completing the work of this SECTION.

1.06 SAMPLES

.1 Submit samples of materials used in the work of this Section as requested by the Architect.

2.0.1 MATERIALS

.1 Asphalt Shingles: Shingles shall be similar in quality to ____________________ or ____________________. Shingles shall be fire-resistant with a minima U.L. Glass "C" rating and self-sealing wind resistance rating.

.2 Underlayment shall be ____ lb. asphalt saturated felt.

.3 Gutters shall be of ____ gauge galvanized steel, 5″ × 3-3/4″, Ogee design. Gutters to be furnished in ____ sections with required soldered end caps and hangers.

.4 Downspouts shall be of ____ gauge galvanized steel, in ten foot lengths where possible. Size shall be as noted on the drawings and type shall be corrugated rectangular with locked seam longitudinal joint. End joints shall telescope into each other. Provide elbow at bottom.

.5 Downspout hangers shall be of ____ gauge galvanized steel, ____ wide and be formed to hold downspout off the wall and have ends flanged out on wall. Straps shall be soldered to downspout at ____ maximum spacing and bolted to wall with machine bolts and expansion shields.

.6 Rain diverters on roof shall be of ____ gauge galvanized steel, formed on a sheet metal brake to rise ____ above roof level as indicated on drawings. Diverters shall be shop primed and painted prior to installation.

.7 Metal base flashing, where lower roof meets a vertical surface, shall be formed of ____ gauge galvanized steel maximum ____ lengths. Extend onto roof below shingles a minimum of ____ and rise against vertical wall a minimum of ____, top edge of which shall be covered with cap flashing or parapet wall cap.

2.02 DISSIMILAR MATERIALS

.1 Where sheet metals abut or member into adjacent dissimilar metals, the juncture surfaces shall be painted with one heavy coat of bituminous paint or treated in a manner satisfactory to the Architect to prevent galvanic action between the two metals.

.2 Surfaces to which roof shingles or sheet metal are to be applied shall be even, smooth, sound, thoroughly clean and dry, and free from all defects that might affect application. Any unsatisfactory surfaces will constitute acceptance of condition of surfaces to receive roofing and sheet metal work.

2.04 MATERIALS TO BE BUILT-IN

.1 Materials furnished under this section which are to be built-in by other trades shall be delivered to the site in time to avoid delays to construction process.

2.05 CUTTING AND FITTING

.1 All cutting, fitting, drilling, and other operations in connection with sheet metal required to accommodate work of other trades shall be performed under this section.

3.01 SHEET METAL WORKSHOP

.1 Except as otherwise noted or shown on drawings or specified, workmanship of sheet metal work, method of forming joints, anchoring, cleating, provisions for expansion, etc., shall conform to standard details, design principles and techniques of the industry.

.2 Parapet wall cap flashing shall be shop formed from long sections of ____ gauge galvanized sheet metal with flat lock seam joints. Provide expansion joints at ____. Attachment to wood plate shall be made with continuous cleats nailed to plate.

.3 Cap flashing where required over metal base flashing shall be formed from ____ gauge galvanized sheet metal projecting into masonry wall and turned up ____. Turn down a minimum of ____ to cover top of base flashing as detailed.

.4 All items related to gutters and downspouts herein before specified shall be installed in accordance with the Sheet Metal and Air Conditioning Contractors National Association, Inc. recommendations.

3.02 ASPHALT SHINGLES

.1 Shingles shall be applied over one layer of ____ pound asphalt saturated felt with all edges lapped ____ inches.

.2 Each shingle shall be securely nailed with 4 galvanized large head roofing nails. One nail 1 inch from each end and one nail approximately ____ inches on each side of center.

.3 All nails to be positioned ____ inch above a line, even with top of cut outs.

.4 The shingles shall be laid with the ends (not to be confused with front or back edges) barely touching each other.

.5 All shingles shall be laid with a ____ inch exposure and an inch head lap.

.6 Application shall be in accordance with the manufacturer's instructions.

C. [§ 3.42] Specification List-Customer Decorating and Selection Sheet

(This Exhibit is to be used for illustrative purposes only and the completeness of same is not warranted)

Date ___________

SPECIFICATION LIST

Buyer ____________________________ Phone __________________

Address ____

Job Location ____

Model ____

HOME TO CONSIST OF kitchen, living room, dining room, family room, foyer, ____ bedrooms, ____ baths, laundry facilities in ____________________________________

____

Basement ____

Garage, Carport____

EXTERIOR:

Balcony is ______________________________.

Portico is ______________________________.

Asphalt seal tab roof shingles.

Brick allowance___________________ per thousand ____________________________

____.

If more than one kind/type or size of brick is used on any one residence, a flat fee of $25 will be charged. This charge is not included in your contract price.

Pointing (recessing) of brick mortar joints is _______ per thousand extra, to be billed later if requested by buyer.

If colored mortar is used, a flat fee of $25 will be charged plus the additional cost of colored mortar. This charge is not included in your contract price.

Siding to be ____.

Shutters on front and side windows. (Total ________ pair.)

Exterior painting by ______________ which includes spot sanding, caulking, putty, and filling of nail holes, etc.

Exterior basement entrance ____.

Exterior basement areaway and steps ____________________________________.

Gutters and downspouts to be____.

Well allowance ___ feet, additional footage at ___ per foot plus cost of larger pump if needed. Filter, water conditioners, etc. are not included. Wells at any depth are not guaranteed at all for any period of time against production of water and/or quality of water. This is beyond the Builder's control.

Front sidewalk to driveway and concrete landing pads at all exterior doors and steps is included.

Patio size ____________________________ Location ___________________________.

Driveway to be _________ not to exceed _________ sq. yds._________ tone.

All concrete and driveway work is not guaranteed—the above is subject to weather conditions such as freezing, thawing, settlement, etc. beyond the Builder's control.

Grading of _________ on. ft. is included.

Seeding by ________ not to exceed _________ sq.ft. (No seeding before April 15th and after October 1st.).

Seeding and grading work is not guaranteed at all once completed against growth, wash out, erosion, etc.

Tree Removal ____
exterior hose connections are included.

Percolation test is ____.

Staking of all corners of lot is Buyer's responsibility.

Installation of the septic system is not to exceed the cost of $_________. The septic system is guaranteed to be installed as per county specifications which is also inspected by the county. However, guarantee ends here as ground conditions, although not likely, can change.

INTERIOR:

Walls and ceilings to be ____.

Cracks, nailpops, ridging, etc. are characteristic of all plaster and drywall work and therefore not the responsibility of the Builder. There is no known method of eliminating this condition.

Wood paneling allowance________ per 4 × 8 ft. sheet, to be installed in the following locations: ____. We recommend the use of plywood paneling above and below grade, therefore we do not guarantee nor stand behind at all the use of masonite paneling.

Kitchen floor allowance _________ per sq. yd.

Foyer floor to be ____.

Recreation room floor allowance _________ per sq. ft.

Family bath floor to ____.

Master bath floor to ____.

Powder room floor to be ____.

Balance of floors to be ____.

Family bath to have ________ fixtures with ___________________________. 4 feet high on walls and 6 feet high at tub.

Master bath to have ________ fixtures with ________ in stall shower complete with shower door, ____.

Powder room to have ___________ fixtures with sidewalls and a ___________ ceiling ___________ ceramic tile.

Fireplace to be in ____.

Second fireplace to be in ____.

Interior painting by _________________ which includes spot sanding, spackling of nicks and filling of nail holes, etc.

Interior doors to be ________ type ________ finish.

Attic stairway is ________________.

Windows by ___________________________ with _______________________. glass (________windows) (screens are ________) (grids are ________).

Bow window by ________ with ________ glass.

Picture window by ________ with ________ glass.

Sliding patio doors (________ ft.) to be tempered, insulated glees to be installed ______ ____.

Storm windows are _________________ (________units). We do not install aluminum storm doors.

Front entrance to be _________________. We do not guarantee a double door entrance to be water and/or air tight. Builder's responsibility ends at the original installation—buyer assumes all responsibility.

Sidelights are _______________________ with standard glass.

Kitchen cabinets, equipment, etc. and bathroom vanity purchasing Allowance _________________. Installation by _______________________.

Installation of disposals, charcoal grille, radar ranges, ice cube, makers, venting of duct type hoods, etc. are not included. If a buyer exceeds the allowance, overages must be paid directly to the supplier at time of ordering.

Heat to be ____.

Oil tank to be ______________ gallons. Installed ___________________________.

Humidifier ____________________. Air Conditioning ______________________.

Hot water heater is to be ___________________, _______________________ gallon.

Home to be insulated and weather-stripped.

Complete drain tile system under basement floor.

ELECTRIC:

_____________ sets of dual exterior flood lights are included complete with fixtures.

Porcelain type fixtures is unfinished basements are included.

________ exterior outlet included.

Lamp post ____________________ with no more than ___________ feet of exterior trenching. Additional trenching at ________ per foot.

Door bell system _________________.

All recessed fixtures to be supplied by builder, but to be charged against Buyer's fixture allowance at ________ each.

Intercom _________________________. Total Locations ____________________.

Bathroom fans are included in bath without windows.

Attic exhaust fan ____________________. Timer _________________________.

Dryer outlet ____.

All dimensions of recessed medicine cabinets must be verified with Builder prior to starting of home.

Light fixtures, light bulbs, and medicine cabinet purchasing allowance ________. If a buyer exceeds the allowance, overages must be paid directly to the supplier at time of ordering.

All electric work to be as per local code requirements ___________________________ ____.

WARRANTY:

A new home has been constructed in accordance with good, accepted home-building practices. It has also been inspected where required by building department of municipality in which it is situated.

WARRANTABLE ITEMS:	All complaints having to do with faulty workmanship.
	All complaints having to do with faulty materials.
	All complaints having to do with failure to complete in accordance with the specification section of this contract.
UNWARRANTABLE ITEMS:	Complaints arising from damages due to Acts of God.
	Variations in color grain and shrinkage of woods.
	Those as spelled out in the above specifications.

The provisions of this warranty shall cover a period of one year from date of occupancy or date of completion whichever occurs first. This warranty is non-transferable and any obligation under it terminates if the property is resold or shall cease to be occupied by the Home Owner to whom it is originally issued.

Complete cost of home ___________ as stated above.

Cost of lot ___________.

Price remains in effect until ___________.

Construction and finishes of home to be an per home located at ___________ unless noted differently above.

The Builder and Buyer do hereby agree to the above terms, specifications, and conditions and they therefore become a part of this contract.

Date ________________________

____________________	____________________
Witness	Builder
____________________	____________________
Witness	Buyer
____________________	____________________
Witness	Buyer

D. [§ 3.43] Notice to Buyer

NOTICE TO BUYER

The following types and thicknesses of insulation will be installed in the dwelling which is subject of the attached Contract of Sale. The insulation will be installed in the areas specified below. Each type and thickness of insulation has the "R" value listed below.

TYPE	R-VALUE	THICKNESS	REMARKS
Flat Ceilings	Fiberglass	R-30	9"
Sloped Ceilings	Fiberglass	R-30	9"
Garage Ceilings	Fiberglass	R-30	9"
Exterior Walls	Fiberglass	R-19	6"
Overhangs	Fiberglass	R-19	6"
Band Joists	Fiberglass	R-19	6"
Basement	Fiberglass	R-11	3-1/2"
Crawl Space only under habitable area	Fiberglass	R-30	9"
Cantilever for overhangs at Bay or Projected window	Fiberglass	R-30	

E. [§ 3.44] Sample Escrow Agreement

ESCROW AGREEMENT

THIS ESCROW AGREEMENT, made this ___________ day of ___________ 20__, between ___________ (the "Seller"), and ___________ (the "Buyer"), witnesseth:

1. In connection with the sale of ___________, Baltimore City, Maryland, the Seller has allowed the Buyer to place $___________ of the purchase price in escrow, (the "Deposit") to be held by ______________________ attorneys, as Escrowee.
2. Seller will substantially complete those items set forth in Exhibit A attached hereto (the "Improvements"), on or before the date specified for each item.
3. Buyer agrees that Seller shall be paid the amount set forth for each item when the item is substantially completed, and upon request of Seller, Buyer will sign an authorization to Escrowee instructing Escrowee to pay such amount to Seller. Upon receipt by Escrowee of the authorization from Buyer, that amount shall be made by the Escrowee to Seller.
4. Seller agrees that Buyer shall be paid the amount set forth for any item which is not substantially completed by the specified date, and upon request of Buyer, Seller will sign an authorization to Escrowee instructing Escrowee to pay such amount to Buyer. The Escrowee will pay such amount to Buyer upon receipt of such authorization from Seller. However, if Seller has been delayed in completing any item by any cause other than its own willful default or neglect, and if Seller is, on such date set for completion, proceeding to complete such item, then the date for completion shall be extended so long as Seller is proceeding diligently to complete such item.
5. Buyer and Seller agree that Escrowee shall have no obligation to disburse any part of the Deposit to either Buyer or Seller except upon the written authorization of the party to which the disbursement is not being made.
6. No interest shall be payable on the Deposit or any part thereof. No claim shall be made by the Seller or Buyer upon the Escrowee for or on account of any matter or thing in excess of the balance of the Deposit remaining in its hands and undisposed of from time to time other than for the Escrowee's own willful default hereunder. The Escrowee shall be protected in acting upon any notice, request, consent, demand, statement, note or other paper or document believed by it to be genuine and to have been signed by the party or parties purporting to sign the same.
7. If the Escrowee has not disbursed all of the Deposit on or before ______ __, 20__, then at its sole option Escrowee may place any part of the Deposit into the registry of a Circuit Court of Baltimore City. All parties hereto consent to be sued in interpleader in a Circuit Court of Baltimore City in the event of a dispute concerning the Deposit and all parties acknowledge the jurisdiction and appropriateness of venue of such Courts and consent to the service of process by registered or certified mail or personal delivery.

IN WITNESS WHEREOF, Buyer and Seller have duly executed this Escrow Agreement.

SELLER:

By

____

BUYER:

By

____

__________________ hereby agrees to act as Escrowee under the terms and conditions set forth above, and acknowledges receipt of a check for $______ drawn on the account of __________________

By

____

CHAPTER FOUR

TITLE INSURANCE IN THE RESIDENTIAL TRANSACTION*

Amin Khakpouri, Esq.
Bhavin Patel, Esq.
Samantha B. La Mell, Esq.[1]

Universal Title/The Mason Law Firm

* MSBA gratefully acknowledges the contributions to this chapter by original and previous updating authors Sherri R. Heyman, Esq., and David H. Fishman, Esq.

TABLE OF CONTENTS

I. INTRODUCTION[1]

A. [§ 4.1] Overview

Most homebuyers in Maryland are aware of the existence of title insurance. Most lenders now require that title to property that is the security for their mortgages be insured by a title insurance policy. In addition, many attorneys have withdrawn from the business of title examination and have turned to title insurers to furnish the service of examining and insuring titles, if not also abstracting them. It has been the trend over recent years that title insurance has completely taken over from the lawyer's opinion system in large cities and metropolitan areas.[2] The reasons stated by Johnstone many years ago still seem to be valid: "Especially in the large cities, most lawyers in private practice no longer want to search or examine titles; the practice is unremunerative, and lawyers cannot compete with the mass production techniques of the large title insurers. In addition, the lawyer who examines a title assumes a heavy burden and significant risk of liability for negligence."[3] This risk is illustrated in Maryland in the case of *Myerberg, Sawyer & Rue, P.A. v. Agee*,[4] where a landowner was unable to close on a house construction loan because of the lender's determination that title was unmarketable. The Appellate Court of Maryland (formerly known as the Court of Special Appeals) upheld a judgment against the law firm which examined title for the landowner for the increased costs of construction and financing between the date the loan was originally scheduled to close, and the date suit was brought. Title to the property was unmarketable because there was no recorded means of access between the property and a public right of way, a condition which subjected the landowner to the hazards of litigation to establish an easement by necessity. Because of the failure to disclose this fact to the landowner, the law firm was held liable for breach of its contract to examine title to property.

Despite the fact that most lawyers now do not search or examine titles, the lawyer still has an important function to perform in protecting a client in a real estate transaction in which title insurance is involved.

---

1 In the Second Edition of this publication, author David Fishman, acknowledged, with thanks, the permission of the American Bar Association to make use of portions of an article by Michael J. Rooney, Esq., appearing at 14 REAL PROPERTY, PROBATE & TRUST J. 581 (1979).

2 Quinton Johnstone, *Title Insurance*, 66 YALE L.J. 492 (1957).

3 Comment, *Liability of Abstracting Attorneys and Title Examiners*, 17 ALA. L. REV. 83 (1954); Note, *Title Insurance: The Duty to Search*, 77 YALE L.J. 1161 (1962).

4 51 Md. App. 711, 446 A.2d 69 (1982).

B. [§ 4.2] Scope

The role of the attorney today is to assist in obtaining the correct type of insurance needed to cover the client's particular interest adequately. It is likewise incumbent upon the attorney to explain to the client the importance of having adequate insurance coverage, the meaning of the provisions in the insurance policy purchased, the alternative options available, the extent and nature of the risks dealt with in the policy, and the reputation, security, and financial stability of the title insurance company selected. It is the purpose of this chapter to assist the lawyer in properly carrying out these functions.

II. BASIC FUNCTIONS OF TITLE INSURANCE

A. [§ 4.3] Risk Spreading

The issuance of a title insurance policy serves two basic functions. As with most other types of casualty insurance, one function is risk assumption, which in turn leads to risk spreading. Unlike most other types of casualty insurance, however, the second function is risk elimination.

The essence of all types of insurance is that the company assumes the risk and then spreads that risk evenly among all of its policy-holding customers. The insurance company is able to calculate its premiums by multiplying the projected size of the average loss by the number of average size losses which will occur and dividing that by the number of policyholders; to that figure, of course, must be added the administrative cost of running the company and a fair return on investment as profit. In the end, each individual is left with a choice of paying a nominal sum in order to be protected against a large loss or running the risk of assuming the full loss without any protection. The relatively small one-time premium paid for the title insurance policy means that each individual insured need not worry about suffering a catastrophic loss, since the risk of that loss is assumed by the company and spread among its policyholders.

B. [§ 4.4] Risk Elimination

Few insurers in other fields are able to say that one of the functions of the issuance of their policies is risk elimination. Title insurers, therefore, enjoy certain advantages over fire, auto, life, and other insurers. To be sure, risk elimination can be a factor in fire, auto, and life insurance situations, but in those instances, it is the insured who must, generally speaking, eliminate the risk. They must take the necessary steps to prevent fire; they are responsible for their own safe driving; and they are responsible for taking care of their own health. The title insurance company itself, on the other hand, plays the key role in risk elimination, since its own personnel or its agents conduct the search of the records so that all known title defects may be noted and cured. Thus, before the company issues its policy, these various record defects will, to the extent that they can be ascertained, be eliminated. In instances where the risk is not eliminated the title insurance company will make a determination to voluntarily assume a known risk.

C. [§ 4.5] Hidden Defects

It must be recognized, however, that it is impossible to eliminate all risks. There are a number of "hidden defects," which cannot be discovered by simply examining the public record. These include forgeries, false impersonations, lack of delivery of a deed, missing heirs, and errors by public officials, just to name a few. These hidden defects are the risk that the title insurer assumes and spreads among the policyholders. Moreover, the company may choose not to eliminate a risk but to assume it voluntarily as a known risk, since it may be more economical for the company to assume the risk than to take the steps necessary to ascertain whether defects exist. This is especially true in those instances in which the insurance company is able to charge an "additional risk" premium, as in the case of insurance against restrictive covenants. An examination of the public records, no matter how careful, provides no protection against errors in the record or forgeries.[5] One of the most important characteristics of title insurance is that some title insurance policies protect against these risks.[6]

D. [§ 4.6] Off-Record Risks

The term "off-record risks" includes a tremendous range of eventualities. The following is a list of potential off-record risks that are covered by enhanced title insurance policies:

1. Forgeries and Fraud
   a. Forged Instruments
   b. Fraudulent Releases
   c. Defrauding of a Grantor
2. Incapacity of a Grantor
   a. Mental Incapacity of a Grantor
   b. Infant Grantor
   c. Legal Incapacity

---

5 *Harding v. Ja Laur Corp.*, 20 Md. App. 209, 212–13, 315 A.2d 132 (1974).

6 In connection with potential title defects that can affect property even after title has been searched, see *The History of a Maryland Title: A Conveyancer's Romance Renewed*, 42 Md. L. Rev. 496 (1983), which contains a humorous treatment of the many problems that can crop up in a chain of title.

3. Lack of an Essential Formality in the Execution of an Instrument
    a. Lack of Delivery
    b. Lack of Acknowledgement
4. Mechanics' Liens
5. Unrecorded Family Rights
    a. Dower
    b. Rights of Pretermitted or After-Born Children
    c. Community Property Rights
6. Prior Adverse Possession and Undisclosed Easements[7]
    a. Prior Adverse Possession
    b. Undisclosed Prescriptive Easements
    c. Undisclosed Implied Easements
7. Failure to Inquire with Respect to Possession Not on its Face Inconsistent with Purchaser's Rights
8. Tolled Limitations Periods
9. Prior Holder in a Chain of Title Senior in Record but Junior in Time of Actual Notice
10. Rights of Prior Transferees under Recording Acts with Grace Periods for Filing
11. Void Judgments and Court Orders
12. Subsequently Discovered Will
13. Foreclosure Sale Stayed under Soldiers' and Sailors' Civil Relief Act
14. Instrument Given as Security for Usurious Loan
15. Recording Errors
16. Estoppel by Deed
17. Destruction of Records
18. Conveyances Void Because of § 544 of the Bankruptcy Code, 11 U.S.C. § 544 (1978)[8]

---

7 *Cheverly Terrace P'ship v. Ticor Title Ins. Co.*, 100 Md. App. 606, 642 A.2d 285 (1994).

8 Ralph L. Straw, Jr., *Off-Record Risks for Bona Fide Purchasers of Interests in Real Property*, 72 DICK. L. REV. 35 (1967).

E. [§ 4.7] The Commitment—Generally

Assuming that the decision has been made to utilize title insurance in a particular transaction, the attorney or lender will normally refer the matter to a title insurance company or an authorized agent for an abstract of the title, an examination of the abstract, and issuance of a title report or commitment for the title insurance policy. The commitment or binder for issuance of title insurance[9] normally recites the record owner of the property, all existing liens, a list of matters to be dealt with in order that the title may be insured in the buyer (requirements), and a list of exceptions which will appear in the final insurance policy. However, the issuance of such a commitment imposes no duty on the title insurer to see that the preconditions to insurance are complied with.[10]

F. [§ 4.8] The Commitment—Recordation Precondition

The commitment has only one pre-printed requirement or precondition that must be complied with: namely, that any instruments which are to be recorded (e.g., the deed and deed of trust) be executed, delivered, and filed for record. Even though the title company has no duty to see that the preconditions are satisfied, in actual practice, the title company ordinarily prepares these instruments and, in conjunction with the settlement, which a representative of the title company conducts, makes sure that the requirements are satisfied.

G. [§ 4.9] The Commitment—Other Requirements

Examples of other matters that typically appear on a commitment as requirements to be complied with are the release of any open mortgages or other liens encumbering the property (the title company will obtain the release information and disburse to the lienholder the payoff funds); the payment of open real estate taxes and other assessments (if taxes are unpaid, the title company will collect sufficient funds and apportion the liability for payment thereof between buyer and seller at settlement); and the presentation by the seller at settlement of a death certificate if the property is in title to spouses as tenants by the entirety, and only the living spouse has executed the contract of sale, entity documents if the seller is an entity, trust documents if the seller holds title in trust. In any event, the attorney for the buyer should contact the title company and verify which requirements listed in the commitment will be completed by the title company.

Moreover, communication between the buyer's attorney and the title company, or the closing attorney, is crucial to protect the buyer from unforeseeable damages.

---

9 *See* § **4.46** of this chapter.

10 *District-Realty Title Ins. Corp. v. Jack Spicer Real Estate, Inc.*, 280 Md. 422, 429, 373 A.2d 952, 959 (1977).

The Supreme Court of Maryland formerly known as the Maryland Court of Appeals has ruled that a closing attorney, or title company, who fails to complete a closing requirement is liable only for the buyer's reasonably foreseeable damages resulting from such failure.[11] If there are special circumstances which might subject the buyer to damages in the event of the title company's failure to complete a requirement, the buyer will not be protected unless such circumstances are disclosed.

H. [§ 4.10] The Attorney's Role

Regardless of whether the title insurance company is voluntarily assuming a known risk or is simply assuming the risk of those hidden defects that are present in every transaction, the exact nature of the risk assumed and, therefore, the coverage afforded under the policy cannot be clearly ascertained and understood in the absence of an in-depth analysis of the language of the policy itself. Although many title insurance companies use a "standard" form, careful examination of the policy is in order in each instance so that the attorney may assure themselves that they properly understand its terms before an attempt is made to explain its contents to the client. The attorney for the buyer should examine the commitment to see that the liens and encumbrances on the property that must be satisfied will not require the expenditure of a sum more than the purchase price for the property. Reading an existing encumbrance on the property may reveal that there is no right of prepayment and that the mortgagee may refuse to accept payoff of the encumbrances at closing of the purchase transaction.

Next, the buyer's attorney should examine all documents listed as exceptions to the title. The importance of this cannot be overemphasized. Such a review will often show that listed exceptions do not apply to the subject property. Certain exceptions may raise serious questions as to the desirability of purchasing the property and may be grounds for cancellation of the purchase contract. Examples of exceptions that could pose a negative impact on the property are deferred water and sewer facilities charges, easements burdening the property, shared driveway and/or maintenance agreements.

It is essential that the policies being considered be read in their entirety with the client's interest in mind so that the final product can be negotiated to reflect the best possible protection for the purchaser. The attorney, with sole responsibility for the client's interest, is best equipped to assure that this will happen.

In dealing with problems revealed by the commitment, it will become clear to the practicing attorney that one of their most important functions is the selection of the insurer. There are several reputable title insurers doing business in Maryland, but the services available from specific insurers may vary greatly. The accessibility

---

11 *Stone v. Chi. Title Ins. Co.*, 330 Md. 329, 624 A.2d 496 (1993).

of necessary decision-making personnel may become important where title problems are encountered. Therefore, it is useful to have relationships with more than one title insurance company. It often happens that one company will eliminate an exception from a policy while another company insists upon including the same exception.

I. [§ 4.11] Insured Closing Letters

Insured closing letters, also known as closing protection letters, have been determined to expand the protections offered by the title insurance policy. In a spate of cases, the New Jersey courts found title companies liable for certain acts of attorneys conducting closings not only to third party lenders, the intended beneficiary of the insured closing letter, but also to purchasers. In the companion cases of *Sears Mortgage Corp. v. Rose*[12] and *Clients' Security Fund of the Bar of New Jersey v. Security Title & Guaranty Co.*,[13] the Supreme Court of New Jersey determined that title companies should bear purchasers' losses resulting from the theft of closing funds by the closing attorney. The basis for such liability is that the title company is in the best position to prevent the loss. Moreover, the court ruled that closing attorneys were, in fact, agents of the title companies even in those instances in which the closing attorneys were engaged by the purchaser. Insured closing letters were ruled to have evidenced the agency relationship, and to have established the title companies' knowledge of the potential for losses from attorney misconduct. All consumer lenders and most private lenders require Insured Closing Letters also known as closing protection letters.

In order to provide a means of policing the management of funds of real estate settlements, the title insurance law in Maryland was revised in 1995, to require title insurers to conduct on-site reviews of each title agent authorized by the insurer to sell title insurance and to conduct settlements.[14] This legislation was inspired by and in response to the occurrence of financial irregularities at the settlement table, including embezzlement of escrowed funds.

III. TITLE INSURANCE POLICIES

A. [§ 4.12] Standard Form

The American Land Title Association (ALTA), a Washington-based trade group of title insurance underwriters and agents, has created standard policies for use by its members. Since the introduction of the 1970 ALTA Loan Policy, the ALTA forms

---

12 634 A.2d 74 (N.J. 1993).

13 634 A.2d 90 (N.J. 1993).

14 MD. CODE ANN., INSURANCE I § 10-121(j) (2017 & Supp. 2022).

are the most commonly used title insurance forms in the United States.[15] Residential homeowners and lenders have a choice as to the extent of coverage offered in a title insurance policy, which was provided by either a standard coverage policy or an expanded coverage policy. In most jurisdictions, including Maryland, the standard form of coverage prior to June 17, 2007, was provided by the 1992 ALTA Owner's Policy and Loan Policies (hereinafter the 1992 Policies). As of June 17, 2007, ALTA withdrew the 1992 Policies as the official ALTA Forms and adopted new and updated versions of the 1992 Policies (hereinafter the 2006 Policies), which will be discussed in § **4.34** of this chapter. Effective July 30, 2021, the 2021 ALTA Policy Forms collection went into effect and, although the 2006 forms are still being used by most underwriters, beginning January 2024 the 2021 Forms will be required. The 2021 Policies insure the owner, subject to exclusions and exceptions, against loss due to:

(1) Title being vested other than as stated in Schedule A;

(2) A defect in or lien or encumbrance on the title. Covered Risk 2 includes, but is not limited to, insurance against loss from:

  a. a defect in the Title caused by:

    i. forgery, fraud, undue influence, duress, incompetency, incapacity, or impersonation;

    ii. the failure of a person or Entity to have authorized a transfer or conveyance;

    iii. a document affecting the Title not properly authorized, created, executed, witnessed, sealed, acknowledged, notarized (including by remote online notarization), or delivered;

    iv. a failure to perform those acts necessary to create a document by electronic means authorized by law;

    v. a document executed under a falsified, expired, or otherwise invalid power of attorney;

    vi. a document not properly filed, recorded, or indexed in the Public Records, including the failure to have performed those acts by electronic means authorized by law;

    vii. a defective judicial or administrative proceeding; or

    viii. the repudiation of an electronic signature by a person that executed a document because the electronic signature on the document was not valid under applicable electronic transactions law.

---

15 Practicing Law Institute, *Title Insurance: Enhanced Protection for Residential Homeowners*, REAL ESTATE LAW AND PRAC. COURSE HANDBOOK NO. 462 (2000).

b. the lien of real estate taxes or assessments imposed on the Title by a governmental authority due or payable, but unpaid

c. the effect on the Title of an encumbrance, violation, variation, adverse circumstance, boundary line overlap, or encroachment (including an encroachment of an improvement across the boundary lines of the Land), but only if the encumbrance, violation, variation, adverse circumstance, boundary line overlap, or encroachment would have been disclosed by an accurate and complete land title survey of the Land

(3) Unmarketable title; and

(4) No right of access to and from the land.

(5) A violation or enforcement of a law, ordinance, permit, or governmental regulation (including those relating to building and zoning), but only to the extent of the violation or enforcement described by the enforcing governmental authority in an Enforcement Notice that identifies a restriction, regulation or prohibition relating to:

a. the occupancy, use, or enjoyment of the Land;

b. the character, dimensions, or location of an improvement on the Land;

c. the subdivision of the Land; or

d. environmental remediation or protection on the Land.

(6) An enforcement of a governmental forfeiture, police, regulatory, or national security power, but only to the extent of the enforcement described by the enforcing governmental authority in an Enforcement Notice.

(7) An exercise of the power of eminent domain, but only to the extent:

a. of the exercise described in an Enforcement Notice; or

b. the taking occurred and is binding on a purchaser for value without Knowledge.

(8) An enforcement of a PACA-PSA Trust, but only to the extent of the enforcement described in an Enforcement Notice.

(9) The Title being vested other than as stated in Schedule A, the Title being defective, or the effect of a court order providing an alternative remedy:

a. resulting from the avoidance, in whole or in part, of any transfer of all or any part of the Title to the Land or any interest in the Land occurring prior to the transaction vesting the Title because that prior transfer constituted a:

i. fraudulent conveyance, fraudulent transfer, or a preferential transfer under federal bankruptcy, state insolvency, or similar state or federal creditors' rights law; or

ii. voidable transfer under the Uniform Voidable Transactions Act; or

b. because the instrument vesting the Title constitutes a preferential transfer under federal bankruptcy, state insolvency, or similar state or federal creditors' rights law by reason of the failure:

i. to timely record the instrument vesting the Title in the Public Records after execution and delivery of the instrument to the Insured; or

ii. of the recording of the instrument vesting the Title in the Public Records to impart notice of its existence to a purchaser for value or to a judgment or lien creditor.

(10) Any defect in or lien or encumbrance on the Title or other matter included in Covered Risks 1 through 9 that has been created or attached or has been filed or recorded in the Public Records subsequent to the Date of Policy and prior to the recording of the deed or other instrument vesting the Title in the Public Records.

One of the most important aspects of the insurance policy from the point of view of the buyer is the list of matters not insured against, known as "exclusions" and "exceptions." The printed exclusions from policy coverage and their explanations are discussed in §§ **4.13–4.16** of this chapter. Exceptions are discussed in §§ **4.17–4.19** of this chapter.

B. [§ 4.13] Exclusions—Government regulations

(a) Any law, ordinance, permit or governmental regulation (including those relating to building and zoning) that restricts, regulates, prohibits, or relates to:

(i) the occupancy, use, or enjoyment of the Land;

(ii) the character, dimensions or location of any improvement on the Land;

(iii) the subdivision of land; or

(iv) environmental remediation or protection.

(b) Any governmental forfeiture, police, regulatory, or national security power.[16]

(c) The effect of a violation or enforcement of any matter excluded under Exclusion 1.a. or 1.b.

This exclusion is designed primarily to indicate that matters of zoning are not insured against by the policy. Beyond that, however, the exclusion also relates to building and other use restrictions, moratoria, and restrictions concerning the right of occupancy and any government regulation concerning further subdivision

---

[16] *See* 2021 Policies at **§ 4.47** of this chapter.

of the property. This exclusion reflects the fact that all ownership of property is subject ultimately to control and regulation by the government. The attorney for the purchaser is well advised to ascertain from their client what use is intended to be made of the property. The attorney must then ascertain whether that use is permitted by the zoning ordinance and other government restrictions (as well as by any applicable restrictive covenants). For example, a home buyer may want to use part of the house for a business or professional office, and the zoning for the property must be known to enable the attorney to advise the client whether or not such use is allowed.

Also excluded from coverage under the policy is any impact upon the property resulting from state or federal environmental statutes, and the rights and powers conferred upon third parties as a result of these statutes. An example of this would be the rights and powers conferred upon the Environmental Protection Agency with respect to hazardous waste sites. However, this is not generally a problem in residential transactions, with a few notable exceptions, such as the Love Canal area in New York State.

Another situation that commonly involves zoning problems concerns boundary line setbacks. Landowners must be aware that most properties are subject to two categories of front, rear, and side yard setback requirements: those set forth in the applicable zoning regulations and those set forth in recorded covenants or subdivision plats. These two categories of setbacks do not necessarily bear any relationship to one another. Compliance with the setback requirements recorded among the Land Records which, of the two categories, is the one with which the title company is concerned, does not guarantee compliance with setbacks required by zoning regulations. Therefore, the attorney needs to consider the necessity of independently verifying compliance with zoning regulations, because the spectre of a judicially forced removal of improvements can haunt the unwitting attorney unfortunate enough to be caught in its trap. (Needless to say, the client who is faced with such a prospect will find little comfort in the attorney's explanation that the title policy does not insure against such risks).

Subsection (b) is a catch-all section that excludes from coverage under the policy any impact on the property emanating from the exercise of governmental police powers to the extent that notice of such exercise has not been previously recorded in the public records.

C. [§ 4.14] Exclusions—Eminent domain

> Any power of eminent domain. Exclusion 2 does not modify or limit the coverage provided under Covered Risk 7.

This exclusion recognizes that ownership of private property is subject not only to government control, but also to a government taking in eminent domain or regulation under the police power. Of course, if a notice of the exercise of such rights appears in the public records at or before the effective date of the policy, as, for example, would be the case if a condemnation action has been filed, then the title insurance policy would cover a loss resulting from the condemnation, unless an exception were taken in Schedule B.

D. [§ 4.15] Exclusions—Defects, liens, etc.

Any defect, lien, encumbrance, adverse claim, or other matter:

(a) created, suffered, assumed or agreed to by the Insured Claimant;

(b) not known to the Company, not recorded in the public records at the Date of Policy, but known to the Insured Claimant and not disclosed in writing to the Company by the Insured Claimant prior to the date the Insured Claimant became an Insured under this policy;

(c) resulting in no loss or damage to the Insured Claimant;

(d) attaching or created subsequent to the Date of Policy (Exclusion 3.d. does not modify or limit the coverage provided under Covered Risk 9 or 10); or

(e) resulting in loss or damage that would not have been sustained if consideration sufficient to qualify the Insured named in Schedule A as a bona fide purchaser had been given for the Title at the Date of Policy.[17]

The first subpart of this exclusion exculpates the company from liability where the condition creating the defect results from the acts of the insured.[18] Matters excluded by Paragraph 3(a) have been the subject of numerous court cases and annotations.[19] The title insurance company does not insure against any defects that the policyholder voluntarily undertook to assume. However, if that concept is simply stated in the policy, the cases and annotations indicate that it is more difficult to apply in practice. It is safe to say that, by and large, courts that have considered this language have construed it against the company.

The exclusion expressed in Paragraph 3(b) is designed to protect the company in those situations involving a hidden defect (one dehors the record), which is known to the insured at the time he or she acquires the interest but which, because of the very nature of it, is not susceptible of being discovered by a title search. This provision expressly places the burden upon the insured to disclose known defects in writing to the company.

---

17 *See* 2021 Policies at § **4.42** of this chapter.

18 *See* § **4.47** of this chapter.

19 *See* § **4.45** of this chapter. Annotation, *Title Insurance Exclusion of Liability*, 87 A.L.R. 3D 515 (1978).

In Paragraph 9(a) of the Conditions and Stipulations Section of the Owner's Policy,[20] the insurer reserves the right to perfect the title as insured should it prove to be defective. This protects the insurance company from being forced to pay a substantial sum in the case where an easily eliminated cloud on the title is discovered. Such action is ordinarily more economical than waiting until the insured suffers actual loss which results in a costly claim upon the company. This does not, of course, obligate the insurer to act in such a manner when it believes that no actual loss or damage will occur. Exclusion 3(c) provides that the insurer is only obligated to pay in the event of an actual, provable loss, but in no event will it be forced to pay more than the sum specified in the policy.

The title insurance policy is not an absolute guarantee that the insured's possession of the premises will not be disturbed, since there is always the possibility that the insured will lose possession by reason of some title defect, and they may be reimbursed only for their actual loss up to the limit fixed in the policy. On the other hand, the policy does obligate the title insurer to pay the costs and expenses incurred in defending an action challenging an insured's title.[21] In the event the company's defense is successful, the insured will have received a significant benefit in saving the cost of defending the action which they would not have received without the policy. If the defense is unsuccessful, the company, of course, must pay. On the other hand, if there is no insurance and the purchaser successfully defends an action challenging the title, no recovery would be permitted against the seller for the expenses incurred in defending the action under the covenants in a warranty deed, because the title which was warranted was good, as demonstrated by the successful defense. Thus, without title insurance the owner would lose both ways if the title is attacked.

Because the title insurance policy is issued as of a certain date and the title insurance company has no way of predicting future events, Paragraph 3(d) is an exclusion that informs the insured that title is of a stated quality as of the date the policy is issued and does not provide protection as to events occurring thereafter. The enhanced title insurance policies do protect from some post-settlement defects. Again, though the concept is simply stated, its application may be more difficult. For example, suppose a municipality adopted an ordinance stating that special assessments would be made in the future and that, as of the date of the policy, the original resolution was in effect, but no assessments had actually been made. The Appellate Court of Maryland

---

20 *See* § **4.47** of this chapter.

21 *See Gildenhorn v. Columbia Real Estate Title Ins. Co.,* 271 Md. 387, 396, 317 A.2d 836 (1974). See also *Stewart Title Guar. Co. v. West,* 110 Md. App. 114, 676 A.2d 953 (1996), where the Court of Special Appeals considered the nature of the protection offered by title insurance. The court concluded that title insurance does not operate as a guaranty or warranty of title, but rather as a contract of indemnity. 110 Md. App. at 128.

(formerly known as the Court of Special Appeals) has held that the company is not liable for failing to note the possibility of such future assessments.[22]

Paragraph 3(e) excludes from coverage any loss which the insured would not have sustained had they paid a valuable consideration for the estate or interest insured. In some jurisdictions, failure to pay any consideration for a deed, as would be the case if one were a donee may prevent the donee from claiming the protection of the state's Recording Act. In Maryland, a donee may claim the protection of the Recording Act. The exclusion embodied in Paragraph 3(e) simply states that if the insured is not entitled to the protection of the Recording Act, generally or as to specific liens, then they are likewise not entitled to the protection of the policy.

E. [§ 4.16] Exclusions—Creditor's rights/PACA-PSA/Taxes/Acreage

Exclusion 4: Any claim, by reason of the operation of federal bankruptcy, state insolvency, or similar creditors' rights law, that the transaction vesting the Title as shown in Schedule A is a:

(a) fraudulent conveyance or fraudulent transfer; or

(b) voidable transfer under the Uniform Voidable Transactions Act; or

(c) preferential transfer

(i) to the extent the instrument of transfer vesting the Title as shown in Schedule A is not a transfer made as a contemporaneous exchange for new value; or

(ii) for any other reason not stated in Covered Risk 9.b.

This exclusion seeks to protect the insurer from claims which arise from the fact that the underlying transaction is a preferential transfer or fraudulent conveyance. This exclusion would not, however, shield the title insurance company from liability should the transaction be deemed a preferential transfer solely because of the failure to timely record the instrument of transfer, or the failure of the recorded document to provide notice.

Exclusion 5: Any claim of a PACA-PSA Trust. Exclusion 5 does not modify or limit the coverage provided under Covered Risk 8.

This exclusion seeks to protect the insurer from claims which arise from the Perishable Agricultural Communities Act (PACA) and the Packers and Stockyards Act (PSA), which include trust provisions for the benefit of unpaid sellers and suppliers of perishable agricultural commodities (PACA Trust), and can apply to all assets, including real estate and sale proceeds thereof. No notice, lien, lis pendens or other claim is required to be filed in the Public Records to enforce the trust. These risks

---

22 *Strass v. District-Realty Title Ins. Corp.*, 31 Md. App. 690, 701, 358 A.2d 251 (1976).

were previously addressed by an exception in Schedule B in transactions involving agricultural land but are now addressed in Exclusion 5. This exclusion does not, however, limit the coverage afforded through Covered Risk 8, under which the title insurance company would have liability for enforcement of a PACA-PSA trust if an Enforcement Notice had been recorded in the Public Records prior to the date the policy was issued, but such liability would be limited to the enforcement described in said notice

Exclusion 6: Any lien on the Title for real estate taxes or assessments imposed or collected by a governmental authority that becomes due and payable after the Date of Policy. Exclusion 6 does not modify or limit the coverage provided under Covered Risk 2.b.

Whereas Covered Risk 2.b provides coverage for real estate taxes and assessments that became due and payable during the Gap period but were unpaid, this exclusion shields the title insurance company from taxes and assessments that become due and payable after the date the policy is issued.

Exclusion 7: Any discrepancy in the quantity of the area, square footage, or acreage of the Land or of any improvement to the Land.

This exclusion protects the insurer from claims arising from inaccuracies or discrepancies between the exact acreage of the land or improvements, and the legal description of the insured land. A legal description need only be sufficient to locate and identify the land being conveyed in order to be insurable. Whether the description is made by a metes and bounds, or a reference to a lot on a recorded plat, there is always the possibility that a subsequent surveyor might discover variances, no matter how slight. Given the advances in precision measurement and mapping technologies alone over the past few decades, such discrepancies are to be expected. These risks have traditionally been addressed through exceptions, whether by broad survey exceptions, or by separate exception as to the exact acreage.

1. [§ 4.17] Exceptions contained in Schedule B—Generally

The first sentence of the 2006 Policy reads" SUBJECT TO THE EXCLUSIONS FROM COVERAGE, THE EXCEPTIONS FROM COVERAGE CONTAINED IN *SCHEDULE B*, AND THE *CONDITIONS*, BLANK TITLE INSURANCE COMPANY, a Blank corporation (the Company) insures, as of Date of Policy and, to the extent stated in Covered Risks 9 and 10, after Date of Policy, against loss or damage, not exceeding the Amount of Insurance, sustained or incurred by the Insured by reason of:" The first sentence of the 2021 Policy reads "SUBJECT TO THE EXCLUSIONS FROM COVERAGE, THE EXCEPTIONS FROM COVERAGE CONTAINED IN *SCHEDULE B*, AND THE *CONDITIONS*, [Blank Title Insurance Company], a [Blank] corporation (the Company), insures as of the Date of Policy and, to the extent stated in Covered Risks 9 and 10, after the Date of

Policy, against loss or damage, not exceeding the Amount of Insurance, sustained or incurred by the Insured by reason of." It also contains in bold the following language **"This policy, when issued by the Company with a Policy Number and the Date of Policy, is valid even if this policy or any endorsement to this policy is issued electronically or lacks any signature. Any notice of claim and any other notice or statement in writing required to be given to the Company under this policy must be given to the Company at the address shown in Condition 17."** The policy will contain both Standard (or preprinted) Exceptions and Special Exceptions which are typed onto each policy form. The Standard Exceptions are generally six in number. A waiver of most or even all of the Standard Exceptions is normally possible provided the title insurance company is furnished with evidence to justify such a waiver. Many title insurance companies routinely allow for removal of the Standard Exceptions from the lender's policy.

The exceptions in Schedule B of the ALTA standard form are divided into "Standard Exceptions" and "Special Exceptions." The Standard Exceptions and their explanations are discussed in **§ 4.18**; the Special Exceptions and their explanations are discussed in **§ 4.19**.

2. *[§ 4.18] Standard exceptions in Schedule B*

(a) Claims of parties in possession

The first Standard Exception relates to claims of parties in possession not shown by the public records.

Since it is incumbent upon the purchaser to ascertain who is in possession of the property, and since it is generally more economical for the purchaser to conduct such an investigation than it is for the title company, the title insurance policy excepts loss or damage suffered by reason of the fact that other persons are in possession of the property when such possession is not disclosed by the public records. "Possession" may, in some cases, be more in the nature of what is commonly understood as "constructive possession" than actual possession as in the case of residency. For example, where a power company maintains an electrical transmission line on tall towers across the property, it is in "possession" of the property for purposes of this exception.[23] Most title insurers in Maryland are willing to delete the first Standard Exceptions from a loan policy based upon a combination of an owner's affidavit as to the lack of possession by others (such as tenants) in the property and a location drawing or additional certification as to other forms of possession such as a neighbor's encroachment.[24]

---

23 *McDaniel v. Lawyers' Title Guar. Fund*, 327 So. 2d 852, 856 (Fla. Dist. Ct. App. 2d Dist. 1976).

24 *See* **§ 4.18**(b) as to location drawings.

(b) Easements not shown by public record

The second Standard Exception relates to easements not shown by the public records, such as in a case where a neighboring landowner has acquired an easement by prescription by virtue of the fact that the neighbor has driven an automobile across the land for the requisite number of years, especially where such use of the property is shown by physical evidence such as tire tracks. Moreover, those tire tracks are matters that would probably be best disclosed by a personal inspection of the premises and would constitute an easement or claim of easement not shown by the public records. However, this exception would relieve the title insurer from liability even where no surface physical evidence of an easement exists, or where no claims of easement are shown of record.

The second Standard Exception also deals with encroachments, overlaps, or other matters which an accurate survey or an inspection would disclose. The lack of an accurate survey can only lead to trouble for the purchaser, since the insurer will not insure that the title is defect-free with respect to matters that would be revealed by a survey. If the defects are latent or undiscoverable on inspection, the purchaser has no protection. It thus becomes important for the lawyer to insist that the buyer inspect the property and make inquiry of persons in possession other than the seller to see if there are any unrecorded rights in the property which are excluded from the title insurance coverage. A boundary survey by a licensed surveyor, accompanied by a properly completed report or certification, may be used to eliminate part or all of the first two Standard Exceptions. However, even if there is no survey exception in the title policy, the insured will not be allowed to recover if the insured knew or should have known of discrepancies in the area (acreage content) of the land. This is the case even when the discrepancies are revealed by a survey.[25]

At this point, some discussion on the use of surveys is necessary. In residential real estate transactions, institutional lenders will ordinarily refuse to accept the second Standard Exception in their lender's title insurance policy. In order to remedy this and to remove the second Standard Exception, the title companies may require the prospective purchaser to purchase an ALTA Boundary Survey, a location drawing will not remove this exception (in fact, some lenders, independently of this aspect, require the title company to deliver a location drawing, at the purchaser's expense, for the lender's independent review). The location drawing typically costs between $150 to $250 in 2004. Its purpose is to show that the improvements on a particular property are located within the boundary lines, and whether any obvious encroachments exist. Under no circumstance is the location drawing to be considered

---

[25] *Malkin v. Realty Title Ins. Co.*, 244 Md. 112, 118–19, 223 A.2d 155 (1966). See also *Lawyers Title Ins. Corp. v. Knopf*, 109 Md. App. 134, 674 A.2d 65 (1996), for discussion of the survey exception in the context of judicial construction of title policies, generally.

as establishing or correctly depicting the property's boundary lines. The attorney representing the landowner is well advised to make sure the client understands the limited purpose for which such a "survey" is used. Stories of landowners relying on location drawings years after settlement for purposes of determining that a shed can be built on what the landowner mistakenly believes is an area within the boundary lines of the property are all too familiar. These risks must be weighed against the cost of a boundary survey which for a residential property can be $1,000 or more.

In recent years, title insurers have relaxed the traditional underwriting requirements for deleting the second Standard Exception (the "survey" exception from loan policies). Most title insurers doing business in Maryland no longer require a location drawing for "straightforward" residential deals, where there are no known survey or boundary issues. If the owner had obtained a location drawing in connection with the acquisition or later refinancing of the property, most title insurers would accept the existing location drawing, along with an affidavit from the owner certifying that the owner made no subsequent improvements to the land and, otherwise, has no knowledge of boundary line disputes or encroachments with respect to the land. Even without a prior location drawing, most title insurers are, nevertheless, willing to delete the second Standard Exception from the lender's policy only, based solely upon receipt of an appropriate owner's affidavit.

While this approach to the second Standard Exception works for lenders, most title companies, as a matter of policy, have taken the position that the owner will not be accorded the same treatment. So, the removal of this Exception from the lender's title insurance policy does not result in its removal from the owner's title insurance policy.

If the location drawing discloses an encroachment onto the adjoining property or into an easement, the title companies are usually willing to offer lenders affirmative insurance against any loss or damage resulting from the encroachment depending upon the nature and severity of the encroachment. Again, this coverage, as a matter of policy, is usually not extended to the owner. In fact, the title company will take a specific exception for the encroachment. The purchaser of the property is then left to work the matter out with the seller, possibly through requiring the removal of the encroachment (this is practical when the encroachment involves an old wooden fence or something of like nature), or through the seller's indemnification of the purchaser for any resulting loss or damage. If the encroachment is on the property being purchased due to improvements on adjoining property, the lender should not be concerned unless the encroachment materially threatens the value of the property—and hence the value of the security. The title company will most certainly take a specific exception to such an encroachment, and it is up to the purchaser to decide the extent of concern the encroachment, or exception, causes. Again, further negotiations with the seller may be in order.

The Maryland Board for Professional Land Surveyors has promulgated regulations, codified at COMAR 09.13.06–09.13.06.14. (Effective Mar. 1, 1995), which require, in relevant part, that surveyors provide to the property owner or prospective property owner to whom survey services are rendered the following disclosure:

APPROVAL FORM

In connection with (your) (the) purchase or refinancing of the property located at ________________, (this office has been requested) (a licensed Maryland surveyor will be engaged) to prepare a location drawing. A location drawing is generally satisfactory for purposes of either purchase or refinancing.

Since a location drawing is not a boundary survey and does not identify property boundary lines, State Regulations require us to have your approval. Therefore, please return the original form promptly so that there will be no delay in settlement. If you wish, (we can) (a surveyor can be engaged to) perform a boundary survey which includes a location drawing described above. This survey will identify property boundary lines and will mark property boundary corners, and can be used for various purposes, for example: erecting a fence, a garage, or other improvements on the property. A location survey will cost approximately $_________. A boundary survey which includes a location drawing will cost approximately $___________.

Very truly yours,

____

Check appropriate lines:

________ I/We approve the preparation of the location drawing. I/We have read and understand that, in the absence of any problem revealed by or during the preparation of this drawing, it will be all that is required for settlement.

________ I/We request a boundary survey that will include a location drawing and will identify and mark the property boundary. I/We have read and understand that this may not be required for settlement purposes and will increase the cost of the services.

____

____

The regulations are designed to protect consumers by (i) establishing minimum performance levels to be exercised by all Maryland surveyors; and (ii) requiring surveyors to provide the above disclosures to property owners and potential purchasers of property to clarify the limitations of location drawings and the differences between location drawings and boundary surveys. The new rules, however, do not appear to affect the appropriateness of location drawings for use in connection with most home purchases and refinances.

(c) Unrecorded mechanics' liens

The third Standard Exception generally relates to unrecorded mechanics' liens. In many jurisdictions, mechanics' liens or claims for liens may be filed at a subsequent date and yet have priority from an earlier date, such as the date of visible commencement of the improvement. In this type of situation, the mechanics' lien claimant is entitled to superiority and has, in effect, an inchoate lien for a period of time. Since there is no public record of the existence of the lien, the company would have no liability for it when the existence of the lien becomes known. In Maryland, however, in light of the decision of the Supreme Court of Maryland in *Barry Properties v. Fick Brothers Roofing Co.*,[26] and the enactment of a revised mechanics' lien law,[27] some title companies, if asked, will remove the mechanics' lien exception from the lenders and owner's title insurance policy. This is a covered risk in the enhanced title insurance policy.

The attorney must alert the client to the hazards involved with issues relating to the Standard Exceptions. Either the client must assume the risks without protection, or other means must be contemplated to minimize the risks, such as negotiating with the insurer a waiver of some or all of the exceptions.

3. [§ 4.19] Special exceptions in Schedule B

(a) Generally

In addition to the Standard Exceptions, there is a place on Schedule B of the policy for the listing of Special Exceptions which, in the case of the ALTA form, starts with real estate taxes and then leaves room for the insertion on the form of other items dealt with as Special Exceptions in certain situations and localities. These include defects, encumbrances, liens, covenants, restrictions, or other matters affecting the particular property being insured; for example, prior mortgages which are not yet released will be listed under the Special Exceptions section of Schedule B of the policy. In some instances, the Special Exceptions will relate to matters subject to which purchasers ordinarily take title, such as subdivision plats, covenants and restrictions, public utility easements, and the like. Nonetheless, even

---

26 277 Md. 15, 353 A.2d 222 (1976). For an analysis of Maryland mechanics' lien law post-*Barry*, see *York Roofing v. Adcock*, 333 Md. 158, 634 A.2d 39 (1993). See also *Wolf Org. v. Oles*, 119 Md. App. 357, 705 A.2d 40 (1998), in which the Supreme Court of Maryland held that one who executed a contract with an owner/builder to purchase real property improved by a dwelling to be constructed during the executory period, is not an "owner" of the property within the meaning of the Maryland Mechanic's Lien Statute, and the contract purchaser's equitable interest in the property was not subject to mechanic's lien, because the contract purchaser was not a party to the contract for doing the work or furnishing the material for the dwelling, which may give rise to a lien. 119 Md. App. at 372.

27 MD. CODE ANN., REAL PROPERTY §§ 9-101–9-114 (2015 & Supp. 2022) (hereinafter REAL PROP. §).

though it is customary for the purchaser to take title subject to these matters, the attorney must, as always, be certain that the consequences of doing so are pointed out to the client. In other cases, Schedule B may contain Special Exceptions that are not acceptable to the purchaser. These may relate to prior mortgages and judgments which need to be released, or they may relate to specific title defects involving prior owners. When such matters are shown in the Special Exceptions section of the policy, the attorney for the purchaser must follow up with the company and with the seller's attorney to assure that the matters will be cleared up prior to closing.

In order to better understand the types of typical exceptions which appear in a title insurance policy, set forth below is a list of typical title exceptions that an attorney would find in the Special Exceptions section to a title insurance policy. These exceptions and their explanations are as follows:

(b) Taxes

> Real estate taxes, municipal charges and other public charges, taxes and assessments for the year ____ and all subsequent years, not due and payable at Date of Policy.

Basically, this exception excludes from coverage under the policy any liens resulting from the non-payment of future real estate taxes and other municipal charges and assessments. Note that the exception is written in such a manner to insure the insured that taxes which are due and payable have been paid for the appropriate half of the fiscal year in which settlement occurs. The exception limits the coverage to exclude any assessments or levies which the taxing authority issues during the remainder of the tax year, or in future years. An example of a tax levy which could be issued during the tax year in which settlement occurs is the so-called "new improvements tax bill." It is not uncommon for the purchaser of a newly constructed home to receive an updated tax bill for a portion of the fiscal year in which settlement occurred when the property's assessed value as of settlement only reflected the value of the land. In those instances, the title company has no way of knowing at settlement when the tax assessment office will reassess the land to include the value of the improvements constructed thereon. A prudent purchaser's attorney might include a provision in the purchase contract obligating the seller to pay their prorated share of any such bill relating back to the seller's period of ownership. As for future tax years, real estate taxes can rise to the level of a lien superior to a purchase money mortgage, and the title company has no control over their payment for any year subsequent to the year in which settlement occurred.

(c) Restrictive covenants

Subject to restrictions against the manufacture or sale or traffic of intoxicating liquors as contained in deed from George Gelbach, Jr., and wife to Margaret Ruth

Spencer dated Oct. 10, 1855, and recorded among the Land Records of Baltimore County in Liber H.M.F. No. 13, folio 203.

A large proportion of residential properties are subject to restrictive covenants of various degrees and import. Most, as with the covenant shown above, are concerned with preventing the property from being used in an offensive or noxious manner, such as for raising farm animals, erecting an outhouse, or manufacturing liquor. It is also quite common to find covenants that purport to restrict the race or creed of the purchasers to which the property can be sold, but since such covenants are unenforceable and repugnant to public policy, the title companies will not take exception to them. In fact, the 2021 Policy Schedule B begins, "Some historical land records contain Discriminatory Covenants that are illegal and unenforceable by law. This policy treats any Discriminatory Covenant in a document referenced in Schedule B as if each Discriminatory Covenant is redacted, repudiated, removed, and not republished or recirculated."

Generally, restrictive covenants should be viewed as being beneficial to the property owner because they are usually applicable to surrounding properties in the neighborhood as well as to the subject property. Therefore, they will benefit the property by assuring a standard of compliance and uniformity of use in the neighborhood—all of which is designed to ensure stability in property values. However, care must be taken to make sure that the covenants will not prevent the purchaser from using the property as he or she intends.

(d) Public use

"Subject to the right of the public to use that portion of the property lying within the bed of Helendale Street, formerly Third Street, 25 feet wide, running from the south side of Sulgrave Avenue to the north side of South Road."

Many legal descriptions contain calls which run to the middle of the street or alley on which the property binds. The title company will take exception to so much of the property as lies within the bed of the street or alley. This exception then puts the landowner on notice that despite the fact the property's legal description literally includes a portion of the adjoining road or alley, the landowner's use of that portion of the property is subject to the public's rights of unrestricted passage and use.

(e) Recorded plat

"Subject to a 10-foot widening of the strip along South Road as shown on Amended Sheet No. 1, of James D. Davidson Plat recorded among the Land Records of Baltimore City in Plat Pocket Folder J.F.C. No. 2031."

It is also standard for the title company to take exception to any matters disclosed on a recorded plat of the property. In the plat referred to above, there was a provision wherein the developer reserved for the municipality the right to widen a public street. The exception is necessary to put the landowner on notice that a portion of the property has been reserved for the potential widening of the adjacent public street. The attorney needs to verify that the widening, if it occurs, will not interfere with existing or proposed improvements. It is unlikely that the proposed widening would interfere with any improvements on the property because applicable setback requirements generally prohibit the construction of improvements too close to the boundary lines of the property.

In addition to these types of exceptions, it is quite common to find special exceptions for building setback requirements (as noted earlier in this chapter) and utility easements. Utility easements are generally located along the boundary lines of properties and are, therefore, not problems for the landowner. In fact, they can be viewed as beneficial to the landowner because the utility company has the legal capacity to bring its service to the property.

The basic policy of title insurance written on the "standard form" may be varied by endorsement.[28] The endorsement form may also be a "standard form," such as an ALTA form, or it may be specially designed to fit the needs of a particular situation. In some instances, endorsement of the policy will be a matter of negotiation between the insured and the company, whereas in others it may be handled as a matter of course. Some forms of endorsement will add coverage and protection to the insured while others will exculpate the company and insulate it from liability. Consequently, the attorney must inform the client as to the effect of the endorsement.

Perhaps the most common form of endorsement to the owner's policy is a waiver of one or more of the three Standard Exceptions contained in Schedule B of the policy.[29] For example, if the property is a residence and is occupied solely by the seller who is willing to give the company an affidavit to that effect, the company will ordinarily waive the exception for rights of parties in possession other than the insured in the insured's owner's policy. If a recent boundary survey of the property discloses no encroachments, overlaps, or boundary line disputes, the company will generally also waive this exception in the insured's owner's policy.

Obtaining an endorsement waiving the standard exceptions for the lender's policy can be a simple matter since all that is needed in most cases is a buyer's and/or seller's affidavit and/or location drawing designed to provide the company with basic information needed to assist it in determining whether to waive any or all of the standard exceptions by endorsement. In any event, waiver of the exceptions by endorsement is a matter of negotiation between the insured and the company.

---

28 *See* § **4.51** of this chapter.

29 See § **4.51** of this chapter for a form on which such a waiver is given.

Sometimes endorsement may be mandated by an uncertainty as to the applicable law involved in a particular transaction. For example, in many jurisdictions it is customary for the company to issue a series of endorsements when the title to be insured involves a condominium unit. Endorsements are required because the law applicable to condominium units varies substantially from the law regarding traditional fee simple ownership. An example of this is an affirmative declaration that the entire condominium project complies with the applicable condominium statute. If the company seeks to limit its liability as to specific matters arising because of the nature of condominium ownership, those matters will generally be set forth as special exceptions in Schedule B of the policy, e.g., a lien for Council of Unit Owners' or Homeowners' Association assessments, or right of first refusal, if any, in the Council of Unit Owners' or Homeowners' Association. Most forms of endorsement expand coverage afforded under the policy and frequently require the payment of an additional premium. A form of Condominium Endorsement is included in § **4.51** of this chapter. When the house is part of a planned unit development (as an increasing number of homes are), the same matters are covered by the Planned Unit Development Endorsement included in § **4.52**.

These instances are merely illustrative of special types of endorsements, but there are many other possible types which are adjusted to the needs of each transaction.

In recent years, most title insurers have relaxed traditional underwriting requirements as to the scope of the underlying title search used to identify and eliminate title risks. The customary "60 year" title search has given way to greatly reduced search periods, particularly for refinance and second mortgage loan transactions. Most lenders are satisfied in receiving the ALTA "Short Form Loan Policy," which includes "generic" exceptions as to typical matters affecting title, such as restrictions and easements. Affirmative coverage with respect to the particular generic exception is automatically provided by the Short Form policy, satisfactory to the lenders' needs. This approach means that there is no longer a requirement to identify the specific title exceptions applicable to the residential property at issue. Most title insurers, utilizing this type of approach for refinances and second mortgages, require the title searcher to "bring to date" the title from the date of the title deed, provided such deed represents the acquisition of title by the current owner for valuable consideration and not as a "gift" or "no consideration" transfer.[30]

Surprisingly, title insurers in Maryland are also trying similar approaches for underwriting owners' title insurance; however, most insurers have guidelines requiring at least a 60-year search.

---

30 See § **4.50** in this chapter for an example of the ALTA Short Form Loan Policy.

B. [§ 4.20] Enhanced Policies

Many title insurance underwriters began to offer policies that provided expanded coverage beyond the standard coverage of the 1992, 2006, and 2021 ALTA Owner's Policy. Most expanded policies, sometimes referred to as "enhanced policies," contain new types of coverage dealing with post-policy occurrences; improved access; improved coverage regarding violation of covenants, conditions, and restrictions; and zoning subdivision coverage, to name a few. Previously, such coverage was available only by endorsement. On Oct. 17, 1998, in response to the confusion caused by the variety of coverages offered in expanded policies by different title insurers, ALTA approved and adopted an expanded coverage policy for use on one-to-four family residential properties. This policy is known as the ALTA Homeowner's Policy of Title Insurance, and for purposes of this chapter shall be referred to as the "ALTA Homeowner's Policy." The goal of this policy is to provide not only enhanced coverage, but coverage written in plain English that can be reasonably understood by a homeowner. Unlike the 1992, 2006, and 2021 ALTA Owner's Policy that covers only those risks occurring before the policy date and the limited post-policy Covered Risks, the ALTA Homeowner's Policy contains coverages more closely associated with risk assumption, since the risk cannot be eliminated by either examination of a carefully prepared title search or inspection of the property. In addition, the ALTA Homeowner's Policy contains deductibles and limitations on liability applicable to certain coverage provisions. A sample ALTA Homeowner's Policy is provided in § **4.50** of this chapter. A summary of the new expanded coverage follows.

1. [§ 4.21] Post-policy coverage

This insurance covers loss arising from certain covered risks which first occur or mature after the Policy date. These risks include defects and adverse interests in the title, forgeries or impersonations, easements and restrictions on the land, and rights to limit the insured's use of the land. This coverage, however, is subject to Exclusion 4(a), therein for matters created, allowed, or agreed to by the insured.

2. [§ 4.22] Access

Access coverage specifically refers to loss if the insured does not have actual vehicular and pedestrian access to the land, based upon a legal right (i.e. an easement over a private way or a public way). Under the 1992 ALTA Owner's Policy, an insurer could avoid liability as long as the insured had some legal means of access to the land.

3. [§ 4.23] Restrictive covenants

This coverage insures against loss in the event the insured is required to correct or remove a violation of any covenant or restriction affecting the land, which occurred prior to the date the insured acquired the interest in the land.

4. [§ 4.24] Subdivision

Subdivision coverage not only insures the homeowner in the event a building permit cannot be obtained, but also covers the loss suffered by the insured required to remove or correct the subdivision violation. This covered risk is subject to deductibles or monetary limitations.

5. [§ 4.25] Building permit

Coverage is provided to the homeowner in the event the homeowner is forced to remove an existing structure because it was built without obtaining a permit from the proper government office issuing such building permits. This covered risk is subject to deductibles or monetary limitations.

6. [§ 4.26] Zoning

Zoning coverage insures against loss in the event the insured cannot use the land as a residence because such use violates an existing zoning law or regulation. It also covers loss if the insured is required to remove or correct existing structures because they violate an existing zoning law or regulation. This covered risk is subject to deductibles or monetary limitations.

7. [§ 4.27] Encroachments

There are four insuring provisions dealing with encroachments: (a) loss incurred as a result of removal of a structure encroaching on a neighbor's land; (b) encroachments of a neighbor's structure onto the insured land resulting in the unmarketability of the insured land; (c) future encroachments by a neighbors structures erected after the policy date; and (d) removal by the insured of structures encroaching onto an easement or over a set back line. The encroachment risks are subject to deductibles or monetary limitations.

8. [§ 4.28] Easements

This coverage insures against loss arising from damage to existing structures as a result of the use of any easement affecting the land.

9. [§ 4.29] Extraction or development of minerals

The homeowner is insured against loss if existing improvements, including lawns, trees, or shrubbery, are damaged because of a right to use the surface of the land for extraction or development of minerals, water, or other substances.

10. [§ 4.30] Supplemental tax assessments

This coverage insures the homeowner against loss from supplemental taxes which become due after the policy date for improvements constructed prior to purchase.

11. [§ 4.31] Street address

Schedule "A" of the policy now lists the street address, and the insured is covered against loss in the event there is no residence on the land, or if the residence on the described land does not correspond to the address listed in Schedule "A."

12. [§ 4.32] Continuation of coverage

This provision continues coverage to (a) recipients of the land who acquire title upon the death of the insured by operation of law; (b) a spouse who receives title upon dissolution of marriage; (c) the estate planning entity to which title is transferred after the date of the policy; (d) the beneficiaries of such an estate planning entity upon the insured's death; (e) anyone who receives title by a transfer effective on the death of the insured as authorized by law; and (f) any other named insured in Schedule A. Many individuals with a high net worth often transfer residences to trusts for estate planning purposes. Under the 1992 ALTA Owner's Policy, such individuals would have to purchase an additional title policy or obtain an endorsement; however, under the ALTA Homeowner's Policy, this additional expense is avoided.

13. [§ 4.33] Increased policy amount

The ALTA Homeowner's Policy provides automatic increase in the policy amount of 10% per year for the first five years following the policy date, to a maximum 150% of the initial policy amount.

The ALTA Homeowner's Policy and similar "Enhanced" policy forms used locally by Maryland title insurers provide enhanced coverage, but as would be expected, the premium for such coverage is higher than that charged for the ALTA Owner's Policy, due to the increased risks assumed by the insurer. Typically, rates range from a surcharge of 10-to-30% additional premium over the standard ALTA Owner's Policy. When recommending which type of policy the client should obtain, the attorney should consider the client's ability to pay the additional premium charged in order to obtain the superior form of policy coverage.

C. [§ 4.34] 2006 Policies

The 2006 ALTA forms that phased out the 1992 forms became obsolete effective January 2024 with the adoption of the 2021 ALTA forms collection. The coverage offered by both the 2006 and 1992 Policies are similar, but much of the legalese used in the 1992 Policies was replaced with a more user-friendly language, and the format had been streamlined for ease of use. Schedule A of the 2006 Policies includes: (1) the name and address of the insurer; (2) the address of the insured property; (3) and in the loan policy, a Check-the-Box list of endorsements. The 2006 Policies offered a few new covered risks, but the most notable difference from the

1992 Policies was the removal of the "Exclusions" to the "Exclusions From Coverage" provisions of that earlier policy. Listed below are the most noteworthy of the additional "Covered Risks" of the 2006 Policies:

1. [§ 4.35] Covered risks

a. *Gap coverage*—Both the owners' and lenders' forms of the 2006 Policies include coverage for losses that occur post-closing or after the date of the policy, but prior to the recording. This new coverage effectively shifts the risk from the insured to the insurer for any deeds, liens, judgment, or mortgages recorded during the "Gap" between closing and document recording.

b. *Survey coverage*—The 1992 Policies only covered the land described in the policies and did not include any property beyond the boundary liens of the property described in Schedule "A" and Schedule "C" of that policy. The 2006 Policies expand coverage for losses sustained as a result of encroachments of the insured's improvements onto neighboring land. The new policies now clearly provide coverage to encroachments onto the insured's land and encroachments off the insured's land onto a neighbor's land.

c. *Creditor's right coverage*—The 2006 Policies offer coverage for two types of creditors' rights risks where the 1992 exclusion contained an exception for claims arising as a result of an allegation of a fraudulent conveyance in a bankruptcy action. The first coverage protects against an attack by the prior chain of conveyances as fraudulent transfers while the second protects against an attack against the present transaction due to failure to record, or failure of the recording to give legally binding notice of its existence to a purchaser for value, a judgment, or a lien creditor.[31]

2. [§ 4.36] Conditions

The 2006 Policies refer to the obligations of the insurer and the insured as "Conditions." The major change in the Conditions provisions from the 1992 Policies include the following:

a. Changes in defined terms

i. *Amount of Insurance.* The 1992 Policies defined the amount of insurance available to pay claims as the dollar amount set forth in Schedule A. The 2006 Policies now determine the amount of insurance to be the amount

31 *See* Practicing Law Institute, *Title Insurance 2007: Mastering Critical Issues Facing Buyers, Sellers and Lenders*, Real Estate, Law & Prac. Course Handbook No. 11403 (2007).

provided in Schedule A, as such amount is increased or decreased by policy endorsements.

ii. *Insured.* The definition of "Insured" was expanded in the 2006 Policies which represent a significant change and improvement to the 1992 Policies. The new definition recognizes the following as an Insured:

1. A successor to the title by operation of law which includes heirs, devisees, survivors and personal representatives;
2. A successor by dissolution, merger, consolidation, and reorganization;
3. A successor to the Insured by conversion to another type of entity;
4. A grantee of the Insured by deed without payment of actual valuable consideration;
    (i) Where the equity interests of the grantee are wholly owned by the Insured;
    (ii) Where the grantee owns the Insured;
    (iii) Where the grantee is wholly owned by an affiliate of the Insured and the affiliate and Insured share a common parent; and
    (iv) Where the grantee is the trustee or beneficiary of a trust created by the Insured for estate planning reasons.

b. Public records

The 2006 Policies take into account the records of the U.S. District Court having jurisdiction where the land is located, which includes the recorded notices of environmental protection law violations.

3. [§ 4.37] Proof of loss

The 1992 Policies required the Insured to submit a written claim, or "Proof of Loss" describing the defect in title and the calculation of the loss suffered. If the Insured failed to submit such proof, the Insurer's obligation to indemnify and defend the Insured was terminated. The 2006 Policies effectively shift the burden of determining loss suffered from the Insured to the Insurer; however, the notice of a claim being made remains the duty of the Insured.

4. [§ 4.38] Compensation of insured for loss

The 2006 Policies add two more changes to benefit the Insured. In the event the Insurer is unsuccessful in defending or prosecuting the claim in order to avoid loss to the insured the 2006 Policies provide for an increase in the amount of insurance by 10% and, the Insured can choose to determine loss when the claim was made or at the conclusion of litigation.

5. [§ 4.39] Coinsurance

The 1992 Policies provided that if the Insured purchased title insurance in an amount that was less than the value of the land and improvements, the Insured became a coinsurer in the event of a partial loss. The Insurer would only pay the loss pro rata in the proportion that the amount of insurance at the date of the Policy bears to the value of the insured interest of the date of the Policy. The 2006 Policies have now eliminated this "Coinsurance" provision which provision would have been used to reduce the amount recoverable under an Insured's claim.

6. [§ 4.40] Apportionment

The 2006 Policies also eliminated the "Apportionment" provisions of the 1992 Policies which applied to a single policy that covered two or more parcels, not used as a single site. Such apportionment provisions limited the recovery available in the event loss occurred on fewer than all parcels. The 1992 Policies computed the loss on a pro rata basis, as if the amount of insurance was divided *pro rata*, as to the value of each separate parcel to the whole. The 2006 Policies permit the application of the entire amount of insurance to any separate parcel on which a loss occurs.

7. [§ 4.41] Arbitration

There were two changes made to the "Arbitration Provision" of the 1992 Policies by the 2006 Policies. First, the Insurer or the Insured may demand binding arbitration when the amount of insurance listed on Schedule A of the Policy is two million dollars or less, as opposed to the previous one million dollar threshold. Secondly, the rules applicable to the arbitration proceeding are the Title Insurance Arbitration Rules of the ALTA, which are set out on the ALTA website, and not the American Arbitration Association rules applied under the 1992 Policies. This clause is usually deleted upon request by the Insurer if requested by the proposed insured.

8. [§ 4.42] 2021 Policies

The 2021 ALTA forms became effective as of July 1, 2021, and while the 2006 forms were scheduled for decertification on December 31, 2022, the 2006 forms are still available for use if requested. The changes range from refinements of grammar and punctuation, new or amended defined terms, and amending existing coverages and exclusions, to new coverages and exclusions. Listed below are some of the more notable changes adopted:

1 The Policy Jacket now includes language that incorporates the coverage provided by the ALTA 39 endorsement. A policy, once issued with a Policy Number and Date of Policy, is valid even if issued electronically and/or without any signatures.

2 Covered Risk 2 adds new examples of title defects that can cause a covered loss. Remote Online Notarization (RON) having become available in many

jurisdictions, Covered Risk 2 now includes coverage for loss resulting from improper execution of documents affecting Titel by RON, as well as "repudiation of an electronic signature by a person who signed the document because the electronic signature was not valid under applicable electronic transactions law." Covered Risk 9 of the 2021 Loan Policy adds the same coverage for the lender resulting from improper execution of the Insured Mortgage. Additionally, the survey coverage was enhanced to specifically include boundary line overlaps (if they would have shown up on a survey).

3 Covered Risk 10 of the 2021 Loan Policy was updated to enumerate the components of the Indebtedness that would benefit from "priority" coverage, including: the principal disbursed as of the Date of Policy; the interest on the obligation secured by the Insured Mortgage; reasonable expense of foreclosure; amounts advanced for insurance premiums; and taxes and association fees advanced. While the principal is limited to the amount disbursed as of the policy date, this can be expanded by obtaining an ALTA 14 endorsement to cover future advances.

4 The definition of the "Insured" has been expanded in the both the 2021 Loan and Owner's policies to include "Affiliates." An Affiliate is defined as an Entity that: is wholly owned by the Insured; that wholly owns the insured; or if that Entity and the Insured are both wholly owned by the same person or Entity. Therefore, under the 2021 Loan Policy, an Affiliate who acquired title through a foreclosure or a deed-in-lieu of foreclosure would be an Insured under the policy, whether or not the Affiliate owned or held the indebtedness.

5 One notable change to the Exclusions is found in Exclusion 3(e) of the 2021 Owner's Policy, which was updated to clarify the purpose of the 2006 Exclusion 3(e): to exclude losses or damage that would not have been sustained had the Insured paid consideration sufficient to qualify as a bona fide purchaser, as opposed to paying "value" or "fair market value."

6 A new exclusion, numbered 7 in the Owner's Policy and numbered 9 in the Loan policy, excludes loss caused by "any discrepancy in the quantity of the area, square footage, or acreage of the Land or of any improvement to the Land." While technically new to the Exclusions, discrepancies in area have generally always been excluded from coverage by Schedule B exceptions.

7 Schedule A has been updated to add an optional "Transaction Identification Data" header, which includes fields for the Issuing Agent, Issuing Office, the Issuing Office's ALTA Registry ID, the Issuing Office's File Number, and the Property Address. While none of this information would be an insured matter, it is intended to serve as easily identifiable reference information to improve communication for post-closing inquiries.

8 Coverage Limits have been increased in Condition 8. The 2006 Owner's Policy Condition 8(b)(i) stated that if the insurer is unsuccessful in establishing the Title as insured, the Amount of Insurance would be increased by 10%. The 2021 Owner's Policy Condition 8(d) increased the Amount of Insurance by 15% if the insurer is unsuccessful.

IV. [§ 4.43] NEGOTIATING COVERAGE AND RATES

It is not only possible but highly likely that the attorney will be able to negotiate additional coverage for the client should the need arise. The attorney for the insured may request that any or all of the standard exceptions contained in Schedule B of the policy be waived or eliminated by endorsement. In some instances, such a request will be complied with perfunctorily, but in others, the attorney may be requested to obtain documentation and submit it to the company. Additional coverage may also be requested where the situation involves encroachments, or any other circumstances in which the attorney is of the opinion that the client needs additional protection. The cost of certain endorsements representing special risks can be the subject of negotiation; however, the Maryland Insurance Commissioner requires that filed rates be charged for standard title insurance risks.

Where policy is required for a lender at the same time an owner's policy is purchased, most companies will issue the lender's policy for a nominal simultaneous issue fee provided that the purchaser obtains an owner's title insurance policy, usually $175-$200.00.

V. [§ 4.44] THE NEEDS OF THE CLIENT

Assuming that the title insurance commitment is in order, the survey reveals no problems, and inspection of the property and inquiry of persons in the vicinity reveal nothing out of order, the transaction will close and a policy of title insurance will be issued in due course in accordance with the terms of the commitment or binder. Some attorneys representing purchasers at closing have a representative of the title insurer mark up the binder to show the exact provisions of the final policy and initial all changes. Of course, when the actual title insurance policy is received, the attorney must compare it with the binder to make sure that no additional exceptions have been added and that the documents otherwise conform to one another. The lender in a residential deed obtains similar "at closing" coverage by having the "gap exception"[32] marked so as to be deleted from the final loan policy.

At the outset, the attorney should advise the client whether an owner's policy of title insurance is desirable, or if the purchaser should "rely" upon the title

[32] See § **4.50** in this chapter for an example of the ALTA Short Form Loan Policy.

insurance company's willingness to issue a policy to the lender (mortgagee). Bear in mind that the lender's policy does not adequately protect the purchaser/borrower, even when it is the latter who pays for the policy. While a lender's title insurance policy relates both to the validity of the mortgage and to the quality of the landowner's title, it does not do so for the benefit of the landowner. It is possible, moreover, that the quality of the landowner's title which might be acceptable to a lender would not be acceptable to the landowner, although this possibility becomes remote when the amount of the loan constitutes a high percentage of the total value of the land. In any event, it is both unsafe and unwise for the purchaser or the attorney to assume that the title insurance company is willing to issue a policy to the owner which contains only those exceptions and exclusions appearing in a lender's policy.

Furthermore, the Supreme Court of Maryland[33] has held that a document is considered "recorded" and effective for purposes of REAL PROP § 3-203 despite the fact that the Clerk has failed to properly index the document. This places prospective purchasers of real estate in a very difficult position. For example, even if the lender's title insurance policy reveals no open liens or encumbrances, the landowner is ill-advised to rely on this because the owner will nonetheless be subject to the legal operation and effect of any liens and encumbrances which have been "recorded"—i.e., documents received by the Clerk and stamped with a liber and folio number—but not properly indexed. The landowner's only method of assuring protection against these types of hidden defects is to shift the burden onto the title company by purchasing an owner's policy of title insurance. Then, even though the title company's title search fails to locate the recorded but unindexed document, the owner's title insurance policy will protect the landowner against claims from the lienholder or encumbrancer.[34]

Once it is determined that the situation requires an owner's policy of title insurance, the attorney should explain the coverage afforded by that policy to the client. In the same way that a competent attorney would never permit a client to accept a title abstract without examining it and issuing an opinion as to its impact on the title, the attorney should not permit the client to accept an owner's title insurance policy without a full explanation of its terms as they affect the title being acquired.

The attorney's next involvement with the title insurance policy will not come until a title problem arises during his client's ownership of the property or when the contract to sell the property is made. If the client suffers a loss due to a matter

---

33 *Frank v. Storer*, 308 Md. 194, 204, 517 A.2d 1098 (1986), *overruled in part as stated in Greenpoint Mortgage Funding, Inc. v. Schlossberg*, 390 Md. 211, 888 A.2d 297 (2005).

34 *See* Michele Gilligan, *The Role of Indexing in Record Notice under the Maryland Recording Statutes*, U. BALT. L.F. 18 (Spring 1987).

not excluded or excepted from the title insurance policy, the question of damages becomes very important. One of the most important functions of the title policy is to give the property owner someone to look to for defense of attacks on the title. Once advised of a title problem, the insurer has the option of:

(A) paying the insured's loss;

(B) clearing the defects within a reasonable time, or

(C) showing that the defects do not exist.

While the insurer may decide to pursue a course of litigation concerning a title that it agrees is defective, litigation to final judgment is not a condition precedent to the insured's right to recover from the insurer.[35] Title companies are generally very diligent in defending clients, and their services represent a valuable part of the insurance coverage. However, if an adverse decision is rendered, it is important to know the measure of damages which will be applied. One rule is to measure damages by the difference between the value of the premises as they are, compared to the value as insured on the date of the policy. Another approach is to look at the loss measured as of the time of discovery.[36]

If title to only part of the insured premises is defective, damages are not limited to the value of the part so affected but include any additional expenses flowing from the title defect. Thus, if the property owner makes a bona fide agreement to allow a purchaser an abatement to the purchase price should title fail as to a certain part of the property, this abatement will be the measure of damage rather than the actual value of the portion of the property as a percentage of the entire property. However, there must be "actual damage" to the insured if there is to be recovery under the policy.

VI. [§ 4.45] BIBLIOGRAPHY

This chapter includes only a general treatment of the subject of title insurance. The attorney who wishes to explore the subject in more detail is referred to the law review articles cited in this chapter and to the following:

1. ABA Section of Real Property, Probate and Trust Law, *Title Insurance and You: What Every Lawyer Should Know* (1979).
2. American Land Title Ass'n, *The Title Industry: White Papers*, Vol. 1 (1976).
3. Haymond, *Title Insurance Risks of Which the Public Records Give No Notice*, 1 So. Cal. L. Rev. 422 (1928).
4. Practicing Law Institute, *Title Insurance in Major Real Estate Transactions*, Real Estate Law & Prac. Course Handbook No. 144 (1978).

---

[35] *Stewart Title Guar. Co. v. West*, 110 Md. App. 114, 676 A.2d 953 (1996).

[36] Note, *The Insured's Rights against the Title Insurer*, 6 Case W. Res. L. Rev. 49 (1954).

5. Practicing Law Institute, *Title Insurance: The Attorney's Role*, REAL ESTATE LAW & PRAC. COURSE HANDBOOK NO. 158 (1979).
6. Practicing Law Institute, *Title Insurance: Beyond the Basics.*
7. REAL ESTATE LAW & PRAC. COURSE HANDBOOK NO. 204 (1981).
8. Practicing Law Institute, *Title Insurance: Choosing a Title insurance Policy Form,* REAL ESTATE LAW AND PRAC. COURSE HANDBOOK NO. 448 (1999).
9. Practicing Law Institute, *Title Insurance: Enhanced Protection for Residential Homeowners*, REAL ESTATE LAW & PRAC. COURSE HANDBOOK NO. (462) (2000).
10. Rieger, the *Issue of Real Property—Evolution to Revolution: Enhanced Title Insurance Protection.* XXXIV MD. BAR J., NO. 5, p. 25 (September/October 2001).
11. Practicing Law Institute, *Title Insurance 2007: Mastering Critical Issues Facing Buyers, Sellers & Lenders*, REAL ESTATE LAW AND PRAC. COURSE HANDBOOK NO. 11403 (2007).
12. American Law Institute-American Bar Association, *The New 2006 Alta Policies: The Industry Listens!*, SN001 ALI-ABI 1025 (2007).

VII. APPENDIX

The Appendix begins on the next page.

A. [§ 4.46] Commitment for Title Insurance

ALTA COMMITMENT FOR TITLE INSURANCE
issued by
BLANK TITLE INSURANCE COMPANY

NOTICE

IMPORTANT—READ CAREFULLY: THIS COMMITMENT IS AN OFFER TO ISSUE ONE OR MORE TITLE INSURANCE POLICIES. ALL CLAIMS OR REMEDIES SOUGHT AGAINST THE COMPANY INVOLVING THE CONTENT OF THIS COMMITMENT OR THE POLICY MUST BE BASED SOLELY IN CONTRACT.

THIS COMMITMENT IS NOT AN ABSTRACT OF TITLE, REPORT OF THE CONDITION OF TITLE, LEGAL OPINION, OPINION OF TITLE, OR OTHER REPRESENTATION OF THE STATUS OF TITLE. THE PROCEDURES USED BY THE COMPANY TO DETERMINE INSURABILITY OF THE TITLE, INCLUDING ANY SEARCH AND EXAMINATION, ARE PROPRIETARY TO THE COMPANY, WERE PERFORMED SOLELY FOR THE BENEFIT OF THE COMPANY, AND CREATE NO EXTRACONTRACTUAL LIABILITY TO ANY PERSON, INCLUDING A PROPOSED INSURED.

THE COMPANY'S OBLIGATION UNDER THIS COMMITMENT IS TO ISSUE A POLICY TO A PROPOSED INSURED IDENTIFIED IN SCHEDULE A IN ACCORDANCE WITH THE TERMS AND PROVISIONS OF THIS COMMITMENT. THE COMPANY HAS NO LIABILITY OR OBLIGATION INVOLVING THE CONTENT OF THIS COMMITMENT TO ANY OTHER PERSON.

COMMITMENT TO ISSUE POLICY

Subject to the Notice; Schedule B, Part I—Requirements; Schedule B, Part II—Exceptions; and the Commitment Conditions, [Blank Title Insurance Company], a [Blank] (the "Company"), commits to issue the Policy according to the terms and provisions of this Commitment. This Commitment is effective as of the Commitment Date shown in Schedule A for each Policy described in Schedule A, only when the Company has entered in Schedule A both the specified dollar amount as the Proposed Amount of Insurance and the name of the Proposed Insured.

If all of the Schedule B, Part I—Requirements have not been met within ______ *(Insert the time period)* after the Commitment Date, this Commitment terminates and the Company's liability and obligation end.

COMMITMENT CONDITIONS

1. DEFINITIONS

a. "Discriminatory Covenant": Any covenant, condition, restriction, or limitation that is unenforceable under applicable law because it illegally discriminates against a class of individuals based on personal characteristics such as race, color, religion, sex, sexual orientation, gender identity, familial status, disability, national origin, or other legally protected class.

b. "Knowledge" or "Known": Actual knowledge or actual notice, but not constructive notice imparted by the Public Records.

c. "Land": The land described in Item 5 of Schedule A and improvements located on that land that by State law constitute real property. The term "Land" does not include any property beyond that described in Schedule A, nor any right, title, interest, estate, or easement in any abutting street, road, avenue, alley, lane, right-of-way, body of water, or waterway, but does not modify or limit the extent that a right of access to and from the Land is to be insured by the Policy.

d. "Mortgage": A mortgage, deed of trust, trust deed, security deed, or other real property security instrument, including one evidenced by electronic means authorized by law.

e. "Policy": Each contract of title insurance, in a form adopted by the American Land Title Association, issued or to be issued by the Company pursuant to this Commitment.

f. "Proposed Amount of Insurance": Each dollar amount specified in Schedule A as the Proposed Amount of Insurance of each Policy to be issued pursuant to this Commitment.

g. "Proposed Insured": Each person identified in Schedule A as the Proposed Insured of each Policy to be issued pursuant to this Commitment.

h. "Public Records": The recording or filing system established under State statutes in effect at the Commitment Date under which a document must be recorded or filed to impart constructive notice of matters relating to the Title to a purchaser for value without Knowledge. The term "Public Records" does not include any other recording or filing system, including any pertaining to environmental remediation or protection, planning, permitting, zoning, licensing, building, health, public safety, or national security matters.

i. "State": The state or commonwealth of the United States within whose exterior boundaries the Land is located. The term "State" also includes the District of Columbia, the Commonwealth of Puerto Rico, the U.S. Virgin Islands, and Guam.

j. "Title": The estate or interest in the Land identified in Item 3 of Schedule A.

2. If all of the Schedule B, Part I—Requirements have not been met within the time period specified in the Commitment to Issue Policy, this Commitment terminates and the Company's liability and obligation end.
3. The Company's liability and obligation is limited by and this Commitment is not valid without:
   a. the Notice;
   b. the Commitment to Issue Policy;
   c. the Commitment Conditions;
   d. Schedule A;
   e. Schedule B, Part I—Requirements;[and]
   f. Schedule B, Part II—Exceptions[; and
   g. a counter-signature by the Company or its issuing agent that may be in electronic form].
4. COMPANY'S RIGHT TO AMEND

   The Company may amend this Commitment at any time. If the Company amends this Commitment to add a defect, lien, encumbrance, adverse claim, or other matter recorded in the Public Records prior to the Commitment Date, any liability of the Company is limited by Commitment Condition 5. The Company is not liable for any other amendment to this Commitment.
5. LIMITATIONS OF LIABILITY
   a. The Company's liability under Commitment Condition 4 is limited to the Proposed Insured's actual expense incurred in the interval between the Company's delivery to the Proposed Insured of the Commitment and the delivery of the amended Commitment, resulting from the Proposed Insured's good faith reliance to:
      i. comply with the Schedule B, Part I—Requirements;
      ii. eliminate, with the Company's written consent, any Schedule B, Part II—Exceptions; or
      iii. acquire the Title or create the Mortgage covered by this Commitment.
   b. The Company is not liable under Commitment Condition 5.a. if the Proposed Insured requested the amendment or had Knowledge of the matter and did not notify the Company about it in writing.
   c. The Company is only liable under Commitment Condition 4 if the Proposed Insured would not have incurred the expense had the Commitment included the added matter when the Commitment was first delivered to the Proposed Insured.
   d. The Company's liability does not exceed the lesser of the Proposed Insured's actual expense incurred in good faith and described in Commitment Condition 5.a. or the Proposed Amount of Insurance.

e. The Company is not liable for the content of the Transaction Identification Data, if any.

f. The Company is not obligated to issue the Policy referred to in this Commitment unless all of the Schedule B, Part I—Requirements have been met to the satisfaction of the Company.

g. The Company's liability is further limited by the terms and provisions of the Policy to be issued to the Proposed Insured.

6. LIABILITY OF THE COMPANY MUST BE BASED ON THIS COMMITMENT; CHOICE OF LAW AND CHOICE OF FORUM

a. Only a Proposed Insured identified in Schedule A, and no other person, may make a claim under this Commitment.

b. Any claim must be based in contract under the State law of the State where the Land is located and is restricted to the terms and provisions of this Commitment. Any litigation or other proceeding brought by the Proposed Insured against the Company must be filed only in a State or federal court having jurisdiction.

c. This Commitment, as last revised, is the exclusive and entire agreement between the parties with respect to the subject matter of this Commitment and supersedes all prior commitment negotiations, representations, and proposals of any kind, whether written or oral, express or implied, relating to the subject matter of this Commitment.

d. The deletion or modification of any Schedule B, Part II—Exception does not constitute an agreement or obligation to provide coverage beyond the terms and provisions of this Commitment or the Policy.

e. Any amendment or endorsement to this Commitment must be in writing[and authenticated by a person authorized by the Company].

f. When the Policy is issued, all liability and obligation under this Commitment will end and the Company's only liability will be under the Policy.

7. IF THIS COMMITMENT IS ISSUED BY AN ISSUING AGENT

The issuing agent is the Company's agent only for the limited purpose of issuing title insurance commitments and policies. The issuing agent is not the Company's agent for closing, settlement, escrow, or any other purpose.

8. PRO-FORMA POLICY

The Company may provide, at the request of a Proposed Insured, a pro-forma policy illustrating the coverage that the Company may provide. A pro-forma policy neither reflects the status of Title at the time that the pro-forma policy is delivered to a Proposed Insured, nor is it a commitment to insure.

9. CLAIMS PROCEDURES

This Commitment incorporates by reference all Conditions for making a claim in the Policy to be issued to the Proposed Insured. Commitment Condition 9 does not modify the limitations of liability in Commitment Conditions 5 and 6.

10. CLASS ACTION

ALL CLAIMS AND DISPUTES ARISING OUT OF OR RELATING TO THIS COMMITMENT, INCLUDING ANY SERVICE OR OTHER MATTER IN CONNECTION WITH ISSUING THIS COMMITMENT, ANY BREACH OF A COMMITMENT PROVISION, OR ANY OTHER CLAIM OR DISPUTE ARISING OUT OF OR RELATING TO THE TRANSACTION GIVING RISE TO THIS COMMITMENT, MUST BE BROUGHT IN AN INDIVIDUAL CAPACITY. NO PARTY MAY SERVE AS PLAINTIFF, CLASS MEMBER, OR PARTICIPANT IN ANY CLASS OR REPRESENTATIVE PROCEEDING. ANY POLICY ISSUED PURSUANT TO THIS COMMITMENT WILL CONTAIN A CLASS ACTION CONDITION.

[**11.** ARBITRATION

The Policy contains an arbitration clause. All arbitrable matters when the Proposed Amount of Insurance is $2,000,000 or less may be arbitrated at the election of either the Company or the Proposed Insured as the exclusive remedy of the parties. A Proposed Insured may review a copy of the arbitration rules at http://www.alta.org/arbitration.]

[Transaction Identification Data, for which the Company assumes no liability as set forth in Commitment Condition 5.e.:

Issuing Agent:

Issuing Office:

Issuing Office's ALTA® Registry ID:

Loan ID Number:

Commitment Number:

Issuing Office File Number:

Property Address:]

[Revision Number:]

SCHEDULE A

1. Commitment Date:

2. Policy to be issued:

a. [2021 ALTA® Owner's Policy][2021 ALTA® Loan Policy][_____ ALTA® _________ Policy]

Proposed Insured: _______________

Proposed Amount of Insurance: $_______________

The estate or interest to be insured: _______________

[b. [2021 ALTA® Owner's Policy][2021 ALTA® Loan Policy][_____ ALTA® _________ Policy]

Proposed Insured: _______________

Proposed Amount of Insurance: $_______________

The estate or interest to be insured: _______________]

[c. [2021 ALTA® Owner's Policy][2021 ALTA® Loan Policy][_____ ALTA® _________ Policy]

Proposed Insured: _______________

Proposed Amount of Insurance: $_______________

The estate or interest to be insured: _______________]

3. The estate or interest in the Land at the Commitment Date is: *(Identify each estate or interest covered, i.e., fee, leasehold, etc.)*

4. The Title is, at the Commitment Date, vested in[:] *(Identify vesting for each estate or interest identified in Item 3 above)*[and, as disclosed in the Public Records, has been since *(Date)*]

5. The Land is described as follows:

BLANK TITLE INSURANCE COMPANY

By:_________________________

[Authorized Signatory]

SCHEDULE B, PART I—Requirements

All of the following Requirements must be met:

1. The Proposed Insured must notify the Company in writing of the name of any party not referred to in this Commitment who will obtain an interest in the Land or who will make a loan on the Land. The Company may then make additional Requirements or Exceptions.

2. Pay the agreed amount for the estate or interest to be insured.

3. Pay the premiums, fees, and charges for the Policy to the Company.

4. Documents satisfactory to the Company that convey the Title or create the Mortgage to be insured, or both, must be properly authorized, executed, delivered, and recorded in the Public Records.

(Documents to be listed here)

(Additional Requirements may be listed here by number)

SCHEDULE B, PART II—Exceptions

Some historical land records contain Discriminatory Covenants that are illegal and unenforceable by law. This Commitment and the Policy treat any Discriminatory Covenant in a document referenced in Schedule B as if each Discriminatory Covenant is redacted, repudiated, removed, and not republished or recirculated. Only the remaining provisions of the document will be excepted from coverage.

The Policy will not insure against loss or damage resulting from the terms and conditions of any lease or easement identified in Schedule A, and will include the following Exceptions unless cleared to the satisfaction of the Company:

[**1.** Any defect, lien, encumbrance, adverse claim, or other matter that appears for the first time in the Public Records or is created, attaches, or is disclosed between the Commitment Date and the date on which all of the Schedule B, Part I—Requirements are met.]

(Additional Exceptions may be listed here by number)

B. [§ 4.47] ALTA Owner's Title Insurance Policy (2021)

ALTA OWNER'S POLICY OF TITLE INSURANCE
issued by
BLANK TITLE INSURANCE COMPANY

This policy, when issued by the Company with a Policy Number and the Date of Policy, is valid even if this policy or any endorsement to this policy is issued electronically or lacks any signature.

Any notice of claim and any other notice or statement in writing required to be given to the Company under this policy must be given to the Company at the address shown in Condition 17.

COVERED RISKS

SUBJECT TO THE EXCLUSIONS FROM COVERAGE, THE EXCEPTIONS FROM COVERAGE CONTAINED IN SCHEDULE B, AND THE CONDITIONS, [Blank Title Insurance Company], a [Blank] corporation (the "Company"), insures as of the Date of Policy and, to the extent stated in Covered Risks 9 and 10, after the Date of Policy, against loss or damage, not exceeding the Amount of Insurance, sustained or incurred by the Insured by reason of:

1. The Title being vested other than as stated in Schedule A.

2. Any defect in or lien or encumbrance on the Title. Covered Risk 2 includes, but is not limited to, insurance against loss from:

a. a defect in the Title caused by:

i. forgery, fraud, undue influence, duress, incompetency, incapacity, or impersonation;

ii. the failure of a person or Entity to have authorized a transfer or conveyance;

iii. a document affecting the Title not properly authorized, created, executed, witnessed, sealed, acknowledged, notarized (including by remote online notarization), or delivered;

iv. a failure to perform those acts necessary to create a document by electronic means authorized by law;

v. a document executed under a falsified, expired, or otherwise invalid power of attorney;

vi. a document not properly filed, recorded, or indexed in the Public Records, including the failure to have performed those acts by electronic means authorized by law;

vii. a defective judicial or administrative proceeding; or

viii. the repudiation of an electronic signature by a person that executed a document because the electronic signature on the document was not valid under applicable electronic transactions law.

b. the lien of real estate taxes or assessments imposed on the Title by a governmental authority due or payable, but unpaid.

c. the effect on the Title of an encumbrance, violation, variation, adverse circumstance, boundary line overlap, or encroachment (including an encroachment of an improvement across the boundary lines of the Land), but only if the encumbrance, violation, variation, adverse circumstance, boundary line overlap, or encroachment would have been disclosed by an accurate and complete land title survey of the Land.

3. Unmarketable Title.

4. No right of access to and from the Land.

5. A violation or enforcement of a law, ordinance, permit, or governmental regulation (including those relating to building and zoning), but only to the extent of the violation or enforcement described by the enforcing governmental authority in an Enforcement Notice that identifies a restriction, regulation, or prohibition relating to:

a. the occupancy, use, or enjoyment of the Land;

b. the character, dimensions, or location of an improvement on the Land;

c. the subdivision of the Land; or

d. environmental remediation or protection on the Land.

6. An enforcement of a governmental forfeiture, police, regulatory, or national security power, but only to the extent of the enforcement described by the enforcing governmental authority in an Enforcement Notice.

7. An exercise of the power of eminent domain, but only to the extent:

a. of the exercise described in an Enforcement Notice; or

b. the taking occurred and is binding on a purchaser for value without Knowledge.

8. An enforcement of a PACA-PSA Trust, but only to the extent of the enforcement described in an Enforcement Notice.

9. The Title being vested other than as stated in Schedule A, the Title being defective, or the effect of a court order providing an alternative remedy:

a. resulting from the avoidance, in whole or in part, of any transfer of all or any part of the Title to the Land or any interest in the Land occurring prior to the transaction vesting the Title because that prior transfer constituted a:

i. fraudulent conveyance, fraudulent transfer, or preferential transfer under federal bankruptcy, state insolvency, or similar state or federal creditors' rights law; or

ii. voidable transfer under the Uniform Voidable Transactions Act; or

b. because the instrument vesting the Title constitutes a preferential transfer under federal bankruptcy, state insolvency, or similar state or federal creditors' rights law by reason of the failure:

   i. to timely record the instrument vesting the Title in the Public Records after execution and delivery of the instrument to the Insured; or

   ii. of the recording of the instrument vesting the Title in the Public Records to impart notice of its existence to a purchaser for value or to a judgment or lien creditor.

10. Any defect in or lien or encumbrance on the Title or other matter included in Covered Risks 1 through 9 that has been created or attached or has been filed or recorded in the Public Records subsequent to the Date of Policy and prior to the recording of the deed or other instrument vesting the Title in the Public Records.

DEFENSE OF COVERED CLAIMS

The Company will also pay the costs, attorneys' fees, and expenses incurred in defense of any matter insured against by this policy, but only to the extent provided in the Conditions.

[Witness clause]

BLANK TITLE INSURANCE COMPANY

By: ______________________________
[Authorized Signatory]

By: ______________________________
[Authorized Signatory]

EXCLUSIONS FROM COVERAGE

The following matters are excluded from the coverage of this policy, and the Company will not pay loss or damage, costs, attorneys' fees, or expenses that arise by reason of:

1. a. any law, ordinance, permit, or governmental regulation (including those relating to building and zoning) that restricts, regulates, prohibits, or relates to:

   i. the occupancy, use, or enjoyment of the Land;

   ii. the character, dimensions, or location of any improvement on the Land;

   iii. the subdivision of land; or

   iv. environmental remediation or protection.

b. any governmental forfeiture, police, regulatory, or national security power.

c. the effect of a violation or enforcement of any matter excluded under Exclusion 1.a. or 1.b.

Exclusion 1 does not modify or limit the coverage provided under Covered Risk 5 or 6.

2. Any power of eminent domain. Exclusion 2 does not modify or limit the coverage provided under Covered Risk 7.
3. Any defect, lien, encumbrance, adverse claim, or other matter:
   a. created, suffered, assumed, or agreed to by the Insured Claimant;
   b. not Known to the Company, not recorded in the Public Records at the Date of Policy, but Known to the Insured Claimant and not disclosed in writing to the Company by the Insured Claimant prior to the date the Insured Claimant became an Insured under this policy;
   c. resulting in no loss or damage to the Insured Claimant;
   d. attaching or created subsequent to the Date of Policy (Exclusion 3.d. does not modify or limit the coverage provided under Covered Risk 9 or 10); or
   e. resulting in loss or damage that would not have been sustained if consideration sufficient to qualify the Insured named in Schedule A as a bona fide purchaser had been given for the Title at the Date of Policy.
4. Any claim, by reason of the operation of federal bankruptcy, state insolvency, or similar creditors' rights law, that the transaction vesting the Title as shown in Schedule A is a:
   a. fraudulent conveyance or fraudulent transfer;
   b. voidable transfer under the Uniform Voidable Transactions Act; or
   c. preferential transfer:
      i. to the extent the instrument of transfer vesting the Title as shown in Schedule A is not a transfer made as a contemporaneous exchange for new value; or
      ii. for any other reason not stated in Covered Risk 9.b.
5. Any claim of a PACA-PSA Trust. Exclusion 5 does not modify or limit the coverage provided under Covered Risk 8.
6. Any lien on the Title for real estate taxes or assessments imposed or collected by a governmental authority that becomes due and payable after the Date of Policy. Exclusion 6 does not modify or limit the coverage provided under Covered Risk 2.b.
7. Any discrepancy in the quantity of the area, square footage, or acreage of the Land or of any improvement to the Land.

[Transaction Identification Data, for which the Company assumes no liability as set forth in Condition 9.d.:

Issuing Agent:

Issuing Office:

Issuing Office's ALTA® Registry ID:

Issuing Office File Number:

Property Address:]

SCHEDULE A

Name and Address of Title Insurance Company:

Policy Number:

Amount of Insurance: $ [Premium: $]

Date of Policy: [at a.m./p.m.]

1. The Insured is:
2. The estate or interest in the Land insured by this policy is:
3. The Title is vested in:
4. The Land is described as follows:

[5. This policy incorporates by reference the endorsements designated below, adopted by the [American Land Title Association][_______________] as of the Date of Policy:]

SCHEDULE B

Policy Number:

EXCEPTIONS FROM COVERAGE

Some historical land records contain Discriminatory Covenants that are illegal and unenforceable by law. This policy treats any Discriminatory Covenant in a document referenced in Schedule B as if each Discriminatory Covenant is redacted, repudiated, removed, and not republished or recirculated. Only the remaining provisions of the document are excepted from coverage.

This policy does not insure against loss or damage and the Company will not pay costs, attorneys' fees, or expenses resulting from the terms and conditions of any lease or easement identified in Schedule A, and the following matters:

(Insert Schedule B exceptions here)

CONDITIONS

1. DEFINITION OF TERMS

In this policy, the following terms have the meanings given to them below. Any defined term includes both the singular and the plural, as the context requires:

a. "Affiliate": An Entity:

i. that is wholly owned by the Insured;

ii. that wholly owns the Insured; or

iii. if that Entity and the Insured are both wholly owned by the same person or entity.

b. "Amount of Insurance": The Amount of Insurance stated in Schedule A, as may be increased by Condition 8.d. or decreased by Condition 10 or 11; or increased or decreased by endorsements to this policy.

c. "Date of Policy": The Date of Policy stated in Schedule A.

d. "Discriminatory Covenant": Any covenant, condition, restriction, or limitation that is unenforceable under applicable law because it illegally discriminates against a class of individuals based on personal characteristics such as race, color, religion, sex, sexual orientation, gender identity, familial status, disability, national origin, or other legally protected class.

e. "Enforcement Notice": A document recorded in the Public Records that describes any part of the Land and:

   i. is issued by a governmental agency that identifies a violation or enforcement of a law, ordinance, permit, or governmental regulation;

   ii. is issued by a holder of the power of eminent domain or a governmental agency that identifies the exercise of a governmental power; or

   iii. asserts a right to enforce a PACA-PSA Trust.

f. "Entity": A corporation, partnership, trust, limited liability company, or other entity authorized by law to own title to real property in the State where the Land is located.

g. "Insured":

   i. (a). The Insured named in Item 1 of Schedule A;

      (b). the successor to the Title of an Insured by operation of law as distinguished from purchase, including heirs, devisees, survivors, personal representatives, or next of kin;

      (c). the successor to the Title of an Insured resulting from dissolution, merger, consolidation, distribution, or reorganization;

      (d). the successor to the Title of an Insured resulting from its conversion to another kind of Entity; or

      (e). the grantee of an Insured under a deed or other instrument transferring the Title, if the grantee is:

         (1). an Affiliate;

         (2). a trustee or beneficiary of a trust created by a written instrument established for estate planning purposes by an Insured;

         (3). a spouse who receives the Title because of a dissolution of marriage;

         (4). a transferee by a transfer effective on the death of an Insured as authorized by law; or

         (5). another Insured named in Item 1 of Schedule A.

ii. The Company reserves all rights and defenses as to any successor or grantee that the Company would have had against any predecessor Insured.

h. "Insured Claimant": An Insured claiming loss or damage arising under this policy.

i. "Knowledge" or "Known": Actual knowledge or actual notice, but not constructive notice imparted by the Public Records.

j. "Land": The land described in Item 4 of Schedule A and improvements located on that land at the Date of Policy that by State law constitute real property. The term "Land" does not include any property beyond that described in Schedule A, nor any right, title, interest, estate, or easement in any abutting street, road, avenue, alley, lane, right-of-way, body of water, or waterway, but does not modify or limit the extent that a right of access to and from the Land is insured by this policy.

k. "Mortgage": A mortgage, deed of trust, trust deed, security deed, or other real property security instrument, including one evidenced by electronic means authorized by law.

l. "PACA-PSA Trust": A trust under the federal Perishable Agricultural Commodities Act or the federal Packers and Stockyards Act or a similar State or federal law.

m. "Public Records": The recording or filing system established under State statutes in effect at the Date of Policy under which a document must be recorded or filed to impart constructive notice of matters relating to the Title to a purchaser for value without Knowledge. The term "Public Records" does not include any other recording or filing system, including any pertaining to environmental remediation or protection, planning, permitting, zoning, licensing, building, health, public safety, or national security matters.

n. "State": The state or commonwealth of the United States within whose exterior boundaries the Land is located. The term "State" also includes the District of Columbia, the Commonwealth of Puerto Rico, the U.S. Virgin Islands, and Guam.

o. "Title": The estate or interest in the Land identified in Item 2 of Schedule A.

p. "Unmarketable Title": The Title affected by an alleged or apparent matter that would permit a prospective purchaser or lessee of the Title or a lender on the Title to be released from the obligation to purchase, lease, or lend if there is a contractual condition requiring the delivery of marketable title.

2. CONTINUATION OF COVERAGE

This policy continues as of the Date of Policy in favor of an Insured, so long as the Insured:

a. retains an estate or interest in the Land;

b. owns an obligation secured by a purchase money Mortgage given by a purchaser from the Insured; or

c. has liability for warranties given by the Insured in any transfer or conveyance of the Insured's Title.

Except as provided in Condition 2, this policy terminates and ceases to have any further force or effect after the Insured conveys the Title. This policy does not continue in force or effect in favor of any person or entity that is not the Insured and acquires the Title or an obligation secured by a purchase money Mortgage given to the Insured.

3. NOTICE OF CLAIM TO BE GIVEN BY INSURED CLAIMANT

The Insured must notify the Company promptly in writing if the Insured has Knowledge of:

a. any litigation or other matter for which the Company may be liable under this policy; or

b. any rejection of the Title as Unmarketable Title.

If the Company is prejudiced by the failure of the Insured Claimant to provide prompt notice, the Company's liability to the Insured Claimant under this policy is reduced to the extent of the prejudice.

4. PROOF OF LOSS

The Company may, at its option, require as a condition of payment that the Insured Claimant furnish a signed proof of loss. The proof of loss must describe the defect, lien, encumbrance, adverse claim, or other matter insured against by this policy that constitutes the basis of loss or damage and must state, to the extent possible, the basis of calculating the amount of the loss or damage.

5. DEFENSE AND PROSECUTION OF ACTIONS

a. Upon written request by the Insured and subject to the options contained in Condition 7, the Company, at its own cost and without unreasonable delay, will provide for the defense of an Insured in litigation in which any third party asserts a claim covered by this policy adverse to the Insured. This obligation is limited to only those stated causes of action alleging matters insured against by this policy. The Company has the right to select counsel of its choice (subject to the right of the Insured to object for reasonable cause) to represent the Insured as to those covered causes of action. The Company is not liable for and will not pay the fees of any other counsel. The Company will not pay any fees, costs, or expenses incurred by the Insured in the defense of any cause of action that alleges matters not insured against by this policy.

b. The Company has the right, in addition to the options contained in Condition 7, at its own cost, to institute and prosecute any action or proceeding or to do any other act that, in its opinion, may be necessary or desirable to establish the Title, as insured, or to prevent or reduce loss or damage to the Insured. The Company may take any appropriate action under the terms of this policy, whether or not it is liable to the Insured. The Company's exercise of these rights is not an admission of liability or waiver of any provision of this policy. If the Company exercises its rights under Condition 5.b., it must do so diligently.

c. When the Company brings an action or asserts a defense as required or permitted by this policy, the Company may pursue the litigation to a final determination by a court having jurisdiction. The Company reserves the right, in its sole discretion, to appeal any adverse judgment or order.

6. DUTY OF INSURED CLAIMANT TO COOPERATE

a. When this policy permits or requires the Company to prosecute or provide for the defense of any action or proceeding and any appeals, the Insured will secure to the Company the right to prosecute or provide defense in the action or proceeding, including the right to use, at its option, the name of the Insured for this purpose.

   When requested by the Company, the Insured, at the Company's expense, must give the Company all reasonable aid in:

   i. securing evidence, obtaining witnesses, prosecuting or defending the action or proceeding, or effecting settlement; and

   ii. any other lawful act that in the opinion of the Company may be necessary or desirable to establish the Title or any other matter, as insured.

   If the Company is prejudiced by any failure of the Insured to furnish the required cooperation, the Company's liability and obligations to the Insured under this policy terminate, including any obligation to defend, prosecute, or continue any litigation, regarding the matter requiring such cooperation.

b. The Company may reasonably require the Insured Claimant to submit to examination under oath by any authorized representative of the Company and to produce for examination, inspection, and copying, at such reasonable times and places as may be designated by the authorized representative of the Company, all records, in whatever medium maintained, including books, ledgers, checks, memoranda, correspondence, reports, e-mails, disks, tapes, and videos, whether bearing a date before or after the Date of Policy, that reasonably pertain to the loss or damage. Further, if requested by any authorized representative of the Company, the Insured Claimant must grant its permission, in writing, for any authorized representative of the Company to examine, inspect, and copy all the records in the custody or control of a third party that reasonably pertain to the loss or damage. No information designated in writing as confidential by the Insured Claimant provided to the Company pursuant to Condition 6 will be later disclosed to others unless, in the reasonable judgment of the Company, disclosure is necessary in the administration of the claim or required by law. Any failure of the Insured Claimant to submit for examination under oath, produce any reasonably requested information, or grant permission to secure reasonably necessary information from third parties as required in Condition 6.b., unless prohibited by law, terminates any liability of the Company under this policy as to that claim.

7. OPTIONS TO PAY OR OTHERWISE SETTLE CLAIMS; TERMINATION OF LIABILITY

In case of a claim under this policy, the Company has the following additional options:

a. *To Pay or Tender Payment of the Amount of Insurance*

To pay or tender payment of the Amount of Insurance under this policy. In addition, the Company will pay any costs, attorneys' fees, and expenses incurred by the Insured Claimant that were authorized by the Company up to the time of payment or tender of payment and that the Company is obligated to pay.

Upon the exercise by the Company of this option provided for in Condition 7.a., the Company's liability and obligations to the Insured under this policy terminate, including any obligation to defend, prosecute, or continue any litigation.

b. *To Pay or Otherwise Settle with Parties other than the Insured or with the Insured Claimant*

i. To pay or otherwise settle with parties other than the Insured for or in the name of the Insured Claimant. In addition, the Company will pay any costs, attorneys' fees, and expenses incurred by the Insured Claimant that were authorized by the Company up to the time of payment and that the Company is obligated to pay; or

ii. To pay or otherwise settle with the Insured Claimant the loss or damage provided for under this policy. In addition, the Company will pay any costs, attorneys' fees, and expenses incurred by the Insured Claimant that were authorized by the Company up to the time of payment and that the Company is obligated to pay.

Upon the exercise by the Company of either option provided for in Condition 7.b., the Company's liability and obligations to the Insured under this policy for the claimed loss or damage terminate, including any obligation to defend, prosecute, or continue any litigation.

8. CONTRACT OF INDEMNITY; DETERMINATION AND EXTENT OF LIABILITY

This policy is a contract of indemnity against actual monetary loss or damage sustained or incurred by an Insured Claimant who has suffered loss or damage by reason of matters insured against by this policy. This policy is not an abstract of the Title, report of the condition of the Title, legal opinion, opinion of the Title, or other representation of the status of the Title. All claims asserted under this policy are based in contract and are restricted to the terms and provisions of this policy. The Company is not liable for any claim alleging negligence or negligent misrepresentation arising from or in connection with this policy or the determination of the insurability of the Title.

a. The extent of liability of the Company for loss or damage under this policy does not exceed the lesser of:

   i. the Amount of Insurance; or
   ii. the difference between the fair market value of the Title, as insured, and the fair market value of the Title subject to the matter insured against by this policy.

b. Except as provided in Condition 8.c. or 8.d., the fair market value of the Title in Condition 8.a.ii. is calculated using the date the Insured discovers the defect, lien, encumbrance, adverse claim, or other matter insured against by this policy.

c. If, at the Date of Policy, the Title to all of the Land is void by reason of a matter insured against by this policy, then the Insured Claimant may, by written notice given to the Company, elect to use the Date of Policy as the date for calculating the fair market value of the Title in Condition 8.a.ii.

d. If the Company pursues its rights under Condition 5.b. and is unsuccessful in establishing the Title, as insured:
   i. the Amount of Insurance will be increased by 15%; and
   ii. the Insured Claimant may, by written notice given to the Company, elect, as an alternative to the dates set forth in Condition 8.b. or, if it applies, 8.c., to use either the date the settlement, action, proceeding, or other act described in Condition 5.b. is concluded or the date the notice of claim required by Condition 3 is received by the Company as the date for calculating the fair market value of the Title in Condition 8.a.ii.

e. In addition to the extent of liability for loss or damage under Conditions 8.a. and 8.d., the Company will also pay the costs, attorneys' fees, and expenses incurred in accordance with Conditions 5 and 7.

9. LIMITATION OF LIABILITY

a. The Company fully performs its obligations and is not liable for any loss or damage caused to the Insured if the Company accomplishes any of the following in a reasonable manner:
   i. removes the alleged defect, lien, encumbrance, adverse claim, or other matter;
   ii. cures the lack of a right of access to and from the Land; or
   iii. cures the claim of Unmarketable Title,

   all as insured. The Company may do so by any method, including litigation and the completion of any appeals.

b. The Company is not liable for loss or damage arising out of any litigation, including litigation by the Company or with the Company's consent, until a State or federal court having jurisdiction makes a final, non-appealable determination adverse to the Title.

c. The Company is not liable for loss or damage to the Insured for liability voluntarily assumed by the Insured in settling any claim or suit without the prior written consent of the Company.

d. The Company is not liable for the content of the Transaction Identification Data, if any.

10. REDUCTION OR TERMINATION OF INSURANCE

All payments under this policy, except payments made for costs, attorneys' fees, and expenses, reduce the Amount of Insurance by the amount of the payment.

11. LIABILITY NONCUMULATIVE

The Amount of Insurance will be reduced by any amount the Company pays under any policy insuring a Mortgage to which exception is taken in Schedule B or to which the Insured has agreed, assumed, or taken subject, or which is executed by an Insured after the Date of Policy and which is a charge or lien on the Title, and the amount so paid will be deemed a payment to the Insured under this policy.

12. PAYMENT OF LOSS

When liability and the extent of loss or damage are determined in accordance with the Conditions, the Company will pay the loss or damage within 30 days.

13. COMPANY'S RECOVERY AND SUBROGATION RIGHTS UPON SETTLEMENT AND PAYMENT

a. If the Company settles and pays a claim under this policy, it is subrogated and entitled to the rights and remedies of the Insured Claimant in the Title and all other rights and remedies in respect to the claim that the Insured Claimant has against any person, entity, or property to the fullest extent permitted by law, but limited to the amount of any loss, costs, attorneys' fees, and expenses paid by the Company. If requested by the Company, the Insured Claimant must execute documents to transfer these rights and remedies to the Company. The Insured Claimant permits the Company to sue, compromise, or settle in the name of the Insured Claimant and to use the name of the Insured Claimant in any transaction or litigation involving these rights and remedies.

b. If a payment on account of a claim does not fully cover the loss of the Insured Claimant, the Company defers the exercise of its subrogation right until after the Insured Claimant fully recovers its loss.

c. The Company's subrogation right includes the Insured's rights to indemnity, guaranty, warranty, insurance policy, or bond, despite any provision in those instruments that addresses recovery or subrogation rights.

14. POLICY ENTIRE CONTRACT

a. This policy together with all endorsements, if any, issued by the Company is the entire policy and contract between the Insured and the Company. In interpreting any provision of this policy, this policy will be construed as a whole. This policy and any endorsement to this policy may be evidenced by electronic means authorized by law.

b. Any amendment of this policy must be by a written endorsement issued by the Company. To the extent any term or provision of an endorsement is inconsistent with any term or provision of this policy, the term or provision of the endorsement controls. Unless the endorsement expressly states, it does not:

i. modify any prior endorsement,

ii. extend the Date of Policy,

iii. insure against loss or damage exceeding the Amount of Insurance, or

iv. increase the Amount of Insurance.

15. SEVERABILITY

In the event any provision of this policy, in whole or in part, is held invalid or unenforceable under applicable law, this policy will be deemed not to include that provision or the part held to be invalid, but all other provisions will remain in full force and effect.

16. CHOICE OF LAW AND CHOICE OF FORUM

a. *Choice of Law*

The Company has underwritten the risks covered by this policy and determined the premium charged in reliance upon the State law affecting interests in real property and the State law applicable to the interpretation, rights, remedies, or enforcement of policies of title insurance of the State where the Land is located.

The State law of the State where the Land is located, or to the extent it controls, federal law, will determine the validity of claims against the Title and the interpretation and enforcement of the terms of this policy, without regard to conflicts of law principles to determine the applicable law.

b. *Choice of Forum*

Any litigation or other proceeding brought by the Insured against the Company must be filed only in a State or federal court having jurisdiction.

17. NOTICES

Any notice of claim and any other notice or statement in writing required to be given to the Company under this policy must be given to the Company at:
(fill in) .

18. CLASS ACTION

ALL CLAIMS AND DISPUTES ARISING OUT OF OR RELATING TO THIS POLICY, INCLUDING ANY SERVICE OR OTHER MATTER IN CONNECTION WITH ISSUING THIS POLICY, ANY BREACH OF A POLICY PROVISION, OR ANY OTHER CLAIM OR DISPUTE ARISING OUT OF OR RELATING TO THE TRANSACTION GIVING RISE TO THIS POLICY, MUST

BE BROUGHT IN AN INDIVIDUAL CAPACITY. NO PARTY MAY SERVE AS PLAINTIFF, CLASS MEMBER, OR PARTICIPANT IN ANY CLASS, REPRESENTATIVE, OR PRIVATE ATTORNEY GENERAL PROCEEDING.

[**19.** ARBITRATION

a. All claims and disputes arising out of or relating to this policy, including any service or other matter in connection with issuing this policy, any breach of a policy provision, or any other claim or dispute arising out of or relating to the transaction giving rise to this policy, may be resolved by arbitration. If the Amount of Insurance is $2,000,000 or less, any claim or dispute may be submitted to binding arbitration at the election of either the Company or the Insured. If the Amount of Insurance is greater than $2,000,000, any claim or dispute may be submitted to binding arbitration only when agreed to by both the Company and the Insured. Arbitration must be conducted pursuant to the Title Insurance Arbitration Rules of the American Land Title Association ("ALTA Rules"). The ALTA Rules are available online at www.alta.org /arbitration. The ALTA Rules incorporate, as appropriate to a particular dispute, the Consumer Arbitration Rules and Commercial Arbitration Rules of the American Arbitration Association ("AAA Rules"). The AAA Rules are available online at www.adr.org.

b. ALL CLAIMS AND DISPUTES MUST BE BROUGHT IN AN INDIVIDUAL CAPACITY. NO PARTY MAY SERVE AS PLAINTIFF, CLASS MEMBER, OR PARTICIPANT IN ANY CLASS, REPRESENTATIVE, OR PRIVATE ATTORNEY GENERAL PROCEEDING IN ANY ARBITRATION GOVERNED BY CONDITION 19. The arbitrator does not have authority to conduct any class action arbitration, private attorney general arbitration, or arbitration involving joint or consolidated claims under any circumstance.

c. *If there is a final judicial determination that a request for particular relief cannot be arbitrated in accordance with this Condition 19, then only that request for particular relief may be brought in court. All other requests for relief remain subject to this Condition 19.*

d. [The Company will pay all AAA filing, administration, and arbitrator fees of the consumer when the arbitration seeks relief of $100,000 or less. Other fees][Fees] will be allocated in accordance with the applicable AAA Rules. The results of arbitration will be binding upon the parties. The arbitrator may consider, but is not bound by, rulings in prior arbitrations involving different parties. The arbitrator is bound by rulings in prior arbitrations involving the same parties to the extent required by law. The arbitrator must issue a written decision sufficient to explain the findings and conclusions on which the award is based. Judgment upon the award rendered by the arbitrator may be entered in any State or federal court having jurisdiction.]

NOTE: Bracketed ***[ ]*** *material optional*

C. [§ 4.48] ALTA Owner's Title Insurance Policy (2006)

OWNER'S POLICY OF TITLE INSURANCE
Issued by
BLANK TITLE INSURANCE COMPANY

Any notice of claim and any other notice or statement in writing required to be given to the Company under this Policy must be given to the Company at the address shown in Section 18 of the Conditions.

COVERED RISKS

SUBJECT TO THE EXCLUSIONS FROM COVERAGE, THE EXCEPTIONS FROM COVERAGE CONTAINED IN SCHEDULE B, AND THE CONDITIONS, BLANK TITLE INSURANCE COMPANY, a Blank corporation (the "Company") insures, as of Date of Policy and, to the extent stated in Covered Risks 9 and 10, after Date of Policy, against loss or damage, not exceeding the Amount of Insurance, sustained or incurred by the Insured by reason of:

1. Title being vested other than as stated in Schedule A.
2. Any defect in or lien or encumbrance on the Title. This Covered Risk includes but is not limited to insurance against loss from
   (a) A defect in the Title caused by
      (i) forgery, fraud, undue influence, duress, incompetency, incapacity, or impersonation;
      (ii) failure of any person or Entity to have authorized a transfer or conveyance;
      (iii) a document affecting Title not properly created, executed, witnessed, sealed, acknowledged, notarized, or delivered;
      (iv) failure to perform those acts necessary to create a document by electronic means authorized by law;
      (v) a document executed under a falsified, expired, or otherwise invalid power of attorney;
      (vi) a document not properly filed, recorded, or indexed in the Public Records including failure to perform those acts by electronic means authorized by law; or
      (vii) a defective judicial or administrative proceeding.
   (b) The lien of real estate taxes or assessments imposed on the Title by a governmental authority due or payable, but unpaid.
   (c) Any encroachment, encumbrance, violation, variation, or adverse circumstance affecting the Title that would be disclosed by an accurate and complete land survey of the Land. The term "encroachment" includes encroachments of

existing improvements located on the Land onto adjoining land, and encroachments onto the Land of existing improvements located on adjoining land.

3. Unmarketable Title.
4. No right of access to and from the Land.
5. The violation or enforcement of any law, ordinance, permit, or governmental regulation (including those relating to building and zoning) restricting, regulating, prohibiting, or relating to
   (a) the occupancy, use, or enjoyment of the Land;
   (b) the character, dimensions, or location of any improvement erected on the Land;
   (c) the subdivision of land; or
   (d) environmental protection

   if a notice, describing any part of the Land, is recorded in the Public Records setting forth the violation or intention to enforce, but only to the extent of the violation or enforcement referred to in that notice.
6. An enforcement action based on the exercise of a governmental police power not covered by Covered Risk 5 if a notice of the enforcement action, describing any part of the Land, is recorded in the Public Records, but only to the extent of the enforcement referred to in that notice.
7. The exercise of the rights of eminent domain if a notice of the exercise, describing any part of the Land, is recorded in the Public Records.
8. Any taking by a governmental body that has occurred and is binding on the rights of a purchaser for value without Knowledge.
9. Title being vested other than as stated in Schedule A or being defective
   (a) as a result of the avoidance in whole or in part, or from a court order providing an alternative remedy, of a transfer of all or any part of the title to or any interest in the Land occurring prior to the transaction vesting Title as shown in Schedule A because that prior transfer constituted a fraudulent or preferential transfer under federal bankruptcy, state insolvency, or similar creditors' rights laws; or
   (b) because the instrument of transfer vesting Title as shown in Schedule A constitutes a preferential transfer under federal bankruptcy, state insolvency, or similar creditors' rights laws by reason of the failure of its recording in the Public Records
      (i) to be timely, or
      (ii) to impart notice of its existence to a purchaser for value or to a judgment or lien creditor.

10. Any defect in or lien or encumbrance on the Title or other matter included in Covered Risks 1 through 9 that has been created or attached or has been filed or recorded in the Public Records subsequent to Date of Policy and prior to the recording of the deed or other instrument of transfer in the Public Records that vests Title as shown in Schedule A.

The Company will also pay the costs, attorneys' fees, and expenses incurred in defense of any matter insured against by this Policy, but only to the extent provided in the Conditions.

[Witness clause optional]

BLANK TITLE INSURANCE COMPANY

BY: PRESIDENT

BY: SECRETARY

EXCLUSIONS FROM COVERAGE

The following matters are expressly excluded from the coverage of this policy, and the Company will not pay loss or damage, costs, attorneys' fees, or expenses that arise by reason of:

1. (a) Any law, ordinance, permit, or governmental regulation (including those relating to building and zoning) restricting, regulating, prohibiting, or relating to
   (i) the occupancy, use, or enjoyment of the Land;
   (ii) the character, dimensions, or location of any improvement erected on the Land;
   (iii) the subdivision of land; or
   (iv) environmental protection;

   or the effect of any violation of these laws, ordinances, or governmental regulations. This Exclusion 1(a) does not modify or limit the coverage provided under Covered Risk 5.

   (b) Any governmental police power. This Exclusion 1(b) does not modify or limit the coverage provided under Covered Risk 6.
2. Rights of eminent domain. This Exclusion does not modify or limit the coverage provided under Covered Risk 7 or 8.
3. Defects, liens, encumbrances, adverse claims, or other matters
   (a) created, suffered, assumed, or agreed to by the Insured Claimant;
   (b) not Known to the Company, not recorded in the Public Records at Date of Policy, but Known to the Insured Claimant and not disclosed in writing to

the Company by the Insured Claimant prior to the date the Insured Claimant became an Insured under this policy;

(c) resulting in no loss or damage to the Insured Claimant;

(d) attaching or created subsequent to Date of Policy (however, this does not modify or limit the coverage provided under Covered Risk 9 and 10); or

(e) resulting in loss or damage that would not have been sustained if the Insured Claimant had paid value for the Title.

4. Any claim, by reason of the operation of federal bankruptcy, state insolvency, or similar creditors' rights laws, that the transaction vesting the Title as shown in Schedule A, is

   (a) a fraudulent conveyance or fraudulent transfer; or

   (b) a preferential transfer for any reason not stated in Covered Risk 9 of this policy.

5. Any lien on the Title for real estate taxes or assessments imposed by governmental authority and created or attaching between Date of Policy and the date of recording of the deed or other instrument of transfer in the Public Records that vests Title as shown in Schedule A.

SCHEDULE A

Name and Address of Title Insurance Company:

[File No.:] Policy No.:

Address Reference:

Amount of Insurance: $ [Premium: $]

Date of Policy: [at a.m./p.m.]

1. Name of Insured:
2. The estate or interest in the Land that is insured by this policy is:
3. Title is vested in:
4. The Land referred to in this policy is described as follows:

SCHEDULE B

[File No.] Policy No.

EXCEPTIONS FROM COVERAGE

This policy does not insure against loss or damage, and the Company will not pay costs, attorneys' fees, or expenses that arise by reason of:

1. [Policy may include regional exceptions if so desired by the issuing Company.]
2. [Variable exceptions such as taxes, easements, CC&R's, etc., shown here]

CONDITIONS

1. DEFINITION OF TERMS

The following terms when used in this policy mean:

(a) "Amount of Insurance": The amount stated in Schedule A, as may be increased or decreased by endorsement to this policy, increased by Section 8(b), or decreased by Sections 10 and 11 of these Conditions.

(b) "Date of Policy": The date designated as "Date of Policy" in Schedule A.

(c) "Entity": A corporation, partnership, trust, limited liability company, or other similar legal entity.

(d) "Insured": The Insured named in Schedule A.

(i) the term "Insured" also includes

(A) successors to the Title of the Insured by operation of law as distinguished from purchase, including heirs, devisees, survivors, personal representatives, or next of kin;

(B) successors to an Insured by dissolution, merger, consolidation, distribution, or reorganization;

(C) successors to an Insured by its conversion to another kind of Entity;

(D) a grantee of an Insured under a deed delivered without payment of actual valuable consideration conveying the Title

(1) if the stock, shares, memberships, or other equity interests of the grantee are wholly-owned by the named Insured,

(2) if the grantee wholly owns the named Insured,

(3) if the grantee is wholly-owned by an affiliated Entity of the named Insured, provided the affiliated Entity and the named Insured are both wholly-owned by the same person or Entity, or

(4) if the grantee is a trustee or beneficiary of a trust created by a written instrument established by the Insured named in Schedule A for estate planning purposes.

(ii) with regard to (A), (B), (C), and (D) reserving, however, all rights and defenses as to any successor that the Company would have had against any predecessor Insured.

(e) "Insured Claimant": An Insured claiming loss or damage.

(f) "Knowledge" or "Known": Actual knowledge, not constructive knowledge or notice that may be imputed to an Insured by reason of the Public Records or any other records that impart constructive notice of matters affecting the Title.

(g) "Land": The land described in Schedule A, and affixed improvements that by law constitute real property. The term "Land" does not include any property beyond the lines of the area described in Schedule A, nor any right, title, interest, estate, or easement in abutting streets, roads, avenues, alleys, lanes, ways, or waterways, but this does not modify or limit the extent that a right of access to and from the Land is insured by this policy.

(h) "Mortgage": Mortgage, deed of trust, trust deed, or other security instrument, including one evidenced by electronic means authorized by law.

(i) "Public Records": Records established under state statutes at Date of Policy for the purpose of imparting constructive notice of matters relating to real property to purchasers for value and without Knowledge. With respect to Covered Risk 5(d), "Public Records" shall also include environmental protection liens filed in the records of the clerk of the United States District Court for the district where the Land is located.

(j) "Title": The estate or interest described in Schedule A.

(k) "Unmarketable Title": Title affected by an alleged or apparent matter that would permit a prospective purchaser or lessee of the Title or lender on the Title to be released from the obligation to purchase, lease, or lend if there is a contractual condition requiring the delivery of marketable title.

2. CONTINUATION OF INSURANCE

The coverage of this policy shall continue in force as of Date of Policy in favor of an Insured, but only so long as the Insured retains an estate or interest in the Land, or holds an obligation secured by a purchase money Mortgage given by a purchaser from the Insured, or only so long as the Insured shall have liability by reason of warranties in any transfer or conveyance of the Title. This policy shall not continue in force in favor of any purchaser from the Insured of either (i) an estate or interest in the Land, or (ii) an obligation secured by a purchase money Mortgage given to the Insured.

3. NOTICE OF CLAIM TO BE GIVEN BY INSURED CLAIMANT

The Insured shall notify the Company promptly in writing (i) in case of any litigation as set forth in Section 5(a) of these Conditions, (ii) in case Knowledge shall come to an Insured hereunder of any claim of title or interest that is adverse to the Title, as insured, and that might cause loss or damage for which the Company may be liable by virtue of this policy, or (iii) if the Title, as insured, is rejected as Unmarketable Title. If the Company is prejudiced by the failure of the Insured Claimant to provide prompt notice, the Company's liability to the Insured Claimant under the policy shall be reduced to the extent of the prejudice.

4. PROOF OF LOSS

In the event the Company is unable to determine the amount of loss or damage, the Company may, at its option, require as a condition of payment that the Insured Claimant furnish a signed proof of loss. The proof of loss must describe the defect, lien, encumbrance, or other matter insured against by this policy that constitutes the basis of loss or damage and shall state, to the extent possible, the basis of calculating the amount of the loss or damage.

5. DEFENSE AND PROSECUTION OF ACTIONS

(a) Upon written request by the Insured, and subject to the options contained in Section 7 of these Conditions, the Company, at its own cost and without unreasonable delay, shall provide for the defense of an Insured in litigation in which any third party asserts a claim covered by this policy adverse to the Insured. This obligation is limited to only those stated causes of action alleging matters insured against by this policy. The Company shall have the right to select counsel of its choice (subject to the right of the Insured to object for reasonable cause) to represent the Insured as to those stated causes of action. It shall not be liable for and will not pay the fees of any other counsel. The Company will not pay any fees, costs, or expenses incurred by the Insured in the defense of those causes of action that allege matters not insured against by this policy.

(b) The Company shall have the right, in addition to the options contained in Section 7 of these Conditions, at its own cost, to institute and prosecute any action or proceeding or to do any other act that in its opinion may be necessary or desirable to establish the Title, as insured, or to prevent or reduce loss or damage to the Insured. The Company may take any appropriate action under the terms of this policy, whether or not it shall be liable to the Insured. The exercise of these rights shall not be an admission of liability or waiver of any provision of this policy. If the Company exercises its rights under this subsection, it must do so diligently.

(c) Whenever the Company brings an action or asserts a defense as required or permitted by this policy, the Company may pursue the litigation to a final determination by a court of competent jurisdiction, and it expressly reserves the right, in its sole discretion, to appeal any adverse judgment or order.

6. DUTY OF INSURED CLAIMANT TO COOPERATE

(a) In all cases where this policy permits or requires the Company to prosecute or provide for the defense of any action or proceeding and any appeals, the Insured shall secure to the Company the right to so prosecute or provide defense in the action or proceeding, including the right to use, at its option, the name of the Insured for this purpose. Whenever requested by the Company, the Insured, at the Company's expense, shall give the Company all reasonable aid (i) in securing evidence, obtaining witnesses, prosecuting or defending the action or proceeding, or effecting settlement, and (ii) in any other lawful act that in the opinion of the Company may be necessary or desirable to establish the Title or any other matter as insured. If the Company is prejudiced by the failure of the Insured to furnish the required cooperation, the Company's obligations to the Insured under the policy shall terminate, including any liability or obligation to defend, prosecute, or continue any litigation, with regard to the matter or matters requiring such cooperation.

(b) The Company may reasonably require the Insured Claimant to submit to examination under oath by any authorized representative of the Company and to produce for examination, inspection, and copying, at such reasonable times and places as may be designated by the authorized representative of the Company, all records, in whatever medium maintained, including books, ledgers, checks, memoranda, correspondence, reports, e-mails, disks, tapes, and videos whether bearing a date before or after Date of Policy, that reasonably pertain to the loss or damage. Further, if requested by any authorized representative of the Company, the Insured Claimant shall grant its permission, in writing, for any authorized representative of the Company to examine, inspect, and copy all of these records in the custody or control of a third party that reasonably pertain to the loss or damage. All information designated as confidential by the Insured Claimant provided to the Company pursuant to this Section shall not be disclosed to others unless, in the reasonable judgment of the Company, it is necessary in the administration of the claim. Failure of the Insured Claimant to submit for examination under oath, produce any reasonably requested information, or grant permission to secure reasonably necessary information from third parties as required in this subsection, unless prohibited by law or governmental regulation, shall terminate any liability of the Company under this policy as to that claim.

7. OPTIONS TO PAY OR OTHERWISE SETTLE CLAIMS; TERMINATION OF LIABILITY

In case of a claim under this policy, the Company shall have the following additional options:

(a) To Pay or Tender Payment of the Amount of Insurance.

To pay or tender payment of the Amount of Insurance under this policy together with any costs, attorneys' fees, and expenses incurred by the Insured Claimant that were authorized by the Company up to the time of payment or tender of payment and that the Company is obligated to pay.

Upon the exercise by the Company of this option, all liability and obligations of the Company to the Insured under this policy, other than to make the payment required in this subsection, shall terminate, including any liability or obligation to defend, prosecute, or continue any litigation.

(b) To Pay or Otherwise Settle With Parties Other Than the Insured or With the Insured Claimant.

(i) to pay or otherwise settle with other parties for or in the name of an Insured Claimant any claim insured against under this policy. In addition, the Company will pay any costs, attorneys' fees, and expenses incurred by the Insured Claimant that were authorized by the Company up to the time of payment and that the Company is obligated to pay; or

(ii) to pay or otherwise settle with the Insured Claimant the loss or damage provided for under this policy, together with any costs, attorneys' fees, and expenses incurred by the Insured Claimant that were authorized by the Company up to the time of payment and that the Company is obligated to pay.

Upon the exercise by the Company of either of the options provided for in subsections (b)(i) or (ii), the Company's obligations to the Insured under this policy for the claimed loss or damage, other than the payments required to be made, shall terminate, including any liability or obligation to defend, prosecute, or continue any litigation.

8. DETERMINATION AND EXTENT OF LIABILITY

This policy is a contract of indemnity against actual monetary loss or damage sustained or incurred by the Insured Claimant who has suffered loss or damage by reason of matters insured against by this policy.

(a) The extent of liability of the Company for loss or damage under this policy shall not exceed the lesser of

(i) the Amount of Insurance; or

(ii) the difference between the value of the Title as insured and the value of the Title subject to the risk insured against by this policy.

(b) If the Company pursues its rights under Section 5 of these Conditions and is unsuccessful in establishing the Title, as insured,

(i) the Amount of Insurance shall be increased by 10%, and

(ii) the Insured Claimant shall have the right to have the loss or damage determined either as of the date the claim was made by the Insured Claimant or as of the date it is settled and paid.

(c) In addition to the extent of liability under (a) and (b), the Company will also pay those costs, attorneys' fees, and expenses incurred in accordance with Sections 5 and 7 of these Conditions.

9. LIMITATION OF LIABILITY

(a) If the Company establishes the Title, or removes the alleged defect, lien, or encumbrance, or cures the lack of a right of access to or from the Land, or cures the claim of Unmarketable Title, all as insured, in a reasonably diligent manner by any method, including litigation and the completion of any appeals, it shall have fully performed its obligations with respect to that matter and shall not be liable for any loss or damage caused to the Insured.

(b) In the event of any litigation, including litigation by the Company or with the Company's consent, the Company shall have no liability for loss or damage until there has been a final determination by a court of competent jurisdiction, and disposition of all appeals, adverse to the Title, as insured.

(c) The Company shall not be liable for loss or damage to the Insured for liability voluntarily assumed by the Insured in settling any claim or suit without the prior written consent of the Company.

10. REDUCTION OF INSURANCE; REDUCTION OR TERMINATION OF LIABILITY

All payments under this policy, except payments made for costs, attorneys' fees, and expenses, shall reduce the Amount of Insurance by the amount of the payment.

11. LIABILITY NONCUMULATIVE

The Amount of Insurance shall be reduced by any amount the Company pays under any policy insuring a Mortgage to which exception is taken in Schedule B or to which the Insured has agreed, assumed, or taken subject, or which is executed by an Insured after Date of Policy and which is a charge or lien on the Title, and the amount so paid shall be deemed a payment to the Insured under this policy.

12. PAYMENT OF LOSS

When liability and the extent of loss or damage have been definitely fixed in accordance with these Conditions, the payment shall be made within 30 days.

13. RIGHTS OF RECOVERY UPON PAYMENT OR SETTLEMENT

(a) Whenever the Company shall have settled and paid a claim under this policy, it shall be subrogated and entitled to the rights of the Insured Claimant in the Title and all other rights and remedies in respect to the claim that the Insured Claimant has against any person or property, to the extent of the amount of any loss, costs, attorneys' fees, and expenses paid by the Company. If requested by the Company, the Insured Claimant shall execute documents to evidence the transfer to the Company of these rights and remedies. The Insured Claimant shall permit the Company to sue, compromise, or settle in the name of the Insured Claimant and to use the name of the Insured Claimant in any transaction or litigation involving these rights and remedies.

If a payment on account of a claim does not fully cover the loss of the Insured Claimant, the Company shall defer the exercise of its right to recover until after the Insured Claimant shall have recovered its loss.

(b) The Company's right of subrogation includes the rights of the Insured to indemnities, guaranties, other policies of insurance, or bonds, notwithstanding any terms or conditions contained in those instruments that address subrogation rights.

14. ARBITRATION

Either the Company or the Insured may demand that the claim or controversy shall be submitted to arbitration pursuant to the Title Insurance Arbitration Rules of the American Land Title Association ("Rules"). Except as provided in the Rules, there shall be no joinder or consolidation with claims or controversies of other persons. Arbitrable matters may include, but are not limited to, any controversy or claim between the Company and the Insured arising out of or relating to this policy, any service in connection with its issuance or the breach of a policy provision, or to any other controversy or claim arising out of the transaction giving rise to this policy. All arbitrable matters when the Amount of Insurance is $2,000,000 or less shall be arbitrated at the option of either the Company or the Insured. All arbitrable matters when the Amount of Insurance is in excess of $2,000,000 shall be arbitrated only when agreed to by both the Company and the Insured. Arbitration pursuant to this policy and under the Rules shall be binding upon the parties. Judgment upon the award rendered by the Arbitrator(s) may be entered in any court of competent jurisdiction.

15. LIABILITY LIMITED TO THIS POLICY; POLICY ENTIRE CONTRACT

(a) This policy together with all endorsements, if any, attached to it by the Company is the entire policy and contract between the Insured and the Company. In interpreting any provision of this policy, this policy shall be construed as a whole.

(b) Any claim of loss or damage that arises out of the status of the Title or by any action asserting such claim shall be restricted to this policy.

(c) Any amendment of or endorsement to this policy must be in writing and authenticated by an authorized person, or expressly incorporated by Schedule A of this policy.

(d) Each endorsement to this policy issued at any time is made a part of this policy and is subject to all of its terms and provisions. Except as the endorsement expressly states, it does not (i) modify any of the terms and provisions of the policy, (ii) modify any prior endorsement, (iii) extend the Date of Policy, or (iv) increase the Amount of Insurance.

16. SEVERABILITY

In the event any provision of this policy, in whole or in part, is held invalid or unenforceable under applicable law, the policy shall be deemed not to include that provision or such part held to be invalid, but all other provisions shall remain in full force and effect.

17. CHOICE OF LAW; FORUM

(a) Choice of Law: The Insured acknowledges the Company has underwritten the risks covered by this policy and determined the premium charged therefor in reliance upon the law affecting interests in real property and applicable to the interpretation, rights, remedies, or enforcement of policies of title insurance of the jurisdiction where the Land is located.

Therefore, the court or an arbitrator shall apply the law of the jurisdiction where the Land is located to determine the validity of claims against the Title that are adverse to the Insured and to interpret and enforce the terms of this policy. In neither case shall the court or arbitrator apply its conflicts of law principles to determine the applicable law.

(b) Choice of Forum: Any litigation or other proceeding brought by the Insured against the Company must be filed only in a state or federal court within the United States of America or its territories having appropriate jurisdiction.

18. NOTICES, WHERE SENT

Any notice of claim and any other notice or statement in writing required to be given to the Company under this policy must be given to the Company at [fill in].

NOTE: Bracketed [ ] material optional

D. [§ 4.49] Endorsement Deleting "Parties in Possession"

ENDORSEMENT

(Deleting 1st Standard Exception)

To be annexed to and form a part of Policy No. insuring as set forth in said Policy.

The said Policy is hereby amended in the following manner:

Schedule B, Item No. 1. "Rights or claims of parties other than Insured in actual possession of any or all of the property" is hereby deleted.

Except as modified this Policy shall remain the same and unchanged.

The total liability of the Company under said policy and any endorsements attached thereto shall not exceed, in the aggregate, the face amount of said policy and costs which the Company is obligated under the provisions of said policy to pay.

This endorsement is made a part of said policy and is subject to the exclusions, schedules, endorsements, conditions, stipulations and terms thereof, except as modified by the provisions hereof.

Nothing herein contained shall be construed as extending or changing the effective date of said Policy, unless otherwise expressly stated.

TITLE INSURANCE COMPANY

Dated: ____________________ BY: _____

(Authorized Signatory)

E. [§ 4.50] ALTA Short Form Loan Policy (2021)

ALTA SHORT FORM RESIDENTIAL LOAN POLICY—CURRENT ASSESSMENTS
ONE-TO-FOUR FAMILY
issued by
BLANK TITLE INSURANCE COMPANY

[Transaction Identification Data, for which the Company assumes no liability as set forth in Condition 9.e.:

Issuing Agent:

Issuing Office:

Issuing Office's ALTA® Registry ID:

Loan ID Number:

Issuing Office File Number:

Property Address:]

SCHEDULE A

Name and Address of Title Insurance Company:

Policy Number:

Amount of Insurance: $ [Premium: $]

Mortgage Amount: $ Mortgage Date:

Date of Policy:

Property Address:

1. Name of Insured:
2. Name of Borrower(s):
3. The estate or interest in the Land identified in this Schedule A and which is encumbered by the Insured Mortgage is fee simple and is, at the Date of Policy, vested in the Borrower(s) identified in the Insured Mortgage and named above.
4. The Land referred to in this policy is described as set forth in the Insured Mortgage.
5. This policy consists of [one] page(s), [including its reverse side,] unless an addendum is attached and indicated below:

   □ Addendum attached

[6. This policy incorporates by reference the endorsements selected below, if any, adopted by the [American Land Title Association][________________] as of the Date of Policy:

- □ ALTA 4.1 Condominium—Current Assessments endorsement, if the Land or estate or interest is referred to in the Insured Mortgage as a condominium
- □ ALTA 5.1 Planned Unit Development—Current Assessments endorsement
- □ ALTA 6 Variable Rate Mortgage endorsement, if the Insured Mortgage contains provisions which provide for an adjustable interest rate
- □ ALTA 6.2 Variable Rate Mortgage—Negative Amortization endorsement, if the Insured Mortgage contains provisions which provide for both an adjustable interest rate and negative amortization
- □ ALTA 7 Manufactured Housing Unit endorsement, if a manufactured housing unit is located on the Land at the Date of Policy
- □ ALTA 7.1 Manufactured Housing—Conversion—Loan Policy endorsement
- □ ALTA 8.1 Environmental Protection Lien endorsement—Paragraph b refers to the following State statute(s):
- □ ALTA 9.6.1 Private Rights—Current Assessments—Loan Policy endorsement
- □ ALTA 9.10 Restrictions, Encroachments, Minerals—Current Violations—Loan Policy endorsement
- □ ALTA 14 Future Advance—Priority endorsement
- □ ALTA 14.1 Future Advance—Knowledge endorsement
- □ ALTA 14.3 Future Advance—Reverse Mortgage endorsement
- □ ALTA 22 Location endorsement, if the type of improvement is a one-to-four family residential structure and the Property Address is as shown above
- □ ALTA 30 Shared Appreciation Mortgage endorsement]

[Witness clause]

BLANK TITLE INSURANCE COMPANY

By: __________________________
[Authorized Signatory]

By: __________________________
[Authorized Signatory]

NOTE: Bracketed [ ] material optional

SUBJECT TO THE EXCEPTIONS FROM COVERAGE CONTAINED IN SCHEDULE B BELOW, AND ANY ADDENDUM ATTACHED HERETO, [BLANK TITLE INSURANCE COMPANY], A [BLANK] CORPORATION, (THE "COMPANY"), HEREBY INSURES THE INSURED IN ACCORDANCE WITH AND SUBJECT TO THE TERMS, EXCLUSIONS, AND CONDITIONS SET FORTH IN THE AMERICAN LAND TITLE ASSOCIATION (ALTA) LOAN POLICY (07-01-2021), ALL OF WHICH

ARE INCORPORATED HEREIN. ALL REFERENCES TO SCHEDULES A AND B REFER TO SCHEDULES A AND B OF THIS POLICY.

SCHEDULE B

EXCEPTIONS FROM COVERAGE

Some historical land records contain Discriminatory Covenants that are illegal and unenforceable by law. This policy treats any Discriminatory Covenant in a document referenced in Schedule B as if each Discriminatory Covenant is redacted, repudiated, removed, and not republished or recirculated. Only the remaining provisions of the document are excepted from coverage.

Except to the extent set forth below, this policy does not insure against loss or damage and the Company will not pay costs, attorneys' fees, or expenses arising by reason of:

1. Those taxes and assessments that become due or payable subsequent to the Date of Policy. Exception 1 does not modify or limit the coverage provided in Covered Risk 11.b.

2. Covenants, conditions, restrictions, or limitations, if any, appearing in the Public Records; however, this policy insures against loss or damage arising from:

a. the violation of those covenants, conditions, restrictions, or limitations on or prior to the Date of Policy;

b. a forfeiture or reversion of Title from a violation at the Date of Policy of those covenants, conditions, restrictions, or limitations, including those relating to environmental protection; and

c. the invalidation, subordination, or other impairment of the lien of the Insured Mortgage because of a violation at the Date of Policy of any provisions in those covenants, conditions, restrictions, or limitations, including those relating to environmental protection.

As used in Exception 2.a., the words "covenants, conditions, restrictions, or limitations" do not refer to or include any covenant, condition, restriction, or limitation (i) relating to obligations of any type to perform maintenance, repair, or remediation on the Land; or (ii) pertaining to environmental protection of any kind or nature, including hazardous or toxic matters, conditions, or substances, except to the extent that an Enforcement Notice as of the Date of Policy identifies a violation or alleged violation affecting the Land and is not referenced in an Addendum attached to this policy.

3. Any easements or servitudes appearing in the Public Records; however, this policy insures against loss or damage arising from:

a. the encroachment, at the Date of Policy, of the improvements on any easement; and

b. any interference with or damage to existing improvements, including lawns, shrubbery, and trees, resulting from the use of the easements for the purposes granted or reserved.

4. Any lease, grant, exception, or reservation of minerals or mineral rights or other subsurface substances appearing in the Public Records; however, this policy insures against loss or damage arising from:

a. any effect on or impairment of the use of the Land for one-to-four family residential purposes by reason of such lease, grant, exception, or reservation of minerals or mineral rights or other subsurface substances; and

b. any damage to existing improvements, including lawns, shrubbery, and trees, resulting from the future exercise of any right to use the surface of the Land for the extraction or development of the minerals or mineral rights or other subsurface substances so leased, granted, excepted, or reserved.

Nothing herein insures against loss or damage resulting from contamination, explosion, fire, flooding, vibration, fracturing, earthquake, or subsidence.

NOTICES, WHERE SENT: Any notice of claim and any other notice or statement in writing required to be given to the Company under this policy must be given to the Company at: *(fill in)* .

ADDENDUM
ALTA SHORT FORM RESIDENTIAL LOAN POLICY—CURRENT ASSESSMENTS ONE-TO-FOUR FAMILY

Policy Number:

SCHEDULE B
(Continued)

In addition to the matters set forth in Schedule B of the policy to which this Addendum is attached, this policy does not insure against loss or damage and the Company will not pay costs, attorneys' fees, or expenses that arise by reason of the following:

F. [§ 4.51] ALTA Endorsement Form 4—Condominium

CONDOMINIUM—ASSESSMENTS PRIORITY ENDORSEMENT
Issued by
First American Title Insurance Company

Attached to Policy No.: File No.:

The Company insures against loss or damage sustained by the Insured by reason of:

1. The failure of the unit identified in Schedule A and its common elements to be part of a condominium within the meaning of the condominium statutes of the jurisdiction in which the unit and its common elements are located.
2. The failure of the documents required by the condominium statutes to comply with the requirements of the statutes to the extent that such failure affects the Title to the unit and its common elements.
3. Present violations of any restrictive covenants that restrict the use of the unit and its common elements and that are contained in the condominium documents or the forfeiture or reversion of Title by reason of any provision contained in the restrictive covenants. As used in this paragraph 3, the words "restrictive covenants" do not refer to or include any covenant, condition, or restriction (a) relating to obligations of any type to perform maintenance, repair, or remediation on the Land, or (b) pertaining to environmental protection of any kind or nature, including hazardous or toxic matters, conditions, or substances, except to the extent that a notice of a violation or alleged violation affecting the Land has been recorded in the Public Records at Date of Policy and is not excepted in Schedule B.
4. The priority of any lien for charges and assessments provided for in the condominium statutes and condominium documents at Date of Policy over the lien of any Insured Mortgage identified in Schedule A.
5. The failure of the unit and its common elements to be entitled by law to be assessed for real property taxes as a separate parcel.
6. Any obligation to remove any improvements that exist at Date of Policy because of any present encroachments or because of any future unintentional encroachment of the common elements upon any unit or of any unit upon the common elements or another unit.
7. The failure of the Title by reason of a right of first refusal, to purchase the unit and its common elements that was exercised or could have been exercised at Date of Policy.

This endorsement is issued as part of the policy. Except as it expressly states, it does not (i) modify any of the terms and provisions of the policy, (ii) modify any prior endorsements, (iii) extend the Date of Policy, or (iv) increase the Amount of Insurance. To the extent a provision of the policy or a previous endorsement is inconsistent with an express provision of this endorsement, this endorsement controls. Otherwise, this endorsement is subject to all of the terms and provisions of the policy and of any prior endorsements.

Date:

First American Title Insurance Company

Dennis J. Gilmore, President   Greg L. Smith, Secretary

____
Name of Agent

By: ______________________
Authorized Countersignature

G. [§ 4.52] ALTA Endorsement Form 5—Planned Unit Development

PLANNED UNIT DEVELOPMENT
ENDORSEMENT
Issued by
First American Title Insurance Company

Attached to Policy No.:

File No.:

The Company insures against loss or damage sustained by the Insured by reason of:

1. Present violations of any restrictive covenants referred to in Schedule B that restrict the use of the Land or the forfeiture or reversion of Title by reason of any provision contained in the restrictive covenants. As used in this paragraph 1, the words "restrictive covenants" do not refer to or include any covenant, condition or restriction (a) relating to obligations of any type to perform maintenance, repair or remediation on the Land, or (b) pertaining to environmental protection of any kind or nature, including hazardous or toxic matters, conditions, or substances, except to the extent that a notice of a violation or alleged violation affecting the Land has been recorded in the Public Records at Date of Policy and is not excepted in Schedule B.
2. The priority of any lien for charges and assessments in favor of any association of homeowners that are provided for in any document at Date of Policy and referred to in Schedule B over the lien of any Insured Mortgage identified in Schedule A.
3. The enforced removal of any existing structure on the Land (other than a boundary wall or fence) because it encroaches onto adjoining land or onto any easements.
4. The failure of the Title by reason of a right of first refusal to purchase the Land that was exercised or could have been exercised at Date of Policy.

This endorsement is issued as part of the policy. Except as it expressly states, it does not (i) modify any of the terms and provisions of the policy, (ii) modify any prior endorsements, (iii) extend the Date of Policy, or (iv) increase the Amount of Insurance. To the extent a provision of the policy or a previous endorsement is inconsistent with an express provision of this endorsement, this endorsement controls. Otherwise, this endorsement is subject to all of the terms and provisions of the policy and of any prior endorsements.

Date:

First American Title Insurance Company

Dennis J. Gilmore, President   Greg L. Smith, Secretary

By: ____________________

Authorized Countersignature

H. [§ 4.53] ALTA Homeowner's Policy (2021)

ALTA HOMEOWNER'S POLICY OF TITLE INSURANCE
issued by
BLANK TITLE INSURANCE COMPANY

This policy, when issued by Us with a Policy Number and the Date of Policy, is valid even if this policy or any endorsement to this policy is issued electronically or lacks any signature.

As soon as You Know of anything that might be covered by this policy, You must notify Us promptly in writing at the address shown in Condition 3.

COVERAGE STATEMENT

SUBJECT TO THE PROVISIONS SET FORTH BELOW, We insure You against loss or damage resulting from one or more of the Covered Risks if the matter creating the risk exists on the Date of Policy or, to the extent expressly stated in any Covered Risk, after the Date of Policy. We will also pay the costs, attorneys' fees, and expenses provided for under this policy.

Your insurance is effective on the Date of Policy.

This policy covers You only if the Land is improved with an existing one-to-four family residence and each party named in Item 1 of Schedule A is a Natural Person or Estate Planning Entity.

Your insurance is further limited by all of the following:

- Amount of Insurance
- For Covered Risks 16, 18, 19, and 21, Your Deductible Amount and Our Maximum Dollar Limit of Liability shown in Schedule A
- Exceptions from Coverage in Schedule B
- Our Duty to Defend against Legal Actions
- Exclusions from Coverage
- Conditions

COVERED RISKS

1. Someone else owns an interest in Your Title.

2. Someone else has a right affecting Your Title because of a lease, contract, or option.

3. Someone else claims to have a right affecting Your Title because of forgery or impersonation.

4. Someone else has an Easement on the Land.

5. Any of Covered Risks 1 through 4 occurring after the Date of Policy.

6. Someone else has a right to enforce a Covenant to limit Your use of the Land.

7. Your Title is defective. Some examples of title defects are:

  a. someone else's failure to have authorized a transfer or conveyance of Your Title.

  b. a defective judicial or administrative proceeding.

  c. a document, including an electronic document, on which Your Title is based:

    i. was signed using a falsified, expired, or otherwise invalid power of attorney;

    ii. was not properly authorized, executed, created, signed, witnessed, sealed, acknowledged, notarized (including by remote online notarization), or delivered; or

    iii. was not properly filed, recorded, or indexed in the Public Records.

  d. the repudiation of an electronic signature by a person that executed a document because the electronic signature on the document was not valid under applicable electronic transactions law.

8. Someone else has a lien on Your Title. Some examples of liens are:

  a. a lien of real estate taxes or assessments imposed on Your Title by a governmental authority due or payable, but unpaid;

  b. a Mortgage;

  c. a judgment lien;

  d. a State or federal tax lien;

  e. a charge by a homeowner's or condominium association; or

  f. a statutory lien, attaching before or after the Date of Policy, for service, labor, material, or equipment in connection with an improvement or work related to the Land and furnished before the Date of Policy.

9. Someone else has an encumbrance on Your Title.

10. Someone else claims to have a right affecting Your Title because of fraud, duress, incompetency, or incapacity.

11. You do not have actual vehicular and pedestrian access to and from the Land, based on a legal right.

12. You are forced to remove or remedy a violation, existing at the Date of Policy, of any Covenant, even if the Covenant is excepted in Schedule B. You are not covered for any violation of an obligation contained in a Covenant:

  a. to perform maintenance or repair on the Land; or

  b. relating to environmental protection of any kind, including hazardous or toxic conditions or substances;

unless there is a notice of either of these violations recorded in the Public Records at the Date of Policy, and then, Our liability for Covered Risk 12 is limited to the extent of the violation described in that notice.

13. Your Title is lost or taken because of a violation, existing at the Date of Policy, of any Covenant, even if the Covenant is excepted in Schedule B.

14. A violation or enforcement of any law, ordinance, permit, or governmental regulation (including those relating to building and zoning), but only to the extent of the violation or enforcement described by the enforcing governmental authority in an Enforcement Notice that identifies a restriction, regulation, or prohibition relating to:

a. the occupancy, use, or enjoyment of the Land;

b. the character, dimensions, or location of an improvement on the Land;

c. the subdivision of the Land; or

d. environmental remediation or protection on the Land.

15. An enforcement of a governmental forfeiture, police, regulatory, or national security power, but only to the extent of the enforcement described by the enforcing governmental authority in an Enforcement Notice.

16. Because of a violation existing at the Date of Policy of a State or Municipal subdivision law or State or Municipal subdivision regulation affecting the Land:

a. You are unable to obtain a building permit from a Municipal authority;

b. You are ordered by a State or Municipal authority to remove or remedy the violation; or

c. someone else refuses to perform a contract to purchase the Land, lease the Land, or make a mortgage loan on the Land, based on that violation.

The Amount of Insurance for Covered Risk 16 is subject to Your Deductible Amount and Our Maximum Dollar Limit of Liability shown in Schedule A.

17. You lose Your Title to any portion of the Land to an enforcement authority because of an exercise of the power to take the Land by condemnation, but only to the extent:

a. of the taking described in an Enforcement Notice; or

b. the taking occurred before the Date of Policy and is binding on You, if You purchased the Land without Knowledge of the taking.

18. You are ordered by a State or Municipal authority to remove or remedy any portion of Your existing structures—other than boundary walls or fences—because any portion of Your existing structures was built without obtaining a building permit from the proper Municipal authority. The Amount of Insurance for Covered Risk 18 is subject to Your Deductible Amount and Our Maximum Dollar Limit of Liability shown in Schedule A.

19. You are ordered by a State or Municipal authority to remove or remedy any portion of Your existing structures, because they violate an existing State or Municipal zoning law or State or Municipal zoning regulation. The Amount of Insurance for Covered Risk 19 is subject to Your Deductible Amount and Our Maximum Dollar Limit of Liability shown in Schedule A.

20. You are not able to use the Land because use as a single-family residence violates an existing State or Municipal zoning law or State or Municipal zoning regulation.

21. You are forced to remove any portion of Your existing structures because they encroach onto Your neighbor's land. If the encroaching structures are boundary walls or fences, the Amount of Insurance for Covered Risk 21 is subject to Your Deductible Amount and Our Maximum Dollar Limit of Liability shown in Schedule A.

22. Someone else exercises a legal right refusing to perform a contract to purchase, lease, or make a mortgage loan on the Land because Your neighbor's existing structures encroach onto the Land.

23. You are forced to remove any portion of Your existing structures that encroach onto an Easement or over a building set-back line, even if the Easement or building set-back line is excepted in Schedule B.

24. Your existing structures are damaged because of the exercise of the right to maintain or use any Easement affecting Your Title, even if the Easement is excepted in Schedule B.

25. Your existing improvements (or a replacement or modification made to them after the Date of Policy), including lawns, shrubbery, or trees, are damaged because of the future exercise of the right to use the surface of the Land for the extraction or development of oil, gas, minerals, groundwater, or any other subsurface substance, even if those rights are excepted or reserved from the description of the Land or excepted in Schedule B.

26. Someone else tries to enforce a Discriminatory Covenant that they claim affects Your Title.

27. A State or Municipal taxing authority assesses supplemental real estate taxes not previously assessed against the Land for any period before the Date of Policy because of construction or change of ownership or use, that occurred before the Date of Policy.

28. Your neighbor builds any structures after the Date of Policy—other than boundary walls or fences—that encroach onto the Land.

29. Your Title is unmarketable, which allows someone else to refuse to perform a contract to purchase, lease, or make a mortgage loan on the Land.

30. Someone else owns an interest in Your Title because a court order invalidates a prior transfer of the Title under federal bankruptcy, state insolvency, or similar state or federal creditors' rights law.

31. The residence with the Property Address shown in Schedule A is not located on the Land at the Date of Policy.

32. Any defect in or lien or encumbrance on the Title that has been created or attached or has been filed or recorded in the Public Records subsequent to the Date of Policy and prior to the recording of the deed or other instrument vesting the Title in the Public Records.

33. The map, if any, attached to this policy does not show the correct location of the Land according to the Public Records.

OUR DUTY TO DEFEND AGAINST LEGAL ACTIONS

We will defend Your Title in any legal action, only as to that portion of the legal action for a matter that is based on a Covered Risk and that is not excepted or excluded from coverage in this policy. We will pay the costs, attorneys' fees, and expenses We incur in that defense.

We will not pay for any portion of the legal action for a matter that is not based on a Covered Risk or that is excepted or excluded from coverage in this policy.

We can end Our duty to defend Your Title under Condition 4.

THIS POLICY IS NOT COMPLETE WITHOUT SCHEDULE A AND SCHEDULE B.

[Witness clause]

BLANK TITLE INSURANCE COMPANY

By: ______________________________
[Authorized Signatory]

By: ______________________________
[Authorized Signatory]

EXCLUSIONS FROM COVERAGE

The following matters are excluded from the coverage of this policy and We will not pay loss or damage, costs, attorneys' fees, or expenses that arise by reason of:

1. a. any law, ordinance, permit, or governmental regulation (including those relating to building and zoning) that restricts, regulates, prohibits, or relates to:

i. the occupancy, use, or enjoyment of the Land;

ii. the character, dimensions, or location of any improvement on the Land;

iii. the subdivision of land; or

iv. environmental remediation or protection.

b. any governmental forfeiture, police, or regulatory, or national security power.

c. the effect of a violation or enforcement of any matter excluded under Exclusion 1.a. or 1.b.

Exclusion 1 does not modify or limit the coverage provided under Covered Risk 8.a., 14, 15, 16, 18, 19, 20, 23, or 27.

2. Any power to take the Land by condemnation. Exclusion 2 does not modify or limit the coverage provided under Covered Risk 17.
3. Any defect, lien, encumbrance, adverse claim, or other matter:
   a. created, suffered, assumed, or agreed to by You;
   b. not Known to Us, not recorded in the Public Records at the Date of Policy, but Known to You and not disclosed in writing to Us by You prior to the date You became an Insured under this policy;
   c. resulting in no loss or damage to You;
   d. attaching or created subsequent to the Date of Policy (Exclusion 3.d. does not modify or limit the coverage provided under Covered Risk 5, 8.f., 25, 26, 27, 28, or 32); or
   e. resulting in loss or damage that would not have been sustained if You paid consideration sufficient to qualify You as a bona fide purchaser of the Title at the Date of Policy.
4. Lack of a right:
   a. to any land outside the area specifically described and referred to in Item 3 of Schedule A; and
   b. in any street, road, avenue, alley, lane, right-of-way, body of water, or waterway that abut the Land.

   Exclusion 4 does not modify or limit the coverage provided under Covered Risk 11 or 21.
5. The failure of Your existing structures, or any portion of Your existing structures, to have been constructed before, on, or after the Date of Policy in accordance with applicable building codes. Exclusion 5 does not modify or limit the coverage provided under Covered Risk 14 or 15.
6. Any claim, by reason of the operation of federal bankruptcy, state insolvency, or similar creditors' rights law, that the transfer of the Title to You is a:
   a. fraudulent conveyance or fraudulent transfer;
   b. voidable transfer under the Uniform Voidable Transactions Act; or
   c. preferential transfer:
      i. to the extent the instrument of transfer vesting the Title as shown in Schedule A is not a transfer made as a contemporaneous exchange for new value; or
      ii. for any other reason not stated in Covered Risk 30.
7. Contamination, explosion, fire, flooding, vibration, fracturing, earthquake, or subsidence.

8. Negligence by a person or an entity exercising a right to extract or develop oil, gas, minerals, groundwater, or any other subsurface substance.

9. Any lien on Your Title for real estate taxes or assessments imposed or collected by a governmental authority that becomes due and payable after the Date of Policy. Exclusion 9 does not modify or limit the coverage provided under Covered Risk 8.a. or 27.

10. Any discrepancy in the quantity of the area, square footage, or acreage of the Land or of any improvement to the Land.

CONDITIONS

1. DEFINITIONS

a. "Amount of Insurance": The Amount of Insurance stated in Schedule A, as may be increased by Condition 6.d. or 10 or decreased by Condition 7.d. or 7.e.; or increased or decreased by endorsements to this policy.

b. "Covenant": A covenant, condition, restriction, or limitation affecting the Title in a document or instrument in effect at the Date of Policy.

c. "Date of Policy": The Date of Policy stated in Schedule A.

d. "Discriminatory Covenant": Any covenant, condition, restriction, or limitation that is unenforceable under applicable law because it illegally discriminates against a class of individuals based on personal characteristics such as race, color, religion, sex, sexual orientation, gender identity, familial status, disability, national origin, or other legally protected class.

e. "Easement": The right of someone else to use any part of the Land for a specified purpose.

f. "Enforcement Notice": A document recorded in the Public Records at the Date of Policy that describes any part of the Land and:

   i. is issued by a governmental agency that identifies a violation or enforcement of a law, ordinance, permit, or governmental regulation; or

   ii. is issued by a holder of the power of condemnation or a governmental agency that identifies the exercise of a governmental power.

g. "Estate Planning Entity": A legal entity, a trust, or a trustee of a trust, if the entity or trust is established by a Natural Person for the purpose of planning the disposition of that person's estate.

h. "Insured": The Insured named in Item 1 of Schedule A and also the parties identified in Condition 2.b.

i. "Knowledge" or "Known": Actual knowledge or actual notice, but not constructive notice imparted by Public Records.

j. "Land": The land or condominium unit described in Item 3 of Schedule A and improvements located on that Land at the Date of Policy that by State law constitute real property. The term "Land" does not include any property beyond that described in Schedule A, nor any right, title, interest, estate, or easement in any abutting street, road, avenue, alley, lane, right-of-way, body of water, or waterway, but does not modify or limit the extent that a right of access to and from the Land is insured by this policy.

k. "Mortgage": A mortgage, deed of trust, trust deed, security deed, or other real property security instrument, including one evidenced by electronic means authorized by law.

l. "Municipal": A political subdivision of a State, such as a city, county, parish, town, or village.

m. "Natural Person": A human being, not a commercial or legal organization or entity.

n. "Public Records": The recording or filing system established under State statutes in effect at the Date of Policy under which a document must be recorded or filed to impart constructive notice of matters relating to the Title to a purchaser for value without Knowledge. The term "Public Records" does not include any other recording or filing system, including any pertaining to environmental remediation or protection, planning, permitting, zoning, licensing, building, health, public safety, or national security matters.

o. "State": The state or commonwealth of the United States within whose exterior boundaries the Land is located. The term "State" also includes the District of Columbia, the Commonwealth of Puerto Rico, the U.S. Virgin Islands, and Guam.

p. "Title": The estate or interest in the Land identified in Item 2 of Schedule A.

q. "We," "Our," or "Us": *Blank Title Insurance Company*.

r. "You" or "Your": The Insured.

2. CONTINUATION OF COVERAGE

a. Your coverage under this policy continues as of the Date of Policy, so long as You:

i. own Your Title;

ii. own an obligation secured by a purchase money Mortgage given by a purchaser from You; or

iii. have liability for warranties of title given by You in any transfer or conveyance of Your Title.

b. This policy also insures:

i. anyone who receives Your Title by operation of law upon Your death;

ii. Your spouse who receives Your Title because of a dissolution of Your marriage;

iii. Your Estate Planning Entity to which You transfer Your Title after the Date of Policy;

iv. any beneficiary or distributee of Your Estate Planning Entity who receives Your Title;

v. anyone who receives Your Title by a transfer effective upon Your death as provided by law; or

vi. another Insured named in Item 1 of Schedule A.

c. We may assert against any Insured identified in Condition 2.b. any rights and defenses that We have against any previous Insured under this policy.

3. HOW TO MAKE A CLAIM

a. *Prompt Notice of Your Claim*

i. You must notify Us promptly in writing as soon as You Know of anything that might be covered by this policy.

ii. Send Your notice to:

Blank Title Insurance Company

____

____

Attention: Claims Department

Please include Your Policy Number shown in Schedule A and the county and State where the Land is located. Please enclose a copy of this policy, if available.

iii. If You do not give Us prompt notice, Your coverage may be reduced or ended, but only to the extent Your failure affects Our ability to resolve the claim or defend You.

b. *Proof of Your Loss*

i. We may require You to give Us a written statement signed by You describing Your loss that includes:

(a). the facts supporting Your claim;

(b). the Covered Risks that apply to Your claim;

(c). the dollar amount of Your loss; and

(d). the method You used to compute the amount of Your loss.

ii. We may require You to make available to Us records, checks, letters, contracts, insurance policies, and other papers relating to Your claim. We may make copies of these papers.

iii. We may require You to answer questions about Your claim under oath.

iv. If You fail or refuse to give Us a statement of loss, answer Our questions under oath, or make available to Us the papers We request, Your coverage may be reduced or ended, but only to the extent Your failure or refusal affects Our ability to resolve the claim or defend You.

4. OUR CHOICES WHEN WE LEARN OF A CLAIM

a. After We receive Your notice or otherwise learn of a claim covered by this policy, and after subtracting Your Deductible Amount, if it applies, Our choices include one or more of the following:

   i. pay the claim;

   ii. negotiate a settlement;

   iii. bring or defend a legal action related to the claim;

   iv. pay You the amount required by this policy;

   v. end the coverage of this policy for the claim by paying You Your loss determined in Condition 6.a., as applicable, resulting from the Covered Risk;

   vi. end the coverage described in Covered Risk 16, 18, 19, or 21 by paying You Our Maximum Dollar Limit of Liability then in force for the particular Covered Risk;

   vii. end all coverage of this policy by paying You the Amount of Insurance then in force; or

   viii.take other appropriate action, including to cure or otherwise resolve the covered matter giving rise to the claim.

b. When We choose the options in Condition 4.a.v., 4.a.vi., or 4.a.vii., all Our liability and obligations to You under this policy terminate, including Our obligation to defend or continue any legal action. In addition, We will pay any costs, attorneys' fees, and expenses that were authorized by Us up to that time and that We are obligated to pay.

c. Whether or not We agree there is coverage, We may choose one or more of the options above. By doing so, We do not give up any rights.

5. HANDLING A CLAIM OR LEGAL ACTION

a. You must cooperate with Us in handling any claim or legal action and give Us all relevant information.

b. If You fail or refuse to cooperate with Us, Your coverage may be reduced or ended, but only to the extent Your failure or refusal affects Our ability to resolve the claim or defend You.

c. We are only required to repay You for amounts, including settlement costs, attorneys' fees, and expenses, that We approve in advance.

d. We have the right to choose the attorney when We bring or defend a legal action on Your behalf. We can appeal any decision to the highest level. We do not have to pay Your claim until a State or federal court having jurisdiction makes a final, non-appealable determination adverse to the Title.

6. CONTRACT OF INDEMNITY; DETERMINATION AND EXTENT OF LIABILITY

This policy is a contract of indemnity against actual monetary loss or damage sustained or incurred by You by reason of matters insured against by this policy. This policy is not an abstract of the Title, report of the condition of the Title, legal opinion, opinion of the Title, or other representation of the status of the Title. All claims asserted under this policy are based in contract and are restricted to the terms and provisions of this policy. We are not liable for any claim alleging negligence or negligent misrepresentation arising from or in connection with this policy or the determination of the insurability of the Title.

a. After subtracting Your Deductible Amount, if it applies, Our liability for Your loss or damage is limited to the least of:

   i. the difference between the fair market value of Your Title, as insured, and the fair market value of Your Title subject to the matter insured against by this policy;

   ii. Our Maximum Dollar Limit of Liability then in force for the particular Covered Risk, for claims covered only under Covered Risk 16, 18, 19, or 21; or

   iii. the Amount of Insurance then in force.

b. Except as provided in Condition 6.c. or 6.d., the fair market value of Your Title in Condition 6.a.i. is calculated using the date You discover the defect, lien, encumbrance, adverse claim, or other matter insured against by this policy.

c. If, at the Date of Policy, the Title to all of the Land is void by reason of a matter insured against by this policy, then You may, by providing Us written notice, elect to use the Date of Policy as the date for calculating the fair market value of Your Title in Condition 6.a.i.

d. If We pursue Our rights under Conditions 4.a.iii. and 4.a.viii. and are unsuccessful in establishing Your Title, as insured:

   i. the Amount of Insurance then in force will be increased by 15% of the Amount of Insurance shown in Schedule A; and

   ii. You may, by providing Us written notice, elect, as an alternative to the dates set forth in Condition 6.b. or, if it applies, 6.c., to use either the date the settlement, action, proceeding, or other act described in Conditions 4.a.iii. and 4.a.viii. is concluded or the date the notice of claim required by Condition 3 is received by Us as the date for calculating the fair market value of Your Title in Condition 6.a.i.

e. In addition to the extent of liability for loss or damage under Conditions 6.a.:

   i. We will also pay the costs, attorneys' fees, and expenses incurred in accordance with Conditions 4 and 5; and

ii. if You are unable to use the Land because of a claim covered by this policy:

(a). You may rent a reasonably equivalent substitute residence and We will repay You for the actual rent You pay, until the earlier of:

(1). the cause of the claim is removed; or

(2). We pay You the amount required by this policy. If Your claim is covered only under Covered Risk 16, 18, 19, or 21, that payment is the Amount of Insurance then in force for the particular Covered Risk.

(b). We will pay reasonable costs You pay to relocate any personal property You have the right to remove from the Land, including transportation of that personal property for up to fifty (50) miles from the Land, and repair of any damage to that personal property because of the relocation. The amount We will pay You under Condition 6.e.ii.(b). is limited to the value of the personal property before You relocate it.

7. LIMITATION OF OUR LIABILITY

a. Other than as provided in Condition 6.e., if We remove the cause of the claim after receiving notice of the claim, all Our obligations for the claim end, including any obligation for loss You had while We were removing the cause of the claim.

b. We are not liable for loss or damage arising out of any litigation, including litigation by Us or with Our consent, until a State or federal court having jurisdiction makes a final, non-appealable determination adverse to the Title.

c. We are not liable for loss or damage to You for liability voluntarily assumed by You in settling any claim or suit without Our prior written consent.

d. All payments under this policy reduce the Amount of Insurance then in force, except for costs, attorneys' fees, and expenses. All payments for claims covered only under Covered Risk 16, 18, 19, or 21 also reduce Our Maximum Dollar Limit of Liability for the particular Covered Risk, except for costs, attorneys' fees, and expenses.

e. If We issue, or have issued, a policy to the owner of a Mortgage that is on Your Title and We have not given You any coverage against the Mortgage, then:

i. We have the right to pay any amount due to You under this policy to the owner of the Mortgage, and any amount paid will be treated as a payment to You under this policy, including under Condition 4.a.;

ii. any amount paid to the owner of the Mortgage will be subtracted from the Amount of Insurance then in force; and

iii. if Your claim is covered only under Covered Risk 16, 18, 19, or 21, any amount paid to the owner of the Mortgage will also be subtracted from Our Maximum Dollar Limit of Liability for the particular Covered Risk.

f. If You do anything to affect any right of recovery You may have against someone else, We can subtract from Our liability the amount by which You reduced the value of that right.

g. We are not liable for the content of the Transaction Identification Data, if any. Condition 7.g. does not modify or limit the coverage provided under Covered Risk 31.

8. TRANSFER OF YOUR RIGHTS TO US

a. If We settle and pay Your claim, We have all the rights and remedies You have against any person, entity, or property related to the claim. You must not do anything to affect these rights and remedies. If We ask, You must execute documents to transfer these rights and remedies to Us. You must let Us use Your name in enforcing these rights and remedies.

b. We will not be liable to You if We do not pursue these rights and remedies or if We do not recover any amount that might be recoverable.

c. We will pay any money We collect from enforcing these rights and remedies in the following order:

i. to Us for the costs, attorneys' fees, and expenses We paid to enforce these rights and remedies;

ii. to You for Your loss that You have not already collected;

iii. to Us for any money We paid out under this policy on account of Your claim; and

iv. to You whatever is left.

d. If You have rights and remedies under contracts (such as indemnities, guaranties, warranties, insurance policies, or bonds) to recover all or part of Your loss, then We have all of those rights and remedies, even if those contracts provide that those obligated have all of Your rights and remedies under this policy.

9. POLICY ENTIRE CONTRACT

a. This policy together with all endorsements, if any, issued by Us is the entire policy and contract between You and Us. In interpreting any provision of this policy, this policy will be construed as a whole. This policy and any endorsement to this policy may be issued by electronic means authorized by law.

b. Any claim You make against Us must be made under this policy and is subject to its terms.

c. Any amendment of this policy must be by a written endorsement issued by Us. To the extent any term or provision of an endorsement is inconsistent with any term or provision of this policy, the term or provision of the endorsement controls. Unless the endorsement expressly states, it does not:

i. modify any prior endorsement,

ii. extend the Date of Policy,

iii. insure against loss or damage exceeding the Amount of Insurance, or

iv. increase the Amount of Insurance.

10. INCREASED AMOUNT OF INSURANCE

The Amount of Insurance then in force will increase by ten percent (10%) of the Amount of Insurance shown in Schedule A each year for the first five years following the Date of Policy shown in Schedule A, up to one hundred fifty percent (150%) of the Amount of Insurance shown in Schedule A. The increase each year will happen on the anniversary of the Date of Policy shown in Schedule A.

11. SEVERABILITY

In the event any provision of this policy, in whole or in part, is held invalid or unenforceable under applicable law, both You and We can still enforce the rest of this policy.

12. CHOICE OF LAW AND CHOICE OF FORUM

The State law of the State where the Land is located, or to the extent it controls, federal law, applies to this policy. A court or arbitrator must not apply conflict of law principles to determine the applicable law. Any litigation or other proceeding brought by You against Us must be filed only in a State or federal court having jurisdiction.

13. CLASS ACTION

ALL CLAIMS AND DISPUTES ARISING OUT OF OR RELATING TO THIS POLICY, INCLUDING ANY SERVICE OR OTHER MATTER IN CONNECTION WITH ISSUING THIS POLICY, ANY BREACH OF A POLICY PROVISION, OR ANY OTHER CLAIM OR DISPUTE ARISING OUT OF OR RELATING TO THE TRANSACTION GIVING RISE TO THIS POLICY, MUST BE BROUGHT IN AN INDIVIDUAL CAPACITY. NO PARTY MAY SERVE AS PLAINTIFF, CLASS MEMBER, OR PARTICIPANT IN ANY CLASS, REPRESENTATIVE, OR PRIVATE ATTORNEY GENERAL PROCEEDING.

[**14.** ARBITRATION

a. All claims and disputes arising out of or relating to this policy, including any service or other matter in connection with issuing this policy, any breach of a policy provision, or any other claim or dispute arising out of or relating to the transaction giving rise to this policy, may be resolved by arbitration. If the Amount of Insurance is $2,000,000 or less, any claim or dispute may be submitted to binding arbitration at the election of either You or Us. If the Amount of Insurance is greater than $2,000,000, any claim or dispute may be submitted to binding arbitration only when agreed to by both You and Us. Arbitration must be conducted pursuant to the Title Insurance Arbitration Rules of the American Land Title Association ("ALTA Rules"). The ALTA Rules are available online at www.alta.org/arbitration . The ALTA Rules incorporate, as appropriate to a particular dispute, the Consumer Arbitration Rules and Commercial Arbitration Rules of the American Arbitration Association ("AAA Rules"). The AAA Rules are available online at www.adr.org .

b. ALL CLAIMS AND DISPUTES MUST BE BROUGHT IN AN INDIVIDUAL CAPACITY. NO PARTY MAY SERVE AS PLAINTIFF, CLASS MEMBER, OR PARTICIPANT IN ANY CLASS, REPRESENTATIVE, OR PRIVATE ATTORNEY GENERAL PROCEEDING IN ANY ARBITRATION GOVERNED BY CONDITION 14. The arbitrator does not have authority to conduct any class action arbitration, private attorney general arbitration, or arbitration involving joint or consolidated claims under any circumstance.

c. *If there is a final judicial determination that a request for particular relief cannot be arbitrated in accordance with this Condition 14, then only that request for particular relief may be brought in court. All other requests for relief remain subject to this Condition 14.*

d. [We will pay all AAA filing, administration, and arbitrator fees of the consumer when the arbitration seeks relief of $100,000 or less. Other fees][Fees] will be allocated in accordance with the applicable AAA Rules. The results of arbitration will be binding upon the parties. The arbitrator may consider, but is not bound by, rulings in prior arbitrations involving different parties. The arbitrator is bound by rulings in prior arbitrations involving the same parties to the extent required by law. The arbitrator must issue a written decision sufficient to explain the findings and conclusions on which the award is based. Judgment upon the award rendered by the arbitrator may be entered in any State or federal court having jurisdiction.]

[Transaction Identification Data, for which the Company assumes no liability as set forth in Condition 7.g.:

Issuing Agent:

Issuing Office:

Issuing Office's ALTA® Registry ID:

Issuing Office File Number:

Property Address:]

SCHEDULE A

Name and Address of Title Insurance Company:

Policy Number: [Premium: $]

Amount of Insurance: $

Date of Policy: [at a.m./p.m.]

Deductible Amounts and Maximum Dollar Limits of Liability for Covered Risks 16, 18, 19, and 21:

	Your Deductible Amount	**Our Maximum Dollar Limit of Liability**
Covered Risk 16:	___% of Amount of Insurance shown in Schedule A or $___________ *(whichever is less)*	$___________
Covered Risk 18:	___% of Amount of Insurance shown in Schedule A or $___________ *(whichever is less)*	$___________
Covered Risk 19:	___% of Amount of Insurance shown in Schedule A or $___________ *(whichever is less)*	$___________
Covered Risk 21:	___% of Amount of Insurance shown in Schedule A or $___________ *(whichever is less)*	$___________

Property Address of the Land:

1. The Insured is:
2. Your interest in the Land covered by this policy is:
3. The Land referred to in this policy is described as:

SCHEDULE B

EXCEPTIONS FROM COVERAGE

Policy Number:

Some historical land records contain Discriminatory Covenants that are illegal and unenforceable by law. This policy treats any Discriminatory Covenant in a document referenced in Schedule B as if each Discriminatory Covenant is redacted, repudiated, removed, and not republished or recirculated. Only the remaining provisions of the document are excepted from coverage.

In addition to the Exclusions from Coverage, this policy does not insure You against loss or damage and We will not pay costs, attorneys' fees, or expenses resulting from the terms and conditions of any lease or easement identified in Schedule A, and the following matters:

(Insert Schedule B exceptions here)

I. [§ 4.54] ALTA Loan Policy of Title Insurance (2006)

LOAN POLICY OF TITLE INSURANCE
Issued By
BLANK TITLE INSURANCE COMPANY

Any notice of claim and any other notice or statement in writing required to be given to the Company under this Policy must be given to the Company at the address shown in Section 17 of the Conditions.

COVERED RISKS

SUBJECT TO THE EXCLUSIONS FROM COVERAGE, THE EXCEPTIONS FROM COVERAGE CONTAINED IN SCHEDULE B, AND THE CONDITIONS, BLANK TITLE INSURANCE COMPANY, a Blank corporation (the "Company") insures as of Date of Policy and, to the extent stated in Covered Risks 11, 13, and 14, after Date of Policy, against loss or damage, not exceeding the Amount of Insurance, sustained or incurred by the Insured by reason of:

1. Title being vested other than as stated in Schedule A.
2. Any defect in or lien or encumbrance on the Title. This Covered Risk includes but is not limited to insurance against loss from
   (a) A defect in the Title caused by
      (i) forgery, fraud, undue influence, duress, incompetency, incapacity, or impersonation;
      (ii) failure of any person or Entity to have authorized a transfer or conveyance;
      (iii) a document affecting Title not properly created, executed, witnessed, sealed, acknowledged, notarized, or delivered;
      (iv) failure to perform those acts necessary to create a document by electronic means authorized by law;
      (v) a document executed under a falsified, expired, or otherwise invalid power of attorney;
      (vi) a document not properly filed, recorded, or indexed in the Public Records including failure to perform those acts by electronic means authorized by law; or
      (vii) a defective judicial or administrative proceeding.
   (b) The lien of real estate taxes or assessments imposed on the Title by a governmental authority due or payable, but unpaid.
   (c) Any encroachment, encumbrance, violation, variation, or adverse circumstance affecting the Title that would be disclosed by an accurate and complete land survey of the Land. The term "encroachment" includes encroachments of

existing improvements located on the Land onto adjoining land, and encroachments onto the Land of existing improvements located on adjoining land.

3. Unmarketable Title.
4. No right of access to and from the Land.
5. The violation or enforcement of any law, ordinance, permit, or governmental regulation (including those relating to building and zoning) restricting, regulating, prohibiting, or relating to
   (a) the occupancy, use, or enjoyment of the Land;
   (b) the character, dimensions, or location of any improvement erected on the Land;
   (c) the subdivision of land; or
   (d) environmental protection

   if a notice, describing any part of the Land, is recorded in the Public Records setting forth the violation or intention to enforce, but only to the extent of the violation or enforcement referred to in that notice.
6. An enforcement action based on the exercise of a governmental police power not covered by Covered Risk 5 if a notice of the enforcement action, describing any part of the Land, is recorded in the Public Records, but only to the extent of the enforcement referred to in that notice.
7. The exercise of the rights of eminent domain if a notice of the exercise, describing any part of the Land, is recorded in the Public Records.
8. Any taking by a governmental body that has occurred and is binding on the rights of a purchaser for value without Knowledge.
9. The invalidity or unenforceability of the lien of the Insured Mortgage upon the Title. This Covered Risk includes but is not limited to insurance against loss from any of the following impairing the lien of the Insured Mortgage
   (a) forgery, fraud, undue influence, duress, incompetency, incapacity, or impersonation;
   (b) failure of any person or Entity to have authorized a transfer or conveyance;
   (c) the Insured Mortgage not being properly created, executed, witnessed, sealed, acknowledged, notarized, or delivered;
   (d) failure to perform those acts necessary to create a document by electronic means authorized by law;
   (e) a document executed under a falsified, expired, or otherwise invalid power of attorney;
   (f) a document not properly filed, recorded, or indexed in the Public Records including failure to perform those acts by electronic means authorized by law; or
   (g) a defective judicial or administrative proceeding.

10. The lack of priority of the lien of the Insured Mortgage upon the Title over any other lien or encumbrance.
11. The lack of priority of the lien of the Insured Mortgage upon the Title
    (a) as security for each and every advance of proceeds of the loan secured by the Insured Mortgage over any statutory lien for services, labor, or material arising from construction of an improvement or work related to the Land when the improvement or work is either
        (i) contracted for or commenced on or before Date of Policy; or
        (ii) contracted for, commenced, or continued after Date of Policy if the construction is financed, in whole or in part, by proceeds of the loan secured by the Insured Mortgage that the Insured has advanced or is obligated on Date of Policy to advance; and
    (b) over the lien of any assessments for street improvements under construction or completed at Date of Policy.
12. The invalidity or unenforceability of any assignment of the Insured Mortgage, provided the assignment is shown in Schedule A, or the failure of the assignment shown in Schedule A to vest title to the Insured Mortgage in the named Insured assignee free and clear of all liens.
13. The invalidity, unenforceability, lack of priority, or avoidance of the lien of the Insured Mortgage upon the Title
    (a) resulting from the avoidance in whole or in part, or from a court order providing an alternative remedy, of any transfer of all or any part of the title to or any interest in the Land occurring prior to the transaction creating the lien of the Insured Mortgage because that prior transfer constituted a fraudulent or preferential transfer under federal bankruptcy, state insolvency, or similar creditors' rights laws; or
    (b) because the Insured Mortgage constitutes a preferential transfer under federal bankruptcy, state insolvency, or similar creditors' rights laws by reason of the failure of its recording in the Public Records
        (i) to be timely, or
        (ii) to impart notice of its existence to a purchaser for value or to a judgment or lien creditor.
14. Any defect in or lien or encumbrance on the Title or other matter included in Covered Risks 1 through 13 that has been created or attached or has been filed or recorded in the Public Records subsequent to Date of Policy and prior to the recording of the Insured Mortgage in the Public Records.

The Company will also pay the costs, attorneys' fees, and expenses incurred in defense of any matter insured against by this Policy, but only to the extent provided in the Conditions.

[Witness clause optional]

BLANK TITLE INSURANCE COMPANY

BY: PRESIDENT

BY: SECRETARY

EXCLUSIONS FROM COVERAGE

The following matters are expressly excluded from the coverage of this policy, and the Company will not pay loss or damage, costs, attorneys' fees, or expenses that arise by reason of:

1. (a) Any law, ordinance, permit, or governmental regulation (including those relating to building and zoning) restricting, regulating, prohibiting, or relating to

   (i) the occupancy, use, or enjoyment of the Land;

   (ii) the character, dimensions, or location of any improvement erected on the Land;

   (iii) the subdivision of land; or

   (iv) environmental protection;

   or the effect of any violation of these laws, ordinances, or governmental regulations. This Exclusion 1(a) does not modify or limit the coverage provided under Covered Risk 5.

   (b) Any governmental police power. This Exclusion 1(b) does not modify or limit the coverage provided under Covered Risk 6.

2. Rights of eminent domain. This Exclusion does not modify or limit the coverage provided under Covered Risk 7 or 8.

3. Defects, liens, encumbrances, adverse claims, or other matters

   (a) created, suffered, assumed, or agreed to by the Insured Claimant;

   (b) not Known to the Company, not recorded in the Public Records at Date of Policy, but Known to the Insured Claimant and not disclosed in writing to the Company by the Insured Claimant prior to the date the Insured Claimant became an Insured under this policy;

   (c) resulting in no loss or damage to the Insured Claimant;

   (d) attaching or created subsequent to Date of Policy (however, this does not modify or limit the coverage provided under Covered Risk 11, 13, or 14); or

   (e) resulting in loss or damage that would not have been sustained if the Insured Claimant had paid value for the Insured Mortgage.

4. Unenforceability of the lien of the Insured Mortgage because of the inability or failure of an Insured to comply with applicable doing-business laws of the state where the Land is situated.

5. Invalidity or unenforceability in whole or in part of the lien of the Insured Mortgage that arises out of the transaction evidenced by the Insured Mortgage and is based upon usury or any consumer credit protection or truth-in-lending law.
6. Any claim, by reason of the operation of federal bankruptcy, state insolvency, or similar creditors' rights laws, that the transaction creating the lien of the Insured Mortgage, is
   (a) a fraudulent conveyance or fraudulent transfer, or
   (b) a preferential transfer for any reason not stated in Covered Risk 13(b) of this policy.
7. Any lien on the Title for real estate taxes or assessments imposed by governmental authority and created or attaching between Date of Policy and the date of recording of the Insured Mortgage in the Public Records. This Exclusion does not modify or limit the coverage provided under Covered Risk 11(b).

SCHEDULE A

Name and Address of Title Insurance Company:

[File No.:] Policy No.:

Loan No.:

Address Reference:

Amount of Insurance: $ [Premium: $]

Date of Policy: [at a.m./p.m.]

1. Name of Insured:

2. The estate or interest in the Land that is encumbered by the Insured Mortgage is:

3. Title is vested in:

4. The Insured Mortgage and its assignments, if any, are described as follows:

5. The Land referred to in this policy is described as follows:

[6. This policy incorporates by reference those ALTA endorsements selected below:

4-06	(Condominium)
4.1-06	
5-06	(Planned Unit Development)
5.1-06	
6-06	(Variable Rate)
6.2-06	(Variable Rate—Negative Amortization)

8.1-06	(Environmental Protection Lien) Paragraph b refers to the following state statute(s):
9-06	(Restrictions, Encroachments, Minerals)
13.1-06	(Leasehold Loan)
14-06	(Future Advance-Priority)
14.1-06	(Future Advance-Knowledge)
14.3-06	(Future Advance-Reverse Mortgage)
22-06	(Location) The type of improvement is a _______________, and the street address is as shown above.]

SCHEDULE B

[File No.   ] Policy No.

EXCEPTIONS FROM COVERAGE

[Except as provided in Schedule B - Part II,] t[or T]his policy does not insure against loss or damage, and the Company will not pay costs, attorneys' fees, or expenses that arise by reason of:

[PART I

PART II

In addition to the matters set forth in Part I of this Schedule, the Title is subject to the following matters, and the Company insures against loss or damage sustained in the event that they are not subordinate to the lien of the Insured Mortgage:]

CONDITIONS

1. DEFINITION OF TERMS

The following terms when used in this policy mean:

(a) "Amount of Insurance": The amount stated in Schedule A, as may be increased or decreased by endorsement to this policy, increased by Section 8(b) or decreased by Section 10 of these Conditions.

(b) "Date of Policy": The date designated as "Date of Policy" in Schedule A.

(c) "Entity": A corporation, partnership, trust, limited liability company, or other similar legal entity.

(d) "Indebtedness": The obligation secured by the Insured Mortgage including one evidenced by electronic means authorized by law, and if that obligation is the payment of a debt, the Indebtedness is the sum of

(i) the amount of the principal disbursed as of Date of Policy;

(ii) the amount of the principal disbursed subsequent to Date of Policy;

(iii) the construction loan advances made subsequent to Date of Policy for the purpose of financing in whole or in part the construction of an improvement to the Land or related to the Land that the Insured was and continued to be obligated to advance at Date of Policy and at the date of the advance;

(iv) interest on the loan;

(v) the prepayment premiums, exit fees, and other similar fees or penalties allowed by law;

(vi) the expenses of foreclosure and any other costs of enforcement;

(vii) the amounts advanced to assure compliance with laws or to protect the lien or the priority of the lien of the Insured Mortgage before the acquisition of the estate or interest in the Title;

(viii) the amounts to pay taxes and insurance; and

(ix) the reasonable amounts expended to prevent deterioration of improvements;

but the Indebtedness is reduced by the total of all payments and by any amount forgiven by an Insured.

(e) "Insured": The Insured named in Schedule A.

(i) The term "Insured" also includes

(A) the owner of the Indebtedness and each successor in ownership of the Indebtedness, whether the owner or successor owns the Indebtedness for its own account or as a trustee or other fiduciary, except a successor who is an obligor under the provisions of Section 12(c) of these Conditions;

(B) the person or Entity who has "control" of the "transferable record," if the Indebtedness is evidenced by a "transferable record," as these terms are defined by applicable electronic transactions law;

(C) successors to an Insured by dissolution, merger, consolidation, distribution, or reorganization;

(D) successors to an Insured by its conversion to another kind of Entity;

(E) a grantee of an Insured under a deed delivered without payment of actual valuable consideration conveying the Title

(1) if the stock, shares, memberships, or other equity interests of the grantee are wholly-owned by the named Insured,

(2) if the grantee wholly owns the named Insured, or

(3) if the grantee is wholly-owned by an affiliated Entity of the named Insured, provided the affiliated Entity and the named Insured are both wholly-owned by the same person or Entity;

(F) any government agency or instrumentality that is an insurer or guarantor under an insurance contract or guaranty insuring or guaranteeing the Indebtedness secured by the Insured Mortgage, or any part of it, whether named as an Insured or not;

(ii) With regard to (A), (B), (C), (D) , and (E) reserving, however, all rights and defenses as to any successor that the Company would have had against any predecessor Insured, unless the successor acquired the Indebtedness as a purchaser for value without Knowledge of the asserted defect, lien, encumbrance, or other matter insured against by this policy.

(f) "Insured Claimant": An Insured claiming loss or damage.

(g) "Insured Mortgage": The Mortgage described in paragraph 4 of Schedule A.

(h) "Knowledge" or "Known": Actual knowledge, not constructive knowledge or notice that may be imputed to an Insured by reason of the Public Records or any other records that impart constructive notice of matters affecting the Title.

(i) "Land": The land described in Schedule A, and affixed improvements that by law constitute real property. The term "Land" does not include any property beyond the lines of the area described in Schedule A, nor any right, title, interest, estate, or easement in abutting streets, roads, avenues, alleys, lanes, ways, or waterways, but this does not modify or limit the extent that a right of access to and from the Land is insured by this policy.

(j) "Mortgage": Mortgage, deed of trust, trust deed, or other security instrument, including one evidenced by electronic means authorized by law.

(k) "Public Records": Records established under state statutes at Date of Policy for the purpose of imparting constructive notice of matters relating to real property to purchasers for value and without Knowledge. With respect to

Covered Risk 5(d), "Public Records" shall also include environmental protection liens filed in the records of the clerk of the United States District Court for the district where the Land is located.

(l) "Title": The estate or interest described in Schedule A.

(m) "Unmarketable Title": Title affected by an alleged or apparent matter that would permit a prospective purchaser or lessee of the Title or lender on the Title or a prospective purchaser of the Insured Mortgage to be released from the obligation to purchase, lease, or lend if there is a contractual condition requiring the delivery of marketable title.

2. CONTINUATION OF INSURANCE

The coverage of this policy shall continue in force as of Date of Policy in favor of an Insured after acquisition of the Title by an Insured or after conveyance by an Insured, but only so long as the Insured retains an estate or interest in the Land, or holds an obligation secured by a purchase money Mortgage given by a purchaser from the Insured, or only so long as the Insured shall have liability by reason of warranties in any transfer or conveyance of the Title. This policy shall not continue in force in favor of any purchaser from the Insured of either (i) an estate or interest in the Land, or (ii) an obligation secured by a purchase money Mortgage given to the Insured.

3. NOTICE OF CLAIM TO BE GIVEN BY INSURED CLAIMANT

The Insured shall notify the Company promptly in writing (i) in case of any litigation as set forth in Section 5(a) of these Conditions, (ii) in case Knowledge shall come to an Insured of any claim of title or interest that is adverse to the Title or the lien of the Insured Mortgage, as insured, and that might cause loss or damage for which the Company may be liable by virtue of this policy, or (iii) if the Title or the lien of the Insured Mortgage, as insured, is rejected as Unmarketable Title. If the Company is prejudiced by the failure of the Insured Claimant to provide prompt notice, the Company's liability to the Insured Claimant under the policy shall be reduced to the extent of the prejudice.

4. PROOF OF LOSS

In the event the Company is unable to determine the amount of loss or damage, the Company may, at its option, require as a condition of payment that the Insured Claimant furnish a signed proof of loss. The proof of loss must describe the defect, lien, encumbrance, or other matter insured against by this policy that constitutes the basis of loss or damage and shall state, to the extent possible, the basis of calculating the amount of the loss or damage.

5. DEFENSE AND PROSECUTION OF ACTIONS

(a) Upon written request by the Insured, and subject to the options contained in Section 7 of these Conditions, the Company, at its own cost and without unreasonable delay, shall provide for the defense of an Insured in litigation in which any third party asserts a claim covered by this policy adverse to the Insured. This obligation is limited to only those stated causes of action alleging matters insured against by this policy. The Company shall have the right to select counsel of its choice (subject to the right of the Insured to object for reasonable cause) to represent the Insured as to those stated causes of action. It shall not be liable for and will not pay the fees of any other counsel. The Company will not pay any fees, costs, or expenses incurred by the Insured in the defense of those causes of action that allege matters not insured against by this policy.

(b) The Company shall have the right, in addition to the options contained in Section 7 of these Conditions, at its own cost, to institute and prosecute any action or proceeding or to do any other act that in its opinion may be necessary or desirable to establish the Title or the lien of the Insured Mortgage, as insured, or to prevent or reduce loss or damage to the Insured. The Company may take any appropriate action under the terms of this policy, whether or not it shall be liable to the Insured. The exercise of these rights shall not be an admission of liability or waiver of any provision of this policy. If the Company exercises its rights under this subsection, it must do so diligently.

(c) Whenever the Company brings an action or asserts a defense as required or permitted by this policy, the Company may pursue the litigation to a final determination by a court of competent jurisdiction, and it expressly reserves the right, in its sole discretion, to appeal any adverse judgment or order.

6. DUTY OF INSURED CLAIMANT TO COOPERATE

(a) In all cases where this policy permits or requires the Company to prosecute or provide for the defense of any action or proceeding and any appeals, the Insured shall secure to the

Company the right to so prosecute or provide defense in the action or proceeding, including the right to use, at its option, the name of the Insured for this purpose.

Whenever requested by the Company, the Insured, at the Company's expense, shall give the Company all reasonable aid (i) in securing evidence, obtaining witnesses, prosecuting or defending the action or proceeding, or effecting settlement, and (ii) in any other lawful act that in the opinion of the Company may be necessary or desirable to establish the Title, the lien of the Insured Mortgage, or any other matter as insured. If the Company is prejudiced by the failure of the Insured to furnish the required cooperation, the Company's obligations to the Insured under the policy shall terminate, including any liability or obligation to defend, prosecute, or continue any litigation, with regard to the matter or matters requiring such cooperation.

(b) The Company may reasonably require the Insured Claimant to submit to examination under oath by any authorized representative of the Company and to produce for examination, inspection, and copying, at such reasonable times and places as may be designated by the authorized representative of the Company, all records, in whatever medium maintained, including books, ledgers, checks, memoranda, correspondence, reports, e-mails, disks, tapes, and videos whether bearing a date before or after Date of Policy, that reasonably pertain to the loss or damage. Further, if requested by any authorized representative of the Company, the Insured Claimant shall grant its permission, in writing, for any authorized representative of the Company to examine, inspect, and copy all of these records in the custody or control of a third party that reasonably pertain to the loss or damage. All information designated as confidential by the Insured Claimant provided to the Company pursuant to this Section shall not be disclosed to others unless, in the reasonable judgment of the Company, it is necessary in the administration of the claim. Failure of the Insured Claimant to submit for examination under oath, produce any reasonably requested information, or grant permission to secure reasonably necessary information from third parties as required in this subsection, unless prohibited by law or governmental regulation, shall terminate any liability of the Company under this policy as to that claim.

7. **OPTIONS TO PAY OR OTHERWISE SETTLE CLAIMS; TERMINATION OF LIABILITY**

In case of a claim under this policy, the Company shall have the following additional options:

(a) To Pay or Tender Payment of the Amount of Insurance or to Purchase the Indebtedness.

(i) To pay or tender payment of the Amount of Insurance under this policy together with any costs, attorneys' fees, and expenses incurred by the Insured Claimant that were authorized by the Company up to the time of payment or tender of payment and that the Company is obligated to pay; or

(ii) To purchase the Indebtedness for the amount of the Indebtedness on the date of purchase, together with any costs, attorneys' fees, and expenses incurred by the Insured Claimant that were authorized by the Company up to the time of purchase and that the Company is obligated to pay.

When the Company purchases the Indebtedness, the Insured shall transfer, assign, and convey to the Company the Indebtedness and the Insured Mortgage, together with any collateral security.

Upon the exercise by the Company of either of the options provided for in subsections (a)(i) or (ii), all liability and obligations of the Company to the Insured under this policy, other than to make the payment required in those subsections, shall terminate, including any liability or obligation to defend, prosecute, or continue any litigation.

(b) To Pay or Otherwise Settle With Parties Other Than the Insured or With the Insured Claimant.

(i) to pay or otherwise settle with other parties for or in the name of an Insured Claimant any claim insured against under this policy. In addition, the Company will pay any costs, attorneys' fees, and expenses incurred by the Insured Claimant that were authorized by the Company up to the time of payment and that the Company is obligated to pay; or

(ii) to pay or otherwise settle with the Insured Claimant the loss or damage provided for under this policy, together with any costs, attorneys' fees, and expenses incurred by the Insured Claimant that were authorized by the Company up to the time of payment and that the Company is obligated to pay.

Upon the exercise by the Company of either of the options provided for in subsections (b)(i) or (ii), the Company's obligations to the Insured under this policy for the claimed loss or damage, other than the payments required to be made, shall terminate, including any liability or obligation to defend, prosecute, or continue any litigation.

8. DETERMINATION AND EXTENT OF LIABILITY

This policy is a contract of indemnity against actual monetary loss or damage sustained or incurred by the Insured Claimant who has suffered loss or damage by reason of matters insured against by this policy.

(a) The extent of liability of the Company for loss or damage under this policy shall not exceed the least of

(i) the Amount of Insurance,

(ii) the Indebtedness,

(iii) the difference between the value of the Title as insured and the value of the Title subject to the risk insured against by this policy, or

(iv) if a government agency or instrumentality is the Insured Claimant, the amount it paid in the acquisition of the Title or the Insured Mortgage in satisfaction of its insurance contract or guaranty.

(b) If the Company pursues its rights under Section 5 of these Conditions and is unsuccessful in establishing the Title or the lien of the Insured Mortgage, as insured,

(i) the Amount of Insurance shall be increased by 10%, and

(ii) the Insured Claimant shall have the right to have the loss or damage determined either as of the date the claim was made by the Insured Claimant or as of the date it is settled and paid.

(c) In the event the Insured has acquired the Title in the manner described in Section 2 of these Conditions or has conveyed the Title, then the extent of liability of the Company shall continue as set forth in Section 8(a) of these Conditions.

(d) In addition to the extent of liability under (a), (b), and (c), the Company will also pay those costs, attorneys' fees, and expenses incurred in accordance with Sections 5 and 7 of these Conditions.

9. LIMITATION OF LIABILITY

(a) If the Company establishes the Title, or removes the alleged defect, lien, or encumbrance, or cures the lack of a right of access to or from the Land, or cures the claim of Unmarketable Title, or establishes the lien of the Insured Mortgage, all as insured, in a reasonably diligent manner by any method, including litigation and the completion of any appeals, it shall have fully performed its obligations with respect to that matter and shall not be liable for any loss or damage caused to the Insured.

(b) In the event of any litigation, including litigation by the Company or with the Company's consent, the Company shall have no liability for loss or damage until there has been a final determination by a court of competent jurisdiction, and disposition of all appeals, adverse to the Title or to the lien of the Insured Mortgage, as insured.

(c) The Company shall not be liable for loss or damage to the Insured for liability voluntarily assumed by the Insured in settling any claim or suit without the prior written consent of the Company.

10. REDUCTION OF INSURANCE; REDUCTION OR TERMINATION OF LIABILITY

(a) All payments under this policy, except payments made for costs, attorneys' fees, and expenses, shall reduce the Amount of Insurance by the amount of the payment. However, any payments made prior to the acquisition of Title as provided in Section 2 of these Conditions shall not reduce the Amount of Insurance afforded under this policy except to the extent that the payments reduce the Indebtedness.

(b) The voluntary satisfaction or release of the Insured Mortgage shall terminate all liability of the Company except as provided in Section 2 of these Conditions.

11. PAYMENT OF LOSS

When liability and the extent of loss or damage have been definitely fixed in accordance with these Conditions, the payment shall be made within 30 days.

12. RIGHTS OF RECOVERY UPON PAYMENT OR SETTLEMENT

(a) The Company's Right to Recover

Whenever the Company shall have settled and paid a claim under this policy, it shall be subrogated and entitled to the rights of the Insured Claimant in the Title or Insured Mortgage and all other rights and remedies in respect to the claim that the Insured Claimant has against any person or property, to the extent of the amount of any loss, costs, attorneys' fees, and expenses paid by the Company. If requested by the Company, the Insured Claimant shall execute documents to evidence the transfer to the Company of these rights and remedies. The Insured Claimant shall permit the Company to sue, compromise, or settle in the name of the Insured Claimant and to use the name of the Insured Claimant in any transaction or litigation involving these rights and remedies.

If a payment on account of a claim does not fully cover the loss of the Insured Claimant, the Company shall defer the exercise of its right to recover until after the Insured Claimant shall have recovered its loss.

(b) The Insured's Rights and Limitations

(i) The owner of the Indebtedness may release or substitute the personal liability of any debtor or guarantor, extend or otherwise modify the terms of payment, release a portion of the Title from the lien of the Insured Mortgage, or release any collateral security for the Indebtedness, if it does not affect the enforceability or priority of the lien of the Insured Mortgage.

(ii) If the Insured exercises a right provided in (b)(i), but has Knowledge of any claim adverse to the Title or the lien of the Insured Mortgage insured against by this policy, the Company shall be required to pay only that part of any losses insured against by this policy that shall exceed the amount, if any, lost to the Company by reason of the impairment by the Insured Claimant of the Company's right of subrogation.

(c) The Company's Rights Against Noninsured Obligors

The Company's right of subrogation includes the Insured's rights against noninsured obligors including the rights of the Insured to indemnities, guaranties, other policies of insurance, or bonds, notwithstanding any terms or conditions contained in those instruments that address subrogation rights.

The Company's right of subrogation shall not be avoided by acquisition of the Insured Mortgage by an obligor (except an obligor described in Section 1(e)(i)(F) of these Conditions) who acquires the Insured Mortgage as a result of an indemnity, guarantee, other policy of insurance, or bond, and the obligor will not be an Insured under this policy.

13. ARBITRATION

Either the Company or the Insured may demand that the claim or controversy shall be submitted to arbitration pursuant to the Title Insurance Arbitration Rules of the American Land Title Association ("Rules"). Except as provided in the Rules, there shall be no joinder or consolidation with claims or controversies of other persons. Arbitrable matters may include, but are not limited to, any controversy or claim between the Company and the Insured arising out of or relating to this policy, any service in connection with its issuance or the breach of a policy provision, or to any other controversy or claim arising out of the transaction giving rise to this policy. All arbitrable matters when the Amount of Insurance is $2,000,000 or less shall be arbitrated at the option of either the Company or the Insured. All arbitrable matters when the Amount of Insurance is in excess of $2,000,000 shall be arbitrated only when agreed to by both the Company and the Insured. Arbitration pursuant to this policy and under the Rules shall be binding upon the parties. Judgment upon the award rendered by the Arbitrator(s) may be entered in any court of competent jurisdiction.

14. LIABILITY LIMITED TO THIS POLICY; POLICY ENTIRE CONTRACT

(a) This policy together with all endorsements, if any, attached to it by the Company is the entire policy and contract between the Insured and the Company. In interpreting any provision of this policy, this policy shall be construed as a whole.

(b) Any claim of loss or damage that arises out of the status of the Title or lien of the Insured Mortgage or by any action asserting such claim shall be restricted to this policy.

(c) Any amendment of or endorsement to this policy must be in writing and authenticated by an authorized person, or expressly incorporated by Schedule A of this policy.

(d) Each endorsement to this policy issued at any time is made a part of this policy and is subject to all of its terms and provisions. Except as the endorsement expressly states, it does not (i) modify any of the terms and provisions of the policy, (ii) modify any prior endorsement, (iii) extend the Date of Policy, or (iv) increase the Amount of Insurance.

15. SEVERABILITY

In the event any provision of this policy, in whole or in part, is held invalid or unenforceable under applicable law, the policy shall be deemed not to include that provision or such part held to be invalid, but all other provisions shall remain in full force and effect.

16. CHOICE OF LAW; FORUM

(a) Choice of Law: The Insured acknowledges the Company has underwritten the risks covered by this policy and determined the premium charged therefor in reliance upon the law affecting interests in real property and applicable to the interpretation, rights, remedies, or enforcement of policies of title insurance of the jurisdiction where the Land is located.

Therefore, the court or an arbitrator shall apply the law of the jurisdiction where the Land is located to determine the validity of claims against the Title or the lien of the Insured Mortgage that are adverse to the Insured and to interpret and enforce the terms of this policy. In neither case shall the court or arbitrator apply its conflicts of law principles to determine the applicable law.

(b) Choice of Forum: Any litigation or other proceeding brought by the Insured against the Company must be filed only in a state or federal court within the United States of America or its territories having appropriate jurisdiction.

17. NOTICES, WHERE SENT

Any notice of claim and any other notice or statement in writing required to be given to the Company under this policy must be given to the Company at [fill in].

NOTE: Bracketed [ ] material optional

J. [§ 4.55] ALTA Loan Policy of Title Insurance (2021)

ALTA LOAN POLICY OF TITLE INSURANCE
issued by
BLANK TITLE INSURANCE COMPANY

This policy, when issued by the Company with a Policy Number and the Date of Policy, is valid even if this policy or any endorsement to this policy is issued electronically or lacks any signature.

Any notice of claim and any other notice or statement in writing required to be given to the Company under this policy must be given to the Company at the address shown in Condition 16.

COVERED RISKS

SUBJECT TO THE EXCLUSIONS FROM COVERAGE, THE EXCEPTIONS FROM COVERAGE CONTAINED IN SCHEDULE B, AND THE CONDITIONS, [Blank Title Insurance Company], a [Blank] corporation (the "Company"), insures as of the Date of Policy and, to the extent stated in Covered Risks 11, 13, and 14, after the Date of Policy, against loss or damage, not exceeding the Amount of Insurance, sustained or incurred by the Insured by reason of:

1. The Title being vested other than as stated in Schedule A.

2. Any defect in or lien or encumbrance on the Title. Covered Risk 2 includes, but is not limited to, insurance against loss from:

   a. a defect in the Title caused by:

      i. forgery, fraud, undue influence, duress, incompetency, incapacity, or impersonation;

      ii. the failure of a person or Entity to have authorized a transfer or conveyance;

      iii. a document affecting the Title not properly authorized, created, executed, witnessed, sealed, acknowledged, notarized (including by remote online notarization), or delivered;

      iv. a failure to perform those acts necessary to create a document by electronic means authorized by law;

      v. a document executed under a falsified, expired, or otherwise invalid power of attorney;

      vi. a document not properly filed, recorded, or indexed in the Public Records, including the failure to have performed those acts by electronic means authorized by law;

      vii. a defective judicial or administrative proceeding; or

viii. the repudiation of an electronic signature by a person that executed a document because the electronic signature on the document was not valid under applicable electronic transactions law.

b. the lien of real estate taxes or assessments imposed on the Title by a governmental authority due or payable, but unpaid.

c. the effect on the Title of an encumbrance, violation, variation, adverse circumstance, boundary line overlap, or encroachment (including an encroachment of an improvement across the boundary lines of the Land), but only if the encumbrance, violation, variation, adverse circumstance, boundary line overlap, or encroachment would have been disclosed by an accurate and complete land title survey of the Land.

3. Unmarketable Title.

4. No right of access to and from the Land.

5. A violation or enforcement of a law, ordinance, permit, or governmental regulation (including those relating to building and zoning), but only to the extent of the violation or enforcement described by the enforcing governmental authority in an Enforcement Notice that identifies a restriction, regulation, or prohibition relating to:

a. the occupancy, use, or enjoyment of the Land;

b. the character, dimensions, or location of an improvement on the Land;

c. the subdivision of the Land; or

d. environmental remediation or protection on the Land.

6. An enforcement of a governmental forfeiture, police, regulatory, or national security power, but only to the extent of the enforcement described by the enforcing governmental authority in an Enforcement Notice.

7. An exercise of the power of eminent domain, but only to the extent:

a. of the exercise described in an Enforcement Notice; or

b. the taking occurred and is binding on a purchaser for value without Knowledge.

8. An enforcement of a PACA-PSA Trust, but only to the extent of the enforcement described in an Enforcement Notice.

9. The invalidity or unenforceability of the lien of the Insured Mortgage upon the Title. Covered Risk 9 includes, but is not limited to, insurance against loss caused by:

a. forgery, fraud, undue influence, duress, incompetency, incapacity, or impersonation;

b. the failure of a person or Entity to have authorized a transfer or conveyance;

c. the Insured Mortgage not being properly authorized, created, executed, witnessed, sealed, acknowledged, notarized (including by remote online notarization), or delivered;

d. a failure to perform those acts necessary to create an Insured Mortgage by electronic means authorized by law;

e. a document having been executed under a falsified, expired, or otherwise invalid power of attorney;

f. the Insured Mortgage not having been properly filed, recorded, or indexed in the Public Records, including the failure to have performed those acts by electronic means authorized by law;

g. a defective judicial or administrative proceeding; or

h. invalidity or unenforceability of the lien of the Insured Mortgage as a result of the repudiation of an electronic signature by a person that executed the Insured Mortgage because the electronic signature on the Insured Mortgage was not valid under applicable electronic transactions law.

10. The lack of priority of the lien of the Insured Mortgage upon the Title over any other lien or encumbrance on the Title as security for the following components of the Indebtedness:

a. the amount of the principal disbursed as of the Date of Policy;

b. the interest on the obligation secured by the Insured Mortgage;

c. the reasonable expense of foreclosure;

d. amounts advanced for insurance premiums by the Insured before the acquisition of the estate or interest in the Title; and

e. the following amounts advanced by the Insured before the acquisition of the estate or interest in the Title to protect the priority of the lien of the Insured Mortgage:

i. real estate taxes and assessments imposed by a governmental taxing authority; and

ii. regular, periodic assessments by a property owners' association.

11. The lack of priority of the lien of the Insured Mortgage upon the Title:

a. as security for each advance of proceeds of the loan secured by the Insured Mortgage over any statutory lien for service, labor, material, or equipment arising from construction of an improvement or work related to the Land when the improvement or work is:

i. contracted for or commenced on or before the Date of Policy; or

ii. contracted for, commenced, or continued after the Date of Policy if the construction is financed, in whole or in part, by proceeds of the loan secured by the Insured Mortgage that the Insured has advanced or is obligated on the Date of Policy to advance; and

b. over the lien of any assessments for street improvements under construction or completed at the Date of Policy.

12. The invalidity or unenforceability of any assignment of the Insured Mortgage, provided the assignment is shown in Schedule A, or the failure of the assignment shown in Schedule A to vest title to the Insured Mortgage in the named Insured assignee free and clear of all liens.
13. The invalidity, unenforceability, lack of priority, or avoidance of the lien of the Insured Mortgage upon the Title, or the effect of a court order providing an alternative remedy:
    a. resulting from the avoidance, in whole or in part, of any transfer of all or any part of the Title to the Land or any interest in the Land occurring prior to the transaction creating the lien of the Insured Mortgage because that prior transfer constituted a:
        i. fraudulent conveyance, fraudulent transfer, or preferential transfer under federal bankruptcy, state insolvency, or similar state or federal creditors' rights law; or
        ii. voidable transfer under the Uniform Voidable Transactions Act; or
    b. because the Insured Mortgage constitutes a preferential transfer under federal bankruptcy, state insolvency, or similar state or federal creditors' rights law by reason of the failure:
        i. to timely record the Insured Mortgage in the Public Records after execution and delivery of the Insured Mortgage to the Insured; or
        ii. of the recording of the Insured Mortgage in the Public Records to impart notice of its existence to a purchaser for value or to a judgment or lien creditor.
14. Any defect in or lien or encumbrance on the Title or other matter included in Covered Risks 1 through 13 that has been created or attached or has been filed or recorded in the Public Records subsequent to the Date of Policy and prior to the recording of the Insured Mortgage in the Public Records.

DEFENSE OF COVERED CLAIMS

The Company will also pay the costs, attorneys' fees, and expenses incurred in defense of any matter insured against by this policy, but only to the extent provided in the Conditions.

[Witness clause]

BLANK TITLE INSURANCE COMPANY

By: ______________________________

[Authorized Signatory]

By: ______________________________

[Authorized Signatory]

EXCLUSIONS FROM COVERAGE

The following matters are excluded from the coverage of this policy, and the Company will not pay loss or damage, costs, attorneys' fees, or expenses that arise by reason of:

1. a. any law, ordinance, permit, or governmental regulation (including those relating to building and zoning) that restricts, regulates, prohibits, or relates to:

i. the occupancy, use, or enjoyment of the Land;

ii. the character, dimensions, or location of any improvement on the Land;

iii. the subdivision of land; or

iv. environmental remediation or protection.

b. any governmental forfeiture, police, regulatory, or national security power.

c. the effect of a violation or enforcement of any matter excluded under Exclusion 1.a. or 1.b.

Exclusion 1 does not modify or limit the coverage provided under Covered Risk 5 or 6.

2. Any power of eminent domain. Exclusion 2 does not modify or limit the coverage provided under Covered Risk 7.

3. Any defect, lien, encumbrance, adverse claim, or other matter:

a. created, suffered, assumed, or agreed to by the Insured Claimant;

b. not Known to the Company, not recorded in the Public Records at the Date of Policy, but Known to the Insured Claimant and not disclosed in writing to the Company by the Insured Claimant prior to the date the Insured Claimant became an Insured under this policy;

c. resulting in no loss or damage to the Insured Claimant;

d. attaching or created subsequent to the Date of Policy (Exclusion 3.d. does not modify or limit the coverage provided under Covered Risk 11, 13, or 14); or

e. resulting in loss or damage that would not have been sustained if consideration sufficient to qualify the Insured named in Schedule A as a bona fide purchaser or encumbrancer had been given for the Insured Mortgage at the Date of Policy.

4. Unenforceability of the lien of the Insured Mortgage because of the inability or failure of an Insured to comply with applicable doing-business law.

5. Invalidity or unenforceability of the lien of the Insured Mortgage that arises out of the transaction evidenced by the Insured Mortgage and is based upon usury law or Consumer Protection Law.

6. Any claim, by reason of the operation of federal bankruptcy, state insolvency, or similar creditors' rights law, that the transaction creating the lien of the Insured Mortgage is a:

  a. fraudulent conveyance or fraudulent transfer;
  b. voidable transfer under the Uniform Voidable Transactions Act; or
  c. preferential transfer:
    i. to the extent the Insured Mortgage is not a transfer made as a contemporaneous exchange for new value; or
    ii. for any other reason not stated in Covered Risk 13.b.

7. Any claim of a PACA-PSA Trust. Exclusion 7 does not modify or limit the coverage provided under Covered Risk 8.

8. Any lien on the Title for real estate taxes or assessments imposed by a governmental authority and created or attaching between the Date of Policy and the date of recording of the Insured Mortgage in the Public Records. Exclusion 8 does not modify or limit the coverage provided under Covered Risk 2.b. or 11.b.

9. Any discrepancy in the quantity of the area, square footage, or acreage of the Land or of any improvement to the Land.

[Transaction Identification Data, for which the Company assumes no liability as set forth in Condition 9.e.:

Issuing Agent:

Issuing Office:

Issuing Office's ALTA® Registry ID:

Loan ID Number:

Issuing Office File Number:

Property Address:]

SCHEDULE A

Name and Address of Title Insurance Company:

Policy Number:

Amount of Insurance: $ [Premium: $]

Date of Policy: [at a.m./p.m.]

1. The Insured is:

2. The estate or interest in the Land encumbered by the Insured Mortgage is:

3. The Title encumbered by the Insured Mortgage is vested in:

4. The Insured Mortgage and its assignments, if any, are described as follows:

5. The Land is described as follows:

[6. This policy incorporates by reference the endorsements designated below, adopted by the [American Land Title Association]**[**________________] as of the Date of Policy:]

SCHEDULE B

Policy Number:

EXCEPTIONS FROM COVERAGE

Some historical land records contain Discriminatory Covenants that are illegal and unenforceable by law. This policy treats any Discriminatory Covenant in a document referenced in Schedule B as if each Discriminatory Covenant is redacted, repudiated, removed, and not republished or recirculated. Only the remaining provisions of the document are excepted from coverage.

[This policy does not insure against loss or damage and the Company will not pay costs, attorneys' fees, or expenses resulting from the terms and conditions of any lease or easement identified in Schedule A, and the following matters:

(Insert Schedule B exceptions here)]

[This policy does not insure against loss or damage and the Company will not pay costs, attorneys' fees, or expenses resulting from the terms and conditions of any lease or easement identified in Schedule A, and the following matters:

PART I

(Insert Schedule B exceptions here)

PART II

Covered Risk 10 insures against loss or damage sustained by the Insured by reason of the lack of priority of the lien of the Insured Mortgage over the matters listed in Part II, subject to the terms and conditions of any subordination provision in a matter listed in Part II:]

CONDITIONS

1. DEFINITION OF TERMS

In this policy, the following terms have the meanings given to them below. Any defined term includes both the singular and the plural, as the context requires:

a. "Affiliate": An Entity:

   i. that is wholly owned by the Insured;

   ii. that wholly owns the Insured; or

   iii. if that Entity and the Insured are both wholly owned by the same person or entity.

b. "Amount of Insurance": The Amount of Insurance stated in Schedule A, as may be increased by Condition 8.c.; decreased by Condition 10; or increased or decreased by endorsements to this policy.

c. "Consumer Protection Law": Any law regulating trade, lending, credit, sale, and debt collection practices involving consumers; any consumer financial law; or any other law relating to truth-in-lending, predatory lending, or a borrower's ability to repay a loan.

d. "Date of Policy": The Date of Policy stated in Schedule A.

e. "Discriminatory Covenant": Any covenant, condition, restriction, or limitation that is unenforceable under applicable law because it illegally discriminates against a class of individuals based on personal characteristics such as race, color, religion, sex, sexual orientation, gender identity, familial status, disability, national origin, or other legally protected class.

f. "Enforcement Notice": A document recorded in the Public Records that describes any part of the Land and:

    i. is issued by a governmental agency that identifies a violation or enforcement of a law, ordinance, permit, or governmental regulation;

    ii. is issued by a holder of the power of eminent domain or a governmental agency that identifies the exercise of a governmental power; or

    iii. asserts a right to enforce a PACA-PSA Trust.

g. "Entity": A corporation, partnership, trust, limited liability company, or other entity authorized by law to own title to real property in the State where the Land is located.

h. "Government Mortgage Agency or Instrumentality": Any government agency or instrumentality that is the owner of the Indebtedness, an insurer, or a guarantor under an insurance contract or guaranty insuring or guaranteeing the Indebtedness, or any part of it, whether named as an Insured or not.

i. "Indebtedness": Any obligation secured by the Insured Mortgage, including an obligation evidenced by electronic means authorized by law. If that obligation is the payment of a debt, the Indebtedness is:

    i. the sum of:

        (a). principal disbursed as of the Date of Policy;

        (b). principal disbursed subsequent to the Date of Policy;

        (c). the construction loan advances made subsequent to the Date of Policy for the purpose of financing, in whole or in part, the construction of an improvement to the Land or related to the Land that the Insured was and continues to be obligated to advance at the Date of Policy and at the date of the advance;

        (d). interest on the loan;

        (e). prepayment premiums, exit fees, and other similar fees or penalties allowed by law;

        (f). expenses of foreclosure and any other costs of enforcement;

(g). advances for insurance premiums;

(h). advances to assure compliance with law or to protect the validity, enforceability, or priority of the lien of the Insured Mortgage before the acquisition of the estate or interest in the Title; including, but not limited to:

(1). real estate taxes and assessments imposed by a governmental taxing authority, and

(2). regular, periodic assessments by a property owners' association; and

(i). advances to prevent deterioration of improvements before the Insured's acquisition of the Title, but

ii. reduced by the sum of all payments and any amounts forgiven by an Insured.

j. "Insured":

i. (a). The Insured named in Item 1 of Schedule A or future owner of the Indebtedness other than an Obligor, if the named Insured or future owner of the Indebtedness owns the Indebtedness, the Title, or an estate or interest in the Land as provided in Condition 2, but only to the extent the named Insured or the future owner either:

(1). owns the Indebtedness for its own account or as a trustee or other fiduciary, or

(2). owns the Title after acquiring the Indebtedness;

(b). the person or Entity who has "control" of the "transferable record," if the Indebtedness is evidenced by a "transferable record," as defined by applicable electronic transactions law;

(c). the successor to the Title of an Insured resulting from dissolution, merger, consolidation, distribution, or reorganization;

(d). the successor to the Title of an Insured resulting from its conversion to another kind of Entity;

(e). the grantee of an Insured under a deed or other instrument transferring the Title, if the grantee is an Affiliate;

(f). an Affiliate that acquires the Title through foreclosure or deed-in-lieu of foreclosure of the Insured Mortgage; or

(g). any Government Mortgage Agency or Instrumentality.

ii. With regard to Conditions 1.j.i.(a). and 1.j.i.(b)., the Company reserves all rights and defenses as to any successor that the Company would have had against any predecessor Insured, unless the successor acquired the Indebtedness as a purchaser for value without Knowledge of the asserted defect, lien, encumbrance, adverse claim, or other matter insured against by this policy.

iii. With regard to Conditions 1.j.i.(c)., 1.j.i.(d)., 1.j.i.(e)., and 1.j.i.(f)., the Company reserves all rights and defenses as to any successor or grantee that the Company would have had against any predecessor Insured.

k. "Insured Claimant": An Insured claiming loss or damage arising under this policy.

l. "Insured Mortgage": The Mortgage described in Item 4 of Schedule A.

m. "Knowledge" or "Known": Actual knowledge or actual notice, but not constructive notice imparted by the Public Records.

n. "Land": The land described in Item 5 of Schedule A and improvements located on that land at the Date of Policy that by State law constitute real property. The term "Land" does not include any property beyond that described in Schedule A, nor any right, title, interest, estate, or easement in any abutting street, road, avenue, alley, lane, right-of-way, body of water, or waterway, but does not modify or limit the extent that a right of access to and from the Land is insured by this policy.

o. "Mortgage": A mortgage, deed of trust, trust deed, security deed, or other real property security instrument, including one evidenced by electronic means authorized by law.

p. "Obligor": A person or entity that is or becomes a maker, borrower, or guarantor as to all or part of the Indebtedness or other obligation secured by the Insured Mortgage. A Government Mortgage Agency or Instrumentality is not an Obligor.

q. "PACA-PSA Trust": A trust under the federal Perishable Agricultural Commodities Act or the federal Packers and Stockyards Act or a similar State or federal law.

r. "Public Records": The recording or filing system established under State statutes in effect at the Date of Policy under which a document must be recorded or filed to impart constructive notice of matters relating to the Title to a purchaser for value without Knowledge. The term "Public Records" does not include any other recording or filing system, including any pertaining to environmental remediation or protection, planning, permitting, zoning, licensing, building, health, public safety, or national security matters.

s. "State": The state or commonwealth of the United States within whose exterior boundaries the Land is located. The term "State" also includes the District of Columbia, the Commonwealth of Puerto Rico, the U.S. Virgin Islands, and Guam.

t. "Title": The estate or interest in the Land identified in Item 2 of Schedule A.

u. "Unmarketable Title": The Title affected by an alleged or apparent matter that would permit a prospective purchaser or lessee of the Title, a lender on the Title, or a prospective purchaser of the Insured Mortgage to be released from the obligation to purchase, lease, or lend if there is a contractual condition requiring the delivery of marketable title.

2. CONTINUATION OF COVERAGE

This policy continues as of the Date of Policy in favor of an Insured:

a. after the Insured's acquisition of the Title, so long as the Insured retains an estate or interest in the Land; and

b. after the Insured's conveyance of the Title, so long as the Insured:

   i. retains an estate or interest in the Land;

   ii. owns an obligation secured by a purchase money Mortgage given by a purchaser from the Insured; or

   iii. has liability for warranties given by the Insured in any transfer or conveyance of the Insured's Title.

Except as provided in Condition 2, this policy terminates and ceases to have any further force or effect after the Insured conveys the Title. This policy does not continue in force or effect in favor of any person or entity that is not the Insured and acquires the Title or an obligation secured by a purchase money Mortgage given to the Insured.

3. NOTICE OF CLAIM TO BE GIVEN BY INSURED CLAIMANT

The Insured must notify the Company promptly in writing if the Insured has Knowledge of:

a. any litigation or other matter for which the Company may be liable under this policy; or

b. any rejection of the Title or the lien of the Insured Mortgage as Unmarketable Title.

If the Company is prejudiced by the failure of the Insured Claimant to provide prompt notice, the Company's liability to the Insured Claimant under this policy is reduced to the extent of the prejudice.

4. PROOF OF LOSS

The Company may, at its option, require as a condition of payment that the Insured Claimant furnish a signed proof of loss. The proof of loss must describe the defect, lien, encumbrance, adverse claim, or other matter insured against by this policy that constitutes the basis of loss or damage and must state, to the extent possible, the basis of calculating the amount of the loss or damage.

5. DEFENSE AND PROSECUTION OF ACTIONS

a. Upon written request by the Insured and subject to the options contained in Condition 7, the Company, at its own cost and without unreasonable delay, will provide for the defense of an Insured in litigation in which any third party asserts a claim covered by this policy adverse to the Insured. This obligation is limited to only those stated causes of action alleging matters insured against by this policy. The Company has the right to select counsel of its choice (subject to the right of the Insured to object for reasonable cause) to represent the Insured as to those covered causes of action. The Company is not liable for and will not pay the fees of any other counsel. The Company will not pay any fees, costs, or expenses incurred by the Insured in the defense of any cause of action that alleges matters not insured against by this policy.

b. The Company has the right, in addition to the options contained in Condition 7, at its own cost, to institute and prosecute any action or proceeding or to do any other act that, in its opinion, may be necessary or desirable to establish the Title or the lien of the Insured Mortgage, as insured, or to prevent or reduce loss or damage to the Insured. The Company may take any appropriate action under the terms of this policy, whether or not it is liable to the Insured. The Company's exercise of these rights is not an admission of liability or waiver of any provision of this policy. If the Company exercises its rights under Condition 5.b., it must do so diligently.

c. When the Company brings an action or asserts a defense as required or permitted by this policy, the Company may pursue the litigation to a final determination by a court having jurisdiction. The Company reserves the right, in its sole discretion, to appeal any adverse judgment or order.

6. DUTY OF INSURED CLAIMANT TO COOPERATE

a. When this policy permits or requires the Company to prosecute or provide for the defense of any action or proceeding and any appeals, the Insured will secure to the Company the right to prosecute or provide defense in the action or proceeding, including the right to use, at its option, the name of the Insured for this purpose.

   When requested by the Company, the Insured, at the Company's expense, must give the Company all reasonable aid in:

   i. securing evidence, obtaining witnesses, prosecuting or defending the action or proceeding, or effecting settlement; and

   ii. any other lawful act that in the opinion of the Company may be necessary or desirable to establish the Title, the lien of the Insured Mortgage, or any other matter, as insured.

   If the Company is prejudiced by any failure of the Insured to furnish the required cooperation, the Company's liability and obligations to the Insured under this policy terminate, including any obligation to defend, prosecute, or continue any litigation, regarding the matter requiring such cooperation.

b. The Company may reasonably require the Insured Claimant to submit to examination under oath by any authorized representative of the Company and to produce for examination, inspection, and copying, at such reasonable times and places as may be designated by the authorized representative of the Company, all records, in whatever medium maintained, including books, ledgers, checks, memoranda, correspondence, reports, e-mails, disks, tapes, and videos, whether bearing a date before or after the Date of Policy, that reasonably pertain to the loss or damage. Further, if requested by any authorized representative of the Company, the Insured Claimant must grant its permission, in writing, for any authorized representative of the Company to examine, inspect, and copy all the records in the custody or control of a third party that reasonably pertain to the loss or damage. No information designated in writing as confidential by the Insured Claimant provided to the Company pursuant to Condition 6 will be later disclosed to others unless, in the reasonable judgment of the Company, disclosure is necessary in the administration of the claim or required by law. Any failure of the Insured Claimant to submit for examination under oath, produce any reasonably requested information, or grant permission to secure reasonably necessary information from third parties as required in Condition 6.b., unless prohibited by law, terminates any liability of the Company under this policy as to that claim.

7. OPTIONS TO PAY OR OTHERWISE SETTLE CLAIMS; TERMINATION OF LIABILITY

   In case of a claim under this policy, the Company has the following additional options:

   a. *To Pay or Tender Payment of the Amount of Insurance or to Purchase the Indebtedness*

      i. To pay or tender payment of the Amount of Insurance under this policy. In addition, the Company will pay any costs, attorneys' fees, and expenses incurred by the Insured Claimant that were authorized by the Company up to the time of payment or tender of payment and that the Company is obligated to pay; or

      ii. To purchase the Indebtedness for the amount of the Indebtedness on the date of purchase. In addition, the Company will pay any costs, attorneys' fees, and expenses incurred by the Insured Claimant that were authorized by the Company up to the time of purchase and that the Company is obligated to pay.

         If the Company purchases the Indebtedness, the Insured must transfer, assign, and convey to the Company the Indebtedness and the Insured Mortgage, together with any collateral security.

      Upon the exercise by the Company of either option provided for in Condition 7.a., the Company's liability and obligations to the Insured under this policy terminate, including any obligation to defend, prosecute, or continue any litigation.

   b. *To Pay or Otherwise Settle with Parties other than the Insured or with the Insured Claimant*

      i. To pay or otherwise settle with parties other than the Insured for or in the name of the Insured Claimant. In addition, the Company will pay any costs, attorneys' fees, and expenses incurred by the Insured Claimant that were authorized by the Company up to the time of payment and that the Company is obligated to pay; or

ii. To pay or otherwise settle with the Insured Claimant the loss or damage provided for under this policy. In addition, the Company will pay any costs, attorneys' fees, and expenses incurred by the Insured Claimant that were authorized by the Company up to the time of payment and that the Company is obligated to pay.

Upon the exercise by the Company of either option provided for in Condition 7.b., the Company's liability and obligations to the Insured under this policy for the claimed loss or damage terminate, including any obligation to defend, prosecute, or continue any litigation.

8. CONTRACT OF INDEMNITY; DETERMINATION AND EXTENT OF LIABILITY

This policy is a contract of indemnity against actual monetary loss or damage sustained or incurred by an Insured Claimant who has suffered loss or damage by reason of matters insured against by this policy. This policy is not an abstract of the Title, report of the condition of the Title, legal opinion, opinion of the Title, or other representation of the status of the Title. All claims asserted under this policy are based in contract and are restricted to the terms and provisions of this policy. The Company is not liable for any claim alleging negligence or negligent misrepresentation arising from or in connection with this policy or the determination of the insurability of the Title.

a. The extent of liability of the Company for loss or damage under this policy does not exceed the least of:

   i. the Amount of Insurance;

   ii. the Indebtedness;

   iii. the difference between the fair market value of the Title, as insured, and the fair market value of the Title subject to the matter insured against by this policy; or

   iv. if a Government Mortgage Agency or Instrumentality is the Insured Claimant, the amount it paid in the acquisition of the Title or the Insured Mortgage or in satisfaction of its insurance contract or guaranty relating to the Title or the Insured Mortgage.

b. Fair market value of the Title in Condition 8.a.iii. is calculated using either:

   i. the date the Insured acquires the Title as a result of a foreclosure or deed in lieu of foreclosure of the Insured Mortgage; or

   ii. the date the lien of the Insured Mortgage or any assignment set forth in Item 4 of Schedule A is extinguished or rendered unenforceable by reason of a matter insured against by this policy.

c. If the Company pursues its rights under Condition 5.b. and is unsuccessful in establishing the Title or the lien of the Insured Mortgage, as insured:

   i. the Amount of Insurance will be increased by 15%; and

   ii. the Insured Claimant may, by written notice given to the Company, elect, as an alternative to the dates set forth in Condition 8.b., to use either the date the settlement, action, proceeding, or other act described in Condition 5.b. is concluded or the date the notice of claim required by Condition 3 is received by the Company as the date for calculating the fair market value of the Title in Condition 8.a.iii.

d. In addition to the extent of liability for loss or damage under Conditions 8.a. and 8.c., the Company will also pay the costs, attorneys' fees, and expenses incurred in accordance with Conditions 5 and 7.

9. LIMITATION OF LIABILITY

a. The Company fully performs its obligations and is not liable for any loss or damage caused to the Insured if the Company accomplishes any of the following in a reasonable manner:

   i. removes the alleged defect, lien, encumbrance, adverse claim, or other matter;

   ii. cures the lack of a right of access to and from the Land;

   iii. cures the claim of Unmarketable Title; or

   iv. establishes the lien of the Insured Mortgage,

   all as insured. The Company may do so by any method, including litigation and the completion of any appeals.

b. The Company is not liable for loss or damage arising out of any litigation, including litigation by the Company or with the Company's consent, until a State or federal court having jurisdiction makes a final, non-appealable determination adverse to the Title or to the lien of the Insured Mortgage.

c. The Company is not liable for loss or damage to the Insured for liability voluntarily assumed by the Insured in settling any claim or suit without the prior written consent of the Company.

d. An Insured Claimant must own the Indebtedness or have acquired the Title at the time that a claim under this policy is paid.

e. The Company is not liable for the content of the Transaction Identification Data, if any.

10. REDUCTION OR TERMINATION OF INSURANCE

a. All payments under this policy, except payments made for costs, attorneys' fees, and expenses, reduce the Amount of Insurance by the amount of the payment. However, any payment made by the Company prior to the acquisition of the Title as provided in Condition 2 does not reduce the Amount of Insurance afforded under this policy, except to the extent that the payment reduces the Indebtedness.

b. When the Title is acquired by the Insured as a result of foreclosure or deed in lieu of foreclosure, the amount credited against the Indebtedness does not reduce the Amount of Insurance.

c. The voluntary satisfaction or release of the Insured Mortgage terminates all liability of the Company, except as provided in Condition 2.

11. PAYMENT OF LOSS

When liability and the extent of loss or damage are determined in accordance with the Conditions, the Company will pay the loss or damage within 30 days.

12. COMPANY'S RECOVERY AND SUBROGATION RIGHTS UPON SETTLEMENT AND PAYMENT

a. *Company's Right to Recover*

   i. If the Company settles and pays a claim under this policy, it is subrogated and entitled to the rights and remedies of the Insured Claimant in the Title or Insured Mortgage and all other rights and remedies in respect to the claim that the Insured Claimant has against any person, entity, or property to the fullest extent permitted by law, but limited to the amount of any loss, costs, attorneys' fees, and expenses paid by the Company. If requested by the Company, the Insured Claimant must execute documents to transfer these rights and remedies to the Company. The Insured Claimant permits the Company to sue, compromise, or settle in the name of the Insured Claimant and to use the name of the Insured Claimant in any transaction or litigation involving these rights and remedies.

   ii. If a payment on account of a claim does not fully cover the loss of the Insured Claimant, the Company defers the exercise of its subrogation right until after the Insured Claimant fully recovers its loss.

b. *Company's Subrogation Rights against Obligors*

The Company's subrogation right includes the Insured's rights against Obligors including the Insured's rights to repayment under a note, indemnity, guaranty, warranty, insurance policy, or bond, despite any provision in those instruments that addresses recovery or subrogation rights. An Obligor cannot avoid the Company's subrogation right by acquiring the Indebtedness as a result of an indemnity, guaranty, warranty, insurance policy, or bond, or in any other manner. The Obligor is not an Insured under this policy. The Company may not exercise its rights under Condition 12.b. against a Government Mortgage Agency or Instrumentality.

c. *Insured's Rights and Limitations*

   i. The owner of the Indebtedness may release or substitute the personal liability of any debtor or guarantor, extend or otherwise modify the terms of payment, release a portion of the Title from the lien of the Insured Mortgage, or release any collateral security for the Indebtedness, if the action does not affect the enforceability or priority of the lien of the Insured Mortgage.

ii. If the Insured exercises a right provided in Condition 12.c.i. but has Knowledge of any claim adverse to the Title or the lien of the Insured Mortgage insured against by this policy, the Company is required to pay only that part of the loss insured against by this policy that exceeds the amount, if any, lost to the Company by reason of the impairment by the Insured Claimant of the Company's subrogation right.

13. POLICY ENTIRE CONTRACT

a. This policy together with all endorsements, if any, issued by the Company is the entire policy and contract between the Insured and the Company. In interpreting any provision of this policy, this policy will be construed as a whole. This policy and any endorsement to this policy may be evidenced by electronic means authorized by law.

b. Any amendment of this policy must be by a written endorsement issued by the Company. To the extent any term or provision of an endorsement is inconsistent with any term or provision of this policy, the term or provision of the endorsement controls. Unless the endorsement expressly states, it does not:

i. modify any prior endorsement,

ii. extend the Date of Policy,

iii. insure against loss or damage exceeding the Amount of Insurance, or

iv. increase the Amount of Insurance.

14. SEVERABILITY

In the event any provision of this policy, in whole or in part, is held invalid or unenforceable under applicable law, this policy will be deemed not to include that provision or the part held to be invalid, but all other provisions will remain in full force and effect.

15. CHOICE OF LAW AND CHOICE OF FORUM

a. *Choice of Law*

The Company has underwritten the risks covered by this policy and determined the premium charged in reliance upon the State law affecting interests in real property and the State law applicable to the interpretation, rights, remedies, or enforcement of policies of title insurance of the State where the Land is located.

The State law of the State where the Land is located, or to the extent it controls, federal law, will determine the validity of claims against the Title or the lien of the Insured Mortgage and the interpretation and enforcement of the terms of this policy, without regard to conflicts of law principles to determine the applicable law.

b. *Choice of Forum*

Any litigation or other proceeding brought by the Insured against the Company must be filed only in a State or federal court having jurisdiction.

16. NOTICES

Any notice of claim and any other notice or statement in writing required to be given to the Company under this policy must be given to the Company at: ____*(fill in)*____.

17. CLASS ACTION

ALL CLAIMS AND DISPUTES ARISING OUT OF OR RELATING TO THIS POLICY, INCLUDING ANY SERVICE OR OTHER MATTER IN CONNECTION WITH ISSUING THIS POLICY, ANY BREACH OF A POLICY PROVISION, OR ANY OTHER CLAIM OR DISPUTE ARISING OUT OF OR RELATING TO THE TRANSACTION GIVING RISE TO THIS POLICY, MUST BE BROUGHT IN AN INDIVIDUAL CAPACITY. NO PARTY MAY SERVE AS PLAINTIFF, CLASS MEMBER, OR PARTICIPANT IN ANY CLASS OR REPRESENTATIVE PROCEEDING.

[**18.** ARBITRATION

a. All claims and disputes arising out of or relating to this policy, including any service or other matter in connection with issuing this policy, any breach of a policy provision, or any other claim or dispute arising out of or relating to the transaction giving rise to this policy, may be resolved by arbitration. If the Amount of Insurance is $2,000,000 or less, any claim or dispute may be submitted to binding arbitration at the election of either the Company or the Insured. If the Amount of Insurance is greater than $2,000,000, any claim or dispute may be submitted to binding arbitration only when agreed to by both the Company and the Insured. Arbitration must be conducted pursuant to the Title Insurance Arbitration Rules of the American Land Title Association ("ALTA Rules"). The ALTA Rules are available online at www.alta.org/arbitration. The ALTA Rules incorporate, as appropriate to a particular dispute, the Consumer Arbitration Rules and Commercial Arbitration Rules of the American Arbitration Association ("AAA Rules"). The AAA Rules are available online at www.adr.org.

b. ALL CLAIMS AND DISPUTES MUST BE BROUGHT IN AN INDIVIDUAL CAPACITY. NO PARTY MAY SERVE AS PLAINTIFF, CLASS MEMBER, OR PARTICIPANT IN ANY CLASS OR REPRESENTATIVE PROCEEDING IN ANY ARBITRATION GOVERNED BY CONDITION 18. The arbitrator does not have authority to conduct any class action arbitration or arbitration involving joint or consolidated claims under any circumstance.

c. *If there is a final judicial determination that a request for particular relief cannot be arbitrated in accordance with this Condition 18, then only that request for particular relief may be brought in court. All other requests for relief remain subject to this Condition 18.*

d. [The Company will pay all AAA filing, administration, and arbitrator fees of the consumer when the arbitration seeks relief of $100,000 or less. Other fees][Fees] will be allocated in accordance with the applicable AAA Rules. The results of arbitration will be binding upon the parties. The arbitrator may consider, but is not bound by, rulings in prior arbitrations involving different parties. The arbitrator is bound by rulings in prior arbitrations involving the same parties to the extent required by law. The arbitrator must issue a written decision sufficient to explain the findings and conclusions on which the award is based. Judgment upon the award rendered by the arbitrator may be entered in any State or federal court having jurisdiction.]

NOTE: Bracketed [ ] material optional

CHAPTER FIVE

THE LENDER'S ROLE*

* This chapter was updated by MSBA staff attorneys. MSBA gratefully acknowledges the contributions to this chapter from previous authors Wingrove S. Lynton, Esq., Elizabeth M. Huffman, Esq., and Douglas Scott MacGregor, Esq.

TABLE OF CONTENTS

I. INTRODUCTION[1]

A. [§ 5.1] Methods of Financing the Purchase of a House

After the owner of a house or a condominium unit has agreed to sell their home to a willing buyer and the parties have executed a contract,[2] the buyer individually or through their real estate agent or attorney typically arranges to finance the purchase. There are several ways that a buyer who cannot or chooses not to pay the entire purchase price with their own resources may acquire financing:

1. The seller may agree to deed the property to the buyer in exchange for a portion of the sales price in cash at or before settlement and the buyer's obligation to pay the balance over a period of time, secured by a purchase money mortgage, which may either be a first or subordinate mortgage.
2. Upon receipt of less than the full purchase price of the property, the buyer and seller may enter into a land installment contract, which will enable the buyer to have possession of the property without having legal title to it.[3]
3. The buyer may have friends or relatives who will give or lend the buyer sufficient funds to enable them to purchase the property.
4. The most common method of financing residential real estate transactions is for the buyer to obtain the balance of the purchase price from a lending institution.

B. Types of Loans

1. [§ 5.2] Generally

First mortgage loans may generally be categorized as "conventional," "insured," or "guaranteed." In a conventional loan, which is neither insured nor guaranteed by a government agency, the institutional lender bears the risk of loss in the event the borrower defaults on the mortgage obligation. Generally, institutional lenders will not make a conventional loan for more than 80% of the appraised value of the residential real property unless the loan is insured by a private mortgage insurance company. To induce the institutional lender to make a mortgage loan by reducing the lender's risk of loss, the borrower, under certain circumstances, may obtain a

---

1 NOTE: This chapter is written primarily for the benefit of counsel to purchasers of real property. It attempts to set forth the positions and attitudes of lenders who make loans secured by real property and the reasons for such positions and attitudes.

2 *See* Chapter 2, Contracts of Sale: Resale of Existing Residences.

3 This method of financing must comply with the provisions of MD. CODE ANN., REAL PROPERTY §§ 10-101–10-108 (2005 & Supp. 2022) (hereinafter REAL PROP. §).

loan that is guaranteed by the Veterans Administration (VA) or insured by either the Federal Housing Administration of the Department of Housing and Urban Development (FHA) or a private mortgage insurer (PMI).

2. [§ 5.3] *Insurance and guarantee limitations*

While PMI coverage is generally limited to 20 or 25% of the amount of a loan, the VA will guarantee up to 50% depending on the loan amount, and the FHA will insure the entire amount of a loan.[4] All FHA loans must be made by approved lenders. They are generally limited to 95% of the median house price in the area for single-family dwellings but in most cases shall not exceed 97% of the estimated cost of acquisition.[5] Current FHA loan limits for applicable areas of Maryland are available online at *https://entp.hud.gov/idapp/html/hicostlook.cfm* (last visited Jan. 4, 2024). By their own choice, individual lenders often limit the size of VA or PMI loans that they will make.

3. [§ 5.4] *Alternative mortgage instruments (AMIs)*

Traditional first mortgage loans are written on a straight amortized basis with a fixed rate of interest over the term of the loan. Payments of principal and interest on such a loan are made in equal monthly installments, and the loan is fully amortized (paid off) with the last payment. However, other types of loans gained popularity during the late 1970s and early 1980s, and such alternative mortgage instruments (AMIs) are still sometimes used today. The common types of AMIs include:

a. Graduated payment mortgages (GPMs), which have a constant interest rate over the life of the loan but provide for increases in the monthly payment of principal and interest over time in fixed amounts.
b. Variable rate mortgages (VRMs) or adjustable rate mortgages (ARMs), the interest rates of which vary over the life of the loan based on an external standard, often within fixed limits. These loans appear to be the most popular conventional AMIs.
c. Renegotiable rate mortgages (RRMs), which are a series of short-term loans that the lender is obligated to make as each of the prior loans in the series matures.
d. Rollover mortgages (ROMs), which are amortized over a long term, such as 30 years, but have a fixed interest rate for a much shorter term (for example, three years) after which time the rate will change based on the then-current market interest rate.

---

4 *Compare* 38 C.F.R. § 36.4302 *with* 24 C.F.R. § 203.255.

5 24 C.F.R. §§ 203.18, 203.19.

e. Reduction option loans (ROLs), which permit borrowers to take advantage of declining interest rates by exercising a one-time option to reduce the interest rate at any time after the first year of the loan.

4. [§ 5.5] *Authority for and regulation of AMIs*

Some GPMs, VRMs, and ARMs currently are insurable by the FHA.[6] The Office of the Comptroller of the Currency (OCC) has promulgated regulations concerning the making of ARMs by national banks.[7] The National Credit Union Administration (NCUA) has done the same for federal credit unions.[8] Maryland institutions are authorized to make ARMs, subject to applicable usury limitations.[9] The Alternative Mortgage Transaction Parity Act of 1982[10] authorizes non-federally chartered "housing creditors," as defined in the statute, to enter alternative mortgage transactions in accordance with federal regulations despite contrary state law. Banks may comply with either state law or OCC regulations. Credit unions may comply with either state law or NCUA regulations. Other "housing creditors" may comply with either state law or OTS regulations.

5. [§ 5.6] *Other types of loans*

Lending institutions also make loans to borrowers who have equity in their homes by granting second mortgage or home equity loans (discussed in Part V, *infra*). Lending institutions also will provide construction loans to individuals to finance the construction of new homes. Lenders frequently structure construction loans so that during the construction period the borrower pays only interest on the loan proceeds advanced to pay the construction costs, and upon completion of the house the borrower begins to repay the principal. Such loans may either be written so that they convert by their own terms to permanent loans upon completion of construction, or they become due and payable when the house is finished. A borrower should be advised to arrange for the financing of both the permanent and construction loan before accepting a construction loan. This approach should enable the borrower to know the total financial burden before becoming too financially involved. Lenders may be reluctant, however, to set a rate on the permanent portion of a construction/permanent loan since, during times of wide fluctuations in interest

---

[6] 24 C.F.R. §§ 203.45, 203.49.

[7] 12 C.F.R. §§ 34.20–34.25.

[8] 12 C.F.R. § 701.21.

[9] MD. CODE ANN., COMMERCIAL LAW II §§ 12-118, 12-904, 12-1004 (2013 & Supp. 2022) (hereinafter COM. LAW I or II § __).

[10] 12 U.S.C. §§ 3801–3806 (2009). *See Grunbeck v. Dime Sav. Bank, FSB,* 74 F.3d 331 (1st Cir. 1996); *First Gibraltar Bank, FSB v. Morales,* 19 F.3d 1032 (5th Cir. 1994), *aff'd*, 42 F.3d 895 (5th Cir. 1995) (Texas homestead law preempted by federal statute).

rates, fixing a rate many months in the future may make the loan unmarketable on the secondary market or unattractive in the lender's own portfolio.

C. [§ 5.7] Marketability of Loans

Lending institutions increasingly want to be able to sell the loans they originate to other investors on the "secondary market." Therefore, they have a strong interest in making sure that the entire loan package is marketable. This generally means that they must comply with the requirements of the Federal National Mortgage Association (FNMA), the Federal Home Loan Mortgage Corporation (FHLMC), and/or the Government National Mortgage Association (GNMA). FNMA, FHLMC, and GNMA are federal corporations that either issue or guarantee securities backed by mortgage loans and sold to investors.

D. [§ 5.8] Standardization of Forms

The development of the secondary market for residential loans has led to the national standardization of loan application and security instrument forms, with special provisions provided when required by individual state laws. Also, lending institutions that want to maintain the ability to sell their Maryland loans generally use deeds of trust rather than mortgages. When deeds of trust are used, the right to receive repayment of the loan can be transferred solely upon endorsement and delivery of the note.[11] If a mortgage form is used, it is prudent to record an assignment among the land records of the jurisdiction where the property is located. It is also advisable to require a title examination from the date that the mortgage is recorded to the date that the assignment is recorded to determine whether another assignment had previously been recorded. Title to a promissory note secured by a mortgage is conclusively presumed to be held by the mortgagee of record.[12]

E. Cost of Obtaining a Loan; Interest Rates

1. [§ 5.9] Borrower's cost—generally

The borrower's cost of obtaining a loan will vary depending upon the lender and type of loan sought. Generally, lending institutions pass on to their borrowers as a separate charge all of the costs of making a loan other than their overhead. These costs frequently include costs of appraisals, credit reports, surveys, title examination, mortgagee title insurance premiums, recording fees, and fees of lender's counsel. These costs are in addition to the costs that the borrower is obligated to pay to acquire title to the property, such as recordation and transfer taxes. Furthermore, in some instances a lending institution may charge an origination fee to the buyer/

---

11 *Billingsley v. Mitchell,* 257 Md. 301, 307, 262 A.2d 746, 749 (1970); *Le Brun v. Prosise,* 197 Md. 466, 474, 79 A.2d 543, 548 (1951).

12 REAL PROP. § 7-103.

borrower and/or a mortgage discount fee to the seller as a precondition to making a loan. These fees are generally called "points"; a point is equal to 1% of the loan amount. Although the imposition of points is prohibited by Maryland law in many cases, preemptive federal legislation allows the charging of points in federally-related first mortgage loans.[13]

Some of the costs of obtaining a mortgage loan are the same regardless of the size of the loan (for example, the charge for the credit report) while others will vary with the size of the loan (for example, points and the cost of mortgagee title insurance).

2. [§ 5.10] Settlement Expense Loan Fund

In 1988, Maryland established the Settlement Expense Loan Fund to provide funds for those people who are unable to save sufficient funds to pay for the up-front costs of purchasing a home but are able to make monthly principal and interest payments.[14] Under the Settlement Expense Loan Program, purchasers of real property who have not owned any residential real property within the previous three years are able to borrow money to pay for their settlement costs. The Secretary of the Maryland Department of Housing and Community Development shall establish maximum income levels for purchasers who wish to use this fund.

3. [§ 5.11] Payment of costs

If the loan is insured by the FHA or a PMI, the borrower must pay the first year's FHA or PMI insurance premium at settlement, and they must pay additional premiums during the term of the loan. If the borrower is required to pay a mortgage insurance premium only once, they must pay the premium at settlement. Certain loan programs permit the insurance premium to be included in the amount financed. Lenders frequently require that real property taxes, insurance premiums, homeowners association or condominium assessments, and ground rent, if any, be escrowed so that sufficient funds are available to pay those items when they become due. The amount of initial deposits for those accounts, which is collected at settlement, depends upon the lender's estimate of the following year's taxes and premiums and upon the month in which the loan closes. The required initial escrow deposits become larger as the time when the payments for those items draws closer. If the lender requires that an escrow account be established for real property taxes, at settlement the buyer/borrower will either have to reimburse the seller or pay the city or county where the land is located for the current fiscal year's taxes plus make an initial deposit into the lender's escrow for the next fiscal year's taxes, which total

---

13 See § **5.49** of this chapter for a discussion of usury laws.

14 Md. Code Ann., Housing and Community Development §§ 9-101–9-501 (2019 & Supp. 2022).

sum will be an amount sufficient to pay the subsequent semi-annual tax payment, regardless of when the loan closes. Although collecting escrows increases closing costs, real property taxes and insurance premiums must be paid at the time of purchase whether or not a loan is made; therefore, these prepaid items are not true costs of the loan. As discussed in § **5.40** of this chapter, certain lenders are required to pay interest on these items that are escrowed.

4. [§ 5.12] Interest rates

The interest rate on an individual loan by a particular lending institution will generally depend on the type of loan requested, the security offered, and the amount of the buyer's down payment. For loans insured by the FHA or guaranteed by the VA, the maximum interest rate is set by federal regulation. The buyer who borrows 90% or more of the sale price will more than likely have to pay the maximum interest rate charged by a lender and will generally have to obtain private mortgage insurance as well. Often, if a borrower makes a deposit of 20% or more of the purchase price, they will get the benefit of the lender's lowest interest rate.

II. PROCESS OF OBTAINING LOANS

A. Initial Contact and Application

1. [§ 5.13] Form

Before signing a contract to purchase a home, a prospective buyer who must borrow money to finance the purchase should inquire as to the availability of mortgage money and its cost (both closing costs and monthly payments must be considered) to determine whether they will be able to afford the purchase. Lenders generally require, however, that prospective borrowers execute purchase contracts before they can formally apply for a loan. Therefore, buyers are well advised to include in their purchase contracts a clause permitting them to terminate the purchase contracts without any liability if they are unable to secure the kind of mortgage financing they need. Also, if the buyer is seeking a Veterans Administration (VA) or Federal Housing Administration of the Department of Housing and Urban Development (FHA) loan, it is necessary that the purchase contract contain particular language.[15] If the lender is going to require that the seller pay any points, that fact should be indicated in the purchase contract. To determine the different types of financing available, the borrower may discuss financing with their realtor or review the Maryland Mortgage Rates published in the Wednesday and Sunday editions of the *Baltimore Sun*.

When the purchase contract has been signed by all parties to it, the buyer should take a copy to the lending institution and apply for a particular type and size loan.

---

15 *See* Chapter 2, Contracts of Sale: Resale of Existing Residences.

The Federal National Mortgage Association (FNMA)/Federal Home Loan Mortgage Corporation (FHLMC) Residential Loan Application Form, which is frequently used by lending institutions throughout the country, is set forth in § **5.77** of this chapter.

2. *[§ 5.14] Credit reports, appraisals, and customer identification*

(a) Credit reports

Lenders are concerned about both the creditworthiness of their applicants and the value of the property that will serve as security. A lending institution will not make a loan unless it is satisfied that its borrower has the ability to repay the loan and that its risk of loss, if it has to liquidate the security upon the borrower's default, is small. In order to check the credit of an applicant, lenders generally obtain a credit report from a credit bureau for a cost that may range between $25 and $100.

(b) Appraisals

To determine the value of the property, an appraisal is made, either by an employee of the lender or by an outside appraiser. When the borrower seeks an FHA, VA, or private mortgage insurer (PMI) loan, the appraisal must also be satisfactory to the insurer or guarantor of the loan. The cost of an appraisal is typically $200 to $500. The borrower usually pays the cost of the credit report and appraisal when the initial loan application is made.

(c) Customer identification

Following the tragedy of September 11, 2001, President Bush's Executive Order No. 13224, 66 Fed. Reg. 49079 (Sept. 23, 2001) had the effect of freezing ("blocking") the property of, and prohibiting transactions with, persons and/or entities who commit, threaten to commit, or support terrorism. The U.S. Treasury maintains a searchable list of "Specially Designated Nationals" found at *https://www.treasury.gov/ofac/downloads/sdnlist.pdf* (last visited July 12, 2023). Searching the Treasury's database (or utilizing a service that certifies the results of an "SDN" search) has become part of a lender's routine due diligence. Additionally, final rules issued on May 9, 2003, under § 326 of the U.S. Patriot Act,[16] require a financial institution to develop a customer identification program (CIP) that would enable the financial institution to form a reasonable belief that it knows the true identity of the customer. The rules under the Patriot Act require the CIP to provide for obtaining the following:

- Borrower's name(s)
- Borrower's date(s) of birth

[16] Pub. L. No. 107-56, 115 Stat. 272 (2001).

- Address(es)
  — For an individual, collect a street address.
  — For an individual without a street address, collect a military P.O. Box number, or street address of next of kin or another contact individual.
  — For a customer other than an individual (business, trust, or partnership), collect an identification number from an official government-issued, non-expired picture identification.
  — For non-U.S. persons, collect one or more of the following: a taxpayer ID number, collect a passport number with country of issuance, alien ID card number, or other foreign-issued picture ID.

3. [§ 5.15] Initial RESPA requirements

At the time of application, the lender must provide to the prospective borrower a disclosure indicating whether the loan may be assigned, sold, or transferred during its term. Within three business days after the prospective borrower submits an application, the lender must give the applicant a copy of the Special Information Booklet, which is in a form prescribed by the Secretary of the U.S. Department of Housing and Urban Development (HUD) and explains the nature of a residential real estate transaction.[17]

Also within three business days after receipt of an application, the lender must supply the borrower with a "good faith estimate" of the borrower's closing costs of the residential real estate transaction, based on the lender's general experience.[18] Sellers are prohibited under the Real Estate Settlement Procedures Act of 1974 (RESPA)[19] from requiring that particular providers of settlement services be used,[20] but lenders are not. If a lender makes such a designation, however, it is obliged under RESPA to inform the borrower of any business relationship it has with the designated provider.[21]

4. [§ 5.16] Truth-in-Lending disclosures

Good faith estimates of all of the loan disclosures required pursuant to Regulation Z of the Federal Reserve Board, 12 C.F.R. Part 226 (2008), which implements the federal Truth-in-Lending Act, 15 U.S.C. §§ 1601 *et seq.* (2008), must be

---

17 Real Estate Settlement Procedures Act of 1974 (RESPA), as amended, 12 U.S.C. §§ 2604, 2605; Regulation X, 24 C.F.R. §§ 3500.6, 3500.21.

18 Regulation X, 24 C.F.R. § 3500.7.

19 12 U.S.C. §§ 2601–2617 (2009).

20 RESPA, 12 U.S.C. § 2608.

21 Regulation X, 24 C.F.R. § 3500.7. This may be done on the good faith estimate sheet. The good faith estimate need not be in any particular form; an example is set forth in § **5.78** of this chapter.

delivered or mailed within three business days after a lender receives an application from a borrower or be delivered before consummation of the loan, whichever is earlier.[22]

Giving the disclosures required by Regulation Z satisfies Maryland statutory disclosure requirements.[23] Special Regulation Z disclosure requirements are applicable to variable rate mortgages (VRM) and adjustable rate mortgages (ARM).[24] The lender must provide more detailed disclosures, including the Consumer Handbook on Adjustable Rate Mortgages, to any applicant at the time an application is provided but no later than when the applicant pays a non-refundable fee, if the VRMs and ARMs have terms greater than one year, are secured by the borrower's principal residence, and have interest rates that may increase after consummation.[25] Additional disclosures also are required before an adjustment in the monthly payment occurs and at least once a year if there is an adjustment in the interest rate without a corresponding adjustment in the monthly payment.[26]

5. *[§ 5.17] Private mortgage insurance disclosure*

The Homeowners Protection Act of 1998[27] (Act) offers borrowers who secure loans with their primary homes three rights related to private mortgage insurance: disclosure, cancellation, and automatic termination. The Act requires lenders to inform mortgage borrowers of their rights under the Act.[28] The Act also allows borrower-initiated cancellation of private mortgage insurance and requires its termination by the lender when the borrower has accumulated a certain level of equity in the home.[29]

The Act covers all lenders that grant "residential mortgages." A residential mortgage is defined as a mortgage, loan, or other evidence of a security interest created with respect to a single-family dwelling that is the primary residence of the borrower.[30] A single-family dwelling is a residence consisting of one family dwelling unit.[31] The Act also requires lenders that refinance or service home mortgages to comply with its terms.

---

22 Regulation Z, 12 C.F.R. § 226.19(a).
23 COM. LAW II § 12-106(b).
24 12 C.F.R. § 226.18(f).
25 12 C.F.R. § 226.19(b).
26 12 C.F.R. § 226.20(c).
27 12 U.S.C. §§ 4901–4910.
28 12 U.S.C. § 4903.
29 12 U.S.C. § 4902.
30 12 U.S.C. § 4901(14).
31 12 U.S.C. § 4901(17).

At a loan closing for a fixed-rate mortgage, the lender must provide an initial amortization schedule with a written notice stating the cancellation date and the automatic termination date.[32] At a loan closing for an adjustable rate mortgage, the lender must provide borrowers with a written notice explaining their right to cancel private mortgage insurance on the cancellation date and the lender's duty to terminate private mortgage insurance on the automatic termination date.[33]

A lender must cancel a borrower's private mortgage insurance when all of the following occur:

(1) The borrower's loan-to-value ratio reaches 80%;

(2) The borrower makes a written request;

(3) The borrower provides, upon the lender's request, information showing that the property has not declined in value and is not encumbered by any subordinate lien; and

(4) The borrower has a good payment history.[34]

Upon receiving a borrower's written request for cancellation, a lender may require the borrower to prove that the property securing the mortgage has not declined in value and is unencumbered by any subordinate lien.[35] If the property has depreciated or is subject to a subordinate lien, the Act does not compel the lender to cancel the private mortgage insurance. In addition, the borrower must have a "good payment history," meaning he or she has neither:

(1) Made a mortgage payment that was 60 days or longer past due during the 12-month period beginning 24 months before the date on which the mortgage reaches the cancellation date, nor

(2) Made a mortgage payment that was 30 days or longer past due during the 12-month period preceding the date on which the mortgage reaches the cancellation date.[36]

A lender must automatically terminate private mortgage insurance when all of the following occur:

(1) The loan-to-value ratio reaches 78%; and

(2) The borrower is current on the payments required by the terms of the loan.[37]

---

32 12 U.S.C. § 4903(a)(1)(A).
33 12 U.S.C. § 4903(a)(1)(B).
34 12 U.S.C. § 4902.
35 12 U.S.C. § 4902(a)(4).
36 12 U.S.C. § 4901(4).
37 12 U.S.C. § 4902(b).

Automatic termination differs from cancellation in two important ways. First, the borrower is not required to have a good payment history; the payments must only be "current." Second, the lender may not consider whether the property has depreciated. The Act does not define the term "current"; therefore, the lender must determine how to track whether a loan is current as of the termination date. If the borrower's loan is not current on the termination date, as soon as the borrower is current, a lender must terminate private mortgage insurance.

Regardless of the loan-to-value ratio, the lender must terminate private mortgage insurance on the first day of the month after the mid-point of the loan's amortization period if that loan is current.[38] Maryland law requires first mortgage lenders to eliminate all charges to the borrower for mortgage insurance premiums "when the mortgage is reduced to the level at which the federal Homeowners Protection Act of 1998 requires termination of the private mortgage insurance insuring the mortgage."[39]

6. *[§ 5.18] Financing agreement*

If a borrower applies for a purchase money loan from a lender licensed under the Maryland Mortgage Lender Law (MMLL), FINANCIAL INSTITUTIONS Article, Title 11, Subtitle 5, and that loan is to be secured by a first mortgage on a one to four family home, which the borrower occupies or shall occupy as a primary residence, then such a lender must deliver to the borrower a financing agreement executed by the parties within 10 business days after the date the application is completed.[40] A lender must also deliver a financing agreement on a loan that refinances an existing loan that results in or is secured by a first mortgage or deed of trust on residential real property that is to be occupied by the borrower. The type of lender required to be licensed under MMLL is a "mortgage lender," which is defined generally to

---

38 12 U.S.C. § 4902(c).

39 MD. CODE ANN., FINANCIAL INSTITUTIONS § 5-508 (2020 & Supp. 2022) (hereinafter FIN. INST. §).

40 FIN. INST. §§ 11-501–11-524; COM. LAW II § 12-125. Examiners in the Division of Financial Regulation take the position that an application is completed very early in the process. For the examiners, the pivotal event is when the lender obtains a credit report. On May 23, 2008, the Commissioner of Financial Regulation published proposed regulations to clarify when a loan application is complete for purposed of Maryland mortgage broker law. 25 Md. Reg. 1050 (May 23, 2008). Under the proposed regulations, a loan application is completed when a broker receives a borrower's credit report and the borrower has identified to the broker the specific dwelling that will secure the loan. It is likely that the Division of Financial Regulation will look to the mortgage broker regulations for guidance on when an application is received for purposes of the mortgage lending laws.

include persons who broker, make, or service "mortgage loans" (as defined under that Subtitle) and who are not otherwise exempt.[41]

FINANCIAL INSTITUTIONS § 11-502 specifically exempts the following lenders (among others) from the provisions of MMLL:

a. Any Maryland or federally-chartered bank, trust company, savings bank, savings and loan association, credit union, or other regulated financial institution;

b. Any insurance company;

c. Any nonprofit registered charitable organization or nonprofit religious organization;

d. Any person who makes three or fewer mortgage loans per year, and any person who brokers no more than one mortgage loan per calendar year.[42]

The purpose of this financing agreement disclosure is to inform the borrower of the terms of the loan being offered, and COM. LAW II §§ 12-125, 12-922, and 12-1022 require that the financing agreement contain:

a. The term and principal amount of the loan;

b. An explanation of the type of mortgage loan being offered;

c. The rate of interest that will apply to the loan and, if the rate is subject to change, is a variable rate, or is subject to a final determination at a future date based on some objective standard, a specific statement of those facts;

d. The points, if any, to be paid by the borrower or the seller or both; and

e. The term during which the financing agreement remains in effect.

If any of the terms of the financing agreement are subject to change or determination after execution of the financing agreement by the parties, the mortgage lender must provide the borrower with a commitment, executed by the lender, at least 72 hours prior to the time of settlement. The commitment must contain:

a. The effective fixed interest rate or initial interest rate that will be applied to the loan; and

b. A restatement of all the remaining unchanged provisions of the financing agreement.[43]

The licensing and regulatory authority under MMLL is vested in the Commissioner of Financial Regulation. The regulations require certain procedures and

---

41 FIN. INST. §§ 11-501, 11-502.

42 FIN. INST. § 11-502(b).

43 COM. LAW II §§ 12-125(b), (c); 12-922(b), (c); 12-1022(b), (c).

standards of conduct to be followed in the advertising, solicitation, processing, documentation, and closing of a mortgage loan.[44] If a mortgage lender fails to comply with the requirements of COM. LAW II §§ 12-125, 12-922, and 12-1022, that lender shall be subject to the penalties provided under MMLL. These penalties include a fine not to exceed $50,000 and/or imprisonment not to exceed 10 years, and forfeiture of all interest and charges with respect to the loan. The lender may also be subject to suspension or revocation of its license and civil penalties pursuant to an enforcement action brought by the Commissioner. The aggrieved borrower also may sue that lender for damages including reasonable attorneys' fees.[45]

The regulations provide that a financing agreement need not be provided if within 10 business days after initial application the loan is closed or a written commitment containing all material loan terms is furnished to the applicant.[46]

B. [§ 5.19] Timing of Decision by Lender

It may take from two weeks to two months (or even longer in some cases) for some lenders to evaluate fully a loan application and to decide whether to make the loan requested. Of course, when the credit report and appraisal are requested from other persons and they do not arrive in a timely manner, the lender must either delay its decision until it receives those items or issue a commitment to make a loan specifically subject to receipt of any outstanding item in a form satisfactory to it.

Some lenders use computer-based, automated underwriting systems. For example, Desktop Underwriter is Fanny Mae's automated underwriting system. A computer-based, automated underwriting system automates the process for lenders by requesting information online and then analyzing the borrower's loan application and credit history data, as well as the property information. Theoretically, the underwriting process can take minutes.

C. [§ 5.20] Basis for Declination

In the event the lender declines to make a loan, it must notify the applicant of its reasons for denying credit to the applicant.[47] A sample form declination letter including a notice of adverse action, which is required under ECOA, is set forth in § **5.79** of this chapter.

---

44 *See* COMAR 09.03.06.03, .08, .10.

45 COM. LAW II §§ 12-125(d), (e); 12-922(d) ; 12-1022(d), (e) ; Fin. Inst. §§ 11-517, 11-523.

46 COMAR 09.03.06.06.

47 Equal Credit Opportunity Act (ECOA), 15 U.S.C. §§ 1691–1691f; Regulation B, 12 C.F.R. §§ 202.1–202.15. *See also* COM. LAW II §§ 14-1701–14-1706.

Under both ECOA and similar Maryland law,[48] a lender may not discriminate on a prohibited basis and, therefore, may not decline an applicant on such basis. The prohibited bases under federal law are:

1. sex,
2. marital status,
3. race,
4. color,
5. religion,
6. national origin,
7. age,
8. because all or part of an applicant's income derives from a public assistance program, and
9. because an applicant in good faith has exercised any right under the Consumer Credit Protection Act.

Under the Maryland law, a lender may not refuse to lend money to a person solely because of:

1. geographic area or neighborhood,
2. race,
3. creed,
4. color,
5. age,
6. sex,
7. marital status,
8. handicap, or
9. national origin.[49]

Also, the Maryland Equal Credit Opportunity Act,[50] prohibits discrimination on any of the above bases, excluding items one and eight. That act sets forth specific prohibited practices and gives the State Commissioner of Financial Regulation jurisdiction to enforce its provisions.[51]

---

48 Com. Law II § 12-113.

49 Com. Law II § 12-113(a).

50 Com. Law II §§ 12-701–12-708.

51 An amendment by Ch. 326, Acts 1996, substituted the Commissioner of Financial Regulation for the officials who previously held the enforcement authority. *See* Com. Law II § 12-703.

D. Acceptance of Application

1. [§ 5.21] Conditions of loan commitment—generally

If the credit report and appraisal are satisfactory to the lender, the lender will often issue a letter of commitment in which it agrees to lend a stated sum of money at a particular interest rate or rates if certain conditions precedent to the closing of the loan are met. These conditions may include any number of items based on factors which the lender deems relevant. The most frequent conditions are discussed in §§ **5.22–5.27** of this chapter.

2. [§ 5.22] Fire and hazard insurance

Lenders generally insist that they be named as the loss payee on fire and hazard insurance policies and that they hold the original insurance policies. They may not require borrowers to use particular insurers, brokers, or agents or to provide insurance in amounts in excess of the replacement value of the improvements securing their loans.[52] Lenders, however, will frequently require that the insurance companies have at least a minimum rating under an independent rating system and that the policies be in such amounts that the borrowers will not be deemed to be co-insurers. Lenders often require that borrowers provide the insurance policies prior to settlement so that they may be reviewed.

3. [§ 5.23] Flood insurance

If the property is located in an area designated by either the Director of the Federal Emergency Management Agency or the Secretary of the Department of Housing and Urban Development as having special flood hazards (flood prone area), and for which flood insurance has been made available under the National Flood Insurance Act of 1968,[53] as amended, most institutional lenders are required by law to give their borrowers written notice that the property is so located. Such lenders must notify their borrowers whether the property is located in a community participating in the National Flood Insurance Program (NFIP) and, if so, whether federal disaster relief assistance will be available in the event of a federally declared disaster. If the community is participating in the NFIP, federally assisted flood insurance must be obtained.

Federal financial benefits (including loans insured by the FHA, guaranteed by the VA, or direct federal loans) are not available for a loan that is being made,

---

[52] Com. Law II § 12-124.
[53] 42 U.S.C. 4001–4129.

increased, extended, or renewed, if the area has been designated as flood prone for any given year and the community is not participating in the NFIP.[54]

Flood maps may be checked by contacting the insurance agent who will be providing the insurance for the property. Flood maps may be acquired from:

Federal Emergency Management Agency

FEMA Map Service Center

PO Box 1038

Jessup, Md. 20794-1038

Phone: 1-800-358-9616

Email: FEMA-mscservice@dhs.gov

or from the website at *http://msc.fema.gov*.

The location of the property in an area designated as flood prone will not relieve the buyer of his obligation to purchase the house unless there is a provision in the purchase contract permitting termination on that basis. Therefore, it is recommended that a clause be inserted in the purchase contract to allow for this possibility if it may be a problem.

A lender may not require a borrower, as a condition to receiving or maintaining a loan secured by a first mortgage or first deed of trust, to provide or purchase flood insurance coverage in an amount exceeding the replacement value of the improvements on the real property.[55] In determining the replacement value of the improvements on any real property, the lender may: (i) accept the value placed on the improvements by the insurer; or (ii) use the value placed on the improvements that is determined by the lender's appraisal of the real property.[56]

4. *[§ 5.24] Title and appraisal*

Lenders will require that title to the property be good and marketable, and they will often require that a mortgagee title insurance policy be issued in their favor containing no exceptions objectionable to them or their counsel. Since most lenders object to a title policy that contains a survey exception, a location survey, also called

---

54 *See generally* Flood Disaster Protection Act of 1973, as amended by the Housing and Community Development Act of 1977, 42 U.S.C. §§ 4001–4129 and the following regulations issued by the federal instrumentalities responsible for the supervision, approval, regulation, or insuring of lending institutions: 12 C.F.R. §§ 22.1–22.10 (regulations of the Office of the Comptroller of the Currency (OCC)); 12 C.F.R. §§ 339.1–339.10 (regulations of the Federal Deposit Insurance Corporation (FDIC)); and 12 C.F.R. §§ 760.1–760.10 (regulations of the National Credit Union Administration (NCUA)).

55 Com. Law II § 12-124(a)(3).

56 Com. Law II § 12-124(a)(4).

a location drawing, dated within six months prior to the date of closing often will have to be made. The current charge for a location survey of a normal residence on a small lot ranges from $100 to $500.

Lenders also will require that an appraisal of the property be performed by a licensed or certified independent appraiser. The current charge for a typical residential appraisal ranges from $250 to $500. Under Regulation B, 12 C.F.R. § 202.5a, and also under REAL PROP. § 14-104.1, the borrower is entitled to a copy of the appraisal report used by the lender to determine market value.

5. [§ 5.25] Completion and inspection

In the case of a new house or a house in need of repair, the lender will condition settlement of a permanent loan upon completion or repair of the improvements, issuance of a use and occupancy permit, if applicable, and inspection of the property by the lender or its designee.

6. [§ 5.26] Compliance with local requirements

Lenders will require that all local laws and regulations are complied with before settlement, including procurement of abatement notices for housing violations and compliance with the Baltimore City tenant's right of first refusal[57] and the Baltimore County well tests,[58] if applicable.

E. [§ 5.27] The Commitment Letter

The commitment letter probably will state that all loan closing documents must be in a form satisfactory to the lender and its counsel. Copies of the note and mortgage or deed of trust that the lender will use might be attached for the borrower's convenience.

If the lender expects the borrower to pay any or all of the lender's closing costs, the commitment letter should so state. Also, the commitment letter should include the name of the attorney or law firm that will represent the lender in connection with that transaction and the name of the settlement attorney or title company that will conduct the closing if the lender makes such a designation.

F. [§ 5.28] Designation of Title Examiner or Insurer

RESPA does not prohibit a lender from designating the person who will examine title and conduct the closing of the loan transaction unless such person is in a controlled business relationship with the lender, and Maryland law requires a lender to

---

57 *See* § **5.51** of this chapter.

58 *See* § **5.52** of this chapter.

permit the borrower to select the title examiner or insurer.[59] Maryland law further prohibits lenders from requiring that any insurance, including title insurance, be purchased through any particular agent, broker, or insurer.[60]

COMMERCIAL LAW II requires a lender that designates an attorney or other person to perform settlement services to disclose to the applicant within three days after the taking of the application the lender's requirements concerning selection of such person, the fact of borrower's ability to choose, and a good faith estimate of the fee or fees that the borrower will be charged.[61] If the lender requires the borrower to pay the lender's attorney's fees, the lender's attorney may only charge for those services attributable to the processing and closing of the particular loan. An attorney whose fees exceed $100 must provide the borrower at settlement with a statement in form that satisfies the requirements set forth in COM. LAW II § 12-120(b).

G. [§ 5.29] Amendments and Acceptance of Conditions by the Borrower

Commitment letters generally provide that their terms are effective only for a given time period (frequently from 60 to 180 days). They also may provide that the borrower must formally accept the commitment within a shorter time period (perhaps two weeks) or else it will expire by its own terms. If such is the case, the lender is not contractually bound to make the loan until the borrower accepts the terms of the commitment.

Upon acceptance of the commitment, the borrower becomes obligated to accept the loan in accordance with the terms set forth therein. If the commitment so provides, the borrower assumes liability for all expenses incurred by the lender or its designees in connection with the preparation for the loan closing, including attorneys' fees and fees for title examinations, judgment reports, lien sheets, and location surveys. Therefore, before accepting a commitment the borrower should determine that the terms of the loan are satisfactory in all respects. If, for example, the borrower wants to have the right to change the terms of the loan at some future time, but the commitment letter does not so provide, or if one of the persons named as a borrower does not want to be personally liable for repayment of the loan, the commitment letter should not be accepted until the outstanding issues are resolved.

---

59 *See* Regulation X, 24 C.F.R. § 3500.7; COM. LAW II § 12-120. Notwithstanding the Maryland requirement, a lender may reject for good cause the borrower's choice of attorney or title insurance company. A lender also may require a borrower to pay for the preparation of loan closing documents, the issuance of title insurance, the review of documents prepared by the borrower's attorney, or attendance at settlement by the lender's attorney, provided that the disclosure requirements of COM. LAW II § 12-120(b) are met. The provisions of COM. LAW II § 12-120 do not apply to commercial loans. *See* COM. LAW II § 12-120(a).

60 MD. CODE ANN., INSURANCE II § 27-214 (2017 & Supp. 2022).

61 COM. LAW II § 12-119.

Alternatively, the commitment may be accepted subject to the requested change or changes; however, the amended commitment will not bind the lender until it has accepted the amended commitment.

III. SETTLEMENT OF THE LOAN

A. [§ 5.30] Title Examination and Title Insurance Binder

Once the borrower has accepted the commitment, or earlier if the lender chooses, the lender will refer the matter to its counsel or to a title company that employs an attorney so that the necessary title work can begin. The land records of the jurisdiction in which the property is located must be searched to determine whether the seller of the property (or, in the case of a refinance or junior mortgage loan, the borrower) is in title, what the legal description of the property is, and what encumbrances and restrictions are of record. The court dockets of that jurisdiction must be examined to determine whether there are any judgments against the owner of the property or a predecessor which have created liens against the property and to find out if there is a lis pendens concerning the property. A typical judgment search service will also pick up any federal district court docket or bankruptcy court docket entries. Additionally, lien sheets must be obtained to determine if there are any charges due to the municipality, county, or state that must be paid before title can be transferred.[62] In the event that there are liens of record against the property, pay-off statements must be obtained.

The lender may be satisfied to rely upon a certificate of an approved attorney regarding the status of title, in which case such a certificate will be issued to the lender after the title examination is completed. However, if the lender requires that a policy of title insurance be issued to protect its interests, either an officer, agent, approved attorney, or authorized issuing agent of a title company will prepare before settlement a commitment of that title company to issue a mortgagee title insurance policy subject only to items enumerated therein, or such a person will prepare a title insurance binder containing the same exceptions. Although approved attorneys may certify the status of titles, they do not have the authority to issue either a title report or a commitment to issue a title insurance policy that is binding on the title insurance company. When the lender will not rely on a certificate regarding the status of title, approved attorneys must submit their title examination to the title company which in turn issues the commitment. Therefore, a title report or a purported commitment that has not been countersigned by the title company or an authorized issuing agent should not be accepted.

---

[62] A lien certificate is only required to be obtained in Baltimore City and in Baltimore, Carroll, Harford, and Howard Counties. In all other counties, a lien certificate is either not required or not used.

The lender and the title company have an inherent conflict with respect to the form of the title insurance policy. Since the protection of a title insurance policy is limited by the items listed as exceptions, it is to the benefit of the lender to have the commitment or binder contain as few exceptions as possible. In many instances, the lender will also want to obtain specific guarantees in the title insurance policy regarding certain exceptions as well as affirmative coverage concerning other items that affect title. Counsel for the lender is responsible for evaluating the legal risks posed by the final form of the commitment or binder so that the lender can make the business decision of whether to make the loan in light of those risks.

B. Closing Papers

1. [§ 5.31] Generally

Unlike commercial loans, the form of residential loan closing papers is almost never negotiable in any material respect. At the settlement when the lender advances the loan funds, the borrower executes a promissory note evidencing the obligation to repay the loan and a deed of trust or mortgage as security for the loan. With a mortgage, the borrower conveys legal title to and the right of possession of the property to the lender for security purposes. When a deed of trust is used, the borrower conveys, subject to the terms of the trust, such title and right to one or more individuals named by the lender (who are called trustees) for the benefit of the lender and the borrower. Although the trustees, who may be easily removed and replaced in the discretion of the holder of the note, are usually under the control of the lender, they owe a fiduciary duty to the borrower as well as the lender.

There is no substantive difference with respect to the lender's security between a deed of trust and a mortgage. But many lenders prefer to use deeds of trust, because the security for a loan may be assigned by the mere endorsement and delivery of the note without the need to record an assignment among the land records (as is the case with a mortgage) and without the need to obtain a title bring-to-date; i.e., a title search from the date the mortgage was recorded to the present. Such a bring-to-date is necessary when assigning a mortgage in order to determine that the seller of the loan has not previously sold it and assigned the mortgage of record.

2. [§ 5.32] Standard form notes and security documents

To enhance the marketability of loans, many lenders use the FNMA/FHLMC form notes and deeds of trust for conventional loans. A copy of the FNMA/FHLMC form note for fixed-rate loans is set forth in § **5.80** of this chapter, and a copy of the corresponding deed of trust is set forth in § **5.80** of this chapter. A copy of a FNMA form adjustable rate note for an adjustable rate mortgage (ARM) annually adjusted to one year United States Treasury securities and a copy of the corresponding FNMA adjustable rate rider to the deed of trust are set forth in §§ **5.82–5.83** of this chapter. Additionally, if the property is a condominium unit or part of a planned unit development (PUD), a condominium or PUD rider, as applicable, may be attached to the deed of trust to give the lender some additional security. Copies of these riders are set forth in §§ **5.84–5.85** of this chapter.

3. [§ 5.33] Authorized changes to the standard forms

Deeds of trust securing property in Maryland may be changed only in certain limited respects and still be considered FNMA/FHLMC uniform instruments. For example, lenders may add legends to identify the preparer(s) of the instrument, consistent with the requirements of Real Prop. § 3-104(f); they need not require borrowers to provide social security numbers on the security instrument; they may insert initial lines at the bottom of each page for borrowers to initial; and they may modify certain covenant language dealing with use of the property when a second home is involved.

4. [§ 5.34] Riders

If lenders are not concerned with selling the loans they originate, they may attach other riders, make other changes, or use different forms altogether. For example, a lender may want to prohibit junior encumbrances of the property, which encumbrances are permitted by the FNMA/FHLMC form. Moreover, a lender may not want to be obliged to give 30 days' notice by certified mail to a borrower in default of an obligation in the note or deed of trust before it may exercise its remedies or to be forced to reinstate a loan that it has accelerated as the FNMA/FHLMC forms require. Sometimes lenders attach riders that state that all or certain provisions of the riders terminate upon sale of the loan to FNMA or FHLMC.

5. [§ 5.35] Right of possession provision

In the absence of a provision to the contrary, the mortgage or deed of trust conveys the right to possession of the property to the mortgagee or trustee, because Maryland is a title state.[63] For this reason, the mortgage or deed of trust usually contains a provision that gives to the borrower the right of possession and the right to profits until default.

C. Escrow and Building Loan Agreements

1. [§ 5.36] New construction

If the purpose of the loan is to finance the construction of a new house, the borower generally will need the loan proceeds (or a large portion thereof) only

[63] *Commercial Bldg. & Loan Ass'n v. Robinson,* 90 Md. 615, 618, 45 A. 449, 450 (1900).

as the construction progresses. At the settlement of such loans, the borrower and the lender typically execute a building loan agreement, according to the terms of which the lender agrees to advance funds as construction progresses as long as no default has occurred. Alternatively, the lender may advance at settlement the full loan proceeds to the borrower, which the borrower immediately deposits in an escrow account under the terms of an escrow agreement. While the lender customarily appoints the escrowees, they owe a fiduciary duty to both the lender and borrower. Regardless of whether a building loan agreement or an escrow agreement is used, the loan proceeds are disbursed as construction advances and specified conditions are satisfied. Generally, the borrower is charged interest only on the funds that are disbursed from the escrow account or under the building loan agreement. If the borrower were charged interest on the full amount of the loan even though it has not been completely disbursed from escrow, a possible usury problem might arise, particularly if the escrowees are not independent of the lender.[64] It should be noted, however, that lenders are no longer governed by an interest rate ceiling on first mortgage loans as they were when the loan described in the *Hoffman* case was settled.[65]

2. [§ 5.37] Property in need of repair or incomplete house (early settlement)

Occasionally, if the property is in need of repair or construction has not been completed by the scheduled settlement date, the lender may be willing to lend the borrower less than the original loan amount at the time of settlement and to advance the remaining portion of the loan proceeds upon completion of the repairs or construction.

In such situations, the lender might require that these funds be placed in an escrow account to be made available upon completion of the repairs or construction. Although the buyer/borrower may have contracted with the seller or another person to make the improvements that the lender is requiring as a condition to advance some of the loan proceeds, the lender may choose to deal solely with its borrower in connection with such an escrow arrangement.

Should the person with the contractual obligation to make the improvements need assurances that the borrower will make his or her payments, that person and the borrower might enter into either an escrow agreement or other arrangement. For example, the borrower might assign his interest in the escrow agreement prepared by the lender unless the lender prohibits such an assignment.

---

64 *Hoffman v. Key Fed. Sav. & Loan Ass'n,* 286 Md. 28, 416 A.2d 1265 (1979).

65 *See* § **5.50** of this chapter.

IV. FEDERAL, STATE, AND LOCAL LAWS AND REGULATIONS

A. Real Estate Settlement Procedures Act (RESPA)

1. [§ 5.38] Background

RESPA[66] controls many of the practices and procedures in connection with federally-related mortgage loan transactions, as defined therein. Enacted by Congress in 1974, RESPA was designed to reform certain practices in connection with residential real estate transactions and to ensure that home buyers would be given certain information about such settlements and certain disclosures about their closing costs. As part of the original act, sellers were required in certain cases to disclose to their buyers the previous sales prices of their homes, and lenders were required to make particular disclosures in advance of settlement. These requirements made RESPA unworkable, however, and they were eliminated or substantially modified by the 1975 amendments.

2. [§ 5.39] Current requirements

As indicated in § **5.16** of this chapter, the current forms of RESPA and Regulation X require that lenders give good faith estimates and copies of special information booklets to all first mortgage loan applicants and inform them of the lender's business relationships with settlement providers.[67] The person conducting settlement must use the settlement sheet form known as HUD-1, which is set forth in § **5.86** of this chapter. Upon borrower's request the settlement agent must give the borrower an opportunity to inspect the settlement sheet, completed to the fullest extent possible, one day prior to settlement.[68]

3. [§ 5.40] Escrow accounts

Although RESPA permits lenders to establish and maintain escrow accounts to assure payment of taxes, other charges against the property, and insurance premiums, RESPA limits the initial and monthly deposits into such accounts so that the amount held at any time does not exceed the proportionate amount necessary to pay those charges from the last date they would have been paid to the due date of the first full installment payment under the mortgage, plus one-sixth of those estimated annual charges.[69]

Maryland law has eliminated the one-sixth cushion at the end of each year by requiring notice to the borrower and an opportunity to elect to receive all overages in

---

66 12 U.S.C. §§ 2601–2617 (2009).

67 RESPA, 12 U.S.C. § 2604; Regulation X, 24 C.F.R. §§ 3500.6, 3500.7.

68 RESPA, 12 U.S.C. § 2603; Regulation X, 24 C.F.R. §§ 3500.8, 3500.10.

69 RESPA, 12 U.S.C. § 2609.

the escrow account.[70] Borrowers must receive interest on the escrowed funds at the greater of 3% per year or the lender's passbook rate of interest if the loans are from banks, savings banks, or savings and loan associations that do business in Maryland or from an out-of-state lender, which places the loan with a Maryland lender for servicing.[71] If, however, a loan is purchased from a lender that is not required to pay interest on the escrowed funds, then the purchasing lender is not required to pay interest on the escrowed funds.[72] Lenders that require escrow accounts for real property taxes are required to pay the taxes in a timely fashion, provided sufficient funds are available therefor.[73]

4. [§ 5.41] Prohibitions—kickbacks

No person may give or accept a kickback, thing of value, or unearned fee in connection with the referral of real estate settlement services for a mortgage transaction covered by RESPA. There is a criminal penalty for violation of that statute.[74]

Until recently, lenders could offer programs that provide either monetary benefits or benefits in kind to real estate agents that direct their clients to the lender, based upon two federal court cases, which supported the position that "real estate settlement services" did not include mortgage lending and that helping a borrower obtain a mortgage was a service for which a fee may be charged.[75] Congress and the U.S. Department of Housing and Urban Development (HUD), however, have since amended the anti-kickback provisions of RESPA and Regulation X to effectively circumvent the *Graham* case and its progeny. "Settlement services" now include the origination of a federally related mortgage loan.[76]

5. [§ 5.42] Prohibitions—title companies

Sellers may not require that title insurance be purchased from any particular title company. The penalty for violating this prohibition is three times the cost of the title insurance.[77] Although RESPA does not impose a similar limitation on lenders, Maryland law imposes certain restrictions on the lender's ability to select a title examiner or insurer.[78]

---

70 Com. Law II § 12-109(c)

71 Com. Law II § 12-109.

72 67 Op. Att'y Gen. 104 (1982).

73 Real Prop. § 7-107.

74 RESPA, 12 U.S.C. § 2607 (2004); Regulation X, 24 C.F.R. § 3500.14.

75 *United States v. Graham Mortgage Corp.,* 740 F.2d 414 (6th Cir. 1984); *Eisenberg v. Comfed Mortgage Co.,* 629 F. Supp. 1157 (D. Mass. 1986).

76 12 U.S.C. § 2602; Regulation X, 24 C.F.R. § 3500.2.

77 RESPA, 12 U.S.C. § 2608.

78 *See* § **5.29**, *supra*, for discussion of limitations on a lender's right to designate a settlement provider.

6. [§ 5.43] Prohibitions—charges

No fee or charge may be imposed for the preparation of the HUD-1 settlement sheet or any disclosures required by the federal Truth-in-Lending Act.[79]

B. Federal Truth-in-Lending Act

1. [§ 5.44] Disclosures

As indicated in § **5.17** of this chapter, in a residential mortgage transaction subject to RESPA, good faith estimates of all of the disclosures required by the federal Truth-in-Lending Act[80] must be given before consummation of the transaction, or they must be delivered or mailed not later than three business days after the lender receives the borrower's application, whichever is earlier.[81] If the lender determines within the three-day period that the application should be declined on the terms requested, these "early disclosures" need not be given.

2. [§ 5.45] Right of rescission

The lender must give the borrower three business days from the later of (a) consummation of the loan; (b) delivery to the borrower of a notice of its right to rescind; or (c) delivery of the material disclosures required under 12 C.F.R. § 226.18 to rescind the borrower's obligations in any credit transaction in which a security interest is given in real property that is, or is expected to be, the principal residence of the borrower, except:

- when the transaction involves a mortgage loan to finance the acquisition or initial construction of the borrower's residence, or
- when the mortgage loan is a refinance or consolidation by the same lender of a loan or loans already secured by the borrower's residence.[82]

Nevertheless, the right to rescind does apply in the latter case to the extent that the new amount financed exceeds the unpaid balance and any earned, but unpaid, finance charges of the loan or loans being refinanced or consolidated and costs attributable solely to the refinancing or consolidation.[83]

In those cases in which a right of rescission exists, the lender must provide the borrower with a notice that sets forth in prescribed form the right to rescind and the effect of rescission. A copy of the notice required under Regulation Z is set forth in § **5.87** of this chapter. If the borrower elects to cancel the transaction within the three-day period, any lien placed on that real property as a result of the transaction

---

79 RESPA, 12 U.S.C. § 2610; Regulation X, 24 C.F.R. § 3500.12.

80 15 U.S.C. §§ 1601 *et seq.* (2008).

81 Regulation Z, 12 C.F.R. § 226.19(a).

82 Truth-in-Lending Act, 15 U.S.C. § 1635; Regulation Z, 12 C.F.R. § 226.23.

83 Regulation Z, 12 C.F.R. § 226.23.

becomes void. If such notice is not given, the borrower's right to rescind the transaction extends for three years after consummation, giving the borrower an interest-free loan for that period.[84]

A lender may not fund a loan until the rescission period has passed unless the borrower has waived his right to rescind because of a bona fide personal financial emergency.[85] A borrower refinancing a loan secured by his principal residence should request the lender to provide the notice of the right to rescind more than three days in advance of settlement so that the borrower may receive the new money at settlement and not pay interest on two loans.

C. [§ 5.46] Equal Credit Opportunity Acts

Lenders must be aware of the federal and state equal credit opportunity acts.[86] Lenders may not discriminate on any prohibited basis, and their loan application forms and their credit approval systems must not violate these acts. If an applicant is sufficiently creditworthy to be able to borrow the sum requested in his or her own name, the lender may not require his or her spouse to execute either the note or a guaranty and thereby become personally liable to repay the loan. Notwithstanding this restriction, a lender may require the spouse who is a co-tenant to execute the deed of trust or mortgage in order to convey their interest in the land although the lender did not rely upon that spouse's credit.

D. [§ 5.47] Community Reinvestment Act

Although it may not directly affect individual loans, the Community Reinvestment Act of 1977 (Act)[87] requires that lenders regulated by the Federal Reserve System, Office of the Comptroller of the Currency (OCC), Federal Deposit Insurance Corporation (FDIC) and Office of Thrift Supervision (OTS) meet the credit needs of their entire community, including low and moderate income neighborhoods. Affected lenders must be aware of the Act's impact on them.

E. [§ 5.48] Regulation by Chartering or Insuring Agencies

Lenders must, of course, be aware of the additional requirements of the state and/or federal agencies that insure them or otherwise regulate their activities. Certain lenders are prohibited from making particular types of loans (such as those

---

84 Truth-in-Lending Act, 15 U.S.C. § 1635(d); Regulation Z, 12 C.F.R. § 226.23 (c), (e). Under 12 C.F.R. § 226.23(a)(2), the consumer must notify the creditor of rescission in writing. The filing of a complaint constitutes statutory notice of rescission. *Taylor v. Domestic Remodeling*, 97 F.3d 96, 100 (5th Cir. 1996).

85 Truth-in-Lending Act, 15 U.S.C. § 1635(d); Regulation Z, 12 C.F.R. § 226.23(c), (e).

86 *See* § **5.21** of this chapter, *supra*.

87 12 U.S.C. §§ 2901–2908.

with less than a specified loan-to-value ratio), and others may have limitations on the types of loans that they may keep in their own portfolios.

Lending institutions must be cognizant of the separate adjustable rate mortgages disclosure requirements and related limitations issued by federal agencies[88]—OCC,[89] HUD[90] and the Federal Reserve Board (FRB).[91] The OCC requires only those disclosures dictated by Regulation Z.[92]

F. [§ 5.49] Usury Laws

Lenders may make loans secured by first mortgages or deeds of trust on residential real property at any stated rate of interest provided they do not impose a prepayment penalty.[93] Prior to passage of the Depository Institutions Deregulation and Monetary Control Act of 1980 (DIDA),[94] Com. Law II § 12-108 prohibited a lender in Maryland from charging points to a borrower or any other person except in connection with (1) loans that the lender planned to sell to a federal, state, or local agency or that were made under a federal program, and (2) certain other specified situations. DIDA has preempted state law and constitutional limitations on interest rates, points, and other charges in connection with federally-related first mortgage loans on residential real property and residential manufactured homes and in connection with loans secured by first liens on stock in residential cooperative housing corporations that are granted to finance the acquisition of that stock. Between April 1, 1980 and April 1, 1983 states were permitted to override DIDA's preemption by enacting or reenacting state limitations. Maryland did not act within that window.

DIDA also permits states to override at any time the federal preemption of state limitations on discount points and such other charges. Since Maryland has not reenacted Com. Law II § 12-108 subsequent to the passage of DIDA, the limitation on the charging of points set forth at Com. Law II § 12-108 remains preempted by DIDA.

It should be noted, however, that Veterans Administration (VA) and Federal Housing Administration of the Department of Housing and Urban Development (FHA) regulations permit lenders to charge only one point to their borrowers for VA or FHA loans, but do not restrict the numbers of points lenders may receive from the seller.[95]

---

88 *See* discussion in 82 Op. Att'y Gen. 18 (1997).

89 12 C.F.R. §§ 34.20–34.25.

90 *See* 24 C.F.R. §§ 34.5–34.12.

91 Regulation Z, 12 C.F.R. §§ 226.18, 226.19.

92 12 C.F.R. § 34.20; Regulation Z, 12 C.F.R. § 226.19.

93 Com. Law II § 12-103(b)(1)(iii).

94 12 U.S.C. § 1735f-7a.

95 38 C.F.R. § 36.4312 (2008); 24 C.F.R § 203.27 (2008) (note that two and one-half points may be charged with respect to construction financing).

In 1986 the Maryland General Assembly amended Com. Law II § 12-103(b) to prohibit lenders from requiring borrowers to pay interest in advance. Although Com. Law II § 12-103(b) currently reflects this change, the Office of General Counsel of the Federal Home Loan Bank Board (FHLBB) opined in a letter, dated May 8, 1987, to the Maryland Office of the Attorney General that DIDA preempted and prohibited that amendment.

There is no ceiling on interest rates on first mortgage loans in Maryland, and the federal law has the effect in this state of permitting lenders to charge points on all first mortgage loans. Although it may be argued that by amending Com. Law II § 12-103(c) in 1983 and 1985 Maryland overrode DIDA's preemption of Com. Law II § 12-103(c), which permitted a lender to charge simple interest at a rate no greater than 24% per year, the regulations of the FHLBB preempt any Maryland override of DIDA and permit lenders to charge interest above the rate of 24% per year for loans secured by a first lien on either residential real property or cooperative stock purchased with the loan proceeds.[96]

G. [§ 5.50] Fair Housing Laws

Title VIII of the Civil Rights Act of 1968,[97] as amended, establishes a Fair Housing Assistance Program and directs the Secretary of HUD to cooperate with state and local public agencies carrying on programs to prevent or eliminate discriminatory housing practices. Maryland is one of the states currently designated as having substantially equivalent rights and remedies.[98] Therefore, the federal government provides Maryland the first opportunity to process complaints and contributes federal funds for such purpose.[99]

H. [§ 5.51] Baltimore City Tenant's Right of First Refusal

Landlords must give the tenants of single family residences in Baltimore City the right for 30 days to purchase the houses in which they live on the same terms as

---

96 12 C.F.R. § 590.3 (2008); FHLBB Interpretation No. 590-6, 45 Fed. Reg. 8000 (Feb. 6, 1980). *See also* 73 Op. Att'y Gen. 144 (1988). *Note Pac. Mortgage & Inv. Group v. Horn,* 100 Md. App. 311, 641 A.2d 913 (1994) (to meet the requirements of § 12-103, the lender must show the loan was insured or guaranteed by a federal agency or instrumentality). *But see Lampros v. Gelb & Gelb, P.C.,* 153 Md. App. 447, 837 A.2d 229 (2003); *Bowie v. Rose Shanis Fin. Serv., LLC,* 160 Md. App. 227, 62 A.2d 102 (2004); and *Parham v. Numax Mortgage Corp.*, No. 24-C-02-000151, 2006 Md. Cir. Ct. LEXIS 17 (Aug. 1, 2006).

97 42 U.S.C. §§ 3601–3619.

98 It has been so certified because of Md. Ann. Code, art. 49B, §§ 19–39 (2003 & Supp. 2008), pursuant to the standards set forth in 24 C.F.R. §§ 115.200–115.212 (1996).

99 24 C.F.R. §§ 111.101–111.123 (1994). Part 111 of 24 C.F.R. was removed in 61 F.R. 7625, Feb. 28, 1996.

those offered to third parties.[100] This right of first refusal is limited to those people who have been tenants for not less than six months.[101] A tenant's refusal to accept a landlord's offer of sale does not automatically terminate the tenant's right of first refusal. The landlord must provide the tenant with the opportunity to accept any subsequent contract that contains terms more favorable to a buyer than the terms in the landlord's offer of sale.[102]

To determine that these provisions are complied with, lenders should require that their borrowers, who purchase homes in Baltimore City that were previously occupied by tenants, present written evidence to them that the tenants did not choose to exercise their rights. Also, every deed conveying title to a residence located in Baltimore City should include a certification by the seller that either the subject property was not occupied by a tenant within the prior six months or that the tenant did not choose or was unable to match the purchase contract of the buyer.

I. [§ 5.52] Baltimore County Well Tests

Improved and unimproved lots in Baltimore County, which are not served by a public or community water supply system, may not be conveyed unless the requirements of Title 35, Article II of the Baltimore County Code are met. Unless the buyer provides a written waiver, which must be filed with the Baltimore County Department of Environmental Protection and Resource Management at least six days prior to settlement, all such lots must be served by wells having a recovery rate of at least one gallon of water per minute. The water supply on improved lots also must meet the bacteriological and chemical quality requirements of the State Department of Health and Mental Hygiene.[103] In order to determine that these provisions are complied with, lenders should require that their borrowers who purchase lots in Baltimore County present copies of the applicable waivers or written evidence of satisfactory test results, as the case may be.

J. [§ 5.53] High Cost Loans

Maryland enacted a new high cost mortgage statute on May 16, 2002. The statute applies the same restrictions and duties on mortgage lenders who originate their

---

100 Baltimore City, Md. Code, art. 13, §§ 6-1–6-10 (2007) (hereinafter Balt. City Code §).

101 Balt. City Code, art. 13, § 6-2(b).

102 Balt. City Code, art. 13, § 6-4(b).

103 Baltimore County, Md., Code, tit. §§ 34-2-102–34-2-105 (2004). Note that a well test generally may not be waived if an unimproved lot is located within any delineated county critical water area. *See* § 34-2-103(b), (e). If the water supply for an improved lot fails to meet the minimum yield requirements, the buyer may execute a waiver accepting the lesser yield. *See* § 34-2-104(e).

loans under the Interest and Usury Subtitle of Title 12 of the Commercial Law II Article (Subtitle 1), the Maryland Secondary Mortgage Loan Law (Subtitle 4), or the Credit Grantor Closed End Credit Provisions (Subtitle 10).

The restrictions and duties apply to lenders who make a "covered loan." "Covered loan" means a mortgage loan that satisfies the criteria for a loan subject to the Federal Home Ownership Equity Protection Act set forth in 15 U.S.C. § 1602(AA), as modified from time to time by Regulation Z, except that the comparison percentages for the mortgage loan must be one percentage point less than those specified in 15 U.S.C. § 1602(AA), as modified from time to time by Regulation Z.[104]

A lender making a "covered loan" may not finance as a part of the covered loan transaction single premium coverage for credit health insurance, credit involuntary unemployment benefit insurance, or credit life insurance.[105] "Single premium coverage" means "insurance for which the total premium is payable in one lump sum at or before the time coverage commences."[106]

When the borrower completes an application for a "covered loan," the lender must provide the buyer with the following: (a) a written recommendation that the borrower seek home buyer education or housing counseling; and (b) a list of agencies and organizations approved by the county in which the residential real property securing the covered loan is located to provide home buyer education or housing counseling.[107] A loan application is completed at the time of the initial application.[108] If a lender receives an application by mail, telephone, or other electronic means, a lender may satisfy the requirement that the lender provide a written recommendation that the borrower seek home buyer education or housing counseling and a list of approved agencies if the recommendation and list are mailed or otherwise provided to the borrower at the time of the initial application or within three business days after completion of the initial application.[109]

Except for five potentially broad exceptions, the statute provides that only the State of Maryland may enact a law that purports to regulate extensions of credit made by a financial institution.[110] This preemption does not:

(1) affect federal law preemption of state law;

(2) restrict or otherwise affect local laws that establish property ownership or the rights and obligations of property owners;

---

104 Com. Law II §§ 12-124.1(a)(2);12-409.1(a)(2); 12-410(a)(2); 12-1007(a)(2); 12-1029(a)(2).

105 Com. Law II §§ 12-124.1(b)(1); 12-410(e); 12-1007(b)(3)(i).

106 Com. Law II §§ 12-124.1(a)(9); 12-410(a)(8); 12-1007(a)(3).

107 Com. Law II §§ 12-124.l(c)(2); 12-409.1(d)(2); 12-1029(d)(2).

108 COMAR 09.03.06.18(C)(1)(a).

109 COMAR 09.03.06.18(C)(1)(b).

110 Fin. Inst. § 1-209(a).

(3) restrict or otherwise affect a local government's ability to regulate its fiscal economic or community development policy;

(4) restrict or otherwise affect a local government's ability to enact laws or adopt regulations relating to fair housing or other civil rights; or

(5) restrict or otherwise affect a local government's ability to establish or administer loan programs to assist residents with financial needs.[111]

K. [§ 5.54] Underwriting Guidance

A lender may not make a mortgage loan[112] without giving due regard to the borrower's ability to repay the mortgage loan in accordance with its terms, including the fully indexed rate[113] of the mortgage loan, if applicable, and property taxes and homeowners' insurance whether or not an escrow account is established for the collection and payment of these expenses.[114] Due regard to a borrowers ability to repay a mortgage loan must include: (i) consideration of the borrower's debt-to-income ratio, including existing debts and other obligations and (ii) verification of the borrower's gross monthly income and assets by review of third-party written documentation reasonably believed by the credit grantor to be accurate and complete.[115]

Acceptable third-party written documentation includes: (1) the borrower's internal revenue service form W-2; (2) a copy of the borrower's income tax return; (3) payroll receipts; (4) the records of a financial institution; or (5) other third-party discounts that provide reasonable reliable evidence of the borrower's income or assets.[116]

L. [§ 5.55] Prepayment Penalty Prohibited

A lender who originates a first mortgage loan under the Interest and Usury Subtitle may not charge a prepayment penalty.[117]

In addition, a lender may not require or authorize the imposition of a penalty, fee, premium, or other charge if a mortgage loan is prepaid in whole or in part.[118]

"Mortgage loan" means any loan primarily for personal, family, or household use that is secured by a mortgage, deed of trust, or other equivalent

---

111 Fin. Inst. § 1-209(b).

112 *See* § **5.55**, *infra*. "Mortgage Loan" does not include a reverse mortgage loan. Com. Law II §§ 12-127(a)(3), 12-1029(a)(5).

113 "Fully indexed rate" means "the index rate, as defined in the mortgage loan documents, prevailing at the time the mortgage loan is approved by the lender, plus the margin that will apply after the expiration of an introductory rate." Com. Law II §§ 12-127(a)(2), 12-409.1(a)(3), 12-1029(a)(3).

114 Com. Law II §§ 12-127(b), 12-409.1(b), 12-1029(b).

115 Com. Law II §§ 12-127(c), 12-409.1(c), 12-1029(c).

116 Com. Law II §§ 12-127(c)(2), 12-409.1(c)(2), 12-1029(c).

117 Com. Law II § 12-103(b)(iii).

118 Com. Law II § 12-105(d).

consensual security interest on a dwelling or residential real estate on which a dwelling is constructed or intended to be constructed.[119]

A prepayment charge is also prohibited under the Credit Grantor Closed End Credit Provisions.[120]

Finally, a lender originating second mortgage loans under the Maryland Secondary Mortgage Loan Law must permit a borrower to prepay a loan in full or in part at any time, without penalty.[121]

M. [§ 5.56] A Lender's Recapture of Deferred Closing Cost is Not a Prohibited Prepayment Penalty

In a specific response to *Bednar v. Provident Bank of Maryland*[122] where the Supreme Court of Maryland held that the recapture of closing costs constituted a prohibited prepayment charge under Subtitle 10 of Title 12 of COM. LAW II, the Maryland General Assembly amended Subtitle 10. A credit grantor under Subtitle 10 may charge and collect the additional fees and charges permitted under COM. LAW II § 12-1005(d) at *any time*.[123]

V. SECOND MORTGAGE LOANS

A. [§ 5.57] Applicable State Law

Knowledgeable Maryland lenders originate their loans that are secured by subordinate liens on residential property under the Credit Grantor Closed-End Credit Provisions of Com. Law II Title 12, Subtitle 10. Unless a lender specifically elects to make a second mortgage loan pursuant to Subtitle 10, however, the lender who makes second mortgage loans must comply with the Maryland Secondary Mortgage Loan Law (SMLL) under COM. LAW II Title 12, Subtitle 4.[124] The SMLL defines a secondary mortgage loan as a loan or deferred purchase price secured by a lien on real property located in Maryland (a mortgage, deed of trust, security agreement, sale and leaseback agreement, or other agreements containing a confession of judgment clause for the purpose of acquiring a lien), on which is located a one to four family dwelling, which is already subject to one or more prior encumbrances, not including a lease or ground lease.[125]

---

119 FIN. INST. § 11-501(l); *see also* COM. LAW II §§ 12-105(a), 12-127(a)(3); 12-1029(a)(5).

120 COM. LAW II § 12-1009(e).

121 COM. LAW II § 12-407(d).

122 *Bednar v. Provident Bank of Md., Inc.*, 402 Md. 532, 937 A.2d 210 (2007).

123 COM. LAW II § 12-1005(d)(2).

124 *See* COM. LAW II § 12-1013.1.

125 COM. LAW II § 12-401.

B. [§ 5.58] Licensing Provisions

In either case, unless a specific exemption applies, the lender must comply with the licensing provisions of the Maryland Mortgage Lender Law. A lender who elects to make the loan under subtitle 10 is not required to comply with the Installment Loan Licensing provisions if the lender is only engaged in the mortgage lending business.[126]

Installment loan licenses are not required for the following persons, if organized under Maryland law or otherwise qualified to do business in the state:

1. banking institutions, national banking associations, and federal or state savings and loan associations or credit unions;
2. licensees under the Maryland Consumer Loan Law;
3. sellers of goods and/or services not engaged in making loans or acting as credit services businesses;[127]
4. an other-state bank having a branch in Maryland;

or

5. licensees under the Maryland Mortgage Lender Law that are engaged solely in the mortgage lending business.

C. Credit Provisions

1. [§ 5.59] Interest and charges

For a new second mortgage loan subject to the SMLL, the maximum simple interest rate is 24% per year on the unpaid principal balance if no interest is charged in advance or compounded.[128]

Additionally, in accordance with COM. LAW II § 12-405, the aggregate amount of the loan originating fee imposed by a lender when combined with any finder's fee imposed by a mortgage broker may not exceed the greater of $250 or 10% of the net proceeds on a second mortgage loan. Lenders may require that their borrowers pay clerks' fees for recording and satisfying instruments. Also, a lender may charge all fees, points, and other charges permitted pursuant to either federal, Maryland, or local programs for mortgage purchases or Maryland and local loan programs,

---

126 *See* COM. LAW II §§ 12-402, 12-1015; FIN. INST. §§ 11-302(b)(7), 11-501, 11-504.

127 FIN. INST. § 11-302(b). For a discussion of entities not subject to the Maryland Mortgage Lender Law, see § **5.18**.

128 COM. LAW II § 12-404(d). Note that if the loan is a renewal or refinancing of a loan made prior to July 1, 1982, the requirements of COM. LAW II § 12-116 must also be met. Also, if the loan provides for an adjustable interest rate, the lender must comply with COM. LAW II § 12-118.

provided that the sum of all fees, points, other charges, and interest does not exceed 24% per annum and such charges and the interest rate do not exceed those permitted by the applicable federal mortgage purchase program.[129] Any additional points, commissions, or finder's fees must be paid by the lender and may only be paid to licensed real estate brokers, attorneys licensed to practice law in Maryland, or persons licensed under the Maryland Mortgage Lender Law.[130]

As a condition to making second mortgage loans, lenders may require that borrowers obtain fire and extended coverage and title insurance on the property and life insurance on any person obligated to repay the loan, but the insurance on the property must be limited to its value and must be reasonably related to the risk of loss. The amount of life insurance may not exceed the amount of the loan. The amount of accident and health insurance may not exceed the total of unpaid scheduled payments of the loan.[131]

In accordance with COM. LAW II § 12-405(c), if an installment is delinquent 10 or more days, lenders may collect a late or delinquency charge of not more than $2 or 5% of the late payment, whichever is greater. Such charges must be deducted from the next payment made by the borrower.

A lender may not receive any interest, fee, points, commissions, or charges in excess of those permitted by the credit provisions of the SMLL, nor may a lender make a false or misleading statement regarding second mortgage loans or their availability.[132]

For a new second mortgage loan made under COM. LAW II, Title 12, Subtitle 10, the following credit provisions apply:

- the maximum effective rate of simple interest that may be charged is 24% per year;
- the agreement or note may provide for a variable rate of interest in accordance with an index readily available to and verifiable by the borrower and beyond the credit grantor's control;
- loan fees, points, finder's fees imposed by a mortgage broker, and other changes are permitted, but all such charges when combined with any finder's fee may not exceed 10% of the original extension of credit;
- fees may be charged for actual and verifiable expenses of the credit grantor paid (i) to attorneys for services rendered in connection with preparation, closing, or disbursement of the loan, (ii) to governmental agencies, (iii) for

---

129 COM. LAW II § 12-404.1.
130 COM. LAW II § 12-406.
131 COM. LAW II § 12-410(f)(3)(i).
132 COM. LAW II §§ 12-403, 12-411.

title examinations, appraisals, and other costs necessary or appropriate to the security of the loan, and (iv) for insurance premiums; and

- late or delinquency charge may be collected on any payment not made when due.[133]

None of the foregoing fees or charges may be assessed unless the credit agreement provides for them. The purchase of property insurance, title insurance, and credit loss insurance from an insurer of the borrower's choice may be required if the loan is secured.[134]

2. [§ 5.60] Provisions of loan instruments

Normally, mortgage loans must be amortized in equal or substantially equal monthly installments without a balloon payment at maturity. However, under the SMLL, a second mortgage loan may be structured so that the payments are reduced or suspended until all prior liens or encumbrances are partially or fully paid off.[135]

Under Com. Law II Title 12, Subtitle 10, a credit grantor, and under the SMLL, a seller who takes back a second mortgage in the sale of his residence or a lender that takes a second mortgage to aid the borrower in the sale of his residence or the purchase of his new house, may create a balloon payment at maturity under the following circumstances. The balloon payment must be expressly disclosed to the borrower and agreed to in writing. Furthermore, the borrower must have the opportunity to require the lender/seller to postpone the balloon payment once for no more than six months without additional costs to the borrower as long as the borrower continues to pay the monthly installments as provided in the original agreement.[136]

Second mortgage loan instruments may not contain any provision that:

a. permits acceleration of the loan, under Subtitle 10, because the credit grantor deems itself insecure, or, under the SMLL, for any reason except for a nonpayment or other default in the loan instrument;

b. purports to waive any of the borrower's rights under the provisions of the SMLL or Subtitle 10, as the case may be;

c. gives an assignment of wages to the lender, whether earned or to be earned;

d. under Subtitle 10 only, a confession of judgment provision; or

e. under Subtitle 10 only, a provision whereby an agent of the holder is treated also as an agent of the borrower for formation or execution purposes.[137]

---

133 Com. Law II §§ 12-1003–12-1005, 12-1008.
134 Com. Law II § 12-1007(b)(2).
135 Com. Law II § 12-404(c)(1).
136 Com. Law II §§ 12-1003(c)(2), 12-404(c)(2).
137 Com. Law II §§ 12-1023(b), 12-409.

3. *[§ 5.61] Disclosures*

Pursuant to COM. LAW II § 12-407(b), SMLL lenders must provide borrowers with a statement that complies with applicable disclosure requirements of the federal Truth-in-Lending Act.[138]

Also, as noted in § **5.46** of this chapter, borrowers must be given notice of a three-day right to rescind their obligation to accept a second mortgage loan and their responsibilities thereunder, pursuant to the provisions of the federal Truth-in-Lending Act, unless the second mortgage loan is a purchase money transaction.[139]

Under the SMLL, lenders must furnish borrowers with a disclosure notifying them of the rights that they will forfeit if the loan proceeds are used for commercial purposes.[140]

Pursuant to COM. LAW II § 12-1013.1, a lender who wishes to originate a loan under Subtitle 10 rather than the SMLL must make a written election in the agreement, note, or other evidence of the loan. All too many lenders mistakenly fail to make this election.

4. *[§ 5.62] Refinances*

A lender may refinance a second mortgage loan under the SMLL only once in any 12-month period and only twice in any five-year period of the loan. Under Subtitle 10, the only limitations applicable with respect to refinancing transactions of second mortgage loans are that refinancing charges may not be imposed more often than once in any 12-month period of the loan if the loan is made to cure a default that existed for more than 30 days on the loan being refinanced.[141]

D. [§ 5.63] Home Equity Loans

Home Equity Loans (HELs), which are revolving lines of credit secured by the borrower's residence, became very popular with the enactment of the Tax Reform Act of 1986.[142] This Act limited taxpayers' ability to deduct their interest payments. They were able to do so only to the extent that such payments were in connection with loans secured by mortgages or deeds of trust on their residential properties, provided that the total loan proceeds did not exceed the sum of the purchase price and the cost of all home improvements. However, the Tax Reform Act of 1986 did provide special treatment for certain debts incurred to pay educational or medical expenses.

---

138 COM. LAW II § 12-106(b)(4).

139 15 U.S.C. § 1635; Regulation Z, 12 C.F.R. § 226.23.

140 COM. LAW II § 12-407.1.

141 COM. LAW II §§ 12-408, 12-1010(c).

142 Pub. L. No. 99-514, 100 Stat. 2085 (1986).

Congress amended the Internal Revenue Code again in 1987 to partially restore interest deductions. Under the Omnibus Budget Reconciliation Act of 1987[143] a taxpayer may deduct interest on indebtedness secured by a principal or second residence provided the total indebtedness on the taxpayer's principal and second residence does not exceed the lesser of $1 million or the total debt incurred in connection with the acquisition and improvement of the residences (the "acquisition indebtedness"). The Omnibus Budget Reconciliation Act of 1987 also permits taxpayers to deduct interest on that portion of the indebtedness secured by either the principal or second residence and incurred to meet personal expenditures (the "home equity indebtedness"), provided that the home equity indebtedness does not exceed the lesser of $100,000 or the difference between the fair market value of the qualified residences and the acquisition indebtedness. The 1987 Act, however, did take away the special treatment that the Tax Reform Act of 1986 gave debt incurred to meet educational or medical expenses.[144]

Lenders usually make HELs under the Credit Grantor Revolving Credit Provisions, Com. Law II, Title 12, Subtitle 9. With certain exceptions, including the following, the credit provisions under Com. Law II, Title 12, Subtitle 9 are similar to the credit provisions in Com. Law II, Title 12, Subtitle 10, discussed in §§ **5.56–5.61** of this chapter. Under Com. Law II, Title 12, Subtitle 9, lenders may not require borrowers to make balloon payments at maturity.[145] Interest may be calculated on an amount not greater than the average outstanding unpaid indebtedness for the applicable billing period or an amount calculated by another balance computation method set forth in the agreement.[146]

E. [§ 5.64] Disclosure Requirements

With respect to HELs, the surge in their popularity prompted Congress to enact the Home Equity Consumer Protection Act of 1988,[147] pursuant to which lenders are required to provide certain disclosures at the time of application, as well as certain disclosures at the time the HEL plan is opened. First, at the time of application, the lender must provide a pamphlet published by the Federal Reserve Board (FRB), entitled "When Your Home Is on the Line: What You Should Know About Home Equity Lines of Credit," or a substantially similar substitute, which contains a general description of HELs, the terms and conditions under which such loans are generally extended, and a discussion of the potential advantages and disadvantages of

143 Pub. L. No. 100-203, 101 Stat. 1330 (1987).

144 *See* I.R.C. § 163.

145 Com. Law II § 12-903(a).

146 Com. Law II § 12-903(b). *See also* Com. Law II § 12-903(a), regarding charges for borrower points, loan origination, discount fees, and other similar fees.

147 Pub. L. No. 100-709, 102 Stat. 4725 (1988).

such plans, including how to compare them and how they compare with closed-end credit plans.[148]

In addition, the lender must provide certain disclosures commonly referred to as the "Important Terms" of its HEL, which include a description of the fees imposed, payment terms, transaction requirements, and conditions under which the plan may be terminated, suspended, or amended; tax-implications information; variable- or fixed-rate information; and certain examples and historical information to help the applicant anticipate how the plan would operate.[149]

Second, at the time the plan is opened, the lender must also include much of the above-described information as part of the Truth-in-Lending disclosure.[150]

In addition to those HEL disclosures required under federal law, a lender also must make certain disclosures to the borrower regarding the payment of recordation tax under Title 12 of the Tax-Property Article. At the time that the deed of trust securing the HEL is recorded, the borrower may pay the recordation tax due on the entire amount of the loan or on only so much as the lender has actually advanced to date. If the borrower chooses to defer the payment of the recordation tax, the borrower has a continuing responsibility for the payment of such tax as amounts are advanced under the HEL. The lender must disclose that failure to pay the tax when due may subject the borrower to criminal penalties provided under Tax-Prop. § 14-1011.[151]

With respect to both HELs and second mortgage loans, Congress also amended the Real Estate Settlement Procedures Act[152] in 1992 to extend its scope to subordinate lien transactions.[153] The Good Faith Estimate and Special Information Booklet are not required for HELs as long as the Important Terms disclosure and FRB pamphlet are provided.[154] The Good Faith Estimate is required for second mortgage loans; however, the Special Information Booklet is not.[155] The disclosure related to the assignment, sale, or transfer of servicing is not required currently for any subordinate lien transactions.[156] Finally, use of a HUD-1 Settlement Sheet is required for all subordinate lien transactions involving a borrower and a seller. If no seller is involved, the lender has the option of utilizing either the borrower's side only of the HUD-1 form or an alternative HUD-1A Settlement Sheet (the form of which is

---

148 Pub. L. No. 100-709, § 4; 15 U.S.C. § 1637a(b)(1)(A), (e); Regulation Z, 12 C.F.R. § 226.5b(b), (e); 24 C.F.R. § 3500.6(a)(2).

149 15 U.S.C. § 1637a(a), (b)(1)(A); Regulation Z, 12 C.F.R. § 226.5b(b), (d).

150 Regulation Z, 12 C.F.R. § 226.6(e).

151 MD. CODE ANN., TAX-PROPERTY § 12-105(f) (2019 & Supp. 2022) (hereinafter TAX-PROP. §).

152 12 U.S.C. §§ 2601–2617 (2009).

153 Pub. L. No. 102-550 (1992); *see* 12 U.S.C. § 2602(1); Regulation X, 24 C.F.R. § 3500.2.

154 24 C.F.R. §§ 3500.6(a)(2), 3500.7(f).

155 24 C.F.R. §§ 3500.6(a)(3)(ii), 3500.7(a).

156 *See* 59 Fed. Reg. 6509 (1994), at ¶ 4.

reproduced in **§ 5.88** of this chapter). Neither the HUD-1 nor the HUD-1A Settlement sheet is required, however, for HELs.[157]

If a non-purchase-money second mortgage loan or HEL will be co-signed by a natural person who will not receive any of the loan proceeds or any contractual right to obtain extensions of credit under the plan, that person must receive a disclosure statement prior to becoming obligated that advises the person of the responsibility to be undertaken and the potential consequences of that undertaking.[158]

VI. OTHER TYPES OF FINANCING

A. [§ 5.65] Assumptions

If the seller of property has a mortgage or deed of trust on property that he is selling, the purchaser might want to assume the loan if the interest rate the seller is obligated to pay his lender is less than the current market interest rate. Many mortgages and deeds of trust, however, have "due-on-sale clauses," which permit the lender to accelerate the outstanding indebtedness upon a conveyance of the property.

Historically, due-on-sale clauses have been held enforceable in Maryland.[159] Although such provisions had been rendered unenforceable in some states either by statute or judicial action, federal law has since preempted all such state limitations on due-on-sale clauses.[160] Office of Thrift Supervision regulations, for example, permit lenders to include due-on-sale clauses in loan instruments used in connection with loans secured by a lien on real property, the stock or membership certificate allocated to a dwelling unit of a cooperative housing corporation, or a residential manufactured home.[161] In the following circumstances, however, a lender may not exercise its rights under a due-on-sale clause with respect to any loan on the security of a home occupied or to be occupied by the borrower:

1. the borrower creates a subordinate lien that does not relate to the transfer of the rights of occupancy in the property, provided that such lien is not created pursuant to a contract for deed;
2. the borrower creates a purchase money security interest for household appliances;
3. the property transfers by devise, descent, or operation of law on the death of a joint tenant or tenant by the entirety;

---

157 Regulation X, 24 C.F.R. § 3500.8.

158 12 C.F.R. §§ 227.12(a), (b), 227.14(b).

159 *Chapman v. Ford,* 246 Md. 42, 227 A.2d 26 (1967).

160 Garn-St. Germain Depository Institutions Act of 1982, as amended, 12 U.S.C. § 1701j-3.

161 12 C.F.R. §§ 591.1–591.6.

4. the borrower grants a leasehold interest for a term of not longer than three years and the lease does not contain an option to purchase;
5. the borrower transfers the property to a person who occupies or will occupy the property and the transfer is
   (a) to a relative resulting from the borrower's death;
   (b) to the spouse or child(ren) who becomes an owner of the property; or
   (c) to the spouse who becomes the owner of the property because of a decree of dissolution of the marriage, legal separation agreement, or incidental property separation agreement; or
6. the borrower transfers the property into an *inter vivos* trust in which the borrower remains the beneficiary and occupant of the property, provided that the lender is given reasonable means acceptable to the lender by which it may be assured of timely notice of any subsequent transfer of the beneficial interest or a change in occupancy.[162]

Even if the mortgage or deed of trust contains a due-on-sale clause, in certain instances the lender might permit an outstanding loan to be assumed by a buyer if the interest rate of the loan is raised and/or points are paid to the lender. The lender may choose to release the seller (its original borrower) from personal liability on the loan if the buyer obligates himself to repay the loan balance. At the time of the assumption, the seller should assign to the buyer any monies held in escrow by the lender for payment of property taxes, charges, or insurance premiums.

A lender that accepts a buyer as a new obligor must give the disclosures required by the federal Truth-in-Lending Act.[163] A lender that releases its original borrower and requires that the interest rate on the loan be raised should be concerned that there might be a novation, which would cause it to lose the priority of its mortgage or deed of trust. In such cases, the lender should have title brought to date to determine if there are any intervening lienors and should have the effective date of its title policy brought forward to the date of the assumption.

B. [§ 5.66] Wrap-Around Mortgages

Residential property may be subject to an assumable first mortgage that is in an amount substantially less than the sale price of the property. In many such situations the buyer who plans to assume the first mortgage will have to borrow a portion of the difference between the sale price and the mortgage balance. This may be done by obtaining a second mortgage loan or by obtaining a loan secured by a wrap-around mortgage.

---

162 12 C.F.R. § 591.5(b).

163 Regulation Z, 12 C.F.R. § 226.20(b)(3).

A wrap-around mortgage is a lien (either in the form of a mortgage or deed of trust) on real property that is already subject to one or more prior liens (the first mortgage) and is in the face amount of the unpaid balance of the first mortgage plus the amount of new money advanced. Since the first mortgage is not released, the property may appear to be encumbered by mortgages in excess of the purchase price.

When a wrap-around mortgage is used, the mortgagor pays the wrap-around mortgagee the periodic amount necessary to repay the total amount of principal advanced under both the first mortgage and the wrap-around mortgage, plus interest thereon, plus sums for escrow when required. The wrap-around mortgagee remits to the first mortgagee the sums required under the first mortgage, and it retains the balance for itself.

Because the first mortgage remains of record, interest generally accrues on a portion of the debt secured by the property at less than the current market rate. A wrap-around mortgage is written with an interest rate applicable to the full debt, and typically that rate is higher than the rate under the first mortgage but lower than the current market interest rate for second mortgages. Therefore, the interest yield on the sums advanced by the wrap-around mortgagee, based on the sums retained after paying the first mortgagee, will be higher, and often significantly higher, than the interest rate stated in the wrap-around mortgage or the note it secures.

An additional benefit of a wrap-around mortgage is that it enables the wrap-around mortgagee to monitor the borrower's payments under the first mortgage. The wrap-around mortgagee will immediately be aware of the borrower's inability to make the payments due under the first mortgage, whereas a second mortgagee might learn of the borrower's default under the first mortgage only after the first mortgagee has commenced foreclosure proceedings.

By definition, a wrap-around mortgage loan involves an encumbrance on property that is subject to a prior lien. Therefore, when it involves residential property under Maryland law, it is a second mortgage loan. Consequently, all requirements of the Secondary Mortgage Loan Law (SMLL) or Subtitle 10, as the case may be, must be met, including the limitation on interest to 24% simple interest per year on the unpaid principal balance of the loan.[164]

C. [§ 5.67] Seller Take-Back Mortgages

To assist in selling his residence, a seller may take back a mortgage or deed of trust to secure the portion of the purchase price not paid at settlement. The affidavit of disbursement, otherwise required to be completed in mortgage transactions, does

---

164 *See* §§ **5.56–5.71** of this chapter.

not apply to such a purchase money mortgage.[165] However, the affidavit of consideration still must be given.[166] Also, a person selling his own house and taking back a first mortgage as an isolated transaction does not have to comply with the Real Estate Settlement Procedures Act[167] or give any loan disclosures; however, absurd as it may seem, if the mortgage that a seller takes back is subordinate to another lien, the disclosure requirements under the SMLL would nevertheless apply.[168]

D. Land Installment Contracts

1. [§ 5.68] Definition

A seller may finance the sale of their home by entering into a land installment contract under which they retain legal title as security for the buyer's obligation to pay the balance of the purchase price. If the subject property is improved by a dwelling in which an individual buyer lives or intends to live, and the buyer agrees to pay the purchase price in five or more installments in addition to the down payment, the agreement is a "land installment contract" as defined by REAL PROP. § 10-101(b). Hence, it is subject to the provisions of REAL PROP., Title 10, Subtitle 1. A "land installment contract" controlled by that statute also may involve an unimproved subdivided lot or lots intended to be improved for residential purposes.[169]

2. [§ 5.69] Form of land installment contracts

All land installment contracts must be in writing, signed by all parties, and must contain the following information:

(1) the names, residences, and mailing addresses of all parties thereto;

(2) the date signed by the buyer;

(3) a legal description of the subject property;

(4) a disclosure of all transfers of title within six months prior to the date of the contract, the sales prices of such transfers, and the cost of repairs or improvements made by the seller within that period;

(5) a statement that the buyer has the right to pay any installment in advance;

(6) a statement describing any collateral security taken;

---

165 REAL PROP. § 4-106(b).

166 REAL PROP. § 4-106(a).

167 12 U.S.C. §§ 2601–2617 (2009).

168 *See* MD. CODE ANN., COMMERCIAL LAW II §§ 12-407(b), 12-106(b)(1)(i)—(iii) (2013 & Supp. 2022) (hereinafter COM. LAW II §) (even though the provisions of COM. LAW II § 12-106 do not apply to seller take-back financing transactions, the SMLL does apply).

169 REAL PROP. § 10-101(d). When used herein, the term "land installment contract" refers only to those contracts which are subject to REAL PROP., Title 10, Subtitle 1.

(7) a statement whether the seller has received any written notice from any public agency requiring that repairs or improvements be made to the subject property;

(8) a statement that the seller must record the contract among the land records of the jurisdiction where the property is located and mail a copy of the recorder's receipt to the buyer;

(9) a notice in at least 12-point bold type placed directly above the signature line of the buyer reading as follows: "Notice to Purchaser, You are entitled to a copy of this contract at the time you sign it"; and

(10) a notice in at least 12-point bold type placed directly below the separate signature line of the buyer acknowledging receipt of a copy of the contract, reading as follows: "In the event of default, the purchaser may be liable to a default judgment."[170]

The following items must be shown in simple tabular form:

(1) the cash price of the property;

(2) any additional charge or fee included in the contract;

(3) if credit is extended to the buyer for the payment of any insurance premium, the cost to the buyer of such insurance coverage, the amount or extent and expiration date of the coverage, a description of the type of coverage and every party to whom the insurance proceeds are payable;

(4) the sum of items 1, 2, and 3;

(5) the amount of the down payment;

(6) the balance owed (item 4 minus item 5);

(7) the amount and time of each installment payment and the total number of periodic installments;

(8) the interest on the unpaid balance; and

(9) any ground rent, taxes, and other public charges.[171]

3. [§ 5.70] Delivery and recordation of contracts

The seller under a land installment contract is required to give the buyer a duplicate of the land installment contract signed by the seller within 15 days after he receives notice that the buyer has signed it. The buyer has a right to cancel the contract and receive a full refund of all payments until he has received a copy of the contract.[172]

---

[170] REAL PROP. §§ 10-102(a), (c), (f), 10-103(a).

[171] REAL PROP. § 10-103(b).

[172] REAL PROP. § 10-102(b), (d).

Within 15 days after both seller and buyer have signed the contract, the seller must record the contract among the land records of the jurisdiction where the property is located and mail a copy of the recorder's receipt to the buyer. Failure to disclose this duty in the contract or to record the contract within that time-frame gives the buyer a right to cancel the contract and receive a full refund of all payments, exercisable at any time before the seller records the contract.[173]

The recordation of the land installment contract is exempt from recordation and transfer taxes.[174] However, recordation of the deed conveying the property to the buyer is subject to recordation and transfer taxes unless the conveyance is otherwise exempt from these taxes.

4. *[§ 5.71] Interest allowable under installment contracts*

Interest on the unpaid balance due under a land installment contract may not exceed that allowed by COM. LAW II § 12-404(b) (under the SMLL). That section limits interest to an effective rate of simple interest of 24% per annum. Additionally, no points may be charged.[175]

5. *[§ 5.72] Conversion to purchase money mortgage*

Unless a land installment contract sets an earlier time, after a buyer has paid 40% or more of the original cash price for the property, the buyer is entitled to a deed giving him legal title on condition that he executes a purchase money mortgage in favor of the seller or a mortgagee procured by the buyer. The buyer must pay all of the costs of recordation of the deed and conversion to a purchase money mortgage, including title examination costs, except that the seller must pay one-half of the recordation taxes.[176] The purchase money mortgage may contain the usual covenants that require the buyer/mortgagor to pay the debt, property taxes, insurance premiums, and ground rent. Additionally, the mortgage may give the mortgagee the usual remedies to sell the property after default pursuant to a power of sale or assent to decree.[177]

A seller may not place or hold a mortgage on property subject to a land installment contract in an amount greater than the balance due thereunder. The mortgage may not require periodic payments of principal and interest in amounts greater than the payments required under the land installment contract.[178]

---

173 REAL PROP. § 10-102(f).

174 TAX-PROP. §§ 12-108(r), 13-207(a)(11).

175 REAL PROP. § 10-103(b)(8).

176 REAL PROP. § 10-105(a).

177 REAL PROP. § 10-105(c).

178 REAL PROP. § 10-103(d).

6. [§ 5.73] Statements from seller

Sellers under land installment contracts must furnish buyers with periodic statements showing the total amount paid for insurance, taxes, other periodic charges, and ground rent, if any; the amount credited to principal and interest; and the balance due. The seller must provide such statements when 40% of the original cash price has been paid as well as in January of each year or on demand by the buyer, but not more than twice per year.[179]

7. [§ 5.74] Default and remedies

Should a buyer default in his obligations under the land installment contract, a seller may neither merely terminate the contract nor seek to regain possession of the property in accordance with landlord-tenant law. A seller, however, may foreclose the rights of the buyer thereunder in accordance with Maryland Rules that govern foreclosure of mortgages and deeds of trust[180] as if the seller were the mortgagee and the buyer were the mortgagor.[181]

Since a seller must provide a buyer with no more than 30 days and not less than 10 days notice prior to the date of the sale, a buyer may cure a default in a land installment contract by the date of the sale set forth in the notice from the seller.[182] If the buyer does cure the default, the land installment contract continues in full force and effect, notwithstanding any provision therein to the contrary.[183]

VII. PAYOFF OF LOAN

A. [§ 5.75] Early Payoff

Notwithstanding the fact that residential loans are typically written on a 15-, 25-, or 30-year basis, lenders anticipate that borrowers pay off their loans within eight to twelve years from the date of settlement. The reasons for paying off a loan early include:

1. the ability to refinance the loan at a lower rate of interest;
2. the desire to refinance in order to take advantage of the equity that has accumulated in the real property; and
3. the borrower's sale of his house and purchase of a new home.

---

179 Real Prop. § 10-107.

180 Maryland Rules, Title 14, Chapter 200, Rules 14-201–14-210 (hereinafter Md. Rule).

181 Md. Rule 14-203.

182 Real Prop. § 7-105(b).

183 Real Prop. § 10-106.

B. [§ 5.76] Release

Once the borrower has paid off the loan, the lien of the mortgage or deed of trust securing the loan must be released. A trustee of a deed of trust may not charge more than $15 for executing either a partial or complete release unless the deed of trust or mortgage specifies otherwise.[184]

A lender must deliver the release to the person responsible for the disbursement of funds, on written request, within seven days after it has received all amounts due under the deed of trust or mortgage and all other instruments secured thereby.[185] When a mortgage loan is being paid off in connection with a refinance or sale of a house, the settlement officer for the new loan may bring an action to enforce REAL PROP. § 7-106(d), if the prior lender does not deliver the release to the settlement officer within 30 days after satisfaction of the debt and demand for the release.[186]

C. [§ 5.77] Recording the Release

REAL PROP. § 3-105 sets forth the requirements for the form of a release. If the lender does not execute a release, the borrower may present his cancelled check evidencing final payment to the clerk for indexing and recording provided:

1. the lender has not delivered a release within 60 days from the date that the borrower satisfied the loan;
2. the borrower has sent the lender a copy of REAL PROP. § 3-105 and a notice stating that he or she will obtain a release under this section if the lender does not provide a release within 30 days;
3. the borrower has waited 30 days from the date of mailing the notice for the lender to send the release;
4. the cancelled check contains the borrower's name, the loan account number, if any, and words to the effect that payment in full is intended; and
5. an affidavit of a Maryland attorney is attached to the check, certifying that the loan has been satisfied and the requisite notice has been sent to the lender, and specifying the recording reference of the lien instrument.[187]

Even if a release is never recorded, the deed of trust or mortgage is presumed to have been paid off:

1. 12 years from the maturity date or last payment date set forth in the recorded instrument and no continuation statement has been filed; or

---

184 REAL PROP. § 7-106(a).

185 REAL PROP. § 7-106(d).

186 REAL PROP. § 7-106(e).

187 REAL PROP. § 3-105(d)(3).

2. 40 years from the date of recordation if the instrument does not set forth either a maturity date or last payment date and no continuation statement has been filed; or
3. 12 years from the date of recordation of the last continuation statement.[188]

The legal operation and effect of the deed of trust or mortgage will be automatically extinguished if no action to enforce the lien is brought within the 12- or 40-year period, whichever is applicable.

Within a reasonable time after a loan secured by an existing mortgage or deed of trust has been paid in full and there is no further commitment by the holder to make an advance or by the borrower to incur an obligation secured by that mortgage or deed of trust, the holder must

(1) (i) Indelibly mark with the word "paid" or "cancelled" and return to the borrower each payment, note, or other evidence of the loan secured by that mortgage or deed of trust; or

(ii) Furnish the borrower with a written statement that identifies the loan secured by that mortgage or deed of trust and states that the loan has been paid in full; and

(2) Release any recorded mortgage or deed of trust securing the loan.

The release must be in writing and prepared at the expense of the holder. If the holder does not record the release or provide the release to a responsible person for recording within 45 days following payoff, the holder must furnish the borrower with the release in a recordable form and a notice disclosing the location where the release should be recorded and the estimated amount if any fee required to be paid to a governmental entity in order to record the release. If the holder records the release, the holder must furnish the borrower with a copy of the release. If a fee is collected for the recording of a release the holder must record the release and the holder must refund to the borrower any portion of the fee not paid to a governmental entity for recording the release that exceeds $15. If the holder does not collect a fee for recording the release, the holder is not required to record the release.[189]

VIII. APPENDIX

The Appendix begins on the next page.

---

[188] Real Prop. § 7-106(c).

[189] Real Prop. § 3-105.1.

A. [§ 5.78] FNMA/FHLMC Application Form

To be completed by the **Lender:**
Lender Loan No./Universal Loan Identifier ______________________ Agency Case No. ______________

Uniform Residential Loan Application — Lender Loan Information

This section is completed by your Lender.

L1. Property and Loan Information

Community Property State
☐ At least one borrower lives in a community property state.
☐ The property is in a community property state.

Transaction Detail
☐ Conversion of Contract for Deed or Land Contract
☐ Renovation
☐ Construction-Conversion/Construction-to-Permanent
○ Single-Closing ○ Two-Closing
Construction/Improvement Costs $ ______________
Lot Acquired Date ____/____/______ *(mm/dd/yyyy)*
Original Cost of Lot $ ______________

Refinance Type
○ No Cash Out
○ Limited Cash Out
○ Cash Out

Refinance Program
○ Full Documentation
○ Interest Rate Reduction
○ Streamlined without Appraisal
○ Other ______________

Energy Improvement
☐ Mortgage loan will finance energy-related improvements.
☐ Property is currently subject to a lien that could take priority over the first mortgage lien, such as a clean energy lien paid for through property taxes *(e.g., the Property Assessed Clean Energy program).*

Project Type ☐ Condominium ☐ Cooperative ☐ Planned Unit Development (PUD) ☐ Property is not located in a project

L2. Title Information

Title to the Property **Will** be Held in What Name(s):

For Refinance: Title to the Property is **Currently** Held in What Name(s):

Estate Will be Held in
○ Fee Simple
○ Leasehold Expiration Date ____/____/______ *(mm/dd/yyyy)*

Manner in Which Title Will be Held
○ Sole Ownership ○ Joint Tenancy with Right of Survivorship
○ Life Estate ○ Tenancy by the Entirety
○ Tenancy in Common ○ Other

Trust Information
○ Title Will be Held by an *Inter Vivos (Living)* Trust
○ Title Will be Held by a Land Trust

Indian Country Land Tenure
○ Fee Simple On a Reservation
○ Individual Trust Land *(Allotted/Restricted)*
○ Tribal Trust Land On a Reservation
○ Tribal Trust Land Off Reservation
○ Alaska Native Corporation Land

L3. Mortgage Loan Information

Mortgage Type Applied For
○ Conventional ○ USDA-RD
○ FHA ○ VA ○ Other: ______________

Terms of Loan
Note Rate ________ %
Loan Term ________ *(months)*

Mortgage Lien Type
○ First Lien
○ Subordinate Lien

Amortization Type
○ Fixed Rate ○ Other *(explain)*: ______________
○ Adjustable Rate

If Adjustable Rate:
Initial Period Prior to First Adjustment ________ *(months)*
Subsequent Adjustment Period ________ *(months)*

Loan Features
☐ Balloon/ Balloon Term ______ *(months)*
☐ Interest Only / Interest Only Term ______ *(months)*
☐ Negative Amortization
☐ Prepayment Penalty / Prepayment Penalty Term ______ *(months)*
☐ Temporary Interest Rate Buydown/Initial Buydown Rate ______ %
☐ Other *(explain)*: ______________

Proposed Monthly Payment for Property

First Mortgage *(P & I)*	$
Subordinate Lien(s) *(P & I)*	$
Homeowner's Insurance	$
Supplemental Property Insurance	$
Property Taxes	$
Mortgage Insurance	$
Association/Project Dues *(Condo, Co-Op, PUD)*	$
Other	$
TOTAL	$ **0.00**

Borrower Name(s):
Uniform Residential Loan Application — Lender Loan Information
Freddie Mac Form 65 • Fannie Mae Form 1003
Effective 1/2021

L4. Qualifying the Borrower – Minimum Required Funds or Cash Back

DUE FROM BORROWER(S)		
A. Sales Contract Price	$	
B. Improvements, Renovations, and Repairs	$	
C. Land *(if acquired separately)*	$	
D. For Refinance: Balance of Mortgage Loans on the Property to be paid off in the Transaction *(See Table 3a. Property You Own)*	$	
E. Credit Cards and Other Debts Paid Off *(See Table 2c. Liabilities — Credit Cards, Other Debts, and Leases that You Owe)*	$	
F. Borrower Closing Costs *(including Prepaid and Initial Escrow Payments)*	$	
G. Discount Points	$	
H. TOTAL DUE FROM BORROWER(s) (Total of A thru G)	$	**0.00**
TOTAL MORTGAGE LOANS		
I. Loan Amount Loan Amount Excluding Financed Mortgage Insurance *(or Mortgage Insurance Equivalent)* $ ____________ Financed Mortgage Insurance *(or Mortgage Insurance Equivalent)* Amount $ ____________	$	0.00
J. Other New Mortgage Loans on the Property the Borrower(s) is Buying or Refinancing *(See Table 4b. Other New Mortgage Loans on the Property You are Buying or Refinancing)*	$	
K. TOTAL MORTGAGE LOANS (Total of I and J)	$	**0.00**
TOTAL CREDITS		
L. Seller Credits *(Enter the amount of Borrower(s) costs paid by the property seller)*	$	
M. Other Credits *(Enter the sum of all other credits — Borrower Paid Fees, Earnest Money, Employer Assisted Housing, Lease Purchase Fund, Lot Equity, Relocation Funds, Sweat Equity, Trade Equity, Other)*	$	
N. TOTAL CREDITS (Total of L and M)	$	**0.00**
CALCULATION		
TOTAL DUE FROM BORROWER(s) *(Line H)*	$	**0.00**
LESS TOTAL MORTGAGE LOANS *(Line K)* AND TOTAL CREDITS *(Line N)*	– $	**0.00**
Cash From/To the Borrower (Line H minus Line K and Line N) **NOTE: This amount does not include reserves or other funds that may be required by the Lender to be verified.**	$	**0.00**

Borrower Name(s): ____________________

Uniform Residential Loan Application — Lender Loan Information
Freddie Mac Form 65 • Fannie Mae Form 1003
Effective 1/2021

To be completed by the **Lender:**
Lender Loan No./Universal Loan Identifier ______________________ Agency Case No. ____________

Uniform Residential Loan Application

Verify and complete the information on this application. If you are applying for this loan with others, each additional Borrower must provide information as directed by your Lender.

Section 1: Borrower Information.

This section asks about your personal information and your income from employment and other sources, such as retirement, that you want considered to qualify for this loan.

1a. Personal Information

Name *(First, Middle, Last, Suffix)*

Social Security Number ____ - ____ - ____
(or Individual Taxpayer Identification Number)

Alternate Names – *List any names by which you are known or any names under which credit was previously received (First, Middle, Last, Suffix)*

Date of Birth *(mm/dd/yyyy)* ____/____/____

Citizenship
- ○ U.S. Citizen
- ○ Permanent Resident Alien
- ○ Non-Permanent Resident Alien

Type of Credit
- ○ I am applying for **individual credit.**
- ○ I am applying for **joint credit.** Total Number of Borrowers: __
  Each Borrower intends to apply for joint credit. **Your initials:** ____

List Name(s) of Other Borrower(s) Applying for this Loan
(First, Middle, Last, Suffix) – Use a separator between names

Marital Status
- ○ Married
- ○ Separated
- ○ Unmarried
  (Single, Divorced, Widowed, Civil Union, Domestic Partnership, Registered Reciprocal Beneficiary Relationship)

Dependents *(not listed by another Borrower)*
Number __
Ages ______________

Contact Information
Home Phone (___) ___ - ____
Cell Phone (___) ___ - ____
Work Phone (___) ___ - ____ **Ext.** ____
Email ______________

Current Address
Street ______________ Unit # ____
City ______________ State ____ ZIP ____ Country ____
How Long at Current Address? ___ Years ___ Months **Housing** ○ No primary housing expense ○ Own ○ Rent ($ ______ /month)

If at Current Address for LESS than 2 years, list Former Address ☐ ***Does not apply***
Street ______________ Unit # ____
City ______________ State ____ ZIP ____ Country ____
How Long at Former Address? ___ Years ___ Months **Housing** ○ No primary housing expense ○ Own ○ Rent ($ ______ /month)

Mailing Address – *if different from Current Address* ☐ ***Does not apply***
Street ______________ Unit # ____
City ______________ State ____ ZIP ____ Country ____

1b. Current Employment/Self-Employment and Income

☐ ***Does not apply***

Employer or Business Name ______________ Phone (___) ___ - ____
Street ______________ Unit # ____
City ______________ State ____ ZIP ____ Country ____

Position or Title ______________
Start Date ____/____/____ *(mm/dd/yyyy)*
How long in this line of work? ___ Years ___ Months

Check if this statement applies:
☐ I am employed by a family member, property seller, real estate agent, or other party to the transaction.

☐ **Check if you are the Business Owner or Self-Employed**
- ○ I have an ownership share of less than 25%.
- ○ I have an ownership share of 25% or more.

Monthly Income (or Loss) $ ______

Gross Monthly Income

Base	$ ______	/month
Overtime	$ ______	/month
Bonus	$ ______	/month
Commission	$ ______	/month
Military Entitlements	$ ______	/month
Other	$ ______	/month
TOTAL $	**0.00**	**/month**

Uniform Residential Loan Application
Freddie Mac Form 65 • Fannie Mae Form 1003
Effective 1/2021

1c. IF APPLICABLE, Complete Information for Additional Employment/Self-Employment and Income ☐ ***Does not apply***

Employer or Business Name ____________ Phone (___) ___ – ____
Street ____________ Unit # ____
City ____________ State ____ ZIP ____ Country ____

Position or Title ____________
Start Date ___ / ___ / ____ *(mm/dd/yyyy)*
How long in this line of work? ___ Years ___ Months

Check if this statement applies:
☐ I am employed by a family member, property seller, real estate agent, or other party to the transaction.

☐ **Check if you are the Business Owner or Self-Employed**
◯ I have an ownership share of less than 25%.
◯ I have an ownership share of 25% or more.
Monthly Income (or Loss) $ ____________

Gross Monthly Income

Base	$ ____	/month
Overtime	$ ____	/month
Bonus	$ ____	/month
Commission	$ ____	/month
Military Entitlements	$ ____	/month
Other	$ ____	/month
TOTAL $	**0.00**	**/month**

1d. IF APPLICABLE, Complete Information for Previous Employment/Self-Employment and Income ☐ ***Does not apply***

Provide at least 2 years of current and previous employment and income.

Employer or Business Name ____________
Street ____________ Unit # ____
City ____________ State ____ ZIP ____ Country ____

Position or Title ____________
Start Date ___ / ___ / ____ *(mm/dd/yyyy)*
End Date ___ / ___ / ____ *(mm/dd/yyyy)*

☐ **Check if you were the Business Owner or Self-Employed**

Previous Gross Monthly Income $ ____ **/month**

1e. Income from Other Sources ☐ ***Does not apply***

Include income from other sources below. Under Income Source, choose from the sources listed here:

- Alimony
- Automobile Allowance
- Boarder Income
- Capital Gains
- Child Support
- Disability
- Foster Care
- Housing or Parsonage
- Interest and Dividends
- Mortgage Credit Certificate
- Mortgage Differential Payments
- Notes Receivable
- Public Assistance
- Retirement *(e.g., Pension, IRA)*
- Royalty Payments
- Separate Maintenance
- Social Security
- Trust
- Unemployment Benefits
- VA Compensation
- Other

NOTE: *Reveal alimony, child support, separate maintenance, or other income ONLY IF you want it considered in determining your qualification for this loan.*

Income Source – *use list above*	**Monthly Income**
	$
	$
	$
Provide TOTAL Amount Here	**$ 0.00**

Borrower Name: ____________
Uniform Residential Loan Application
Freddie Mac Form 65 • Fannie Mae Form 1003
Effective 1/2021

Section 2: Financial Information — Assets and Liabilities.

This section asks about things you own that are worth money and that you want considered to qualify for this loan. It then asks about your liabilities (or debts) that you pay each month, such as credit cards, alimony, or other expenses.

2a. Assets – Bank Accounts, Retirement, and Other Accounts You Have

Include all accounts below. Under Account Type, choose from the types listed here:

- Checking
- Savings
- Money Market
- Certificate of Deposit
- Mutual Fund
- Stocks
- Stock Options
- Bonds
- Retirement *(e.g., 401k, IRA)*
- Bridge Loan Proceeds
- Individual Development Account
- Trust Account
- Cash Value of Life Insurance *(used for the transaction)*

Account Type – *use list above*	**Financial Institution**	**Account Number**	**Cash or Market Value**
			$
			$
			$
			$
			$
		Provide TOTAL Amount Here	**$ 0.00**

2b. Other Assets and Credits You Have ☐ *Does not apply*

Include all other assets and credits below. Under Asset or Credit Type, choose from the types listed here:

Assets

- Proceeds from Real Estate Property to be sold on or before closing
- Proceeds from Sale of Non-Real Estate Asset
- Secured Borrowed Funds
- Unsecured Borrowed Funds
- Other

Credits

- Earnest Money
- Employer Assistance
- Lot Equity
- Relocation Funds
- Rent Credit
- Sweat Equity
- Trade Equity

Asset or Credit Type – *use list above*	**Cash or Market Value**
	$
	$
	$
	$
Provide TOTAL Amount Here	**$ 0.00**

2c. Liabilities – Credit Cards, Other Debts, and Leases that You Owe ☐ *Does not apply*

List all liabilities below (except real estate) and include deferred payments. Under Account Type, choose from the types listed here:

- Revolving *(e.g., credit cards)*
- Installment *(e.g., car, student, personal loans)*
- Open 30-Day *(balance paid monthly)*
- Lease *(not real estate)*
- Other

Account Type – *use list above*	**Company Name**	**Account Number**	**Unpaid Balance**	*To be paid off at or before closing*	**Monthly Payment**
			$	☐	$
			$	☐	$
			$	☐	$
			$	☐	$
			$	☐	$

2d. Other Liabilities and Expenses ☐ *Does not apply*

Include all other liabilities and expenses below. Choose from the types listed here:

- Alimony
- Child Support
- Separate Maintenance
- Job Related Expenses
- Other

	Monthly Payment
	$
	$
	$

Borrower Name: ______________________

Uniform Residential Loan Application
Freddie Mac Form 65 • Fannie Mae Form 1003
Effective 1/2021

Section 3: Financial Information — Real Estate.

This section asks you to list all properties you currently own and what you owe on them. ☐ ***I do not own any real estate***

3a. Property You Own **If you are refinancing, list the property you are refinancing FIRST.**

Address Street ______ Unit # ______
City ______ State ______ ZIP ______ Country ______

Property Value	**Status:** Sold, Pending Sale, or Retained	**Intended Occupancy:** Investment, Primary Residence, Second Home, Other	**Monthly Insurance,Taxes, Association Dues, etc.** *if not included in Monthly Mortgage Payment*	**For 2-4 Unit Primary or Investment Property** **Monthly Rental Income**	**For LENDER to calculate:** Net Monthly Rental Income
$			$	$	$

Mortgage Loans on this Property ☐ ***Does not apply***

Creditor Name	**Account Number**	**Monthly Mortgage Payment**	**Unpaid Balance**	*To be paid off at or before closing*	**Type:** FHA, VA, Conventional, USDA-RD, Other	**Credit Limit** *(if applicable)*
		$	$	☐		$
		$	$	☐		$

3b. IF APPLICABLE, Complete Information for Additional Property ☐ ***Does not apply***

Address Street ______ Unit # ______
City ______ State ______ ZIP ______ Country ______

Property Value	**Status:** Sold, Pending Sale, or Retained	**Intended Occupancy:** Investment, Primary Residence, Second Home, Other	**Monthly Insurance, Taxes, Association Dues, etc.** *if not included in Monthly Mortgage Payment*	**For 2-4 Unit Primary or Investment Property** **Monthly Rental Income**	**For LENDER to calculate:** Net Monthly Rental Income
$			$	$	$

Mortgage Loans on this Property ☐ ***Does not apply***

Creditor Name	**Account Number**	**Monthly Mortgage Payment**	**Unpaid Balance**	*To be paid off at or before closing*	**Type:** FHA, VA, Conventional, USDA-RD, Other	**Credit Limit** *(if applicable)*
		$	$	☐		$
		$	$	☐		$

3c. IF APPLICABLE, Complete Information for Additional Property ☐ ***Does not apply***

Address Street ______ Unit # ______
City ______ State ______ ZIP ______ Country ______

Property Value	**Status:** Sold, Pending Sale, or Retained	**Intended Occupancy:** Investment, Primary Residence, Second Home, Other	**Monthly Insurance, Taxes, Association Dues, etc.** *if not included in Monthly Mortgage Payment*	**For 2-4 Unit Primary or Investment Property** **Monthly Rental Income**	**For LENDER to calculate:** Net Monthly Rental Income
$			$	$	$

Mortgage Loans on this Property ☐ ***Does not apply***

Creditor Name	**Account Number**	**Monthly Mortgage Payment**	**Unpaid Balance**	*To be paid off at or before closing*	**Type:** FHA, VA, Conventional, USDA-RD, Other	**Credit Limit** *(if applicable)*
		$	$	☐		$
		$	$	☐		$

Borrower Name: ______
Uniform Residential Loan Application
Freddie Mac Form 65 • Fannie Mae Form 1003
Effective 1/2021

Section 4: Loan and Property Information. This section asks about the loan's purpose and the property you want to purchase or refinance.

4a. Loan and Property Information

Loan Amount $ ____________ **Loan Purpose** ○ Purchase ○ Refinance ○ Other *(specify)* ____________

Property Address Street ____________ Unit # ____________

City ____________ State ______ ZIP ______ County ______

Number of Units ______ **Property Value $** ____________

Occupancy ○ Primary Residence ○ Second Home ○ Investment Property **FHA Secondary Residence** ☐

1. Mixed-Use Property. If you will occupy the property, will you set aside space within the property to operate your own business? *(e.g., daycare facility, medical office, beauty/barber shop)* ○ NO ○ YES

2. Manufactured Home. Is the property a manufactured home? *(e.g., a factory built dwelling built on a permanent chassis)* ○ NO ○ YES

4b. Other New Mortgage Loans on the Property You are Buying or Refinancing ☐ *Does not apply*

Creditor Name	Lien Type	Monthly Payment	Loan Amount/ Amount to be Drawn	Credit Limit *(if applicable)*
	○ First Lien ○ Subordinate Lien	$	$	$
	○ First Lien ○ Subordinate Lien	$	$	$

4c. Rental Income on the Property You Want to Purchase **For Purchase Only** ☐ *Does not apply*

Complete if the property is a 2-4 Unit Primary Residence or an Investment Property	Amount
Expected Monthly Rental Income	$
For LENDER to calculate: Expected Net Monthly Rental Income	$

4d. Gifts or Grants You Have Been Given or Will Receive for this Loan ☐ *Does not apply*

Include all gifts and grants below. Under Source, choose from the sources listed here:

- Community Nonprofit
- Employer
- Federal Agency
- Local Agency
- Relative
- Religious Nonprofit
- State Agency
- Unmarried Partner
- Lender
- Other

Asset Type: Cash Gift, Gift of Equity, Grant	Deposited/Not Deposited	**Source** – *use list above*	Cash or Market Value
	○ Deposited ○ Not Deposited		$
	○ Deposited ○ Not Deposited		$

Borrower Name: ____________

Uniform Residential Loan Application
Freddie Mac Form 65 • Fannie Mae Form 1003
Effective 1/2021

Section 5: Declarations. This section asks you specific questions about the property, your funding, and your past financial history.

5a. About this Property and Your Money for this Loan

A. Will you occupy the property as your primary residence? If YES, have you had an ownership interest in another property in the last three years? If YES, complete (1) and (2) below: (1) What type of property did you own: primary residence (PR), FHA secondary residence (SR), second home (SH), or investment property (IP)? (2) How did you hold title to the property: by yourself (S), jointly with your spouse (SP), or jointly with another person (O)?	◯ NO ◯ YES ◯ NO ◯ YES ________ ________
B. If this is a Purchase Transaction: Do you have a family relationship or business affiliation with the seller of the property?	◯ NO ◯ YES
C. Are you borrowing any money for this real estate transaction *(e.g., money for your closing costs or down payment)* or obtaining any money from another party, such as the seller or realtor, that you have not disclosed on this loan application? If YES, what is the amount of this money?	◯ NO ◯ YES $________
D. 1. Have you or will you be applying for a mortgage loan on another property (not the property securing this loan) on or before closing this transaction that is not disclosed on this loan application? 2. Have you or will you be applying for any new credit *(e.g., installment loan, credit card, etc.)* on or before closing this loan that is not disclosed on this application?	◯ NO ◯ YES ◯ NO ◯ YES
E. Will this property be subject to a lien that could take priority over the first mortgage lien, such as a clean energy lien paid through your property taxes *(e.g., the Property Assessed Clean Energy Program)*?	◯ NO ◯ YES

5b. About Your Finances

F. Are you a co-signer or guarantor on any debt or loan that is not disclosed on this application?	◯ NO ◯ YES
G. Are there any outstanding judgments against you?	◯ NO ◯ YES
H. Are you currently delinquent or in default on a Federal debt?	◯ NO ◯ YES
I. Are you a party to a lawsuit in which you potentially have any personal financial liability?	◯ NO ◯ YES
J. Have you conveyed title to any property in lieu of foreclosure in the past 7 years?	◯ NO ◯ YES
K. Within the past 7 years, have you completed a pre-foreclosure sale or short sale, whereby the property was sold to a third party and the Lender agreed to accept less than the outstanding mortgage balance due?	◯ NO ◯ YES
L. Have you had property foreclosed upon in the last 7 years?	◯ NO ◯ YES
M. Have you declared bankruptcy within the past 7 years? If YES, identify the type(s) of bankruptcy: ☐ Chapter 7 ☐ Chapter 11 ☐ Chapter 12 ☐ Chapter 13	◯ NO ◯ YES

Borrower Name: ____________________
Uniform Residential Loan Application
Freddie Mac Form 65 • Fannie Mae Form 1003
Effective 1/2021

Section 6: Acknowledgments and Agreements. This section tells you about your legal obligations when you sign this application.

Acknowledgments and Agreements

Definitions:
- "Lender" includes the Lender's agents, service providers, and any of their successors and assigns.
- "Other Loan Participants" includes (i) any actual or potential owners of a loan resulting from this application (the "Loan"), (ii) acquirers of any beneficial or other interest in the Loan, (iii) any mortgage insurer, (iv) any guarantor, (v) any servicer of the Loan, and (vi) any of these parties' service providers, successors or assigns.

I agree to, acknowledge, and represent the following:

(1) The Complete Information for this Application
- The information I have provided in this application is true, accurate, and complete as of the date I signed this application.
- If the information I submitted changes or I have new information before closing of the Loan, I must change and supplement this application, including providing any updated/supplemented real estate sales contract.
- For purchase transactions: The terms and conditions of any real estate sales contract signed by me in connection with this application are true, accurate, and complete to the best of my knowledge and belief. I have not entered into any other agreement, written or oral, in connection with this real estate transaction.
- The Lender and Other Loan Participants may rely on the information contained in the application before and after closing of the Loan.
- Any intentional or negligent misrepresentation of information may result in the imposition of:
  - (a) civil liability on me, including monetary damages, if a person suffers any loss because the person relied on any misrepresentation that I have made on this application, and/or
  - (b) criminal penalties on me including, but not limited to, fine or imprisonment or both under the provisions of Federal law (18 U.S.C. §§ 1001 *et seq.*).

(2) The Property's Security
The Loan I have applied for in this application will be secured by a mortgage or deed of trust which provides the Lender a security interest in the property described in this application.

(3) The Property's Appraisal, Value, and Condition
- Any appraisal or value of the property obtained by the Lender is for use by the Lender and Other Loan Participants.
- The Lender and Other Loan Participants have not made any representation or warranty, express or implied, to me about the property, its condition, or its value.

(4) Electronic Records and Signatures
- The Lender and Other Loan Participants may keep any paper record and/or electronic record of this application, whether or not the Loan is approved.
- If this application is created as (or converted into) an "electronic application", I consent to the use of "electronic records" and "electronic signatures" as the terms are defined in and governed by applicable Federal and/or state electronic transactions laws.
- I intend to sign and have signed this application either using my:
  - (a) electronic signature; or
  - (b) a written signature and agree that if a paper version of this application is converted into an electronic application, the application will be an electronic record, and the representation of my written signature on this application will be my binding electronic signature.
- I agree that the application, if delivered or transmitted to the Lender or Other Loan Participants as an electronic record with my electronic signature, will be as effective and enforceable as a paper application signed by me in writing.

(5) Delinquency
- The Lender and Other Loan Participants may report information about my account to credit bureaus. Late payments, missed payments, or other defaults on my account may be reflected in my credit report and will likely affect my credit score.
- If I have trouble making my payments I understand that I may contact a HUD-approved housing counseling organization for advice about actions I can take to meet my mortgage obligations.

(6) Authorization for Use and Sharing of Information
By signing below, in addition to the representations and agreements made above, I expressly authorize the Lender and Other Loan Participants to obtain, use, and share with each other (i) the loan application and related loan information and documentation, (ii) a consumer credit report on me, and (iii) my tax return information, as necessary to perform the actions listed below, for so long as they have an interest in my loan or its servicing:
- (a) process and underwrite my loan;
- (b) verify any data contained in my consumer credit report, my loan application and other information supporting my loan application;
- (c) inform credit and investment decisions by the Lender and Other Loan Participants;
- (d) perform audit, quality control, and legal compliance analysis and reviews;
- (e) perform analysis and modeling for risk assessments;
- (f) monitor the account for this loan for potential delinquencies and determine any assistance that may be available to me; and
- (g) other actions permissible under applicable law.

Borrower Signature ______________________ Date *(mm/dd/yyyy)* ___/___/_____

Additional Borrower Signature ______________________ Date *(mm/dd/yyyy)* ___/___/_____

Borrower Name: ______________________
Uniform Residential Loan Application
Freddie Mac Form 65 • Fannie Mae Form 1003
Effective 1/2021

Section 7: Military Service. This section asks questions about your (or your deceased spouse's) military service.

Military Service of Borrower

Military Service – Did you (or your deceased spouse) ever serve, or are you currently serving, in the United States Armed Forces? ◯ **NO** ◯ **YES**

If YES, check all that apply:
- ☐ Currently serving on active duty with projected expiration date of service/tour ___/___/______ *(mm/dd/yyyy)*
- ☐ Currently retired, discharged, or separated from service
- ☐ Only period of service was as a non-activated member of the Reserve or National Guard
- ☐ Surviving spouse

Section 8: Demographic Information. This section asks about your ethnicity, sex, and race.

Demographic Information of Borrower

The purpose of collecting this information is to help ensure that all applicants are treated fairly and that the housing needs of communities and neighborhoods are being fulfilled. For residential mortgage lending, Federal law requires that we ask applicants for their demographic information (ethnicity, sex, and race) in order to monitor our compliance with equal credit opportunity, fair housing, and home mortgage disclosure laws. You are not required to provide this information, but are encouraged to do so. You may select one or more designations for "Ethnicity" and one or more designations for "Race." **The law provides that we may not discriminate** on the basis of this information, or on whether you choose to provide it. However, if you choose not to provide the information and you have made this application in person, Federal regulations require us to note your ethnicity, sex, and race on the basis of visual observation or surname. The law also provides that we may not discriminate on the basis of age or marital status information you provide in this application. If you do not wish to provide some or all of this information, please check below.

Ethnicity: *Check one or more*
- ☐ Hispanic or Latino
  - ☐ Mexican ☐ Puerto Rican ☐ Cuban
  - ☐ Other Hispanic or Latino – *Print origin:*

    ____

    For example: Argentinean, Colombian, Dominican, Nicaraguan, Salvadoran, Spaniard, and so on.
- ☐ Not Hispanic or Latino
- ☐ I do not wish to provide this information

Sex
- ☐ Female
- ☐ Male
- ☐ I do not wish to provide this information

Race: *Check one or more*
- ☐ American Indian or Alaska Native – *Print name of enrolled or principal tribe*: ______________________
- ☐ Asian
  - ☐ Asian Indian ☐ Chinese ☐ Filipino
  - ☐ Japanese ☐ Korean ☐ Vietnamese
  - ☐ Other Asian – *Print race:* ______________________

    For example: Hmong, Laotian, Thai, Pakistani, Cambodian, and so on.
- ☐ Black or African American
- ☐ Native Hawaiian or Other Pacific Islander
  - ☐ Native Hawaiian ☐ Guamanian or Chamorro ☐ Samoan
  - ☐ Other Pacific Islander – *Print race:*

    ____

    For example: Fijian, Tongan, and so on.
- ☐ White
- ☐ I do not wish to provide this information

To Be Completed by Financial Institution (for application taken in person):

Was the ethnicity of the Borrower collected on the basis of visual observation or surname? ◯ NO ◯ YES
Was the sex of the Borrower collected on the basis of visual observation or surname? ◯ NO ◯ YES
Was the race of the Borrower collected on the basis of visual observation or surname? ◯ NO ◯ YES

The Demographic Information was provided through:

◯ Face-to-Face Interview *(includes Electronic Media w/ Video Component)* ◯ Telephone Interview ◯ Fax or Mail ◯ Email or Internet

Borrower Name: ______________________

Uniform Residential Loan Application
Freddie Mac Form 65 • Fannie Mae Form 1003
Effective 1/2021

Section 9: Loan Originator Information. To be completed by your **Loan Originator**.

Loan Originator Information

Loan Originator Organization Name ______________________________

Address ______________________________

Loan Originator Organization NMLSR ID# ______________ State License ID# ______________

Loan Originator Name ______________________________

Loan Originator NMLSR ID# ______________ State License ID# ______________

Email ______________________________ Phone (_____) _____ – _________

Signature ______________________________ Date *(mm/dd/yyyy)* _____ / _____ / _________

B. [§ 5.79] Good Faith Estimate of Settlement Costs

OMB No. xxxx-xxxx
Approval Expires mm/dd/yyyy

Good Faith Estimate (GFE)

Name of Originator		Borrower	
Originator Address		Property Address	
Originator Phone Number			
Originator email		Date of GFE	

Instructions

This GFE gives you an estimate of your settlement charges and loan terms if you are approved for this loan. See page 3 for more detailed instructions.

Important dates

1. The interest rate for this GFE is available until . After that date, the interest rate, some of your Loan Origination Charges, and the monthly payment shown below can change until you lock your interest rate.
2. This estimate for all other settlement charges is available until .
3. If you proceed with this loan, you must go to settlement in days. You must lock the interest rate at least days before settlement.

Summary of your loan terms

Your Loan Details		
Your initial loan balance is	$	
Your loan term is		years
Your initial interest rate is		%
Your initial monthly amount owed for principal, interest, and any mortgage insurance is	$	per month
Your rate lock period is *After you lock in your interest rate, you must go to settlement within this number of days to guarantee this interest rate.*		days
Can your interest rate rise?	☐ No	☐ Yes, it can rise to a maximum of %
Can your loan balance rise?	☐ No	☐ Yes, it can rise to a maximum of $
Can your monthly amount owed for principal, interest, and any mortgage insurance rise?	☐ No	☐ Yes, it can rise to a maximum of $
Does your loan have a prepayment penalty?	☐ No	☐ Yes, your maximum prepayment penalty is $
Does your loan have a balloon payment?	☐ No	☐ Yes, you have a balloon payment of $ due in years.
Does your loan include a monthly escrow payment for property taxes and, possibly, other obligations?	☐ No	☐ Yes

Summary of your settlement charges

A	Your Adjusted Origination Charges *(Table A, page 2)*	$
B	Your Charges for All Other Settlement Services *(Table B, page 2)*	$
A + B	Total Estimated Settlement Charges	$

Good Faith Estimate (GFE) 1

Understanding your estimated settlement charges

Your Loan Details	
1. Our service charge These charges are for the services we provide when we get and process this loan for you.	
2. Your credit or charge for the specific interest rate chosen (points) ☐ The credit or charge for the interest rate you have chosen is included in "Our service charge." (See item 1 above.) ☐ You receive a credit of $ for this interest rate of %. This credit reduces your upfront charges. ☐ You pay a charge of $ for this interest rate of %. This payment (discount points) increases your upfront charges. (See the table on page 3 to see how you can change this charge or credit by choosing a different interest rate.)	
A Your Adjusted Origination Charges	$

Your Charges for All Other Settlement Services	
3. Required services that we select These charges are for services we require to complete your settlement. We will choose the providers of these services. *Service* *Charge*	
4. Title services and lender's title insurance This charge includes the services of a title agent, for example, and title insurance to protect the lender, if required.	
5. Required services that you can shop for These charges are for other services that are required to complete your settlement. We can refer you to providers of these services or you can shop for them yourself. Our estimates for providing these services are below. *Service* *Charge*	
6. Government recording and transfer charges This includes state and local charges on mortgages and home sales.	
7. Reserves or escrow This charge is held in an escrow account to pay recurring charges on your property, such as property taxes or insurance.	
8. Daily interest charges This charge is for the daily interest on your loan from the day of your settlement until the first day of the next month or the first day of your normal mortgage payment cycle. For this loan, this amount is $ per day for days (if your closing date is).	
9. Homeowner's insurance This charge is for the insurance you must buy for the property to protect from a loss, such as fire.	
10. Optional owner's title insurance This charge is for additional insurance you can choose to buy to protect yourself from title defects.	
B Your Charges for All Other Settlement Services	$
A + B Total Estimated Settlement Charges	$

Good Faith Estimate (GFE) 2

Important Information and Instructions

Shopping for a loan offer

Only you can shop for the best loan for you. Compare this GFE with other loan offers, so you can find the best loan. Use the table on page 4 to compare all the offers you receive.

Understanding which charges can change at settlement

The GFE estimates your settlement charges. At your settlement, you will receive a HUD-1. Compare the charges on the HUD-1 with the charges on this GFE. Charges can change if you select your own provider and do not use the companies your lender suggests.

The list below shows you how much the estimated charges on this GFE can change at your closing.

These charges ***cannot increase*** at settlement:	The total of these charges ***can increase up to 10%*** at settlement:	These charges ***can change*** at settlement:
• Our service charge • Your charge or credit for the specific interest rate chosen *(after you lock in your interest rate)* • Government recording and transfer charges	• Required services that we select • Title services and lender's title insurance *(if we select them or you use providers identified by us)* • Required services that you can shop for *(if you use providers identified by us)* • Optional owner's title insurance *(if you use providers identified by us)*	• Required services that you can shop for *(if you do not use providers identified by us)* • Title services and lender's title insurance *(if you do not use providers identified by us)* • Reserves or escrow • Daily interest rate charges • Homeowner's insurance • Optional owner's title insurance *(if you do not use providers identified by us)*

Looking at trade-offs

In this GFE, we offered you a particular interest rate and estimated settlement charges. But, you could choose other loans to get a lower interest rate or lower settlement charges.

- If you want to choose a loan with a **lower interest rate,** then you will have **higher settlement charges.**
- If you want to choose a loan with **lower settlement charges,** then you will have a **higher interest rate.**

The table below shows how the loan for this GFE compares to two other options. If you decide you want to make one of these trade-offs, you must ask us for a new GFE.

	The loan in this GFE	A loan with a lower interest rate	A loan with lower settlement charges
Your loan amount	$	$	$
Your interest rate	%	%	%
How much your monthly payment will be	$	$	$
How much more or less in monthly payments from this GFE	No Change	You will pay $ less every month	You will pay $ more every month
How much more or less you will pay at settlement with this interest rate	No Change	Your lower interest rate will raise your settlement charges by $	Your higher interest rate will lower your settlement charges by $
How much your total estimated settlement charges will be	$	$	$

If this loan offer is for an adjustable rate loan, the comparisons in the table are for the initial interest rate before any adjustments are made.

Your financial responsibilities as a homeowner

In addition to your monthly amount owed for principal, interest, and mortgage insurance, you may need to pay other required annual charges to keep your property. We must provide an estimate for annual property taxes along with homeowner's, flood, and other required property protection insurance, but we are not required to provide estimates for the other charges. You may have to identify the other charges and ask for additional estimates from others.

Different sources might use different techniques to estimate these charges, but the actual charges will be the same in the end. Therefore, do not use these estimates to compare settlement charges from different loan originators.

Annual property taxes	
Annual homeowner's insurance	
Annual flood insurance	
Annual homeowners association/condominium fees	
Other	
Total Other Annual Charges	

Applying for this loan

If you decide you would like to apply for this loan, contact us at .
You must pay a fee of $. This fee will be subtracted from your settlement charges.

Getting more information

The type of loan you choose can affect your current and future monthly payments. You can ask us for more information about loan types. You can also look at several government publications: HUD's *Special Information Booklet* on settlement charges, your *Truth-in-Lending Disclosures,* and consumer information publications of the Federal Reserve Board.

Using the shopping chart

Use this chart to compare Good Faith Estimates (GFEs) from different loan originators. Fill in the information by using a different column for each GFE you receive.

By comparing loan offers, you can shop for the best loan.

	Loan 1	Loan 2	Loan 3	Loan 4
Loan Originator Name				
Initial Loan Balance				
Loan Term				
Initial Interest Rate				
Initial Monthly Amount Owed				
Rate Lock Period				
Can Interest Rate Rise?				
Can Loan Balance Rise?				
Can Monthly Amount Owed Rise?				
Prepayment Penalty?				
Balloon Payment?				
Total Estimated Settlement Charges				

If your loan is sold in the future

Lenders can receive additional fees by selling your loan at some future date after settlement. Once you have obtained your loan at settlement, however, your loan terms, adjusted origination charges, and total settlement charges cannot change. After settlement, any fees lenders receive in the future cannot change the loan you received or the charges you paid at settlement.

C. [§ 5.80] ECOA Declination Letter

Adverse Action Form

Sample Notice of Action Taken and Statement of Reasons

Date

Dear Applicant: Thank you for your recent application. Your request for [a loan/a credit card/an increase in your credit limit] was carefully considered, and we regret that we are unable to approve your application at this time, for the following reason(s):

Your Income:
__is below our minimum requirement.
__is insufficient to sustain payments on the amount of credit requested.
__could not be verified.

Your Employment:
__is not of sufficient length to qualify.
__could not be verified.

Your Credit History:
__of making payments on time was not satisfactory.
__could not be verified.

Your Application:
__lacks a sufficient number of credit references.
__lacks acceptable types of credit references.
__reveals that current obligations are excessive in relation to income.

Other:

The consumer reporting agency contacted that provided information that influenced our decision in whole or in part was [name, address and [toll-free] telephone number of the reporting agency]. The reporting agency played no part in our decision and is unable to supply specific reasons why we have denied credit to you. You have a right under the Fair Credit Reporting Act to know the information contained in your credit file at the consumer reporting agency. You also have a right to a free copy of your report from the reporting agency, if you request it no later than 60 days after you receive this notice. In addition, if you find that any information contained in the report you receive is inaccurate or incomplete, you have the right to dispute the matter with the reporting agency. Any questions regarding such information should be directed to [consumer reporting agency]. If you have any questions regarding this letter, you should contact us at [creditor's name, address and telephone number].

[We also obtained your credit score from this consumer reporting agency and used it in making our credit decision. Your credit score is a number that reflects the information in your consumer report. Your credit score can change, depending on how the information in your consumer report changes.
Your credit score:
Date:
Scores range from a low of______to a high of______
Key factors that adversely affected your credit score:

[Number of recent inquiries on consumer report, as a key factor]
[If you have any questions regarding your credit score, you should contact [entity that provided the credit score] at:
Address:
[Toll-free] Telephone number:__________]]

Notice: The federal Equal Credit Opportunity Act prohibits creditors from discriminating against credit applicants on the basis of race, color, religion, national origin, sex, marital status, age (provided the applicant has the capacity to enter into a binding contract); because all or part of the applicant's income derives from any public assistance program; or because the applicant has in good faith exercised any right under the Consumer Credit Protection Act. The federal agency that administers compliance with this law concerning this creditor is [INSERT name and address as specified by the appropriate agency listed in Appendix A of Regulation B].

D. [§ 5.81] FNMA/FHLMC Note

NOTE

____________________, _________ ______________________________, ______________________________

[Note Date] [City] [State]

____

[Property Address]

1. BORROWER'S PROMISE TO PAY

In return for a loan in the amount of U.S. $ _________ (the "Principal") that I have received from ______________________ (the "Lender"), I promise to pay the Principal, plus interest, to the order of the Lender. I will make all payments under this Note in U.S. currency in the form of cash, check, money order, or other payment method accepted by Lender.

I understand that the Lender may transfer this Note. The Lender or anyone who takes this Note by transfer and who is entitled to receive payments under this Note is called the "Note Holder."

2. INTEREST

Interest will be charged on unpaid Principal until the full amount of the Principal has been paid. I will pay interest at a yearly rate of ________________%.

The interest rate required by this Section 2 is the rate I will pay both before and after any default described in Section 6(B) of this Note.

3. PAYMENTS

(A) Time and Place of Payments

I will pay principal and interest by making a payment every month. This amount is called my "Monthly Payment."

I will make my Monthly Payment on the _________ day of each month beginning on ___________________, ______. I will make these payments every month until I have paid all of the Principal and interest and any other charges described below that I may owe under this Note. Each Monthly Payment will be applied as of its scheduled due date and will be applied to interest before the Principal. If, on _________________________________, ______, I still owe amounts under this Note, I will pay those amounts on that date, which is called the "Maturity Date."

I will make my Monthly Payments at ____ or at a different place if required by the Note Holder.

(B) Amount of Monthly Payments

My Monthly Payment will be in the amount of U.S. $___________________________________. This payment amount does not include any property taxes, insurance, or other charges that I may be required to pay each month.

4. BORROWER'S RIGHT TO PREPAY

I have the right to make payments of principal at any time before they are due. A payment of principal only is known as a "Prepayment." When I make a Prepayment, I will notify the Note Holder in writing that I am doing so. I may not designate a payment as a Prepayment if I have not made all the Monthly Payments then due under this Note.

I may make a full Prepayment or partial Prepayments without paying a Prepayment charge. The Note Holder will use my Prepayments to reduce the amount of Principal that I owe under this Note. However, the Note Holder may apply my Prepayment to the accrued and unpaid interest on the Prepayment amount, before applying my Prepayment to reduce the Principal amount of the Note. If I make a partial Prepayment, there will be no changes in the due date or in the amount of my Monthly Payment unless the Note Holder agrees in writing to those changes.

5. LOAN CHARGES

If applicable law sets maximum loan charges, and that law is finally interpreted so that the interest or other loan charges collected or to be collected in connection with the loan exceed the permitted limits, then (a) any such loan charge will be reduced by the amount necessary to reduce the charge to the permitted limit, and (b) any sums already collected from me that exceeded permitted limits will be refunded to me. The Note Holder may choose to make this refund by reducing the Principal I owe under this Note or by making a direct payment to me. If a refund reduces Principal, the reduction will be treated as a partial Prepayment.

6. BORROWER'S FAILURE TO PAY AS REQUIRED

(A) Late Charges for Overdue Payments

If the Note Holder has not received the full amount of any Monthly Payment by the end of ___________ calendar days after the date it is due, I will pay a late charge to the Note Holder. The amount of the charge will be _____% of my overdue Monthly Payment. I will pay this late charge promptly but only once on each late payment.

(B) Default

If I do not pay the full amount of each Monthly Payment on the date it is due, I will be in default.

(C) Notice of Default

If I am in default, the Note Holder may send me a written notice telling me that if I do not pay the overdue amount by a certain date, the Note Holder may require me to pay immediately the full amount of unpaid Principal, all the interest that I owe on that amount, and other charges due under this Note (the "Default Balance"). That date must be at least 30 days after the date on which the notice is mailed to me or delivered by other means.

(D) No Waiver By Note Holder

If I am in default and the Note Holder does not require me to pay the Default Balance immediately as described above, the Note Holder will still have the right to do so if I continue to be in default or if I am in default at a later time.

(E) Payment of Note Holder's Costs and Expenses

If the Note Holder has required me to pay the Default Balance immediately as described above, the Note Holder will have the right to be paid back by me for all of its costs and expenses in enforcing this Note to the extent not prohibited by applicable law. Those expenses include, for example, reasonable attorneys' fees and costs.

7. GIVING OF NOTICES

(A) Notice to Borrower

Unless applicable law requires a different method, any notice that must be given to me under this Note will be given by delivering it, or by mailing it by first class mail, to me at the Property Address above or at a different address if I give the Note Holder a notice of my different address. I will promptly notify the Note Holder of any change to my physical address and of any change to my mailing address. Unless applicable law requires otherwise, notice may instead be sent by e-mail or other electronic communication if agreed to by me and the Note Holder in writing and if I have provided the Note Holder with my current e-mail address or other electronic address. If I have agreed with the Note Holder that notice may be given by e-mail or other electronic communication, I will promptly notify the Note Holder of any changes to my e-mail address or other electronic address.

(B) Notice to Note Holder

Any notice that I must give to the Note Holder under this Note will be delivered by first class mail to the Note Holder at the address stated in Section 3(A) above or at a different address if I am given a notice of that different address.

8. OBLIGATIONS OF PERSONS UNDER THIS NOTE

If more than one person signs this Note, each person is fully and personally obligated to keep all of the promises made in this Note, including the promise to pay the full amount owed. Any person who is a guarantor, surety, or endorser of this Note is also obligated to do these things. Any person who takes over these obligations, including the obligations of a guarantor, surety, or endorser of this Note, is also obligated to keep all of the promises made in this Note. The Note Holder may enforce its rights under this Note against each person individually or against all of us together. This means that any one of us may be required to pay all of the amounts owed under this Note.

9. WAIVERS

I and any other person who has obligations under this Note waive the rights of Presentment and Notice of Dishonor. "Presentment" means the right to require the Note Holder to demand payment of amounts due. "Notice of Dishonor" means the right to require the Note Holder to give notice to other persons that amounts due have not been paid.

10. UNIFORM SECURED NOTE

This Note is a uniform instrument with limited variations in some jurisdictions. In addition to the protections given to the Note Holder under this Note, a Mortgage, Mortgage Deed, Deed of Trust, or Security Deed (the "Security Instrument"), dated the same date as this Note, protects the Note Holder from possible losses that might result if I do not keep the promises that I make in this Note. That Security Instrument also describes how and under what conditions I may be required to make immediate payment of all amounts I owe under this Note. Some of those conditions are described as follows:

> If all or any part of the Property or any Interest in the Property is sold or transferred (or if Borrower is not a natural person and a beneficial interest in Borrower is sold or transferred) without Lender's prior written consent, Lender may require immediate payment in full of all sums secured by this Security Instrument. However, Lender will not exercise this option if such exercise is prohibited by Applicable Law.
>
> If Lender exercises this option, Lender will give Borrower notice of acceleration. The notice will provide a period of not less than 30 days from the date the notice is given in accordance with Section 16 within which Borrower must pay all sums secured by this Security Instrument. If Borrower fails to pay these sums prior to, or upon, the expiration of this period, Lender may invoke any remedies permitted by this Security Instrument without further notice or demand on Borrower and will be entitled to collect all expenses incurred in pursuing such remedies, including, but not limited to: (a) reasonable attorneys' fees and costs; (b) property inspection and valuation fees; and (c) other fees incurred to protect Lender's Interest in the Property and/or rights under this Security Instrument.

WITNESS THE HAND(S) AND SEAL(S) OF THE UNDERSIGNED.

____(Seal)
- Borrower

____(Seal)
- Borrower

____(Seal)
- Borrower

[Sign Original Only]

E. [§ 5.82] FNMA/FHLMC Deed of Trust

After Recording Return To:

____
____
____
____

__________________ **[Space Above This Line For Recording Data]** ________________

DEED OF TRUST

DEFINITIONS

Words used in multiple sections of this document are defined below and other words are defined under the caption TRANSFER OF RIGHTS IN THE PROPERTY and in Sections 3, 4, 10, 11, 12, 16, 19, 24, and 25. Certain rules regarding the usage of words used in this document are also provided in Section 17.

Parties

(A) **"Borrower"** is ____, currently residing at ___________________________________. Borrower is the trustor under this Security Instrument.

(B) **"Lender"** is ____. Lender is a _____________ organized and existing under the laws of _________________________. Lender's address is ___________________________. Lender is the beneficiary under this Security Instrument. The term "Lender" includes any successors and assigns of Lender.

(C) **"Trustee"** is ____. Trustee's address is ____. The term "Trustee" includes any substitute/successor Trustee.

Documents

(D) **"Note"** means the promissory note dated _______________, ____, and signed by each Borrower who is legally obligated for the debt under that promissory note, that is in either (i) paper form, using Borrower's written pen and ink signature, or (ii) electronic form, using Borrower's adopted Electronic Signature in accordance with the UETA or E-SIGN, as applicable. The Note evidences the legal obligation of each Borrower who signed the Note to pay Lender ______________________________ Dollars (U.S. $_________________) plus interest. Each Borrower who signed the Note has promised to pay this debt in regular monthly payments and to pay the debt in full not later than ______________, _______.

(E) "Riders" means all Riders to this Security Instrument that are signed by Borrower. All such Riders are incorporated into and deemed to be a part of this Security Instrument. The following Riders are to be signed by Borrower [check box as applicable]:

□ Adjustable Rate Rider □ Condominium Rider □ Other(s) [specify]

□ 1-4 Family Rider □ Planned Unit Development Rider ____________

□ Second Home Rider

(F) "Security Instrument" means this document, which is dated ____________, _______, together with all Riders to this document.

Additional Definitions

(G) "Applicable Law" means all controlling applicable federal, state, and local statutes, regulations, ordinances, and administrative rules and orders (that have the effect of law) as well as all applicable final, non-appealable judicial opinions.

(H) "Community Association Dues, Fees, and Assessments" means all dues, fees, assessments, and other charges that are imposed on Borrower or the Property by a condominium association, homeowners association, or similar organization.

(I) "Default" means: (i) the failure to pay any Periodic Payment or any other amount secured by this Security Instrument on the date it is due; (ii) a breach of any representation, warranty, covenant, obligation, or agreement in this Security Instrument; (iii) any materially false, misleading, or inaccurate information or statement to Lender provided by Borrower or any persons or entities acting at Borrower's direction or with Borrower's knowledge or consent, or failure to provide Lender with material information in connection with the Loan, as described in Section 8; or (iv) any action or proceeding described in Section 12(e).

(J) "Electronic Fund Transfer" means any transfer of funds, other than a transaction originated by check, draft, or similar paper instrument, which is initiated through an electronic terminal, telephonic instrument, computer, or magnetic tape so as to order, instruct, or authorize a financial institution to debit or credit an account. Such term includes, but is not limited to, point-of-sale transfers, automated teller machine transactions, transfers initiated by telephone or other electronic device capable of communicating with such financial institution, wire transfers, and automated clearinghouse transfers.

(K) "Electronic Signature" means an "Electronic Signature" as defined in the UETA or E-SIGN, as applicable.

(L) "E-SIGN" means the Electronic Signatures in Global and National Commerce Act (15 U.S.C. § 7001 *et seq.*), as it may be amended from time to time, or any applicable additional or successor legislation that governs the same subject matter.

(M) "Escrow Items" means: (i) taxes and assessments and other items that can attain priority over this Security Instrument as a lien or encumbrance on the Property;

(ii) leasehold payments or ground rents on the Property, if any; (iii) premiums for any and all insurance required by Lender under Section 5; (iv) Mortgage Insurance premiums, if any, or any sums payable by Borrower to Lender in lieu of the payment of Mortgage Insurance premiums in accordance with the provisions of Section 11; and (v) Community Association Dues, Fees, and Assessments if Lender requires that they be escrowed beginning at Loan closing or at any time during the Loan term.

(N) **"Loan"** means the debt obligation evidenced by the Note, plus interest, any prepayment charges, costs, expenses, and late charges due under the Note, and all sums due under this Security Instrument, plus interest.

(O) **"Loan Servicer"** means the entity that has the contractual right to receive Borrower's Periodic Payments and any other payments made by Borrower, and administers the Loan on behalf of Lender. Loan Servicer does not include a sub-servicer, which is an entity that may service the Loan on behalf of the Loan Servicer.

(P) **"Miscellaneous Proceeds"** means any compensation, settlement, award of damages, or proceeds paid by any third party (other than insurance proceeds paid under the coverages described in Section 5) for: (i) damage to, or destruction of, the Property; (ii) condemnation or other taking of all or any part of the Property; (iii) conveyance in lieu of condemnation; or (iv) misrepresentations of, or omissions as to, the value and/or condition of the Property.

(Q) **"Mortgage Insurance"** means insurance protecting Lender against the nonpayment of, or Default on, the Loan.

(R) "**Partial Payment**" means any payment by Borrower, other than a voluntary prepayment permitted under the Note, which is less than a full outstanding Periodic Payment.

(S) **"Periodic Payment"** means the regularly scheduled amount due for (i) principal and interest under the Note, plus (ii) any amounts under Section 3.

(T) **"Property"** means the property described below under the heading "TRANSFER OF RIGHTS IN THE PROPERTY."

(U) "**Rents"** means all amounts received by or due Borrower in connection with the lease, use, and/or occupancy of the Property by a party other than Borrower.

(V) **"RESPA"** means the Real Estate Settlement Procedures Act (12 U.S.C. § 2601 *et seq.*) and its implementing regulation, Regulation X (12 C.F.R. Part 1024), as they may be amended from time to time, or any additional or successor federal legislation or regulation that governs the same subject matter. When used in this Security Instrument, "RESPA" refers to all requirements and restrictions that would apply to a "federally related mortgage loan" even if the Loan does not qualify as a "federally related mortgage loan" under RESPA.

(W) **"Successor in Interest of Borrower"** means any party that has taken title to the Property, whether or not that party has assumed Borrower's obligations under the Note and/or this Security Instrument.

(X) "UETA" means the Uniform Electronic Transactions Act, as enacted by the jurisdiction in which the Property is located, as it may be amended from time to time, or any applicable additional or successor legislation that governs the same subject matter.

TRANSFER OF RIGHTS IN THE PROPERTY

This Security Instrument secures to Lender (i) the repayment of the Loan, and all renewals, extensions, and modifications of the Note, and (ii) the performance of Borrower's covenants and agreements under this Security Instrument and the Note. For this purpose, Borrower irrevocably grants and conveys to Trustee, in trust, with power of sale, the following described property located in the ________________________________ of ______ ____________________________:

[Type of Recording Jurisdiction] [Name of Recording Jurisdiction]

which currently has the address of ____

[Street]

____________________________, Maryland _______________ ("Property Address");

[City] [Zip Code]

TOGETHER WITH all the improvements now or subsequently erected on the property, including replacements and additions to the improvements on such property, all property rights, including, without limitation, all easements, appurtenances, royalties, mineral rights, oil or gas rights or profits, water rights, and fixtures now or subsequently a part of the property. All of the foregoing is referred to in this Security Instrument as the "Property."

BORROWER REPRESENTS, WARRANTS, COVENANTS, AND AGREES that: (i) Borrower lawfully owns and possesses the Property conveyed in this Security Instrument in fee simple or lawfully has the right to use and occupy the Property under a leasehold estate; (ii) Borrower has the right to grant and convey the Property or Borrower's leasehold interest in the Property; and (iii) the Property is unencumbered, and not subject to any other ownership interest in the Property, except for encumbrances and ownership interests of record. Borrower warrants generally the title to the Property and covenants and agrees to defend the title to the Property against all claims and demands, subject to any encumbrances and ownership interests of record as of Loan closing.

THIS SECURITY INSTRUMENT combines uniform covenants for national use with limited variations and non-uniform covenants that reflect specific Maryland state requirements to constitute a uniform security instrument covering real property.

UNIFORM COVENANTS. Borrower and Lender covenant and agree as follows:

1. Payment of Principal, Interest, Escrow Items, Prepayment Charges, and Late Charges. Borrower will pay each Periodic Payment when due. Borrower will also pay any prepayment charges and late charges due under the Note, and any other amounts due under this Security Instrument. Payments due under the Note and this Security Instrument must be made in U.S. currency. If any check or other instrument received by Lender as payment under the Note or this Security Instrument is returned to Lender unpaid, Lender may require that any or all subsequent payments due under the Note and this Security Instrument be made in one or more of the following forms, as selected by Lender: (a) cash; (b) money order; (c) certified check, bank check, treasurer's check, or cashier's check, provided any such check is drawn upon an institution whose deposits are insured by a U.S. federal agency, instrumentality, or entity; or (d) Electronic Fund Transfer.

Payments are deemed received by Lender when received at the location designated in the Note or at such other location as may be designated by Lender in accordance with the notice provisions in Section 16. Lender may accept or return any Partial Payments in its sole discretion pursuant to Section 2.

Any offset or claim that Borrower may have now or in the future against Lender will not relieve Borrower from making the full amount of all payments due under the Note and this Security Instrument or performing the covenants and agreements secured by this Security Instrument.

2. Acceptance and Application of Payments or Proceeds.

(a) Acceptance and Application of Partial Payments. Lender may accept and either apply or hold in suspense Partial Payments in its sole discretion in accordance with this Section 2. Lender is not obligated to accept any Partial Payments or to apply any Partial Payments at the time such payments are accepted, and also is not obligated to pay interest on such unapplied funds. Lender may hold such unapplied funds until Borrower makes payment sufficient to cover a full Periodic Payment, at which time the amount of the full Periodic Payment will be applied to the Loan. If Borrower does not make such a payment within a reasonable period of time, Lender will either apply such funds in accordance with this Section 2 or return them to Borrower. If not applied earlier, Partial Payments will be credited against the total amount due under the Loan in calculating the amount due in connection with any foreclosure proceeding, payoff request, loan modification, or reinstatement. Lender may accept any payment insufficient to bring the Loan current without waiver of any rights under this Security Instrument or prejudice to its rights to refuse such payments in the future.

(b) Order of Application of Partial Payments and Periodic Payments. Except as otherwise described in this Section 2, if Lender applies a payment, such payment will be applied to each Periodic Payment in the order in which it became due, beginning with the oldest outstanding Periodic Payment, as follows: first to interest and then to principal due under the Note, and finally to Escrow Items. If all outstanding Periodic Payments then due are paid in full, any payment amounts remaining may be applied to late charges and to any amounts then due under this Security Instrument. If all sums then due under the Note and this Security Instrument are paid in full, any remaining payment amount may be applied, in Lender's sole discretion, to a future Periodic Payment or to reduce the principal balance of the Note.

If Lender receives a payment from Borrower in the amount of one or more Periodic Payments and the amount of any late charge due for a delinquent Periodic Payment, the payment may be applied to the delinquent payment and the late charge.

When applying payments, Lender will apply such payments in accordance with Applicable Law.

(c) Voluntary Prepayments. Voluntary prepayments will be applied as described in the Note.

(d) No Change to Payment Schedule. Any application of payments, insurance proceeds, or Miscellaneous Proceeds to principal due under the Note will not extend or postpone the due date, or change the amount, of the Periodic Payments.

3. Funds for Escrow Items.

(a) Escrow Requirement; Escrow Items. Borrower must pay to Lender on the day Periodic Payments are due under the Note, until the Note is paid in full, a sum of money to provide for payment of amounts due for all Escrow Items (the "Funds"). The amount of the Funds required to be paid each month may change during the term of the Loan. Borrower must promptly furnish to Lender all notices or invoices of amounts to be paid under this Section 3.

(b) Payment of Funds; Waiver. Borrower must pay Lender the Funds for Escrow Items unless Lender waives this obligation in writing. Lender may waive this obligation for any Escrow Item at any time. In the event of such waiver, Borrower must pay directly, when and where payable, the amounts due for any Escrow Items subject to the waiver. If Lender has waived the requirement to pay Lender the Funds for any or all Escrow Items, Lender may require Borrower to provide proof of direct payment of those items within such time period as Lender may require. Borrower's obligation to make such timely payments and to provide proof of payment is deemed to be a covenant and agreement of Borrower under this Security Instrument. If Borrower is obligated to pay Escrow Items directly pursuant to a waiver, and Borrower fails to pay timely the amount due for an Escrow Item, Lender may exercise its rights under Section 9 to pay such amount and Borrower will be obligated to repay to Lender any such amount in accordance with Section 9.

Lender may withdraw the waiver as to any or all Escrow Items at any time by giving a notice in accordance with Section 16; upon such withdrawal, Borrower must pay to Lender all Funds for such Escrow Items, and in such amounts, that are then required under this Section 3.

(c) Amount of Funds; Application of Funds. Lender may, at any time, collect and hold Funds in an amount up to, but not in excess of, the maximum amount a lender can require under RESPA. Lender will estimate the amount of Funds due in accordance with Applicable Law.

The Funds will be held in an institution whose deposits are insured by a U.S. federal agency, instrumentality, or entity (including Lender, if Lender is an institution whose deposits are so insured) or in any Federal Home Loan Bank. Lender will apply the Funds to pay the Escrow Items no later than the time specified under RESPA. Lender may not charge Borrower for: (i) holding and applying the Funds; (ii) annually analyzing the escrow account; or (iii) verifying the Escrow Items, unless Lender pays Borrower interest on the Funds and Applicable Law permits Lender to make such a charge. Unless Lender and Borrower agree in writing or Applicable Law requires interest to be paid on the Funds, Lender will not be required to pay Borrower any interest or earnings on the Funds. Lender will give to Borrower, without charge, an annual accounting of the Funds as required by RESPA.

(d) Surplus; Shortage and Deficiency of Funds. In accordance with RESPA, if there is a surplus of Funds held in escrow, Lender will account to Borrower for such surplus. If Borrower's Periodic Payment is delinquent by more than 30 days, Lender may retain the surplus in the escrow account for the payment of the Escrow Items. If there is a shortage or deficiency of Funds held in escrow, Lender will notify Borrower and Borrower will pay to Lender the amount necessary to make up the shortage or deficiency in accordance with RESPA.

Upon payment in full of all sums secured by this Security Instrument, Lender will promptly refund to Borrower any Funds held by Lender.

4. Charges; Liens. Borrower must pay (a) all taxes, assessments, charges, fines, and impositions attributable to the Property which have priority or may attain priority over this Security Instrument, (b) leasehold payments or ground rents on the Property, if any, and (c) Community Association Dues, Fees, and Assessments, if any. If any of these items are Escrow Items, Borrower will pay them in the manner provided in Section 3.

Borrower must promptly discharge any lien that has priority or may attain priority over this Security Instrument unless Borrower: (aa) agrees in writing to the payment of the obligation secured by the lien in a manner acceptable to Lender, but only so long as Borrower is performing under such agreement; (bb) contests the lien in good faith by, or defends against enforcement of the lien in, legal proceedings which Lender determines, in its sole discretion, operate to prevent the enforcement of the lien while those proceedings are pending, but only until such proceedings are concluded; or (cc) secures from the holder of the lien an agreement satisfactory to Lender that subordinates the lien to this Security Instrument (collectively, the "Required Actions"). If Lender determines that any part of the Property is subject to a lien that has priority or may attain priority over this Security Instrument and Borrower has not taken any of the Required Actions in regard to such lien, Lender may give Borrower a notice identifying the lien. Within 10 days after the date on which that notice is given, Borrower must satisfy the lien or take one or more of the Required Actions.

5. Property Insurance.

(a) Insurance Requirement; Coverages. Borrower must keep the improvements now existing or subsequently erected on the Property insured against loss by fire, hazards included within the term "extended coverage," and any other hazards including, but not limited to, earthquakes, winds, and floods, for which Lender requires insurance. Borrower must maintain the types of insurance Lender requires in the amounts (including deductible levels) and for the periods that Lender requires. What Lender requires pursuant to the preceding sentences can change during the term of the Loan, and may exceed any minimum coverage required by Applicable Law. Borrower may choose the insurance carrier providing the insurance, subject to Lender's right to disapprove Borrower's choice, which right will not be exercised unreasonably.

(b) Failure to Maintain Insurance. If Lender has a reasonable basis to believe that Borrower has failed to maintain any of the required insurance coverages described above, Lender may obtain insurance coverage, at Lender's option and at Borrower's expense.

Unless required by Applicable Law, Lender is under no obligation to advance premiums for, or to seek to reinstate, any prior lapsed coverage obtained by Borrower. Lender is under no obligation to purchase any particular type or amount of coverage and may select the provider of such insurance in its sole discretion. Before purchasing such coverage, Lender will notify Borrower if required to do so under Applicable Law. Any such coverage will insure Lender, but might not protect Borrower, Borrower's equity in the Property, or the contents of the Property, against any risk, hazard, or liability and might provide greater or lesser coverage than was previously in effect, but not exceeding the coverage required under Section 5(a). Borrower acknowledges that the cost of the insurance coverage so obtained may significantly exceed the cost of insurance that Borrower could have obtained. Any amounts disbursed by Lender for costs associated with reinstating Borrower's insurance policy or with placing new insurance under this Section 5 will become additional debt of Borrower secured by this Security Instrument. These amounts will bear interest at the Note rate from the date of disbursement and will be payable, with such interest, upon notice from Lender to Borrower requesting payment.

(c) Insurance Policies. All insurance policies required by Lender and renewals of such policies: (i) will be subject to Lender's right to disapprove such policies; (ii) must include a standard mortgage clause; and (iii) must name Lender as mortgagee and/or as an additional loss payee. Lender will have the right to hold the policies and renewal certificates. If Lender requires, Borrower will promptly give to Lender proof of paid premiums and renewal notices. If Borrower obtains any form of insurance coverage, not otherwise required by Lender, for damage to, or destruction of, the Property, such policy must include a standard mortgage clause and must name Lender as mortgagee and/or as an additional loss payee.

(d) Proof of Loss; Application of Proceeds. In the event of loss, Borrower must give prompt notice to the insurance carrier and Lender. Lender may make proof of loss if not made promptly by Borrower. Any insurance proceeds, whether or not the underlying insurance was required by Lender, will be applied to restoration or repair of the Property, if Lender deems the restoration or repair to be economically feasible and determines that Lender's security will not be lessened by such restoration or repair.

If the Property is to be repaired or restored, Lender will disburse from the insurance proceeds any initial amounts that are necessary to begin the repair or restoration, subject to any restrictions applicable to Lender. During the subsequent repair and restoration period, Lender will have the right to hold such insurance proceeds until Lender has had an opportunity to inspect such Property to ensure the work has been completed to Lender's satisfaction (which may include satisfying Lender's minimum eligibility requirements for persons repairing the Property, including, but not limited to, licensing, bond, and insurance requirements) provided that such inspection must be undertaken promptly. Lender may disburse proceeds for the repairs and restoration in a single payment or in a series of progress payments as the work is completed, depending on the size of the repair or restoration, the terms of the repair agreement, and whether Borrower is in Default on the Loan. Lender may make such disbursements directly to Borrower, to the person repairing or restoring the Property, or payable jointly to both. Lender will not be required to pay Borrower any interest or earnings on such insurance proceeds unless Lender and Borrower agree in writing or Applicable Law requires otherwise. Fees for public adjusters, or other third parties, retained by Borrower will not be paid out of the insurance proceeds and will be the sole obligation of Borrower.

If Lender deems the restoration or repair not to be economically feasible or Lender's security would be lessened by such restoration or repair, the insurance proceeds will be applied to the sums secured by this Security Instrument, whether or not then due, with the excess, if any, paid to Borrower. Such insurance proceeds will be applied in the order that Partial Payments are applied in Section 2(b).

(e) Insurance Settlements; Assignment of Proceeds. If Borrower abandons the Property, Lender may file, negotiate, and settle any available insurance claim and related matters. If Borrower does not respond within 30 days to a notice from Lender that the insurance carrier has offered to settle a claim, then Lender may negotiate and settle the claim. The 30-day period will begin when the notice is given. In either event, or if Lender acquires the Property under Section 26 or otherwise, Borrower is unconditionally assigning to Lender (i) Borrower's rights to any insurance proceeds in an amount not to exceed the amounts unpaid under the Note and this Security Instrument, and (ii) any other of Borrower's rights (other than the right to any refund of unearned premiums paid by Borrower) under all insurance policies covering the Property, to the extent that such rights are applicable to the coverage of the Property. If Lender files, negotiates, or settles a claim, Borrower agrees that any insurance proceeds may be made payable directly to Lender without the need to include Borrower as an additional loss payee. Lender may use the insurance proceeds either to repair or restore the Property (as provided in Section 5(d)) or to pay amounts unpaid under the Note or this Security Instrument, whether or not then due.

6. Occupancy. Borrower must occupy, establish, and use the Property as Borrower's principal residence within 60 days after the execution of this Security Instrument and must continue to occupy the Property as Borrower's principal residence for at least one year after the date of occupancy, unless Lender otherwise agrees in writing, which consent will not be unreasonably withheld, or unless extenuating circumstances exist that are beyond Borrower's control.

7. Preservation, Maintenance, and Protection of the Property; Inspections. Borrower will not destroy, damage, or impair the Property, allow the Property to deteriorate, or commit waste on the Property. Whether or not Borrower is residing in the Property, Borrower must maintain the Property in order to prevent the Property from deteriorating or decreasing in value due to its condition. Unless Lender determines pursuant to Section 5 that repair or restoration is not economically feasible, Borrower will promptly repair the Property if damaged to avoid further deterioration or damage.

If insurance or condemnation proceeds are paid to Lender in connection with damage to, or the taking of, the Property, Borrower will be responsible for repairing or restoring the Property only if Lender has released proceeds for such purposes. Lender may disburse proceeds for the repairs and restoration in a single payment or in a series of progress payments as the work is completed, depending on the size of the repair or restoration, the terms of the repair agreement, and whether Borrower is in Default on the Loan. Lender may make such disbursements directly to Borrower, to the person repairing or restoring the Property, or payable jointly to both. If the insurance or condemnation proceeds are not sufficient to repair or restore the Property, Borrower remains obligated to complete such repair or restoration.

Lender may make reasonable entries upon and inspections of the Property. If Lender has reasonable cause, Lender may inspect the interior of the improvements on the Property. Lender will give Borrower notice at the time of or prior to such an interior inspection specifying such reasonable cause.

8. Borrower's Loan Application. Borrower will be in Default if, during the Loan application process, Borrower or any persons or entities acting at Borrower's direction or with Borrower's knowledge or consent gave materially false, misleading, or inaccurate information or statements to Lender (or failed to provide Lender with material information) in connection with the Loan, including, but not limited to, overstating Borrower's income or assets, understating or failing to provide documentation of Borrower's debt obligations and liabilities, and misrepresenting Borrower's occupancy or intended occupancy of the Property as Borrower's principal residence.

9. Protection of Lender's Interest in the Property and Rights Under this Security Instrument.

(a) Protection of Lender's Interest. If: (i) Borrower fails to perform the covenants and agreements contained in this Security Instrument; (ii) there is a legal proceeding or government order that might significantly affect Lender's interest in the Property and/or rights under this Security Instrument (such as a proceeding in bankruptcy, probate, for condemnation or forfeiture, for enforcement of a lien that has priority or may attain priority over this Security Instrument, or to enforce laws or regulations); or (iii) Lender reasonably believes that Borrower has abandoned the Property, then Lender may do and pay for whatever is reasonable or appropriate to protect Lender's interest in the Property and/or rights under this Security Instrument, including protecting and/or assessing the value of the Property, and securing and/or repairing the Property. Lender's actions may include, but are not limited to: (I) paying any sums secured by a lien that has priority or may attain priority over this Security Instrument; (II) appearing in court; and (III) paying: (A) reasonable attorneys' fees and costs; (B) property inspection and valuation fees; and (C) other fees incurred for the purpose of protecting Lender's interest in the Property and/or rights under this Security Instrument, including its secured position in a bankruptcy proceeding. Securing the Property includes, but is not limited to, exterior and interior inspections of the Property, entering the Property to make repairs, changing locks, replacing or boarding up doors and windows, draining water from pipes, eliminating building or other code violations or dangerous conditions, and having utilities turned on or off. Although Lender may take action under this Section 9, Lender is not required to do so and is not under any duty or obligation to do so. Lender will not be liable for not taking any or all actions authorized under this Section 9.

(b) Avoiding Foreclosure; Mitigating Losses. If Borrower is in Default, Lender may work with Borrower to avoid foreclosure and/or mitigate Lender's potential losses, but is not obligated to do so unless required by Applicable Law. Lender may take reasonable actions to evaluate Borrower for available alternatives to foreclosure, including, but not limited to, obtaining credit reports, title reports, title insurance, property valuations, subordination agreements, and third-party approvals. Borrower authorizes and consents to these actions. Any costs associated with such loss mitigation activities may be paid by Lender and recovered from Borrower as described below in Section 9(c), unless prohibited by Applicable Law.

(c) Additional Amounts Secured. Any amounts disbursed by Lender under this Section 9 will become additional debt of Borrower secured by this Security Instrument. These amounts may bear interest at the Note rate from the date of disbursement and will be payable, with such interest, upon notice from Lender to Borrower requesting payment.

(d) Leasehold Terms. If this Security Instrument is on a leasehold, Borrower will comply with all the provisions of the lease. If Borrower acquires fee title to the Property, the leasehold and the fee title will not merge unless Lender agrees to the merger in writing.

10. Assignment of Rents.

(a) Assignment of Rents. If the Property is leased to, used by, or occupied by a third party ("Tenant"), Borrower is unconditionally assigning and transferring to Lender any Rents, regardless of to whom the Rents are payable. Borrower authorizes Lender to collect the Rents, and agrees that each Tenant will pay the Rents to Lender. However, Borrower will receive the Rents until (i) Lender has given Borrower notice of Default pursuant to Section 26, and (ii) Lender has given notice to the Tenant that the Rents are to be paid to Lender. This Section 10 constitutes an absolute assignment and not an assignment for additional security only.

(b) Notice of Default. If Lender gives notice of Default to Borrower: (i) all Rents received by Borrower must be held by Borrower as trustee for the benefit of Lender only, to be applied to the sums secured by the Security Instrument; (ii) Lender will be entitled to collect and receive all of the Rents; (iii) Borrower agrees to instruct each Tenant that Tenant is to pay all Rents due and unpaid to Lender upon Lender's written demand to the Tenant; (iv) Borrower will ensure that each Tenant pays all Rents due to Lender and will take whatever action is necessary to collect such Rents if not paid to Lender; (v) unless Applicable Law provides otherwise, all Rents collected by Lender will be applied first to the costs of taking control of and managing the Property and collecting the Rents, including, but not limited to, reasonable attorneys' fees and costs, receiver's fees, premiums on receiver's bonds, repair and maintenance costs, insurance premiums, taxes, assessments, and other charges on the Property, and then to any other sums secured by this Security Instrument; (vi) Lender, or any judicially appointed receiver, will be liable to account for only those Rents actually received; and (vii) Lender will be entitled to have a receiver appointed to take possession of and manage the Property and collect the Rents and profits derived from the Property without any showing as to the inadequacy of the Property as security.

(c) Funds Paid by Lender. If the Rents are not sufficient to cover the costs of taking control of and managing the Property and of collecting the Rents, any funds paid by Lender for such purposes will become indebtedness of Borrower to Lender secured by this Security Instrument pursuant to Section 9.

(d) Limitation on Collection of Rents. Borrower may not collect any of the Rents more than one month in advance of the time when the Rents become due, except for security or similar deposits.

(e) No Other Assignment of Rents. Borrower represents, warrants, covenants, and agrees that Borrower has not signed any prior assignment of the Rents, will not make any further assignment of the Rents, and has not performed, and will not perform, any act that could prevent Lender from exercising its rights under this Security Instrument.

(f) Control and Maintenance of the Property. Unless required by Applicable Law, Lender, or a receiver appointed under Applicable Law, is not obligated to enter upon, take control of, or maintain the Property before or after giving notice of Default to Borrower. However, Lender, or a receiver appointed under Applicable Law, may do so at any time when Borrower is in Default, subject to Applicable Law.

(g) Additional Provisions. Any application of the Rents will not cure or waive any Default or invalidate any other right or remedy of Lender. This Section 10 does not relieve Borrower of Borrower's obligations under Section 6.

This Section 10 will terminate when all the sums secured by this Security Instrument are paid in full.

11. Mortgage Insurance.

(a) Payment of Premiums; Substitution of Policy; Loss Reserve; Protection of Lender. If Lender required Mortgage Insurance as a condition of making the Loan, Borrower will pay the premiums required to maintain the Mortgage Insurance in effect. If Borrower was required to make separately designated payments toward the premiums for Mortgage Insurance, and (i) the Mortgage Insurance coverage required by Lender ceases for any reason to be available from the mortgage insurer that previously provided such insurance, or (ii) Lender determines in its sole discretion that such mortgage insurer is no longer eligible to provide the Mortgage Insurance coverage required by Lender, Borrower will pay the premiums required to obtain coverage substantially equivalent to the Mortgage Insurance previously in effect, at a cost substantially equivalent to the cost to Borrower of the Mortgage Insurance previously in effect, from an alternate mortgage insurer selected by Lender.

If substantially equivalent Mortgage Insurance coverage is not available, Borrower will continue to pay to Lender the amount of the separately designated payments that were due when the insurance coverage ceased to be in effect. Lender will accept, use, and retain these payments as a non-refundable loss reserve in lieu of Mortgage Insurance. Such loss reserve will be non-refundable, even when the Loan is paid in full, and Lender will not be required to pay Borrower any interest or earnings on such loss reserve.

Lender will no longer require loss reserve payments if Mortgage Insurance coverage (in the amount and for the period that Lender requires) provided by an insurer selected by Lender again becomes available, is obtained, and Lender requires separately designated payments toward the premiums for Mortgage Insurance.

If Lender required Mortgage Insurance as a condition of making the Loan and Borrower was required to make separately designated payments toward the premiums for

Mortgage Insurance, Borrower will pay the premiums required to maintain Mortgage Insurance in effect, or to provide a non-refundable loss reserve, until Lender's requirement for Mortgage Insurance ends in accordance with any written agreement between Borrower and Lender providing for such termination or until termination is required by Applicable Law. Nothing in this Section 11 affects Borrower's obligation to pay interest at the Note rate.

(b) Mortgage Insurance Agreements. Mortgage Insurance reimburses Lender for certain losses Lender may incur if Borrower does not repay the Loan as agreed. Borrower is not a party to the Mortgage Insurance policy or coverage.

Mortgage insurers evaluate their total risk on all such insurance in force from time to time, and may enter into agreements with other parties that share or modify their risk, or reduce losses. These agreements may require the mortgage insurer to make payments using any source of funds that the mortgage insurer may have available (which may include funds obtained from Mortgage Insurance premiums).

As a result of these agreements, Lender, another insurer, any reinsurer, any other entity, or any affiliate of any of the foregoing, may receive (directly or indirectly) amounts that derive from (or might be characterized as) a portion of Borrower's payments for Mortgage Insurance, in exchange for sharing or modifying the mortgage insurer's risk, or reducing losses. Any such agreements will not: (i) affect the amounts that Borrower has agreed to pay for Mortgage Insurance, or any other terms of the Loan; (ii) increase the amount Borrower will owe for Mortgage Insurance; (iii) entitle Borrower to any refund; or (iv) affect the rights Borrower has, if any, with respect to the Mortgage Insurance under the Homeowners Protection Act of 1998 (12 U.S.C. § 4901 *et seq.*), as it may be amended from time to time, or any additional or successor federal legislation or regulation that governs the same subject matter ("HPA"). These rights under the HPA may include the right to receive certain disclosures, to request and obtain cancellation of the Mortgage Insurance, to have the Mortgage Insurance terminated automatically, and/or to receive a refund of any Mortgage Insurance premiums that were unearned at the time of such cancellation or termination.

12. Assignment and Application of Miscellaneous Proceeds; Forfeiture.

(a) Assignment of Miscellaneous Proceeds. Borrower is unconditionally assigning the right to receive all Miscellaneous Proceeds to Lender and agrees that such amounts will be paid to Lender.

(b) Application of Miscellaneous Proceeds upon Damage to Property. If the Property is damaged, any Miscellaneous Proceeds will be applied to restoration or repair of the Property, if Lender deems the restoration or repair to be economically feasible and Lender's security will not be lessened by such restoration or repair. During such repair and restoration period, Lender will have the right to hold such Miscellaneous Proceeds until Lender has had an opportunity to inspect the Property to ensure the work has been completed to Lender's satisfaction (which may include satisfying Lender's minimum eligibility requirements for persons repairing the Property, including, but not limited to, licensing, bond, and insurance requirements) provided that such inspection must be undertaken promptly. Lender may pay for the repairs and restoration in a single disbursement or in a series of progress payments as the work is completed, depending on the size of the repair or restoration, the terms of the repair agreement, and whether Borrower is in Default on the Loan. Lender may make such disbursements directly to Borrower, to the person repairing or restoring the Property, or payable jointly to both. Unless Lender and Borrower agree in writing or Applicable Law requires interest to be paid on such Miscellaneous Proceeds, Lender will not be required to pay Borrower any interest or earnings on such Miscellaneous Proceeds. If Lender deems the restoration or repair not to be economically feasible or Lender's security would be lessened by such restoration or repair, the Miscellaneous Proceeds will be applied to the sums secured by this Security Instrument, whether or not then due, with the excess, if any, paid to Borrower. Such Miscellaneous Proceeds will be applied in the order that Partial Payments are applied in Section 2(b).

(c) Application of Miscellaneous Proceeds upon Condemnation, Destruction, or Loss in Value of the Property. In the event of a total taking, destruction, or loss in value of the Property, all of the Miscellaneous Proceeds will be applied to the sums secured by this Security Instrument, whether or not then due, with the excess, if any, paid to Borrower.

In the event of a partial taking, destruction, or loss in value of the Property (each, a "Partial Devaluation") where the fair market value of the Property immediately before the Partial Devaluation is equal to or greater than the amount of the sums secured by this Security Instrument immediately before the Partial Devaluation, a percentage of the Miscellaneous Proceeds will be applied to the sums secured by this Security Instrument unless Borrower and Lender otherwise agree in writing. The amount of the Miscellaneous Proceeds that will be so applied is determined by multiplying the total amount of the Miscellaneous Proceeds by a percentage calculated by taking (i) the total amount of the sums secured immediately before the Partial Devaluation, and dividing it by (ii) the fair market value of the Property immediately before the Partial Devaluation. Any balance of the Miscellaneous Proceeds will be paid to Borrower.

In the event of a Partial Devaluation where the fair market value of the Property immediately before the Partial Devaluation is less than the amount of the sums secured immediately before the Partial Devaluation, all of the Miscellaneous Proceeds will be applied to the sums secured by this Security Instrument, whether or not the sums are then due, unless Borrower and Lender otherwise agree in writing.

(d) Settlement of Claims. Lender is authorized to collect and apply the Miscellaneous Proceeds either to the sums secured by this Security Instrument, whether or not then due, or to restoration or repair of the Property, if Borrower (i) abandons the Property, or (ii) fails to respond to Lender within 30 days after the date Lender notifies Borrower that the Opposing Party (as defined in the next sentence) offers to settle a claim for damages. "Opposing Party" means the third party that owes Borrower the Miscellaneous Proceeds or the party against whom Borrower has a right of action in regard to the Miscellaneous Proceeds.

(e) Proceeding Affecting Lender's Interest in the Property. Borrower will be in Default if any action or proceeding begins, whether civil or criminal, that, in Lender's judgment, could result in forfeiture of the Property or other material impairment of Lender's interest in the Property or rights under this Security Instrument. Borrower can cure such a Default and, if acceleration has occurred, reinstate as provided in Section 20, by causing the action or proceeding to be dismissed with a ruling that, in Lender's judgment, precludes forfeiture of the Property or other material impairment of Lender's interest in the Property or rights under this Security Instrument. Borrower is unconditionally assigning to Lender the proceeds of any award or claim for damages that are attributable to the impairment of Lender's interest in the Property, which proceeds will be paid to Lender. All Miscellaneous Proceeds that are not applied to restoration or repair of the Property will be applied in the order that Partial Payments are applied in Section 2(b).

13. Borrower Not Released; Forbearance by Lender Not a Waiver. Borrower or any Successor in Interest of Borrower will not be released from liability under this Security Instrument if Lender extends the time for payment or modifies the amortization of the sums secured by this Security Instrument. Lender will not be required to commence proceedings against any Successor in Interest of Borrower, or to refuse to extend time for payment or otherwise modify amortization of the sums secured by this Security Instrument, by reason of any demand made by the original Borrower or any Successors in Interest of Borrower. Any forbearance by Lender in exercising any right or remedy including, without limitation, Lender's acceptance of payments from third persons, entities, or Successors in Interest of Borrower or in amounts less than the amount then due, will not be a waiver of, or preclude the exercise of, any right or remedy by Lender.

14. Joint and Several Liability; Signatories; Successors and Assigns Bound. Borrower's obligations and liability under this Security Instrument will be joint and several. However, any Borrower who signs this Security Instrument but does not sign the Note: (a) signs this Security Instrument to mortgage, grant, and convey such Borrower's interest in the Property under the terms of this Security Instrument; (b) signs this Security Instrument to waive any applicable inchoate rights such as dower and curtesy and any available homestead exemptions; (c) signs this Security Instrument to assign any Miscellaneous Proceeds, Rents, or other earnings from the Property to Lender; (d) is not personally obligated to pay the sums due under the Note or this Security Instrument; and (e) agrees that Lender and any other Borrower can agree to extend, modify, forbear, or make any accommodations with regard to the terms of the Note or this Security Instrument without such Borrower's consent and without affecting such Borrower's obligations under this Security Instrument.

Subject to the provisions of Section 19, any Successor in Interest of Borrower who assumes Borrower's obligations under this Security Instrument in writing, and is approved by Lender, will obtain all of Borrower's rights, obligations, and benefits under this Security Instrument. Borrower will not be released from Borrower's obligations and liability under this Security Instrument unless Lender agrees to such release in writing.

15. Loan Charges.

(a) Tax and Flood Determination Fees. Lender may require Borrower to pay (i) a one-time charge for a real estate tax verification and/or reporting service used by Lender in connection with this Loan, and (ii) either (A) a one-time charge for flood zone determination, certification, and tracking services, or (B) a one-time charge for flood zone determination and certification services and subsequent charges each time remappings or similar changes occur that reasonably might affect such determination or certification. Borrower will also be responsible for the payment of any fees imposed by the Federal Emergency Management Agency, or any successor agency, at any time during the Loan term, in connection with any flood zone determinations.

(b) Default Charges. If permitted under Applicable Law, Lender may charge Borrower fees for services performed in connection with Borrower's Default to protect Lender's interest in the Property and rights under this Security Instrument, including: (i) reasonable attorneys' fees and costs; (ii) property inspection, valuation, mediation, and loss mitigation fees; and (iii) other related fees.

(c) Permissibility of Fees. In regard to any other fees, the absence of express authority in this Security Instrument to charge a specific fee to Borrower should not be construed as a prohibition on the charging of such fee. Lender may not charge fees that are expressly prohibited by this Security Instrument or by Applicable Law.

(d) Savings Clause. If Applicable Law sets maximum loan charges, and that law is finally interpreted so that the interest or other loan charges collected or to be collected in connection with the Loan exceed the permitted limits, then (i) any such loan charge will be reduced by the amount necessary to reduce the charge to the permitted limit, and (ii) any sums already collected from Borrower which exceeded permitted limits will be refunded to Borrower. Lender may choose to make this refund by reducing the principal owed under the Note or by making a direct payment to Borrower. If a refund reduces principal, the reduction will be treated as a partial prepayment without any prepayment charge (whether or not a prepayment charge is provided for under the Note). To the extent permitted by Applicable Law, Borrower's acceptance of any such refund made by direct payment to Borrower will constitute a waiver of any right of action Borrower might have arising out of such overcharge.

16. Notices; Borrower's Physical Address. All notices given by Borrower or Lender in connection with this Security Instrument must be in writing.

(a) Notices to Borrower. Unless Applicable Law requires a different method, any written notice to Borrower in connection with this Security Instrument will be deemed to have been given to Borrower when (i) mailed by first class mail, or (ii) actually delivered to Borrower's Notice Address (as defined in Section 16(c) below) if sent by means other than first class mail or Electronic Communication (as defined in Section 16(b) below). Notice to any one Borrower will constitute notice to all Borrowers unless Applicable Law expressly requires otherwise. If any notice to Borrower required by this Security Instrument is also required under Applicable Law, the Applicable Law requirement will satisfy the corresponding requirement under this Security Instrument.

(b) Electronic Notice to Borrower. Unless another delivery method is required by Applicable Law, Lender may provide notice to Borrower by e-mail or other electronic communication ("Electronic Communication") if: (i) agreed to by Lender and Borrower in writing; (ii) Borrower has provided Lender with Borrower's e-mail or other electronic address ("Electronic Address"); (iii) Lender provides Borrower with the option to receive notices by first class mail or by other non-Electronic Communication instead of by Electronic Communication; and (iv) Lender otherwise complies with Applicable Law. Any notice to Borrower sent by Electronic Communication in connection with this Security Instrument will be deemed to have been given to Borrower when sent unless Lender becomes aware that such notice is not delivered. If Lender becomes aware that any notice sent by Electronic Communication is not delivered, Lender will resend such communication to Borrower by first class mail or by other non-Electronic Communication. Borrower may withdraw the agreement to receive Electronic Communications from Lender at any time by providing written notice to Lender of Borrower's withdrawal of such agreement.

(c) Borrower's Notice Address. The address to which Lender will send Borrower notice ("Notice Address") will be the Property Address unless Borrower has designated a different address by written notice to Lender. If Lender and Borrower have agreed that notice may be given by Electronic Communication, then Borrower may designate an Electronic Address as Notice Address. Borrower will promptly notify Lender of Borrower's change of Notice Address, including any changes to Borrower's Electronic Address if designated as Notice Address. If Lender specifies a procedure for reporting Borrower's change of Notice Address, then Borrower will report a change of Notice Address only through that specified procedure.

(d) Notices to Lender. Any notice to Lender will be given by delivering it or by mailing it by first class mail to Lender's address stated in this Security Instrument unless Lender has designated another address (including an Electronic Address) by notice to Borrower. Any notice in connection with this Security Instrument will be deemed to have been given to Lender only when actually received by Lender at Lender's designated address (which may include an Electronic Address). If any notice to Lender required by this Security Instrument is also required under Applicable Law, the Applicable Law requirement will satisfy the corresponding requirement under this Security Instrument.

(e) Borrower's Physical Address. In addition to the designated Notice Address, Borrower will provide Lender with the address where Borrower physically resides, if different from the Property Address, and notify Lender whenever this address changes.

17. Governing Law; Severability; Rules of Construction. This Security Instrument is governed by federal law and the law of the State of Maryland. All rights and obligations contained in this Security Instrument are subject to any requirements and limitations of Applicable Law. If any provision of this Security Instrument or the Note conflicts with Applicable Law (i) such conflict will not affect other provisions of this Security Instrument or the Note that can be given effect without the conflicting provision, and (ii) such conflicting provision, to the extent possible, will be considered modified to comply with Applicable Law. Applicable Law might explicitly or implicitly allow the parties to agree by contract or it might be silent, but such silence should not be construed as a prohibition against agreement by contract. Any action required under this Security Instrument to be made in accordance with Applicable Law is to be made in accordance with the Applicable Law in effect at the time the action is undertaken.

As used in this Security Instrument: (a) words in the singular will mean and include the plural and vice versa; (b) the word "may" gives sole discretion without any obligation to take any action; (c) any reference to "Section" in this document refers to Sections contained in this Security Instrument unless otherwise noted; and (d) the headings and captions are inserted for convenience of reference and do not define, limit, or describe the scope or intent of this Security Instrument or any particular Section, paragraph, or provision.

18. Borrower's Copy. One Borrower will be given one copy of the Note and of this Security Instrument.

19. Transfer of the Property or a Beneficial Interest in Borrower. For purposes of this Section 19 only, "Interest in the Property" means any legal or beneficial interest in the Property, including, but not limited to, those beneficial interests transferred in a bond for deed, contract for deed, installment sales contract, or escrow agreement, the intent of which is the transfer of title by Borrower to a purchaser at a future date.

If all or any part of the Property or any Interest in the Property is sold or transferred (or if Borrower is not a natural person and a beneficial interest in Borrower is sold or transferred) without Lender's prior written consent, Lender may require immediate payment in full of all sums secured by this Security Instrument. However, Lender will not exercise this option if such exercise is prohibited by Applicable Law.

If Lender exercises this option, Lender will give Borrower notice of acceleration. The notice will provide a period of not less than 30 days from the date the notice is given in accordance with Section 16 within which Borrower must pay all sums secured by this Security Instrument. If Borrower fails to pay these sums prior to, or upon, the expiration of this period, Lender may invoke any remedies permitted by this Security Instrument without further notice or demand on Borrower and will be entitled to collect all expenses incurred in pursuing such remedies, including, but not limited to: (a) reasonable attorneys' fees and costs; (b) property inspection and valuation fees; and (c) other fees incurred to protect Lender's Interest in the Property and/or rights under this Security Instrument.

20. Borrower's Right to Reinstate the Loan after Acceleration. If Borrower meets certain conditions, Borrower will have the right to reinstate the Loan and have enforcement of this Security Instrument discontinued at any time up to the later of (a) five days before any foreclosure sale of the Property, or (b) such other period as Applicable Law might specify for the termination of Borrower's right to reinstate. This right to reinstate will not apply in the case of acceleration under Section 19.

To reinstate the Loan, Borrower must satisfy all of the following conditions: (aa) pay Lender all sums that then would be due under this Security Instrument and the Note as if no acceleration had occurred; (bb) cure any Default of any other covenants or agreements under this Security Instrument or the Note; (cc) pay all expenses incurred in enforcing this Security Instrument or the Note, including, but not limited to: (i) reasonable attorneys' fees and costs; (ii) property inspection and valuation fees; and (iii) other fees incurred to protect Lender's interest in the Property and/or rights under this Security Instrument or the Note; and (dd) take such action as Lender may reasonably require to assure that Lender's interest in the Property and/or rights under this Security Instrument or the Note, and Borrower's obligation to pay the sums secured by this Security Instrument or the Note, will continue unchanged.

Lender may require that Borrower pay such reinstatement sums and expenses in one or more of the following forms, as selected by Lender: (aaa) cash; (bbb) money order; (ccc) certified check, bank check, treasurer's check, or cashier's check, provided any such check is drawn upon an institution whose deposits are insured by a U.S. federal agency, instrumentality, or entity; or (ddd) Electronic Fund Transfer. Upon Borrower's reinstatement of the Loan, this Security Instrument and obligations secured by this Security Instrument will remain fully effective as if no acceleration had occurred.

21. Sale of Note. The Note or a partial interest in the Note, together with this Security Instrument, may be sold or otherwise transferred one or more times. Upon such a sale or other transfer, all of Lender's rights and obligations under this Security Instrument will convey to Lender's successors and assigns.

22. Loan Servicer. Lender may take any action permitted under this Security Instrument through the Loan Servicer or another authorized representative, such as a sub-servicer. Borrower understands that the Loan Servicer or other authorized representative of Lender has the right and authority to take any such action.

The Loan Servicer may change one or more times during the term of the Note. The Loan Servicer may or may not be the holder of the Note. The Loan Servicer has the right and authority to: (a) collect Periodic Payments and any other amounts due under the Note and this Security Instrument; (b) perform any other mortgage loan servicing obligations; and (c) exercise any rights under the Note, this Security Instrument, and Applicable Law on behalf of Lender. If there is a change of the Loan Servicer, Borrower will be given written notice of the change which will state the name and address of the new Loan Servicer, the address to which payments should be made, and any other information RESPA requires in connection with a notice of transfer of servicing.

23. Notice of Grievance. Until Borrower or Lender has notified the other party (in accordance with Section 16) of an alleged breach and afforded the other party a reasonable period after the giving of such notice to take corrective action, neither Borrower nor Lender may commence, join, or be joined to any judicial action (either as an individual litigant or a member of a class) that (a) arises from the other party's actions pursuant to this Security Instrument or the Note, or (b) alleges that the other party has breached any provision of this Security Instrument or the Note. If Applicable Law provides a time period that must elapse before certain action can be taken, that time period will be deemed to be reasonable for purposes of this Section 23. The notice of Default given to Borrower pursuant to Section 26(a) and the notice of acceleration given to Borrower pursuant to Section 19 will be deemed to satisfy the notice and opportunity to take corrective action provisions of this Section 23.

24. Hazardous Substances.

(a) Definitions. As used in this Section 24: (i) "Environmental Law" means any Applicable Laws where the Property is located that relate to health, safety, or environmental protection; (ii) "Hazardous Substances" include (A) those substances defined as toxic or hazardous substances, pollutants, or wastes by Environmental Law, and (B) the following substances: gasoline, kerosene, other flammable or toxic petroleum products, toxic pesticides and herbicides, volatile solvents, materials containing asbestos or formaldehyde, corrosive materials or agents, and radioactive materials; (iii) "Environmental Cleanup" includes any response action, remedial action, or removal action, as defined in Environmental Law; and (iv) an "Environmental Condition" means a condition that can cause, contribute to, or otherwise trigger an Environmental Cleanup.

(b) Restrictions on Use of Hazardous Substances. Borrower will not cause or permit the presence, use, disposal, storage, or release of any Hazardous Substances, or threaten to release any Hazardous Substances, on or in the Property. Borrower will not do, nor allow anyone else to do, anything affecting the Property that: (i) violates Environmental Law; (ii) creates an Environmental Condition; or (iii) due to the presence, use, or release of a Hazardous Substance, creates a condition that adversely affects or could adversely affect the value of the Property. The preceding two sentences will not apply to the presence, use, or storage on the Property of small quantities of Hazardous Substances that are generally recognized to be appropriate to normal residential uses and to maintenance of the Property (including, but not limited to, hazardous substances in consumer products).

(c) Notices; Remedial Actions. Borrower will promptly give Lender written notice of: (i) any investigation, claim, demand, lawsuit, or other action by any governmental or regulatory agency or private party involving the Property and any Hazardous Substance or Environmental Law of which Borrower has actual knowledge; (ii) any Environmental Condition, including but not limited to, any spilling, leaking, discharge, release, or threat of release of any Hazardous Substance; and (iii) any condition caused by the presence, use, or release of a Hazardous Substance that adversely affects the value of the Property. If Borrower learns, or is notified by any governmental or regulatory authority or any private party, that any removal or other remediation of any Hazardous Substance affecting the Property is necessary, Borrower will promptly take all necessary remedial actions in accordance with Environmental Law. Nothing in this Security Instrument will create any obligation on Lender for an Environmental Cleanup.

25. Electronic Note Signed with Borrower's Electronic Signature. If the Note evidencing the debt for this Loan is electronic, Borrower acknowledges and represents to Lender that Borrower: (a) expressly consented and intended to sign the electronic Note using an Electronic Signature adopted by Borrower ("Borrower's Electronic Signature") instead of signing a paper Note with Borrower's written pen and ink signature; (b) did not withdraw Borrower's express consent to sign the electronic Note using Borrower's Electronic Signature; (c) understood that by signing the electronic Note using Borrower's Electronic Signature, Borrower promised to pay the debt evidenced by the electronic Note in accordance with its terms; and (d) signed the electronic Note with Borrower's Electronic Signature with the intent and understanding that by doing so, Borrower promised to pay the debt evidenced by the electronic Note in accordance with its terms.

NON-UNIFORM COVENANTS. Borrower and Lender further covenant and agree as follows:

26. Acceleration; Remedies.

(a) Notice of Default. Lender will give a notice of Default to Borrower prior to acceleration following Borrower's Default, except that such notice of Default will not be sent when Lender exercises its right under Section 19 unless Applicable Law provides otherwise. The notice will specify, in addition to any other information required by Applicable Law: (i) the Default; (ii) the action required to cure the Default; (iii) a date, not less than 30 days (or as otherwise specified by Applicable Law) from the date the notice is given to Borrower, by which the Default must be cured; (iv) that failure to cure the Default on or before the date specified in the notice may result in acceleration of the sums secured by this Security Instrument and sale of the Property; (v) Borrower's right to reinstate after acceleration; and (vi) Borrower's right to deny in the foreclosure proceeding the existence of a Default or to assert any other defense of Borrower to acceleration and sale.

(b) Acceleration; Power of Sale; Expenses. If the Default is not cured on or before the date specified in the notice, Lender may require immediate payment in full of all sums secured by this Security Instrument without further demand and may, in accordance with the requirements set forth under Applicable Law, invoke the power of sale, assent to decree, and/or any other remedies permitted by Applicable Law. Lender will be entitled to collect all expenses incurred in pursuing the remedies provided in this Section 26 as permitted under Applicable Law, including, but not limited to: (i) reasonable attorneys' fees and costs; (ii) property inspection and valuation fees; and (iii) other fees incurred to protect Lender's interest in the Property and/or rights under this Security Instrument.

(c) Notice of Sale; Sale of Property. If Lender invokes the power of sale, Lender will mail or cause Trustee to mail a notice of sale to Borrower and to other required recipients in the manner prescribed by Applicable Law. Trustee will give notice of sale by public advertisement and by such other means as required by Applicable Law. Trustee, without further demand on Borrower, will sell the Property at public auction to the highest bidder at the time and place and under the terms designated in the notice of sale in one or more parcels and in any order Trustee determines. Trustee may postpone sale of all or any parcel of the Property by public announcement at the time and place of any previously scheduled sale and by notice to any other persons as required by Applicable Law. Lender or its designee may purchase the Property at any sale.

(d) Trustee's Deed; Proceeds of Sale. Trustee will deliver to the purchaser a Trustee's deed conveying the Property without any covenant or warranty, expressed or implied. The recitals in the Trustee's deed will be prima facie evidence of the truth of the statements made in that deed. Trustee will apply the proceeds of the sale in the following order: (i) to all expenses of the sale, including, but not limited to, Trustee's fees of ____________________% of the gross sale price and reasonable attorneys' fees and costs; (ii) to all sums secured by this Security Instrument; and (iii) any excess to the person or persons legally entitled to it.

Borrower, in accordance with Title 14, Chapter 200 of the Maryland Rules of Procedure, does hereby declare and assent to the passage of a decree to sell the Property in one or more parcels by the equity court having jurisdiction for the sale of the Property, and consents to the granting to any trustee appointed by the assent to decree of all the rights, powers, and remedies granted to the Trustee in this Security Instrument together with any and all rights, powers, and remedies granted by the decree. Neither the assent to decree nor the power of sale granted in this Section 26 will be exhausted in the event the proceeding is dismissed before the payment in full of all sums secured by this Security Instrument.

27. Release. Upon payment of all sums secured by this Security Instrument, Lender or Trustee will release this Security Instrument and mark the Note "paid" and return the Note to Borrower. Borrower will pay any recordation costs associated with such release. Lender may charge Borrower a fee for releasing this Security Instrument only if the fee is paid to a third party for services rendered and is permitted under Applicable Law.

28. Substitute Trustee. Lender may, from time to time, by itself or through the Loan Servicer, remove Trustee and appoint a successor trustee to any Trustee appointed under this Security Instrument by an instrument recorded in the city or county in which this Security Instrument is recorded. Without conveyance of the Property, the successor trustee will succeed to all the rights, title, power, and duties conferred upon Trustee in this Security Instrument and by Applicable Law.

29. Possession of the Property. Borrower will have possession of the Property until Lender has given Borrower notice of Default pursuant to Section 26.

BY SIGNING BELOW, Borrower accepts and agrees to the terms and covenants contained in this Security Instrument and in any Rider signed by Borrower and recorded with it.

Witnesses:

______________________________ ______________________________ (Seal)

- Borrower

______________________________ ______________________________ (Seal)

- Borrower

________________ **[Space Below This Line For Acknowledgment]** ______________

F. [§ 5.83] FNMA Adjustable Rate Note

ADJUSTABLE RATE NOTE

(30-day Average SOFR Index (As Published by the Federal Reserve Bank of New York)–Rate Caps)

THIS NOTE CONTAINS PROVISIONS ALLOWING FOR CHANGES IN MY INTEREST RATE AND MY MONTHLY PAYMENT. THIS NOTE LIMITS THE AMOUNT MY ADJUSTABLE INTEREST RATE CAN CHANGE AT ANY ONE TIME AND THE MINIMUM AND MAXIMUM RATES I MUST PAY.

________________, ________ ____________________, ____________________

[Note Date] [City] [State]

____

[Property Address]

1. BORROWER'S PROMISE TO PAY

In return for a loan in the amount of U.S. $________________ (the "Principal") that I have received from ________________ (the "Lender"), I promise to pay the Principal, plus interest, to the order of the Lender. I will make all payments under this Note in U.S. currency in the form of cash, check, money order, or other payment method accepted by Lender.

I understand that the Lender may transfer this Note. The Lender or anyone who takes this Note by transfer and who is entitled to receive payments under this Note is called the "Note Holder."

2. INTEREST

Interest will be charged on unpaid Principal until the full amount of the Principal has been paid. I will pay interest at a yearly rate of __________%. The interest rate I will pay will change in accordance with Section 4 of this Note.

The interest rate required by this Section 2 and Section 4 of this Note is the rate I will pay both before and after any default described in Section 7(B) of this Note.

3. PAYMENTS

(A) Time and Place of Payments

I will pay principal and interest by making a payment every month. This amount is called my "Monthly Payment."

I will make my Monthly Payment on the first day of each month beginning on ______________, ______. I will make these payments every month until I have paid all of the Principal and interest and any other charges described below that I may owe under this Note. Each Monthly Payment will be applied as of its scheduled due date and will be applied to interest before the Principal. If, on ____________________, ____, I still owe amounts under this Note, I will pay those amounts on that date, which is called the "Maturity Date."

I will make my Monthly Payments at ____ or at a different place if required by the Note Holder.

(B) Amount of My Initial Monthly Payments

Each of my initial Monthly Payments will be in the amount of U.S. $____________________. This amount may change. This payment amount does not include any property taxes, insurance, or other charges that I may be required to pay each month.

(C) Monthly Payment Changes

Changes in my Monthly Payment will reflect changes in the unpaid Principal of my loan and in the interest rate that I must pay. The Note Holder will determine my new interest rate and the changed amount of my Monthly Payment in accordance with Section 4 of this Note.

4. INTEREST RATE AND MONTHLY PAYMENT CHANGES

(A) Change Dates

The interest rate I will pay may change on the first day of ______________________, _______, and on the first day of the month every 6th month thereafter. Each date on which my interest rate could change is called a "Change Date."

(B) The Index

Beginning with the first Change Date, my interest rate will be based on an Index that is calculated and provided to the general public by an administrator (the "Administrator"). The "Index" is a benchmark, known as the 30-day Average SOFR index. The Index is currently published by the Federal Reserve Bank of New York. The most recent Index value available as of the date 45 days before each Change Date is called the "Current Index," provided that if the Current Index is less than zero, then the Current Index will be deemed to be zero for purposes of calculating my interest rate.

If the Index is no longer available, it will be replaced in accordance with Section 4(G) below.

(C) Calculation of Changes

Before each Change Date, the Note Holder will calculate my new interest rate by adding _______ percentage points (___________%) (the "Margin") to the Current Index. The Margin may change if the Index is replaced by the Note Holder in accordance with Section 4(G)(2) below. The Note Holder will then round the result of the Margin plus the Current Index to the nearest one-eighth of one percentage point (0.125%). Subject to the limits stated in Section 4(D) below, this rounded amount will be my new interest rate until the next Change Date.

The Note Holder will then determine the amount of the Monthly Payment that would be sufficient to repay the unpaid Principal that I am expected to owe at the Change Date on the Maturity Date at my new interest rate in substantially equal payments. The result of this calculation will be the new amount of my Monthly Payment.

(D) Limits on Interest Rate Changes

The interest rate I am required to pay at the first Change Date will not be greater than _____________% or less than _____________%. Thereafter, my interest rate will never be increased or decreased on any single Change Date by more than one percentage point (1.0%) from the rate of interest I have been paying for the preceding 6 months, and will never be greater than _____________% or less than ___________%.

(E) Effective Date of Changes

My new interest rate will become effective on each Change Date. I will pay the amount of my new Monthly Payment beginning on the first Monthly Payment date after the Change Date until the amount of my Monthly Payment changes again.

(F) Notice of Changes

The Note Holder will deliver or mail to me a notice of any changes in my interest rate and the amount of my Monthly Payment before the effective date of any change. The notice will include information required by law to be given to me and also the title and telephone number of a person who will answer any question I may have regarding the notice.

(G) Replacement Index and Replacement Margin

The Index is deemed to be no longer available and will be replaced if any of the following events (each, a "Replacement Event") occur: (i) the Administrator has permanently or indefinitely stopped providing the Index to the general public; or (ii) the Administrator or its regulator issues an official public statement that the Index is no longer reliable or representative.

If a Replacement Event occurs, the Note Holder will select a new index (the "Replacement Index") and may also select a new margin (the "Replacement Margin"), as follows:

(1) If a replacement index has been selected or recommended for use in consumer products, including residential adjustable-rate mortgages, by the Board of Governors of the Federal Reserve System, the Federal Reserve Bank of New York, or a committee endorsed or convened by the Board of Governors of the

Federal Reserve System or the Federal Reserve Bank of New York at the time of a Replacement Event, the Note Holder will select that index as the Replacement Index.

(2) If a replacement index has not been selected or recommended for use in consumer products under Section (G)(1) at the time of a Replacement Event, the Note Holder will make a reasonable, good faith effort to select a Replacement Index and a Replacement Margin that, when added together, the Note Holder reasonably expects will minimize any change in the cost of the loan, taking into account the historical performance of the Index and the Replacement Index.

The Replacement Index and Replacement Margin, if any, will be operative immediately upon a Replacement Event and will be used to determine my interest rate and Monthly Payments on Change Dates that are more than 45 days after a Replacement Event. The Index and Margin could be replaced more than once during the term of my Note, but only if another Replacement Event occurs. After a Replacement Event, all references to the "Index" and "Margin" will be deemed to be references to the "Replacement Index" and "Replacement Margin."

The Note Holder will also give me notice of my Replacement Index and Replacement Margin, if any, and such other information required by applicable law and regulation.

5. BORROWER'S RIGHT TO PREPAY

I have the right to make payments of principal at any time before they are due. A payment of principal only is known as a "Prepayment." When I make a Prepayment, I will notify the Note Holder in writing that I am doing so. I may not designate a payment as a Prepayment if I have not made all the Monthly Payments then due under this Note.

I may make a full Prepayment or partial Prepayments without paying a Prepayment charge. The Note Holder will use my Prepayments to reduce the amount of Principal that I owe under this Note. However, the Note Holder may apply my Prepayment to the accrued and unpaid interest on the Prepayment amount, before applying my Prepayment to reduce the Principal amount of the Note. If I make a partial Prepayment, there will be no changes in the due date of my Monthly Payment unless the Note Holder agrees in writing to those changes. My partial Prepayment may reduce the amount of my Monthly Payments after the first Change Date following my partial Prepayment. However, any reduction due to my partial Prepayment may be offset by an interest rate increase.

6. LOAN CHARGES

If applicable law sets maximum loan charges, and that law is finally interpreted so that the interest or other loan charges collected or to be collected in connection with the loan exceed the permitted limits, then (a) any such loan charge will be reduced by the amount necessary to reduce the charge to the permitted limit, and (b) any sums already collected from me that exceeded permitted limits will be refunded to me. The Note Holder may choose to make this refund by reducing the Principal I owe under this Note or by making a direct payment to me. If a refund reduces Principal, the reduction will be treated as a partial Prepayment.

7. BORROWER'S FAILURE TO PAY AS REQUIRED

(A) Late Charges for Overdue Payments

If the Note Holder has not received the full amount of any Monthly Payment by the end of ______________ calendar days after the date it is due, I will pay a late charge to the Note Holder. The amount of the charge will be ______________% of my overdue Monthly Payment. I will pay this late charge promptly but only once on each late payment.

(B) Default

If I do not pay the full amount of each Monthly Payment on the date it is due, I will be in default.

(C) Notice of Default

If I am in default, the Note Holder may send me a written notice telling me that if I do not pay the overdue amount by a certain date, the Note Holder may require me to pay immediately the full amount of unpaid Principal, all the interest that I owe on that amount, and other charges due under this Note (the "Default Balance"). That date must be at least 30 days after the date on which the notice is mailed to me or delivered by other means.

(D) No Waiver By Note Holder

If I am in default and the Note Holder does not require me to pay the Default Balance immediately as described above, the Note Holder will still have the right to do so if I continue to be in default or if I am in default at a later time.

(E) Payment of Note Holder's Costs and Expenses

If the Note Holder has required me to pay the Default Balance immediately as described above, the Note Holder will have the right to be paid back by me for all of its costs and expenses in enforcing this Note to the extent not prohibited by applicable law. Those expenses include, for example, reasonable attorneys' fees and costs.

8. GIVING OF NOTICES

(A) Notice to Borrower

Unless applicable law requires a different method, any notice that must be given to me under this Note will be given by delivering it, or by mailing it by first class mail, to me at the Property Address above or at a different address if I give the Note Holder a notice of my different address. I will promptly notify the Note Holder of any change to my physical address and of any change to my mailing address. Unless applicable law requires otherwise, notice may instead be sent by e-mail or other electronic communication if agreed to by me and the Note Holder in writing and if I have provided the Note Holder with my current e-mail address or other electronic address. If I have agreed with the Note Holder that notice may be given by e-mail or other electronic communication, I will promptly notify the Note Holder of any changes to my e-mail address or other electronic address.

(B) Notice to Note Holder

Any notice that I must give to the Note Holder under this Note will be delivered by first class mail to the Note Holder at the address stated in Section 3(A) above or at a different address if I am given a notice of that different address.

9. OBLIGATIONS OF PERSONS UNDER THIS NOTE

If more than one person signs this Note, each person is fully and personally obligated to keep all of the promises made in this Note, including the promise to pay the full amount owed. Any person who is a guarantor, surety, or endorser of this Note is also obligated to do these things. Any person who takes over these obligations, including the obligations of a guarantor, surety, or endorser of this Note, is also obligated to keep all of the promises made in this Note. The Note Holder may enforce its rights under this Note against each person individually or against all of us together. This means that any one of us may be required to pay all of the amounts owed under this Note.

10. WAIVERS

I and any other person who has obligations under this Note waive the rights of Presentment and Notice of Dishonor. "Presentment" means the right to require the Note Holder to demand payment of amounts due. "Notice of Dishonor" means the right to require the Note Holder to give notice to other persons that amounts due have not been paid.

11. UNIFORM SECURED NOTE

This Note is a uniform instrument with limited variations in some jurisdictions. In addition to the protections given to the Note Holder under this Note, a Mortgage, Mortgage Deed, Deed of Trust, or Security Deed, as amended by the Adjustable Rate Rider (the "Security Instrument"), dated the same date as this Note, protects the Note Holder from possible losses that might result if I do not keep the promises that I make in this Note. That Security Instrument also describes how and under what conditions I may be required to make immediate payment of all amounts I owe under this Note. Some of those conditions are described as follows:

> If all or any part of the Property or any Interest in the Property is sold or transferred (or if Borrower is not a natural person and a beneficial interest in Borrower is sold or transferred) without Lender's prior written consent, Lender may require immediate payment in full of all sums secured by this Security Instrument. However, Lender will not exercise this option if such exercise is prohibited by Applicable Law. Lender also will not exercise this option if (a) Borrower causes to be submitted to Lender information required by Lender to evaluate the intended transferee as if a new loan were being made to the

transferee, and (b) Lender reasonably determines that Lender's security will not be impaired by the loan assumption and that the risk of a breach of any covenant or agreement in this Security Instrument is acceptable to Lender.

To the extent permitted by Applicable Law, Lender may charge a reasonable fee as a condition to Lender's consent to the loan assumption. Lender may also require the transferee to sign an assumption agreement that is acceptable to Lender and that obligates the transferee to keep all the promises and agreements made in the Note and in this Security Instrument. Borrower will continue to be obligated under the Note and this Security Instrument unless Lender releases Borrower in writing.

If Lender exercises this option to require immediate payment in full, Lender will give Borrower notice of acceleration. The notice will provide a period of not less than 30 days from the date the notice is given in accordance with Section 16 within which Borrower must pay all sums secured by this Security Instrument. If Borrower fails to pay these sums prior to, or upon, the expiration of this period, Lender may invoke any remedies permitted by this Security Instrument without further notice or demand on Borrower and will be entitled to collect all expenses incurred in pursuing such remedies, including, but not limited to: (a) reasonable attorneys' fees and costs; (b) property inspection and valuation fees; and (c) other fees incurred to protect Lender's Interest in the Property and/or rights under this Security Instrument.

WITNESS THE HAND(S) AND SEAL(S) OF THE UNDERSIGNED.

_______________________________(Seal)
-Borrower

_______________________________(Seal)
-Borrower

_______________________________(Seal)
-Borrower

[Sign Original Only]

G. [§ 5.84] FNMA Adjustable Rate Rider to Deed of Trust

FIXED/ADJUSTABLE RATE RIDER

(30-day Average SOFR Index (As Published by the Federal Reserve Bank of New York) – Rate Caps)

THIS FIXED/ADJUSTABLE RATE RIDER is made this ____ day of ________________, ______, and is incorporated into and amends and supplements the Mortgage, Mortgage Deed, Deed of Trust, or Security Deed (the "Security Instrument") of the same date given by the undersigned (the "Borrower") to secure Borrower's Fixed/Adjustable Rate Note (the "Note") to _______________________ (the "Lender") of the same date and covering the property described in the Security Instrument and located at:

____

[Property Address]

THE NOTE CONTAINS PROVISIONS ALLOWING FOR A CHANGE IN BORROWER'S FIXED INTEREST RATE TO AN ADJUSTABLE INTEREST RATE. THE NOTE LIMITS THE AMOUNT THE BORROWER'S ADJUSTABLE INTEREST RATE CAN CHANGE AT ANY ONE TIME AND THE MINIMUM AND MAXIMUM RATES THE BORROWER MUST PAY.

ADDITIONAL COVENANTS. In addition to the representations, warranties, covenants, and agreements made in the Security Instrument, Borrower and Lender further covenant and agree as follows:

A. INTEREST RATE AND MONTHLY PAYMENT CHANGES

The Note provides for monthly payments of interest and a portion of the principal ("Monthly Payment") and an initial fixed interest rate of ___________%. The Note also provides for a change in the initial fixed interest rate to an adjustable interest rate, as follows:

4. ADJUSTABLE INTEREST RATE AND MONTHLY PAYMENT CHANGES

(A) Change Dates

The initial fixed interest rate I will pay will change to an adjustable interest rate on the first day of __________, ______, and the adjustable interest rate I will pay may change on the first day of the month every 6th month thereafter. The date on which my initial fixed interest rate changes to an adjustable interest rate, and each date on which my adjustable interest rate could change is called a "Change Date."

(B) The Index

Beginning with the first Change Date, my adjustable interest rate will be based on an Index that is calculated and provided to the general public by an administrator (the "Administrator"). The "Index" is a benchmark, known as the 30-day Average SOFR index. The Index is currently published by the Federal Reserve Bank of New York. The most recent Index value available as of the date 45 days before each Change Date is called the "Current Index," provided that if the Current Index is less than zero, then the Current Index will be deemed to be zero for purposes of calculating my interest rate.

If the Index is no longer available, it will be replaced in accordance with Section 4(G) below.

(C) Calculation of Changes

Before each Change Date, the Note Holder will calculate my new interest rate by adding ____________ percentage points (___________%) (the "Margin") to the Current Index. The Margin may change if the Index is replaced by the Note Holder in accordance with Section 4(G)(2) below. The Note Holder will then round the result of the Margin plus the Current Index to the nearest one-eighth of one percentage point (0.125%). Subject to the limits stated in Section 4(D) below, this rounded amount will be my new interest rate until the next Change Date.

The Note Holder will then determine the amount of the Monthly Payment that would be sufficient to repay the unpaid Principal that I am expected to owe at the Change Date on the Maturity Date at my new interest rate in substantially equal payments. The result of this calculation will be the new amount of my Monthly Payment.

MULTISTATE FIXED/ADJUSTABLE RATE RIDER—30-day Average SOFR Form 3142 07/2021
—Single Family— Fannie Mae/Freddie Mac Uniform Instrument *Page 1 of 4*

(D) Limits on Interest Rate Changes

The interest rate I am required to pay at the first Change Date will not be greater than __________% or less than ___________%. Thereafter, my adjustable interest rate will never be increased or decreased on any single Change Date by more than one percentage point (1.0%) from the rate of interest I have been paying for the preceding 6 months, and will never be greater than ___________% or less than _________%.

(E) Effective Date of Changes

My new interest rate will become effective on each Change Date. I will pay the amount of my new Monthly Payment beginning on the first Monthly Payment date after the Change Date until the amount of my Monthly Payment changes again.

(F) Notice of Changes

The Note Holder will deliver or mail to me a notice of any changes in my initial fixed interest rate to an adjustable interest rate and of any changes in my adjustable interest rate before the effective date of any change. The notice will include the amount of my Monthly Payment, any information required by law to be given to me and also the title and telephone number of a person who will answer any question I may have regarding the notice.

(G) Replacement Index and Replacement Margin

The Index is deemed to be no longer available and will be replaced if any of the following events (each, a "Replacement Event") occur: (i) the Administrator has permanently or indefinitely stopped providing the Index to the general public; or (ii) the Administrator or its regulator issues an official public statement that the Index is no longer reliable or representative.

If a Replacement Event occurs, the Note Holder will select a new index (the "Replacement Index") and may also select a new margin (the "Replacement Margin"), as follows:

(1) If a replacement index has been selected or recommended for use in consumer products, including residential adjustable-rate mortgages, by the Board of Governors of the Federal Reserve System, the Federal Reserve Bank of New York, or a committee endorsed or convened by the Board of Governors of the Federal Reserve System or the Federal Reserve Bank of New York at the time of a Replacement Event, the Note Holder will select that index as the Replacement Index.

(2) If a replacement index has not been selected or recommended for use in consumer products under Section (G)(1) at the time of a Replacement Event, the Note Holder will make a reasonable, good faith effort to select a Replacement Index and a Replacement Margin that, when added together, the Note Holder reasonably expects will minimize any change in the cost of the loan, taking into account the historical performance of the Index and the Replacement Index.

The Replacement Index and Replacement Margin, if any, will be operative immediately upon a Replacement Event and will be used to determine my interest rate and Monthly Payments on Change Dates that are more than 45 days after a Replacement Event. The Index and Margin could be replaced more than once during the term of my Note, but only if another Replacement Event occurs. After a Replacement Event, all references to the "Index" and "Margin" will be deemed to be references to the "Replacement Index" and "Replacement Margin."

The Note Holder will also give me notice of my Replacement Index and Replacement Margin, if any, and such other information required by applicable law and regulation.

B. TRANSFER OF THE PROPERTY OR A BENEFICIAL INTEREST IN BORROWER

1. Until Borrower's initial fixed interest rate changes to an adjustable interest rate under the terms stated in Section A above, Section 19 of the Security Instrument will read as follows:

Transfer of the Property or a Beneficial Interest in Borrower. For purposes of this

Section 19 only, "Interest in the Property" means any legal or beneficial interest in the Property, including, but not limited to, those beneficial interests transferred in a bond for deed, contract for deed, installment sales contract or escrow agreement, the intent of which is the transfer of title by Borrower to a purchaser at a future date.

If all or any part of the Property or any Interest in the Property is sold or transferred (or if Borrower is not a natural person and a beneficial interest in Borrower is sold or transferred) without Lender's prior written consent, Lender may require immediate payment in full of all sums secured by this Security Instrument. However, Lender will not exercise this option if such exercise is prohibited by Applicable Law.

If Lender exercises this option, Lender will give Borrower notice of acceleration. The notice will provide a period of not less than 30 days from the date the notice is given in accordance with Section 16 within which Borrower must pay all sums secured by this Security Instrument. If Borrower fails to pay these sums prior to, or upon, the expiration of this period, Lender may invoke any remedies permitted by this Security Instrument without further notice or demand on Borrower and will be entitled to collect all expenses incurred in pursuing such remedies, including, but not limited to: (a) reasonable attorneys' fees and costs; (b) property inspection and valuation fees; and (c) other fees incurred to protect Lender's Interest in the Property and/or rights under this Security Instrument.

2. When Borrower's initial fixed interest rate changes to an adjustable interest rate under the terms stated in Section A above, Section 19 of the Security Instrument described in Section B1 above will then cease to be in effect, and the provisions of Section 19 of the Security Instrument will be amended to read as follows:

Transfer of the Property or a Beneficial Interest in Borrower. For purposes of this Section 19 only, "Interest in the Property" means any legal or beneficial interest in the Property, including, but not limited to, those beneficial interests transferred in a bond for deed, contract for deed, installment sales contract or escrow agreement, the intent of which is the transfer of title by Borrower to a purchaser at a future date.

If all or any part of the Property or any Interest in the Property is sold or transferred (or if Borrower is not a natural person and a beneficial interest in Borrower is sold or transferred) without Lender's prior written consent, Lender may require immediate payment in full of all sums secured by this Security Instrument. However, Lender will not exercise this option if such exercise is prohibited by Applicable Law. Lender also will not exercise this option if (a) Borrower causes to be submitted to Lender information required by Lender to evaluate the intended transferee as if a new loan were being made to the transferee, and (b) Lender reasonably determines that Lender's security will not be impaired by the loan assumption and that the risk of a breach of any covenant or agreement in this Security Instrument is acceptable to Lender.

To the extent permitted by Applicable Law, Lender may charge a reasonable fee as a condition to Lender's consent to the loan assumption. Lender may also require the transferee to sign an assumption agreement that is acceptable to Lender and that obligates the transferee to keep all the promises and agreements made in the Note and in this Security Instrument. Borrower will continue to be obligated under the Note and this Security Instrument unless Lender releases Borrower in writing.

If Lender exercises this option to require immediate payment in full, Lender will give Borrower notice of acceleration. The notice will provide a period of not less than 30 days from the date the notice is given in accordance with Section 16 within which Borrower must pay all sums secured by this Security Instrument. If Borrower fails to pay these sums prior to, or upon, the expiration of this period, Lender may invoke any remedies permitted by this Security Instrument without further notice or demand on Borrower and will be entitled to collect all expenses incurred in pursuing such remedies, including, but not limited to: (a) reasonable attorneys' fees and costs; (b) property inspection and valuation fees; and (c) other fees incurred to protect Lender's Interest in the Property and/or rights under this Security Instrument.

BY SIGNING BELOW, Borrower accepts and agrees to the terms and covenants contained in this Fixed/Adjustable Rate Rider.

.... (Seal)
-Borrower

.... (Seal)
-Borrower

H. [§ 5.85] Condominium Rider

CONDOMINIUM RIDER

THIS CONDOMINIUM RIDER is made this __________ day of ____________________________________,
__________, and is incorporated into and amends and supplements the Mortgage, Mortgage Deed, Deed of Trust, or Security Deed (the "Security Instrument") of the same date given by the undersigned (the "Borrower") to secure Borrower's Note to ____ (the "Lender") of the same date and covering the Property described in the Security Instrument and located at:

____
[Property Address]

The Property includes a unit in, together with an undivided interest in the common elements of, a condominium project known as:

____
[Name of Condominium Project]

(the "Condominium Project"). If the owners association or other entity which acts for the Condominium Project (the "Owners Association") holds title to property for the benefit or use of its members or shareholders, the Property also includes Borrower's interest in the Owners Association and the uses, proceeds, and benefits of Borrower's interest.

CONDOMINIUM COVENANTS. In addition to the representations, warranties, covenants, and agreements made in the Security Instrument, Borrower and Lender further covenant and agree as follows:

A. Condominium Obligations. Borrower will perform all of Borrower's obligations under the Condominium Project's Constituent Documents. The "Constituent Documents" are the: (i) Declaration or any other document which creates the Condominium Project; (ii) by-laws; (iii) code of regulations; and (iv) other equivalent documents. Borrower will promptly pay, when due, all dues and assessments imposed pursuant to the Constituent Documents.

B. Property Insurance. So long as the Owners Association maintains, with a generally accepted insurance carrier, a "master" or "blanket" policy on the Condominium Project which is satisfactory to Lender and which provides insurance coverage in the amounts (including deductible levels), for the periods, and against loss by fire, hazards included within the term "extended coverage," and any other hazards, including, but not limited to, earthquakes, winds, and floods, for which Lender requires insurance, then (i) Lender waives the provision in Section 3 for the portion of the Periodic Payment made to Lender consisting of the yearly premium installments for property insurance on the Property, and (ii) Borrower's obligation under Section 5 to maintain property insurance coverage on the Property is deemed satisfied to the extent that the required coverage is provided by the Owners Association policy.

What Lender requires as a condition of this waiver can change during the term of the loan.

Borrower will give Lender prompt notice of any lapse in required property insurance coverage provided by the master or blanket policy.

In the event of a distribution of property insurance proceeds in lieu of restoration or repair following a loss to the Property, whether to the unit or to common elements, any proceeds payable to Borrower are hereby assigned and will be paid to Lender for application to the sums secured by the Security Instrument, whether or not then due, with the excess, if any, paid to Borrower.

C. Public Liability Insurance. Borrower will take such actions as may be reasonable to insure that the Owners Association maintains a public liability insurance policy acceptable in form, amount, and extent of coverage to Lender.

D. Condemnation. The proceeds of any award or claim for damages, direct or consequential, payable to Borrower in connection with any condemnation or other taking of all or any part of the Property, whether of the unit or of the common elements, or for any conveyance in lieu of condemnation, are hereby assigned and will be paid to Lender. Such proceeds will be applied by Lender to the sums secured by the Security Instrument as provided in Section 12.

E. Lender's Prior Consent. Borrower will not, except after notice to Lender and with Lender's prior written consent, either partition or subdivide the Property or consent to: (i) the abandonment or termination of the Condominium Project, except for abandonment or termination required by law in the case of substantial destruction by fire or other casualty or in the case of a taking by condemnation or eminent domain; (ii) any amendment to any provision of the Constituent Documents unless the provision is for the

MULTISTATE CONDOMINIUM RIDER--Single Family--**Fannie Mae/Freddie Mac UNIFORM INSTRUMENT** **Form 3140** 07/2021
Page 1 of 2

express benefit of Lender; (iii) termination of professional management and assumption of self-management of the Owners Association; or (iv) any action which would have the effect of rendering the public liability insurance coverage maintained by the Owners Association unacceptable to Lender.

F. Remedies. If Borrower does not pay condominium dues and assessments when due, then Lender may pay them. Any amounts disbursed by Lender under this paragraph F will become additional debt of Borrower secured by the Security Instrument. Unless Borrower and Lender agree to other terms of payment, these amounts will bear interest from the date of disbursement at the Note rate and will be payable, with interest, upon notice from Lender to Borrower requesting payment.

BY SIGNING BELOW, Borrower accepts and agrees to the terms and covenants contained in this Condominium Rider.

_______________________________________ (Seal)
- Borrower

_______________________________________ (Seal)
- Borrower

I. [§ 5.86] PUD Rider

PLANNED UNIT DEVELOPMENT RIDER

THIS PLANNED UNIT DEVELOPMENT RIDER is made this ___________ day of ______________________, __________, and is incorporated into and amends and supplements the Mortgage, Mortgage Deed, Deed of Trust, or Security Deed (the "Security Instrument") of the same date, given by the undersigned (the "Borrower") to secure Borrower's Note to ____ (the "Lender") of the same date and covering the Property described in the Security Instrument and located at:

____

[Property Address]

The Property includes, but is not limited to, a parcel of land improved with a dwelling, together with other such parcels and certain common areas and facilities, as described in ____ (the "Declaration"). The Property is a part of a planned unit development known as ____

[Name of Planned Unit Development]

(the "PUD"). The Property also includes Borrower's interest in the homeowners association or equivalent entity owning or managing the common areas and facilities of the PUD (the "Owners Association") and the uses, benefits, and proceeds of Borrower's interest.

PUD COVENANTS. In addition to the representations, warranties, covenants, and agreements made in the Security Instrument, Borrower and Lender further covenant and agree as follows:

A. PUD Obligations. Borrower will perform all of Borrower's obligations under the PUD's Constituent Documents. The "Constituent Documents" are the: (i) Declaration; (ii) articles of incorporation, trust instrument, or any equivalent document which creates the Owners Association; and (iii) any by-laws or other rules or regulations of the Owners Association. Borrower will promptly pay, when due, all dues and assessments imposed pursuant to the Constituent Documents.

B. Property Insurance. So long as the Owners Association maintains, with a generally accepted insurance carrier, a "master" or "blanket" policy insuring the Property which is satisfactory to Lender and which provides insurance coverage in the amounts (including deductible levels), for the periods, and against loss by fire, hazards included within the term "extended coverage," and any other hazards, including, but not limited to, earthquakes, winds, and floods, for which Lender requires insurance, then (i) Lender waives the provision in Section 3 for the portion of the Periodic Payment made to Lender consisting of the yearly premium installments for property insurance on the Property, and (ii) Borrower's obligation under Section 5 to maintain property insurance coverage on the Property is deemed satisfied to the extent that the required coverage is provided by the Owners Association policy.

What Lender requires as a condition of this waiver can change during the term of the loan.

Borrower will give Lender prompt notice of any lapse in required property insurance coverage provided by the master or blanket policy.

In the event of a distribution of property insurance proceeds in lieu of restoration or repair following a loss to the Property, or to common areas and facilities of the PUD, any proceeds payable to Borrower are hereby assigned and will be paid to Lender. Lender will apply the proceeds to the sums secured by the Security Instrument, whether or not then due, with the excess, if any, paid to Borrower.

C. Public Liability Insurance. Borrower will take such actions as may be reasonable to insure that the Owners Association maintains a public liability insurance policy acceptable in form, amount, and extent of coverage to Lender.

D. Condemnation. The proceeds of any award or claim for damages, direct or consequential, payable to Borrower in connection with any condemnation or other taking of all or any part of the Property or the common areas and facilities of the PUD, or for any conveyance in lieu of condemnation, are hereby assigned and will be paid to Lender. Such proceeds will be applied by Lender to the sums secured by the Security Instrument as provided in Section 12.

E. Lender's Prior Consent. Borrower will not, except after notice to Lender and with Lender's prior written consent, either partition or subdivide the Property or consent to: (i) the abandonment or termination of the PUD, except for abandonment or termination required by law in the case of substantial destruction by fire or other casualty or in the case of a taking by condemnation or eminent domain; (ii) any amendment to any provision of the Constituent Documents unless the provision is for the express benefit of Lender; (iii) termination of professional management and assumption of self-management of the Owners Association; or (iv) any action which would have the effect of rendering the public liability insurance coverage maintained by the Owners Association unacceptable to Lender.

F. Remedies. If Borrower does not pay PUD dues and assessments when due, then Lender may pay them. Any amounts disbursed by Lender under this paragraph F will become additional debt of Borrower secured by the Security Instrument. Unless Borrower and Lender agree to other terms of payment, these amounts will bear interest from the date of disbursement at the Note rate and will be payable, with interest, upon notice from Lender to Borrower requesting payment.

BY SIGNING BELOW, Borrower accepts and agrees to the terms and covenants contained in this PUD Rider.

_______________________________________ (Seal)
- Borrower

_______________________________________ (Seal)
- Borrower

J. [§ 5.87] HUD-1 Settlement Sheet

OMB Approval No. 2502-0265

A. Settlement Statement (HUD-1)

B. Type of Loan			
1. ☐ FHA 2. ☐ RHS 3. ☐ Conv. Unins. 4. ☐ VA 5. ☐ Conv. Ins.	6. File Number:	7. Loan Number:	8. Mortgage Insurance Case Number:

C. Note: This form is furnished to give you a statement of actual settlement costs. Amounts paid to and by the settlement agent are shown. Items marked "(p.o.c.)" were paid outside the closing; they are shown here for informational purposes and are not included in the totals.

D. Name & Address of Borrower:	E. Name & Address of Seller:	F. Name & Address of Lender:
G. Property Location:	H. Settlement Agent:	I. Settlement Date:
	Place of Settlement:	

J. Summary of Borrower's Transaction		K. Summary of Seller's Transaction	
100. Gross Amount Due from Borrower		**400. Gross Amount Due to Seller**	
101. Contract sales price		401. Contract sales price	
102. Personal property		402. Personal property	
103. Settlement charges to borrower (line 1400)		403.	
104.		404.	
105.		405.	
Adjustment for items paid by seller in advance		**Adjustment for items paid by seller in advance**	
106. City/town taxes to		406. City/town taxes to	
107. County taxes to		407. County taxes to	
108. Assessments to		408. Assessments to	
109.		409.	
110.		410.	
111.		411.	
112.		412.	
120. Gross Amount Due from Borrower		**420. Gross Amount Due to Seller**	
200. Amount Paid by or in Behalf of Borrower		**500. Reductions In Amount Due to seller**	
201. Deposit or earnest money		501. Excess deposit (see instructions)	
202. Principal amount of new loan(s)		502. Settlement charges to seller (line 1400)	
203. Existing loan(s) taken subject to		503. Existing loan(s) taken subject to	
204.		504. Payoff of first mortgage loan	
205.		505. Payoff of second mortgage loan	
206.		506.	
207.		507.	
208.		508.	
209.		509.	
Adjustments for items unpaid by seller		**Adjustments for items unpaid by seller**	
210. City/town taxes to		510. City/town taxes to	
211. County taxes to		511. County taxes to	
212. Assessments to		512. Assessments to	
213.		513.	
214.		514.	
215.		515.	
216.		516.	
217.		517.	
218.		518.	
219.		519.	
220. Total Paid by/for Borrower		**520. Total Reduction Amount Due Seller**	
300. Cash at Settlement from/to Borrower		**600. Cash at Settlement to/from Seller**	
301. Gross amount due from borrower (line 120)		601. Gross amount due to seller (line 420)	
302. Less amounts paid by/for borrower (line 220)	( )	602. Less reductions in amounts due seller (line 520)	( )
303. Cash ☐ **From** ☐ **To Borrower**		**603. Cash** ☐ **To** ☐ **From Seller**	

The Public Reporting Burden for this collection of information is estimated at 35 minutes per response for collecting, reviewing, and reporting the data. This agency may not collect this information, and you are not required to complete this form, unless it displays a currently valid OMB control number. No confidentiality is assured; this disclosure is mandatory. This is designed to provide the parties to a RESPA covered transaction with information during the settlement process.

Previous edition are obsolete | Page 1 of 3 | HUD-1

L. Settlement Charges

700. Total Real Estate Broker Fees			Paid From Borrower's Funds at Settlement	Paid From Seller's Funds at Settlement
Division of commission (line 700) as follows :				
701. $ to				
702. $ to				
703. Commission paid at settlement				
704.				
800. Items Payable In Connection with Loan				
801. Our origination charge	$	(from GFE #1)		
802. Your credit or charge (points) for the specific interest rate chosen	$	(from GFE #2)		
803. Your adjusted origination charges		(from GFE #A)		
804. Appraisal fee to		(from GFE #3)		
805. Credit report to		(from GFE #3)		
806. Tax service to		(from GFE #3)		
807. Flood certification to		(from GFE #3)		
808.				
809.				
810.				
811.				
900. Items Required by Lender to be Paid in Advance				
901. Daily interest charges from to @ $ /day		(from GFE #10)		
902. Mortgage insurance premium for months to		(from GFE #3)		
903. Homeowner's insurance for years to		(from GFE #11)		
904.				
1000. Reserves Deposited with Lender				
1001. Initial deposit for your escrow account		(from GFE #9)		
1002. Homeowner's insurance months @ $ per month	$			
1003. Mortgage insurance months @ $ per month	$			
1004. Property Taxes months @ $ per month	$			
1005. months @ $ per month	$			
1006. months @ $ per month	$			
1007. Aggregate Adjustment	-$			
1100. Title Charges				
1101. Title services and lender's title insurance		(from GFE #4)		
1102. Settlement or closing fee	$			
1103. Owner's title insurance		(from GFE #5)		
1104. Lender's title insurance	$			
1105. Lender's title policy limit $				
1106. Owner's title policy limit $				
1107. Agent's portion of the total title insurance premium to	$			
1108. Underwriter's portion of the total title insurance premium to	$			
1109.				
1110.				
1111.				
1200. Government Recording and Transfer Charges				
1201. Government recording charges		(from GFE #7)		
1202. Deed $ Mortgage $ Release $				
1203. Transfer taxes		(from GFE #8)		
1204. City/County tax/stamps Deed $ Mortgage $				
1205. State tax/stamps Deed $ Mortgage $				
1206.				
1300. Additional Settlement Charges				
1301. Required services that you can shop for		(from GFE #6)		
1302.	$			
1303.	$			
1304.				
1305.				
1400. Total Settlement Charges (enter on lines 103, Section J and 502, Section K)				

Previous edition are obsolete Page 2 of 3 HUD-1

Comparison of Good Faith Estimate (GFE) and HUD-1 Charrges		Good Faith Estimate	HUD-1
Charges That Cannot Increase	**HUD-1 Line Number**		
Our origination charge	# 801		
Your credit or charge (points) for the specific interest rate chosen	# 802		
Your adjusted origination charges	# 803		
Transfer taxes	# 1203		

Charges That In Total Cannot Increase More Than 10%		Good Faith Estimate	HUD-1
Government recording charges	# 1201		
	#		
	#		
	#		
	#		
	#		
	#		
	#		
	Total		
	Increase between GFE and HUD-1 Charges	$ or	%

Charges That Can Change		Good Faith Estimate	HUD-1
Initial deposit for your escrow account	# 1001		
Daily interest charges $ /day	# 901		
Homeowner's insurance	# 903		
	#		
	#		
	#		

Loan Terms

Your initial loan amount is	$
Your loan term is	years
Your initial interest rate is	%
Your initial monthly amount owed for principal, interest, and any mortgage insurance is	$ includes ☐ Principal ☐ Interest ☐ Mortgage Insurance
Can your interest rate rise?	☐ No ☐ Yes, it can rise to a maximum of %. The first change will be on and can change again every after . Every change date, your interest rate can increase or decrease by %. Over the life of the loan, your interest rate is guaranteed to never be **lower** than % or **higher** than %.
Even if you make payments on time, can your loan balance rise?	☐ No ☐ Yes, it can rise to a maximum of $
Even if you make payments on time, can your monthly amount owed for principal, interest, and mortgage insurance rise?	☐ No ☐ Yes, the first increase can be on and the monthly amount owed can rise to $. The maximum it can ever rise to is $
Does your loan have a prepayment penalty?	☐ No ☐ Yes, your maximum prepayment penalty is $
Does your loan have a balloon payment?	☐ No ☐ Yes, you have a balloon payment of $ due in years on .
Total monthly amount owed including escrow account payments	☐ You do not have a monthly escrow payment for items, such as property taxes and homeowner's insurance. You must pay these items directly yourself. ☐ You have an additional monthly escrow payment of $ that results in a total initial monthly amount owed of $. This includes principal, interest, any mortagage insurance and any items checked below: ☐ Property taxes ☐ Homeowner's insurance ☐ Flood insurance ☐ ☐ ☐

Note: If you have any questions about the Settlement Charges and Loan Terms listed on this form, please contact your lender.

Previous edition are obsolete | Page 3 of 3 | HUD-1

K. [§ 5.88] HUD-1A Settlement Sheet

OMB Approval No. 2502-0265

Settlement Statement (HUD-1A)

Optional Form for Transactions without Sellers

Name and Address of Borrower:	Name and Address of Lender:
Property Location: (if different from above)	Settlement Agent:
	Place of Settlement:
Loan Number:	Settlement Date:

L. Settlement Charges	
800. Items Payable in Connection with Loan	
801. Our origination charge (from GFE #1) $	
802. Your credit or charge (points) for the specific interest rate chosen (from GFE #2) $	
803. Your adjusted origination charges (from GFE A)	
804. Appraisal fee to (from GFE #3)	
805. Credit report to (from GFE #3)	
806. Tax service to (from GFE #3)	
807. Flood certification (from GFE #3)	
808.	
900. Items Required by Lender to Be Paid in Advance	
901. Daily interest charges from to @ $ /day (from GFE #10)	
902. Mortgage insurance premium for months to ☐ (from GFE #3)	
903. Homeowner's insurance for years to ☐ (from GFE #11)	
904.	
1000. Reserves Deposited with Lender	
1001. Initial deposit for your escrow account (from GFE #9)	
1002. Homeowner's insurance months @ $ per month $	
1003. Mortgage insurance months @ $ per month $	
1004. Property taxes months @ $ per month $	
1005. months @ $ per month $	
1006. months @ $ per month $	
1007. Aggregate Adjustment –$	
1100. Title Charges	
1101. Title services and lender's title insurance (from GFE #4)	
1102. Settlement or closing fee $	
1103. Owner's title insurance (from GFE #5)	
1104. Lender's title insurance $	
1105. Lender's title policy limit $	
1106. Owner's title policy limit $	
1107. Agent's portion of the total title insurance premium $	
1108. Underwriter's portion of the total title insurance premium $	
1200. Government Recording and Transfer Charges	
1201. Government recording charges (from GFE #7)	
1202. Deed $ Mortgage $ Releases $	
1203. Transfer taxes (from GFE #8)	
1204. City/County tax/stamps Deed $ Mortgage $	
1205. State tax/stamps Deed $ Mortgage $	
1206.	
1300. Additional Settlement Charges	
1301. Required services that you can shop for (from GFE #6)	
1302. $	
1303. $	
1304.	
1305.	
1400. Total Settlement Charges (enter on line 1602, Section N)	

M. Disbursements to Others	
1501.	
1502.	
1503.	
1504.	
1505.	
1506.	
1507.	
1508.	
1509	
1510.	
1511.	
1512.	
1513.	
1514.	
1515.	
1520. Total Disbursed (enter on line 1603)	

N. Net Settlement	
1600. Loan Amount	$
1601. **Plus** Cash/Check from Borrower	$
1602. **Minus** Total Settlement Charges (line 1400)	$
1603. **Minus** Total Disbursements to Others (line 1520)	$
1604. **Equals** Total Disbursements to Borrower (after expiration of any applicable rescission period required by law)	**$**

The Public Reporting Burden for this collection of information is estimated at 35 minutes per response for collecting, reviewing, and reporting the data. This agency may not collect this information, and you are not required to complete this form, unless it displays a currently valid OMB control number. No confidentiality is assured; this disclosure is mandatory. This is designed to provide the parties to a RESPA covered transaction with information during the settlement process.

Previous editions are obsolete Page 1 of 2 HUD-1A

Comparison of Good Faith Estimate (GFE) and HUD-1A Charges		Good Faith Estimate	HUD-1A
Charges That Cannot Increase	**HUD-1A Line Number**		
Our origination charge	# 801		
Your credit or charge (points) for the specific interest rate chosen	# 802		
Your adjusted origination charges	# 803		
Transfer taxes	#1203		

Charges That in Total Cannot Increase More Than 10%		Good Faith Estimate	HUD-1A
Government recording charges	# 1201		
	#		
	#		
	#		
	#		
	#		
	#		
	#		
	Total		
	Increase between GFE and HUD-1A Charges	$ or %	

Charges That Can Change		Good Faith Estimate	HUD-1A
Initial deposit for your escrow account	#1001		
Daily interest charges	# 901 $ /day		
Homeowner's insurance	# 903		
	#		
	#		
	#		

Loan Terms

Your initial loan amount is	$
Your loan term is	years
Your initial interest rate is	%
Your initial monthly amount owed for principal, interest, and and any mortgage insurance is	$ includes ☐ Principal ☐ Interest ☐ Mortgage Insurance
Can your interest rate rise?	☐ No. ☐ Yes, it can rise to a maximum of %. The first change will be on and can change again every after . Every change date, your interest rate can increase or decrease by %. Over the life of the loan, your interest rate is guaranteed to never be lower than % or higher than %.
Even if you make payments on time, can your loan balance rise?	☐ No. ☐ Yes, it can rise to a maximum of $.
Even if you make payments on time, can your monthly amount owed for principal, interest, and mortgage insurance rise?	☐ No. ☐ Yes, the first increase can be on and the monthly amount owed can rise to $. The maximum it can ever rise to is $.
Does your loan have a prepayment penalty?	☐ No. ☐ Yes, your maximum prepayment penalty is $.
Does your loan have a balloon payment?	☐ No. ☐ Yes, you have a balloon payment of $ due in years on .
Total monthly amount owed including escrow account payments	☐ You do not have a monthly escrow payment for items, such as property taxes and homeowner's insurance. You must pay these items directly yourself. ☐ You have an additional monthly escrow payment of $ that results in a total initial monthly amount owed of $. This includes principal, interest, any mortgage insurance and any items checked below: ☐ Property taxes ☐ Homeowner's insurance ☐ Flood insurance ☐ ☐ ☐

Note: If you have any questions about the Settlement Charges and Loan Terms listed on this form, please contact your lender.

Previous editions are obsolete Page 2 of 2 HUD-1A

CHAPTER SIX

PRE-CLOSING PROBLEMS*

Matthew D. Alegi, Esq.
Erin M. August, Esq.
Danielle M. Dolch, Esq.
Kyle Kirby, Esq.
Hope Gouterman

Shulman Rogers, P.A.

* MSBA gratefully acknowledges the contributions to this chapter from previous authors Jeffrey H. Scherr, Esq., Herbert Burgunder, III, Esq. and Nichole M. Galvin, Esq.

ABOUT THE AUTHOR

Matthew D. Alegi, Esq.

Matthew D. Alegi, Esq. is a Shareholder at Shulman Rogers where he serves on the firm's Executive Committee and Board of Directors, and Co-Chairs the Real Estate Department. In his practice he advises real estate brokers, title insurance agents, mortgage loan originators, builders, and home improvement contractors regarding regulatory compliance, dispute resolution and day-to-day operations. Mr. Alegi also represents companies and individuals in buying, selling, financing and operating commercial and residential real estate, including related dispute resolution. He is a graduate of the Catholic University of America, Columbus School of Law (J.D. 2004) where he was an associate law journal editor and moot court associate, a past Member of the Section Council for the Real Property Section of the Maryland State Bar Association where he served as the inaugural Chair of its Title and Closings Committee, a Fellow of the Maryland Bar Foundation, and served as Chair or Co-Chair of the Bar Association of Montgomery County's Real Estate Law Section for over a decade.

Erin M. August, Esq.

Erin M. August, Esq. is an Associate in the Real Estate Department of Shulman Rogers. Her practice concentrates on residential and commercial real estate transactions, title insurance and closings, landlord-tenant, and real estate litigation. Ms. August received her law degree, with cum laude honors, from the University of Baltimore in 2012 and received her Bachelor of Arts in Psychology and Criminal Justice in 2001 from the University of Maryland. She is admitted to practice in Maryland, Washington, D.C., and Virginia and the U.S. District Court for the District of Maryland and the Eastern District of Virginia. Ms. August is a licensed Maryland, D.C. and Virginia title insurance producer; Member of the Maryland State Bar Association, American Bar Association and Montgomery County Bar Association.

Danielle M. Dolch, Esq.

Danielle M. Dolch, Esq. is a Shareholder in the Real Estate Department of Shulman Rogers. Her practice concentrates on commercial and residential real estate transactions, title insurance and closings, and advising real estate brokers on day-to-day operations and regulatory compliance. Ms. Dolch is a graduate of Gettysburg College (B.A. 2009) and the University of Maryland Francis King Carey School of Law (J.D. 2014). She is admitted to practice in Maryland, Pennsylvania, and the U.S. District Court for the Middle District of Pennsylvania. She is a licensed title insurance producer in Maryland, the District of Columbia, and Virginia. Ms. Dolch is a Member of the Section Council for the Real Property Section of the Maryland State Bar Association where she serves as Chair of the Real Estate Discussion Group Committee, a Fellow of the Maryland Bar Foundation, and a Fellow of the American Bar Association Section of Real Property, Trust and Estate Law where she serves as Vice-Chair of the Purchase and Sale Committee of the Commercial Real Estate Transactions Group.

Kyle Kirby, Esq.

Kyle Kirby, Esq. is an Associate in the Real Estate Department of Shulman Rogers. His practice concentrates on residential and commercial real estate transactions, title insurance and closings, leasing, real estate litigation, and financing. Mr. Kirby earned his law degree, with cum laude honors, from the University of Baltimore in 2012 and he obtained a Bachelor of Arts in Business Management in 2009 from James Madison University in Harrisonburg, VA. He is admitted to practice in Maryland and the U.S. District Court for the District of Maryland. Mr. Kirby is a licensed Maryland title insurance producer; Member of the Maryland State Bar Association, American Bar Association and Montgomery County Bar Association; Board Member on the Eastern Shore Revolving Loan Fund Committee; and Board Member on the Citizens Review Board for Children, Kent and Queen Anne's County, serving as the Chairman.

Hope Gouterman

Hope Gouterman is a current 3L at The Catholic University of America, Columbus School of Law. Hope is a Co-Lead Articles Editor on the Catholic University Law Review; a Member of the National Mock Trial Team; Member of the Students for Public Interest Law; and Student Member of the American Bar Association, D.C. Bar Law Student Community, Maryland State Bar Association and Virginia Bar Association. Hope was a Summer Associate with Shulman Rogers during 2023. Upon graduation from law school, Hope will be an Associate in the Real Estate Department of Shulman Rogers.

TABLE OF CONTENTS

I. [§ 6.1] INTRODUCTION

The period of time between contract and closing presents a number of challenges to a buyer and seller of residential real property. The problems that arise typically revolve around the condition of the property, damage to the property during the period, fulfilling the financing contingency, title insurance, and issues related to moving in or moving out. For most people, buying a home is the single largest investment they will ever make. Unlike the process of buying a car, buying a house does not involve a test drive. Issues will likely arise between the date of contract and the date of closing and buyers and sellers should be prepared to address any such issues that arise.

Most issues will be resolved by compromise. Once the parties have agreed on the terms of sale, they are usually motivated to proceed to closing. If a resolution cannot be negotiated, then litigation may result. This chapter describes common problems that arise before closing. It is intended to serve as both a guide to navigating a client's way through unexpected circumstances and as a practical approach to drafting a contract so that typical problems are anticipated and avoided.

Most "form" contracts cover the basics for typical deals. They do not, however, adequately anticipate all potential problems. The careful practitioner will customize a "form" contract to meet the needs of the situation. For example, a more thorough inspection might be needed for an older home. If financing might be difficult, the parties might want to broaden the language of the financing addendum to incorporate specific timetables for application, appraisal, and non-contingent approval. If the buyer needs to move in before closing or the seller needs to stay after closing, careful drafting can help your client to avoid occupancy problems.

Precise drafting will help your clients know what to do if any of these problems arise. While a contract cannot account for every potential problem (or it would be 50 pages long), simple drafting techniques and broad language that addresses common problem areas will resolve most disputes before they begin.

II. CONDITION OF THE PROPERTY

A. Responsibility for Condition of Property

1. [§ 6.2] Generally

Typically, the seller retains possession of the property until settlement. The party in possession (again, typically, the seller) is in the best position to guard against damage or injury to the property. Moreover, the seller typically has insurance on the property. For practical reasons (discussed below), it ordinarily makes sense for the seller to continue the existing insurance coverage during the contract period until closing. Therefore, most standardized form contracts used by realtors provide that the property shall be held at the risk of seller until execution and delivery of the deed at settlement or until the buyer takes possession. Accordingly, under most standardized form contracts, the seller remains responsible for maintenance of the property during the contract period. Some standardized form contracts provide that the seller shall deliver the property at settlement in substantially the same condition as existed on the date of contract ratification or acceptance. Other standardized form contracts allow for negotiation of this provision by giving the parties the option to select that the seller shall deliver the property at settlement in substantially the same condition to be determined as of (i) the date of the offer, (ii) the date of home inspection, or (iii) another date selected by the parties. The parties should be mindful of these options when negotiating the contract.

A thorough inspection near the date of contract will help reduce the chance of a dispute over any perceived change in condition. Therefore, the buyer might choose to negotiate for a home inspection contingency. Even if there is no contingency and the home inspection is for informational purposes only (i.e., the buyer has no right to terminate the contract or to negotiate for changes such as repairs, a closing credit, or a reduction in the purchase price), the home inspection may still be valuable, particularly in the event of a dispute. If there is a home inspection, then the parties will have a written report, prepared by an independent third party (the home inspector), that they may look to as evidence of the condition of the property in the event of a dispute. If there is a home inspection, then the parties might select "the date of home inspection" as the date for determining the condition of the property.

Most standardized form contracts attempt to differentiate between the general condition of the improvements and the condition of the systems. While most residential contracts convey property in "as is" condition, the inclusion of a clause requiring systems (electrical, heating, plumbing, etc.) to be in "working order" can cause a problem. Not everyone agrees about what constitutes "working order." A toilet that has a small leak but still flushes might or might not be in "working order." To avoid a dispute, a lawyer representing a seller should seek to delete such a phrase in favor of a strict "as is" clause. The strict "as is" clause is also consistent with the Disclaimer Statement that the seller might provide to prospective buyers as part of seller's disclosure obligations.

Responsibility for damage or loss occurring between execution of the contract and settlement depends on the type of loss and the specific terms of the contract. Unless modified by contract, the general rule in Maryland transfers the risk of loss to the buyer, notwithstanding that the seller typically retains possession of the property until settlement.[1] The following are examples of losses that occur after the contract is executed: a boiler "blows up," a settlement crack appears, paint begins to crack or peel, or trees are removed. If the damage is ordinary wear and tear, the buyer is responsible for the loss.[2] If the loss constitutes waste, then the seller is responsible.[3] Losses resulting from catastrophic events are discussed in Subtitle III.

2. *[§ 6.3] Ordinary wear and tear*

The buyer is responsible for damage or loss that is ordinary wear and tear.[4] Ordinary wear and tear is natural deterioration that occurs from usual and proper use of the premises.[5] In Maryland, "a present possessor is required to preserve the property essentially unchanged in value and character, in anticipation of the time when the future interest ripens into possession."[6] Buyers of vacant houses should be careful about determining the condition of the house at the time of contract ratification. If the air conditioning is turned off or the house has been "winterized," the house's condition might change substantially between the date of the contract and the date of closing. If the air conditioning system cannot be tested, then the buyer

---

1 *See Royal Ins. Co. v. Drury*, 150 Md. 211, 221, 132 A. 635, 639 (1926) ("Whatever the rule may be elsewhere, it has been repeatedly decided and is now definitely established in Maryland that, in equity, 'from the time the owner of an estate enters into a binding agreement for its sale he holds the same in trust for the purchaser, and the latter becomes a trustee of the purchase money for the vendor, and being thus, in equity, the owner, the vendee must bear any loss which may happen, and is entitled to any benefit which may accrue to the estate in the interim between the agreement and the conveyance.'" (quoting *Brewer v. Herbert*, 30 Md. 301, 308 (1869))); 19A Maryland Law Encyclopedia *Sales of Realty* § 63 (2017) ("Unless there is an agreement providing otherwise, the consequences of an accidental loss pending a contract of sale of real estate fall on the person who is the owner at the time of the loss and since the purchaser under a contract of sale is regarded in equity as the owner, the property sold is at the risk of the purchaser, who must bear all subsequent losses and is entitled to all subsequent gains.").

2 2 Milton R. Friedman & James Charles Smith, Friedman and Smith on Contracts and Conveyances of Real Property §18:1.6 (8th ed. 2017).

3 11 Thompson on Real Property, Third Thomas Edition § 96.06(b)(8) (David A. Thompson ed., 2015); 77 Am. Jur. 2d *Vendor and Purchaser* §§ 297, 299 (2016); Friedman & Smith, *supra* note 2.

4 14 Michael Allan Wolf, Powell on Real Property § 81.03 (2023).

5 77 Am. Jur. 2d *Vendor and Purchaser* § 299 (2016); *see also* Friedman & Smith, *supra* note 2 ("All property necessarily deteriorates in the interval between the date of contract and the closing. This is usually the gradual and virtually imperceptible effect of ordinary use and exposure to weather.").

6 *Boucher Invs., L.P. v. Annapolis-West Ltd. P'ship*, 141 Md. App. 1, 15, 784 A.2d 39, 47 (2001) (citation omitted); *see also* 8 Thompson on Real Property, Third Thomas Edition § 70.02 (David A. Thompson ed., 2016).

might consider negotiating for a post-settlement inspection contingency for the air conditioning system, which is an optional inspection contingency included in some standardized form contracts. Some standardized form contracts also include an optional inspection contingency for a post-settlement pool inspection.

3. [§ 6.4] Waste

The seller is responsible for loss or damage that constitutes waste.[7] Waste occurs when one physically damages the real estate, whether negligently or intentionally, or fails to maintain and repair the real estate in a reasonable manner, except for repair of casualty damage or acts of third parties not the fault of the seller.[8]

Waste is prohibited by statute in Maryland.[9] Thus, the seller has a duty to take reasonable care of the premises and, if ordinary maintenance is necessary to prevent waste, the seller is responsible for resultant damage for failure to do so.[10] Two types of waste recognized in Maryland cases are voluntary waste and permissive waste.[11] Voluntary waste is an act of destruction such as damaging the property or removing something fixed or attached to the property.[12] Permissive waste is the failure of the seller to exercise the care of a reasonable person to preserve and protect the property for the benefit of the buyer.[13]

The seller is liable to the buyer for actual damages caused to the property when the seller commits waste.[14] There are two principal ways the buyer may recover damages when the seller commits waste. The buyer may seek abatement of the purchase price based on the damages, which damages may be measured by diminution in property value or cost of restoration, as appropriate.[15] Otherwise, the buyer may bring an action for damages against the seller pursuant to REAL PROP.

---

7 WOLF, *supra* note 4.

8 *Boucher Invs., L.P.*, 141 Md. App. at 17, 784 A.2d at 48.

9 MD. CODE ANN., REAL PROPERTY (hereinafter REAL PROP.) § 14-102 (providing that a mortgagor, tenant, or any other person in possession of land who, without express or implied authorization, commits or permits waste is liable for actual damages suffered by the property).

10 *Coutant v. Coutant*, 86 Md. App. 581, 596, 587 A.2d 1125, 1132 (1991) (holding that wife's failure to repair the septic system was neglect constituting permissive waste for which the wife was responsible for the cost of repair); *see also* WOLF, *supra* note 4.

11 *Boucher Invs., L.P.*, 141 Md. App. 1, 784 A.2d 39.

12 *Id.* at 18, 784 A.2d at 49; *see also* 8 MICHAEL ALLAN WOLF, POWELL ON REAL PROPERTY § 56.05 (2023) ("The main situations involving affirmative waste continue to be (1) cutting down trees for timber; (2) removing minerals, including oil and gas; and (3) destroying or altering improvements located on the property.").

13 *Boucher Invs., L.P.*, 141 Md. App. at 18, 784 A.2d at 49; *see also* 78 AM. JUR. 2D *Waste* § 5 (2016) ("Permissive waste results from negligence or the omission to do that which would prevent injury.") (internal quotation marks omitted).

14 REAL PROP. § 14-102.

15 THOMPSON ON REAL PROPERTY, *supra* note 6, § 70.13(d).

§ 14-102. The buyer may be able to seek injunctive relief pursuant to REAL PROP. § 14-102.[16] Also, if the contract includes a covenant to not commit or permit waste, then the buyer may have a breach of contract claim against the seller.[17]

The general rule of merger is that all negotiations and agreements leading up to delivery of the deed are merged into it.[18] However, the doctrine of merger is not absolute, and one exception to the presumption of merger is "where the agreement contains covenants collateral to the deed or where the deed appears to be only a partial execution of the contract."[19] In other words, collateral conditions do not merge into the deed where such conditions are not incorporated into the deed and are not otherwise inconsistent with the deed.[20] In Maryland, the rule of merger does not prevent the buyer from bringing an action after settlement with respect to non-merged terms.[21] Therefore, it might be possible for a buyer to bring an action for waste committed by the seller during the interim occupancy, if assent to seller's waste is not manifest at settlement.[22] The practical solution, however, is to appropriately adjust

---

16 *See Beesley v. Hanish*, 70 Md. App. 482, 493, 521 A.2d 1235, 1240 (1987) ("The right to sue for waste generally encompasses the right to restrain its commission."); *Redwood Hotel, Inc. v. Korbien*, 195 Md. 402, 73 A.2d 468 (1950) (noting that landlord has a right to seek an injunction to preclude tenant from committing waste).

17 THOMPSON ON REAL PROPERTY, *supra* note 6, § 70.13(d).

18 *Dorsey v. Beads*, 288 Md. 161, 170, 416 A.2d 739, 744 (1980) ("It is an accepted rule that a *prima facie* presumption arises from the acceptance of a deed that it is an execution of the entire agreement for the sale of the realty, and the rights of the parties in relation to the agreement are to be determined by the deed." (quoting *Barrie v. Abate*, 209 Md. 578, 583, 121 A.2d 862, 864 (1956))); *Rosenthal v. Heft*, 155 Md. 410, 418, 142 A. 598, 602 (1928) (noting the general rule that "a contract for the sale of land becomes null and void when a deed conveying the property to the purchaser is executed and accepted").

19 *Prime Venturers v. OneWest Bank Group, LLC*, 213 Md. App. 122, 137, 73 A.3d 361, 370 (2013) (quoting *Levin v. Cook*, 186 Md. 535, 539, 47 A.2d 505, 507 (1946)); *see also* Barry M. Goldman & Victoria Smouse Berghel, *Common Law Doctrine of Merger: The Exceptions Are the Rule*, 13 U. BALT. L. REV. 19, 22-23, 25 (1983) (noting that collateral covenants "are interpreted narrowly to mean any agreements contained in a contract that are not directly related to the agreement to sell or buy real estate" and "[t]he distinction between a partial execution and a collateral covenant is a subtle one").

20 *Barrie v. Abate*, 209 Md. 578, 583, 121 A.2d 862, 864 (1956) (noting that "parol evidence may be given of collateral facts relating to an agreement for the sale of realty, even though a deed has been executed, if the facts are consistent with the deed and do not tend to contradict it"); *Dorsey*, 288 Md. at 170-71, 416 A.2d at 744-45 ("Generally, contract provisions as to title, possession, quantity, or emblements of land are conclusively presumed to be merged into the subsequently delivered and accepted deed, even though the contract and deed vary." (internal citation omitted)).

21 *See Dorsey*, 288 Md. 161, 416 A.2d 739; *Laurel Realty Co. v. Himelfarb*, 194 Md. 672, 72 A.2d 23 (1950); *Stevens v. Milestone*, 190 Md. 61, 57 A.2d 292 (1948); *Levin v. Cook*, 186 Md. 535, 47 A.2d 505 (1946); *see generally* Goldman & Berghel, *supra* note 19.

22 THOMPSON ON REAL PROPERTY, *supra* note 6, § 70.09(h).

the purchase price at settlement. Note, however, that the settlement agent may not be willing to proceed to closing or insure title to the property if the parties do not reach an agreement in writing prior to settlement and in such case, litigation may be appropriate.

B. Agreements to Repair

1. [§ 6.5] Generally

In the event the contract provides for a home inspection, attorneys for the parties should specifically state within the contract the rights, obligations, timelines and contingencies of the parties relative to any home inspection. The typical inspection is limited to major systems (electrical, heating, air conditioning, plumbing, etc.) and structural items (roof, walls, foundation, etc.). This does not stop buyers from naming every defect in the house in hopes that the seller will agree to make some of the repairs. Lawyers representing sellers try to limit the list of repairs, and lawyers representing buyers try to expand the list. In an attempt to be universal, the standardized form contracts do not adequately provide for an easy resolution of these competing desires. A better drafted provision for sellers would limit the repair requests to specific areas or items agreed upon by the parties in advance. A better drafted provision for buyers would permit a more open-ended list of items.

Oftentimes, the home inspection contingency gives the buyer one or more of the following rights based on the results of the home inspection: (i) the right to terminate the contract; (ii) the right to request repairs; or (iii) the right to request a purchase price reduction or a closing credit. After the home inspection and buyer's notice (offer) to the seller related to the home inspection results, the seller typically agrees to make none, some, or all of the repairs, or, in lieu of repairs, agrees to a credit towards the purchase price. Alternatively, the seller may refuse to make any repairs or give any purchase price reduction or closing credit. After seller's notice (counteroffer) to buyer, the buyer generally has the right to elect to accept the seller's counteroffer or to terminate the contract. The parties must be careful to adhere to the notice requirements and deadlines set forth in the home inspection contingency, as failure to do so may result in adverse consequences.

If the parties agree that the seller will perform repairs, the parties should execute an addendum that specifically addresses the items that will be repaired. The addendum might include provisions setting forth matters such as the materials, quality, cost, and timeline of repairs. If the repairs are to be completed before settlement, then the buyer should require an additional pre-settlement inspection. Additionally, the buyer should require receipts or invoices for the repair work and assignment of any warranty or rights related to the repair work. Typically, the seller selects the contractor and oversees the repair work. If the buyer would prefer to make the repairs—so that the buyer can select the contractor and oversee the repair work to ensure it meets their satisfaction—then a purchase price reduction or closing credit may be appropriate as an alternative to the seller making the repairs. If the parties agree to a purchase price reduction or closing credit, they should execute an addendum memorializing their agreement. Also, if financing is involved, the buyer should check with the lender to confirm that the closing credit is allowed under the buyer's loan program, as some loan programs have a maximum allowable credit amount. The risk for a buyer trading repair work for a reduction in the purchase price or closing credit is the potential that the work will be more extensive (and, thus, expensive) than anticipated, which the buyer will not discover until after settlement when the work is performed.

2. *[§ 6.6] Quality of repairs*

The importance of precise drafting is crucial to protect the interests of the parties. For example, if the seller contracts under broad language to "fix leak in roof," then they take on broad responsibility. If the leak can only be fixed by replacing the roof, the seller is obligated to replace the roof.[23] Conversely, where the seller contracted to "replace wooden toilet seat," the buyer's damages were limited to the reasonable cost of a new toilet seat, not the entire toilet, even where it was impossible to obtain a replacement seat to fit the toilet.[24]

To avoid a problem at closing, the parties should plan to have the repairs done far enough in advance to permit an additional pre-settlement inspection. The buyer's attorney should anticipate that some of the work might not be completed and structure a method by which the purchase price could be adjusted or a credit could be given at settlement to account for the incomplete work, taking into consideration the applicable financing restrictions. If the parties do not agree to a purchase price reduction or closing credit, then as an alternative to extending the settlement date, the parties may choose to escrow funds from the seller's proceeds and execute a post-closing escrow agreement to ensure that the repairs are completed after settlement. When contemplating a post-closing escrow agreement for repairs, attorneys should be aware of the requirements and restrictions of the buyer's financing as some loan programs prohibit post-closing escrow agreements.

3. *[§ 6.7] Timing*

When a breach of contract is discovered after settlement, the buyer is given reasonable time to enforce the provision.[25] In *Levin v. Cook*, for example, sellers

---

23 *Clarke v. Cleckley*, 55 A.2d 287 (Mun. Ct. App. D.C. 1947).

24 *Id.*

25 *See Levin*, 186 Md. at 542, 47 A.2d at 509; *Laurel*, 194 Md. at 680, 72 A.2d at 26; *Gilbert Constr. Co. v. Gross*, 212 Md. 402, 410, 129 A.2d 518, 522 (1957); *Kandalis v. Paul Pet Constr. Co.*, 210 Md. 319, 323, 123 A.2d 345, 347 (1956).

represented in the contract that the heating plant and oil burner at the premises were efficient and in good condition.[26] Settlement occurred in August. In December, the boiler burst. In January, the plumber replacing the system discovered a pre-existing defect that caused the system to fail. In February, the buyer's attorney notified the seller's attorney of the pre-existing defect and demanded payment. This notice was considered reasonable because it was within a reasonable time after the defect was discovered.[27] The rule of merger does not preclude the buyer's right of action after settlement for breach of such contractual covenants, provided the covenants are collateral to and not inconsistent with the deed.[28] To preserve the right of action, however, the buyer must notify the seller promptly after discovery.[29] If the breach is established, the measure of damages is the cost of repairing or remedying the defect, if reasonable or practicable to do so; otherwise, the measure of damages is the difference between the fair market value of the property with the defect and the fair market value of the property without the defect.[30]

III. RISK OF LOSS AND INSURANCE

A. [§ 6.8] Equitable Conversion

As previously noted, the seller typically is in the best position to maintain the property until closing. The seller is likely living in the house, has the keys and complete control of the property, and maintains the insurance. Therefore, the parties

---

26 186 Md. at 537, 47 A.2d at 506.

27 *Id.* at 542, 47 A.2d at 509.

28 *Id.* at 539, 47 A.2d at 507; *Barrie*, 209 Md. at 583, 121 A.2d at 864; *Dorsey*, 288 Md. at 170, 416 A.2d at 744.

29 *Levin*, 186 Md. at 542, 47 A.2d at 509; *Laurel*, 194 Md. at 680, 72 A.2d at 26; *Gilbert Constr. Co.*, 212 Md. at 410, 129 A.2d at 522; *Kandalis*, 210 Md. at 323, 123 A.2d at 347.

30 *Gilbert*, 212 Md. at 411, 129 A.2d at 522 (noting that where seller breached contractual obligation to install heating unit in a good and workmanlike manner, the buyer would be entitled to damages, the measure of which would be the cost of repairing or remedying any defects due to seller's failure, if it were reasonable or practicable to correct such defects; but if it were not reasonable or practicable to do so, then the measure of damages would be the difference between the fair market value of the house with the heating unit as actually installed and the fair market value of the house with the same heating unit installed in a good and workmanlike manner. If there was insufficient evidence as to the cost of repairing or remedying the defects, the buyer would only be entitled to recover nominal damages.); *Laurel Realty Co.*, 194 Md. at 676, 679, 72 A.2d at 24–25 (holding that where seller installed defective sub-flooring in breach of contractual obligation to deliver a house constructed in accordance with certain plans and check-list specifications, the buyer was entitled to damages, the measure of which would be the difference in the value of the house with proper flooring and its value with the improper flooring. It would be impossible to reconstruct the house, especially as to relaying floors, so the only reasonable remedy would be to provide compensation in the form of money damages.).

may expect that the seller bears the risk of loss until closing.[31] However, unless modified by contract, the general rule in Maryland transfers the risk of loss to the buyer.[32] The general rule is an application of the doctrine of equitable conversion. "The doctrine of equitable conversion and, more particularly, by contract is . . . well-established in Maryland."[33] Maryland courts have routinely cited *Thompson on Real Property* for the maxim that:

> The legal cliche, that equity treats that as being done which should be done, is the basis of the theory of equitable conversion. Hence, when the vendee contracts to buy and the vendor to sell, though legal title has not yet passed, in equity the vendee becomes the owner of the land, the vendor of the purchase money. In equity the vendee has a real interest and the vendor a personal interest. Equity treats the executory contract as a conversion, whereby an equitable interest in the land is secured to the purchaser for whom the vendor holds the legal title in trust. This is the doctrine of equitable conversion.[34]

Under Maryland law, the doctrine of equitable conversion provides that once a contract is capable of being specifically enforced against the seller, then, in equity, the seller no longer owns the property but rather retains bare legal title while the buyer becomes the equitable owner.[35] "The [buyer] is in equity the owner of the

---

31 *See* FRIEDMAN & SMITH, *supra* note 2, § 18.1 ("The term 'risk of loss' embraces damages and destruction due to fire or other casualty, an Act of God, or conduct of third parties. Damage or destruction due to the intentional conduct of seller or purchaser, such as the seller's destruction or removal of improvements or fixtures, is not within the scope of the risk-of-loss rules.").

32 *Noor v. Centreville Bank*, 193 Md. App. 160, 171, 996 A.2d 928, 935 (2010), *cert. granted*, 415 Md. 607, 4 A.3d 512 (2010), *case dismissed by joint stipulation*, 417 Md. 500, 10 A.3d 1180 (2011) ("A variety of views have developed regarding which party bears the risk of loss while the contract remains executory, but the general rule seems to be that the risk passes to the buyer.").

33 *DeShields v. Broadwater*, 338 Md. 422, 437, 659 A.2d 300, 307 (1995).

34 *Grant v. Kahn*, 198 Md. App. 421, 428, 18 A.3d 91, 96 (2011) (quoting 11 THOMPSON ON REAL PROPERTY § 96.06(a) (David A. Thomas ed., 2002 & Supp. 2008)); *see also DeShields*, 338 Md. 422, 659 A.2d 300; *Coe v. Hays*, 328 Md. 350, 614 A.2d 576 (1992); *Himmighoefer v. Medallion Indus., Inc.*, 302 Md. 270, 487 A.2d 282 (1985).

35 *Wash. Mut. Bank v. Homan*, 186 Md. App. 372, 392, 974 A.2d 376, 388 (2009) ("Legal title to the property remains with the seller and 'does not pass, other than by operation of law, until a deed is properly executed and recorded.'" (quoting *Kingsley v. Makay*, 253 Md. 24, 27, 251 A.2d 585, 587 (1969))); *Brewer v. Herbert*, 30 Md. 301, 398 (1869) (stating that "from the time the owner of an estate enters into a binding agreement for its sale, he holds the same in trust for the purchaser, and the latter becomes a trustee of the purchase money for the vendor, and being thus in equity the owner, the vendee must bear any loss which may happen, and is entitled to any benefit which may accrue to the estate in the interim between the agreement and the conveyance."); *Royal Ins. Co.*, 150 Md. 211, 132 A. 635; *Linthicum Heights Co. v. Firemen's Ins. Co.*, 134 Md. 62, 106 A. 165 (1919).

estate from the time of the contract of sale, and must sustain the loss if the estate be destroyed between the agreement and the conveyance, and will be entitled to any benefit which may accrue to it in the interim."[36] The general rule may be modified by agreement of the parties.[37] If the contract is silent, the buyer is responsible for payment of the full purchase price and may not rescind the contract, even if the property is damaged or destroyed by events such as fire, floods, windstorm, vandalism, boiler destruction, hurricane, erosion, or collapse of a retaining wall.[38]

Given that the general rule and the parties' expectations may not be aligned, attorneys for the parties should ensure that the contract accurately reflects the intentions and understanding of the parties as to whom bears the risk of loss during the contract period.[39] Most standardized form contracts reverse the general rule by placing the risk of loss on the seller until execution and delivery of the deed at settlement or until the buyer takes possession. The following is a sample provision shifting the risk of loss to the seller:

> The Property is to be held at the risk of Seller until legal title has passed or possession has been given to Buyer. If, prior to the time legal title has passed or possession has been given to Buyer, whichever shall occur first, all or a substantial part of the Property is destroyed or damaged, without fault of Buyer, then this Contract, at the option of Buyer, upon written notice to Seller, shall be null and void and of no further effect, and the deposits shall be disbursed in accordance with the Deposit paragraph of this Contract.[40]

If the parties do not modify the general rule and the risk of loss passes to the buyer by virtue of equitable conversion, then the buyer should attempt to insure the

---

36 *Brewer*, 30 Md. at 307–08, 831 at 528.

37 *White v. Simard*, 152 Md. App. 229, 248, 831 A.2d 517, 528 (2003), *aff'd*, 383 Md. 257, 859 A.2d 168 (2004) (citing *Coolidge & Sicker, Inc. v. Regn*, 7 N.J. 93, 80 A.2d 554, 557 (N.J. 1951) ("It is rather universally recognized that the parties to a contract of sale for real property may allocate the risk of loss for fire or other casualty occurring before the actual transfer of the legal title. . . . If the contract allocates the risk to the vendor, then the doctrine of equitable conversion, which places the risk of loss on the purchaser, is no longer applicable." (citation omitted)); *Noor*, 193 Md. App. 160, 996 A.2d 928 (noting that parties may limit or prelude the operation or consequences of equitable conversion and courts have freely allowed certain aspects of the doctrine to be modified by contract—to permit the buyer to take possession prior to settlement, to shift the risk of loss, to provide for insurance against that risk, to preclude the buyer from assigning the contract or engaging in activities that could result in liens or third party claims against the property).

38 *See* FRIEDMAN & SMITH, *supra* note 2, § 18:1.1.

39 *See generally* Randy R. Koenders, Annotation, *Risk of Loss by Casualty Pending Contract for Conveyance of Real Property—Modern Cases*, 85 A.L.R. 4th 233 (1991); Robert L. Flores, *A Comparison of the Rule and Rationales for Allocating Risks Arising in Realty Sales Using Executory Sale Contracts and Escrows*, 59 MO. L. REV. 307 (1994).

40 1 RUSSELL R. RENO, JR. ET AL., MARYLAND REAL ESTATE FORMS, § 1.1, FORM 1.2.1.1 *Contract of Sale* (2022).

property from the date of contract. This will likely prove difficult, however, as most insurance companies will only insure the buyer up to the extent of the buyer's interest at any time (maybe to the extent of the deposit, if that is all that is paid). Thus, for practical reasons, the parties should consider modifying the general rule by contract. If the seller insists on passing the risk of loss to the buyer, then the buyer should consider requesting that the seller continue the existing insurance coverage on the property and add the buyer as an additional insured on the seller's policy. Of course, if agreed to by the seller, this should be documented in the contract and the buyer should request that the seller provide a certificate of insurance as evidence of the same. On the other hand, if the property is being purchased as a rental or an investment, it might be possible for the purchaser to add the property to a general insurance policy (although not all companies will permit the addition).

B. [§ 6.9] Remedies

Under the general rule, the buyer assumes all risk of loss, damage, or destruction to the property and is obligated to pay the full purchase price and complete settlement.[41] There are some qualifications to the general rule. When the contract is silent and the buyer bears the risk of loss, there are several ways the buyer may defend against a suit for payment of the purchase price. First, the language of the contract may provide a defense. For example, in *Coolidge & Sickler, Inc. v. Regn*, where the contract provided that the house was sold in the condition it was in at the date of contract, reasonable wear and tear excepted, and the house was vandalized during the period between contract and settlement and the seller refused to repair the damage, specific performance against the buyer was denied because the seller failed to perform a material element of the contract.[42] Second, the risk of loss does not pass to the buyer if the contract is conditional.[43] Third, the risk of loss does not pass to the buyer if the seller's title is defective or does not conform to the provisions of the contract.[44]

---

41 *See* FRIEDMAN & SMITH, *supra* note 2, § 18:1.1.

42 7 N.J. 93, 80 A.2d 554 (N.J. 1951).

43 FRIEDMAN & SMITH, *supra* note 2, § 18:1.1; WOLF, *supra* note 4 (noting that "a contract involving a precondition such as adequate financing approval for the purchaser or the prior sale of a residence by one of the parties is not a valid agreement until the precondition has been accomplished.").

44 FRIEDMAN & SMITH, *supra* note 2, § 18:1.1 (noting that "if the purchaser could have defended successfully against an effort by the seller to enforce the contract, he does not lose this position by reason of injury to the premises."). If, as suggested by Friedman and Smith, the defect must be such that the buyer could have successfully defended a suit for specific performance by seller, the availability of this defense seems somewhat diminished by the Supreme Court of Maryland's (formerly the Court of Appeals) statement in *Schlosser v. Creamer*, 263 Md. 583, 589, 284 A.2d 220, 233 (1971), that "[w]hile cases are legion in which no reasonable doubt as to marketability has been found, the number of cases are few in which such reasonable doubt as would excuse a purchaser from taking title has been found."

Fourth, the seller bears the risk of loss if the loss is due to the seller's fault.[45] Finally, if the seller delays the closing and the buyer rightfully objects, the seller bears the risk of loss.[46]

C. [§ 6.10] Insurance

Whenever a risk is involved, the issue of insurance must be considered. As previously noted, most standardized form contracts shift the risk of loss to the seller and obligate the seller to maintain the property, including insurance on the property. Therefore, the buyer's attorney should ensure that the contract requires the seller to maintain insurance for the full value of the property. If there is a casualty, then the contract should specify how the insurance proceeds will be used. A typical provision will give the buyer the option to go to closing and accept the insurance proceeds or to terminate the contract and let the seller retain the proceeds from insurance with buyer receiving a refund of the earnest money deposit. If the seller has insurance and the risk of loss is on the buyer, the seller holds the proceeds of the insurance for the benefit of the buyer.[47] It makes no difference whether the contract obligates the seller to maintain the insurance or whether the contract is silent on the topic, and it makes no difference which party paid the insurance premiums.[48] However, absent a contractual provision to the contrary, the seller is not obligated to provide insurance for the buyer's benefit.[49]

If the contract places the risk of loss on the seller, the seller's insurance policy should be reviewed to see if it requires as a condition of coverage that the seller have sole ownership of the property. If such a provision exists, the seller should notify the

---

45 FRIEDMAN & SMITH, *supra* note 2, § 18:1.1; *see also Coolidge & Sickler, Inc.*, 7 N.J. 93, 80 A.2d 554.

46 FRIEDMAN & SMITH, *supra* note 2, § 18:1.1.

47 *William Skinner & Sons' Ship-Building & Dry-Dock Co. v. Houghton*, 92 Md. 68, 88, 48 A. 85, 88 (1900) ("If property is destroyed between the time of effecting the contract for the sale and delivery of the deed, the proceeds of an insurance policy upon such property belongs to the vendor as between him and the company, but the former is held to act as trustee for the vendee and must therefore account to his *cestui que trust* in equity." (citation omitted)); *Krick v. Dougherty*, 266 Md. 97, 291 A.2d 648 (1972); *Brewer*, 30 Md. 301.

48 FRIEDMAN & SMITH, *supra* note 2, § 18:1.1.

49 *Brewer*, 30 Md. at 313 ("After the contract the vendee had an insurable interest in the house and in the absence of all agreement on the subject, the presumption is, he intended to protect himself by insuring in his own name, or to take the risk of a failure to insure. The vendor was not bound to keep up the insurance or give notice to the vendee of its having expired. If the policy had existed at the time of the loss, the vendor could have recovered from the insurance company, but being trustee of the premises for the vendee, he would be bound in equity to account to the latter for the money so received, . . . but his failure to renew or to give notice cannot deprive him of his right to enforce the contract of sale." (citation omitted)).

insurance company of the executed contract of sale because the doctrine of equitable conversion means that the seller is no longer the sole owner of the property.[50] To provide insurance coverage for both seller's and buyer's interests, the parties may contract for the seller to maintain an insurance policy endorsed to cover both buyer and seller. Both parties should check the limits of such policy to determine if it the coverage is adequate or if additional coverage is needed.

IV. BUYER MOVING IN

A. [§ 6.11] Generally

There are occasions when a buyer desires to move into the house prior to settlement. This can present a problem for the seller if settlement does not occur as planned, but sellers rarely give serious consideration to the ramifications of early occupancy. Perhaps the most serious problem arises when the buyer refuses to settle.[51] The seller has a right of action against the buyer for breach of contract, but the seller's main objective is usually to move the buyer out and quickly place the house back on the market. If the buyer refuses to cooperate, it can be difficult to remove them, unless the contract or a pre-settlement occupancy agreement has appropriate provisions to cover this situation.

B. [§ 6.12] Buyer's Status

Some lawyers suggest that when the buyer moves in prior to settlement, a landlord-tenant relationship is created, and the seller may move the buyer out of the premises in accordance with the summary proceedings provided by the Maryland Code.[52] Others suggest that the seller has given the buyer a license to occupy the premises and may revoke it at any time. If the parties wish to proceed with a pre-settlement occupancy, they should memorialize their agreement in writing, either as part of the contract or as a separate pre-settlement occupancy agreement, and the terms of that agreement should be clear as to the relationship between the parties (landlord-tenant or licensor-licensee) and the property interest granted from seller to the buyer (leasehold or license). Additionally, the pre-settlement occupancy agreement should clearly set forth the rights and responsibilities of the

---

50 *See Royal Ins. Co.*, 150 Md. 211, 132 A. 635; *Linthicum Heights Co.*, 134 Md. 62, 106 A. 165.

51 If a buyer refuses to settle, they are not entitled to remain in possession and must either settle and pay the balance under the contract or not pay and move out. *See Fett v. Sligo Hills Development Corp.*, 226 Md. 190, 196, 172 A.2d 511, 514 (1961), *overruled on other grounds by Paape v. Grimes*, 256 Md. 490, 260 A.2d 644 (1970) (noting that "where there is a contract which the vendee has abandoned or failed to comply with by neglecting or declining to pay or tender the purchase price the vendor may regain possession by ejectment").

52 Real Prop. § 8-401 *et seq.*

parties with respect to maintenance, risk of loss, and insurance. Some local realtor boards have sample agreements for a pre-settlement occupancy. Some of those standardized forms make it clear that seller is granting to buyer a license to occupy the property and that no landlord-tenant relationship is created between the parties.[53] Others, however, set forth a landlord-tenant relationship between the parties and may even require that the parties enter into a separate lease agreement. In entering into any pre-settlement occupancy agreement, the parties should ensure that the terms of the occupancy accurately reflect their intentions and that they understand the rights and responsibilities created by the agreement. Moreover, the parties should ensure that their agreement complies with applicable local laws of the jurisdiction where the property is located, including any requirement for a rental license.

C. [§ 6.13] Seller's Remedies

If the contract or pre-settlement occupancy agreement does not provide a remedy, the seller must file an action for possession.[54] The disadvantage of an action for possession is that it is a lengthy process at the circuit court level, as opposed to the summary nature of a district court ejectment or wrongful detainer action pursuant to REAL PROP. §§ 8-401 and 14-132, respectively.

The parties should clearly dictate the terms of the occupancy, including any rent or adjustments to the purchase price relative to the occupancy. Attorneys for the parties should ensure they are not running afoul of the landlord-tenant provisions of the Maryland Code and other applicable laws when dealing with pre-settlement occupancies and repossession provisions. Also, attorneys should give consideration to any provision in which the buyer waives their right to a jury trial.[55]

---

53 Specifically, some realtor board forms include the following language for a pre-settlement occupancy: (i) seller is granting to buyer a license to the occupy the property; (ii) no landlord-tenant relationship is created between buyer and seller; (iii) no such tenancy shall arise under the agreement or under applicable law; and (iv) buyer shall have no rights afforded to tenants under applicable law by reason of the license granted from seller to buyer.

54 *Fett*, 226 Md. at 196, 172 A.2d at 514 (noting that "where there is a contract which the vendee has abandoned or failed to comply with by neglecting or declining to pay or tender the purchase price the vendor may regain possession by ejectment"). While the right of ejectment is an ancient common law action, such action would be brought pursuant to REAL PROP. § 14-108.1. For an example of a pre-settlement occupancy agreement *see* 2 RUSSELL R. RENO, JR. ET AL., MARYLAND REAL ESTATE FORMS, § 2.26.9.2 *Pre-Settlement Occupancy Agreements* (2022).

55 REAL PROP. § 8-603 ("A provision contained within a residential lease in which tenant is occupying the space as that tenant's primary residence which waives a trial by jury shall be invalid and unenforceable.").

D. [§ 6.14] Measure of Damages

When the buyer is removed in an ejectment action, the seller is entitled to damages assessed against all occupants wrongfully holding over.[56] In *Fett v. Sligo Hills Dev. Corp.*, damages were measured by the fair rental value of the property from the time when the seller demanded the buyers vacate the premises by filing an ejectment suit, which was the first unequivocal demand to vacate the premises.[57] The seller might also consider an action for profits lost on resale but such damages may not be recoverable if they are too speculative.[58] In addition to fair rental value, the seller may recover damages for destruction to the premises if the buyer makes unauthorized improvements that damage or reduce the value of the property.[59] The defaulting buyer does not have a right to recover for improvements.[60] The seller should consider obtaining a substantial deposit to provide a means to recover the damages if the buyer breaches the contract.[61]

---

56 These damages are for the wrongful act of the buyer in holding over and are in addition to any damages collectable for breach of the contract to purchase. *See Fett*, 226 Md. at 197, 172 A.2d at 514; *cf. Van Ruymbeke v. Patapsco Indus. Park*, 261 Md. 470, 276 A.2d 61 (1971) (standing for the proposition that damages may be calculated based on the rental value of the premises wrongfully withheld as well as business profits attributed to the use of the premises which are not uncertain, speculative or remote).

57 226 Md. at 197, 172 A.2d at 514 (noting that when a proper demand to vacate is ignored, an occupancy rightful because permissive becomes tortious, and it is then the occupants become trespassers and damages for their wrongful occupancy begin to accrue).

58 *See Van Ruymbeke*, 261 Md. 470, 276 A.2d 61.

59 *See Baltimore & Philadelphia Steamboat Co. v. Ministers & Trustees of Starr Methodist Protestant Church*, 149 Md. 163, 130 A. 46 (1925); *Beesley*, 70 Md. App. 482, 521 A.2d 1235.

60 Conversely, where the seller is in breach of contract and the buyer has incurred expenses in good faith in making improvements to the property, the buyer should be able to recover for those expenditures. *See Markoff v. Kreiner*, 180 Md. 150, 158-59, 23 A.2d 19, 25 (1941) ("The measure of damages for a vendor's breach of contract for the sale of real estate is ordinarily the purchase money paid under the terms of the contract. . . . But where a purchaser has incurred expenses in good faith in making improvements to the property, he should be allowed to recover for those expenditures. . . . A party who has received benefits under a contract made void by alterations should not be allowed to retain the benefits derived. He must rescind the contract and make reimbursement for whatever he has received before he can be fully discharged from the effect of the alteration.").

61 The seller should be aware that forfeiture of a deposit that exceeds ten percent (10%) of the purchase price may not be allowed if the buyer proves that the deposit exceeds the seller's damages. *See Chas. H. Steffey, Inc. v. Derr*, 275 Md. 121, 126–27, 338 A.2d 262, 265-66 (1975) (citing *Quillen v. Kelley*, 216 Md. 396, 406, 140 A.2d 517, 522 (1958)); *Traylor v. Grafton*, 273 Md. 649, 332 A.2d 651 (1975).

V. SELLER HOLDING OVER

A. [§ 6.15] Generally

The problem of the seller refusing to relinquish possession to the buyer is really a post-closing, not a pre-closing, problem.

Delivery of possession at settlement is absolutely crucial and fundamental to the residential transaction. Yet, there are only a few cases on point, most likely because the problem becomes apparent in advance of settlement and is resolved before it reaches the litigation stage. If it reaches litigation, the seller has breached the contract and the issue in the case often is the right of the buyer to specific performance or damages.

B. [§ 6.16] Remedies

Most contracts provide that the buyer takes possession on the date of settlement. If the contract is silent, the buyer is still entitled to possession at settlement unless they are taking subject to existing tenancies. Unless the contract otherwise provides, if the seller does not relinquish possession, REAL PROP. § 14-109 provides a remedy. The buyer may file an action for possession in the District Court. The District Court will issue a summons to the seller to appear and show cause why possession has not been given. If the court finds the seller is in wrongful possession, it may give a judgment for immediate possession and issue its warrant ordering the sheriff to deliver possession to the buyer.[62] Presumably, the buyer would also be entitled to recover the same measure of damages as the seller plus the additional costs of items such as alternative accommodations and storage charges.[63]

VI. [§ 6.17] TENANTS

The buyer is obligated to inspect the property for tenants. If the buyer wants the property free of tenants, buyer should include a covenant in the contract that the property is to be free of any existing tenancy.[64] If the buyer takes subject to the tenancy, the buyer must determine the tenants' rights and legal status under the lease or occupancy.[65] If the contract provides for possession free of tenants and tenants are still in possession after settlement, the buyer may move them out under the

---

62 REAL PROP. § 14-109.

63 *Murphy v. O'Donnell*, 63 A.2d 340, 342 (Mun. Ct. App. D.C. 1948). See also RENO, *supra* note 54, Form 2.26.10.2, Post-Settlement Occupancy Agreement, for a suggestion concerning post-settlement occupancy agreements.

64 *New Freedom Corp. v. Brown*, 260 Md. 383, 391, 272 A.2d 401, 405 (1971); *Goldberg v. Feldman*, 108 Md. 330, 339, 70 A. 245, 247 (1908).

65 *Cook v. Boehl*, 188 Md. 581, 53 A.2d 555 (1947).

landlord-tenant provisions of the Maryland Code.[66] The buyer then may recover damages from both seller and tenants for the amount paid for alternative accommodation and storage.[67]

The parties to a contract for the purchase of a single-family residence in Baltimore City need to be aware of the tenants' right of first refusal. Tenants living in a single-family rental property have a right of first refusal to purchase the property.[68] The owner must notify the tenants in writing of their right of first refusal and the terms of any proposed offer or any existing offer to third party. The tenant has a 30-day period following the mailing date of the offer or the mailing date regarding notice of an offer to a third party, in which to respond in writing. If the tenant does not respond within the 30-day period, the owner may sell the property to one other than the tenant.[69] Compliance with the requirements of the ordinance is very important, as there are civil and criminal penalties for its violation.[70] Several exceptions apply, such as transfers to spouses and certain family members. Most importantly, if the property is listed with a licensed real estate broker and the tenant is notified in writing within 48 hours of the listing that the tenant may negotiate for the purchase of the property on the same basis as other members of the general public (along with other required information), then the right of first refusal does not apply.[71] Sellers should be aware of other local jurisdictional requirements related to tenants' rights of first refusal.

VII. TITLE PROBLEMS

A. [§ 6.18] Buyer's Burden

The burden of examining title to determine whether defects exist is on the buyer, unless the contract of sale provides otherwise.[72] Title matters are discussed in Chapter 4, Title Insurance in the Residential Transaction, and Chapter 7,

---

66 Real Prop. § 8-402 (providing remedies for tenant's holding over); *Murphy*, 63 A.2d at 343.

67 *Murphy*, 63 A.2d at 343.

68 Baltimore City Code, art. 13, § 6-3 (2000).

69 *Id.* at § 6-4.

70 *Id.* at § 6-8.

71 *Id.* at § 6-11.

72 *Blondell v. Turover*, 195 Md. 251, 257, 72 A.2d 697, 699 (1950) ("The law requires reasonable diligence in a purchaser of real property to ascertain any defect of title. When such defect is brought to his knowledge, no inconvenience will excuse him from the utmost scrutiny."); *see also Heckrotte v. Riddle*, 224 Md. 591, 594, 168 A.2d 879, 881 (1961) (holding that where the seller did not point out the property lines or make any representation as to their location, it was the buyers' duty to ascertain the property lines by an examination of the land records and by causing a location survey to be made; had they done so, they would have discovered the side-yard violation, and they would not have been compelled to perform the contract of sale by accepting a conveyance of the property).

Settlement of Title of Residential Real Estate. This chapter assumes that buyer or seller has asserted that such a title defect exists.

B. [§ 6.19] Marketability

The duty to convey marketable title is implied in every contract unless the parties provide for a different standard.[73] Most standardized form contracts provide for the seller to convey either "marketable" or "merchantable" title, which terms are synonymous.[74] The issue of marketable title often arises when the buyer is trying to avoid the contract or recover damages.[75] The seller is not in breach until they are unable to convey the title as promised on the date of settlement.[76] In Maryland, a marketable title is a title free from encumbrances and reasonable doubt as to its validity, and such as a reasonably intelligent person, who is well informed as to the facts and their legal bearing, and ready and willing to perform the contract, would be willing to accept in the exercise of ordinary business prudence.[77] This precludes buyers from requiring that title be free from "every conceivable technical criticism . . . every possibility of defect or even threat of suit."[78] In other words, "[a] title to be marketable need not be flawless."[79] There are few cases where sufficient reasonable doubt existed to excuse the buyer from settlement.[80]

---

73 WOLF, *supra* note 4; *Ahrens v. Ijams*, 158 Md. 412, 148 A. 816 (1930).

74 *Mayor of Baltimore v. Thornton Mellon*, LLC, 478 Md. 396, 415, 274 A.3d 1079, 1090 (2022).

75 *See Schlosser v. Creamer*, 263 Md. 583, 588, 284 A.2d 220, 223 (1971) ("Whether the suit be one for specific performance or one by a purchaser to recover a down payment made on real estate . . . the test is the same, whether a marketable title can be conveyed.").

76 *Clark v. Kirsner*, 196 Md. 52, 55, 74 A.2d 830, 832 (1950) (noting that "if a vendor is able to give good title at the time for conveyance under the contract, it is immaterial, at least in the absence of bad faith, that he may not have been able to do so at the time the contract was made); *Friedman v. McLane*, 193 Md. 565, 574, 69 A.2d 253, 257 (1949).

77 *Zulver Realty Co. v. Snyder*, 191 Md. 374, 384, 62 A.2d 276, 280 (1948) ("No specific rule can be laid down as to what doubts will be sufficient to make a title unmarketable. The general rule is that the purchaser is entitled to a deed which will enable him to hold the land in peace and, if he wishes to sell it, to be reasonably certain that no flaw will appear to disturb its market value."); *Jefferson v. Jones*, 286 Md. 544, 551, 408 A.2d 1036, 1040 (1979); *New Freedom Corp.*, 260 Md. at 389, 272 A.2d at 404; *Schlosser*, 263 Md. at 588-89, 284 A.2d at 223.

78 *New Freedom Corp.*, 260 Md. at 389, 272 A.2d at 404; *see also Jefferson*, 286 Md. at 553, 408 A.2d at 1041 ("The criteria which have developed essentially require a determination of whether the claim is of such a substantial nature that it may reasonably subject the buyer to serious litigation.").

79 *New Freedom Corp.*, 260 Md. at 389, 272 A.2d at 404.

80 *See Schlosser*, 263 Md. at 593, 284 A.2d at 224.

C. [§ 6.20] Timely Notice of Defect

The buyer must promptly notify the seller of any defects found while searching title.[81] If the contract contains a specific timeframe for notifying the seller of title defects, then the buyer must comply with the timeframe set forth in the contract. Failure to notify the seller may be deemed as a waiver of the defect.[82] When the contract does not provide that time is of the essence, the seller has a reasonable time to cure the defect.[83] If the buyer brings a suit for specific performance, the seller may cure the defect until the time of the decree.[84] If time is of the essence and the buyer promptly notified seller, seller must cure the defect by the date of settlement.[85]

D. Buyer's Remedies

1. [§ 6.21] Generally

A buyer has several legal and equitable remedies against the seller when the seller wrongfully fails or refuses to perform its part of the contract or to convey to the buyer the quality of title required under the contract.[86] A buyer generally may: (1) elect to rescind the contract and seek a return of any payments or deposits already made; (2) sue for damages; or (3) sue for specific performance.[87]

The general rule is that the amount of damages recoverable for seller's breach of contract is that which will place the buyer in as good a position as that in which the buyer would have been, had the contract been performed.[88] These "expectation interest damages" include both losses sustained (i.e., out of pocket damages) and gains lost (i.e., benefit of the bargain damages).[89] An exception to the general rule exists where the seller's breach is in good faith, such as the good faith failure to provide marketable title.[90] Good faith is that "ordinarily exhibited by a seller who

---

81 WOLF, *supra* note 4, § 81.03[f].

82 WOLF, *supra* note 4, § 81.03[g].

83 WOLF, *supra* note 4, § 81.03[f].

84 *Friedman*, 193 Md. at 574, 69 A.2d at 257 ("The rule is that the vendor need not have a marketable title at the time of the agreement, but is only required to be in a position to convey such a title by the time the decree is entered, provided that, as here, time is not of the essence of the contract, and the vendor appears to have acted in good faith." (quoting *Hammer v. Westphal*, 120 Md. 15, 18, 87 A. 488, 489 (1913)).

85 *Zulver Realty Co.*, 191 Md. at 385, 62 A.2d at 281.

86 *See generally* 77 AM. JUR. 2D *Vendor and Purchaser* § 495 (2016).

87 19A MARYLAND LAW ENCYCLOPEDIA *Sales of Realty* § 90 (2017).

88 *Beard v. S/E Joint Venture*, 321 Md. 126, 581 A.2d 1275 (1990).

89 *Id.* at 133, 581 A.2d at 1278; *Hall v. Lovell Regency Homes Ltd. P'ship.* 121 Md. App. 1, 708 A.2d 344 (1998).

90 *Beard*, 321 Md. at 133, 581 A.2d at 1278.

is unable to perform through no fault or fraud of [their] own, while bad faith is that shown by a seller who refuses to perform when able to do so."[91] The amount of damages recoverable for seller's good faith breach is typically the deposit with interest and title search fees, among other potential damages.[92]

If the seller's breach is in bad faith, the buyer is entitled to the benefit of the bargain, and the measure of damages is the value of the land at the time of the breach (i.e., at the time the transfer was to be made).[93] Bad faith is a seller's refusal to perform when able to do so.[94] Examples of seller's bad faith include situations where the seller willfully or arbitrarily refuses to complete the sale, fails to perfect title, or makes it impossible to convey good title.[95]

As a general rule, a buyer who has made payments on the purchase price under a contract may recover the amount of the payments where the contract is invalid or unenforceable.[96] The buyer is entitled, in equity, to a lien on the land to the extent of the payments made on the purchase price.[97] The lien arises only in the event that the contract, through the fault of the seller, is not consummated.[98] The lien is superior to subsequent judgment liens and may not be defeated by a subsequent grantee of the seller who takes with knowledge of the existing contract.[99]

---

91 *Charles County Broadcasting Co. v. Meares*, 270 Md. 321, 326, 311 A.2d 27, 31 (1973) *disapproved on other ground by Beard v. S/E Joint Venture*, 321 Md. 126, 581 A.2d 1275 (1990).

92 *Hupp v. George R. Rembold Bldg. Co.*, 279 Md. 597, 602-03, 369 A.2d 1048, 1051-52 (1977) ("If the vendor acts in bad faith,—as, if having title he refuses to convey, or disables himself from conveying,—the proper measure of damages is the value of the land at the time of the breach; the rule, in such case, being the same in relation to real as to personal property. But, on the other hand, if the contract of sale was made in good faith, and the vendor for any reason is unable to perform it, and is guilty of no fraud, the clear weight of authority is that the vendee is limited in his recovery to the consideration money (paid) and interest, with perhaps in addition, the costs of investigating the title." (quoting *Hartsock v. Mort*, 76 Md. 281, 288, 25 A. 303, 304 (1892))).

93 *Hupp*, 279 Md. at 602, 369 A.2d at 1051-52; *Charles Cty. Broadcasting Co.*, 270 Md. at 326, 311 A.2d at 31.

94 *Charles Cty. Broadcasting Co.*, 270 Md. at 326, 311 A.2d at 31.

95 *See Hartsock v. Mort*, 76 Md. 281, 25 A. 303 (1892); *Horner v. Beasley*, 105 Md. 193, 65 A. 820 (1907).

96 19A Maryland Law Encyclopedia *Sales of Realty* § 91 (2017).

97 *Gribble v. Stearman & Kaplan, Inc.*, 249 Md. 289, 239 A.2d 573 (1968).

98 *Id.*

99 *Id.*, at 296, 239 A.2d at 577; *Colonial Bldg. & Loan Ass'n v. Boden*, 169 Md. 493, 182 A. 665 (1936); *Stahl v. Roulhac*, 50 Md. App. 382, 384–85, 438 A.2d 1366, 1367 (1982) ("[O]ne who purchases real property under an executory contract of sale is entitled, in equity, to a lien on the land to the extent of payments made on the purchase price. This equitable lien is enforceable not only against the seller, but also against any person who subsequently acquires an interest in the property with knowledge of the existing contract. . . .").

2. [§ 6.22] *Specific performance*

After deciding to purchase a home and signing a contract, most buyers are committed to a course of action that will not be completed until occupancy. Thus, when a title defect is relatively minor, the buyer may decide to proceed to closing and take what title the seller can convey. Generally, the buyer is allowed to ignore or waive a defective title and to specifically enforce the contract if the seller breaches.[100] However, before pursuing specific performance, the buyer should consider the title defect's impact on title insurance. Most standardized form contracts provide that in addition to being marketable or merchantable, title shall be insurable with no additional risk premium (i.e., the buyer shall not pay more than the standard rate as filed with the Maryland Insurance Commissioner). If the title defect limits the ability of buyer (and buyer's lender, if financing is involved) to obtain title insurance, then specific performance might not be a desirable or viable option. Instead, the buyer may elect to terminate the contract and receive a return of the deposit, and possibly pursue damages, if available. Monetary encumbrances that have not been released or discharged (such as outstanding mortgages and deeds of trust, judgment liens, and tax obligations) are generally not considered minor title defects, and a title insurance carrier will generally not insure with monetary encumbrances affecting title.[101]

Another situation in which the buyer may pursue specific enforcement is when the seller refuses to perform under the contract. Litigation arises when the seller's motive is to avoid the contractual obligation to convey. The buyer's remedy in such a situation is an action for specific performance.

If the buyer is at all times ready, willing, and able to perform and the contract is unobjectionable, a decree for specific performance should be granted.[102] The buyer

---

[100] WOLF, *supra* note 4, § 81.04; 20 MARYLAND LAW ENCYCLOPEDIA *Specific Performance* § 25 (2016).

[101] *See* WOLF, *supra* note 4, § 81.04 (noting that the parties generally anticipate that the settlement agent will use the purchase money to satisfy outstanding monetary encumbrances before transferring the remaining proceeds to the seller; therefore, the buyer may not insist that the seller eliminate these potential title defects before the purchase price is paid, and the seller is not in breach if monetary encumbrances may be removed by applying a portion of the purchase price to satisfy them at closing).

[102] *DeMar v. Crosco Bldg. Co.*, 179 Md. 161, 168-69, 16 A.2d 884, 887 (1940); *Paape v. Grimes*, 256 Md. 490, 493, 260 A.2d 644 (1970) (noting the general rule that, to be specifically enforced, a contract for the sale of land must be definite and certain in all of its terms, free from ambiguity and in accordance with the Statute of Frauds); *Charles Cty. Broadcasting Co.*, 270 Md. at 324, 311 A.2d at 30 ("The granting of specific performance rests within the sound discretion of the trial court. . . . If a contract is fair, reasonable and certain, specific performance may be granted almost as a matter of course. . . . This is true even if the contract is contingent, if the contingency can be met . . . within the time stated. . . ." (citations omitted)).

must tender performance within the time provided by the contract and promptly go forward after the seller's default.[103] If time is of the essence, then tender must be made by the settlement date provided in the contract; otherwise, if time is not of the essence, then tender must be within a reasonable time of the settlement date.[104] The buyer is not required to tender performance where it is clear that seller will not convey.[105]

Whether or not time is of the essence, a seller that breached in bad faith is estopped from using the requirement of tender as a defense to specific performance.[106] This is also true when the seller waives the time is of the essence provision or reaches an agreement with the buyer to extend the time for settlement.[107] It is within the court's

---

103 *Silver Holding Corp. v. Sheeler*, 231 Md. 35, 37, 188 A.2d 562, 563 (1963) ("The general rule is well established in this State that in order to be entitled to specific performance of a contract for the sale of real estate, the purchaser must be "ready, desirous, prompt and eager" to consummate the contract, whether or not time is of the essence thereunder."); *Chapman v. Thomas*, 211 Md. 102, 108, 126 A.2d 579, 582 (1956) ("Whether time is or is not of the essence in a contract for the sale of real estate, a purchaser who seeks specific performance has two primary obligations. First he must seek relief with due diligence and show that under all the circumstances he was 'ready, desirous, prompt, and eager' . . . . Second, if he delays settlement while attempting to have the seller remedy a claimed defect in the title of the property, he must, when it becomes clear the seller will not meet his demands, either accept the title as it is and promptly tender settlement, or cancel the contract.").

104 *Soehnlein v. Pumphrey*, 183 Md. 334, 338, 37 A.2d 843, 845 (1944) ("The accepted doctrine is that in the ordinary case of contract for the sale of land, even though a certain period of time is stipulated for its consummation, equity treats the provision as formal rather than essential, and permits the purchaser who has suffered the period to elapse to make payments after the prescribed date, and to compel performance by the vendor notwithstanding the delay, unless it appears that time is of the essence of the contract by express stipulation, or by inference from the conduct of the parties, the special purpose for which the sale was made, or other circumstances surrounding the sale. The doctrine is subject to qualifications, one of the most important of which is that the delay must not be willful and must not have worked any harm to the vendor."); *Triton Realty Co. v. Frieman*, 210 Md. 252, 259, 123 A.2d 290, 294 (1956) ("The purchaser, in order to be entitled to a conveyance, must perform all conditions precedent to the vendor's obligation to convey, unless they are waived or their performance excused. . . . Where, by the terms of the contract, the acts of the parties are to be concurrent, or it is provided that the deed is to be delivered on demand, it is the duty of the purchaser, not only to make a tender of the purchase price . . . but also to demand performance from the vendor." (citation omitted)).

105 *Lissau v. Smith*, 215 Md. 538, 545, 138 A.2d 381, 385 (1958) ("In equity, a tender is sufficient if the purchaser is ready to, offers to, and has the ability to pay."); *Darneille v. Geraci*, 237 Md. 51, 57, 205 A.2d 55, 58 (1964) (noting that a tender is not necessary when it would have been futile, such as when a seller repudiates a contract before suit or where is appears the seller would refuse a tender).

106 *Chapman*, 211 Md. 102, 126 A.2d 579; *Budacz v. Fradkin*, 146 Md. 400, 126 A. 220 (1924).

107 *Shoreham Developers, Inc. v. Randolph Hills, Inc.*, 248 Md. 267, 235 A.2d at 735 (1967); *Lissau*, 215 Md. 538, 138 A.2d 381.

discretion to allow time for the seller to obtain clear title in framing a decree for specific performance.[108]

E. Seller's Remedies

1. [§ 6.23] Election

Although, as already noted, title defects rarely excuse performance, some buyers claim that title is defective as a way to get out of the contract. A contract is not specifically enforceable against an unwilling buyer unless the seller is able to convey marketable title.[109] If the seller is ready, willing, and able to convey marketable title and the buyer breaches, the seller may elect either to terminate the contract and retain the buyer's deposit as liquidated damages or to seek actual damages resulting from the breach, but not both.[110] A liquidated damages clause is an enforceable provision as a sum agreed upon by the parties to be paid in the event of a breach, enforceable as any other provision or valid promise in the contract.[111] "If the sum agreed upon is a reasonable forecast of the just and fair compensation for the harm that would result by a breach of the contract and the resultant injury is difficult to estimate accurately or actual damages could not be easily ascertained, such a clause has been held enforceable as liquidated damages."[112] If a deposit is forfeited as liquidated damages, a claim may not then be made for actual damages.[113] In situations where the deposit is not treated as liquidated damages, the deposit may be treated as a fund out of which damages may be paid, with a refund to the buyer if damages are actually less than the deposit and a right in the seller to go after the buyer for

---

108 *Lissau*, 215 Md. at 548, 138 A.2d at 386–87 ("[T]he court can frame a decree which will give sufficient time for the completion of the formal mechanics necessary to effectively discharge the Federal [tax] lien and can condition the obligation of the [buyer] to pay the purchase money upon the release of the lien. If it is necessary to do so, the [seller] can be enjoined from selling the land to anyone else in the meantime. Where specific performance is proper, equity may accomplish the same result permanently or temporarily by the use of injunction.").

109 *See Schlosser*, 263 Md. at 589, 284 A.2d at 224 (holding that violation of the setback requirements contained in the seller's deed was not a reasonable basis for the buyer's rejection of title because the house had been in its location for nearly 50 years, adjacent residences violated the same setbacks, and building within the setbacks would be almost impossible due to shape of the lot).

110 *Alois v. Waldman*, 219 Md. 369, 149 A.2d 406 (1959); *Macon v. Zeiler*, 233 Md. 160, 195 A.2d 687 (1963).

111 *Traylor*, 273 Md. 649, 661, 332 A.2d 651, 660 (1975).

112 *Id.* at 662, 332 A.2d at 660; *see also Blood v. Gibbons*, 288 Md. 268, 274, 418 A.2d 213, 217 (1980) ("A provision for such damages is enforceable unless it is shown that the provision is actually designed as a penalty.").

113 *Alois*, 219 Md. 369, 149 A.2d 406; *Macon*, 233 Md. 160, 195 A.2d 687; *Blood v. Gibbons*, 288 Md. 268, 418 A.2d 213 (1980).

the excess if damages exceed the deposit.[114] If the contract does not specify that forfeiture of the deposit is the seller's sole and exclusive remedy (i.e., the contract provides that the deposit may be forfeited at the option of the seller), then the seller may elect which remedy to pursue in the event of a buyer breach.[115] Most standardized form contracts provide that the seller may accept the deposit as liquidated damages, but if the seller elects not to or if the buyer refuses to sign a release agreement, then the seller shall have all legal and equitable remedies.

Unless the contract provides otherwise, the measure of damages for breach of contract by buyer is the difference between the contract price and the fair market value at the time of the breach.[116] These are "general damages."[117] Damages which a seller may recover for breach of contract by buyer include both those which may fairly and reasonably be considered as arising naturally from the breach (general damages) and those which may reasonably be supposed to have been in the contemplation of both parties at the time of making of the contract (special damages).[118] "Special damages" are sometimes called "consequential damages," and courts may award "incidental damages" as well.[119] The seller may introduce evidence of resale of the property as an alternative means of establishing damages, but in such a case, the burden is upon the seller to establish that the sale was fairly made within a reasonable time.[120] Thus, in the event of a buyer breach, the seller may be able to recover its carrying costs such as insurance, real property taxes, and mortgage interest plus the difference between the contract price and the new sale price of the property when it is resold.

The seller must weigh the tactical considerations in making this election depending on whether damages are likely to amount to more than the deposit. If, however, the deposit is greater than ten percent (10%), it may be considered a penalty.[121] If it is a penalty rather than compensation for injury, the court may order restitution to the buyer for the amount that exceeds actual costs.[122] Also, if the deposit is held by

---

114 *Alois*, 219 Md. 369, 149 A.2d 406; *Macon*, 233 Md. 160, 195 A.2d 687; *Blood*, 288 Md. 268, 418 A.2d 213.

115 *See Blood*, 288 Md. 268, 418 A.2d 213 (involving a forfeiture provision that permitted the sellers either to forfeit the deposit and release the buyers or to pursue any legal or equitable remedies to the exclusion of the right to forfeit the deposit).

116 *Kasten Constr. Co. v. Jolles*, 262 Md. 527, 278 A.2d 48 (1971); *Lake Shore Investors v. Rite Aid Corp.*, 55 Md. App. 171, 461 A.2d 725 (1983), *aff'd*, 298 Md. 611, 471 A.2d 735 (1984). The time of the breach will be when the buyer refuses to settle.

117 *Burson v. Simard*, 424 Md. 318, 35 A.3d 1154 (2012).

118 *Id.*

119 *Id.*

120 *Kasten Constr. Co.*, 262 Md. 527, 278 A.2d 48.

121 *Quillen v. Kelley*, 216 Md. 396, 140 A.2d 517 (1958); *Traylor*, 273 Md. 649, 332 A.2d 651.

122 *Quillen*, 216 Md. 396, 140 A.2d 517.

the settlement agent, the settlement agent most likely will not agree to release the deposit as liquidated damages without a release agreement signed by both the seller and the buyer that authorizes and directs the settlement agent to disburse the deposit to the seller. This could lead to the settlement agent interpleading the deposit into the court without seller being able to immediately exercise its election to accept the deposit as liquidated damages.

Attorneys should ensure that the parties comply with REAL PROP. § 10-802, which provides, among other requirements, that when an escrow agent agrees to hold trust money (i.e., the deposit), the escrow agent shall enter into a written agreement with the parties that contains (among other information) the conditions under which the escrow agent may release the deposit. Some local realtor boards have sample escrow agreement forms that may be used to comply with the requirements of REAL PROP. § 10-802. Typically, in a residential real estate transaction, the escrow agent is the same as the settlement agent selected by the buyer to conduct closing. Sometimes, however, the deposit is held by one of the real estate brokers in the transaction. In that case, the requirements of REAL PROP. § 10-802 do not apply, and instead the real estate broker must handle the deposit in accordance with the Maryland Real Estate Brokers Act.[123] Attorneys should also be aware that if a buyer terminates a real estate transaction under the terms of a contingency clause in accordance with REAL PROP. § 10-803, then the parties and the holder of the trust money (either the escrow agent or real estate broker) must follow the procedures set forth in REAL PROP. § 10-803 for distribution of the deposit.

2. *[§ 6.24] Specific performance*

It is well settled in Maryland that specific performance is an available and preferred remedy for sellers.[124] As previously noted, most standardized form contracts provide that the seller may accept the deposit as liquidated damages, but if the

---

123 MD. CODE ANN., BUSINESS OCCUPATIONS AND PROFESSIONS § 17-101 *et seq.*

124 *Archway Motors, Inc. v. Herman*, 37 Md. App. 674, 681, 378 A.2d 720, 724 (1977) ("Specific performance is considered an extraordinary equitable remedy which may be granted, in the discretion of the chancellor, where more traditional remedies, such as damages, are either unavailable or inadequate. This extraordinary remedy has been particularly recognized as appropriate where the contract is for the sale of land because of the presumed uniqueness of land itself, no parcel being exactly like another. Although it has most frequently been granted at the behest of the buyer to compel the seller to convey the land, the criteria justifying its use have also been found operative where the seller is its seeker."); *Maryland Clay Co. v. Simpers*, 96 Md. 1, 6, 53 A. 424, 425 (1902) (noting that specific performance is permissible under the equitable doctrine that enforcement of contracts must be mutual, and where the buyer would have a right to a decree compelling the conveyance of the land to him, the seller must likewise be permitted in equity to compel the acceptance of the deed and the payment of the consideration for it).

seller elects not to or if the buyer refuses to sign a release agreement, then the seller shall have all legal and equitable remedies. Therefore, the seller has the right to specific performance unless the contract expressly states otherwise.[125] Absent a contractual provision that clearly prohibits specific performance, the contract is specifically enforceable against the buyer if the seller is able to convey good and marketable title.[126] To be in a position to demand performance, the seller must tender performance unless it would be a useless act.[127]

If what the seller can deliver is practically the same as that agreed upon, the court may exercise its discretion and decree specific performance with a proportionate reduction or "abatement" in the purchase price.[128] For example, in *Senick v. Lucas*, after discovering that a tool shed encroached upon the neighbor's property by 1.2 feet, the seller reduced the size of the shed to eliminate the encroachment.[129] The buyer tried to rescind the contract, arguing that the reduction in the size of the shed rendered it too small for the storage of tools. The Supreme Court of Maryland held that the buyer was bound to perform and that the appropriate remedy was an abatement of the purchase price because seller's failure of performance did not go to the root of the contract or defeat the object of the contract (i.e., the property could be utilized for the very purposes for which it was bought and the breach could easily be compensated by damages).[130] In cases involving a question as to the extent of land bargained for, the test is whether the seller can deliver approximately the same amount of land as agreed upon, or whether there is a material difference.[131]

---

125 *Miller v. U.S. Naval Inst.*, 47 Md. App. 426, 435, 423 A.2d 283, 288 (1980) ("The parties' rights to specific performance ought not be foreclosed (thereby confining their remedies to those available at law) absent a clear expression of their intent to do so. . . .").

126 *Coe v. Hays*, 328 Md. 350, 614 A.2d 576 (1992).

127 *Shoreham Developers, Inc.*, 248 Md. at 277–78, 235 A.2d at 742.

128 *Tolchester Beach Improv. Co. v. Boyd*, 161 Md. 269, 276–77, 156 A. 795, 798 (1931) ("When some part even within the bounds of the land contracted to be sold cannot be conveyed by the vendor, from some cause not involving *mala fides* on his part, if such part is of small importance, or is immaterial to the purchaser's enjoyment of that which may be conveyed to him, the vendor may insist on performance with compensation to the purchaser, or a proportionate abatement from the agreed price. But this cannot be done where the part is a considerable portion of the entire subject-matter, or is material to the enjoyment of the other part.").

129 234 Md. 373, 381, 199 A.2d 375, 379 (1964).

130 *Id.*, at 381, 199 A.2d at 379 (holding that buyer was entitled to an abatement of the purchase price in the amount of the value of that portion of the shed used as a tool shed).

131 *Housing Engineering Co. v. David M. Andrew Co.*, 184 Md. 290, 295, 40 A.2d 368, 370 (1945) ("The discretion of the Court will be exercised when it appears that the vendor cannot deliver exactly what he agrees to sell. In that case the question arises whether what he can deliver is practically the same as that agreed upon, or whether there is such a material difference as to render the property purchased unfit for the use for which it was purchased. In the former case, it is generally a question of a lack of acreage or footage, and courts customarily decree performance with a proportionate reduction of the purchase price. . . . Cases of the second

Attorneys for the parties should ensure that the legal description, including any metes and bounds, courses and distances, acreage and other factors, is specifically described in the contract of sale to avoid disputes regarding the land and improvements to be conveyed.

VIII. [§ 6.25] Financing Contingencies

The financing contingency section causes many pre-closing problems. Careful drafting will help your clients avoid most problems. The provisions for financing in the form contracts cause uncertainty. If the buyer is applying for conventional financing, the careful seller will make sure that the interest rate selected by the buyer is not too aggressive or unrealistic so as to give the buyer the ability to terminate the contract for inability to obtain the specified financing. In other words, if current 30-year mortgage rates are 7%, a buyer who must get a loan commitment at 7% or less potentially has a contingency that cannot be fulfilled. While a buyer could waive the contingency and close with a higher interest rate, the seller loses the right to enforce the contract if the buyer cannot obtain the unrealistic or aggressive specified financing. Attorneys should be sure the provisions of the financing contingency clearly state the terms of the financing contingency such as the type of financing, the interest rate, the loan points, the term of the financing, the amortization and the applicable timelines for application, approval, denial, and termination on the basis of such contingency.

The form contracts also leave open the possibility that a buyer might attempt to add the additional requirement of an appraisal to the financing contingency. A stronger financing contingency would provide the following:

a. a specific number of days for the buyer to file a written application;

b. a specific number of days for the buyer to obtain a financing commitment; and

c. a final number of days for all conditions of the financing commitment to be fulfilled (in other words, "within __ days from the date of contract, buyer must have a non-contingent financing commitment.")

By requiring the financing contingency to be completely fulfilled (without additional requirements such as appraisal or inspection), the seller and buyer know what needs to be done before closing and there are timelines for each act. This reduces the possibility that buyer reports, the day before closing, that the lender has rejected buyer's application and attempts to terminate the contract.

---

class are those where it has been held that the defects seriously affect the value of the property to the purchaser.").

IX. MARYLAND STATUTES AFFORDING A REMEDY TO BUYERS

A. [§ 6.26] Generally

Certain provisions of the REAL PROPERTY Article provide remedies for home-buyers both before and after the pre-closing period.

B. [§ 6.27] Express and Implied Warranties

By REAL PROP. § 10-202, with respect to every newly constructed house, its fixtures and structure, a vendor creates an express warranty by making written affirmations of fact or promises, and by including written descriptions and samples or models that relate to an improvement, provided the representation is part of the basis of the bargain. A vendor is a person engaged in the business of erecting or otherwise creating an improvement on realty or to whom a completed improvement has been granted for resale in the course of their business.[132]

By REAL PROP. § 10-203, in every sale of a newly constructed house, its fixtures and structures, an implied warranty exists that the improvement is free from faulty materials; constructed according to sound engineering standards; constructed in a workmanlike manner; and fit for habitation.[133] With new homes, there is a requirement that a new home warranty be provided to buyer under REAL PROP. § 10-604. Certain counties and local jurisdictions may also have heightened new home seller and new home builder warranty requirements such as Montgomery County, under Section 31C of the Montgomery County Code. With regard to the construction of condominiums, the express and implied warranties found in REAL PROP., Title 10 are in addition to the warranties found in REAL PROP., Title 11.[134]

Absent a local requirement for longer coverage under a warranty, with regard to a dwelling completed at delivery of the deed to the original buyer, the express and implied warranties expire one year after delivery or the taking of possession by the original purchaser, whichever comes first, unless an express warranty specifies a longer period of time.[135] In the case of structural defects, the time period is

---

[132] REAL PROP. § 10-201(e), 10-601 *et seq.*

[133] REAL PROP. § 10-203(a), 10-601 *et seq.* The issue of habitability can be determined by the court as a matter of law and in determining whether a dwelling is fit for habitation, applicable regulations or building code requirements act as both a guide in determining the issue of habitability. *Adams v. NVR Homes, Inc.*, 135 F. Supp. 2d 675, 700 (D. Md. 2001) (citing *Loch Hill Constr. Co. v. Fricke*, 284 Md. 708, 715–16, 399 A.2d 883, 888 (1979)) (minor inconveniences resulting from methane detectors do not make a home unfit for habitation).

[134] *Milton Co. v. Council of Unit Owners of Bentley Place Condo.*, 354 Md. 264, 729 A.2d 981 (1999).

[135] REAL PROP. § 10-204(b)(1). In the case of a dwelling not delivered to the original purchaser on the date of the deed, the express and implied warranties extend to one year after the date of completion or the date of possession (whichever comes first). REAL PROP. § 10-204(b)(2).

extended to two years after the date of completion, delivery, or taking of possession, whichever comes first.[136] Actions arising out of an express or implied warranty must be commenced within two years after the defect was discovered or should have been discovered, or within two years after the expiration of the warranty (whichever occurs first). The running of the statute of limitations will commence when homeowners first discover a defect, and not when they discover the cause of the problem.[137]

If the purchaser makes known to the vendor the particular purpose for the improvement, and relies on the vendor's skill and judgment, then an implied warranty of fitness for the particular purpose exists.[138] It should be noted that implied warranties do not apply to any condition that an inspection of the premises would reveal to a reasonably diligent buyer at the time the contract is signed.[139] It should be anticipated that express warranties could be limited in like fashion, although the statute does not so state.

If an express warranty is made, neither words in the contract of sale, the deed, other instrument of grant, nor merger of the contract of sale into the deed, or any other instrument of grant is effective to exclude or modify the warranty.[140] Similar provisions apply to implied warranties.[141] An express warranty or an implied warranty where the improvement is completed may only be modified or excluded by execution of a written instrument setting forth in detail the warranty to be modified or excluded, the purchaser's consent, and the terms of the new agreement.[142]

A buyer who determines during the pre-closing period that an "improvement" does not conform to the warranties should demand that the defect be cured. While the statute does not expressly set forth remedies available to buyers during the pre-closing period, notifying the vendor that the dwelling does not comply with the statutory warranties may be sufficient to spur the vendor to cure the defect. Should the defect not be cured and the buyer nonetheless goes to closing, the statute provides for "legal or equitable relief, or both, as justice requires."[143]

C. [§ 6.28] Maryland Homeowners' Association Act

Real Prop. Title 11B is the Maryland Homeowners Association Act. The Act requires that vendors of residential real property must make certain disclosures to the

---

136 Real Prop. § 10-204(b)(3).

137 *Lumsden v. Design Tech Builders, Inc.*, 358 Md. 435, 452, 749 A.2d 796, 805 (2000).

138 Real Prop. § 10-203(c).

139 *Id.* § 10-203(b).

140 *Id.* § 10-202(c).

141 *Id.* § 10-203(d).

142 *Id.* §§ 10-202(c);10-203(d).

143 *Id.* § 10-204(a).

buyer if the real property is subject to assessment by a homeowners association.[144] In the absence of such disclosures, a buyer is entitled to cancel a contract and to immediately have their deposit returned.[145] Generally, a buyer is likewise entitled to cancel in writing the contract within five calendar days following receipt by the purchaser of the disclosures if the purchaser has not received the disclosures five calendar days or more before the contract was executed.

During the pre-closing period, the buyer of a dwelling subject to assessment by a homeowners association should be aware that they are entitled to the stipulated information, and that the contract is terminable should the requisite disclosure not be made.[146] The buyer should note, however, "if any purchaser proceeds to settlement, the purchaser's right to cancel under this section is terminated."[147] In certain circumstances, the vendor may be held liable for damage proximately caused by untrue statements or material omissions.[148] Buyers should be aware of certain information revealed by the association disclosures such as pending special assessments, capital reserves balance, anticipated major projects, monthly dues and use restrictions within the association.

Sellers and purchasers should also be aware that sellers have an obligation to disclose certain information related to deferred water and sewer charges pursuant to REAL PROPERTY § 14-117. In the event a seller fails to disclose deferred water and sewer charges, the purchaser may have the right to rescind the contract or if discovered after closing, the purchaser may be entitled to recoup from the seller the full amount of remaining deferred water and sewer charges not disclosed pursuant to REAL PROPERTY § 14-117.

D. [§ 6.29] Maryland Condominium Act

A vendor cannot enforce a contract for the initial sale of a condominium unit unless on or before execution of the contract, the buyer is given a public offering statement containing the information required by REAL PROP. § 11-126(b).[149] Under REAL PROP. § 11-126(e), condominium buyers enjoy the right to rescind a sales contract within certain time periods following their receipt of disclosures required by the Condominium Act. If in disclosing the required information the vendor makes an untrue statement of material fact or omits a material fact, the

---

144 *See, e.g.*, REAL PROP. § 11B-105 (relating to disclosures required upon initial sale of a lot in a development containing more than 12 lots to a member of the public who intends to occupy or rent the lot for residential purposes).

145 REAL PROP. § 11B-108(a).

146 *Id.* § 11B-108(a), (b), and (c).

147 *Id.* § 11B-108(d).

148 *Id.* § 11B-109.

149 *Id.* § 11-126(a).

vender is liable to the buyer for damages proximately caused by the untrue statement or omission.

REAL PROP. § 11-131 imposes the express and implied warranties from REAL PROP. §§ 10-202 and 10-203 on developers of condominiums and the common elements when initially sold. If the developer conveys the condominiums to an intermediate purchaser for the purpose of evading warranty liability, REAL PROP. § 11-131(b) now extends the warranties to cover buyers who purchase from intermediate purchasers. These warranties are not exclusive remedies but are in addition to the warranties in REAL PROP. §§ 10-202 and 10-203.[150]

The resale of condominium units by owners other than developers is governed by the provisions of REAL PROP. § 11-135. The seller may only enforce the contract if it contains specified information regarding the unit and if the seller furnishes to the buyer certain documents regarding the unit.[151] Generally, the buyer enjoys the right to rescind the contract for a period of seven days following receipt of all the information required under REAL PROP. § 11-135.[152] The practitioner should read each of the above statutory provisions carefully to determine whether rights and remedies are afforded the buyer in any given case. Buyers should be aware of certain information revealed by the condominium disclosures such as pending special assessments, capital reserves balance, anticipated major projects, monthly dues and use restrictions within the complex.

E. [§ 6.30] Maryland Home Builder Registration Act

BUSINESS REGULATION TITLE 4.5 contains the Maryland Home Builder Registration Act. The Act requires the registration of new home builders. A contract for the performance of any act for which a home builder registration number is required is not enforceable unless the home builder was registered at the time that the contract was signed by the owner.[153]

F. [§ 6.31] Custom Home Protection Act

A "custom home" is a single-family dwelling constructed for the buyer's residence on land currently or previously owned by the buyer.[154] A violation of the Custom Home Protection Act is considered a violation of the Consumer Protection Act.[155]

---

150 *Milton Co. v. Council of Unit Owners of Bentley Place Condo.*, 354 Md. 264, 729 A.2d 981 (1999).

151 REAL PROP. § 11-135(a) and (g); *see Swinson v. Lords Landing Vill. Condo.*, 360 Md. 462, 758 A.2d 1008 (2000).

152 REAL PROP. § 11-135(f).

153 MD. CODE ANN., BUSINESS REGULATION § 4.5-605 (2015 & Supp. 2022).

154 REAL PROP. § 10-501(c). *See also* REAL PROP. §§ 10-505 contracts and 10-506 disclosures.

155 REAL PROP. § 10-507. *See also* COMMERCIAL LAW Article, Title 13.

G. [§ 6.32] Local Requirements

A potential problem could arise before closing if a local requirement is not included in a contract. For example, in Baltimore County, the failure of a seller to provide a notice of the well water law or to obtain a waiver of minimum well test prior to conveyance for either improved or unimproved property not served by public water could subject the conveyance to rescission at the option of the buyer plus compensatory damages including attorneys' fees.[156]

In Howard County, sellers of new or resale homes are required by § 17.502 of the Howard County Code to provide buyers, on or before execution of the contract of sale, with a copy of the current General Plan Maps for Howard County. The General Plan Maps consist of the Policies Maps, the Land Use Map, and the Highways Map as published by the Howard County Department of Planning and Zoning. If the buyer receives the General Plan Maps within less than two days before executing the contract, the buyer shall have the right to rescind the contract in accordance with § 17.502.

Many counties have local requirements. The practitioner cannot rely solely on the state contract requirements enumerated in REAL PROP. §§ 14-117; Title 10, Subtitle 7; and the REAL PROP. Title generally. The state code provisions often do not include local requirements created under local law.

H. [§ 6.33] Disclosures/Disclaimer

REAL PROP. § 10-702 applies only to single family residential real property improved by four or fewer single-family units. The section does not apply to the initial sale of single-family residential real property that has never been occupied or for which a certificate of occupancy has been issued within one year before seller and buyer enter into a contract of sale.[157] For a complete discussion of the statutory disclosure requirements of REAL PROP. § 10-702, see Chapter 2. A purchaser who does not receive the disclosure or disclaimer statement on or before entering into a contract has the unconditional right, upon written notice, to rescind the contract before receiving the disclosure or disclaimer statement or within five days of receiving it.[158] Note, with limited exceptions, a seller is generally required to disclose latent defects, regardless of whether the seller provides a disclosure or disclaimer statement to the purchaser.

For a discussion of the availability of attorneys' fees in an action for false or negligent misrepresentation in a Disclosure Statement, see *Stratakos v. Parcells*.[159]

---

156 BALTIMORE COUNTY CODE §§ 34-2-103, 34-2-104 and 34-2-105.

157 REAL PROP. § 10-702(b)(2).

158 *Id.* § 10-702(h)(1).

159 172 Md. App. 464 (2007).

The Appellate Court of Maryland held that a misrepresentation on the Disclosure Statement arose out of the contract, thus the party was eligible for attorneys' fees.[160] To avoid any dispute about whether the Disclosure Statement is a substantive part of the contract, the carefully drafted contract would incorporate the document into the main body of the contract by reference.

X. MISREPRESENTATION OR FRAUD

A. [§ 6.34] Generally

A buyer may learn of problems after closing that may lead the buyer to believe that the seller failed to disclose a known problem or fraudulently misrepresented the absence of a problem. The following types of problems may lead a buyer to suspect fraud: water problems not in evidence before executing the contract, termites, or inadequate water or septic systems.

B. [§ 6.35] Elements

To prove an intentional misrepresentation by the seller, the buyer must prove:

(i) that the seller asserted a false representation of material fact;

(ii) that the seller knew that the representation was false (or that the representation was made with such reckless disregard for the truth that knowledge of the falsity can be imputed to the seller);

(iii) that the seller made the misrepresentation for the purpose of defrauding the buyer;

(iv) the buyer relied with justification upon the misrepresentation; and

(v) the buyer suffered damages as a direct result of the reliance on the misrepresentation.[161]

Despite the possibility that there may be a cause of action for misrepresentation, the careful buyer will thoroughly inspect the premises as many times as the buyer wants and should also have the premises inspected by a professional inspector who is competent to discover structural defects. Many contracts contain provisions in which the buyer's satisfaction with the results of a termite inspection, home inspection, or contractor inspection are a condition to buyer's obligation to close. See Chapter 2, Contracts of Sale: Resale of Existing Residences, for further discussion of these matters and standard contract terms in general.

---

160 *Id.*

161 *Alleco, Inc. v. Harry & Jeanette Weinberg Found.*, 340 Md. 176, 665 A.2d 1038 (1995); *Lofton v. TLC Laser Eye Ctrs.*, 2001 U.S. Dist. LEXIS 1476, 143 Lab. Cas. (CCH) P59231 (D. Md. Feb. 8, 2001).

To prove a negligent misrepresentation, the buyer must show that:

(i) the seller, owing a duty of care to the buyer, negligently asserted a false statement;

(ii) the seller intended their statement to be acted upon by the buyer;

(iii) the seller had knowledge that the buyer would probably rely on the statement, which, if erroneous, would cause loss or injury;

(iv) the buyer justifiably took action in reliance on the statement; and

(v) the buyer suffered damage proximately caused by the seller's negligence.[162]

Of course, information withheld must be material.[163]

C. [§ 6.36] Remedies

People who discover that they have been induced into a contract by fraud must decide whether to unilaterally rescind the contract or to ratify the contract and seek damages.[164]

XI. [§ 6.37] UNFAIR AND DECEPTIVE TRADE PRACTICES

If there is a problem proving fraud or, perhaps, in addition to proving fraud, counsel for a buyer should always keep in mind the availability of the Maryland Consumer Protection Act.[165] Under the Act, a "consumer" includes an actual or prospective purchaser of "consumer realty," which is real property.[166] The Act does not, however, extend protection to homeowners who purchase homes constructed with consumer goods because the Act covers only goods used primarily for personal, family, or household use.[167] The Act covers false or misleading oral or writ-

---

162 *Ward Dev. Co. v. Ingrao*, 63 Md. App. 645, 654, 493 A.2d 421, 426 (1985).

163 *Id.* at 655, 493 A.2d at 426 (a matter is material if (a) a reasonable man would attach importance to its existence in determining his choice of action in the transaction or (b) the maker of the misrepresentation knows or has reason to know that its recipient regards or is likely to regard the matter as important in determining a choice of action) (internal citation omitted).

164 *Sonnenberg v. Sec. Mgmt. Corp.*, 325 Md. 117, 124, 599 A.2d 820, 823 (1992); *see also Benjamin v. Erk*, 138 Md. App. 459, 771 A.2d 1106 (2001) ("[W]hen a party to a contract discovers a fraud has been perpetrated upon him, he is put to a prompt election to rescind the contract or to ratify it and claim damages.") (quoting *Wolin v. Zenith Homes*, 219 Md. 242, 250, 146 A.2d 197, 202 (1959)).

165 COM. LAW §§ 13-101–13-105, 13-301–13-304. *But see* Comment, *Maryland's Consumer Protection Act: A Private Cause of Action for Unfair or Deceptive Trade Practices*, 38 MD. L. REV. 733 (1979), where the author argues that it is unlikely that an individual selling their house is within the purview of the Act.

166 COM. LAW § 13-101(c) and (d).

167 *Morris v. Osmose Wood Preserving*, 99 Md. App. 646, 639 A.2d 147 (1994), *aff'd as modified*, 340 Md. 519, 667 A.2d 624 (1995).

ten statements that have the capacity, tendency, or effect of deceiving or misleading consumers, including a statement that a condominium when built will conform to the plans presented to the consumer.[168] The Act generally covers unfair or deceptive trade practices, which include representations that consumer realty has a characteristic that it does not have or that consumer realty is of a particular quality that it is not.[169] The Act also covers the failure to state a material fact if the failure deceives or tends to deceive.[170] The Act creates a private action to recover damages for injury or loss caused by an unfair and deceptive trade practice.[171] In addition, any person who is awarded damages under the Act may also seek reasonable attorneys' fees.[172]

XII. ANTICIPATORY BREACH

A. [§ 6.38] Generally

Regardless of the changes either party requests prior to closing, there is no breach of contract until one party refuses to settle on the date of settlement. The exception to this rule is when the buyer or seller anticipatorily repudiates. To prove an anticipatory breach of contract, either the buyer or the seller would need to prove the existence of a contractual obligation and a definite, positive, and unconditional refusal to perform under the contract.[173]

For example, if a buyer writes to seller and requests a rescission of the contract if the deposit is returned, at best there is a request or offer to accept mutual rescission upon certain conditions. The buyer has not repudiated the contract and the seller may not forfeit the buyer's deposit.[174] If, however, a buyer writes to seller stating absolutely the contract is cancelled and demanding a return of the deposit

---

168 *Hartford Accident & Indem. Co. v. Scarlett Harbor Assocs. Ltd. P'ship*, 109 Md. App. 217, 674 A.2d 106 (1996), *aff'd*, 346 Md. 122, 695 A.2d 153 (1997).

169 COM. LAW § 13-301(2).

170 *Id.* § 13-301(3).

171 *Id.* § 13-408.

172 *Id.* § 13-408(b).

173 *RAD Concepts, Inc. v. Wilks Precision Instrument Co.*, 167 Md. App. 132, 891 A.2d 1148 (2006); *C.W. Blomquist & Co. v. Capital Area Realty Investors*, 270 Md. 486, 311 A.2d 787 (1973); *String v. Steven Dev. Corp.*, 269 Md. 569, 578–79, 307 A.2d 713, 719 (1973).

174 *Harrell v. Sea Colony, Inc.*, 35 Md. App. 300, 306, 370 A.2d 119, 123 (1977) ("In 6 Corbin, Contracts, § 973, the standard for determining an anticipatory breach of contract is set forth: 'In order to constitute an anticipatory breach of contract, there must be a definite and unequivocal manifestation of intention on the part of the repudiator that he will not render the promised performance when the time fixed for it in the contract arrives. Doubtful and indefinite statements that the performance may or may not take place and statements that, under certain circumstances that in fact do not yet exist, the performance will not take place, will not be held to create an immediate right of action. A mere request for a change in the terms or a request for cancellation of the contract is not in itself enough to constitute a repudiation.' ").

monies, there is a clear and unequivocal repudiation and seller is entitled to forfeit buyer's deposit.[175] Similarly, there is an anticipatory repudiation where time is of the essence and one party writes to the other stating they will be unable to perform by the date of settlement.[176] It should be noted that unless expressly stated in the contract, there is a presumption that time is not of the essence, and a party may reasonably delay settlement without being in breach.[177] Typically, residential real estate contracts include a provision that time is of the essence. However, even if the contract does not include a provision that time is of the essence, this does not allow a party to do nothing and rely on the presumption that they are entitled to additional time in which to settle. In the face of such conduct, the dilatory party is held to the settlement date and will be in breach if unable to settle at that time.[178] Furthermore, where a party misses a settlement date, the other may in certain circumstances be able to make time of the essence by stipulating it in a letter setting the next settlement date.[179] To avoid instances which may be construed as anticipatory repudiation, the parties should be careful in their communications with the opposing party.

B. [§ 6.39] Remedies

Where there is a clear anticipatory repudiation, the aggrieved party may immediately file suit for anticipatory breach or wait until the time for performance passes and then sue for actual breach. Often it is advantageous to wait until the time for performance passes and until the damages resulting from such breach are fixed or finally calculable prior to filing suit. When a buyer anticipatorily repudiates, the seller's damages may include the carrying costs of the property such as the taxes, insurance and other utilities; the reduction in resale price when seller re-lists the property for sale; and other damages resulting from the buyer's breach. The parties should be mindful of the duty to mitigate damages upon a breach or anticipatory repudiation.

XIII. [§ 6.40] CONCLUSION

Whatever the nature of the pre-closing problem, in deciding what legal remedy to pursue against a breaching party, both seller's and buyer's attorneys must be cognizant of their clients' practical objectives, as well as other areas of the law, such as pleading and practice. If, after buyer's breach, the seller's objective is to turn the

---

175 *String*, 269 Md. at 580–81, 307 A.2d at 720.

176 *Id.* at 579–80, 307 A.2d at 719.

177 *Chirichella v. Erwin*, 270 Md. 178, 310 A.2d 555 (1973); *Kasten Contr. Co. v. Maple Ridge Constr. Co.*, 245 Md. 373, 377, 226 A.2d 341, 344 (1967); *Pines Plaza Ltd. P'ship v. Berkley Trace, LLC*, 431 Md. 652, 66 A.3d 720 (2013).

178 *Chirichella*, 270 Md. at 183, 310 A.2d at 557–58.

179 *Doering v. Fields*, 187 Md. 484, 488–90, 50 A.2d 553, 555 (1947); *Stefanowicz Corp. v. Harris*, 36 Md. App. 136, 144-145, 373 A.2d 54, 60 (1977); *Goldberg v. Feldman*, 108 Md. 330, 70 A. 245 (1908).

property over quickly to another buyer, they do not want the property tied up in litigation (or mediation if required by the terms of the contract).

In any type of lawsuit filed by seller, a buyer might conceivably file a counterclaim that could create a *lis pendens* on the property, so the seller cannot sell it. On the other hand, the buyer may not want to be tied up litigating a claim against the seller for a long time, particularly litigation that could be expensive. If the contract is breached, most of the time, the dispute is resolved by the buyer forfeiting the deposit or the seller returning the deposit, or some compromising combination of both. In the majority of transactions, parties will prefer a pragmatic remedy that completes the sale with minimum problems. Thus, a lawyer faced with pre-closing problems best serves the client by directing efforts toward practical resolutions rather than protracted litigation.

Careful planning and advance communication will likely resolve most pre-closing problems but an attorney representing a residential real estate client should be mindful of the pre-closing problems and solutions.

CHAPTER SEVEN

SETTLEMENT OF TITLE OF RESIDENTIAL REAL ESTATE*

* This chapter was updated by MSBA staff attorneys. MSBA gratefully acknowledges the contributions to this chapter from previous authors Lawrence F. Haislip, Esq., Betsy Grace Cunningham, Esq., Douglas Scott MacGregor, Esq., and Stuart C. Resnick, Esq.

TABLE OF CONTENTS

I. INTRODUCTION

A. [§ 7.1] Overview

The settlement of residential real property is a complex and involved transaction comprised of many stages and subparts. An attorney representing a client at a settlement may be representing either the purchaser, borrower, the lender, and even occasionally the seller. Before any steps are initiated in the settlement process, the attorney must first identify their client and the unique responsibilities the attorney has to that client.

If the attorney decides to handle a settlement in which there is to be a loan to finance or refinance the purchase, they may be obligated to represent the lender's interest, insuring that *all* lender requirements are met, even if one or more of the lender's requirements are adverse to the borrower, buyer, or seller. The attorney should also note that under the Real Estate Settlement Procedures Act (RESPA),[1] the buyer has the right to choose the attorney or title company to handle the settlement. The choice invariably sets up the possibility of a conflict of interest should the attorney decide to represent the buyer and handle the settlement. (*See* **§ 7.7**, *infra*.)

B. [§ 7.2] Scope

This chapter discusses the responsibilities of an attorney who handles a settlement and represents either the borrower, purchaser, or lender at settlement. Since the majority of settlements involve purchasers who borrow in order to finance their purchase, the bulk of this chapter will focus on transactions involving a purchase money mortgage loan. Please note that a three-day right of rescission under the Truth in Lending Act (*See* Chapter 5, § **5.45**) applies to most non-purchase money loan transactions and the practices for such a loan would have to be adjusted accordingly.

C. [§ 7.3] Authority—Title Insurance

Although an attorney admitted to the practice of law in Maryland can conduct a real estate closing, if title insurance is offered in connection with the closing, (which is nearly always the case) the attorney must also hold a title insurance license issued by the Maryland Insurance Administration. MARYLAND CODE ANN., INSURANCE I § 10-125 (2017 & Supp. 2022) (hereinafter INS. §) provides that an attorney (or association of attorneys) who is primarily engaged in the practice of law and who solicits, procures, or negotiates title insurance only as an incident of such law practice, is required to obtain a "limited lines" license as a title insurance "producer" (formerly referred to as an "agent"). Holding the "limited lines" license means that the attorney is not subject to the bonding and continuing education

---

[1] 12 U.S.C. §§ 2601–2617.

requirements that would otherwise apply. However, if the attorney owns an interest in, or is employed by, a title insurance agency, full licensing, bonding, and continuing education requirements apply.

INSURANCE I § 10-103(c) also requires that the attorney-producer hold an "appointment" with a title insurer. This means that the attorney must have an agency agreement with an insurer, allowing the attorney to market and sell title insurance for the insurer.

II. POST CONTRACT AND LOAN COMMITMENT MATTERS—INITIATION OF TRANSACTION

A. [§ 7.4] Generally

This stage of the settlement process focuses on the activities following the negotiation of the contract of sale and the loan arrangements, but prior to preparation of any documents or instruments for the settlement.

Once the contract is negotiated and executed (hopefully, after consultation with an attorney) the buyer must choose the attorney or title company to handle their settlement. Should the buyer retain you to handle his or her settlement, the fee arrangement should be established at the outset.

B. [§ 7.5] Fee Arrangement

There is no set formula for setting a fee with a client. The fee a settlement attorney charges is usually based on a combination of factors: Is the attorney acting as a title insurance agent? Is it a cash transaction or one involving a conventional or an FHA or VA insured loan? What is the custom and practice in the geographical area? Section 8 of the RESPA[2] prohibits kickbacks and unearned fees. Moreover, before a fee arrangement is made, the attorney should be familiar with the U.S. Department of Housing and Urban Development's (HUD) Regulation X[3] to be certain the fee arrangement, whether oral or written, will not violate its prohibitions. Ultimately, the fee must be reasonable in light of the scope of the work involved.

If the attorney will be handling settlement, the standard items to be charged to the client as the attorney's work-product are generally: title examination, title insurance binder preparation, document preparation, notary fee, mortgage release fee, and IRS 1099 tax certification preparation fee.[4] These items and the general range of the charges for these items are discussed more fully in §§ **7.32–7.55** of this chapter.

---

2 12 U.S.C. § 2607.

3 Regulation X, 24 C.F.R. §§ 3500.1–3500.21 and Appendices A–E (1998).

4 Pursuant to 26 U.S.C. § 6045(e).

C. [§ 7.6] Contract of Sale

The entire settlement transaction revolves around the contract of sale. The attorney should obtain one of the original executed contracts their file as early in the representation as possible.

Upon receipt of the contract, the attorney must examine the document to identify the parties to the contract and whether all parties executed the contract, what property is being sold, whether the property is in fee simple or subject to a ground rent, what financing terms are contained in the contract, the identities of the lending institution and of the listing and selling real estate agents.

It is important for the attorney to open a file at this point and check for potential conflicts of interest. The attorney should list the parties to the contract and their phone numbers, as well as identify the real estate agents, the lending institution, the loan office, loan officer, and their individual phone numbers.

Following the tragic events of September 11, 2001, President Bush's Executive Order No. 13224 had the effect of freezing ("blocking") the property of, and prohibiting transactions with, persons and/or entities who commit, threaten to commit, or support terrorism. The U.S. Treasury maintains a searchable list of "Specially Designated Nationals" (SDN) found at *https://sanctionssearch.ofac.treas.gov* (last visited Jan. 4, 2024). Searching the Treasury's database for the names of the parties to the contract (and any other party or parties to the closing) should be part of every title attorney's routine due diligence. The Treasury Department presently maintains a "hotline" at 1-800-540-6322 for reporting name matches.

The consequences of entering into a transaction with a person on the SDN list can be severe. 31 C.F.R. Subpart B, Section 594.202(a) provides that a transfer in violation of the Executive Order or the regulations that involves any property or interest in blocked property "is null and void and shall not be the basis for the assertion or recognition of any interest in or right, remedy, power or privilege with respect to such property or property interest." Section 594.202(d), however, provides that certain transfers that would otherwise be null and void or unenforceable due to the regulation will not be deemed to be null and void or unenforceable in certain limited circumstances which can be generally paraphrased as follows:

(1) The transfer did not represent a willful violation;

(2) The person did not have reasonable cause to know or suspect in view of all available facts and circumstances, that the transaction was blocked and otherwise required a valid license or authorization; and

(3) The person filed a report with the Department of the Treasury's Office of Foreign Assets Control (OFAC) setting forth in full the circumstances

relating to the transfer, promptly upon discovery that the transfer violated the Executive Order or regulation and/or was not validly licensed.

Thus, should the title attorney become aware, after the fact, that they may have engaged in a "blocked" transaction, the attorney must promptly report the transaction to OFAC to prevent the transaction from being null and void. Additionally, § 594.701 outlines the various civil and criminal penalties that may be imposed on persons who violate the Order and/or regulations.

The U.S. Patriot Act,[5] among other things, requires "persons involved in real estate closings and settlements" for closings on or after October 25, 2002, to:

(1) verify the identity of any person seeking to open an account to the extent it is reasonable and practicable to do so;

(2) maintain records of the information used to verify a person's name (including name, address, and other identifying information); and

(3) consult lists of known or suspected terrorists or terrorist organizations provided and maintained by the U.S. government.[6]

Reporting requirements, with respect to persons identified on the SDN list, as well as with respect to "suspicious activities," apply under the statute[7] as well as the implementing regulations.[8]

The provisions of the statute and the draft regulations which focus on customer identification and anti-money laundering measures present obvious ethical issues for an attorney representing a person at closing. The Treasury Department provided advance notice of proposed rulemaking on April 10, 2003, for "persons involved in real estate closings and settlements." In response, the American Bar Association, along with other bar associations and industry groups, expressed concern over the targeting of real estate closings as money-laundering vehicles and the potential for abuse of attorney-client relationship. Despite the advance notice of proposed rulemaking, the Treasury Department has yet to provide notice of proposed rulemaking and has deferred the requirement that "persons involved in real estate closings and settlements" implement programs to meet the anti-money laundering requirements of the U.S. Patriot Act, indefinitely.

However, in the future, attorney-agents will be required to review the statute and implementing regulations and either decide that the Act should be complied

---

5 H.R. 3162, Signed Oct. 26, 2001, Pub. L. No. 107-56; 115 Stat. 272 (2001).

6 See the list of "Specially Designated Nationals" found at *https://sanctionssearch.ofac.treas.gov*.

7 31 U.S.C. 5312(a)(2)(U); 31 U.S.C. 5318(l).

8 31 C.F.R. Part 103.137.

with, obtain their client's limited waiver of the attorney/client privilege for the purposes of concluding the transaction, or else decide to assert the privilege. Where an attorney decides to assert the privilege the attorney-agent should, at a minimum, comply with the identification and record-keeping requirements of the U.S. Patriot Act. Attorney-agents should also be sensitive to the fact that the terms of their agency agreements, and the requirements imposed by their underwriters, as outlined in published underwriting bulletins, may impose separate, contractual obligations upon such attorney-agents as they seek to perform the duties imposed on them as authorized title insurance agents. Counsel should check the contract to determine its expiration date and whether a settlement location is specified. Before the attorney orders the title abstract, they must determine whether there are any contingencies in the contract that could ultimately invalidate it. They must determine when the last contingency should be completed and the calendar should be docketed to order the title at that point. The client should be informed that if a title abstract, survey, and other items in connection with the settlement are ordered and the contract is nullified before settlement, the client will be responsible for out-of-pocket costs. It is advisable, when possible, to have the title abstract, survey, lien report, and judgment reports in hand at least two weeks before settlement.

Counsel must also become familiar with the provisions of the Protection of Homeowners in Foreclosure Act (PHFA) found in §§ 7-301–7-322 of the Real Property Article. PHFA regulates the activities of "foreclosure rescue consultants" and prohibits such a consultant from arranging or entering into a "foreclosure rescue transaction" whereby the owner of a residence in default on a home mortgage transfers title to another party to prevent a foreclosure, in return for the right to continue occupancy of the home and/or repurchase the home at a future time. PHFA also provides the owner of a residence in default with the right to rescind any contract to sell or transfer the home for a three-day period (or potentially longer period in some cases). During the recission period, no conveyancing or related documents may be filed in the Land Records.

D. [§ 7.7] Notification of Representation

The settlement attorney has long borne the difficulty of the question, who does the attorney represent at the closing and how can the attorney protect themselves from inevitable conflicts of interest? Even when the attorney identifies the "client" in the transaction, inevitably, the attorney will be called upon to provide services to other parties involved in the closing, such as the seller by way of paying-off the seller's mortgage and recording a release, or a title insurer, by providing title insurance as the title insurer's agent. The most difficult conflict arises when both the borrower and lender believe that the settlement attorney is "their" attorney. As stated by the Supreme Court of Maryland in *Attorney Grievance Commission v. Lockhart,*[9]

> Settlement lawyers in effect representing all interests, as did Lockhart, must recognize that they have a special duty to all parties to the settlement. This duty includes prompt obtention of appropriate releases of liens. It also includes prompt and proper disbursement of all funds passing through their hands. Such lawyers may not abdicate this responsibility to the seller without the consent of the buyer, the buyer's mortgagee, and the title insurance company insuring the buyer and his mortgagee.

Rule 1.7 of the Maryland Rules of Professional Conduct clearly requires the attorney to disclose and obtain consent from the client and all parties to the closing. Although this may seem difficult in the face of an often crushing settlement workload, ignoring these issues, entirely, will almost certainly lead to disastrous consequences. The form letters appended to this chapter are suggestions; the attorney can certainly choose other means or formats to communicate and obtain consent from the necessary parties.

Additionally, the attorney should inform the listing and selling agents of representation so that any events bearing on the settlement are coordinated through the settlement attorney's office.

E. [§ 7.8] Loan Commitment

Assuming for the purposes of this discussion that the buyer is borrowing in order to finance the purchase, the next step is to procure a copy of the loan commitment from the lender. Unfortunately, in today's fast paced world, the commitment often is presented by the lender in the loan closing package to be accepted and signed by the buyers at the time of settlement.

Regardless of when the attorney first reviews the loan commitment, they must take great care in examining it, as the loan commitment sets out in detail the terms of the loan (interest rate, term of loan, amount of loan), the parties to the loan, the security for the loan, the expiration date of the loan commitment, and special lender requirements that must be satisfied prior to or at the time of settlement.

F. [§ 7.9] Abstract of Title

To obtain the necessary information from the public records regarding the property to be transferred, attorneys in Maryland can search the title themselves or arrange to have the search performed by a title abstractor. The actual title search procedure is beyond the scope of this discussion. It will, therefore, be assumed that

---

9 285 Md. 586, 403 A.2d 1241 (1979).

the services of an abstractor are being utilized. A title abstractor in Maryland may or may not be a member of the Bar. If the abstractor is an attorney, an inquiry should be made to ascertain if they has malpractice coverage. Frequently, non-attorney abstractors carry liability insurance for their errors and omissions. Before establishing a business relationship with an abstractor, it is a good idea for the settlement attorney to check on the reputation of the abstractor. Prices are competitive, as are the services offered.

The title examination a settlement attorney performs is dependent upon the quality of the information received in the abstract of the title. Thus, the abstract must be accurate and legible. In Maryland, an abstractor customarily searches the land records for no less than a 60-year period. However, in recent years, most title insurers have relaxed traditional underwriting requirements as to the scope of the underlying title search. The customary 60-year title search has given way to greatly reduced search periods, particularly for refinance and second mortgage loan transactions. Most insurers offer a "starter letter" service, allowing the insurer's agent to assume a good title in a prior title insurance policy issued by the insurer. Also, because most lenders are satisfied in receiving the ALTA Short Form Loan Policy, (see § 4.**50** for an example) which includes "generic" exceptions as to typical matters affecting title, such as restrictions and easements, the requirement to actually identify the specific title exceptions applicable to the residential property at issue may not be relevant. Most title insurers utilizing a "Short Form" policy approach for refinances and second mortgages require the title searcher to "bring to date" the title from the date of the title deed, provided such deed represents the acquisition of title by the current owner for valuable consideration and not as a "gift" or "no consideration" transfer. Surprisingly, title insurers in Maryland are also trying similar approaches for underwriting owners' title insurance, with guidelines requiring at least a 20-year search.

If a full 60-year search is required, the attorney should allow from two to 10 weeks for the abstractor to produce the search, depending on the location of the property and complexity of the chain of title. It is prudent to discuss timing issues with the abstractor in advance, particularly where the attorney anticipates that the title work will be complex, such as where "raw land" parcels are being assembled for development or where the property is subject to past or ongoing litigation. A limited search abstract or "bring-to-date" can ordinarily be performed and delivered in a matter of days. Many attorneys also take advantage of online resources such as mdlandrec.net, and the Maryland Judiciary Case Search website, casesearch.courts.state.md.us/casesearch/ which provides online court docket information.

In a perfect world, the settlement attorney would request and receive the title abstract weeks before closing, in order to have sufficient time to examine the title.

Unfortunately, the rapidity with which loan commitments can be produced by lenders and the demands for quick turn-arounds by consumers means that title orders are routinely placed on a "rush" basis. This means that the title attorney frequently receives the title abstract only days before (and sometimes on the morning of) the closing.

The title abstract will contain the information needed to prepare documents for settlement. When the title order is made, the attorney should give the abstractor the correct name and spelling of the present owner, the address of the property, the recording reference for the present owner's deed, if known, and any reference to a prior title insurance policy on the property. The attorney should tell the abstractor which copies of court-recorded documents to submit with the abstract (the attorney should expect to be billed separately for copy charges). Examples of copies frequently requested include: the current deed, outstanding mortgages, declaration of restrictions, right-of-way agreements, and the original ground lease if the property has a ground rent.

G. [§ 7.10] Lien Certificate

If a freelance abstractor is searching the title, that abstractor, upon request, will order a lien certificate. The cost of the lien certificate is ordinarily added to the bill submitted from the abstractor. If necessary, the settlement attorney can order a lien certificate directly from the taxing authority. In most counties and Baltimore City, the local jurisdiction has a form that must be filed to place an order for the lien certificate.[10]

Lien certificates supplied by the various counties are generally valid for 45 days from the date of processing. In some jurisdictions an original lien certificate must accompany the deed for recordation.

The lien certificates provide information regarding the status of the real estate taxes, water use information, and often other information regarding monies attributed to the property and paid or monies to be collected by the jurisdiction.

Depending on the jurisdiction, it may take several weeks or more to obtain a lien certificate; hence, it is advisable to order it well in advance.

H. [§ 7.11] Judgments

In most jurisdictions, the judgment records are maintained by the circuit court clerks, and the abstractor runs those indices in the course of preparing the abstract of title. In certain Maryland counties and Baltimore City, independent companies (sometimes title insurers) provide judgment searches for a fee. The abstractor usually

---

10 *See* § 7.**81** of this chapter for the form of application for a lien certificate.

orders judgment reports and requests that the settlement attorney set up an account with the judgment department to facilitate billing. If a judgment report on a name is needed by the settlement attorney, it can be ordered directly by a call to the judgment department of the service-providing company, followed by written confirmation of the name ordered.

The abstractor or attorney handling the settlement must order federal judgment reports in order to obtain a list of all cases filed in the U.S. District Court for Maryland located in Baltimore City or Greenbelt. This report will include bankruptcies filed in either court.

I. [§ 7.12] Survey

Many lenders in Maryland providing residential financing require a current house location survey (now called a "location drawing"). This is not a full boundary survey of the property, or even a "survey" at all, in the technical definition of that term, but is rather a plat or plan which meets certain regulatory standards for accuracy and purports to show the position of improvements on the lot, e.g., house, driveway, detached outbuildings, fence, etc., in relation to lot lines, easements, and setback lines.

If a location drawing is requested by a lender, it should be received in advance of settlement so it can be reviewed along with the title abstract. As with the abstractor, the settlement attorney needs to allow the surveyor sufficient time to complete the job.

In recent years, title insurers have relaxed the traditional underwriting requirements for surveys. Most title insurers doing business in Maryland no longer require a location drawing for residential deals, where there are no known survey or boundary issues. If the owner had obtained a location drawing in connection with the acquisition or later refinancing of the property, most title insurers would accept the existing location drawing, along with an affidavit from the owner certifying that the owner made no subsequent improvements to the land and, otherwise, has no knowledge of boundary line disputes or encroachments with respect to the land. An example of a survey affidavit can be found at § **7.84**. Even without a prior location drawing, most title insurers are, nevertheless, willing to delete the survey exception from the lender's policy, based solely upon receipt of an appropriate owner's affidavit.

The cost of house location drawings are competitive and generally range between $325—$475. The U.S. Department of Veterans Affairs (VA) and the Federal Housing Administration (FHA) have restrictions on the cost of location surveys, and the surveyor should be told whether the loan is an FHA or VA loan when the order is placed.

J. [§ 7.13] Mortgage Pay-Off Statement

Once the title is examined and open mortgages determined, the settlement attorney must order a pay-off from the mortgagee or note holder. The settlement attorney should make every effort to obtain from the seller or borrower the loan account number(s) of the mortgages to be paid off. Many lenders will not allow a caller to order pay-off information over the phone, so the attorney will ordinarily request a pay-off by fax. A minimum of two weeks should be allowed for receipt of the pay-off letter from the lender. When there is an outstanding deed of trust on the property, the note may have been sold (not requiring recordation) and payments may be handled by a loan servicer; in this case, the settlement attorney must request that the seller disclose where monthly payments on the debt are made in order to contact that party for a pay-off letter.

The pay-off letter indicates the amount necessary to satisfy the open mortgage and whether the mortgagee or closing attorney is to prepare the release of the record lien. The letter also indicates a per diem interest rate. If the settlement date is changed, the settlement attorney uses the per diem rate to compute the pay-off figure. Generally mortgagees insist on interest to the day the pay-off check or wire transfer is received. If a pay-off is not hand delivered or wired to the mortgagee on the date of settlement, the settlement attorney should add several days' interest to cover the mailing or overnight delivery time. The settlement attorney also must check the pay-off letter for any additional fees to be collected from the seller at settlement, e.g., attorneys' fee for preparation of release.

K. [§ 7.14] Insurance

The settlement attorney must check the contract and the lender's commitment to determine the insurance coverage requirements. If a new policy is required, lenders frequently require the policy and paid receipt at or prior to settlement. The purchaser is advised to contact an insurance agency to get the necessary coverage in time for settlement. The insurance agent may need to contact with the loan department to determine acceptable language for the loss payee clause.

When flood insurance is required pursuant to the National Flood Insurance Act of 1968,[11] the insurance provided by the National Flood Insurance Association is issued through individual local servicing companies. The carrier issues a countersigned copy of the application and a paid receipt, which serve as a binder until the final flood policy is issued.

L. [§ 7.15] Settlement Date

In considering a settlement date, the attorney and client must keep in mind the date named in the contract, the expiration of the commitment, and the moving

---

[11] 42 U.S.C. §§ 4001 *et seq.*

arrangements of the parties. Depending on the custom and practice in the jurisdiction in which the property was purchased, settlement may be held at one of the real estate offices of the agents involved in the sale, the bank, the title company, or the closing attorney's office. It is not unusual for settlements to be held after 5:00 p.m. or on Saturdays in order to accommodate the parties' schedules.

III. PREPARATION OF CLOSING DOCUMENTS

A. [§ 7.16] Abstract of Title

The abstract of title is a report on the status of title of the property being transferred. The report will identify the person or entity holding title, the reference to the deed which conveyed title to the seller, references to any open encumbrances secured by the property, property tax information, a list of any and all open judgments affecting the title, agreements such as telephone pole agreements and other utility agreements, declarations of covenants and restrictions, applicable condominium declaration and by-law references, homeowners association documents, and other related documents affecting title. The title abstract may also point out any possible title problems. The attorney must examine the title to determine for the client whether the status of title meets the agreed upon standard, i.e. marketable or "as is." If title insurance is requested, the same examination would also focus on whether the title was insurable. Obviously, if any title problems exist, the settlement attorney must report the problem to the client. The seller may be entitled to an opportunity to cure under the contract.

B. [§ 7.17] Survey

The settlement attorney must compare the record description of the deed with the survey description, provided that a location drawing or boundary survey has been obtained. They must check the survey for fence encroachments, violation of set-back lines, etc. If there is a problem, the seller may have a right to cure under the contract. The attorney representing the purchaser should always take appropriate steps to report defects to the seller and demand a cure, where appropriate.

C. [§ 7.18] Judgments

When an open judgment affecting the property appears on the judgment report, the settlement attorney will ordinarily ask the abstractor to get additional details from the court docket including:

(1) the address of the defendant;

(2) the name and address of the attorney for the plaintiff; and

(3) the amount of the judgment and the court costs.

The settlement attorney should then contact the seller's attorney to explain the finding and ask for clarification. Because judgments are listed against a name and not a particular person, judgment questions can sometimes be cleared up by determining that the seller is not the person shown on the report. If the settlement attorney is satisfied that the judgments are against a name identical to that of the seller, but not the seller, he or she should prepare an affidavit and have it executed at the settlement table by seller.[12]

Sometimes the judgment debtor possesses an order of satisfaction which merely needs to be filed. The settlement attorney can arrange to do that at settlement. The seller's attorney can sometimes negotiate the pay-off of an open judgment. If funds for the payment are withheld at settlement, the settlement attorney will need a written pay-off statement from the creditor confirming who is responsible for filing of an order of satisfaction and the amounts necessary for any filing fees, court costs, and interest charges.

D. Lien Certificate

1. [§ 7.19] Generally

The settlement attorney should examine the figures shown on the lien certificate and compare the information to what is already known about the property. For example, if the seller has indicated that there are no leases and the lien sheet shows a payment made for a "multiple family dwelling permit," the discrepancy must be resolved. If the lien sheet discloses a problem and a phone number appears next to any of the items, the settlement attorney should call and keep a record of the conversation and the name of the employee speaking for the department contacted. It is advisable to record this information on the face of the lien certificate so that it is readily available if questions arise at the transfer desk at the time of recording.

2. [§ 7.20] Tax sale posting

If the lien certificate shows a property listed with the tax sale division, the settlement attorney must notify the division of the pending settlement and request a "pay-off" figure as of the date of settlement.

3. [§ 7.21] Personal property taxes

When there is a transfer for value, the usual case in the sale of a residence, personal property taxes must also be paid before a deed will be accepted for recordation.[13] Because the purchaser's unpaid taxes on personal property constitute a lien on the real property being purchased, the settlement attorney must

---

[12] *See* § 7.**85** of this chapter.

[13] Md. Code Ann., Real Property § 3-104(b) (2005 & Supp. 2022) (hereinafter Real Prop. §).

check the appropriate record for the jurisdiction, either the circuit court or local tax office.[14]

E. [§ 7.22] Insured Closing Letter

A title insurer ordinarily will issue an insured closing letter[15] to protect a lender against negligence at settlement or loss of loan proceeds or documents when the closing is being conducted by a title insurance company's approved attorney or licensed agent. The settlement attorney must check the lender's commitment letter to see if an insured closing letter is required for settlement. If so, they must contact the title insurer and have a letter sent directly to the lender. An insured closing letter can only be issued by the insurer.

F. [§ 7.23] Preparation of Title Binder

By following the steps outlined above, the settlement attorney is now ready to prepare a "title insurance binder" (also called a "commitment to insure"). Chapter 4 of this book, Title Insurance in the Residential Transaction, covers substantive title insurance matters in detail but, simply stated, the binder or commitment indicates:

1. the identity of the title-holder,
2. the property being insured,
3. the proposed amount of the insurance coverage,
4. the documents that must be executed and/or recorded in order to convey clear title to the purchaser encumbered only by the new loan, and
5. agreements or encumbrances of record that affect title.

If the settlement attorney has questions concerning a title insurer's instructions on how to prepare a binder, wording for special exceptions, affirmative coverages, special endorsements, or removal of standard exceptions, they should contact the representative of the title insurance underwriter and follow the instructions given.

G. [§ 7.24] Preparation of Deed

Ordinarily the deed is prepared by the settlement attorney or title agent handling the settlement. If more than one purchaser is taking title, the settlement attorney must determine whether the purchasers are taking title as joint tenants, tenants by the entireties, or tenants in common. This information must be set out in the granting clause and should be mirrored in the habendum. The purchase price must be set out as the actual consideration, the description of the property must be set out with particularity and a "being clause" following the description stating the date the

---

14 MD. CODE ANN., TAX-PROPERTY § 14-804 (2019 & Supp. 2022) (hereinafter Tax-Prop. § __).

15 *See* § **7.86** of this chapter.

grantor acquired title and the liber and folio reference of that transaction is a helpful addition in the deed. There must also be signature lines for the seller, and a place following the signatures for the acknowledgement.

Suggested language for various grants and acknowledgements is set forth in Real Prop. §§ 4-202 and 4-204. These forms are useful, but are too abbreviated to represent an accurate depiction of the typical deed used in a residential transaction. A prerequisite to the recording of any deed, mortgage, or deed of trust is that it contain a certification that the document was either prepared by an attorney admitted to practice before the Supreme Court of Maryland, under their supervision, or by one of the parties named in the instrument.[16]

H. [§ 7.25] Preparation of Loan Documents

In conjunction with the preparation of the title binder and deed, the settlement attorney may be required to prepare or complete the partially prepared loan documents. These documents consist of a note and deed of trust or a mortgage. The lender's instructions will inform the settlement attorney whether the lender or the attorney will prepare the loan documents.

If the settlement attorney is required to prepare the note and deed of trust, the lender's instructions will instruct the attorney as to the type of loan, e.g., FHA, VA, conventional insured or uninsured, adjustable rate or fixed rate. The instructions will also set out the principal amount of the loan, the interest rate, the first and last payment dates, and if an adjustable rate mortgage (ARM) is being used, the margin, caps on the rate, and rate change dates.

The lender's instructions will also state whether there are riders required to be attached to and made a part of the note or deed of trust. These include condominium riders, PUD (Planned Unit Development) riders, adjustable rate riders, etc.

I. [§ 7.26] Owner's Affidavit

The settlement attorney prepares the owner's affidavit executed by the seller at settlement. The Affidavit requires the disclosure of any information concerning liens, claims, or encumbrances affecting the property, that may not otherwise appear in the title search.[17] The Affidavit can also be used for specific title insurance requirements, such as a certification as to the facts necessary to issue an "enhanced" title policy.[18]

Additionally, as outlined in **§ 2.70** of this book, statements and affidavits as to the grantor's residency, if applicable, must be collected at closing and made a part of the deed. See **§ 7.95** for an example of a residency/principal residence affidavit.

---

16 Real Prop. § 3-104(f)(1).

17 *See* **§ 7.89** of this chapter.

18 *Id.*

J. [§ 7.27] Insurance § 22-103 Notice[19]

A settlement that includes a purchase money mortgage on which title insurance is issued necessitates certain notices to the purchaser, disclosing:

1. the names of each insured;
2. face amount of the policy;
3. the buyer's right and opportunity to obtain simultaneous title insurance in the buyer's favor;
4. the additional premium required for the purchaser of simultaneous title insurance policy;
5. that the title insurance is subject only to the contingencies and conditions in the binder;
6. the opportunity of the purchaser to review the title insurance commitment or a sample of the form of policy; and
7. the contingencies to be met for the policy to take effect;[20]
8. that the title insurance commitment or sample of the policy (a) constitutes a statement of terms and conditions on which insurer is willing to issue its policy; (b) does not represent as to the state of title; and (3) is not an abstract of title.

All of this material is neatly summarized for the convenience of the settlement attorney on forms available from the title insurer.[21] An original signed statement must be retained by the title insurance company for three years.

K. [§ 7.28] Real Prop. § 7-106(b) Waiver

A settlement attorney is responsible for disbursing funds to the seller's mortgagee and delivering evidence of the recorded release of that mortgage to the purchaser and seller within 30 days of settlement.[22] The settlement attorney must inform the purchaser and seller in writing of this Code requirement. Many times, due to no negligence or omission on the part of the settlement attorney, it takes longer than 30 days to obtain a release and have it recorded. Regardless of delays, the Code requires the attorney to send a letter of explanation to the parties.[23] However, the attorney is not required to deliver evidence of the recorded release if the

---

19 Article 48A was repealed by Chapter 35, § 1, Acts 1997, and replaced with the Insurance Article of the Maryland Annotated Code, effective Oct. 1, 1997. *See* § **7.90** below.

20 Ins. II § 22-103.

21 *See* **§ 7.90.**

22 Real Prop. § 7-106(b).

23 *Id.*

attorney properly disbursed the funds within five days of the date of delivery of the deed.

L. [§ 7.29] State of Maryland Land Intake Sheet

Real Property § 3-104 provides that each deed or other instrument affecting property and presented for recordation (excepting assignments or releases of mortgages or deeds of trust, substitutions of trustees on a deed of trust, powers of attorney; or financing statements or financing statement amendments, continuations, releases, or terminations) shall be accompanied by a complete intake sheet, on the form that the Administrative Office of the Courts provides. A complete intake sheet shall: describe the property by at least one of the enumerated property identifiers; name each grantor, donor, mortgagor, and assignor and each grantee, donee, mortgagee, and assignee; state the type of instrument; state the amount of consideration payable, including the amount of any mortgage or deed of trust indebtedness assumed, or the principal amount of debt secured; state the amount of recording charges due, including the land records surcharge and any transfer and recordation taxes; identify, by citation or explanation, each claimed exemption from recording taxes; for an instrument effecting a change in ownership, state a tax bill mailing address; and indicate the person to whom the instrument is to be returned.[24] An intake sheet may request any other information that the Administrative Office of the Courts considers necessary in expediting transfers of property or recording and indexing of instruments.

M. [§ 7.30] IRS Code Requirements—§§ 6045e—1445

Since January 1, 1987, the individual handling the settlement is required to report the amount of the sale (HUD-1 Form, Line 400) to the Internal Revenue Service.[25] The settlement attorney must obtain each of the sellers' social security numbers, or in the case of a partnership, corporation or limited liability company, the company's Federal Tax I.D. number. The settlement attorney must then send out an IRS 1099 form to the IRS and the seller(s) in January of the year following settlement. Failure to comply may lead to a fine. Filing a Form 1099, however, is not required in certain cases where the transaction is a sale or exchange of a principal residence having a sales price of $250,000 if the seller is an unmarried person, or $500,000 if the sellers are a married couple. The seller(s) must sign a certification with respect to the seller(s)' status, the prior use of the property as the principal residence and not as a business or rental property and the fact that the seller(s) have not sold or exchanged a principal residence in the prior two years.

---

[24] Real Prop. § 3-104. *See* § 7.**88**.

[25] 26 U.S.C. § 6045(e).

Some forms also combine a FIRPTA affidavit. Under 26 U.S.C. § 1445e, the transferee or its agent must withhold tax on the sale from the seller's proceeds if the seller is a foreign person or entity. Effective October 1, 2003, withholding is also required if the seller is not a Maryland resident pursuant to new TAX-GEN. § 10-912. See **§ 2.70** of this book for further discussion.

N. [§ 7.31] Confirmation of Closing

Although the time, date, and place of closing are obvious to the settlement attorney, they may be misunderstood by the purchaser, seller, lender, brokers, and other attorneys. Throughout the contract period, several dates may be discussed and considered for a settlement. It is best for the settlement attorney to confirm the final time, date and place in writing to all parties. Sometimes real estate brokers are willing to send settlement notices to their clients once a firm date is agreed upon.

IV. PREPARATION OF SETTLEMENT SHEET (HUD-1 FORM)

A. [§ 7.32] Introduction to the HUD-1 Form

With the enactment of RESPA came a prescribed Uniform Settlement Statement (hereinafter also referred to as the HUD-1 Form),[26] to be used for closing of a first mortgage, secured by a one-to-four family residential property, made by a federally regulated or insured lender. HUD also issued form HUD-1A for use in non-purchase financing transactions. Line item instructions for completing the form can be found in Regulation X to the RESPA Amendments.[27]

On the HUD-1 settlement statement, the purchaser is known as the "borrower." As much information as possible should be processed, typed, or legibly printed onto the settlement statement before the settlement date. Final calculations can be verified and corrections made at the settlement table. If there is insufficient space on the two sides an extra page may be attached. Under RESPA, a borrower has a right to inspect the statement during the business day immediately prior to the settlement date. Should the borrower make such a request, the settlement attorney will have to press the lender for the various charges the lender wants collected in connection with the loan because the lender's closing packages containing such information generally are not ready until about one-half day prior to settlement.

A settlement attorney is permitted to use the HUD-1 Form for settlements other than those covered by RESPA regulations. For non-RESPA cash transactions,

---

26 *See* **§ 7.87.** These forms are available online at *https://www.hud.gov/program_offices/administration/hudclips/forms/hud1.*

27 24 C.F.R. § 3500.21, App. A (2001). The instructions can also be found at the website in note **31**, *supra.*

commercial loans, second mortgages, etc., the settlement attorney may design another settlement form or use a form preferred by the lender involved.

The settlement attorney should prepare a minimum of four copies of the HUD-1 Form for a purchase and sale closing. Both the buyer and seller receive a copy; the lender is required to keep a copy on file for two years; and the settlement attorney needs a copy in the settlement file.

B. HUD-1 Form, Page 2

1. [§ 7.33] Settlement charges

Before a total can be computed on HUD-1 Form, Page 1, the settlement charges from HUD-1 Form, Page 2 must be totaled. Next to each item listed on HUD-1 Form, Page 2, the settlement attorney should list the name of the person or firm receiving the payment and the amount of the charge.

2. [§ 7.34] Commission (lines 700–04)

This item is normally charged to the seller, although if the buyer engaged their own broker, such charge would be indicated as a buyer expense. The amount is based on the contract or the listing agreement. Line 703 is for the purpose of showing commission paid at settlement, so that if a deposit held by the broker is applied to the commission, only the balance due to the broker appears in the appropriate column. If the deposit is held by the selling broker, that amount is subtracted from the total commission earned, because after settlement, the broker will transfer the deposit funds from its escrow account to its business account. The settlement attorney should either request real estate commission information prior to settlement or at the settlement table before discussing the HUD-1 Form.

3. [§ 7.35] Items in connection with loan (lines 800–11)

Since the name of the lender is shown on HUD-1 Form, Page 1, it is not necessary to repeat that information on the 800 series when the charge is disbursed to the lender. Line 801 might also be called the loan processing fee by lender, and line 802 might also be called the points. The settlement attorney should carefully compare the sales contract language regarding the payment of the points by the buyer and/or seller with the lender's instructions. If the contract is at odds with the lender's instructions, the settlement attorney must resolve the inconsistency to the satisfaction of the lender. The settlement attorney should fill in the percentage and the total on which the percentage is figured. All monies paid by the borrower in connection with the loan must be shown on the HUD-1 Form. Therefore, if certain items such as appraisal and credit reports have been paid prior to closing, the amounts must appear on the settlement sheet as P.O.C., paid outside of closing. The other items appearing in the 800 series are self-explanatory.

4. *[§ 7.36] Items paid in advance (lines 900–05)*

a. Interest—line 901

Interest on the money borrowed begins to accrue on the date of the loan disbursement. Generally, interest may not be collected in advance. Most lenders will submit a bill for the interest payment which is due on the first day of the first month after loan closing, provided that normal monthly payments are to be made on the first of each month. The alternative is that the first payment will be due 30 days after settlement. While Maryland law prohibits the collection of interest in advance (that is, at time of settlement)[28] some out of state lenders will, nevertheless, require the interest payment at settlement claiming that they are governed by federal law, not Maryland law.[29]

Basically, each monthly payment is comprised of principal, interest, and escrow. The payment is apportioned to pay for the use of the money for a 30-day period, to reduce the principal amount of the loan, and to escrow funds for upcoming real estate tax bills, homeowner insurance renewals, ground rents, and mortgage insurance renewals when required. The escrow fund will be explained with more specificity when the 1000 line items are discussed.

When interest is to be paid either in advance or by bill for the period from date of settlement to the first of the first month following settlement, the lender will supply the per diem amount. If the lender does not supply the per diem interest figure it is calculated as in the following example:

Loan Amount—$43,000
Interest Rate—10%
Settlement Date—March 14
First Payment Date—May 1

The May principal and interest payment pays the May principal payment and the April interest payment; therefore, interest on the loan amount must be paid or billed for the balance of March. Counting from March 14, the day of settlement, to March 31 results in 18 days of interest due and owing on April 1. To determine the per diem amount multiply the interest rate times the loan amount and divide that result by 360 (30 days/month times 12 months). This gives the per diem which is then multiplied by the number of days left in the month. Using the example, the calculation is as follows:

$43,000 × 10% divided by 360 = *$11.9444/day*
$11.9444 × 18 = 214.9992 = *$215 due on April 1.*

---

28 MD. CODE ANN., COMMERCIAL LAW II § 12-103(b)(1)(vi) (2013 & Supp. 202) (hereinafter COM. LAW II § __).

29 *See* 73 Op. Atty. Gen. 202 (1988).

b. Insurance, taxes, ground rent

Other items collected or shown in the 900 series include the homeowners insurance policy first year premium (which if paid prior to settlement is shown as P.O.C.), ground rent information, and real estate tax information. There is also a line item for tax credit reimbursement. This line is only used when the seller was awarded a real estate tax reduction. The purchaser will not be entitled to the benefit of the seller's tax credit and, therefore, must pay the appropriate tax amount to the local jurisdiction in which the property is located for the balance of the tax year (which runs from July 1 to June 30). Tax credit information will be found on the lien sheet obtained in connection with the title abstract.

c. Mortgage insurance

Mortgage insurance protects the lender from the possibility of losing money on the sale of its security at foreclosure. Private mortgage insurance (PMI) is purchased in connection with a conventional loan (not government insured) when the loan amount exceeds 80% of the purchase price. The mortgage insurance premium (MIP) is payable in connection with an FHA loan and is paid regardless of the borrower's equity at the time of settlement.

PMI is paid in yearly premium payments collected in advance. In addition to the first-year premium, two months' escrow is collected toward the renewal premium at the time of settlement and shown on Line 1002. PMI is subject to cancellation and termination under the Homeowners Protection Act of 1998 discussed in Chapter 5, **§ 5.17**.

FHA MIP, set out on Line 902, is collected as a one-time premium payment at the time of settlement. The FHA homebuyer has the option of financing most of the premium by increasing the loan amount to cover the premium cost. If the FHA loan is paid off early, the homebuyer may be entitled to a refund of a portion of the mortgage insurance premium paid.[30]

5. [§ 7.37] Reserves deposited with lender (lines 1000–07)

By the terms of the mortgage, most lenders require borrowers to deposit, along with their monthly principal and interest, an amount equal to 1/12th of the annual cost of taxes, insurance, and ground rent when applicable. This money is held in a separate account by the lender. Interest shall be paid on the account unless the loan is sold to an out-of-state lender through the Federal National Mortgage Association (FNMA or Fannie Mae), Government National Mortgage Association (GNMA or Ginnie Mae), or Federal Home Loan Mortgage Corporation and the loan is serviced

---

30 For details, see *https://www.hud.gov/program_offices/housing/comp/refunds/fhafact*. (last visited Jan. 4, 2024).

out of state.[31] In some cases the lender may not require the escrow, but in its place will require proof of tax, insurance, and ground rent payments within 30 to 60 days of the due dates of those items.

The amount of funds placed into escrow with a lender is regulated by Section 10 of RESPA.[32] Due to concerns that traditional lender escrow requirements resulted in overcharges for the consumer, HUD in 1994, changed the accounting method to require an "aggregate analysis" of the escrow account. The lender will, typically, prepare or review lines 1001 through 1006 and then make the necessary adjustment in line 1007 (either zero or a negative number) to reduce the amount of the escrow collected at closing to conform to the 1994 Regulation.

6. *[§ 7.38] Title charges (lines 1100–11)*

The items in this section of the Statement cover the different services provided to the borrower and seller before, during, and after settlement. The settlement attorney may lump several of the title charges together or break down the charge for each line item. There is space available under Line 1108 to show what other line item charges are included in the Line 1108 charge. This should come as no surprise to the borrower at the settlement table, because the attorney should have disclosed this information to the client beforehand.

Locally, many lenders charge for document preparation of the mortgage and a "review fee" by their counsel. If this is the case, on Line 1105, the name of the attorney for the *lender* receiving the fee should be shown. On Line 1107, the name of the attorney for the lender should again be inserted as receiving the fee charged. The fee goes to the lender's attorney for performance of legal services to the lender in connection with the settlement. Another use of Line 1107 could be for collection of the seller's attorneys' fee, in which case the seller's attorney should present a statement to the settlement attorney and ask that it be disbursed from the proceeds of the sale.

7. *[§ 7.39] Government recording and transfer charges (lines 1200–05)*

These rates change, and it is wise for the settlement attorney to call the transfer desk and the recording desk in the jurisdiction where the documents will be recorded to ascertain the current rates. If for any reason the deed and the mortgage are not going to be recorded at the same time or need to be recorded in more than one land record office, the settlement attorney must make arrangements with the appropriate clerks to assure that duplicate tax charges are not made.

---

31 Com. Law II § 12-109.

32 12 U.S.C. § 2609.

It is embarrassing and expensive for a settlement attorney to have to call the borrower and/or seller after closing to try and collect additional monies for taxes and recording. These mistakes can and should be caught before arriving at the settlement table.

8. [§ 7.40] Recording fees (line 1201)

This is the charge made by the clerk's office for putting documents on record in the land record office of the jurisdiction. The charges are: $10 for a release nine pages or less in length; $20 for any other instrument nine pages or less in length or for any instrument regardless of length involving solely a principal residence and $75 for any other instrument 10 pages or more in length. Also, for deeds, leases, mortgages, deeds of trust, releases, easements, declarations, and for most other instruments (other than powers of attorney, plats, notices of sale, and notices of ejectment) there is added a $20 Land Records Improvement Fund Surcharge. "Page" is defined as one side of a leaf not larger than eight-and-one-half inches wide by 14 inches long.[33]

a. The cost of recording the deed is charged to the borrower.
b. The cost of recording the mortgage is charged to the borrower.
c. The cost of recording the release of any existing encumbrances on the property is charged to the seller.
d. If there is a financing statement to be recorded, that cost can be shown on line 1204 or 1205 and charged to the borrower (debtor).

9. [§ 7.41] Taxes (lines 1202–03)

The settlement attorney should review the contract again to ascertain which party is to pay the cost of the transfer taxes and recordation tax. Subject to the "First-time Maryland Home Buyer" provisions in Tax-Prop. § 13-203(b), if the contract is silent, the cost is divided evenly between the borrower and seller.[34] The total of the transfer taxes and recordation tax are shown next to the word "Deed" and then broken out in the proper columns as separate charges to the borrower and the seller.[35]

10. [§ 7.42] Additional settlement charges (lines 1300–05)

The contract terms will also determine which party is to be charged for the cost of the survey and pest inspection. If these items were paid before the settlement, the lines should be marked "P.O.C."

---

33 Real Prop. § 3-601, as amended effective July 1, 1994.

34 For information concerning transfer and recordation taxes, see Chapter 2, § 2.**58**.

35 Tax-Prop. §§ 12-104, 12-105, and 12-108.

The additional lines can be used for such charges as paying open water bills or real estate taxes. Another type of charge that could appear in this space is messenger service for pick-up of the lender's package or delivery of documents to the court house. In most instances the cost is a charge to the borrower. Note that FHA and VA limit imposition of certain charges that would otherwise ordinarily be charged to the borrower.

11. [§ 7.43] Total settlement charges (line 1400)

The fees in the borrower's column titled "Paid from Borrower's Funds at Settlement," are totaled and transferred to Line 103 of Section J on HUD-1 Form, Page 1 of the settlement statement. Likewise, the fees to be paid by the seller are totaled and transferred to Line 502 of Section K on HUD-1 Form, Page 1 of the settlement statement.

In the usual settlement with conventional financing, a quick scan of HUD-1 Form, Page 2 of the uniform settlement statement will only show charges to the seller in the 700, 1200 and 1300 series.

C. Analysis of HUD-1 FORM, Page 1

1. [§ 7.44] Generally

The boxes at the top of the first page of the uniform settlement statement are self-explanatory and should be completed at or prior to settlement.

The rest of the first page summarizes the debits and credits of the borrower's and seller's transaction so that a final tabulation can be made of the transaction for both parties. This discloses how much cash the borrower has to bring to the settlement table and how much cash the seller will realize at the conclusion of the settlement.

Adjustments between the parties require mirror entries to both the borrower's and seller's side of the settlement statement. This is not required for other items. For example, the payoff of a previous mortgage and a release fee are costs to the seller alone, and, therefore, are entered only on the seller's side of the statement. But when the borrower reimburses the seller for real property taxes for the remainder of the tax period, the adjustment figure is entered on both the borrower's and seller's side of the statement.

2. [§ 7.45] Contract sales price (lines 101 and 401)

The exact figure as appears on the contract of sale should be inserted as the contract sales price for the borrower and the seller.

3. [§ 7.46] Settlement charges (lines 103 and 502)

The total settlement charges for the borrower and the seller as totaled on HUD-1 Form, Page 2 are transferred to HUD-1 Form, Page 1 for purposes of computation.

4. *[§ 7.47] Adjustments*

Items which are usually adjusted between the parties include taxes, front foot benefits, water and sewer, and ground rents. The contract of sale may set out other items to be adjusted, e.g., insurance policy premium where the borrower is assuming seller's policy.

Whether items to be adjusted are collected in advance or in arrears, applicable costs for the day of settlement are charged to seller.

There are two sections on HUD-1 Form, page 1 set out for adjustments. The distinction is that, in the 100 and 400 series, the borrower pays the seller. In the 200 and 500 series, the reverse happens—the seller pays the borrower.

The following is an example for calculating the adjustment of real estate taxes keeping in mind that such taxes are paid in advance, i.e., a payment of an entire year's taxes (not just a semi-annual payment), due on July 1, 2024 is for the period July 1, 2004, to June 30, 2025:

Settlement Date—March 14
Date Taxes Paid—July 1 of previous year
Amount Paid—$1,500

An adjustment needs to be made to reimburse the seller for the taxes the seller paid, representing the period of the remainder of the fiscal tax year during which the borrower will be the owner of the property, i.e., March 14 through June 30 of the present tax year. This is done by dividing the amount of taxes paid by 365 to get a daily rate.

$1,500 divided by 365 = $4.1095
Daily Rate $4.1095 × 109 = $447.94 Adjustment Amount

If the taxes are unpaid at the time of settlement the appropriate amount of taxes must be collected at settlement and paid to the appropriate taxing authority. If the settlement attorney collects the open taxes for the current year from the seller, the buyer reimburses seller from the date of settlement through the end of the fiscal year (June 30th). If the open taxes are collected from the buyer, the seller reimburses the buyer from July 1st of the present fiscal year to the date of settlement.

The settlement attorney should enter the amount of open taxes on Line 904 of either the seller's or buyer's side. The settlement attorney must look carefully at the tax bill to determine whether a discount, penalty, or service charge is due on the flat tax amount.

The following is an example for calculating the adjustment of ground rent, keeping in mind that ground rent is paid in arrears:

Settlement Date—March 14
Date Ground Rent Paid—Dec. 1 of previous year
Next Ground Rent Payment Due—June 1
Annual Ground Rent—$92.00

An adjustment must be made to reimburse the borrower for the upcoming June ground rent bill for the time period the seller owned the property, i.e., Dec. 1 through March 14. This is done by dividing the ground rent by 12 to get a monthly rate and by 360 to get a daily rate.

3 months $92 divided by $12 \times 3 =$ $23
14 days $92 divided by $360 \times 14 =$ $3.58
TOTAL ADJUSTMENT = $26.58

The dates of the adjustment period and the total adjustment amount should be entered on Lines 213 and 513 and labeled ground rent.

The following is an example for calculating the adjustment for water. An adjustment for water and sewer charges is only made where the water is supplied and billed by the municipality. The status of water bills for Baltimore City, and Anne Arundel County properties served by Baltimore City water, is shown on the lien sheet. However, in Baltimore County, the lien sheet does not give any information concerning the water. Where there is public water, it is billed through Baltimore City, and the settlement attorney may place a call to the Ashburton Water Division to ascertain the status of the water account. Water bills are sent quarterly and paid in arrears, i.e., after the water has been used by the customer.

Settlement Date—March 14
End of last billing period—Jan. 7
Amount paid—$16.34

An adjustment needs to be made to reimburse the borrower for the bill that will be issued in the borrower's name on April 7, but for which the seller used the water, i.e., Jan. 7 through March 14.

The amount of the quarterly water bill should be divided by 90 to get a daily rate.

68 days $16.34 divided by $90 \times 68 =$ $12.35
TOTAL ADJUSTMENT = $12.35

The dates of the adjustment period and the total adjustment amount are entered on Lines 214 and 514 and labeled water adjustment. This is an estimated adjustment based on the last known bill. The effect of the adjustment is to give the borrower a credit for the water used by the seller during seller's ownership of the property. The borrower must then pay the next water bill in full. If there is an open water bill from a prior billing period, it must be paid by the seller at the time of settlement. The unpaid amount is entered on Line 515 and paid to the appropriate authority.

5. [§ 7.48] Line 120 and line 420

The amounts entered in the 100 and 400 series lines are totaled and entered in the appropriate column.

6. [§ 7.49] Line 201 and line 506

The amount of the deposit on the contract of sale should be confirmed with the party holding the deposit and entered on the borrower's and seller's sides of the settlement sheet.

7. [§ 7.50] Line 202

The amount of the new loan the borrower is making is entered on line 202. Except as hereafter noted, it should not be entered on the seller's side of the statement as it is a credit against the purchase price only for the borrower.

8. [§ 7.51] Line 504

The amount owed on the seller's mortgage is set forth on a pay-off statement by the seller's mortgagee, the amount is entered on line 504. Any additional fees charged by that lender can be described and entered on line 507.

9. [§ 7.52] Line 220 and line 520

The amounts entered in the 200 and 500 series lines should be totaled and entered in the appropriate column.

10. [§ 7.53] Lines 300 and 600

This series of lines summarizes the debits and credits to the amount owed by the borrower and the amount due to the seller. The subtotals should be transferred from the lines above and a final total calculated.

D. [§ 7.54] Estimated Purchaser's Costs

At the same time the settlement attorney gives the purchaser written notice of settlement, an estimate of the costs of closing is made. This can be done by sending a draft copy of the uniform settlement statement (HUD-1 Form) or other format that conveys the information adequately.

The settlement attorney should advise the purchaser of the amount of money needed to close and instruct the purchaser to bring this amount in cash, in a certified check, or in a treasurer's check made payable to the purchaser. This procedure is recommended so that a settlement attorney is not put in the position of personally guaranteeing the purchaser's funds or covering the clearance period local banks are requiring for personal checks.

V. CLOSING OF TITLE

A. [§ 7.55] Generally

This stage of the settlement process focuses on the approximately one hour that is necessary for the parties to the contract of sale to meet at a settlement table, sign instruments, and receive checks. If the settlement attorney follows the steps outlined in §§ **7.32–7.35**, one hour is a realistic figure. If not, this step in the settlement process can take all day.

B. [§ 7.56] Title Bring to Date

The settlement attorney is responsible for insuring that the purchasers obtain clear unencumbered title. In order to determine that all matters of record affecting title are known, the title attorney should call the title abstractor just prior to settlement and have the abstractor run the title from the date of his abstract through date of settlement. Judgment reports should be brought current at the same time.

If any new matters are found affecting title, they must be dealt with and resolved prior to closing.

C. [§ 7.57] Settlement Agenda

In final preparation for the settlement, it is helpful for the settlement attorney to make a list of the order of events that should occur at the settlement table. The items set forth in **§§ 7.16–7.31** of this chapter may serve as a guide. The settlement attorney should update and check the docket control sheet, which should show that everything is ready for settlement. In addition, the agenda reflects particular questions or procedures of the settlement, such as whether a guarantor's signature is needed on the mortgage or whether the seller is supposed to bring a death certificate to settlement. With the help of a settlement agenda, items will not be overlooked in the maze of documents to be executed and the rush of the parties to get away from the settlement table and on with the pressures of moving their possessions.

D. [§ 7.58] Settlement Location

Most settlements take place in the buyer's real estate agent's office. However, some lenders require that settlement take place in their offices. There are areas in the state where it is customary to settle in the settlement attorney's office or in the title company's office.

E. [§ 7.59] Lender's Closing Package

The time of delivery and the contents of the lender's package vary with the practice of the lender. In many instances, after the settlement attorney complies with the instructions received at the time of loan commitment, and after a title insurance binder is submitted to the lender, the lending institution or its attorney will send closing instructions back to the settlement attorney. Usually accompanying the instructions are the mortgage or deed of trust and note, special affidavits, and loan disclosure forms. Depending on the lender's practices, the instructions will list the forms the settlement attorney must complete for settlement. Some larger lenders and mortgage bankers print their own settlement manuals for attorneys closing their loans. The settlement attorney should inquire about the manual and obtain an office copy. If the settlement attorney fills out the mortgage and note forms, a copy of the completed form is returned to the lender for review before settlement.

Unless the funds are wired, the most important item to come from the lender, as far as the borrower is concerned, is the loan check. The settlement attorney must ascertain the local practice of the lender and make arrangements for the check to be picked up or delivered in time for the closing.

It is the practice of some lenders to provide only a net proceeds check or wire for settlement. This means that instead of the attorney disbursing daily interest, amounts for the escrow account, or other charges due the lender from the borrower, the lender deducts these amounts from the amount of the loan check up front. Net checks are permissible as long as the deductions have been agreed upon in advance in writing and the lender provides a schedule of the deductions with the net proceeds check.[36]

F. [§ 7.60] Matters Preliminary to HUD-1 Form Presentation

On a national average, it is only once every five years that a residential purchaser and seller come together at a settlement table. The purchaser and seller may have only met once before during the negotiation of the contract of sale. Therefore, the settlement attorney or one of their staff personnel should greet the parties immediately when they arrive at the office and direct them to the room where the settlement will take place. Introductions should be made of all parties, including real estate brokers and attorneys, and everything possible should be done to put the parties at ease. No matter how well everything is handled, if the clients leave the settlement table with an unfavorable impression of the experience, they may look for a different settlement attorney five years later when they are ready to buy a new home.

Once the parties are comfortable, the settlement attorney should request copies of termite bills and termite reports, real estate commission statements, and original homeowner's insurance policy and paid receipt. Where the parties to the closing are not personally known to the attorney, the attorney must insist on receiving and reviewing identification, such as the parties' driver's licenses.

---

36 Real Prop. § 4-106(2).

Most settlement attorneys make a photocopy of the driver's license or other identification for the file. Once these items are obtained and charges for the invoice are added to the HUD-1 Form, the settlement attorney should ask the parties whether there are any other items which should be accounted for on the HUD-1 Form. When the preliminary matters are complete, the settlement attorney should carefully review the lender's instructions one last time to insure that the lender requirements will be met.

G. [§ 7.61] Presentation of Settlement Statement

The settlement attorney should present the settlement statement to the purchaser, the seller and their agents and review all the figures on HUD-1 Form, Pages 1 and 2, in a manner similar to the way the calculations were set out in **§ 7.47** of this chapter. The easiest way to confirm totals on the settlement sheet is to keep a calculator tape of the figures attached to the original statement. If either party questions the arithmetic, the question can be resolved quickly by reference to the tape. Once the parties agree on the money part of the transaction, they are usually ready to settle; disputes are frequently ended once a monetary adjustment between the parties is made and shown on the settlement sheet.

In explaining the escrow amounts, the settlement attorney should caution the borrower that the monthly accrual for taxes and insurance will change during the life of the loan as taxes and insurance premiums are increased. In many instances, the city or county will send the tax bill directly to the borrower, so the settlement attorney must remind the borrower to send the tax bill to the lender to be paid from the escrow account. In Maryland, the responsibility of the lender to pay the property taxes is set out in REAL PROP. § 7-107. When the borrower and seller have agreed upon all the figures on the settlement statement, the original statement should be signed by all parties. New addresses and phone numbers of the parties involved should be filled in on the acknowledgement page of the HUD-1 Form.

H. [§ 7.62] Execution of Closing Documents

The settlement attorney should date the instruments and ask the Notary Public to be present to acknowledge the signatures. The Notary Public may also act as the witness to the instruments. Enough has been written elsewhere concerning the practices of some lawyers and firms with regard to "getting the notary to sign the acknowledgment." The settlement attorney should avoid asking an employee who acts as Notary Public to compromise ethical standards. In a few instances, the settlement attorney's relationship with the lender may prohibit them from taking the acknowledgement.[37]

---

[37] MD. ANN. CODE, art. 68, § 10 (1995).

Once an acknowledgment is taken on a deed, it has the effect of raising a presumption as to the validity of the execution and delivery of the deed.[38] The Code sets forth certain requirements for execution and acknowledgment of the deed, and calls for affidavits of consideration for mortgages or deeds of trust.[39] An affidavit of disbursement is required for purchase money instruments. The language of the affidavit is pre-printed on the forms instruments commonly utilized, but the blank spaces for the date, names, and amount of mortgage will have to be completed before the Notary Public can sign the affidavit.

The Maryland Code contains a curative statute for instruments that go to record without completion of these formal requisites, as long as the validity of the instrument is not challenged in a judicial proceeding commencing within six months of recordation.[40]

The balance of the documents that must be executed are provided by the lender, such as the Truth-in-Lending Statement, commitment letter, partial interest bill, W-9 Form, seller's and buyer's affidavits, net check certification forms, name affidavits, etc. Check the lender's instructions and check off the documents they need executed and returned as you have them executed.

I. [§ 7.63] Agreements Between Buyer and Seller

Sometimes at settlement matters agreed to in the contract become unperformable, but are not of such significance that the parties want to declare the contract in default or postpone the settlement date. This case frequently arises where the contract calls for immediate possession of the premises, but the seller has been delayed in moving. The seller and the purchaser may come to an agreement wherein the seller rents back the residence for a specified period at a certain price. The seller and purchaser may also request that the settlement attorney hold an additional sum in escrow until the seller vacates and the purchaser is satisfied with the condition of property. Such verbal agreements should be reduced to writing at the settlement table to eliminate problems after settlement when all money has been disbursed. For a form of letter agreement for such a situation, see Chapter 2, **§ 2.77**.

J. [§ 7.64] Utilities and Keys

Arrangements for telephone and gas and electric services are settled between the purchaser and seller outside of settlement. The seller should make advance

---

38 Real Prop. § 4-103.

39 Real Prop. §§ 4-101 and 4-106.

40 Real Prop. § 4-109.

arrangements to have a reading of the meters to the date of settlement and inform the utility company of the change in ownership.

All keys to the property are ordinarily turned over to the purchaser at settlement.

K. [§ 7.65] Disbursement

Before the settlement attorney distributes any checks at the settlement table, the attorney must make certain that the funds received are "good funds," so that the checks and wire transfers to follow will, likewise, be immediately payable.[41] All receipts and disbursements must balance. A disbursement sheet separate from the settlement statement should be used to balance these amounts.[42]

Entered in the upper right portion of the sheet are all checks and cash received, whether from borrower, seller, or lender. Some settlement attorneys keep a photocopy of the checks in their settlement file. The settlement attorney should inspect each check to see that it is properly endorsed and should immediately stamp the check for deposit only to their escrow account.[43]

In the lower portion of the sheet, the payee of the check, the check number, and the amount of the check are listed for each category. The actual check drawn is compared to the amount shown on the disbursement sheet, so that a transposition error does not occur.

At this stage of the settlement all documents are signed and the seller and real estate agent may be a bit impatient to receive their checks. If the receipts and disbursements do not balance to the penny, while it may be tempting for the settlement attorney to draw and issue those two checks and look for the error later, the settlement attorney should not proceed, and no money should be disbursed until the sheet balances.

Some hints for finding mistakes include the following:

1. Reading the receipts and disbursement amounts separately and double checking the calculator tapes.
2. Ascertaining the amount of the difference. Does it equal a particular entry, e.g., the amount of the survey, $125? Has this amount been entered twice or left off completely?
3. Making sure every item to be disbursed from HUD-1 Form, Pages 1 and 2 of the settlement statement was correctly transferred to the disbursement sheet.

---

41 See REAL PROP. § 7-109 for the lender's obligation.

42 *See* **§ 7.94** of this chapter.

43 MD. CODE ANN., BUSINESS OCCUPATIONS AND PROFESSIONS §§ 10-301–10-307 (2018 & Supp. 2022).

4. Enter the amount due from purchaser into the calculator. Deduct all items from both columns of page 2 of the Settlement Statement and any items on HUD-1 Form, Page 1 that are only charged to one party; make sure the seller's proceeds are deducted. If the balance is zero, the mistake occurred in copying information onto the disbursement sheet.

L. [§ 7.66] Copies—Privacy Policy

The settlement attorney should give the purchaser and seller a copy of every document they signed at settlement. In addition, the settlement attorney should give the purchaser a copy of the executed and acknowledged deed and explain that the original, along with the owner's title insurance policy, will be sent after the recorded deed is returned from the record office.

The settlement statement is usually the only document requested by a real estate agent. At the same time a staff person is making these photocopies, a copy of every original instrument or form that will be sent to the record office or returned to the lender should be made for the settlement attorney's file.

The Gramm-Leach-Bliley Financial Services Modernization Act[44] requires title insurers and agents to develop privacy policies to protect the personal information of the parties to a closing. The privacy policy notices of the title agent and insurer are usually provided to the consumers at the closing table along with other documents. It is important to educate staff personnel about the importance of maintaining the contents of settlement files in accordance with the established privacy policy. Similar concerns about privacy also apply to the title attorney representing a party at a closing, based upon attorney-client confidentiality and privilege.

VI. POST-CLOSING MATTERS

A. [§ 7.67] Recordation of Instruments

The deed and mortgage must be recorded in every county where the land affected by the instrument is located.[45] A settlement attorney may make arrangements to have an abstractor handle the recording or may handle the transaction by mail.[46] Before the deed will be accepted for recordation, the proper changes must be made on the tax assessment books. Therefore, the executed deed should be accompanied by the city or county's transfer affidavit, a check made payable to the Director of Finance of the jurisdiction in the amount of the city or county transfer tax, and a valid lien sheet. If there are open taxes, assessments or charges, they must be paid.

---

44 106 Pub. L. 102 (1999)

45 Real Prop. § 3-103.

46 Real Prop. §§ 3-104(a) and 3-110.

When the clerk of the court receives the deed, mortgage, and other documents for recordation, they should be accompanied by a check payable to the clerk in an amount covering the cost of recording, recordation taxes, and the state transfer tax. If the transferee is a non-resident of Maryland, the required amount of withholding and withholding return must also accompany the recording package. All other general and special requirements for the jurisdiction should be complied with, e.g., typing of the grantors' names beneath the signature, correct type of paper, etc.[47]

B. [§ 7.68] Title Policy and Original Deed

After the documents have been recorded, the original deed along with the owner's title insurance policy will be sent to the purchaser. The original recorded deed of trust and lender's title insurance policy must likewise be forwarded to the lender as soon as possible.

VII. [§ 7.69] APPENDIX

The Appendix begins on the next page.

---

47 Real Prop. § 3-104.

A. [§ 7.70] Lender Attorney Engagement Letter to Buyer/Borrower in Refinancing Situation—Settlement Attorney Represents Lender

[Date]

[Buyer/Borrower]

Company

Address

City, State Zip Code

Re: *[Property]*

Dear *[Mr./Ms./Mr. & Mrs.] [Buyer/Borrower]:*

You have obtained a commitment for a mortgage loan on the above property which provides in part that this matter has been referred to this firm for title search, preparation of documents and settlement and that you will be obligated to pay the costs of this loan transaction including our fee as settlement attorney for the Lender.

I wish to notify you that you may be represented by any attorney of your choice and that this firm will represent *[Lender]* as its attorney in this transaction. This representation consists generally of the search of the title to the property which you are offering as security for the loan for the purpose of determining whether or not the title is good and marketable, the kind and amount of any liens against the property which will have to be paid at settlement, consideration of any other exceptions to the title, the handling of the settlement, including the preparation of the settlement sheet, payment of liens, governmental charges and other expenses, disbursement of all funds and the preparation, execution and recording of all necessary documents.

At the conclusion of this transaction, we will *[issue, cause to be issued]* a *[title, certificate, mortgagee title insurance policy]* to protect the interest of the lender.

As the owners of this property you may wish to obtain an owner's *[title certificate, title insurance policy]*. Based on the information now available, this protection will be available for the estimated additional fee of *$___________ (plus $______________ as the premium charge for an owner's policy of title insurance)*. [**Note:** This paragraph is designed to provide for the fee for additional title liability and title premium cost in those situations where the initial attorney fee is based only on the amount of the mortgage.]

A pro forma settlement sheet is included showing our estimate of the cost of the various items which you have agreed *[in the contract of sale and loan commitment]* to pay. Please keep in mind that these figures may vary as more precise figures are obtained.

Please call _________________________________ of this office if you have any questions or wish to discuss this matter further.

Very truly yours,

[Firm]

By:__________________________

Enclosure: Settlement sheet

cc (with enclosure):

[Lender]

B. [§ 7.71] Lender Attorney to Seller Engagement Letter—Settlement Attorney Represents Lender

[Date]

[Seller]

Company

Address

City, State Zip Code

Re: *[Property]*

Dear *[Mr./Ms./Mr. & Mrs.] [Seller]:*

This Firm represents *[Lender]* in connection with the proposed financing of the purchase of the above property by *[Buyer]*, including the title search, preparation of documents and settlement of this transaction.

I wish to notify you that you have the right, if you wish, to be represented by any attorney of your choice, that we represent *[Lender]* as its attorney and may be requested to represent the Buyer for the limited purpose of the settlement of this matter.

This representation consists generally of the search of the title, handling of the settlement, including the disbursement of all settlement funds, payment of any outstanding mortgages, taxes or other liens and charges, the preparation, execution and recording of all necessary documents and the issuance of title certificates or title policies to protect the interest of the Lender and possibly that of the Buyer.

A pro forma settlement sheet is included showing our estimate of the cost of the various items which you have agreed *(in the contract of sale and loan commitment)* to pay. Please keep in mind that these figures may vary as more precise figures are obtained.

Please call ______________________________ of this office if you have any questions or wish to discuss this matter further.

Very truly yours,

[Firm]

By:________________________

Enclosure: (Settlement sheet)

C. [§ 7.72] Buyer Attorney to Lender Engagement Letter—Settlement Attorney Represents Buyer

[Date]

[Lender]

Company

Address

City, State Zip Code

Re: *[Property]*

To Whom it May Concern:

This Firm represents *[Buyer],* to whom you have issued a loan commitment to finance *(the purchase of)* the above property.

You are hereby notified that you have the right to be represented by any attorney of your choice, that our representation of the Buyer will consist generally of the search of the title to the property for the purpose of determining whether or not the title is good and marketable, the kind and amount of any liens against the property which will have to be paid at settlement, consideration of any other exceptions to the title, handling the settlement, including the disbursement of all funds, payment of liens, governmental charges and other expenses and the preparation, execution and recording of all documents.

At the conclusion of this transaction we will issue a *[title certificate, owner's title insurance policy]* to protect the interest of the Buyer and a *[title certificate, mortgagee title insurance policy]* to protect your interests as Lender as required by the loan commitment.

A pro forma settlement sheet is included. Please keep in mind that these figures may vary as more precise figures are obtained.

Please call ______________________________ of this office if you have any questions or wish to discuss this matter further.

Very truly yours,

[Firm]

By:_________________________

Enclosure

D. [§ 7.73] Buyer Attorney to Seller Engagement Letter—Settlement Attorney Represents Buyer

[Date]

[Seller]

Company

Address

City, State Zip Code

Re: *[Property]*

Dear *[Mr./Ms./Mr. & Mrs.] [Seller]:*

This Firm represents *[Buyer]* in connection with their proposed purchase of the above property including the title search, preparation of documents and settlement of this transaction.

I wish to notify you that you have the right, if you wish, to be represented by any attorney of your choice, that we represent *[Buyer]* and may be requested the Lender for the limited purpose of the settlement of this matter.

This representation consists generally of the search of the title, handling of the settlement, including the disbursement of all settlement funds, payment of any outstanding mortgages, taxes or other liens and charges, the preparation, execution and recording of all necessary documents and the issuance of title certificates or title policies to protect the interest of the Buyer and possibly that of the Lender.

A pro forma settlement sheet is included showing our estimate of the cost of the various items which you have agreed *(in the contract of sale and loan commitment)* to pay. Please keep in mind that these figures may vary as more precise figures are obtained.

Please call ______________________________ of this office if you have any questions or wish to discuss this matter further.

Very truly yours,

[Firm]

By:_________________________

Enclosure: (Settlement sheet)

cc (w/enclosure):

[Buyer]

E. [§ 7.74] Seller Attorney to Lender Engagement Letter—Settlement Attorney Represents Seller

[Date]

[Lender]

Company

Address

City, State Zip Code

Re: *[Property]*

Gentlemen:

This Firm represents *[Seller]* of the above property, the purchase of which you have agreed to finance.

You are hereby notified that you have the right to be represented by any attorney of your choice, that our representation of the Seller will consist generally of *[insert here the nature of the representation]*.

A pro forma settlement sheet is included. Please keep in mind that these figures may vary as more precise figures are obtained.

Please call ______________________________ of this office if you have any questions or wish to discuss this matter further.

Very truly yours,

[Firm]

By:_________________________

Enclosure: (Settlement sheet)

F. [§ 7.75] Seller Attorney to Buyer/Borrower Engagement Letter—Settlement Attorney Represents Seller

[Date]

[Buyer/Borrower]

Company

Address

City, State Zip Code

Re: *[Property]*

Dear *[Mr./Ms./Mr. & Mrs.] [Buyer]:*

This Firm represents *[Seller]* from whom you have agreed to purchase the above property.

You are hereby notified that you the right to be represented by any attorney of your choice and that our representation of the Seller will consist generally of [insert here the nature of the representation].

A pro forma settlement sheet is included showing our estimate of the cost of the various items which you have agreed *(in the contract of sale and loan commitment)* to pay. Please keep in mind that these figures may vary as more precise figures are obtained.

Please call ______________________________ of this office if you have any questions or wish to discuss this matter further.

Very truly yours,

[Firm]

By:________________________

Enclosure: (Settlement sheet)

cc (w/enclosure):

[Seller]

G. [§ 7.76] Settlement Attorney to Lender Engagement Letter—Settlement Attorney Represents Buyer/Borrower

[Date]

[Lender]

Company

Address

City, State Zip Code

Re: *[Property]*

To Whom it May Concern:

This Firm has been requested to examine the title, prepare the documents and conduct the settlement of the sale and/or loan on the above property, the Seller being and the Lender being.

I wish to notify you that you may be represented by any attorney of your choice and that the duty of this office will consist generally of the search of the title to the property which is being offered as security for the loan for the purpose or determining whether or not the title is good and marketable, the kind and amount of any liens against the property which will have to be paid at settlement, consideration of any other exceptions to the title, the handling of the settlement, including the preparation of the settlement sheet, payment of liens, governmental charges and other expenses, disbursement of all funds and the preparation, execution and recording of all necessary documents.

At the conclusion of this transaction we will *[issue or cause to be issued]* a *[title certificate, mortgagee title insurance policy]* to protect the interest of the lender.

Committee Note—This paragraph is designed to provide for the fee for additional title liability and title premium cost in those situations where the initial attorney fee is based only on the amount of the mortgage.

A pro forma settlement sheet is included showing our estimate of the cost of the various items which each of you have agreed (in the contract of sale and loan commitment) to pay. Please keep in mind that the figures may vary as more precise figures are obtained.

Please call ______________________________ of this office if you have any questions or wish to discuss this matter further.

Very truly yours,

[Firm]

By:_________________________

H. [§ 7.77] Lender Attorney to Borrower Engagement Letter—Settlement Attorney Represents Lender

[Date]

[Buyer/Borrower]

Company

Address

City, State Zip Code

Re: *[Property]*

Dear *[Mr./Ms./Mr. & Mrs.] [Buyer]:*

This letter will serve to advise you of the basis for the legal fee charged in connection with the review of your loan on the above referenced property. The legal services performed in connection with the loan include the following:

> Review of title examination and binder; review of all plats, easements and restrictions affecting the property; review of the location survey and documents for closing; review of the final Mortgagee title policy.

The fee for these services is a flat fee of *[$___]* for all loans secured by property other than a condominium unit. In the case of condominium units, the fee is *[$___]*. This fee has been determined by averaging the time necessary to not only review these loans but make the necessary communications to both the title company and the bank concerning approvals and/or rectifying problems. The following fees are based on the time required to prepare the documents: preparing Mortgage or Deed of Trust—*[$___]*; preparing Trust Agreements on construction loan—*[$___]*.

You are further advised that the legal services performed are for the institution and not for the Borrower. In any event, however, these services are paid for by the Borrower.

Please call ________________________________ of this office if you have any questions or wish to discuss this matter further.

Very truly yours,

[Firm]

By:__________________________

RECEIPT OF THE ABOVE NOTICE IS HEREBY ACKNOWLEDGED:

By:__________________________

[Buyer/Borrower]

I. [§ 7.78] Buyer Attorney to Buyer Engagement Letter in Routine Real Estate Transaction—Attorney Represents Purchaser

[Date]

Company

Address

City, State Zip Code

Re: *[Property]*; Contract of Sale dated *[date]*

Dear *[Mr./Ms./Mr. & Mrs.] [Purchaser]:*

This is to confirm that you have engaged us to represent you as Purchaser in connection with the purchase from Seller of the above-captioned land and premises. This settlement is scheduled to take place in our *[____________]* offices on *[____________]*, at *[______________ a.m./p.m.]*

We are notifying you that our representation shall consist generally of the title examination, the handling of the settlement process, including the disbursement of all settlement funds (subsequent to the recording of all conveyancing documents), the payment of any outstanding mortgages, taxes or other liens and charges, if any, the preparation, execution and recording of all necessary documents and the issuance of any required title insurance policies.

We intend to conduct the settlement process in conformity with the provisions of your Contract of Sale *[as amended]*, the instructions of the permanent lender, the requirements of *[Title Insurance Company]* and generally accepted methods and practices associated with the transfer of residential realty in the county in which the Property is located.

A pro forma settlement sheet is enclosed showing our estimate of the cost of the various items which you have agreed to pay, in accordance with the terms of your Contract of Sale and the loan commitment, including our fee for professional services that are to be rendered to you, plus out-of-pocket expenses, in connection with this settlement process. Please keep in mind that the amounts shown on the settlement sheet may vary as more precise charges are obtained prior to settlement.

Prior to closing, we will inform you as to the exact amount that will be due from you, to be paid to *[Firm]* at closing, by a certified or cashier's check.

Please sign and return the enclosed copy of this letter to us, in the self-addressed envelope that we have provided for your convenience, indicating your acceptance of the engagement set forth herein.

We look forward to meeting you at the time of settlement, at which time we will be pleased to answer in detail any questions which you may have regarding this transaction.

In the meantime, if you have any questions which you feel cannot be deferred until the time of settlement, please do not hesitate to contact the undersigned.

Very truly yours,

[Firm]

By:__________________________

Enclosure: (Settlement sheet)

ACCEPTED AND APPROVED:

____

[Purchaser]

J. [§ 7.79] Buyer Attorney to Seller Engagement Letter in Routine Real Estate Transaction—Attorney Represents Purchaser

[Date]

[Seller]

Company

Address

City, State Zip Code

Re: *[Property]*; Contract of Sale dated *[date]*

Dear *[Mr./Ms./Mr. & Mrs.] [Seller]:*

This is to inform you that we have been retained by *[Purchaser]* in connection with its purchase from you of the above-captioned land and premises. This settlement is scheduled to take place in our *[___________________]* offices on *[___________________]*, at *[___________________ a.m./p.m.]*

Please be advised that you have the right, if you wish, to be represented by an attorney of your choice, and if you choose to be so represented, please indicate to us the name and address of your attorney.

Our representation of the *[Purchaser]* shall consist generally of the title examination, the handling of the settlement process, including the disbursement of all settlement funds (subsequent to the recording of all conveyancing documents), the payment of any outstanding mortgages, taxes or other liens and charges, if any, the preparation, execution and recording of all necessary documents and the issuance of any required title insurance policies.

We intend to conduct the settlement process in conformity with the provisions of your Contract of Sale *[as amended]*, the instructions of the permanent lender, the requirements of *[Title Insurance Company]* and generally accepted methods and practices associated with the transfer of residential realty in the county in which the Property is located.

A pro forma settlement sheet is enclosed showing our estimate of the cost of the various items which you have agreed to pay, in accordance with the terms of your Contract of Sale, including our fee for professional services that are to be rendered to you, plus out-of-pocket expenses, in connection with this settlement process. Please keep in mind that the amounts shown on the settlement sheet may vary as more precise charges are obtained prior to settlement.

Prior to closing, we will inform you as to the exact amount that will be due from you, to be paid to *[Firm]* at closing, by a certified or cashier's check.

Please sign and return the enclosed copy of this letter to us, in the self-addressed envelope that we have provided for your convenience, indicating your acceptance of the engagement set forth herein.

We look forward to meeting you at the time of settlement, at which time we will be pleased to answer in detail any questions which you may have regarding this transaction.

In the meantime, if you have any questions which you feel cannot be deferred until the time of settlement, please do not hesitate to contact the under-signed.

We look forward to meeting you at the time of settlement, at which time we will be pleased to answer in detail any questions which you may have regarding this transaction. In the meantime, if you have any questions which you feel cannot be deferred until the time of settlement, please do not hesitate to contact the undersigned.

Very truly yours,

[Firm]

By:__________________________

Enclosure: (Settlement sheet)

ACCEPTED AND APPROVED:

____

[Seller]

K. [§ 7.80] Application for Lien Certificate (Baltimore County)

BALTIMORE COUNTY, MARYLAND
OFFICE OF BUDGET & FINANCE
400 WASHINGTON AVENUE-ROOM 150
TOWSON, MARYLAND 21204
410-887-2414

CASHIER'S VALIDATION

APPLICATION FOR LIEN CERTIFICATE

PLEASE ALLOW 3 TO 5 WORKING DAYS FOR A LIEN CERTIFICATE **APPLICATION FEE 55.00**

INSTRUCTIONS

1. PRINT or TYPE the information requested on this form.
2. Write in the spaces provided the EXACT DISTRICT, PROPERTY NUMBER AND DESCRIPTION as recorded on the books of the Department of Assessments.
3. Each application must be accompanied by a fee of $55.00. Make check payable to Baltimore County, MD.
4. A returned check charge of $35.00 will be assessed for checks returned by the bank or financial institution on which it is drawn.
5. This office will not be responsible for errors due to improper or incomplete description or property numbers.

NOTICE: REQUESTS FOR THE PARTITION, CONSOLIDATION OR CHANGE OF DESCRIPTION OF ANY REAL PROPERTY WILL BE DENIED UNTIL ALL TAXES AND OTHER LIENS ARE PAID. CLAIMS WILL NOT BE CONSIDERED UNLESS ALL THE ABOVE INSTRUCTION ARE CARRIED OUT.

DESCRIPTION OF PROPERTY

IS CURRENT OWNER SUBJECT TO A MARYLAND INDIVIDUAL BUSINESS OR CORPORATE PERSONAL PROPERTY TAX?

YES ☐ NO ☐

If a property resubdivision occurred after July 1st, please list
FORMER PROPERTY NUMBER

		----			----						

District

Property Number

		----			----						

Applicant requesting Lien Certificate: ______________________________

Lot and improvements known as ______________________________
HOUSE NUMBER AND STREET ADDRESS

Property owners name(s): ______________________________

☐ **EMAIL** ☐ **MAIL**

EMAIL ADDRESS: ______________________________

Mail to: ______________________ ______________________ ______________
Signature of applicant **Date**

Address: ______________________________
City, State & Zip Code

(Rev. 05/2020)

L. [§ 7.81] Survey Affidavit

SURVEY AFFIDAVIT

Property Address: ____

File No. ______________________

In order to induce **TITLE INSURER** to issue its Loan Policy of Title Insurance free of any exception as to survey matters, I/We hereby certify as follows:

1. I/We are the owners of the captioned property as of the date of this Affidavit.
2. I/We have examined the attached Location Drawing dated _______________.
3. As of today's date, I/We hereby certify that, to the best of my/our knowledge and belief:
    a) No structural changes have been made to any of the buildings or other improvements shown on the attached Location Drawing.
    b) No additional structures or improvements exist on the captioned property which are not also shown on the attached Location Drawing (including, but not limited to, fences, walls, sheds, or other outbuildings, pools, decks, porches, driveways or walks, garages).
    c) I/We have not granted any rights or privileges to any other party to use, cross over, or cross under any portion of the property, other than those rights and/or privileges which are recorded among the Land Records and/or which we have disclosed, in writing, to the Title Insurance Agent an/or Title Insurer handling the real estate closing.
    d) I/We are not aware of any boundary line dispute or disputes involving the captioned property.

I/We understand that Title Insurer will rely on our statements in this Affidavit for the purpose of insuring the title to the captioned property and I/We hereby agree to hold Title Insurer harmless from any loss, claim or damage in the event that my/our statements are not accurate.

____

____

Sworn to and subscribed before me this _____ day of ___________, 20___.

____

NOTARY PUBLIC

My Commission Expires: ______________________

M. [§ 7.82] Judgment Affidavit

JUDGMENT AFFIDAVIT

TO: Title Insurer

DATE: ____________________ FILE NO.: _________________

STATE OF MARYLAND, CITY / COUNTY OF _________________ to wit:

THIS DAY personally appeared before me, a Notary Public, in and for the jurisdiction aforesaid, the undersigned who, having been duly sworn, deposes and states as follows:

(1) THAT _________________ is not the judgment debtor(s) named in the following described judgments:

____

____

(2) THAT the undersigned has never received any notice of any judgments, civil or criminal, having been entered against him/her.

(3) THAT this Affidavit is made for the purpose of inducing Title Insurer to issue its policy or policies insuring the title to said property without exception(s) to the above referenced judgments and said Affiants do hereby jointly and severally agree to indemnify and hold Title Insurer harmless for and from any and all loss, cost, damage, and expenses of every kind, including attorneys' fees, which Title Insurer shall or may suffer or incur or become liable for under its said policy or policies arising directly or indirectly out of or on account upon the accuracy of the foregoing representations, or in connection with the enforcement or its rights under this agreement.

AFFIANTS:

____

____

SUBSCRIBED AND SWORN TO before me this _____ day of _________, 20___.

____

NOTARY PUBLIC

My Commission Expires: _________________________

N. [§ 7.83] Insured Closing Letter

ALTA CLOSING PROTECTION LETTER

(3/27/87)

Name and Address of Addressee

Date:

Re:

To Whom It May Concern:

When title insurance of Title Insurer is specified for your protection in connection with closings of real estate transactions in which you are to be the lessee or purchaser of an interest in land or a lender secured by a mortgage (including any other security instrument) of an interest in land, the Company, subject to the Conditions and Exclusions set forth below, hereby agrees to reimburse you for actual loss incurred by you in connection with such closings when conducted by an Issuing Agent (an agent authorized to issue title insurance for the Company) or an Approved Attorney (an attorney upon whose certification of title the Company issues title insurance) and when such loss arises out of:

1. Failure of the Issuing Agent or Approved Attorney to comply with your written closing instructions to the extent that they relate to (a) the status of the title to said interest in land or the validity, enforceability and priority of the lien of said mortgage on said interest in land, including the obtaining of documents and the disbursement of funds necessary to establish such status of title or lien, (b) the obtaining of any other document, specifically required by you, but not to the extent that said instructions require a determination of the validity, enforceability or effectiveness of such document, or (c) the collection and payment of funds due you, or
2. Fraud or dishonesty of the Issuing Agent or Approved Attorney in handling your funds or documents in connection with such closings.

If you are a lender protected under the foregoing paragraph, your borrower in connection with a loan secured by a mortgage on a one-to-four family dwelling shall be protected as if this letter were addressed to your borrower.

Conditions and Exclusions

A. *The Company will not be liable to you for loss arising out of:*
   1. Failure of the Issuing Agent or Approved Attorney to comply with your closing instructions which require title insurance protection inconsistent with that set forth in the title insurance binder or commitment issued by the Company. Instructions which require the removal of specific exceptions to title or compliance with the requirements contained in said binder or commitment shall not be deemed to be inconsistent.
   2. Loss or impairment of your funds in the course of collecting or while on deposit with a bank due to the bank failure, insolvency or suspension, except

such as shall result from failure of the Issuing Agent or the Approved Attorney to comply with your written closing instructions to deposit the funds in a bank which you designated by name.

3. Mechanics' and materialmen's liens in connection with your purchase or lease or construction loan transactions, except to the extent that protection against such liens is afforded by a title insurance binder, commitment or policy of the Company.

B. *If the closing is to be conducted by an Approved Attorney, a title insurance binder or commitment for the issuance of a policy of title insurance of the Company must have been received by you prior to the transmission of your final closing instructions to the Approved Attorney.*

C. *When the Company shall have reimbursed you pursuant to this letter, it shall be subrogated to all rights and remedies which you would have had against any person or property had you not been so reimbursed. Liability of the Company for such reimbursement shall be reduced to the extent that you have knowingly and voluntarily impaired the value of such right of subrogation.*

D. *Any liability of the Company for loss incurred by you in connection with closings of real estate transactions by an Issuing Agent or Approved Attorney shall be limited to the protection provided by this letter. However, this letter shall not affect the protection afforded by a title insurance binder, commitment or policy of the Company.*

E. *Claims shall be made promptly to the Company at its principal office at _______ _____________. When the failure to give prompt notice shall prejudice the Company, then liability of the Company hereunder shall be reduced to the extent of such prejudice.*

F. *The protection herein offered does not extend to real property transactions in the States of Florida, Iowa, New Hampshire, New Jersey, New Mexico, New York, Pennsylvania, Texas, Vermont and Virginia.*

Any previous Insured Closing Service letter or similar agreement is hereby canceled, except as to closings of your real estate transactions regarding which you have previously sent (or within 30 days hereafter send) written closing instructions to the Issuing Agent or Approved Attorney.

TITLE INSURER

BY:

____

O. [§ 7.84] HUD-1 and HUD-1A Form Settlement Sheets

OMB Approval No. 2502-0265

A. Settlement Statement (HUD-1)

B. Type of Loan

1. ☐ FHA 2. ☐ RHS 3. ☐ Conv. Unins. 4. ☐ VA 5. ☐ Conv. Ins.	6. File Number:	7. Loan Number:	8. Mortgage Insurance Case Number:
C. Note: This form is furnished to give you a statement of actual settlement costs. Amounts paid to and by the settlement agent are shown. Items marked "(p.o.c.)" were paid outside the closing; they are shown here for informational purposes and are not included in the totals.			
D. Name & Address of Borrower:	E. Name & Address of Seller:	F. Name & Address of Lender:	
G. Property Location:	H. Settlement Agent:	I. Settlement Date:	
	Place of Settlement:		

J. Summary of Borrower's Transaction

100. Gross Amount Due from Borrower	
101. Contract sales price	
102. Personal property	
103. Settlement charges to borrower (line 1400)	
104.	
105.	
Adjustment for items paid by seller in advance	
106. City/town taxes to	
107. County taxes to	
108. Assessments to	
109.	
110.	
111.	
112.	
120. Gross Amount Due from Borrower	
200. Amount Paid by or in Behalf of Borrower	
201. Deposit or earnest money	
202. Principal amount of new loan(s)	
203. Existing loan(s) taken subject to	
204.	
205.	
206.	
207.	
208.	
209.	
Adjustments for items unpaid by seller	
210. City/town taxes to	
211. County taxes to	
212. Assessments to	
213.	
214.	
215.	
216.	
217.	
218.	
219.	
220. Total Paid by/for Borrower	
300. Cash at Settlement from/to Borrower	
301. Gross amount due from borrower (line 120)	
302. Less amounts paid by/for borrower (line 220)	( )
303. Cash ☐ From ☐ To Borrower	

K. Summary of Seller's Transaction

400. Gross Amount Due to Seller	
401. Contract sales price	
402. Personal property	
403.	
404.	
405.	
Adjustment for items paid by seller in advance	
406. City/town taxes to	
407. County taxes to	
408. Assessments to	
409.	
410.	
411.	
412.	
420. Gross Amount Due to Seller	
500. Reductions In Amount Due to seller	
501. Excess deposit (see instructions)	
502. Settlement charges to seller (line 1400)	
503. Existing loan(s) taken subject to	
504. Payoff of first mortgage loan	
505. Payoff of second mortgage loan	
506.	
507.	
508.	
509.	
Adjustments for items unpaid by seller	
510. City/town taxes to	
511. County taxes to	
512. Assessments to	
513.	
514.	
515.	
516.	
517.	
518.	
519.	
520. Total Reduction Amount Due Seller	
600. Cash at Settlement to/from Seller	
601. Gross amount due to seller (line 420)	
602. Less reductions in amounts due seller (line 520)	( )
603. Cash ☐ To ☐ From Seller	

The Public Reporting Burden for this collection of information is estimated at 35 minutes per response for collecting, reviewing, and reporting the data. This agency may not collect this information, and you are not required to complete this form, unless it displays a currently valid OMB control number. No confidentiality is assured; this disclosure is mandatory. This is designed to provide the parties to a RESPA covered transaction with information during the settlement process.

Previous edition are obsolete Page 1 of 3 HUD-1

L. Settlement Charges			
700. Total Real Estate Broker Fees		Paid From Borrower's Funds at Settlement	Paid From Seller's Funds at Settlement
Division of commission (line 700) as follows :			
701. $ to			
702. $ to			
703. Commission paid at settlement			
704.			
800. Items Payable in Connection with Loan			
801. Our origination charge $	(from GFE #1)		
802. Your credit or charge (points) for the specific interest rate chosen $	(from GFE #2)		
803. Your adjusted origination charges	(from GFE #A)		
804. Appraisal fee to	(from GFE #3)		
805. Credit report to	(from GFE #3)		
806. Tax service to	(from GFE #3)		
807. Flood certification to	(from GFE #3)		
808.			
809.			
810.			
811.			
900. Items Required by Lender to be Paid in Advance			
901. Daily interest charges from to @ $ /day	(from GFE #10)		
902. Mortgage insurance premium for months to	(from GFE #3)		
903. Homeowner's insurance for years to	(from GFE #11)		
904.			
1000. Reserves Deposited with Lender			
1001. Initial deposit for your escrow account	(from GFE #9)		
1002. Homeowner's insurance months @ $ per month $			
1003. Mortgage insurance months @ $ per month $			
1004. Property Taxes months @ $ per month $			
1005. months @ $ per month $			
1006. months @ $ per month $			
1007. Aggregate Adjustment -$			
1100. Title Charges			
1101. Title services and lender's title insurance	(from GFE #4)		
1102. Settlement or closing fee $			
1103. Owner's title insurance	(from GFE #5)		
1104. Lender's title insurance $			
1105. Lender's title policy limit $			
1106. Owner's title policy limit $			
1107. Agent's portion of the total title insurance premium to $			
1108. Underwriter's portion of the total title insurance premium to $			
1109.			
1110.			
1111.			
1200. Government Recording and Transfer Charges			
1201. Government recording charges	(from GFE #7)		
1202. Deed $ Mortgage $ Release $			
1203. Transfer taxes	(from GFE #8)		
1204. City/County tax/stamps Deed $ Mortgage $			
1205. State tax/stamps Deed $ Mortgage $			
1206.			
1300. Additional Settlement Charges			
1301. Required services that you can shop for	(from GFE #6)		
1302. $			
1303. $			
1304.			
1305.			
1400. Total Settlement Charges (enter on lines 103, Section J and 502, Section K)			

Previous edition are obsolete Page 2 of 3 HUD-1

Comparison of Good Faith Estimate (GFE) and HUD-1 Charrges		Good Faith Estimate	HUD-1
Charges That Cannot Increase	**HUD-1 Line Number**		
Our origination charge	# 801		
Your credit or charge (points) for the specific interest rate chosen	# 802		
Your adjusted origination charges	# 803		
Transfer taxes	# 1203		

Charges That In Total Cannot Increase More Than 10%		Good Faith Estimate	HUD-1
Government recording charges	# 1201		
	#		
	#		
	#		
	#		
	#		
	#		
	#		
	Total		
	Increase between GFE and HUD-1 Charges	$	or %

Charges That Can Change		Good Faith Estimate	HUD-1
Initial deposit for your escrow account	# 1001		
Daily interest charges $ /day	# 901		
Homeowner's insurance	# 903		
	#		
	#		
	#		

Loan Terms

Your initial loan amount is	$
Your loan term is	years
Your initial interest rate is	%
Your initial monthly amount owed for principal, interest, and any mortgage insurance is	$ includes ☐ Principal ☐ Interest ☐ Mortgage Insurance
Can your interest rate rise?	☐ No ☐ Yes, it can rise to a maximum of %. The first change will be on and can change again every after . Every change date, your interest rate can increase or decrease by %. Over the life of the loan, your interest rate is guaranteed to never be **lower** than % or **higher** than %.
Even if you make payments on time, can your loan balance rise?	☐ No ☐ Yes, it can rise to a maximum of $
Even if you make payments on time, can your monthly amount owed for principal, interest, and mortgage insurance rise?	☐ No ☐ Yes, the first increase can be on and the monthly amount owed can rise to $. The maximum it can ever rise to is $.
Does your loan have a prepayment penalty?	☐ No ☐ Yes, your maximum prepayment penalty is $
Does your loan have a balloon payment?	☐ No ☐ Yes, you have a balloon payment of $ due in years on .
Total monthly amount owed including escrow account payments	☐ You do not have a monthly escrow payment for items, such as property taxes and homeowner's insurance. You must pay these items directly yourself. ☐ You have an additional monthly escrow payment of $ that results in a total initial monthly amount owed of $. This includes principal, interest, any mortagage insurance and any items checked below: ☐ Property taxes ☐ Homeowner's insurance ☐ Flood insurance ☐ ☐ ☐

Note: If you have any questions about the Settlement Charges and Loan Terms listed on this form, please contact your lender.

OMB Approval No. 2502-0265

Settlement Statement (HUD-1A)

Optional Form for Transactions without Sellers

Name and Address of Borrower:	Name and Address of Lender:
Property Location: (if different from above)	Settlement Agent:
	Place of Settlement:
Loan Number:	Settlement Date:

L. Settlement Charges		
800. Items Payable In Connection with Loan		
801. Our origination charge	(from GFE #1) $	
802. Your credit or charge (points) for the specific interest rate chosen	(from GFE #2) $	
803. Your adjusted origination charges	(from GFE A)	
804. Appraisal fee to	(from GFE #3)	
805. Credit report to	(from GFE #3)	
806. Tax service to	(from GFE #3)	
807. Flood certification	(from GFE #3)	
808.		
900. Items Required by Lender to Be Paid in Advance		
901. Daily interest charges from to @ $ /day	(from GFE #10)	
902. Mortgage insurance premium for months to	(from GFE #3)	
903. Homeowner's insurance for years to	(from GFE #11)	
904.		
1000. Reserves Deposited with Lender		
1001. Initial deposit for your escrow account	(from GFE #9)	
1002. Homeowner's insurance months @ $ per month	$	
1003. Mortgage insurance months @ $ per month	$	
1004. Property taxes months @ $ per month	$	
1005. months @ $ per month	$	
1006. months @ $ per month	$	
1007. Aggregate Adjustment	-$	
1100. Title Charges		
1101. Title services and lender's title insurance	(from GFE #4)	
1102. Settlement or closing fee	$	
1103. Owner's title insurance	(from GFE #5)	
1104. Lender's title insurance	$	
1105. Lender's title policy limit $		
1106. Owner's title policy limit $		
1107. Agent's portion of the total title insurance premium	$	
1108. Underwriter's portion of the total title insurance premium	$	
1200. Government Recording and Transfer Charges		
1201. Government recording charges	(from GFE #7)	
1202. Deed $ Mortgage $ Releases $		
1203. Transfer taxes	(from GFE #8)	
1204. City/County tax/stamps Deed $ Mortgage $		
1205. State tax/stamps Deed $ Mortgage $		
1206.		
1300. Additional Settlement Charges		
1301. Required services that you can shop for	(from GFE #6)	
1302.	$	
1303.	$	
1304.		
1305.		
1400. Total Settlement Charges (enter on line 1602, Section N)		

M. Disbursements to Others	
1501.	
1502.	
1503.	
1504.	
1505.	
1506.	
1507.	
1508.	
1509.	
1510.	
1511.	
1512.	
1513.	
1514.	
1515.	
1520. Total Disbursed (enter on line 1603)	

N. Net Settlement	
1600. Loan Amount	$
1601. **Plus** Cash/Check from Borrower	$
1602. **Minus** Total Settlement Charges (line 1400)	$
1603. **Minus** Total Disbursements to Others (line 1520)	$
1604. **Equals** Total Disbursements to Borrower (after expiration of any applicable rescission period required by law)	**$**

The Public Reporting Burden for this collection of information is estimated at 35 minutes per response for collecting, reviewing, and reporting the data. This agency may not collect this information, and you are not required to complete this form, unless it displays a currently valid OMB control number. No confidentiality is assured; this disclosure is mandatory. This is designed to provide the parties to a RESPA covered transaction with information during the settlement process.

Previous editions are obsolete | Page 1 of 2 | HUD-1A

Comparison of Good Faith Estimate (GFE) and HUD-1A Charges		Good Faith Estimate	HUD-1A
Charges That Cannot Increase	**HUD-1A Line Number**		
Our origination charge	# 801		
Your credit or charge (points) for the specific interest rate chosen	# 802		
Your adjusted origination charges	# 803		
Transfer taxes	#1203		

Charges That in Total Cannot Increase More Than 10%		Good Faith Estimate	HUD-1A
Government recording charges	# 1201		
	#		
	#		
	#		
	#		
	#		
	#		
	#		
	Total		
	Increase between GFE and HUD-1A Charges	$	or %

Charges That Can Change		Good Faith Estimate	HUD-1A
Initial deposit for your escrow account	#1001		
Daily interest charges	# 901 $ /day		
Homeowner's insurance	# 903		
	#		
	#		
	#		

Loan Terms

Your initial loan amount is	$
Your loan term is	years
Your initial interest rate is	%
Your initial monthly amount owed for principal, interest, and and any mortgage insurance is	$ includes ☐ Principal ☐ Interest ☐ Mortgage Insurance
Can your interest rate rise?	☐ No. ☐ Yes, it can rise to a maximum of %. The first change will be on and can change again every after . Every change date, your interest rate can increase or decrease by %. Over the life of the loan, your interest rate is guaranteed to never be lower than % or higher than %.
Even if you make payments on time, can your loan balance rise?	☐ No. ☐ Yes, it can rise to a maximum of $.
Even if you make payments on time, can your monthly amount owed for principal, interest, and mortgage insurance rise?	☐ No. ☐ Yes, the first increase can be on and the monthly amount owed can rise to $. The maximum it can ever rise to is $.
Does your loan have a prepayment penalty?	☐ No. ☐ Yes, your maximum prepayment penalty is $.
Does your loan have a balloon payment?	☐ No. ☐ Yes, you have a balloon payment of $ due in years on .
Total monthly amount owed including escrow account payments	☐ You do not have a monthly escrow payment for items, such as property taxes and homeowner's insurance. You must pay these items directly yourself. ☐ You have an additional monthly escrow payment of $ that results in a total initial monthly amount owed of $. This includes principal, interest, any mortgage insurance and any items checked below: ☐ Property taxes ☐ Homeowner's insurance ☐ Flood insurance ☐ ☐ ☐

Note: If you have any questions about the Settlement Charges and Loan Terms listed on this form, please contact your lender.

Previous editions are obsolete | Page 2 of 2 | HUD-1A

P. [§ 7.85] Owner's Affidavit

OWNER'S AFFIDAVIT

Agent's File No.: ______________________

Street Address of Subject Property: ____

____

STATE OF MARYLAND, to wit:

THIS DAY, there personally appeared before the undersigned, a Notary Public in and for the State of Maryland, duly commissioned, the undersigned Owner(s) of the captioned property, who, being first duly sworn, depose(s) and say(s) as follows:

1. I/we are a) of legal age, b) have legal capacity to act for myself/ourselves, c) are all of the owners of the subject property, d) are the same persons named in the Title Deed, and e) are citizens of the United States.
2. The property is currently: ____ principal residence; ____ vacant/unimproved; or _____ commercial/investment.
3. The street address of the property is correct as shown at the heading of this Affidavit.
4. No one has ever questioned or disputed my/our ownership of the property.
5. There are no disputes with any adjoining property owners or with any parties or persons as to use or location of any improvements (including fences, driveways, structures, etc.) nor disputes regarding location of property lines.
6. Our access to and from a public street has never been questioned or limited in any way.
7. I/we are not a party to any pending lawsuits in any Court.
8. No proceedings in bankruptcy have been instituted by or against the undersigned in any Court.
9. There are no liens or encumbrances (Mortgages, Deeds of Trust, Judgments, Tax Liens, Mechanics' liens, Unpaid Homeowners or Condominium Association Dues or Assessments, etc.) known to me/us which are not being paid or adjusted for in the current transaction.
10. All labor and materials used in construction of improvements, repairs, or modifications to this property have been paid for, and there are now no unpaid bills for labor or material against the improvements or property. I/we have not received notice of any mechanics' lien claim.
11. There are no unrecorded and/or outstanding leases, contracts, options or agreements affecting this property (other than the contract or option which is the subject of the present transaction) which have not been disclosed to Commonwealth or its agent in writing.

12. I/we know of no violations of subdivision or lot division laws, nor do we know of any violations of any zoning laws regarding this property.
13. All taxes, charges, dues, water and sewer bills and charges, and other assessments payable in connection with this property have been paid through the date of the herein Affidavit unless payment has been provided for on the HUD-1 Settlement Statement used in the current transaction; and the undersigned have not received notice from any Governmental agency that work is required to be done to the subject property which will result in future charges.
14. I/we are not receiving the benefit of any real property tax credits or preferential assessments which may not continue as credits or preferential assessments to any purchaser of this property.
15. No Governmental authority has notified me/us of any violations, abatement notices, or condemnations.
16. I/we have no knowledge of any violations of neighborhood restrictions and/or homeowners or condominium association restrictions or by-laws with respect to this property.
17. I/we are not aware of any problems regarding the issuance of a building permit or failure to obtain a building permit regarding this property.
18. This property is occupied by the undersigned and undersigned's family. No other persons are in possession of this property.
19. None of the improvements to this property are a mobile home or trailer.
20. There are no bodies of water (including ponds, marshlands, or streams) located on or abutting the property.
21. OTHER: ____

    ____
22. OTHER: ____

    ____

Wherever used in this Affidavit, the singular shall be construed to mean the plural, and the plural shall be construed to mean the singular, as the case may be.

NOTE: If any of the statements above are incomplete, inaccurate, or require further explanation or comment, it is the responsibility of the undersigned to place an "X" in the box below and to provide detailed explanation(s) below. Please add an additional page if needed.

EXPLANATION:

____

____

____

____

THE PURPOSE OF THIS AFFIDAVIT is to induce Title Insurance Company or its Agent to make and complete settlement on the subject property, and to issue its Policy(ies) of Title Insurance, and we understand that Title Insurer and/or its Agent will rely upon the accuracy of the statements contained herein. I/we affirm and state under the penalties of perjury that, unless I/we have made written notations on this Affidavit to the contrary, all of the foregoing statements are true and correct to the best of my/our knowledge and belief.

____ (SEAL)

Witness Owner Date

____ (SEAL)

Witness Owner Date

STATE OF MARYLAND, COUNTY OF ____________________, to wit:

Sworn and subscribed to before the undersigned this ____ day of ________, 20 ___.

AS WITNESS my hand and Notarial Seal.

____

NOTARY PUBLIC

My Commission expires: ____________

Q. [§ 7.86] Notice, Insurance II § 22-103

STATUTORY NOTICE TO BUYER

As required by Section 22-103 of the Insurance Article of the Annotated Code of Maryland.

RE: ADDRESS: ______________________________

BORROWERS: ______________________________

PURCHASE PRICE: $______________________________

LOAN AMOUNT: $______________________________

With respect to the real estate transaction involving the purchase of the above property by us and the making of a purchase money mortgage by us on this property, we have been notified by our settlement agent of the following:

1. That the Lender in the captioned transaction has requested a Loan Policy of Title Insurance to be issued by ________________ Title Insurance Company under which Policy the said Lender will be insured as mortgagee of this property.
2. That the face amount of this Loan Policy of Title Insurance is the amount recited above as "Loan Amount." The premium charge for issuance of said Loan Policy is recited hereinbelow.
3. That we, as buyers of this property, have a right to obtain simultaneous title insurance issued in our favor, which will be the issuance of an Owner's Policy of Title Insurance in the amount of the purchase price set forth hereinabove. The additional cost for obtaining an Owner's Policy of Title Insurance is set forth hereinbelow.
4. That any Owner's Policy of Title Insurance issued in our favor will be issued subject only to the contingencies and conditions contained in the title insurance binder/commitment. We understand that we have the right to review a sample of each form of Owner's Policy of Title Insurance in which said contingencies and conditions will be inserted.
5. That if we desire a Policy as buyers, the Owner's Policy of Title Insurance will be effective upon the payment of the additional premium described hereinbelow, and upon the delivery and recordation of the Deed from seller to buyer.

As used herein, plural shall be construed to mean singular, and vice versa.

WE HEREBY ACKNOWLEDGE receipt of this Notice prior to the disbursement of any funds.

We hereby direct that ______________ Title Insurance Company, through its policy-issuing agent, proceed as follows:

(CHOOSE ONE OPTION: INDICATE CHOICE BY PLACING AN "X")

OPTION 1:

_____ISSUE **ONLY** LOAN POLICY: WE DO NOT DESIRE AN OWNER'S POLICY OF TITLE INSURANCE AT THIS TIME.

OPTION 2:

_____ ISSUE LOAN POLICY **AND** 1992 ALTA OWNER'S POLICY. THE ADDITIONAL PREMIUM CHARGE FOR ISSUANCE OF THIS OWNER'S POLICY WILL BE: $___________.

______________________________		______________________________	
Buyer	Date	Buyer	Date

R. [§ 7.87] Statement of Maryland Instrument Intake Sheet

NOTE: As of 5/2007, the gray shading has been removed from the Intake Sheet to improve readability. The Intake Sheet is designed as an 8 1/2" x 14" document. You may need to adjust your printer settings to accomplish this. The Clerk will only accept the Intake Sheet in full 8 1/2" x 14" page size.

This form is fillable and can be completed using your PC. You can save the form to your PC for reuse but the information you input will not save (unless you have installed Adobe Acrobat or Adobe Approval software on your PC). For this reason, you should print the form once it is completed and make the appropriate number of copies - at least 4 copies.

State of Maryland Land Instrument Intake Sheet

❑ Baltimore City ❑ County:________________

Information provided is for the use of the Clerk's Office, State Department of Assessments and Taxation, and County Finance Office Only.

(Type or Print in Black Ink Only—All Copies Must Be Legible)

Space Reserved for Circuit Court Clerk Recording Validation

1 Type(s) of Instruments	(Check Box if addendum Intake Form is Attached.)			
	Deed / Deed of Trust	Mortgage / Lease	Other ______	Other ______
2 Conveyance Type Check Box	Improved Sale Arms-Length *[1]*	Unimproved Sale Arms-Length *[2]*	Multiple Accounts Arms-Length *[3]*	Not an Arms-Length Sale *[9]*
3 Tax Exemptions (if applicable) Cite or Explain Authority	Recordation			
	State Transfer			
	County Transfer			

4 Consideration and Tax Calculations

Consideration Amount		Finance Office Use Only Transfer and Recordation Tax Consideration	
Purchase Price/Consideration	$		
Any New Mortgage	$	Transfer Tax Consideration	$
Balance of Existing Mortgage	$	X ( ) % =	$
Other:	$	Less Exemption Amount −	$
		Total Transfer Tax =	$
Other:	$	Recordation Tax Consideration	$
		X ( ) per $500 =	$
Full Cash Value:	$	TOTAL DUE	$

5 Fees

Amount of Fees	Doc. 1	Doc. 2	
Recording Charge	$	$	Agent:
Surcharge	$	$	
State Recordation Tax	$	$	Tax Bill:
State Transfer Tax	$	$	
County Transfer Tax	$	$	C.B. Credit:
Other	$	$	
Other	$	$	Ag. Tax/Other:

6 Description of Property SDAT requires submission of all applicable information. A maximum of 40 characters will be indexed in accordance with the priority cited in Real Property Article Section 3-104(g)(3)(i).

District	Property Tax ID No. (1)	Grantor Liber/Folio	Map	Parcel No.	Var. LOG (5)

Subdivision Name	Lot (3a)	Block (3b)	Sect/AR (3c)	Plat Ref.	SqFt/Acreage (4)

Location/Address of Property Being Conveyed (2)

Other Property Identifiers (if applicable)	Water Meter Account No.

Residential or Non-Residential Fee Simple or Ground Rent Amount:

Partial Conveyance? Yes No Description/Amt. of SqFt/Acreage Transferred:

If Partial Conveyance, List Improvements Conveyed:

7 Transferred From

Doc. 1 – Grantor(s) Name(s)	Doc. 2 – Grantor(s) Name(s)
Doc. 1 – Owner(s) of Record, if Different from Grantor(s)	Doc. 2 – Owner(s) of Record, if Different from Grantor(s)

8 Transferred To

Doc. 1 – Grantee(s) Name(s)	Doc. 2 – Grantee(s) Name(s)

New Owner's (Grantee) Mailing Address

9 Other Names to Be Indexed

Doc. 1 – Additional Names to be Indexed (Optional)	Doc. 2 – Additional Names to be Indexed (Optional)

10 Contact/Mail Information

Instrument Submitted By or Contact Person

Name:

Firm

Address:

Phone: ( )

☐ Return to Contact Person

☐ Hold for Pickup

☐ Return Address Provided

11 IMPORTANT: *BOTH* THE ORIGINAL DEED *AND* A PHOTOCOPY MUST ACCOMPANY EACH TRANSFER

Assessment Information

Yes No Will the property being conveyed be the grantee's principal residence?

Yes No Does transfer include personal property? If yes, identify:

Yes No Was property surveyed? If yes, attach copy of survey (if recorded, no copy required).

Space Reserved for County Validation

Assessment Use Only – Do Not Write Below This Line

Terminal Verification Agricultural Verification Whole Part Tran. Process Verification

Transfer Number Date Received: Deed Reference: Assigned Property No.:

Year	20	20	Geo.	Map	Sub	Block
Land			Zoning	Grid	Plat	Lot
Buildings			Use	Parcel	Section	Occ. Cd.
Total			Town Cd.	Ex. St.	Ex. Cd.	

REMARKS:

RESET FORM

PRINT FORM on 8 1/2 x 14

Distribution: White – Clerk's Office; Pink – Office of Finance; Canary – SDAT; Goldenrod – Preparer

AOC-CC-300 (5/2007)

Submit 4 copies

S. [§ 7.88] Disbursement Sheet

File No. Settlement Officer_____________

Executive Title Group, Ltd.

Disbursement Sheet

Property: ______________________________(County/City) Date: ___________

Deposit: ____ $_________

____ $_________

____ $_________

TOTAL DEPOSIT . . . . $_________

1. TO SELLER:

_______________________________________ ___________ $_________

_______________________________________ ___________ $_________

2. REAL ESTATE COMMISION TO:

_______________________________________ ___________ $_________

_______________________________________ ___________ $_________

3. TO BUYER:

_______________________________________ ___________ $_________

_______________________________________ ___________ $_________

4. MISCELLANEOUS:

_______________________________________ ___________ $_________

_______________________________________ ___________ $_________

_______________________________________ ___________ $_________

5. OPEN MORTGAGES OR JUDGMENTS:

_______________________________________ ___________ $_________

_______________________________________ ___________ $_________

Release Fee _____________________________ ___________ $_________

6. DOCUMENTARY STAMPS & STATE TRANSFER TAX:

Clerk of the Circuit Court for _______ County/City ___________ $_________

7. TRANSFER TAX:

Director of Finance ___________ $_________

_________________County, Maryland ___________ $_________

8. WATER BILL:

Director of Finance ___________ $_________

9. TAXES:

Director of Finance	________	$________
________County, Maryland	________	$________

10. SURVEY TO:

____________________	________	$________

11. ASSOCIATION OR MORTGAGE BROKER:

____

a.	Origination fee	$________		
b.	Discount Point(s)	$________		
c.	Appraisal Fee or Credit Report	$________		
d.	Inspection Fee/Review Fee	$________		
e.	Amortization Sched/Tax Svc Fee	$________	________	$________
f.	Document Preparation	$________		
g.	Interest Per Diem	$________		
h.	Commitment/Underwriting Fee	$________		
i.	________________	$________		
j.	Escrow:			
	(1) Hazard Insurance	$________		
	(2) Mortgage Insurance	$________		
	(3) Property Taxes	$________		
	(4) Ground Rent	$________		
	(5) ____________	$________	________	$________

12. MORTGAGE INS. (PMI/_ONE TIME MIP)) ________ $________

____

13. REVIEW FEE TO:

____________________	________	$________

14. TERMITE:____________________ ________ $________

15. TITLE INSURANCE TO:

Executive Title Group, Ltd.	________	$________
Mortgagee Policy	________	
Owner's Policy:	________	

16. Resnick & Eidelberg (Rec./Exp.)
    Abs.__ / LR__ / Jdg.__ / Copies__ /
    Rec.__ / Courier__ / Misc.__ __________ $________
17. Executive Title Group, Ltd.
    Title Exam__ / Binder__ / Doc. Prep.__ /
    Notary Fee__ / Rel. Fee__ / Misc.__ __________ $________

T. [§ 7.89] Certification as to Residency/Principal Residence

MARYLAND FORM WH-AR | **Certification of Exemption from Withholding Upon Disposition of Maryland Real Estate Affidavit of Residence or Principal Residence** | **2022**

Based on the certification below, Transferor claims exemption from the tax withholding requirements of §10-912 of the Tax-General Article, Annotated Code of Maryland. Section 10-912 provides that certain tax payments must be withheld and paid when a deed or other instrument that effects a change in ownership of real property is presented for recordation. The requirements of §10-912 do not apply when a transferor provides a certification of Maryland residence or certification that the transferred property is the transferor's principal residence.

---

1. Transferor Information

Name of Transferor ______________________________

2. Description of Property (Street address. If no address is available, include county, district, subdistrict and lot numbers).

____

3. Reasons for Exemption

Resident Status

☐ As of the date this form is signed, I, Transferor, am a resident of the State of Maryland.

☐ Transferor is a resident entity as defined in Code of Maryland Regulations (COMAR)03.04.12.02B(11), I am an agent of Transferor, and I have authority to sign this document on Transferor's behalf.

Principal Residence

☐ Although I am no longer a resident of the State of Maryland, the Property is my principal residence as defined in IRC 121 (principal residence for 2 (two) of the last 5 (five) years) and is currently recorded as such with the State Department of Assessments and Taxation.

Under penalty of perjury, I certify that I have examined this declaration and that, to the best of my knowledge, it is true, correct, and complete.

3a. Individual Transferors

______________________________ Witness

______________________________ Name **Date

______________________________ Signature

3b. Entity Transferors

______________________________ Witness/Attest

______________________________ Name of Entity

______________________________ By

______________________________ Name **Date

______________________________ Title

** Form must be dated to be valid.

Note: Form is only valid if it was executed on the date the Property was transferred and is properly recorded with the Clerk of the Court.

To the Clerk of the Court: Only an un-altered Form WH-AR should be considered a valid certification for purposes of Section 10-912.

01/22

CHAPTER EIGHT

FEDERAL TAX ASPECTS OF THE ACQUISITION, OWNERSHIP, AND SALE OF A TAXPAYER'S PERSONAL RESIDENCE*

Matthew J. Carruth, Esq.
Chelsea B. Riggin, Esq.

Venable LLP

* MSBA gratefully acknowledges the contributions to this chapter by previous authors Robert A. Rombro, Esq., Robert K. Briskin, Esq., and Theodore Hirsh, Esq.

ABOUT THE AUTHORS

Matthew J. Carruth, Esq.

Matthew Carruth is a counsel in the Transactional Tax Group at Venable LLP. He advises clients on federal and state income tax planning, structuring, and compliance matters, and he advises clients on tax controversy matters. Matthew earned his J.D. from The George Washington University Law School, and his LL.M. in Taxation from the Georgetown University Law Center, and he received the Chetwood Prize for finishing first in his LL.M. class.

Chelsea B. Riggin, Esq.

Chelsea Riggin is an associate in the East Coast Wealth Planning Group at Venable LLP. She advises clients on matters related to tax and wealth planning. Chelsea earned her J.D. from William & Mary Law School, where she was executive editor of the William & Mary Journal of Women and the Law. She holds a B.A. in Sociology, cum laude, from Franklin and Marshall College.

TABLE OF CONTENTS

PART 2: THE LAW FOR SALES OR EXCHANGES PRIOR TO MAY 7, 1997

I. [§ 8.1] INTRODUCTION

This chapter covers tax factors to consider in the purchase, ownership, and sale of a home used as the taxpayer's personal residence. This discussion deals largely with the income tax. Estate planning is raised only with respect to title ownership of the home. The real property tax and real property transfer tax are discussed only as they may be considered as income tax deductions.

The federal income tax is a major tool for social engineering. As explained in **§§ 8.16–8.45** of this chapter, the federal government encourages homeownership by underwriting a substantial portion of the carrying costs. This policy maintains, notwithstanding our legislators' penchant for annual tax reform, as seen in the continued deductibility of home mortgage interest. As explained in **§§ 8.46–8.145** of this chapter, homeownership is further encouraged by what may be the best tax shelter available, the provisions for exclusion of taxable gain. Again, this benefit has survived multiple tax reforms even while strenuous effort has been made to police and curtail tax shelters. Also discussed, in **§§ 8.146–8.147** of this chapter, is the tax treatment provided for those sellers who indulged in what has been coined "creative financing" and have repossessed the home when the mortgage taken back was in default.

The planning aspects for owners regarding taking title to, and the transfer of, property and the income tax aspects of settlement costs are discussed in **§§ 8.2–8.15** of this chapter.

II. PURCHASE

A. Forms of Ownership—Estate Planning

1. [§ 8.2] Generally

The automatic taking of title to a married couple's personal residence in joint tenancy or tenancy by the entireties is a prevalent, and sometimes unfortunate, practice. The practice is based, perhaps, on sentiment without recognition of attendant gift and estate tax ramifications. Where title ownership does not match the sources of the purchase money, advisors should be aware of tax consequences so that estate planning in the future does not involve an undoing of what is effected at the settlement of the home purchase. This notwithstanding, it is common knowledge that the rights of survivorship may reduce probate expenses and give some protection to the surviving owner from the decedent's creditors, and, as a general rule, joint ownership by husband and wife may in fact be desirable and advantageous.

However, the tax consequences of this form of ownership should not be overlooked. Basic estate planning seeks to fully utilize both unified credits of a married couple, and the credit of the first to die may be lost if that spouse does not have sufficient assets in their individual name to fund a trust that will keep these assets out of the estate of the second spouse. However, in 2012 relief was provided in Section 2010(c)(4) of the Internal Revenue Code[1], which enacted the concept of "portability." A surviving spouse may now elect to use the deceased spouse's unused estate tax exemption by filing a timely Form 706—United States Estate (and Generation-Skipping Transfer) Tax Return.[2] Transfer of title ownership into the name of one spouse, or the breaking of the rights of survivorship so the will can use the home to fund the credit trust, are alternative methods to electing portability in order to have the estates of both spouses fully utilize the unified credit.

Outside of husband and wife ownership, the taking of title in joint names may have costly gift tax consequences if each title holder does not furnish their ratable share of the purchase price (including down payment and payment on a mortgage, if any). As explained in **§§ 8.3 and 8.4** of this chapter, the failure to recognize the gift at time of settlement could lead to costly estate tax consequences. Present planning should be to have each owner contribute their respective portion of the consideration and the monthly mortgage payment from individual funds. Their separate checks or other evidences of such payments should be preserved to help taxpayers prove what they contributed and what should be excluded from the estate of the non-surviving joint tenant.

For the non-traditional couple, rights of survivorship may cause the estate of the second to die to inflate above the non-taxable floor, and again here severing of the survivorship rights may allow tax saving use of trusts.

The general rule, as stated in § 2040(a) of the I.R.C. and left unchanged by the Tax Reform Act of 1986 (1986 TRA), is that the entire value of property owned by joint tenants or tenants by the entireties must be included in the gross estate of the first to die except to the extent that it can be demonstrated that the survivor contributed toward the purchase. However, property acquired by a husband and wife as tenants by the entireties through gift or bequest from a third party is included only as to one-half in the estate of the first to die.

2. [§ 8.3] Qualified joint interest

Notwithstanding the general rule of I.R.C. § 2040(a), in the case of any "qualified joint interest," one-half of such jointly held property will be included in the estate of the first to die no matter what the source of the purchase price consideration.[3]

---

1 Internal Revenue Code of 1986, 26 U.S.C. §§ 1-9834 (hereinafter I.R.C. § ___).

2 I.R.C. § 2010(c)(4). In addition, in 2019 Maryland enacted its own portability statute allowing the surviving spouse to use the deceased spouse's unused state estate tax exemption by filing a Maryland estate tax return. MD. CODE ANN., TAX-GEN. § 7-309(b).

3 I.R.C. § 2040(b)(1). However, see *Gallenstein v. United States*, 975 F.2d 286 (6th Cir. 1992), *aff'g* 91-2 U.S. Tax Cas. (CCH) ¶60,088 (E.D. Ky. 1991), where certain spousal joint interests created prior to 1977 included 100% in estate, allowing income tax step-up of basis.

The term "qualified joint interest" means any interest in property held by the decedent and the decedent's spouse as tenants by the entirety, or joint tenants with a right of survivorship provided that the decedent and the decedent's spouse are the only joint tenants.[4] This automatic qualification should be considered together with the Federal estate tax marital deduction provided for in I.R.C. § 2056 and any gift tax exclusion. Note that Qualified Joint Interests are not applicable where one spouse is not a U.S. citizen.[5]

3. [§ 8.4] Tax consequences

The tax consequences of taking the deed in joint names is for the surviving spouse to acquire ownership by operation of law with a composite tax basis determined as to one-half by the date of death value and one-half by the carry over basis from the gift. This may not be desirable and consideration should be given to placing title solely in the name of one spouse if age differences or medical situations indicate which will be the first to die.

Property owned jointly by spouses in a common law state like Maryland takes a stepped-up basis on the death of a spouse only as to the decedents' half interest in the property. In a community property state, the interest of each spouse gets stepped-up upon the first death.

4. [§ 8.5] Terminable interest rule—life estate exception

Some consideration should be given in estate planning to the reservation of a life estate by one or both spouses. A life estate is considered a terminable interest and, therefore, generally does not qualify for the marital deduction. I.R.C. § 2056, however, provides five exceptions to the nondeductible terminable interest rule. The exceptions relevant to this discussion include:

(1) the life estate plus power of appointment exception[6] and

(2) the qualified terminable interest exception.[7]

Under the life estate plus power of appointment exception, the marital deduction is allowable with respect to any interest in property passing from the decedent to their surviving spouse in trust, if:

(1) the spouse is entitled for life to all of the income from the entire interest or all the income from the specific portion of the entire interest, and

(2) the spouse has a power to appoint the entire interest or the specific portion, provided certain conditions are met.[8]

---

4 I.R.C. § 2040(b)(2).

5 I.R.C. § 2056(d)(1)(B).

6 I.R.C. § 2056(b)(5).

7 I.R.C. § 2056(b)(7); *see also* I.R.C. § 2056(b)(3), (b)(6), and (b)(8) for additional exceptions.

8 I.R.C. § 2056(b)(5); *see also* 90 A.L.R. 2D 414.

5. [§ 8.6] Terminable interest rule—QTIP exception

Under the qualified terminable interest exception (sometimes referred to as "QTIP"), an executor may elect to have qualified terminable interest property qualify for the unlimited marital deduction in the estate of a decedent spouse.[9] The QTIP is designed to keep the marital deduction available and allow the testator to direct who inherits the remainder interest. Generally, no marital deduction is allowed if a life estate passes to a surviving spouse and, upon the life tenant's death or some other event, a remainder interest passes from the decedent to someone other than the surviving spouse. If, however, a proper QTIP election is made, the value of the property so qualifying for the marital deduction in the estate of the first spouse to die (or for the gift tax martial deduction) will be included in the surviving spouse's estate unless the surviving spouse has made a lifetime transfer of their "qualifying income interest for life," which is treated as a taxable gift by such spouse.[10] If the QTIP election is made, the estate tax allocable to the property at the death of the surviving spouse may be recovered by such spouse's estate from the recipient of the qualified terminable interest property, unless the surviving spouse directs otherwise by will, i.e., the takers of the remainder interest in the QTIP property pay the tax on such property unless the second will directs otherwise.[11]

6. [§ 8.7] Qualified Domestic Trust

Practitioners must be aware that the estate and gift tax marital deduction is not allowable if the surviving spouse is not a U.S. citizen unless the requirements of I.R.C. § 2056A, designed to assure collection of tax from the non-citizen, are satisfied. Determining the client's citizenship is basic.

7. [§ 8.8] Qualified Personal Residence Trust (QPRT)[12]

There may be increasing use of a major exception to I.R.C. § 2702, the Qualified Personal Residence Trust. This trust allows gift of the remainder interest in a principal residence and retention of the use of the property for a period of years. If the donor survives for the retained period of use, the entire property is out of the estate at the gift tax cost measured on the actuarially computed value of the retained use. The actuarial value of the retained use (and therefore the value of the taxable gift) can become nominal by lengthening the term of the QPRT.[13] However, if the grantor

---

9 I.R.C. § 2056(b)(7). Note: the amendment to § 2056(b)(7)(C) is applicable to estates of decedents dying after Aug. 5, 1997.

10 *See* I.R.C. §§ 2044, 2511 and 2519.

11 I.R.C. § 2207A(a). Note: the amendment to I.R.C. § § 2207A(a)(2) is applicable to estates of decedents dying after Aug. 5, 1997.

12 I.R.C. § 2702(a)(3)(A)(ii); TREAS. REG. § 25.2702-5.

13 *See Walton v. Comm'r*, 115 T.C. No. 41.

of the QPRT does not survive the term of the trust, the tax savings is zero because the entire value of the property will be included in the grantor's gross estate.[14] It is for this reason that a viable alternative approach is a sale of the home to a defective grantor trust.[15]

B. [§ 8.9] Forms of Ownership—Divorce

Sections 8-201–8-213 of the FAMILY LAW ARTICLE, ANNOTATED CODE OF MARYLAND, as applicable to petitions for divorce filed after Jan. 1, 1979, sets forth a number of provisions relating to the disposition by a Maryland divorce court of the property of parties to a divorce action. The law gives expanded powers to the court

(1) to grant possession and use of the principal residence of the spouses, and

(2) to determine ownership of real property, however it may be titled, that was acquired other than through inheritance or gift during the marriage.[16]

An antenuptial agreement or the purchase in individual name prior to marriage can defeat these powers.

The transfer of ownership of property to a spouse or incident to a divorce is treated as a gift, not a sale.[17]

C. [§ 8.10] Closing Costs—Generally

The expenses incurred upon the acquisition of residential real estate, just as in the acquisition of any capital asset,[18] may not be taken as deductions against gross income. All of such costs, other than those deductible as "moving costs," must be capitalized and become part of the cost of the asset. In tax jargon, cost is "basis"[19] while "adjusted basis" is the result of increases to basis for the cost of improvements and other capitalized expenditures and reductions to basis for depreciation, amortization, and recovery of capital,[20] such as through a casualty loss deduction. Capitalized closing costs include broker commissions, appraisal fees, attorneys'

---

14 I.R.C. § 2036(a)(1).

15 As used here, a defective trust is one where either the grantor or a beneficiary is treated as the "owner" of the trust for income tax purposes under I.R.C. §§ 671–679, but not for estate, gift, or generation-skipping transfer tax purposes.

16 *See The Effect of 1978 Maryland Divorce Law Reform Upon the Income Taxation of Transfers of Appreciated Property Incident to the Dissolution of Marriage,* 30 MD. BAR J. 78; *see also* Gerson, *Tax Consequences of the New Maryland* `Marital Property Act', 32 MD. BAR J. 34, 36 (1979).

17 *See* § **8.102** of this chapter.

18 I.R.C. § 263.

19 I.R.C. § 1012.

20 I.R.C. §§ 1011, 1016; TREAS. REG. § 1.016-2(a) (casualty losses).

fees, and title insurance. Recording and transfer taxes are not deductible as tax payments and also must be capitalized.[21]

D. [§ 8.11] Closing Costs—Exception for Points

An exception to the requirement to capitalize closing costs is made for certain "points" paid for purchase or improvement of, and secured by, the taxpayer's principal residence. These costs are deductible to the new homeowner when such charges are in the nature of interest, i.e., are for the use of money.[22] In REV. PROC. 94-27,[23] the Internal Revenue Service reversed a long and troublesome position requiring payment of points from funds other than the mortgage proceeds. Now, as an administrative practice, points paid after 1990 will be deductible in the year paid by a cash basis taxpayer if all the following requirements are met:

(1) the HUD-1 Form must identify the points;

(2) the amount must be computed as a percentage of the loan;

(3) the amount paid must conform to the local business practice;

(4) the loan must be for purchase of the principal residence which secures the loan; and

(5) the taxpayer must have paid cash in the transaction at least equal to the points.

REV. PROC. 94-27 also gives guidance on what costs qualify as deductible points. Deductible points must be differentiated from non-deductible service charges (which may be called "points").[24] The essential difference is that deductible charges are for the use of money.[25]

Points that would be deductible upon purchase must be amortized over the term of the mortgage upon a refinancing. In a period of declining interest rates, where there may be successive refinancings, the unamortized points of refinancing may become deductible when refinanced.

---

[21] *Gibbons v. Comm'r*, T.C.M. (CCH) 1976-125 (1976). The liability for the payment of such taxes is a matter for negotiation between the parties, and if the contract is silent, the costs are shared equally. MD. CODE ANN., REAL PROPERTY § 14-104 (2015 & Supp. 202).

[22] I.R.C. § 461(g)(2).

[23] REV. PROC. 94-27, 1994-15 I.R.B. 17. *See also* T.D. 8571.

[24] *See Pacific First Fed. Sav. & Loan Ass'n v. Comm'r*, 79 T.C. 512 (1982) and *Goodwin v. Comm'r*, 75 T.C. 424 (1980), *aff'd*, 691 F.2d 490 (3rd Cir. 1982).

[25] *See* Rev. Rul. 67-297, 1967-2 C.B. 87 (V.A. mortgage); Rev. Rul. 68-650, 1968-2 C.B. 78 (F.H.A. mortgage). But see Rev. Rul. 87-22, 1987-1 C.B. 146 in which the Service held that points paid to refinance an existing mortgage are incurred to repay debt and, hence, are not deductible in full in the year of sale, but must be capitalized and deducted ratably over the term of the loan.

E. [§ 8.12] Closing Costs—Burden of Proof

On the sale of a home, the difference between the adjusted basis and the amount realized would be subject to tax, as discussed in **§§ 8.46–8.125** *infra*. In the presentation of tax liability, the taxpayer has the burden of proof; the buyer should, therefore, be advised to save the settlement sheet, and otherwise document all capitalized expenses, so that the computation of taxable gain can be substantiated. Similarly, costs incurred after settlement which are adjustments to basis, e.g., a new roof or furnace, also should be documented. While profit on sale of a home will likely be sheltered, the amount involved requires adequate accounting.

F. [§ 8.13] Moving Expenses

Certain moving expenses associated with the settlement of a personal residence can have an immediate tax benefit, do not have to be capitalized, and can be deducted if the sale or purchase of the house is associated with the taxpayer's moving to a new job. These costs can be characterized as "moving expenses" pursuant to I.R.C. § 217 if the new "principal place of work" is 50 miles (35 miles prior to 1994) farther from the former residence than was the former principal place of work. There is also a technical period of employment or self-employment requirement after arrival in the general location of the new job.

The qualifying purchaser can deduct their unreimbursed settlement and moving fees and expenses. After 1993, meals consumed while traveling and while living in temporary quarters, pre-move househunting trips, selling expenses, and 30 days of temporary living expenses no longer qualify. After 1986 and before 1994, taxpayers had to itemize expenses to claim these deductions, but after 1993 these deductions are taken in arriving at adjusted gross income. In neither period does the 2% miscellaneous itemized deduction floor apply.

The tax benefits that may be claimed for moving expenses described in this § 8.13 are not available for taxpayers generally for tax years 2018 through 2025, except for members of the Armed Forces described in I.R.C. § 217(g).[26]

G. [§ 8.14] Real Estate Taxes

At settlement, a major item for reconciliation between the buyer and seller are the real estate taxes for the year in which the property is transferred. Unlike the Maryland recording tax and transfer tax, real estate taxes normally are deductible costs[27] and are not capitalized. In Maryland, the real property tax year is July 1

---

26 I.R.C. § 217(k), added as part of the tax legislation informally known as the TAX CUTS AND JOBS ACT, Pub. L. No. 115-97 (TCJA), §11049.

27 I.R.C. § 164; but note the general $10,000 deduction limit on individuals ($5,000 for individuals who are married filing separately) for state and local taxes for tax years 2018 through 2025

through June 30,[28] and the tax is due and the lien attaches on July 1.[29] Since the tax is paid in advance, the normal practice is for the buyer to reimburse the seller for the tax applicable to the portion of the tax year following the sale. Because the tax payment has tax benefits, the parties might bargain for one or the other to pay the entire year's tax with an adjustment in the sales price; but this tactic is forestalled by I.R.C. § 164(d) which provides that the tax benefit or the payment of the current year's tax must be apportioned according to the portion of the fiscal real property tax year that each party owned the property. A buyer or seller who by negotiation actually pays the entire year's tax can deduct only that portion attributable to their period of ownership. This apportionment is according to the number of days each owned the property during the tax year, and it is mandatory. The statute operates to treat the buyer and seller as having had the tax liability separately imposed on each of them. Payment of another person's taxes is not a deductible expense.

Determining the year in which to claim the deduction for such an allocated portion of the tax depends upon the taxpayer's method of accounting. Because the purchaser of a personal residence will almost always be a cash basis individual, the general rule is applicable and the tax is treated as being paid in the year in which the sale takes place.[30] The Maryland calendar for advance payment of the tax and the personal liability of the seller for the tax[31] precludes operation of alternative rules provided in the Regulations.[32]

When a seller has deducted real estate taxes in the calendar year prior to the sale, the excess of the amount deducted over the portion treated as imposed on him by I.R.C. § 164 should be included in their gross income for the year of sale, subject to the provisions of I.R.C. § 111.[33]

H. [§ 8.15] Example

Mr. Ian Genex bought his rowhouse in 1995 for $50,000. Of the $50,000, he paid 5% down ($2,500) and had a 95% mortgage ($47,500). At settlement for the purchase, he incurred costs for title insurance; transfer and recording taxes; his attorneys' fees; and adjustments for water. He paid an amount equal to one year's real property tax, which was split between the reimbursement to the seller and the escrow account required by the mortgagee, and he also paid the seller for a full tank of heating oil. While he owned the property, Mr. Genex did not enlarge the

---

under I.R.C. § 164(b)(6), added as part of the TCJA.

28 MD. CODE ANN., TAX-PROPERTY § 1-101(oo) (hereinafter TAX-PROP. § __).

29 TAX-PROP. §§ 10-102 and 14-805.

30 I.R.C. § 164(d)(2).

31 TAX-PROP. §§ 10-401 and 10-402.

32 TREAS. REG. § 1.164-6(d)(1) and (2).

33 TREAS. REG. § 1.164-6(d)(5).

rowhouse, upgrade the electrical or plumbing systems, or do anything to the property other than routine maintenance.

Mr. Genex has a cost basis for tax purposes equal to:

(1) his purchase price of $50,000 (even though he had actually "paid" only $2,500 and borrowed the rest) plus

(2) his capitalized expenses incurred at settlement and while he owned the property.

Therefore, Mr. Genex would adjust his purchase price of $50,000 upward for the settlement fees paid to the title company, attorneys' fees paid to his attorney, and for transfer and recording taxes. This increase in basis will result in less gain on a subsequent sale of the property.

The payments for water and fuel oil would be personal expenses and would not be deducted or capitalized. On the facts given, no costs after settlement would be capitalized. Residential property costs which are not capitalized, i.e., that do not represent the acquisition of an item or an improvement having a useful life greater than one year, have no tax recognition and are considered personal living expenses. However, the amount of real estate taxes attributable to 1995 would be deductible by Mr. Genex in 1995.

Mr. Genex sold his rowhouse to Ms. Gloria Lowpants for $60,000. At settlement on Dec. 31, 2002, Ms. Lowpants pays to Mr. Genex an amount equal to the real estate taxes for the remaining portion of the tax year, i.e., through June 2003. The real estate tax for the fiscal year July 2002 to June 2003 had been paid by the mortgagee bank in September 2002 from the escrow account Mr. Genex had been required to fund by ratable monthly additions to his payments on the mortgage loan.[34] If settlement were in 2003 after Mr. Genex had claimed a year's real estate tax payment as a 2002 income tax deduction, he would have income in 2002 for the taxes apportioned to the buyer, i.e., until July (to the extent the deduction had a tax benefit).

Mr. Genex realizes taxable gain measured by the difference between $60,000 (reduced by broker commissions and his fixing-up expenses) and the adjusted basis. Fixing-up expenses are costs incurred, e.g., painting, which would not normally have tax recognition to the homeowner, incurred within 90 days of the contract date and paid within 30 days of settlement. The real estate tax reimbursement is not part

---

[34] The year in which the bank, as his agent, makes the actual payment determines the year when Mr. Genex may take the income tax deductions, i.e., if the bank did not pay the tax until January, there would be no income tax deduction until that year. When the escrow is funded does not determine when the tax is paid. Rev. Rul. 78-103, 1978-1 C.B. 58.

of the amount realized.[35] The tax payable upon the sale depends upon whether the realized gain is recognized.[36]

At the December 31, 2002, settlement, Ms. Lowpants reimburses Mr. Genex for the unexpired portion of the tax year, and his lender requires that she fund an escrow for the expired portion of the tax year. From January to June she will make ratable monthly payments to the bank so that by July 1 the bank can pay the next year's tax. Ms. Lowpants is deemed to have paid the tax then escrowed by the bank for which she reimbursed Mr. Genex, and she can take the tax deduction against 2002 income. When the escrow fund is expended to pay the tax for the year beginning July 1, 2003, Ms. Lowpants will have a 2003 income tax deduction for a full year's tax.

III. OWNERSHIP

A. Interest and Taxes

1. [§ 8.16] Generally

As stated in **§ 8.1** of this chapter, the scheme of federal and state income tax is designated to facilitate homeownership, and the government gives an economic incentive through the tax system which encourages the residential renter to become an owner. Homeownership holds a special place in the American taxpayer's psyche and expectations and, therefore, in our legislators' hearts. This is seen again and again in the survival of this social engineering. While severe limitations now generally apply to the deduction of interest, interest on an individual's home mortgage and second home mortgage remains largely protected.[37] The survival of the residential mortgage interest deduction is to be contrasted with the disallowance of "personal interest," i.e., installment debt interest on other consumer purchases, and the matching of the deduction for "investment interest" only against "investment income."

2. [§ 8.17] Personal interest

The 1986 Tax Reform Act added I.R.C. § 163(h) which disallows a deduction for personal interest paid or accrued by noncorporate taxpayers. For purposes of I.R.C. § 163(h), the term "personal interest" generally includes any interest allowable as a deduction for income tax purposes other than a list of exceptions. One important exception is "qualified residence interest."[38] I.R.C. § 163(h)(3) defines "qualified residence interest" as interest paid or accrued during the taxable year on

---

[35] I.R.C. § 1001(b)(1).

[36] This is the subject of §§ **8.126–8.145** *infra.*

[37] I.R.C. § 163(h)(3)(F), enacted as part of the TCJA, imposes additional limitations on the residential mortgage interest deduction for tax years 2018 through 2025.

[38] I.R.C. § 163(h)(2)(D). This section includes other definitions of the term "personal interest" that are beyond the scope of this chapter.

debt that is either (1) "acquisition indebtedness," or (2) "home equity indebtedness" with respect to any qualified residence. Qualified residence interest is limited to an aggregate principal amount of acquisition indebtedness of $1 million ($500,000 for a married individual not filing a joint return), except that for tax years 2018 through 2025, I.R.C. § 163(h)(2)(F), which was added to I.R.C. § 163 as part of the tax legislation informally known as the Tax Cuts and Jobs Act, Pub. L. No. 115-97 ("TCJA"), reduces this amount for certain indebtedness to $750,000 ($375,000 for a married individual not filing a joint return).[39] Home equity indebtedness is limited to the aggregate principal amount of indebtedness of $100,000 ($50,000 for a married individual not filing a joint return), [40] except that for tax years 2018 through 2025, I.R.C. § 163(h)(3)(F)(i)(I) (added as part of the TCJA) bars deductions for interest paid or accrued on home equity indebtedness.

3. *[§ 8.18] Acquisition indebtedness and home equity indebtedness interest*

Subject to the limitations described above, interest paid or accrued on acquisition indebtedness and home equity indebtedness is deductible generally to the extent that the debt does not exceed the purchase price plus improvements. In particular, the term "acquisition indebtedness" means any indebtedness which is incurred in acquiring, constructing, or substantially improving any qualified residence of the taxpayer and is secured by such qualified residence.[41] The term also includes any indebtedness secured by such residence resulting from the refinancing of indebtedness meeting the above requirement, but only to the extent that the amount of the indebtedness resulting from such refinancing does not exceed the amount of the refinanced indebtedness.[42] Thus, acquisition indebtedness cannot be increased by refinancing, but can be increased by amounts expended for substantial improvements to a qualified residence. Similarly, the term "home equity indebtedness" means any indebtedness (other than acquisition indebtedness) secured by a qualified residence to the extent that the aggregate amount of such indebtedness does not exceed the fair market value of such residence, reduced by the amount of acquisition indebtedness with respect to such residence.[43] Thus, interest upon a second mortgage will qualify to the extent the new mortgage is equal to the equity in the home (up to a maximum of $100,000, and subject to the limitations described above). For example, if a taxpayer has an acquisition indebtedness mortgage balance of $80,000 on their home

---

[39] Under I.R.C. § 163(h)(3)(F)(i)(III), for example, the lower threshold does not apply to indebtedness incurred on or before December 15, 2017.

[40] I.R.C. § 163(h)(3)(C); *See also* FSA 200137033.

[41] I.R.C. § 163(h)(3)(B). *See Garrison v. Comm'r*, T.C.M. 1994-200, *aff'd on other issue,* 67 F.3d 299 (6th Cir. 1995).

[42] I.R.C. § 163(h)(3)(B).

[43] I.R.C. § 163(h)(3)(C).

which has a fair market value of $290,000 as of January 1, 2026, and they obtain a home equity indebtedness second mortgage of $150,000, interest on up to $100,000 of the new mortgage is deductible; interest on the remaining $50,000 is personal interest.[44]

4. [§ 8.19] Pre-Oct. 13, 1987 indebtedness

In the case of any pre-Oct. 13, 1987 indebtedness, the $1 million limitation of I.R.C. § 163(h)(3)(B) is subject to further reduction.[45] In such case, the $1 million limitation shall be reduced (but not below zero) by the aggregate amount of outstanding pre-Oct. 13, 1987 indebtedness.[46] Qualified residence interest, computed based upon the above limitations, has no bearing upon the computation of the taxpayer's passive activity loss.[47]

5. [§ 8.20] Recordation and transfer taxes

State and local real property taxes may be deductible,[48] but I.R.C. § 164(b)(6), which was added by the TCJA, limits the deduction that an individual may claim for all state and local taxes under I.R.C. § 164(a) to $10,000 ($5,000 for married taxpayers not filing a joint return) for tax years 2018 through 2025. Real property taxes are deductible by cash basis taxpayers when paid and by accrual basis taxpayers when accrued. In contrast, transfer taxes incurred in buying the home, such as Maryland State Property Transfer Taxes, County Real Estate Transfer Taxes, and County Recordation Taxes are not real property taxes for purposes of I.R.C. § 164.[49] They are capitalized as part of the cost of the home.

6. [§ 8.21] The tax benefits of homeownership

The Internal Revenue Code allows for the reduction of both the costs of financing the purchase and the costs of ownership by allowing, subject to certain limitations such as those discussed above, a dollar-for-dollar reduction from gross income for all sums paid for mortgage interest and real estate taxes. This is available only to taxpayers who itemize deductions (Schedule A to Form 1040), and, since the year of purchase of a home may be the first return for which itemization of deductions would be worthwhile, other planning advice may be simply to identify allowable itemized deductions and the documentation that should be compiled to substantiate them. Since the taxpayer's failure to substantiate claimed deductions can lead

---

44 See Rev. Rul. 96-32, 1996-25 I.R.B. 5 for continued qualification of property destroyed by tornado or earthquake as a qualified residence during the period until sale or rebuilding.

45 I.R.C. § 163(h)(3)(D).

46 I.R.C. § 163(h)(3)(D).

47 I.R.C. § 469 (j)(7).

48 *See* I.R.C. § 164.

49 *See Reinhardt v. Comm'r*, 75 T.C. 47 (1980); *Black v. Commissioner,* 60 T.C. 108 (1973).

to their disallowance, advice on maintaining records is valuable. This same advice should be given for the previously discussed capitalized adjustments to basis.

Where parents, for instance, want to subsidize their children's lifestyle, their payment of mortgage interest and real estate tax on the children's home does not give them the tax deduction. If, however, the parents are part owners of the home, the payments may become deductible.[50] For a taxpayer in the highest individual marginal tax bracket (37% for tax years 2018 through 2025), payment of $100 in mortgage interest or in real estate tax can be seen as effectively costing $63 since $37 would otherwise have been spent as income tax. The income tax system in effect subsidizes the homeowner by this diversion of tax money. The homeowner can live in more expensive surroundings than a renter at the same net cost since the government pays the difference. At the same time the homeowner has a capital asset which historically has been a sound investment.

7. [§ 8.22] *Tax planning strategies*

The subsidy of the two major carrying costs of homeownership and the allowance of a deduction for a casualty loss to a personal residence are major erosions to I.R.C. § 262, which prohibits deductions for "personal, living, or family expenses." This general rule otherwise limits the planning possibilities for seeking tax benefits from operational costs of a residence. Conversely, the sacrosanct deductibility of the home mortgage interest has spawned the "home equity" mortgage (i.e., second mortgage) for use as a revolving line of credit: paying off a credit card balance with a home equity draw makes interest deductible that would otherwise be nondeductible "personal interest." As noted above, however, this strategy is limited by the disallowance of interest deductions on home equity indebtedness under I.R.C. § 163(h)(3)(F)(i)(I) for tax years 2018 through 2025.

Some benefit for cash basis individuals may be achieved by timing one month's mortgage payment to come in the current or the next taxable year. The late payment fee charged by the mortgagee must be considered when evaluating the tax benefits from deferring a payment. Just as with payment of other deductible items, the deferral to a year of higher tax rates or higher marginal bracket makes the deduction save more tax. Conversely, postponement of a deduction delays the tax benefit, and the current tax savings may be more valuable than a greater benefit a year later.

---

[50] *See Daya v. Comm'r*, T.C.M. 2000-360 (stating that "we have held that taxpayers who do not hold legal title to property but who establish they are equitable owners of the property are entitled to deduct mortgage interest paid by them with respect to the property," and citing cases including *Trans v. Comm'r*, T.C. Memo. 1999-233).

An historical, time-honored planning device based upon the ruling[51] of the IRS was to prepay up to five years' interest on a debt. Because interest was deductible, the prepayment would bunch the tax savings in the first year of a transaction and reduce the effective cost of the capital investment. After many years of complacency, the IRS in 1968 reversed its acceptance of this tactic.[52] After a series of litigation victories finding the prepayment a distortion of income,[53] and after the passage of an amendment to the then-current Internal Revenue Code of 1954, the law is now that the interest deduction accrues ratably over the prepaid period, notwithstanding that the taxpayer is on the cash payment method of accounting,[54] subject to the limitations on interest deduction applicable in the year of accrual.

B. Casualty Loss

1. [§ 8.23] Generally

The other area of tax benefit allowed to the homeowner is the deduction for loss arising from "fire, storm, shipwreck, or other casualty, or from theft."[55] The excess of the loss over $100 as to each casualty is a current deduction. While the availability of the tax deduction has been significantly limited (including by a limitation imposed under I.R.C. § 165(h)(5) (codified by the TCJA) for tax years 2018 through 2025 on deductions for personal casualty losses except those attributable to certain disasters designated by the federal government), the system still provides that tax money otherwise payable will underwrite the homeowner.

A casualty loss that gives rise to an income tax deduction must be a loss to property resulting from a sudden, unexpected, or unusual cause.[56] A progressive deterioration is not a casualty even though the property is destroyed. The Internal Revenue Service, in its wisdom, denies a deduction for prolonged termite damage,[57] although there is case law allowing the deduction when the termites had better appetites.[58] Drought or bugs cause deductible loss to the homeowner's ornamental shrubbery only if the drought or the bugs are unusual to the locale.[59]

---

51 I.T. 3740, 1945-1 C.B. 109; *Fackler v. Comm'r*, 39 B.T.A. 395 (1939).

52 Rev. Rul. 68-643, 1968-2 C.B. 76.

53 *See, e.g., Sandor v. Comm'r*, 62 T.C. 469 (1974), *aff'd*, 536 F.2d 874, 875 (9th Cir. 1976).

54 *See* I.R.C. § 461(g); *see also* Rev. Rul. 83-84, 1983-1 C.B. 97, *modified by* Rev. Rul. 86-42, 1986-1 C.B. 82.

55 I.R.C. § 165(c)(3).

56 I.R.C. § 165(c)(3); *see* Rev. Rul. 76-134, 1976-1 C.B. 54.

57 Rev. Rul. 63-232, 1963-2 C.B. 97.

58 *See, e.g., Rosenberg v. Comm'r*, 198 F.2d 46, 51 (8th Cir. 1952).

59 Rev. Rul. 79-174, 1979-1 C.B. 99.

Property loss from storm-caused erosion or high water is deductible, but damage from mere seasonal changes in water level or from gradual erosion is not a casualty loss.[60]

2. [§ 8.24] Computing the casualty loss deduction

The amount of the casualty loss is the lesser of either the reduction in the property's fair market value caused by the casualty or the adjusted basis of the property. Repairs limited to the casualty loss and actually necessary can be a measure of the reduction in fair market value.[61] Any insurance recovery reduces the deduction, and for personal use property there is the $100 floor for each casualty. To arrive at the deductible casualty loss, the Internal Revenue Code requires the offset of the net amount of all otherwise deductible casualty and theft losses for the taxable year by the amount of the casualty gains for that taxable year; and the deduction allowable is only that amount in excess of 10% of the taxpayer's adjusted gross income for that taxable year.[62] Under I.R.C. § 165(h)(5), for tax years 2018 through 2025, personal casualty losses other than those attributable to certain disasters designated by the federal government are generally not deductible, but may be used to offset any personal casualty gain.

3. [§ 8.25] When the loss is deductible—insurance

The loss is deductible in the year sustained except that no loss is allowable in a year when there is a reasonable prospect of recovery of the loss.[63] This possibility of recoupment or reimbursement may derive from the presence of an insurance claim or the pendency of a lawsuit against a party responsible for the loss, and these actions should be coordinated with the tax reporting.[64] A reform enacted by the 1986 TRA requires that, for taxable years beginning after 1986, no deduction for such casualty losses will be allowed unless a timely insurance claim is filed.[65] Under the prior law, a taxpayer could deduct a nonbusiness casualty loss covered by insurance even if he did not file a claim for insurance recovery.[66]

---

60 Rev. Rul. 76-134, 1976-1 C.B. 54. *See Tatham v. Comm'r*, 38 T.C.M. (CCH) 848 (1979).

61 Treas. Reg. § 1.165-7(a) and (b).

62 I.R.C. § 165(h)(2)(A). A casualty loss is deductible as an itemized deduction, but is not subject to the 2% floor for miscellaneous deductions.

63 Treas. Reg. §§ 1.165-1(d) and 1.165-7(a).

64 *Fort Howard Paper Co v. Comm'r*, 36 T.C.M. (CCH) 1711 (1977).

65 I.R.C. § 165(h)(4)(E).

66 *See Hills v. Comm'r*, 76 T.C. 484 (1981), *aff'd*, 691 F.2d 997, 1001 (11th Cir. 1982), 82-2 USTC ¶9969.

4. [§ 8.26] Disaster area

Special provision is made for casualty losses incurred in an area determined by the President of the United States to be a disaster area.[67] An election is available so that the loss can be taken into account for the taxable year immediately preceding the year in which the disaster occurred.[68] Additionally, such casualty losses are not subject to the limitation in I.R.C. § 165(h)(5) discussed above for tax years 2018 through 2025.

C. [§ 8.27] Business Use of Residence—Generally

The Internal Revenue Code severely limits the tax benefits available for business use of personal residence. Deductions for trade or business or investment expenses that would otherwise be allowed are precluded because of their connection to the personal residence unless the business use comes within very limited exceptions. The general disallowance does not apply to deductions, such as interest and tax deductions, which are allowable without regard to the trade or business or investment nexus, but "office-in-home" deductions for depreciation, rent, utilities, and the like must come within the limited exceptions.[69]

The Internal Revenue Code limits the amount of a home office deduction (other than expenses that are deductible without regard to business use, such as home mortgage interest) to the taxpayer's gross income from the activity, reduced by all other deductible expenses attributable to the activity but not allocable to the use of the dwelling unit.[70] Thus, home office deductions are not allowed to the extent that they create or increase a net loss from the business activity to which they relate. The Internal Revenue Code now provides a carryforward for those home office deductions that are disallowed solely due to the income limitation on the amount of an otherwise allowable home office deduction.[71]

The exceptions allow a deduction for the business use of a portion of the residence which, subject to certain requirements, is:

(1) used as a principal place of business;

(2) used as a place for meetings with clients, patients, or customers;

(3) in a separate structure used in connection with the trade or business;

(4) used for inventory storage by a wholesaler or retailer;

(5) used for rental of the dwelling unit or a portion thereof; or

(6) used as a day care facility.

---

[67] I.R.C. § 165(i)(1) and 165(i)(5).

[68] I.R.C. § 165(i)(1).

[69] I.R.C. § 280A.

[70] I.R.C. § 280A(c)(5).

[71] I.R.C. § 280A(c)(5).

D. Business Use of Residence—Exceptions

1. [§ 8.28] Principal place of business

Under the principal place of business exception, only one, if any, place can qualify as the principal place of business, even though activity carried on in the other may be necessary or helpful.[72] The portion of the residence must be used exclusively and on a regular basis to satisfy this exception. For an employee seeking a home office deduction, such use of the dwelling must be for "the convenience of the employer." Business use will not come within this exception if the home office is for personal convenience, for instance if night work at the outside office is too dangerous;[73] and, because of the exclusive use requirement, the exception does not apply to the common situation where both personal and business use is made of a portion of the dwelling. The Supreme Court, in *Commissioner v. Soliman*,[74] articulated a facts and circumstances test to determine a business' principal location based on the relative importance of the activities performed in each location and the amount of time spent at each location. In Rev. Rul. 94-24, 1994-15 I.R.B. 5, the Internal Revenue Service stated that in determining whether a home office is the taxpayer's principal place of business, it will apply the "relative importance" test and only look to the "time" test if this does not lead to a definitive answer. The code has been amended to effectively overrule the factual holding in *Soliman* (but not the facts and circumstances test that *Soliman* articulated) and now provides that for tax years beginning after Dec. 31, 1998, the term *principal place of business* "includes a place of business which is used by the taxpayer for the administrative or management activities of any trade or business of the taxpayer if there is no other fixed location of such trade or business where the taxpayer conducts substantial administrative or management activities of such trade or business."[75] Note that notwithstanding this expanded definition of principal place of business, the taxpayer must still meet the exclusive use test and, in the case of employment-related expenses, the convenience of employer test. The deductions for utilities, insurance, and maintenance must be reduced to reflect the percentage of use in the residence for non-business operations.[76]

---

72 *Baie v. Comm'r*, 74 T.C. 105 (1980); *see generally* INTERNAL REVENUE SERVICE, I.R.S. Pub. 587, BUSINESS USE OF YOUR HOME.

73 *ON-RI-GA Med. Prof'l Ass'n v. Comm'r*, 37 T.C.M. (CCH) 786 (1978).

74 506 U.S. 168, 113 S. Ct. 701 (1993).

75 *See also* Pamela Revak, *Home Office Marches On In Spite of Soliman*, 75 TAXES 549 (1997).

76 *Hefti v. Comm'r*, 54 T.C.M. (CCH) 1555 (1988). See also *Steinberg v. Comm'r*, 69 T.C.M. (CCH) 2131 (1995), for allowance of deduction upon showing of preponderance of importance and of time attributable to home office.

2. [§ 8.29] Place to meet clients, patients, or customers

The exception for a residence used as a place of business to meet clients, patients, or customers requires that the portion of the dwelling be used exclusively and on a regular basis as a place of business in the normal course of the taxpayer's trade or business. The limited availability of the deduction is illustrated by *Chauls v. Commissioner*[77] where the Tax Court held that students were not "patients, clients, or customers," for office-at-home deduction purposes for a music teacher who had a choral group practicing in his house. The Tax Court noted that even if students could be classified as "patients, clients, or customers," this taxpayer had failed to use the music room at home "exclusively" and "on a regular basis" as a place of business.[78]

3. [§ 8.30] Separate structure

The exception for an unattached structure similarly requires regular and exclusive use, and an employee must make such use for "the convenience of the employer." For example, an artist's studio in a structure adjacent, but unattached to their residence, qualifies under this exception.[79]

4. [§ 8.31] Inventory storage

The exception for inventory storage requires that the space be so used on a regular basis and that the dwelling unit be the sole fixed location of the trade or business. A deduction is not available for storage of items other than inventory. Thus, the deduction was not allowed to a lawyer who stored files at home.[80] The space does not, however, have to be used exclusively for storage, but it must be separately identifiable.[81]

5. [§ 8.32] Day care facility

The exception for day care facilities requires that the use be regular, not exclusive, and that the use be primarily for custodial services. Where state law requires licensing, certification, or approval for operation of such a facility, the income tax deduction requires compliance with such regulations. The exception is applicable to a trade or business which provides day care for children, for individuals who obtain

---

77 41 T.C.M. (CCH) 234 (1980).

78 Compare this to *Hewett v. Comm'r*, 71 T.C.M. (CCH) 2350 (1996), where a concert pianist and piano teacher was allowed the deduction on a showing of principal place of business.

79 Prop. Reg. §1.280A-2(d).

80 *Drucker v. Comm'r*, 77 T.C. (CCH) 867 (1981), *aff'd on this issue*, 697 F.2d 46, 52 (2d Cir. 1982).

81 See Prop. Reg. §1.280A-2(e).

the age of 65, or for individuals who are physically or mentally incapable of caring for themselves.[82]

E. Business Use of Residence—Rental

1. [§ 8.33] Generally

In the case of a taxpayer who uses a dwelling unit for personal purposes on any day during the taxable year, the amount deductible under the Internal Revenue Code with respect to expenses attributable to the rental of the unit for the taxable year shall not exceed an amount which bears the same relationship to such expenses as the number of days during each year that the unit (or portion thereof) is rented at a fair rental bears to the total number of days during such year that the unit (or portion thereof) is used.[83] Specific limitations apply to the allowable business deductions that may be taken by a taxpayer who rents out a vacation home or other dwelling unit that they use as their residence during the tax year. The limitations set forth a minimum rental use and a minimum personal use. If the home is used by the taxpayer during the tax year as their residence and it is rented for fewer than 15 days during the taxable year, no deductions attributable to such rental are allowable and no income derived from such rental is includable in gross income.[84] Of course, other allowable deductions in connection with the home, such as mortgage interest and real estate taxes, may still be deducted.

2. [§ 8.34] Hobby loss

Except as provided in I.R.C. § 280A(e)(1), if the home is not used for personal purposes for more than 14 days during the taxable year or, if greater, more than 10% of the number of days during the year for which the home is rented for a fair rental, the limitations of I.R.C. § 280A do not apply. Instead, the so-called "hobby loss" provisions of the Code are used to test the deductibility of the expenses.[85] Under I.R.C. § 280A(e)(1), personal use of a dwelling unit on even a single day during the taxable year requires an allocation of expenses based on days of personal use and days of rental of the property at a fair rental value.

3. [§ 8.35] Shared equity financing

Under the tax rubric of "shared equity financing," the Internal Revenue Code allows a taxpayer to join with other investors in ownership of the taxpayer's principal residence, i.e., the use as a principal residence by one owner does not constitute

---

[82] I.R.C. § 280A(c)(4); see generally Prop. Reg. §1.280A-2(f).

[83] I.R.C. § 280A(e).

[84] I.R.C. § 280A(g).

[85] *See* I.R.C. § 183.

"personal use" for deductions to be disallowed. The user must have an agreement whereby fair market rental is paid[86] and the owners must also have undivided interests for more than 50 years in the entire dwelling unit and the appurtenant land. It might be noted that the "appurtenant land" requirement of I.R.C. § 280A(d)(3)(D) might exclude the common Baltimore ground rent properties, although this is not certain.

F. Business Use of Residence

1. [§ 8.36] Lease to employer

The 1986 Tax Reform Act adopts statutory language, effective for tax years beginning after 1986, that overrules two Tax Court decisions[87] concerning the deductions for the business use of one's home. The Feldman decision held that an employee could deduct expenses associated with the rental of a portion of their home to their employer without regard to the business use requirements of the Internal Revenue Code, thus allowing the employee to deduct home office expenses without requiring the regular and exclusive use of the home either as their principal place of business or as a place to meet customers. I.R.C. § 280A(c)(6) effectively overrules this decision by barring home office deductions where an employee leases a portion of their home to the employer. The rule also extends to an independent contractor who leases to the party for whom he performs the services.

2. [§ 8.37] Home office business expenses not allocable to the use of the home

The *Scott* decision[88] did not require allowable home office expenses to be further reduced by expenditures of the business not allocable to the use of the home. As a result, a taxpayer could use home office deductions to create or increase a net loss from the home office business activity, against which income from unrelated activities could be offset. The 1986 TRA prohibits such result by providing that *all* the deductions allocable to the home office business activity must be utilized to offset the gross income of the business activity.[89] Moreover, the deduction of home office expenses is subject to the 2% floor on miscellaneous itemized deductions. [90] All miscellaneous itemized deductions have been suspended for tax years 2018 through 2025 under I.R.C. § 67(g), which Congress codified in the TCJA.

---

86 I.R.C. § 280A(d)(3).

87 *Feldman v. Comm'r*, 84 T.C. 1 (1985), *aff'd*, 791 F.2d 781 (9th Cir. 1986); *Scott v. Comm'r*, 84 T.C. 683 (1985).

88 *Scott v. Comm'r*, 84 T.C. 683 (1985).

89 I.R.C. § 280A(c)(5)(B)(ii).

90 *See* I.R.C. § 67.

3. [§ 8.38] Conducting business by telephone for convenience of employer

In *Green v. Commissioner,*[91] the Tax Court allowed deduction for a home office maintained exclusively and regularly to handle business telephone calls for the convenience of the taxpayer's employer. The Ninth Circuit reversed this decision in holding that the exception for home office expense deductions based upon the use of a residence exclusively and on a regular basis for use by patients, clients, or customers is not applicable on the basis of regularly conducting business by telephone to such clients. The Tax Court has since adopted the position of the Ninth Circuit in holding that physical presence in the home office while talking on the telephone with clients, customers, etc. will not qualify for the office-at-home deduction.[92]

G. [§ 8.39] Business Use of Residence—Consequences under Internal Revenue Code Provisions for "Residences"

Business use of a portion of a residence denies application of those Internal Revenue Code provisions specifically made applicable to "residences." For instance, allocation of basis and amount realized between residential and business use would be necessary upon sale of the dwelling if the business use is conducted in a place that is separate from the dwelling unit.[93] Gain realized on the business portion would not fall within the rollover[94] or exclusion provisions applicable to gains realized on the residential portion. Conversion of the business portion of the dwelling to residential use prior to sale arguably allows application of the rollover provisions available to principal residences.[95]

H. Improvements to the Residence for Medical Care

1. [§ 8.40] Generally

To a limited extent, deductions may be available to a homeowner for maintenance of or for capital improvements to the personal residence when such costs qualify as medical expenses. A capital expenditure made by the taxpayer may qualify as a medical expense if it has as its primary purpose the medical care

---

91 78 T.C. 428 (1982), *rev'd*, 707 F.2d 404, 83-1 T.C. § 9387 (9th Cir. 1983); *see also Hefti v. Comm'r*, 54 T.C.M. (CCH) 1555 (1988); *Pearson v. Comm'r*, 43 T.C.M. (CCH) 1508 (1982).

92 *Frankel v. Comm'r*, 82 T.C. 318 (1984).

93 Treas. Reg. § 1.121-1(e).

94 See discussion regarding former I.R.C. § 1034 in **§ 8.88** of this chapter.

95 *See* Sang, *Tax Benefits Available on the Purchase, Sale or Rental of Residence or Vacation Homes*, 50 J. TAX'N 23, 26 (1979); Henning, *Personal Residences Planning for Tax-Free and Tax-Deferred Sales and Exchanges*, 4 REV. OF TAX'N OF INDIVIDUALS 22, 32 (1980); and *see* § **8.51** of this chapter.

for the taxpayer, their spouse, or their dependent.[96] For example, the purchase of an air conditioner for an asthmatic can be deducted if it qualifies as a medical expense. Similarly, an expenditure for permanent improvement or betterment of the home that qualifies as a medical expense is deductible to the extent that its cost is in excess of the increase in the property's value. An example would be the cost of an elevator installed for a heart attack victim. Moreover, maintenance expenses for the elevator would be wholly deductible because of the medical expense characterization.[97]

Over the years, Congress has changed the floor for deducting itemized medical expenses as a percentage of adjusted gross income, including by raising the floor from 5% to 7.5% of adjusted gross income in the 1986 TRA, and from 7.5% to 10% of adjusted gross income in the 2010 Patient Protection and Affordable Care Act.[98] Congress again set the floor at 7.5% in the 2020 Taxpayer Certainty and Disaster Tax Relief Act.[99]

The deduction is only allowed for expenses not compensated by insurance or otherwise.[100] The Committee Reports of the 1986 TRA clarify that specific expenses incurred by physically handicapped individuals to remove structural barriers from their residence to accommodate their physical condition constitute deductible medical expenses. These items include railings, support bars, and other modifications.

The deductibility of such expenditure depends on its qualification as a medical care expense and effect on the value of the property rather than on its character as a capital or noncapital expenditure. Thus, the IRS will allow the total cost of the capital improvement as a deductible medical expense to the extent that the cost exceeds an increase in value of the property resulting from the improvement, if the expenditure is related directly to medical care.

The IRS will not issue advance rulings regarding whether a capital expenditure for an item ordinarily used for personal purposes has medical care as its primary purpose or is related directly to medical care.[101]

---

96 Treas. Reg. § 1.213-1(e)(1)(iii). *See Huff v. Comm'r*, 69 T.C.M. (CCH) 2551 (1995); *see also* Rev. Rul. 87-106, 1987-2 C.B. 67.

97 Treas. Reg. § 1.213-1(e)(1)(iii).

98 Pub. L. No. 111-148, Section 9013(a).

99 Included in the Consolidated Appropriations Act, Pub. L. No. 116-260, Division EE, Title I, Subtitle A, Section 101.

100 I.R.C. § 213(a).

101 Rev. Proc. 2023-3, Sec. 3.01(44).

2. *[§ 8.41] How lavish can the improvements be?*

Medical expense deductions have been allowed for the cost of installing special bathroom and bathing facilities for a handicapped person;[102] for special ramps and doors and other facilities for a multiple sclerosis patient;[103] and for a swimming pool for a polio victim.[104] In another swimming pool case,[105] the issue was how lavish a facility could be and still be claimed as a medical cost, i.e., whether the cost of the pool in excess of the property's rise in value was deductible when it was in excess of what had to be expended. The Tax Court allowed the deduction, analogizing the additional costs of making the pool's structure compatible to the architecture of the residence to the difference in cost between a private hospital room and a bed in a ward; but the Seventh Circuit denied the "unnecessary" element as not having "as its primary purpose the medical care" of the taxpayer. This issue of the minimally adequate facility is not fully resolved as of this writing, and, aside from the *Ferris* case discussed below, there does not appear to be another case where a deduction for costs in excess of those needed to create a minimally adequate facility have been disallowed. Maryland taxpayers have the benefit of the Tax Court jurisdiction based on Fourth Circuit precedents rather than Seventh Circuit precedents. The Seventh Circuit in the *Ferris* case suggested two possible ways of figuring the minimum reasonable cost:

(1) start with the taxpayer's actual cost and then subtract costs for materials and methods that are unnecessarily expensive; or

(2) rely on actual costs of other taxpayers who constructed comparable therapeutic facilities in a nearby location (adjusted for inflation).

3. *[§ 8.42] Nature of doctor's recommendation*

In one Private Letter Ruling, the taxpayer suffering from allergies was allowed a deduction for replacing moldy shingles although the amount deductible was left for the taxpayer to substantiate.[106] The Tax Court allowed medical deductions for the cost of central air conditioning to the extent it did not increase the property value, where a doctor recommended that the taxpayer's daughter's medical condition be treated by maintenance of a relatively constant temperature and high humidity.[107] Similarly,

---

[102] Rev. Rul. 70-395, 1970-2 C.B. 65; *see also Keen v. Comm'r*, T.C.M. (CCH) 1981-313 (home health spa); *Haines v. Comm'r*, 71 T.C. 644 (1979).

[103] *Oliver v. Comm'r*, 364 F.2d 575 (8th Cir. 1966); *but see Zipkin v. United States*, 2000-2 U.S. Tax Cas. (CCH) 501863 (2000).

[104] *Mason v. United States*, 52 A.F.T.R. 1593 (1957).

[105] *Ferris v. Comm'r*, 582 F.2d 1112 (7th Cir. 1978), *rev'g and rem'g*, 36 T.C.M. (CCH) 765 (1977)'; *compare Haines v. Comm'r*, 71 T.C. 644 (1979).

[106] I.R.S. Priv. Ltr. Rul. 81-12-069 (Dec. 29, 1980).

[107] *Gerard v. Comm'r*, 37 T.C. 826 (1962).

deduction was allowed for the costs of a weight loss program because two physicians prescribed it for specific health problems.[108] But deduction was not allowed where the weight loss was for general wellbeing.[109] Where the taxpayer, an asthma sufferer, renovated his residence to install forced air heating and central air conditioning, medical expense deductions were disallowed on the grounds that the taxpayer failed to show that the primary purpose for the work was medically related.[110] This conclusion was based upon the absence of evidence that the work was undertaken in response to a recommendation from a physician who was actually treating the taxpayer for a medical condition that the work was assertedly intended to treat.

I. [§ 8.43] Residential Energy Tax Credits

Maryland law provides for a property tax credit under certain circumstances for the use of energy saving devices.[111] The governing body of a county, a municipal corporation, or Baltimore City may grant, by law, a tax credit against that body's property tax imposed on a structure, if to heat or cool the structure, to generate electricity to be used in the structure, or to provide hot water for use in the structure, the structure uses:

(1) a solar energy device,

(2) a geothermal energy device, or

(3) a qualifying energy conservation device.[112]

A county or municipal corporation may provide, by law, for:

(1) the amount of a property tax credit,

(2) the duration of a property tax credit not exceeding three years,

(3) the definition of the aforementioned energy devices, and

(4) any provision necessary to carry out Tax-Prop. § 9-203.[113]

J. Historic Property

1. [§ 8.44] The federal two-tier credit

The 1986 TRA replaced the three-tier rehabilitation credit with a two-tier credit. The 15 and 20% credits for 30-year-old and 40-year-old buildings, respectively, were superseded by a 10% credit that was available only for a building that

---

108 I.R.S. Priv. Ltr. Rul. 80-04-111 (Oct. 31, 1979).

109 Rev. Rul. 79-151, 1979-1 C.B. 116.

110 *Lipson v. Comm'r*, 50 T.C.M. (CCH) 692 (1985).

111 *See* TAX-PROP. § 9-203.

112 TAX-PROP. § 9-203(a).

113 TAX-PROP. § 9-203(b).

was first placed in service before 1936.[114] The 25% credit available for the rehabilitation of certified historic structures was replaced by a 20% credit. The TCJA generally eliminated the 10% credit for any post-December 31, 2017 rehabilitation expenditures.[115]

2. *[§ 8.45] The Maryland property tax credit*

Maryland provides for a property tax credit of up to 25%, for property tax years beginning after June 30, 2013,[116] of a property owner's documented expenses for the restoration and preservation of a structure determined to have historic architectural value. The governing body of a county, a municipal corporation, or Baltimore City is provided the authority to grant this credit against the property tax it imposed.[117] A property tax credit up to 5% of the owner's documented expenses for the construction of an architecturally compatible new structure in a historic district may be granted by the governing body of a county, a municipal corporation, or Baltimore City against such property tax.[118] A property tax credit granted in one year may be applied to any property tax on the structure for up to five subsequent tax years.[119] In addition, Tax-Prop. § 9-204.1 establishes a property tax credit for eligible historic improvements.

IV. FEDERAL INCOME TAX CONSEQUENCES OF SELLING A PRINCIPAL RESIDENCE

PART 1: THE TAXPAYER RELIEF ACT OF 1997 —

THE LAW FOR SALES OR EXCHANGES AFTER MAY 6, 1997

A. [§ 8.46] Introduction

The Taxpayer Relief Act of 1997[120] repealed the rollover gains provision (§ 1034) and the one time $125,000 exclusion for taxpayers over 55 (§ 121). It replaced those provisions with a general exclusion from gain for post-May 6, 1997 sales or exchanges. This part discusses § 121 provisions regarding the general exclusion of gain realized from the sale or exchange of a principal residence after May 6, 1997. Sections **8.86** through **8.125** discuss the previous deferral mechanism which was available under prior § 1034 to taxpayers who "rolled over" a personal residence. Sections **8.126 through 8.145** address the exclusion previously found in prior § 121 for the sale of a principal residence by taxpayers 55 years or older.

---

114 I.R.C. § 47(a).

115 Pub. L. No. 115-97, §13402(c).

116 2013 Md. H.B. 263.

117 TAX-PROP. § 9-204(b).

118 TAX-PROP. § 9-204(c).

119 TAX-PROP. § 9-204(e).

120 *See* Pub. L. No. 105-34, § 312, effective Aug. 5, 1997.

Current § 121 grants an exclusion from gross income from the sale or exchange of property that has been owned and used as the taxpayer's principal residence for periods totaling at least two years during the five-year period ending on the date of the sale or exchange. The exclusion is for up to $250,000 for an individual, and up to $500,000 when a husband and wife file a joint return for the taxable year of the sale or exchange if they meet the following three tests:

(1) either spouse meets the ownership test of § 121(a);

(2) both spouses meet the use test of § 121(a); and

(3) neither spouse is ineligible for the exclusion because of § 121(b)(3).

That paragraph states that the exclusion will not apply if during the two-year period ending on the date of the sale or exchange there was another sale or exchange by the taxpayer to which the exclusion applied. Section 121(d) also addresses property of a deceased or former spouse. In the case of a deceased spouse, § 121(d)(2) provides that an unmarried taxpayer whose spouse is deceased on the date of the sale or exchange is considered to have owned and used the property for a period that includes the period the deceased spouse owned and used it before death. Where property is transferred as part of a divorce, § 121(d)(3) provides that the transferee's ownership includes the period the transferor owned the property. Additionally, a taxpayer is treated as using the property as their principal residence when, pursuant to a divorce, the taxpayer's spouse or former spouse is granted use of the property under a divorce or separation instrument.

Section 121(c) provides hardship relief for taxpayers where a sale or exchange results from a change in the place of employment, health, or unforeseen circumstances to be addressed by regulation. The exception applies where there is a failure to meet the ownership requirements or where, during the two-year period ending on the date of the sale or exchange, there was another sale or exchange by the taxpayer to which the exclusion applied. In such circumstances, the taxpayer may exclude a portion of the gain as set forth in § 121(c)(1).

Where there was a non-recognition of gain under the rollover provisions of prior § 1034, § 121(g) provides that the ownership and use period of previous residences for which the gain was rolled over is included in the period of ownership and use of the residence, the acquisition of which resulted in the nonrecognition of gain.

Other provisions of § 121 pertain to recognition of gain attributable to depreciation, prior tax free exchanges under § 1031, periods of non-qualified use, periods of military service or service with intelligence service or Peace Corps, application of the exclusion to the sale of remainder interests, the determination of use during periods of "out-of-residence" care, and denial of the exclusion to expatriates.

The first part of this section discusses the current law, including as enacted by the Taxpayer Relief Act of 1997. The second part of this section discusses the law in effect for sales or exchanges that occurred prior to May 7, 1997, including the roll-over provisions of prior § 1034 and the exclusion from gross income for sales of principal residences by certain taxpayers age 55 or older.

B. [§ 8.47] General Rule

Section 121(a) of the Internal Revenue Code of 1986, as amended,[121] excludes from gross income gain realized from the sale or exchange of property if, during the five-year period ending on the date of the sale or exchange, the property has been used by the taxpayer as the taxpayer's principal residence for periods aggregating two years or more.[122] The amount excludable is $250,000 for an individual, or $500,000 for spouses who file a joint return and meet certain tests.

C. Principal Residence

1. [§ 8.48] General definition

Whether or not property is used by the taxpayer as the taxpayer's residence, and whether or not property is used by the taxpayer as the taxpayer's principal residence (in the case of a taxpayer using more than one property as a residence), depends upon all the facts and circumstances.[123] If a taxpayer alternates between two properties, using each as a residence for successive periods of time, the property that the taxpayer uses a majority of the time during the year will ordinarily be considered the taxpayer's principal residence.[124]

In addition to the taxpayer's use of the property, relevant factors in determining a taxpayer's principal residence, include, but are not limited to: (i) the taxpayer's place of employment; (ii) the principal place of abode of the taxpayer's family members; (iii) the address listed on the taxpayer's federal and state tax returns, driver's license, automobile registration, and voter registration card; (iv) the taxpayer's mailing address for bills and correspondence; (v) the location of the taxpayer's banks;

---

121 All section references are to the Internal Revenue Code of 1986, as amended, unless otherwise indicated.

122 *See also* Treas. Reg. § 1.121-1(a).

123 Treas. Reg. § 1.121-(b)(1), (b)(2). Some of the factors the courts considered under prior law are similar to those the courts used to determine a person's place of domicile, such as where the taxpayer is registered to vote, has a driver's license, maintains a bank account, files his state income tax return, where his business and family are located, and where he receives his mail.

124 Treas. Reg. § 1.121-(b)(2). *See also* Internal Revenue Serv., I.R.S. Pub. No. 523, Selling Your Home 3 (2022).

and (vi) the location of religious organizations and recreational clubs with which the taxpayer is affiliated.[125] The foregoing factors are nonexclusive.

The income tax regulations provide the following two examples to illustrate the case where the taxpayer owns and occupies more than one residence.[126]

> ***Example 1***—Taxpayer A owns two residences, one in New York and one in Florida. From 1999 through 2004, he lives in the New York residence for seven months and the Florida residence for five months of each year. In the absence of facts and circumstances indicating otherwise, the New York residence is A's principal residence. A would be eligible for the § 121 exclusion of gain from the sale or exchange of the New York residence, but not the Florida residence.
>
> ***Example 2***—Taxpayer B owns two residences, one in Virginia and one in Maine. During 1999 and 2000, she lives in the Virginia residence. During 2001 and 2002, she lives in the Maine residence. During 2003, she lives in the Virginia residence. B's principal residence during 1999, 2000, and 2003 is the Virginia residence. B's principal residence during 2001 and 2002 is the Maine residence. B would be eligible for the § 121 exclusion of gain from the sale or exchange of either residence (but not both) during 2003.

Property used by the taxpayer as the taxpayer's principal residence may include a houseboat, a house trailer, or a house or apartment that the taxpayer is entitled to occupy as a tenant-stockholder in a cooperative housing corporation (as these terms are defined in § 216(b)(1) and (2)) if the dwelling that the taxpayer is entitled to occupy as a stockholder is used by the taxpayer as the taxpayer's principal residence.[127] Property used by the taxpayer as the taxpayer's principal residence does not include personal property that is not a fixture under local law.[128] The principal residence rules are substantially the same rules that applied under prior law for purposes of the rollover rules for sales or exchanges that occurred prior to May 7, 1997.[129]

Under prior law, and current law, to qualify as a principal residence, the residence must be "used" as such. In other words, the taxpayer must physically occupy the residence and live in it.[130] The physical occupancy test is not met where the

---

125 TREAS. REG. § 1.121-1(b)(2).

126 TREAS. REG. § 1.121-1(b)(4). Examples 1 and 2.

127 TREAS. REG. § 1.121-1(b)(1).

128 *Id.*

129 *See* § **8.86**, *infra.*

130 See *Stolk v. Comm'r*, 40 T.C. 345 (1963), *aff'd*, 326 F.2d 760 (2d Cir. 1964) where the Tax Court said "the phrase 'used by the taxpayer as his principal residence' means habitual use of the old residence as the principal residence. The antithesis is nonuse of property as the principal residence." *Stolk*, at 355. *See also Friedman v. Comm'r*, 43 T.C.M. (CCH) 1009 (1982); *McDowell v. Comm'r*, 40 T.C.M. (CCH) 301 (1980); and *Evans v. Comm'r*, 21 T.C.M. (CCH) 339 (1962).

taxpayer's children, and not the taxpayer, occupy the residence.[131] The Internal Revenue Service will not issue an advance ruling or determination letter on whether a residence qualifies as the taxpayer's principal residence.[132]

Taxpayers who demolish a house that is their principal residence and then construct a new house on the same land are not entitled to tack their ownership and use periods for the old house onto the new house for purposes of § 121 if they never actually use the house as their principal residence.[133]

2. *[§ 8.49] Pre-sale rental*

A taxpayer is not required to occupy physically the principal residence up to the date of its sale.[134] Rather, the taxpayer may rent the residence to a third party prior to its sale and still have the gain realized from the sale qualify for tax deferral treatment.[135]

3. *[§ 8.50] Types of residences*

Most types of dwelling houses qualify as a principal residence. For example, single family dwelling units, rowhouses, townhouses, and, as noted earlier, houseboats, trailers, shares of stock by a tenant-stockholder in a cooperative housing corporation,[136] and condominium apartments qualify as a principal residence.[137]

The Internal Revenue Service has also held under prior law that a yacht may qualify as a principal residence if it has cooking, sleeping, and sanitation facilities.[138] This should also apply to current law. On the other hand, property used by the taxpayer as the taxpayer's principal residence does not include personal property, such as furniture, which is not a fixture under local law.[139]

---

131 *Lokan v. Comm'r*, 39 T.C.M. (CCH) 168 (1979); Rev. Rul. 69-434, 1969-2 C.B. 163.

132 Rev. Proc. 2023-3, Sec. 3.01(33).

133 *Gates v. Commissioner*, 135 T.C. 1 (2010).

134 *Aagaard v. Comm'r*, 56 T.C. 191 (1971).

135 Treas. Reg. § 1.121-1(c)(4), Example 1.

136 Treas. Reg. § 1.121-1(b). Exchange of unit in cooperative for shares of stock in corporation not taxable under § 216(e) and prior § 1034(j). *See* I.R.S. Priv. Ltr. Rul. 94-28-006 (Apr. 12, 1994).

137 Rev. Rul. 64-31, 1964-1 C.B. 300. The exchange of stock in a cooperative apartment corporation for legal title to the apartment occupied by the taxpayer as the taxpayer's principal residence for 15 years, when the cooperative apartments converted to a condominium, qualifies for nonrecognition treatment under prior I.R.C. § 1034 if all the other test of prior I.R.C. § 1034 are met. Rev. Rul. 85-132, 1985-2 C.B. 182 (holding that the exchange of stock in cooperative housing corporation for title to condominium and undivided interest in common elements results in nonrecognition of gain). I.R.S. Priv. Ltr. Rul. 8210054 (holding that the exchange of stock in cooperative apartment for title to apartment on conversion to condominium qualifies for nonrecognition treatment).

138 I.R.S. Priv. Ltr. Rul. 83-37-050 (June 14, 1983). A rental apartment converted to condominium ownership may also qualify as a principal residence. Rev. Rul. 80-172, 1980-2 C.B. 56.

139 *See* note **105**, *supra*.

Gain realized from the sale of unimproved residential real estate may not be excluded from Federal income taxation[140] unless:

(i) the vacant land is adjacent to land containing the dwelling unit of the taxpayer's principal residence;

(ii) the taxpayer owned and used the vacant land as part of the taxpayer's principal residence;

(iii) the taxpayer sells or exchanges the dwelling unit in a sale or exchange that meets the requirements of § 121 within two years before, or two years after, the date of the sale or exchange of the vacant land; and

(iv) the requirements of § 121 have otherwise been met with respect to the vacant land.[141]

There are three limitations regarding the sale of vacant land. First, the sale or exchange of the dwelling unit and the vacant land are treated as one sale or exchange. Therefore, only one maximum limitation amount of $250,000 ($500,000 for certain joint returns) applies to the combined sales or exchanges of vacant land and the dwelling unit. In applying the maximum limitation amount to sales or exchanges that occur in different taxable years, gain from the sale or exchange of the dwelling unit, up to the maximum limitation amount, is excluded first, and each spouse is treated as excluding one-half of the gain from a sale or exchange to which § 121(b)(2)(A) and TREAS. REG. § 1.121-(a)(3)(i) (relating to the limitation for certain joint returns) apply.[142]

Second, if a dwelling unit and vacant land are sold or exchanged in separate transactions that qualify for the § 121 exclusion, each of the transactions is disregarded in applying the restriction of § 121(b)(3) (restricting the application of § 121 to only one sale or exchange every two years) to the other transactions, but is taken into account as a sale or exchange of a principal residence on the date of the transaction in applying the § 121(b)(3) restriction of one sale or exchange every two years to that transaction and the sale or exchange of any other principal residence.[143]

Third, if the vacant land is sold or exchanged in a taxable year before the sale or exchange of the dwelling unit occurs and after the date prescribed by law (including extensions) for the filing of the return for the taxable year of the sale or exchange of the vacant land, any gain from the sale or exchange of the vacant land must be reported as taxable on the taxpayer's return for the taxable year of the sale or exchange of

---

140 *O'Barr v. Comm'r*, 44 T.C. 501 (1965); Rev. Rul. 56-420, 1956-2 C.B. 519; TREAS. REG. § 1.121-1(b)(3).

141 TREAS. REG. § 1.121-1(b)(3)(i).

142 TREAS. REG. § 1.121-1(b)(3)(ii)(A).

143 TREAS. REG. § 1.121-1(b)(3)(ii)(B).

the vacant land. If the taxpayer has reported gain from the sale or exchange of the vacant land as taxable, and then determines it is not taxable, the taxpayer may claim the § 121 exclusion with regard to the sale or exchange of the vacant land (for any period for which the period of limitation under § 6511 has not expired) by filing an amended return.[144]

The income tax regulations provide the following two examples to illustrate the situation involving vacant land:

> ***Example 1***—In 1991 Taxpayer C purchased property consisting of a house and 10 acres that they used as their principal residence. In May 2005, C sells eight acres of the land and realizes a gain of $110,000. C does not sell the dwelling unit before the due date for filing C's 2005 return; therefore C is not eligible to exclude the $110,000 of gain. In March 2007, C sells the house and remaining two acres, realizing a gain of $180,000 from the sale of the house. C may exclude the $180,000 of gain. Because the sale of the eight acres occurred within two years from the date of the sale of the dwelling unit, the sale of the eight acres is treated as a sale of the taxpayer's principal residence. C may file an amended return for 2005 to claim an exclusion for $70,000 ($250,000—$180,000 gain previously excluded) of the $110,000 gain from the sale of the eight acres.
>
> ***Example 2***—In 1998 Taxpayer D purchased a house and one acre that they used as their principal residence. In 1999 D purchased 29 acres adjacent to their house and used the vacant land as part of their principal residence. In 2003 D sells the house and one acre, and the 29 acres, in two separate transactions. D sells the house and one acre at a loss of $25,000. D realizes $270,000 of gain from the sale of the 29 acres. D may exclude the $245,000 gain from the two sales.[145]

On the other hand, gain from the sale of a dwelling place only, or gain from the separate sale of a dwelling place and the underlying land, may be excluded from Federal income taxation.[146] These cases, decided under prior law, would appear to apply under current law. But if the taxpayer sells only the land on which their

---

144 TREAS. REG. § 1.121-1(b)(3)(ii)(C).

145 TREAS. REG. § 1.121-1(b)(4). Examples 3 and 4.

146 *Bogley v. Comm'r*, 263 F.2d 746, 747 (4th Cir. 1959), *rev'g*, 30 T.C. 452 (1958), prior I.R.C. § 1034 applied to sale of 10 acres of land where taxpayer had previously sold residence and three of 13 acres surrounding residence. Ten acres had not lost status as principal residence. Rev. Rul. 76-541, 1976-2 C.B. 246 (prior I.R.C. § 1034 applied to gain realized from sale of house and land and sale of contiguous parcel later in same year. Both parcels were used as taxpayer's principal residence) distinguishing Rev. Rul. 56-420, 1956-2 C.B. 519 (Gain recognized where portion of lot sold was only that on which taxpayer had garden, orchard and checking). *Lokan v. Comm'r*, 39 T.C.M. (CCH) 168 (1979) (one-and-one-half acres of land occupied by

principal residence is located, but not the residence, the taxpayer cannot exclude any of the gain from the sale of the land.[147] The Tax Court has ruled that gain from the sale of vacant land adjacent to a principal residence held by a family partnership is not eligible for exclusion under § 121.[148]

4. [§ 8.51] Partial residence

Section 121 exclusionary treatment does not apply to gain allocable to any portion (separate from the dwelling unit) of property sold or exchanged with respect to which the taxpayer does not satisfy the use test. Thus, where property is used, at the time of its sale, partly as a principal residence and partly for business or other purposes, an allocation of basis and amount realized must be made between the two portions of the property, inasmuch as only the gain realized from the part of the property *used* as a principal residence may be excluded from Federal income taxation under I.R.C. § 121.[149] For example, if, at the time of sale, one-half the property is used as a principal residence and the other half is used as a rental apartment or as a law office, the gain attributable to the portion of the property used as an apartment or as a law office does not qualify for I.R.C. § 121 exclusionary treatment.[150] The gain on such portion may, however, qualify for favorable capital gains treatment. No allocation is required if both the residential and non-residential portions of the property are within the same dwelling unit.[151]

A dwelling unit for purposes of the partial use rule is defined by reference to § 280A(f)(1),[152] which provides that a dwelling unit includes a house, condominium, mobile home, boat or similar property, and all structures or other property appurtenant to such dwelling unit, but does not include that portion of a unit which is used exclusively as a hotel, motel, inn, or similar establishment.

For purposes of determining the amount of gain allocable to the residential and non-residential portions of the property, the taxpayer must allocate the basis and the amount realized between the residential and the non-residential portions of the property using the same method of allocation that the taxpayer used to determine depreciation adjustments (as defined in § 1250(b)(3)) if applicable.[153]

---

trailer and used by taxpayer qualified as new principal residence under prior I.R.C. § 1034. Remaining six acres used for farming did not qualify as new principal residence.).

147 Internal Revenue Serv., IRS Pub. No. 523, Selling Your Home 5 (2022).

148 *Farah v. Commissioner*, T.C. Memo. 2007-369.

149 Treas. Reg. § 1.121-1(e).

150 *Id.*

151 Treas. Reg. § 1.121-1(e)(1).

152 Treas. Reg. § 1.121-1(e)(2).

153 Treas. Reg. § 1.121-1(e)(3).

The partial residence rules are illustrated by the following six examples set forth in TREAS. REG. § 1.121-1(e)(4):

Example 1*—Non-residential use of property not within the dwelling unit.* Taxpayer A owns a property that consists of a house, a stable, and 35 acres. A uses the stable and 28 acres for nonresidential purposes for more than three years during the five-year period preceding the sale. A uses the entire house and the remaining seven acres as their principal residence for at least two years during the five-year period preceding the sale. For periods after May 6, 2017, A claims depreciation deductions of $9,000 for the non-residential use of the stable. A sells the entire property in 2024, realizing a gain of $24,000. A has no other § 1231 or capital gains or losses for 2024.

Because the stable and the 28 acres used in the business are separate from the dwelling unit, the allocation rules apply and A must allocate the basis and amount realized between the portion of the property that they used as their principal residence and the portion of the property that they used for nonresidential purposes. A determines that $14,000 of the gain is allocable to the non-residential-use portion of the property and that $10,000 of the gain is allocable to the portion of the property used as their residence. A must recognize the $14,000 of gain allocable to the nonresidential-use portion of the property ($9,000 of which is unrecaptured § 1250 gain within the meaning of § 1(h), and $5,000 of which is adjusted net capital gain). A may exclude $10,000 of the gain from the sale of the property.

Example 2*—Non-residential use of property not within the dwelling unit and rental of the entire property.* In 2018 Taxpayer B purchased a property that included a house, a barn, and two acres. B used the house and two acres as their principal residence and the barn for an antiques business. In 2022, B moves out of the house and rents it to tenants. B sells the property in 2024, realizing a gain of $21,000. Between 1998 and 2004, B claims depreciation deductions of $4,800 attributable to the antiques business. Between 2022 and 2024, B claims depreciation deductions of $3,000 attributable to the house. B has no other § 1231 or capital gains or losses for 2024.

Because the portion of the property used in the antiques business is separate from the dwelling unit, the allocation rules apply. B must allocate basis and amount realized between the portion of the property that they used as their principal residence and the portion of the property that they used for nonresidential purposes. B determines that $4,000 of the gain is allocable to the non-residential portion of the property and that $17,000 of the gain is allocable to the portion of the property that they used as their principal residence.

B must recognize the $4,000 of gain allocable to the non-residential portion of the property (all of which is unrecaptured § 1250 gain within the meaning of § 1(h)). In addition, the § 121 exclusion does not apply to the gain allocable to the residential portion of the property to the extent of the depreciation adjustments attributable to the residential portion of the property for periods after May 6, 2017 ($3,000). Therefore, B may exclude $14,000 of the gain from the sale of the property.

Example 3*—Non-residential use of a separate dwelling unit.* In 2012, Taxpayer C buys a three-story townhouse and converts the basement level, which has a separate entrance, into a separate apartment by installing a kitchen and bathroom and removing the interior stairway that leads from the basement to the upper floors. After the conversion, the property constitutes two dwelling units. C uses the first and second floors of the townhouse as their principal residence and rents the basement level to tenants from 2013 to 2017. C claims depreciation deductions of $2,000 for that period with respect to the basement apartment. C sells the entire property in 2017, realizing gain of $18,000. C has no other § 1231 or capital gains or losses for 2017.

Because the basement apartment and the upper floors of the townhouse are separate dwelling units, C must allocate the gain between the portion of the property that they used as their principal residence and the portion of the property that they used for non-residential purposes. After allocating the basis and the amount realized between the residential and non-residential portions of the property, C determines that $6,000 of the gain is allocable to the non-residential portion of the property and that $12,000 of the gain is allocable to the portion of the property used as their residence. C must recognize the $6,000 of gain allocable to the nonresidential portion of the property ($2,000 of which is unrecaptured § 1250 gain within the meaning of § 1(h), and $4,000 of which is adjusted net capital gain). C may exclude $12,000 of the gain from the sale of the property.

Example 4*—Separate dwelling unit converted to residential use.* The facts are the same as in Example 3 except that in 2017 C incorporates the basement of the townhouse into their principal residence by eliminating the kitchen and building a new interior stairway to the upper floors. C uses all three floors of the townhouse as their principal residence for two full years and sells the townhouse in 2020, realizing a gain of $20,000. Under § 121(d)(6), C must recognize $2,000 of the gain as unrecaptured § 1250 gain within the meaning of § 1(h). Because C used the entire three floors of the townhouse as their principal residence for two of the five years preceding the sale of the property, C may exclude the remaining $18,000 of the gain from the sale of the house.

Example 5*—Non-residential use within the dwelling unit, property depreciated.* Taxpayer D, an attorney, buys a house in 2013. The house constitutes a single dwelling unit but D uses a portion of the house as a law office. D claims depreciation deductions of $2,000 during the period that they owns the house. D sells the house in 2016, realizing a gain of $13,000. D has no other § 1231 or capital gains or losses for 2016. Under § 121(d)(6), D must recognize $2,000 of the gain as unrecaptured § 1250 gain within the meaning of § 1(h). D may exclude the remaining $11,000 of the gain from the sale of their house because tbey are not required to allocate gain to the business use within the dwelling unit.

Example 6*—Non-residential use within the dwelling unit, property not depreciated.* The facts are the same as in Example 5, except that D is not entitled to claim any depreciation deductions with respect to their business use of the house. D may exclude $13,000 of the gain from the sale of their house because they are not required to allocate gain to the business use within the dwelling unit.

The portion of the property used as a rental apartment or as a law office may be converted to residential use prior to the time of sale so that all or part of the gain attributable to such portion of the property would qualify for I.R.C. § 121 exclusionary treatment. Presumably, to convert a portion of the property from business to residential use, the converted portion must be physically occupied by the taxpayer as a residence for more than an insubstantial period of time prior to the sale of the residence.[154] Gain realized on the business portion will reflect depreciation allowed or allowable, and may involve recapture of depreciation and investment tax credit taken on the rehabilitation costs of the structure.[155] According to Rev. Rul. 82-26,[156] however, no allocation is required if the business use of a part of a residence in the year of sale does not meet the requirements of § 280A(c)(1). Thus, where there is minimal business use so that the business portion does not qualify for a deduction, it would appear that the year of minimal business use counts as one of the two of five years.

---

154 TREAS. REG. § 1.121-1(e)(4), Example 4—basement previously used as rental incorporated into townhouse, which taxpayer used as principal residence (in its entirety) for at least two of the five years before selling the townhouse.

155 TREAS. REG. § 1.121-1(d). The § 121 exclusion does not apply to so much of the gain from the sale or exchange of property as does not exceed the portion of the depreciation adjustments (as defined in § 1250(b)(3)) attributable to periods after May 6, 1997, in respect of the property.

156 1982-1 C.B. 114.

5. [§ 8.52] Loss on sale

A loss realized on the sale of a principal residence is not deductible.[157] If, however, the residence is partially used for business or the production of income, any realized loss attributable to such portion of the residence may be recognized.[158] Moreover, if residential property is, prior to its sale, rented or otherwise converted to business or profit use, and is held as such until the time of sale, any loss incurred after conversion may be recognized (i.e., the loss is allowed) to the extent that the adjusted basis of the property at the time of the conversion (which is the lesser of the fair market value of the property at the time of the conversion, or the adjusted basis for loss at the time of conversion) exceeds the amount realized from the sale.[159]

D. [§ 8.53] Ownership and Use Requirements

The requirements of ownership and use for periods aggregating two years or more may be satisfied by establishing ownership and use for 24 full months or for 730 days (365 days × 2).[160] The requirements of ownership and use may be satisfied during non-concurrent periods if both the ownership and use tests are met during the five-year period ending on the date of the sale or exchange.[161] Thus, a taxpayer may satisfy the use and ownership tests during different two-year periods, but must meet the use and ownership test during the same five-year period ending on the date of the sale.

In establishing whether a taxpayer has satisfied the two-year use requirement, occupancy of the residence is required.[162] However, short temporary absences, such as for vacation or other seasonal absence (although accompanied with rental of the residence), are counted as periods of use.[163] An absence of one year or more may not be considered a temporary absence, especially if the residence is sold shortly after the return.[164] On the other hand, an absence of two months of summer vacation is deemed a short absence.[165] The use test can be met where the taxpayer rents the property for at least two years even though he does not own the property at the time.[166]

The owner of a trust characterized as a grantor trust under §§ 671–675 is treated as the owner of the residence owned by the trust because the taxpayer can vest title

---

157 I.R.C. § 165(c); TREAS. REG. § 1.165-9(a).

158 *See Snyder v. Comm'r*, 34 T.C.M. (CCH) 965 (1975); Rev. Rul. 72-111, 1972-1 C.B. 56; Treas. Reg. § 1.165-9(b)(1).

159 TREAS. REG. § 1.165-9(b)(2).

160 TREAS. REG. § 1.121-1(c)(1).

161 *Id.*

162 TREAS. REG. § 1.121-1(c)(2)(i). *See* cases at note **115**, *supra*.

163 TREAS. REG. § 1.121-1(c)(2)(i).

164 *See* TREAS. REG. § 1.121-1(c)(4). Example 3.

165 TREAS. REg. § 1.121-1(c)(4). Example 5.

166 TREAS. REG. § 1.121-1(c)(4). Example 4.

to the residence in themselves at any time.[167] On the other hand, a taxpayer who is the income beneficiary of a trust, established by their mother, which holds fee simple title to a residence is not treated as the owner of the trust because they could not vest title to the residence in themselves, and therefore are not considered the owner of the residence for purposes of satisfying the ownership requirements of § 121.[168]

Where, however, the beneficiary of a trust has the 5+5 power to withdraw principal from the trust annually under § 2041(b)(2), the beneficiary is treated as the owner of a portion of the trust, and hence also the owner of a portion of the residence held by the trust, and thus is entitled to the reduced exclusion.[169] If, however, the beneficiary does not have the power to withdraw principal from the trust, the beneficiary is not treated as the owner of the residence and thus cannot exclude any of the gain realized.[170]

If a taxpayer has become physically or mentally incapable of self-care and the taxpayer sells or exchanges property that the taxpayer owned and used as the taxpayer's principal residence for periods aggregating at least one year during the five-year period preceding the sale or exchange, the taxpayer is treated as using the property as the taxpayer's principal residence for any period of time during the five-year period in which the taxpayer owns the property and resides in any facility (including a nursing home) licensed by a State or political subdivision to care for an individual in the taxpayer's condition.[171]

If a residence is owned by an eligible entity (within the meaning of Treas. Reg. § 301.7701-3(a)) that has a single owner and that is disregarded for Federal tax purposes as an entity separate from its owner under (such as a single member LLC or a qualified subchapter S subsidiary), the owner will be treated as owning the residence for purposes of satisfying the two year ownership requirement of § 121, and the sale or exchange by the entity will be treated as if made by the owner.[172]

On the other hand, a taxpayer is not treated as owning a residence for the period of time that the residence was owned by a partnership of which the taxpayer and a grantor trust established by the taxpayer were the partners.[173]

---

167 TREAS. REG. § 1.121-1(c)(3)(i); Rev. Rul. 85-45, 1985-1 C.B., 183; I.R.S. Priv. Ltr. Rul. 1999-12-026 (Dec. 23, 1998). *See also* I.R.S. Priv. Ltr. Rul. 2001-24-011 (Mar. 15, 2001).

168 I.R.S. Priv. Ltr. Rul. 2000-18-021 (Jan. 21, 2000).

169 I.R.S. Priv. Ltr. Rul. 2001-04-005 (Sept. 11, 2000).

170 I.R.S. Priv. Ltr. Rul. 2000-18-021, *supra* note **151**.

171 TREAS. REG. § 1.121-1(c)(2)(ii).

172 TREAS. REG. § 1.121-1(c)(3)(ii).

173 I.R.S. Priv. Ltr. Rul. 2001-190-14 (Feb. 5, 2001), revoking I.R.S. Priv. Ltr. Rul. 2000-040-22 (Jan. 21, 2000). See also I.R.S. Priv. Ltr. Rul. 2000-290-46 (Apr. 24, 2000) where the Service ruled that § 121 was not applicable to a sale of a residence because the residence was owned by a partnership.

The Tax Relief and Health Care Act of 2006 added § 121(d)(9) that allows individuals serving in the United States Uniformed Services, the Foreign Service, or the intelligence community to elect to suspend the five-year period during which the two-year ownership and use requirement were to be met.[174] This suspension applies for the period of time that the individual or the individual's spouse is serving on "qualified extended duty" as defined in § 121(d)(9)(C).[175] This extended period of time is limited to a maximum of 10 years.[176] This election is available for sales or exchanges made after December 20, 2006.[177]

For the year 2008 and later tax years, the Heroes Earnings Assistance and Relief Tax Act of 2008, provides that the five year period may also be suspended at the election of an individual during a period of time that either the individual or the individual's spouse is serving outside of the United States on a qualified official extended duty as an employee, enrolled volunteer, or volunteer leader of the Peace Corps.[178]

E. [§ 8.54] Examples of Ownership and Use

TREASURY REG. § 1.121-2(c)(4) provides five examples of the ownership and use rules. The examples are illustrated as follows:

> ***Example 1***—Taxpayer A has owned and used their house as their principal residence since 1986. On Jan. 1, 1998, A moves to another state. A leases their house from that date until Apr. 18, 2000, when they sells it. A is eligible for the § 121 exclusion because they have owned and used the house as their principal residence for at least two years out of the five years preceding the sale.
>
> ***Example 2***—Taxpayer B owned and used a house as their principal residence from 1986 to the end of 1997. On Jan. 1, 1998, B moved to another state and ceased to use the house. B's son moved into the house in Mar. 1999 and used the residence until it was sold on July 1, 2001. Taxpayer B may not exclude gain from the sale under § 121 because they did not use the property as their principal residence for at least two years out of the five years preceding the sale. Use of the property by her son alone does not count.

---

174 26 U.S.C. § 121(d)(9)(2007).

175 *Id.*; I.R.C. § 121(d)(9)(A).

176 I.R.C. § 121(d)(9)(B).

177 Under former § 121(d)(9)(A)(iii), the ability to make this election would have ended for tax years after 2010, but § 113 of the Heroes Earnings Assistance and Relief Tax Act of 2008, Pub. L. No. 110-245, repealed this provision.

178 I.R.C. § 121(d)(12).

Example 3—Taxpayer C lived in a townhouse that they rented from 1993 through 1996. On Jan. 18, 1997, they purchased this townhouse. On Feb.1, 1998, C moved into their daughter's home. On May 25, 2000, while still living in their daughter's home, C sold their townhouse. The § 121 exclusion will apply to gain from the sale because C owned the townhouse for at least two years out of the five years preceding the sale (from Jan. 19, 1997, until May 25, 2000) and they used the townhouse as their principal residence for at least two years during the five-year period preceding the sale (from May 25, 1995, until Feb. 1, 1998).

Example 4—Taxpayer D, a college professor, purchased and moved into a house on May 1, 1997. They used the house as their principal residence continuously until Sept. 1, 1998, when they went abroad for a one-year sabbatical leave. On Oct. 1, 1999, one month after returning from the leave, D sold the house. Because their leave is not considered to be a short temporary absence for purposes of § 121, the period of the leave may not be included in determining whether D used the house for periods aggregating two years during the five-year period ending on the date of the sale. Consequently, D is not entitled to exclude gain under § 121 because they did not use the residence for the requisite period.

Example 5—Taxpayer E purchased a house on Feb. 1, 1998 that they used as their principal residence. During 1998 and 1999, E left their residence for a two-month summer vacation. E sold the house on Mar. 1, 2000. Although, in the five-year period preceding the date of sale, the total time E used their residence is less than two years (21 months), the § 121 exclusion will apply to gain from the sale of the residence because the two-month vacations are short temporary absences and are counted as periods of use in determining whether E used the residence for the requisite period.

F. [§ 8.55] Depreciation

The § 121 exclusion does not apply to depreciation adjustments (as defined in § 1250(b)(3)) attributable to the property for periods after May 6, 1997. Depreciation adjustments allocable to any portion of the property to which the § 121 exclusion does not apply are not taken into account for this purpose.[179]

Example—On July 1, 1999, Taxpayer A moved into a house that he owned and had rented to tenants since July 1, 1997. A took depreciation deductions

---

[179] TREAS. REG. § 1.121-1(d)(1).

totaling $14,000 for the period that he rented the property. After using the residence as their principal residence for two full years, A sold the property on Aug. 1, 2001. A's gain realized from the sale is $40,000. A has no other § 1231 or capital gains or losses for 2001. Only $26,000 ($40,000 gain realized—$14,000 depreciation deductions) may be excluded under § 121. Under § 121(d)(6), A must recognize $14,000 of the gain as unrecaptured § 1250 gain.[180]

G. [§ 8.56] Limitations

There are three limitations concerning the amount excluded from gross income. The first limitation sets forth the maximum dollar amount excluded. The second limitation provides for the maximum dollar amount excludible if the parties file a joint return. The third limitation limits the exclusionary rule to one sale or exchange every two years. These three limitations are discussed below.

1. [§ 8.57] Dollar limitations

A taxpayer may exclude from gross income up to $250,000 of gain from the sale or exchange of the taxpayer's principal residence.[181] A taxpayer is eligible for only one maximum exclusion per principal residence.[182] If taxpayers jointly own a principal residence but file separate returns, each taxpayer may exclude from gross income up to $250,000 of gain that is attributable to each taxpayer's interest in the property, if the requirements of § 121 have otherwise been met.[183]

2. [§ 8.58] Special rules for joint returns

a. In general

A husband and wife who make a joint return for the year of the sale or exchange may exclude up to $500,000 of gain realized if the following three tests are met:

(A) Either spouse meets the two-year ownership requirements of § 121(a) and Treas. Reg. § 1.121-1(a) and (c);

(B) Both spouses meet the two-year use requirements of § 121(a) and Treas. Reg. § 1.121-1(a) and (c); and

(C) Neither spouse excluded gain from a prior sale or exchange of property under § 121 within the last two years (as determined under § 121(b)(3) and Treas. Reg. § 1.121-2(c)).[184]

---

180 Treas. Reg. § 1.121-1(d)(2).

181 I.R.C. § 121(b)(1); Treas. Reg. § 1.121-2(a)(1).

182 Treas. Reg. § 1.121-2(a)(1).

183 Treas. Reg. § 1.121-2(a)(2).

184 I.R.C. § 121(b)(2)(A); Treas. Reg. § 1.121-2(a)(3)(i)–(iii).

> ***Example***—Assume the wife owned a house which she sold on June 30 in the third year. Assume the wife and her husband used the house as their principal residence since their marriage on Feb. 1 in year one. The wife has a gain realized on the sale of $300,000. Neither spouse has sold a principal residence within the last two years. The wife can exclude the entire gain realized from the sale of $300,000 since she owned the house, and she and her husband used it as their principal residence for two of the last five years before the sale.

It is important to note that joint filers will meet the $500,000 exclusion only if both spouses meet the use test, although only one spouse has to meet the ownership test.

Pub. Law 110-289, § 3092(a), added § 121(b)(4) effective for sales or exchanges after December 31, 2008. Before this change, the $500,000 exclusion was available only if the spouses filed a joint return for the year of sale. A surviving spouse can file a joint return for the year of death of the decedent and for the following taxable year. Thus, if the principal residence was sold in a tax year following the year of the spouse's death, the maximum exclusions the surviving spouse could claim was $250,000 since no joint return could be filed for the year in which the sale occurred. Under this law, the surviving spouse can qualify for the $500,000 exclusion if the sale occurs not more than two years after the spouse's death, provided that the rules of (A), (B), and (C) above are met immediately before the spouse's death and the surviving spouse is unmarried as of the date of the sale or exchange.[185]

b. Other joint returns

For taxpayers filing jointly, if either spouse fails to meet the above three requirements, the maximum limitation amount to be claimed by the couple will be the sum of each spouse's limitation amount determined on a separate basis as if they had not been married.[186] For this purpose, each spouse will be treated as owning the property during the period that either spouse owned the property.[187] Thus, each spouse will be able to exclude up to $250,000 from gross income on the sale of the principal residence, or the sale of the interest of one of the spouses in the principal residence. Furthermore, the amount each spouse may be able to exclude may be different because of the reduced exclusion rule discussed below:

> For example, assume the spouse sold a house that the wife had owned and lived in for eight years. They sold the house because the husband has accepted another position in another state. The husband had used the house

---

185 I.R.C. § 121(b)(4).
186 TREAS. REG. § 1.121-2(a)(3)(ii).
187 *Id.*

as their principal residence for one year prior to the sale. Neither spouse has previously used the exclusion. Their gain from the sale of the house was $500,000. Because all three tests of § 121(b)(2)(A) were not met, each spouse determines their excludible gain separately. The wife met both the use and ownership tests. Therefore, she can exclude $250,000 of gain from gross income. The husband, on the other hand, is treated as owning the house for the eight years the wife owned the house. However, he did not meet the use test. Thus, the husband cannot exclude $250,000. Rather, he can exclude 50% of the $250,000 exclusion, or $125,000. Thus, the total exclusion available to the spouses is $375,000—$250,000 to the wife and $125,000 to the husband.

c. Examples

Treasury Reg. § 1.121-2(a)(4) provides the following examples to illustrate the special rule for joint returns:

Example 1—Unmarried taxpayers A and B own a house as joint owners, each owning a 50% interest in the house. They sell the house after owning and using it as their principal residence for two full years. The gain realized from the sale is $256,000. A and B are each eligible to exclude $128,000 of gain because the amount of realized gain allocable to each of them from the sale does not exceed each taxpayer's available limitation amount of $250,000.

Example 2—The facts are the same as in Example 1, except that A and B are married taxpayers who file a joint return for the taxable year of the sale. A and B are eligible to exclude the entire amount of realized gain ($256,000) from gross income because the gain realized from the sale does not exceed the limitation amount of $500,000 available to A and B as taxpayers filing a joint return.

Example 3—During 1999, married taxpayers H and W each sell a residence that each had separately owned and used as a principal residence before their marriage. Each spouse meets the ownership and use tests for their respective residence. Neither spouse meets the use requirement for the other spouse's residence. H and W file a joint return for the year of the sales. The gain realized from the sale of H's residence is $200,000. The gain realized from the sale of W's residence is $300,000. Because the ownership and use requirements are met for each residence by each respective spouse, H and W are eligible to exclude up to $250,000 of gain from the sale of each of their residences. However, W may not use H's unused exclusion to exclude gain in excess of her exclusion amount. Therefore, H and W must recognize $50,000 of the gain realized on the sale of W's residence.

Example 4—Married taxpayers H and W sell their residence and file a joint return for the year of the sale. Section 121(c) (relating to the reduced exclusion) does not apply to the sale of their residence. W, but not H, satisfies the requirements of § 121. They are eligible to exclude up to $250,000 of the gain from the sale of the residence because that is the sum of each spouse's dollar limitation amount determined on a separate basis as if they had not been married ($0 for H, $250,000 for W).

Example 5—Married taxpayers H and W have owned and used their principal residence since 1998. On Feb. 16, 2001, H dies. On Sept. 24, 2001, W sells the residence and realizes a gain of $350,000. Pursuant to § 6013(a)(3), W and H's executor make a joint return for 2001. All $350,000 of the gain from the sale of the residence may be excluded from gross income.

Example 6—Assume the same facts as Example 5 except that W does not sell the residence until Jan. 31, 2002. Because W's filing status for the taxable year of the sale is single, the special rules for joint returns under TREAS. REG. § 1.121-2(a)(3) do not apply and W may exclude only $250,000 of the gain.

3. [§ 8.59] Application of § 121 to only one sale or exchange every two years

a. In general

Except as otherwise provided in § 121(c) and TREAS. REG. § 1.121-3(b) (relating to the reduced exclusion) discussed in **§§ 8.60–8.66**, *infra*, a taxpayer may not exclude from gross income gain from the sale or exchange of a principal residence if, during the two-year period ending on the date of the sale or exchange, the taxpayer sold or exchanged other property for which gain was excluded under § 121.[188] For purposes of the above rule, any sale or exchange before May 7, 1997 is disregarded.[189] Thus, there is a limit of one sale every two years to exclude gain from the sale or exchange of a principal residence. If a taxpayer who has never used the exclusion marries someone who has used the exclusion within the two-year period preceding the date of the marriage, the taxpayer who has never used the exclusion is allowed a maximum exclusion of $250,000 for a sale that occurs during the limitations period. After the limitation period has passed and the spouses have met the three tests of the general rule, they may exclude up to $500,000 of gain realized on their joint return. The reduced exclusion discussed *infra* is available for a taxpayer who sells more than one home during the two-year period if the tests discussed therein are met.

According to the Conference Report, the rule limiting the exclusion to one sale every two years does not prevent each spouse from excluding up to $250,000 of

---

[188] I.R.C. § 121(b)(3)(A); TREAS. REG. § 1.121-2(b)(1).

[189] I.R.C. § 121(b)(3)(B); TREAS. REG. § 1.121-2(b)(1).

gain realized from the sale or exchange of each spouse's principal residence, provided each spouse could exclude up to $250,000 of gain realized if they filed separate returns.[190]

b. Example

The following example illustrates the above rules: Taxpayer A owned a townhouse that they used as their principal residence for two full years, 1998 and 1999. A then bought a house in 2000 that they owned and used as their principal residence. A sells the townhouse in 2002 and excludes gain realized on its sale under § 121. A sells the house in the next year, 2003. TREAS. REG. § 1.121-3 (relating to the reduced exclusion) does not apply to the sale of the house. Although A meets the two-year ownership and use requirements of § 121, A is not eligible to exclude gain from the sale of the house because A excluded gain within the last two years under § 121 from the sale of the townhouse. Thus, A must use the reduced exclusion discussed below.[191]

H. Reduced Maximum Exclusion

1. [§ 8.60] Reduced maximum exclusion for taxpayers failing to meet certain requirements

A reduced exclusion is available for a taxpayer who sells or exchanges property used as the taxpayer's principal residence but who fails to satisfy the ownership and use requirements described in § 121(a) and TREAS. REG. § 1.121-1(a) or the one sale every two years limitation described in § 121(b)(3) and TREAS. REG. § 1.121-2(b).[192] This reduced exclusion applies only if the sale or exchange is necessitated by a change in place of employment, health, or, to the extent provided in forms, instructions, or other appropriate guidance including regulations and letter rulings, unforeseen circumstances.[193]

A sale or exchange is necessitated by reason of a change in place of employment, health, or unforeseen circumstances only if the primary reason for the sale or exchange is a change in place of employment, health, or unforeseen circumstances.[194] If the taxpayer meets one of the safe harbor rules discussed below pertaining to employment, health, or unforeseen circumstances, respectively, the taxpayer's primary reason for the sale or exchange is deemed to be a change in place of employment, health, or unforeseen circumstances. If the taxpayer does not meet a

---

190 H.R. Rep. No. 105-220 (1997) (Conf. Rep.).

191 TREAS. REG. § 1.121-3.

192 I.R.C. § 121(c)(2)(A); TREAS. REG. § 1.121-3(a); TREAS. REG. § 1.121-3(b).

193 I.R.C. § 121(c)(2)(B); TREAS. REG. § 1.121-3(g). Worksheet 3 of I.R.S. Pub. No. 523, SELLING YOUR HOME, figures the reduced maximum exclusion. *See* Appendix to this chapter.

194 TREAS. REG. § 1.121-3(b).

safe harbor test, factors that may be relevant in determining the taxpayer's primary reason for the sale or exchange include (but are not limited to) the extent to which:

(a) the sale or exchange and the circumstances giving rise to the sale or exchange are proximate in time;

(b) the suitability of the property as the taxpayer's principal residence materially changes;

(c) the taxpayer's financial ability to maintain the property materially changes;

(d) the taxpayer uses the property as the taxpayer's residence during the period of the taxpayer's ownership of the property;

(e) the circumstances giving rise to the sale or exchange are not reasonably foreseeable when the taxpayer begins using the property as the taxpayer's principal residence; and

(f) the circumstances giving rise to the sale or exchange occur during the period of the taxpayer's ownership and use of the property as the taxpayer's principal residence.[195]

These factors are suggestive only. No single fact or particular combination of facts is determinative of the taxpayer's entitlement to the reduced maximum exclusion.[196]

The following discusses the three grounds for claiming a reduced maximum exclusion. Each ground contains a general rule and a safe harbor test which, if met, establishes that the taxpayer's primary reason for the sale or exchange is deemed to be a change in place of employment, health, or unforeseen circumstances.

2. *[§ 8.61] Sale or exchange by reason of a change in place of employment*

a. General rule

The first ground for a reduced maximum exclusion involves a change in the place of employment. A sale or exchange is by reason of a change in the place of employment if, in the case of a "qualified individual," the primary reason for the sale or exchange is a change in the location of the individual's employment.[197]

b. Definitions

Employment includes the commencement of employment with a new employer, the continuation of employment with the same employer, or the commencement or

---

195 *Id.*

196 TD 9031, 67 Fed. Reg. 78,358, 12/24/02. Preamble.

197 TREAS. REG. § 1.121-3(c)(1).

continuation of self-employment.[198] A "qualified individual" includes the taxpayer, the taxpayer's spouse, a co-owner of the residence, or a person whose principal place of abode is in the same household as the taxpayer.[199]

c. Distance safe harbor rule

The income tax regulations adopt a safe harbor test to establish that a change in location is based upon a change in employment. The primary reason for the sale or exchange is deemed to be a change in place of employment if:

i. The change in place of employment occurs during the period of the taxpayer's ownership and use of the property as the taxpayer's principal residence;[200] and

ii. The individual's new place of employment is at least 50 miles farther from the residence sold or exchanged than was the former place of employment, or, if there was no former place of employment (because, for example, the taxpayer was unemployed), the distance between the individual's new place of employment and the residence sold or exchanged is at least 50 miles.[201] This standard is derived from § 217(c)(1) pertaining to the moving expense deduction. If a sale or exchange does not meet the distance safe harbor test, the taxpayer may still qualify for the reduced maximum exclusion by reason of a change in place of employment if the facts and circumstances indicate that a change in place of employment is the primary reason for the sale or exchange.

d. Examples

The regulations provide the following four examples to illustrate the rules regarding a sale or exchange caused by reason of a change in employment.[202]

> ***Example 1***—A is unemployed and owns a townhouse that she has owned and used as her principal residence since 2003. In 2004, A obtains a job that is 54 miles from her townhouse, and she sells the townhouse. Because the distance between A's new place of employment and the townhouse is at least 50 miles, the sale meets the distance safe harbor rule and A is entitled to claim a reduced maximum exclusion.
>
> ***Example 2***—B is an officer in the U.S. Air Force stationed in Florida. B purchases a house in Florida in 2002. In May 2003, B moves out of the house to take a three-year assignment in Germany. B sells their house in

198 Treas. Reg. § 1.121-3(c)(3).
199 Treas. Reg. § 1.121-3(f).
200 Treas. Reg. § 1.121-3(c)(2)(i).
201 Treas. Reg. § 1.121-3(c)(2)(ii).
202 Treas. Reg. § 1.121-3(c)(4).

January 2004. Because B's new place of employment in Germany is at least 50 miles farther from the residence sold than is B's former place of employment in Florida, the sale is within the distance safe harbor rule and B is entitled to claim a reduced maximum exclusion.

Example 3—C is employed by Employer R at R's Philadelphia office. C purchases a house in February 2002 that is 35 miles from R's Philadelphia office. In May 2002, C begins a temporary assignment at R's Wilmington office that is 72 miles from C's house, and moves out of the house. In June 2015, C is assigned to work in R's London office, and as a result, sells their house in August 2004. The sale of the house is not within the distance safe harbor rule by reason of the change in place of employment from Philadelphia to Wilmington because the Wilmington office is not 50 miles farther from C's house than is the Philadelphia office. Furthermore, the sale is not within the distance safe harbor rule by reason of the change in place of employment to London because C is not using the house as their principal residence when they move to London. However, C is entitled to claim a reduced maximum exclusion because, under the facts and circumstances, the primary reason for the sale is the change in C's place of employment.

Example 4—In July 2003, D buys a condominium that is five miles from their place of employment and uses it as their principal residence. In February 2004, D, who works as an emergency medicine physician, obtains a job that is located 51 miles from D's condominium. D may be called in to work unscheduled hours and, when called, must be able to arrive at work quickly. Therefore, D sells the condominium and buys a townhouse that is four miles from their new place of employment. Because D's new place of employment is only 46 miles farther from the condominium than is D's former place of employment, the sale is not within the distance safe harbor rule. However, D is entitled to claim a reduced maximum exclusion because, under the facts and circumstances, the primary reason for the sale is the change in D's place of employment.

3. [§ 8.62] Sale or exchange by reason of health

The second ground for a reduced maximum exclusion involves a sale or exchange by reason of health.

a. General rule

A sale or exchange is by reason of health if the primary reason for the sale or exchange is:

(1) to obtain, provide, or facilitate the diagnosis, cure, mitigation, or treatment of disease, illness, or injury of a qualified individual, or

(2) to obtain or provide medical or personal care for a qualified individual suffering from a disease, illness, or injury. A sale or exchange that is merely beneficial to the general health or well-being of the individual is not a sale or exchange by reason of health.[203]

b. Qualified individual

A "qualified individual" is an individual who is the taxpayer, the taxpayer's spouse, a co-owner of the residence,[204] a person whose principal place of abode is in the same household as the taxpayer, or a person bearing a relationship specified in § 152(d)(2)(A)-(G)[205] (without regard to qualification as a dependent) to a qualified individual described in this sentence, or a descendent of the taxpayer's grandparent.[206] The inclusion of the list of persons in § 152(d)(2)(A)–(G) in the definition of qualified individual for purposes of the health exception makes the definition broader than the definition of a qualified individual that applies to exclusions by reason of a change in the place of employment or unforeseen circumstances.

c. Physician's recommendation safe harbor rule

The income tax regulations adopt a safe harbor test to determine whether a sale or exchange is by reason of health. The primary reason for the sale or exchange is deemed to be by reason of health if a physician recommends a change of residence for reasons of health as set forth above.[207] A physician is defined by reference to

---

203 Treas. Reg. § 1.121-3(d)(1).

204 I.R.S. Priv. Ltr. Rul. 2006-040-13 (Oct. 18, 2005) (Co-owner, a qualified individual, became ill and was forced to move to an assisted living facility. The other co-owners sold the property. The Service held that the reason for the sale was to obtain health care treatment for the illness of a qualified individual).

205 Section 201 of The Working Families Tax Relief Act of 2004, Pub. L. No. 108-311, amended § 152 to move the relationship descriptions in § 152(a)(1)–(8) to § 152(d)(2)(A)-(G), effective for tax years beginning after 2004.

206 Treas. Reg. § 1.121-3(f). This provision still refers to § 152(a)(1)–(8) for the relationship provisions instead of § 152(d)(2)(A)-(G). The relationships described in § 152(d)(2)(A)–(G) are: (1) a child of the taxpayer (including stepchild, adopted child, or eligible foster child), or a descendant of a child, (2) a brother, sister, stepbrother, or stepsister, (3) the father or mother of the taxpayer, or an ancestor of either, (4) a stepfather or stepmother of the taxpayer, (5) a son or daughter of a brother or sister of the taxpayer, (6) a brother or sister of the father or mother of the taxpayer, and (7) a son-in-law, daughter-in-law, father-in-law, mother-in-law, brother-in-law, or sister-in-law of the taxpayer. In I.R.S. Priv. Ltr. Rul. 2006-260-24 the Service ruled that the mother of the taxpayer is a qualified individual. Thus, the taxpayer met the health exception where the taxpayer was taking care of her partially paralyzed mother and had to purchase a new residence to accommodate the needs of her mother.

207 Treas. Reg. § 1.121-3(d)(2).

§ 213(d)(4), which defines "physician" to mean the term given in § 1861(r) of the Social Security Act.[208]

d. Examples

The following five examples provided by the regulations illustrate the rules for a reduced maximum exclusion of a sale or exchange by reason of health:

> ***Example 1***—In 2003, A buys a house that they uses as their principal residence. A is injured in an accident and is unable to care for themselves. As a result, A sells their house in 2004 and moves in with their daughter so that the daughter can provide the care that A requires as a result of their injury. Because, under the facts and circumstances, the primary reason for the sale of A's house is A's health, A is entitled to claim a reduced maximum exclusion.
>
> ***Example 2***—H's father has a chronic disease. In 2003, H and W purchase a house that they use as their principal residence. In 2004, H and W sell their house in order to move into the house of H's father so that they can provide the care he requires as a result of his disease. Because, under the facts and circumstances, the primary reason for the sale of their house is the health of H's father, H and W are entitled to claim a reduced maximum exclusion.
>
> ***Example 3***—H and W purchase a house in 2003 that they use as their principal residence. Their son suffers from a chronic illness that requires regular medical care. Later that year their doctor recommends that their son begin a new treatment that is available at a medical facility 100 miles away from their residence. In 2004, H and W sell their house to be closer to the medical facility. Because, under the facts and circumstances, the primary reason for the sale is to facilitate the treatment of their son's chronic illness, H and W are entitled to claim a reduced maximum exclusion.
>
> ***Example 4***—B, who has chronic asthma, purchases a house in Minnesota in 2003 that they uses as their principal residence. B's doctor tells B that moving to a warm, dry climate would mitigate B's asthma symptoms. In 2004, B sells the house and moves to Arizona to relieve his asthma symptoms. The sale is within the physician recommendation safe harbor rule. Accordingly, B is entitled to claim a reduced maximum exclusion under § 121(c)(2).
>
> ***Example 5***—In 2003, H and W purchase a house in Michigan that they use as their principal residence. H's doctor tells H that he should get more exercise, but H is not suffering from any disease that can be treated or mitigated by exercise. In 2004, H and W sell their house and move to Florida so

---

208 42 U.S.C. § 1395x(r).

that H can increase his general level of exercise by playing golf year-round. Because the sale of the house is merely beneficial to H's general health, the sale of the house is not by reason of H's health. H and W are not entitled to claim a reduced maximum exclusion.[209]

4. *[§ 8.63] Sale or exchange by reason of unforeseen circumstances*

The third and final ground for a reduced maximum exclusion involves a sale or exchange by reason of unforeseen circumstances.

a. General rule

A sale or exchange is by reason of unforeseen circumstances if the primary reason for the sale or exchange is the occurrence of an event that the taxpayer does not anticipate before purchasing and occupying the residence.[210] The Service has ruled that the following events created an unforeseen circumstance under the statute: marriage involving blended living situations with children,[211] birth of a child,[212] adoption,[213] fear of safety,[214] and noise pollution.[215] A sale or exchange by reason of

---

[209] TREAS. REG. § 1.121-3(d)(3). Examples 1–5.

[210] TREAS. REG. § 1.121-3(e)(1).

[211] I.R.S. Priv. Ltr. Rul. 2008-26-024 (Mar. 19, 2008) (Taxpayer needed larger house to accommodate him, his new wife, and their children from prior marriage); and I.R.S. Priv. Ltr. Rul. 2007-25-018 (Mar. 15, 2007) (Two taxpayers are married and each has children from a prior relationship, and their existing residence is not suitable to accommodate the taxpayer's children and the children of the taxpayer's spouse).

[212] I.R.S. Priv. Ltr. Rul. 2006-52-041 (Sept. 30, 2005) (Taxpayer A and Taxpayer B ended their relationship and it was then determined that Taxpayer B was pregnant. The taxpayers were forced to sell their residence because it was not large enough to accommodate two adults and a child); *see also* I.R.S. Priv. Ltr. Rul. 2016-28-002 (Jul. 8, 2016) (Birth of second child for married couple constituted unforeseen circumstances that materially changed the suitability of the couple's principal residence (a 2 bed 2 bath condominium)).

[213] I.R.S. Priv. Ltr. Rul. 2006-13-009 (Dec. 19, 2005) (Taxpayer, under state law, was required to accommodate adopted daughter with separate living quarters from taxpayer's three sons, and old residence was not suitable to accommodate all the children).

[214] *See* I.R.S. Priv. Ltr. Rul. 2008-20-016 (Feb. 7, 2008) (where the taxpayer decided to move outside of a school district after the taxpayer's daughter suffered from persistent fear because she was subjected to unruly behavior, verbal abuse, and sexual assault while riding the school bus.) I.R.S. Priv. Ltr. Rul. 2006-30-004 (Apr. 28, 2006) (where a taxpayer moved out of the home due to fear after being held at gun point and forced into an automobile after the assailant made repeated threats upon the taxpayer's life); I.R.S. Priv. Ltr. Rul. 2006-15-011 (Dec. 8, 2005) (where taxpayer, a narcotic investigator, made a high-profile drug arrest. The taxpayer moved from the house when the police learned that associates of the arrested individual discovered where the taxpayer lived and planned to kill the taxpayer); and I.R.S. Priv. Ltr. Rul. 2006-04-012 (Oct. 4, 2005) (K-9 police officer who maintained a kennel for his dog was forced to move because the homeowner's association where the taxpayer lived did not allow kennels).

[215] *See* I.R.S. Priv. Ltr. Rul. 2007-02-032 (Sept. 29, 2006) (where a taxpayer was forced to sell a residence because of an extreme amount of noise pollution from airport traffic).

unforeseen circumstances under the specific event safe harbor rule or the designation of additional events as unforeseen circumstances, as described below, does not qualify for the reduced maximum exclusion if the primary reason for the sale or exchange is a preference for a different residence or an improvement in financial circumstances.[216]

b. Specific event safe harbor rule

The regulations[217] adopt a safe harbor test to establish that the primary reason for the sale or exchange is unforeseen circumstances. The primary reason for the sale or exchange is deemed to be unforeseen circumstances if any of the events specified below occur during the period of the taxpayer's ownership and use of the residence as the taxpayer's principal residence:

i. the involuntary conversion of the residence;

ii. natural or man-made disasters or acts of war or terrorism resulting in a casualty to the residence (without regard to deductibility under § 165(h));

iii. in the case of a qualified individual:

  (1) death;

  (2) the cessation of employment as a result of which the individual is eligible for unemployment compensation (as defined in § 85(b));

  (3) a change in employment or self-employment status that results in the taxpayer's inability to pay housing costs and reasonable basic living expenses for the taxpayer's household (including amounts for food, clothing, medical expenses, taxes, transportation, court-ordered payments, and expenses reasonably necessary to the production of income, but not for the maintenance of an affluent or luxurious standard of living);

  (4) divorce or legal separation under a decree of divorce or separate maintenance; or

  (5) multiple births resulting from the same pregnancy.

The Internal Revenue Service may designate other events or situations as unforeseen circumstances in published guidance of general applicability or may issue rulings directed to a specific taxpayer identifying other events or situations as unforeseen circumstances with regard to those taxpayers.[218] A taxpayer who does not qualify for a safe harbor protection may demonstrate that the primary reason for the sale or exchange is unforeseen circumstances under a fact and circumstances test.

---

216 TREAS. REG. § 1.121-3(e)(1).

217 TREAS. REG. § 1.121-3(e)(2).

218 TREAS. REG. § 1.121-3(e)(3).

c. Qualified individual

A qualified individual for purposes of the unforeseen circumstance ground includes the taxpayer, the taxpayer's spouse, a co-owner of the residence, or a person whose principal place of abode is in the same household as the taxpayer.[219] This is the same definition as the one used for sales or exchanges by reason of a change in place of employment.

d. Examples

The income tax regulations provide the following 10 examples to illustrate the foregoing rules:

> ***Example 1***—In 2003, A buys a house in California. After A begins to use the house as their principal residence, an earthquake causes damage to A's house. A sells the house in 2004. The sale is within the specific event safe harbor rule and A is entitled to claim a reduced maximum exclusion.
>
> ***Example 2***—H works as a teacher and W works as a pilot. In 2003, H and W buy a house that they use as their principal residence. Later that year W is furloughed from her job for six months. H and W are unable to pay their mortgage during the period W is furloughed. H and W sell their house in 2004. The sale is within the specific event safe harbor rule, and H and W are entitled to claim a reduced maximum exclusion.
>
> ***Example 3***—In 2003, H and W buy a two-bedroom condominium that they use as their principal residence. In 2004, W gives birth to twins and H and W sell their condominium and buy a four-bedroom house. The sale is within the specific event safe harbor rule, and H and W are entitled to claim a reduced maximum exclusion.
>
> ***Example 4***—B buys a condominium in 2003 and uses it as their principal residence. B's monthly condominium fee is $X. Three months after B moves into the condominium, the condominium association decides to replace the building's roof and heating system. Six months later, B's monthly condominium fee doubles. B sells the condominium in 2004 because B is unable to pay the new condominium fee along with the monthly mortgage payment. The specific event safe harbor rule does not apply. However, under the facts and circumstances ground, the primary reason for the sale is unforeseen circumstances, and B is entitled to claim a reduced maximum exclusion.
>
> ***Example 5***—In 2003, C buys a house that they uses as their principal residence. The property is located on a heavily trafficked road. C sells the property in 2004 because the traffic is more disturbing than they expected. C

---

219 TREAS. REG. § 1.121-3(f).

is not entitled to claim a reduced maximum exclusion because the specific event safe harbor rule does not apply and, under the facts and circumstances ground, the traffic is not an unforeseen circumstance.

Example 6—In 2003, D and her fiancé E buy a house and live in it as their principal residence. In 2004, D and E cancel their wedding plans and E moves out of the house. Because D cannot afford to make the monthly mortgage payments alone, D and E sell the house in 2004. The specific event safe harbor rules do not apply. However, under the facts and circumstances ground, the primary reason for the sale is unforeseen circumstances, and D and E are each entitled to claim a reduced maximum exclusion under § 121(c)(2).

Example 7—In 2003, F buys a small condominium that she uses as her principal residence. In 2005, F receives a promotion and a large increase in her salary. F sells the condominium in 2004 and purchases a house because she can now afford the house. The safe harbors do not apply. Under the facts and circumstances ground, the primary reason for the sale of the house, F's salary increase, is an improvement in F's financial circumstances. Under the rules set forth in § **8.63(a)**, *supra*, an improvement in financial circumstances, even if the result of unforeseen circumstances, does not qualify for the reduced maximum exclusion by reason of unforeseen circumstances.

Example 8—In April 2003, G buys a house that they uses as their principal residence. G sells the house in October 2004 because the house has greatly appreciated in value, mortgage rates have substantially decreased, and G can afford a bigger house. The safe harbors do not apply. Under the facts and circumstances, the primary reasons for the sale of the house, the changes in G's house value and in the mortgage rates, are an improvement in G's financial circumstances. Under the rules set forth in § **8.63(a)**, *supra*, an improvement in financial circumstances, even if the result of unforeseen circumstances, does not qualify for the reduced maximum exclusion by reason of unforeseen circumstances.

Example 9—H works as a police officer for City X. In 2003, H buys a condominium that they uses as their principal residence. In 2004, H is assigned to City X's K-9 unit and is required to care for the police service dog at their home. Because H's condominium association does not permit H to have a dog in his condominium, in 2004 H sells the condominium and buys a house. The safe harbors do not apply. However, under the facts and circumstances ground, the primary reason for the sale, H's assignment to the K-9 unit, is an unforeseen circumstance because H could not reasonably have anticipated the assignment to the K-9 unit at the time they purchased and occupied the condominium. Consequently, the sale of the condominium is by reason of unforeseen circumstances and H is entitled to claim a reduced maximum exclusion under § 121(c)(2).

Example 10—In 2003, J buys a small house that they uses as their principal residence. After J wins the lottery, they sell the small house in 2004 and buys a bigger, more expensive house. The safe harbors do not apply. Under the facts and circumstances, the primary reason for the sale of the house, winning the lottery, is an improvement in J's financial circumstances. Under the rules set forth in § **8.63(a)**, *supra*, an improvement in financial circumstances, even if the result of unforeseen circumstances, does not qualify for the reduced maximum exclusion under § 121(c)(2).[220]

5. [§ 8.64] Election to apply regulations retroactively

Taxpayers who would otherwise qualify under this section to exclude gain from a sale or exchange before December 24, 2002, but on or after May 7, 1997, may elect to apply all of the provisions of this section for any years for which the period of limitations under § 6511 has not expired. The taxpayer makes the election by filing a return for the taxable year of the sale or exchange that does not include the gain from the sale or exchange of the taxpayer's principal residence in the taxpayer's gross income. Taxpayers who have filed a return for the taxable year of the sale or exchange may elect to apply all the provisions of this section for any years for which the period of limitations under § 6511 has not expired by filing an amended return.[221]

---

[220] TREAS. REG. § 1.121-3(e)(3). Examples 1–10. See also I.R.S. Priv. Ltr. Rul. 2004-03-049 (Sept. 23, 2003) where the Service ruled that a sale of house two which the taxpayers owned and used as their principal residence for less than two of the preceding five years qualified for exclusion of gain up to the reduced maximum exclusion amount under § 121(c). The taxpayers sold house one and purchased house two while a family member was at a rehabilitation facility. When released, however, the court ordered the family member to live at house two under house arrest. The neighbors so vehemently protested the family member's presence in the neighborhood that they made living in house two intolerable. They made threats against the family member, insisted that he not spend time outside the yard and interfered with his attempts to find employment. The probation officer believed it to be in the best interest of the family to sell the house and move to a new neighborhood. The Service concluded that the primary reason for the sale of house two was an unforeseen circumstance within the meaning of Treas. Reg. § 1.121-3(e).

Other examples of unforeseen circumstances are illustrated in I.R.S. Priv. Ltr. Rul. 2006-01-009 (Sept. 30, 2005)—criminal activity in neighborhood; I.R.S. Priv. Ltr. Rul. 2006-30-004 (Apr. 28, 2006)—abduction at gunpoint in neighborhood; I.R.S. Priv. Ltr. Rul. 2008-20-016 (Feb. 7, 2008)—sexual assault and abuse on school bus.

[221] TEMP. TREAS. REG. § 1.121-3T(h). TEMP. TREAS. REG. § 1.121-3T was removed by Treasury Decision 9152, effective Aug. 13, 2004.

6. [§ 8.65] Computation of reduced maximum exclusion

The reduced exclusion is computed by multiplying the maximum dollar limitation of $250,000 ($500,000 for certain joint filers) by a fraction. The numerator of the fraction is the shortest of the following three periods of time:

(a) the period of time that the taxpayer owned the property as the taxpayer's principal residence during the five-year period ending on the date of the sale or exchange;

(b) the period of time that the taxpayer used the property as the taxpayer's principal residence during the five-year period ending on the date of the sale or exchange; or

(c) the period of time between the date of a prior sale or exchange of property for which the taxpayer excluded gain under § 121 and the date of the current sale or exchange.

The numerator of the fraction may be expressed in days or months. The denominator of the fraction is 730 days or 24 months (depending on the measure of time used in the numerator).[222] The purpose for this rule is to permit an otherwise qualifying taxpayer who fails to meet the two-year use and ownership requirement to exclude an amount equal to the fraction of $250,000 ($500,000 for joint return filers) limitation, not the fraction of the gain realized which is equal to the fraction of the two years during which the use and ownership requirements are met.[223]

7. [§ 8.66] Examples

The regulations provided the following two examples, which illustrate the reduced exclusion rules:

> ***Example 1***—Taxpayer A purchases a house that they use as their principal residence. Twelve months after the purchase, A sells the house due to a change in place of their employment. A has not excluded gain under § 121 on a prior sale or exchange of property within the last two years. A is eligible to exclude up to $125,000 of the gain from the sale of her house (12/24 × $250,000).[224]
>
> ***Example 2***—
>
> *(A)* Taxpayer H owned a house that they have used as their principal residence since 1996. On Jan. 15, 1999, H and W marry and W

---

[222] I.R.C. § 121(c)(1)(A) & (B); Treas. Reg. § 1.121-3(g).

[223] H.R. Rep. No. 105-356 (1997).

[224] *See* Treas. Reg. § 1.121-3(g)(2). Example 1.

begins to use H's house as their principal residence. On Jan. 15, 2000, H sells the house due to a change in H's and W's places of employment. Neither H nor W has excluded gain under § 121 on a prior sale or exchange of property within the last two years.

(B) Because H and W have not both used the house as their principal residence for at least two years during the five-year period preceding its sale, the maximum dollar limitation amount that may be claimed by H and W will not be $500,000, but the sum of each spouse's limitation amount determined on a separate basis as if they had not been married.

(C) H is eligible to exclude up to $250,000 of gain because he meets the requirements of § 121. W is not eligible to exclude the maximum dollar limitation amount. Instead, W is eligible to claim a reduced exclusion. Because the sale of the house is due to a change in place of employment, W is eligible to exclude up to $125,000 of the gain (365/730 × $250,000). Therefore, H and W are eligible to exclude up to $375,000 of gain ($250,000 + $125,000) from the sale of the house.[225]

I. [§ 8.67] Special Rules

There are 11 special rules for certain circumstances that determine whether the use and/or occupancy tests have been met.

1. [§ 8.68] Joint returns

As noted above at § **8.58**, if a husband and wife file a joint return for the taxable year of the sale or exchange of the property, the general exclusionary rule and the reduced exclusionary rule, as applicable, applies if either spouse meets the use and ownership tests of § 121(a) with respect to the property.[226]

2. [§ 8.69] Property of deceased spouse

a. In general

For purposes of satisfying the ownership and use requirements of § 121, an unmarried taxpayer whose spouse is deceased is treated as owning and using property as the taxpayer's principal residence during any period that the taxpayer's deceased spouse owned and used the property as a principal residence before the deceased spouse's death if:

---

225 TREAS. REG. § 1.121-3(g)(2). Example 2.

226 I.R.C. § 121(d)(1); TREAS. REG. § 1.121-2(a)(3).

(A) the taxpayer's spouse is deceased on the date of the sale or exchange of the property; and

(B) the taxpayer has not remarried at the time of the sale or exchange of the property.[227]

b. Example

This rule is illustrated by the following example:

> Taxpayer H has owned and used a house as their principal residence since 1987. H and W marry on July 1, 1999, and from that date they use H's house as their principal residence. H dies on Aug. 15, 2000, and W inherits the property and continues to use the property as her principal residence. W sells the property on Sept. 1, 2000, at which time she has not remarried. Although W has owned and used the house for less than two years, W is considered to have satisfied the ownership and use requirements of § 121 because W's period of ownership and use includes the period that H owned and used the property before his death.[228]

3. [§ 8.70] Property owned by spouse or former spouse

If a taxpayer obtains property from a spouse or former spouse in a transaction described in § 1041(a), the period that the taxpayer owns the property includes the period that the spouse or former spouse owned the property.[229]

A taxpayer is treated as using property as the taxpayer's principal residence for any period that the taxpayer has an ownership interest in the property and the taxpayer's spouse or former spouse is granted use of the property under a divorce or separation instrument[230] provided that the spouse or former spouse uses the property as a principal residence.[231]

For example, if the spouses are divorced and one spouse retains ownership of the property while the other spouse retains use of the property, the spouse that owns the property can exclude the gain realized from the sale of the property when it is subsequently sold (subject to the dollar limitations) if the one spouse meets the ownership test and the other spouse meets the use test.

---

227 I.R.C. § 121(d)(2); Treas. Reg. § 1.121-4(a).

228 Treas. Reg. § 1.121-4(a)(2).

229 I.R.C. § 121(d)(3)(A); Treas. Reg. § 1.121-4(b)(1).

230 As defined in § 71(b)(2) (generally applicable to instruments executed before 2019) or § 121(d)(3)(C) (generally applicable to instruments executed after 2018). See TCJA §11051(c).

231 I.R.C. § 121(d)(3)(B); Treas. Reg. § 1.121-4(b)(2).

4. *[§ 8.71] Tenant-stockholder in cooperative housing corporation*

A taxpayer who holds stock as a tenant-stockholder in a cooperative housing corporation (as defined in § 216(b)(1) and (2)) may be eligible to exclude gain under § 121 on the sale or exchange of the stock. In determining whether the taxpayer meets the requirements of § 121, the ownership requirements are applied to the holding of the stock and the use requirements are applied to the house or apartment that the taxpayer was entitled to occupy by reason of the taxpayer's stock ownership.[232]

If a taxpayer sells stock in a cooperative housing corporation, the ownership and use tests are met if, during the five-year period ending on the date of the sale, the taxpayer owned the stock for at least two years, and lived in the house or apartment that the stock entitled the taxpayer to occupy as the taxpayer's principal residence for at least two years.

5. *[§ 8.72] Involuntary conversions*

a. In general

For purposes of § 121, the destruction, theft, seizure, requisition, or condemnation of property is treated as a sale of the property.[233]

b. Application of § 1033

In applying § 1033 (relating to involuntary conversions), the amount realized from the sale or exchange of property used as the taxpayer's principal residence is treated as being the amount determined without regard to § 121, reduced by the amount of gain excluded from the taxpayer's gross income under § 121.[234]

A taxpayer whose principal residence is destroyed may apply § 121 to exclude gain that would otherwise result, and may defer any remaining gain under § 1033.[235] The IRS published guidance regarding the treatment of certain tax issues relating to payments from the Federal Emergency Management Agency to persons in New Mexico who suffered losses due to the Cerro Grande Fire.[236] The taxpayers received payments pursuant to an Act of Congress specially enacted to compensate persons whose properties were destroyed by fire.[237] According to the Service, a taxpayer whose residence is destroyed in a fire and who meets all the tests of § 121 may do the following regarding the gain resulting from converting the house into insurance

---

232 I.R.C. § 121(d)(4); TREAS. REG. § 1.121-4(c).

233 I.R.C. § 121(d)(5)(A); TREAS. REG. § 1.121-4(d)(1).

234 I.R.C. § 121(d)(5)(B); TREAS. REG. § 1.121-4(d)(2).

235 I.R.S. Chief Counsel Advice Memorandum 2001-11-056 (Feb. 15, 2001).

236 *Id.*

237 *Id.*

proceeds or recovery under a federal statute: (a) exclude gain to the extent permitted by §121; (b) elect to defer any remaining gain by acquiring replacement property in a manner satisfying § 1033; and (c) if the gain is deferred under § 1033, treat the period of use and ownership of the newly acquired residence as including the period of ownership and use of the destroyed residence.[238]

c. Property acquired after involuntary conversion

If the basis of the property acquired as a result of an involuntary conversion is determined (in whole or in part) under § 1033(b) (relating to the basis of property acquired through involuntary conversion), then for purposes of satisfying the requirements of § 121, the taxpayer will be treated as owning and using the acquired property as the taxpayer's principal residence during any period of time that the taxpayer owned and used the converted property as the taxpayer's principal residence.[239]

d. Example

The involuntary conversion rules are illustrated by the following example: On Feb. 18, 1999, fire destroys Taxpayer A's house that had an adjusted basis of $80,000. A had owned and used this property as her principal residence for 20 years prior to its destruction. A's insurance company paid A $400,000 for the house. Thus, A realized a gain of $320,000 ($400,000—$80,000). On Aug. 27, 1999, A purchases a new house at a cost of $100,000. Because the destruction of the house is treated as a sale for purposes of § 121, A will exclude $250,000 of the realized gain from A's gross income. For purposes of § 1033, the amount realized is then treated as being $150,000 ($400,000—$250,000) and the gain realized is $70,000 ($150,000 amount realized—$80,000 basis). A elects under § 1033 to recognize only $50,000 of the gain ($150,000 amount realized less $100,000 cost of new house). The remaining $20,000 of gain is deferred and A's basis in the new house is $80,000 ($100,000 cost less $20,000 gain not recognized). A will be treated as owning and using the new house as A's principal residence during the 20-year period that A owned and used the destroyed house.[240]

6. *[§ 8.73] Recognition of gain attributable to depreciation*

The general exclusionary rule does not apply to the amount of gain from the sale of any property which does not exceed the portion of depreciation adjustments[241]

---

238 *Id.*

239 I.R.C. § 121(d)(5)(C); TREAS. REG. § 1.121-4(d)(3).

240 TREAS. REG. § 1.121-4(d)(4).

241 I.R.C. § 1250(b)(3).

attributable to periods after May 6, 1997, in respect of such property.[242] Thus, a taxpayer recognizes gain to the extent of any depreciation allowable with respect to the rental or business use of the residence for periods after May 6, 1997. Note that the maximum tax rate for depreciation recapture income is 25%.

7. [§ 8.74] Determination of use during periods of out-of-residence care

If a taxpayer has become physically or mentally incapable of self-care and the taxpayer sells or exchanges property that the taxpayer owned and used as the taxpayer's principal residence for a period aggregating at least one year during the five-year period preceding the sale or exchange, the taxpayer is treated as using the property as the taxpayer's principal residence for any period of time during the five-year period in which the taxpayer owns the property and resides in any facility (including a nursing home) licensed by a State or political subdivision to care for an individual in the taxpayer's condition.[243]

Assume a taxpayer purchases a residence on Jan. 1, 2000, which they occupy for the entire year. Assume that on Jan. 15, 2001, the taxpayer has moved to a State licensed nursing home. The taxpayer continues to reside in the nursing home. On July 1, 2003, the residence is sold. Since the taxpayer owned and used the residence as a principal residence for at least one year during the five-year period preceding the date of sale of the residence, the taxpayer is considered to have used the residence for the period of time during which they were in the nursing home. Thus, the taxpayer can exclude any gain from the sale of his residence, since they are deemed to meet the two year use and ownership rule.

8. [§ 8.75] Sales or exchanges of partial interests

a. Sales or exchanges of remainder interests

i. In general

A taxpayer may elect to have the § 121 exclusion apply to gain from the sale or exchange of a remainder interest in the taxpayer's principal residence.[244]

ii. Limitations

There are two limitations to the general rule permitting § 121 exclusionary treatment for sales or exchanges of remainder interests.

---

242 I.R.C. § 121(d)(6); TREAS. REG. § 1.121-1(d); I.R.S. Rev. Rul. 2014-2 Situation 5 ($1,400 payment received by taxpayer under National Mortgage Settlement due to foreclosure on taxpayer's principal residence not excludable under § 121 where the payment does not result in gain in excess of depreciation deductions).

243 I.R.C. § 121(d)(7); TREAS. REG. § 1.121-1(c)(2)(ii).

244 I.R.C. § 121(d)(8)(A); TREAS. REG. § 1.121-4(e)(2).

(A) Sale or exchange of any other interest

The first limitation provides that if a taxpayer elects to exclude gain from the sale or exchange of a remainder interest in the taxpayer's principal residence, the § 121 exclusion will not apply to a sale or exchange of any other interest in the residence that is sold or exchanged separately.[245]

(B) Sales to related parties

Second, the general rule above permitting the exclusionary rule to apply to the sale or exchange of a remainder interest will not apply to a sale or exchange by any person who bears a relationship to the taxpayer which is described in §§ 267(b) or 707(b).[246]

(C) Election and revocation

The taxpayer makes the election to have the exclusionary rule apply to the sale of a remainder interest by filing a return for the taxable year of the sale or exchange that does not include the gain from the sale or exchange of the remainder interest in the taxpayer's gross income.[247] The election may also be revoked. A taxpayer may make or revoke the election at any time before the expiration of a three-year period beginning on the last date for the filing of the return for the taxable year in which the sale or exchange occurred, determined without regard to extensions.[248]

b. Sales or exchanges of partial interests other than remainder interests

i. General rule

Except for sales or exchanges of remainder interests, a taxpayer may apply the § 121 exclusion to gain from the sale or exchange of an interest in the taxpayer's principal residence that is less than the taxpayer's entire interest if the interest sold or exchanged includes an interest in the dwelling unit.[249]

ii. Limitations

There are two limitations to the general rule.

(A) Maximum limitation amount

The first limitation provides that for purposes of § 121(b)(1) and (2) (relating to the maximum limitation amount of the § 121 exclusion), sales or exchanges of partial interests in the same principal residence are treated as one sale or exchange.

---

245 I.R.C. § 121(d)(8)(A); Treas. Reg. § 1.121-4(e)(2)(ii)(A).

246 I.R.C. § 121(d)(8)(B); Treas. Reg. § 1.121-4(e)(2)(ii)(B).

247 Treas. Reg. § 1.121-4(e)(2)(iii).

248 *Id.*

249 Treas. Reg. § 1.121-4(e)(1)(i).

Therefore, only one maximum limitation amount of $250,000 ($500,000 for certain joint returns) applies to the combined sales or exchanges of the partial interests. In applying the maximum limitation amount to sales or exchanges that occur in different taxable years, a taxpayer may exclude gain from the first sale or exchange of a partial interest up to the taxpayer's full maximum limitation amount and may exclude gain from the sale or exchange of any other partial interest in the same principal residence to the extent of any remaining maximum limitation amount, and each spouse is treated as excluding one-half of the gain from a sale or exchange to which § 121(b)(2)(A) and Treas. Reg. § 1.121-2(a)(3)(i) (relating to the limitation for certain joint returns) apply.[250]

(B) Sale or exchange of more than one principal residence in two-year period

For purposes of applying § 121(b)(3) (restricting the application of § 121 to only one sale or exchange every two years), each sale or exchange of a partial interest is disregarded with respect to other sales or exchanges of partial interests in the same principal residence, but is taken into account as of the date of the sale or exchange in applying § 121(b)(3) to that sale or exchange and the sale or exchange of any other principal residence.[251]

Example—The provisions of sale of a partial interest are illustrated by the following example:

In 1991, Taxpayer A purchased a house that A used as their principal residence. In 2004, A's friend B moves into A's house and A sells B a 50% interest in the house realizing a gain of $136,000. A may exclude the $136,000 of gain. In 2005, A sells their remaining 50% interest in the home to B realizing a gain of $138,000. A may exclude $114,000 ($250,000—$136,000 gain previously excluded) of the $138,000 gain from the sale of the remaining interest.[252]

9. [§ 8.76] Property acquired from a decedent

For estates of a decedent who died during the 2010 calendar year, the executor of decedent's estate was allowed to make an election that would allow certain taxpayers who received the principal residence of the decedent to include the period of decedent's ownership and use of the principal residence for purposes of determining the taxpayer's eligibility for the gain exclusion under § 121 for a sale of such property.

---

250 TREAS. REG. § 1.121-4(e)(1)(ii)(A).
251 TREAS. REG. § 1.121-4(e)(1)(ii)(B).
252 TREAS. REG. § 1.121-4(e)(3).

The exclusionary rule applies to property sold by:

(a) the estate of a decedent;

(b) any individual who acquired such property from the decedent within the meaning of § 1022; and

(c) a trust which, immediately before the death of the decedent, was a qualified revocable trust (as defined in § 645(b)(1)) established by the decedent.[253]

The exclusionary rule applies to those three exceptions because ownership and use by the decedent is attributed to, and taken into account by, those three sellers.[254]

This provision was initially enacted as § 121(d)(9) by Section 542(c), Subtitle E, Title V of the Economic Growth and Tax Relief Reconciliation Act of 2001, Pub. L. 107-16. The provision was retroactively repealed in Section 301(a) of the Tax Relief, Unemployment Insurance Reauthorization, and Job Creation Act of 2010, Pub. L. 111-312. But in Section 301(c) of the 2010 act, Congress allowed the election described above, which effectively may allow a taxpayer to take into account a decedent's period of ownership and use of the decedent's principal residence for purposes of § 121.[255]

10. [§ 8.77] Like-kind exchange

a. Interplay of Sections 121 and 1031

The Jobs Creation Act of 2004[256] added § 121(d)(10), which provides that if a taxpayer acquires property in a like-kind exchange to which § 1031 applies, the $250,000/$500,000 exclusion does not apply to the sale or exchange of that property if the sale or exchange occurs during the five-year period beginning with the date of acquisition of the property.[257] The effect of this provision is to prevent a taxpayer from excluding from gross income previously deferred gain realized, thus permitting the taxpayer to shelter all or some of the gain from income taxation. In addition, because the replacement property may have a low carry-over basis, the taxpayer may have some taxable gain upon the sale or exchange of the replacement property. This provision attempts to balance the concerns associated with the provisions to reduce the tax shelter concern without unduly limiting the exclusion on sales or exchanges of principal residences.

---

253 § 121(d)(11) before repealed by Sec. 301(a) of the Tax Relief, Unemployment Insurance Reauthorization, and Job Creation Act of 2010, Pub. L. 111-312; Chief Counsel Advice Memorandum 2014-29-022 (May 27, 2014).

254 *Id.*

255 Chief Counsel Advice Memorandum 2014-29-022 (May 27, 2014).

256 American Jobs Creation Act of 2004, Pub. L. No. 108-357, § 840, 118 Stat. 1418 (2004).

257 I.R.C. § 121(d)(10).

The Service issued Rev. Proc. 2005-14, 2005-1 C.B. 528, which provides guidance to a single exchange of property that satisfies the requirements for both the exclusion of gain from the exchange of a principal residence under § 121 and the nonrecognition of gain on the exchange of like-kind properties under § 1031. This Revenue Procedure is likely to apply to two situations: first, where the property is used as a residence and then converted to rental property, and second where part of the property is used as rental property and part of the property is used as the taxpayer's principal residence. The Revenue Procedure clarifies four main points: First, § 121 must be applied to gain realized before applying § 1031. Second, the § 121 exclusion does not apply to gain attributable to depreciation deductions for periods after May 6, 1997, claimed with respect to the business or investment portion of a residence, although § 1031 may apply to such gain. Third, boot received in exchange for the relinquished property is only taken into account to the extent that it exceeds the gain excluded under § 121 with respect to the relinquished property. Finally, in determining basis for the replacement property, gain excluded under § 121 is treated as recognized. Thus, under § 131(d), the basis of the replacement property is increased by any gain attributable to the relinquished property that is excluded under § 121. The Revenue Procedure provides six helpful examples that illustrate the application and interplay between §§ 121 and 1031. The Revenue Procedure is effective for sales or exchanges occurring on or after Jan. 27, 2005, although taxpayers may apply the Revenue Procedure in taxable years in which the period of limitations on refund or credit under § 6511 has not expired.

b. Conversion of Principal Residence

Section 1031 does not apply to a principal residence since such property is not held for productive use in a trade or business or for investment. The issue for consideration is whether a taxpayer can acquire property in a like-kind exchange, rent it and then convert it to a principal residence, or convert a principal residence to rental property and then exchange it for property of a like-kind under § 1031.[258]

The Service issued Rev. Proc. 2008-16,[259] which provides a safe harbor under which the IRS will not challenge whether a dwelling unit qualifies as property held for productive use in a trade or business or for investment for purposes of § 1031.

(1) *Relinquished property.* A dwelling unit that a taxpayer intends to be relinquished property in a § 1031 exchange qualifies as property held for productive use in a trade or business or for investment if:

---

258 This later transaction is less likely to occur than the former because a selling taxpayer can avail himself of the benefits of § 121. But if conversion to rental property is necessary or desirable before a sale, then § 1031 may be needed.

259 2008-10 I.R.B. 547.

(a) the dwelling unit is owned by the taxpayer for at least 24 months immediately before the exchange (the "qualifying use period"); and

(b) within the qualifying use period, in each of the two 12-month periods immediately preceding the exchange,

(i) the taxpayer rents the dwelling unit to another person or persons at a fair rental for 14 days or more, and

(ii) the period of the taxpayer's personal use of the dwelling unit does not exceed the greater of 14 days or 10% of the number of days during the 12-month period that the dwelling unit is rented at a fair rental.

For this purpose, the first 12-month period immediately preceding the exchange ends on the day before the exchange takes place (and begins 12 months prior to that day) and the second 12-month period ends on the day before the first 12-month period begins (and begins 12 months prior to that day).

(2) *Replacement property.* A dwelling unit that a taxpayer intends to be replacement property in a § 1031 exchange qualifies as property held for productive use in a trade or business or for investment if:

(a) the dwelling unit is owned by the taxpayer for at least 24 months immediately after the exchange (the "qualifying use period"); and

(b) within the qualifying use period, in each of the two 12-month periods immediately after the exchange,

(i) the taxpayer rents the dwelling unit to another person or persons at a fair rental for 14 days or more, and

(ii) the period of the taxpayer's personal use of the dwelling unit does not exceed the greater of 14 days or 10% of the number of days during the 12-month period that the dwelling unit is rented at a fair rental.

(3) The Revenue Procedure is effective for exchanges of dwelling units occurring on or after Mar. 10, 2008.

11. [§ 8.78] No exclusion for expatriates

The § 121 exclusion does not apply to any sale or exchange by an individual if the treatment provided by § 877(a)(1) (relating to the treatment of expatriates) applies to the individual.[260] For U.S. citizens who relinquish their citizenship or U.S. lawful permanent residents who abandon their "green cards", and who are treated as selling all their property for its fair market value under § 877A, it is unclear

[260] I.R.C. § 121(e); TREAS. REG. § 1.121-4(f).

whether these persons may be entitled to claim the § 121 exclusion to offset gain from the deemed sale of a principal residence.[261]

J. [§ 8.79] Election to Have Section Not Apply

A taxpayer may elect to have the § 121 exclusion not apply to a sale or exchange of property.[262] The taxpayer makes the election by filing a return for the taxable year of the sale or exchange that includes the gain from the sale or exchange of the taxpayer's principal residence in the taxpayer's gross income.[263] A taxpayer may elect out of § 121 exclusionary treatment (or revoke an election to have § 121 not apply) if the taxpayer expects to sell two residences relatively close in time to each other, and the gain from the sale of the first residence will be substantially less than the gain from the sale of the second residence. Under such circumstances, the taxpayer would elect out of § 121 treatment on the sale of the first residence and thus pay tax on the gain realized from the sale of the first property in order to exclude the gain from the sale of the second property. The election or revocation may be made at any time before the expiration of a three-year period beginning on the last date for the filing of the return for the taxable year in which the sale or exchange occurred, determined without regard to extension.[264]

K. [§ 8.80] Residences Acquired in Rollovers under § 1034

If a taxpayer acquired property (§ 121 property) in a transaction that qualified under prior § 1034 for the nonrecognition of gain realized on the sale or exchange of another property (§ 1034 property) and the taxpayer later sells or exchanges the § 121 property, in determining the period of the taxpayer's ownership and use of the sold or exchanged § 121 property, the taxpayer may include the periods that the taxpayer owned and used the § 1034 property as the taxpayer's principal residence (and each prior residence taken into account under § 1223(7) in determining the holding period of the § 1034 property).[265]

L. [§ 8.81] Reserved.

M. [§ 8.82] Election to Apply Regulations Retroactively

Taxpayers who would otherwise qualify under Treas. Reg. §§ 1.121-1–1.121-4 to exclude gain from a sale or exchange of a principal residence before Dec. 24, 2002, but on or after May 7, 1997, may elect to apply Treas. Reg. §§ 1.121-1–1.121-4 for any

---

261 Michael J.A. Karlin and Stanley C. Ruchelman, "Home Thoughts From Abroad: When Foreigners Purchase U.S. Homes," Tax Notes Today International (Sep. 1, 2020), n. 27.

262 I.R.C. § 121(f); Treas. Reg. § 1.121-4(g).

263 *Id.*

264 *Id.*

265 I.R.C. § 121(g); Treas. Reg. § 1.121-4(h).

years for which the period of limitation under § 6511 has not expired. The taxpayer makes the election to have the regulations applied retroactively by filing a return for the taxable year of the sale or exchange that does not include the gain from the sale or exchange of the taxpayer's principal residence in the taxpayer's gross income. Taxpayers who have filed a return for the taxable year of the sale or exchange may elect to apply the provisions of these regulations for any years for which the period of limitation under § 6511 has not expired by filing an amended return.[266]

N. [§ 8.83] Audit Protection

The Internal Revenue Service will not challenge a taxpayer's position that a sale or exchange of a principal residence occurring before Dec. 24, 2002, but on or after May 7, 1997, qualifies for the § 121 exclusion if the taxpayer has made a reasonable, good faith effort to comply with the requirements of § 121. Compliance with the provisions of the regulations project under § 121 (Reg. 105235-99 (2000-2 C.B. 447)) generally will be considered a reasonable, good faith effort to comply with the requirements of § 121.[267]

O. [§ 8.84] Reporting

A taxpayer does not have to report a sale of their principal residence unless the taxpayer has:

(a) gain realized from the sale and cannot exclude all of the gain realized, or

(b) received a Form 1099-S, Proceeds From Real Estate Transactions, or

(c) gain realized and elects not to exclude the gain realized.[268]

Any taxable gain is generally reported on Form 8949, Sales and Other Dispositions of Capital Assets, and Schedule D to Form 1040.[269] To figure gain or loss of the sale of a principal residence, subtract the adjusted basis of the property from the amount realized from the sale of the property (selling price less selling expenses).[270] Worksheets to determine the adjusted basis of the residence sold, and the gain or loss which is excludable or taxable are also included in the Publication.

P. [§ 8.85] Exceptions to Time Limitations

A taxpayer may, at taxpayer's election, be exempt from the time running of the five-year period described in §§ 121(a), (c)(1)(B), and (d)(7) during any period that the

---

266 Treas. Reg. § 1.121-4(j).

267 Treas. Reg. § 1.121-4(k).

268 Internal Revenue Service, IRS Pub. No. 523, Selling Your Home, p. 15 (2022).

269 *Id.* at p. 16.

270 See I.R.S. Pub. No. 523, Selling Your Home, pp. 8-15, in the Appendix to this chapter to determine these components.

taxpayer or the taxpayer's spouse is serving on qualified official extended duty as a member of either the uniformed services, the Foreign Service of the United States, or as an employee of the intelligence community. The five-year period, however, may not be extended more than 10 years.[271] Additionally, at the election of an individual with respect to a property, the running of the five-year period may be suspended during any period that such individual or such individual's spouse is serving outside the United States on qualified official extended duty as an employee of the Peace Corps, or an enrolled volunteer or volunteer leader under §§ 5 or 6 of the Peace Corps Act.[272]

Part 2: The Law for Sales or Exchanges Prior to May 7, 1997

Section A—Deferring Gain Realized

A. [§ 8.86] Introduction

By proper planning, any taxpayer may be able to defer temporarily, and taxpayers age 55 years or over may be able to exclude permanently, from Federal income taxation, all or part of the gain realized from the sale of their personal residences. Considering today's inflated sales price of a residence, and hence inflated taxable gain; the frequency with which taxpayers move, and hence sell residences; the trend to view the residence as an investment; and the return a taxpayer can receive from investing taxes saved, deferral or elimination of Federal income taxes imposed on the gain realized on the sale of a personal residence is of substantial economic benefit to the client.

Sections **8.87–8.125** of this chapter discuss the deferral mechanism available to taxpayers who "roll over" a personal residence. **Sections 8.126–8.145** of this chapter discuss the exclusion from gross income of all or part of the gain realized from the sale of a personal residence by taxpayers 55 years or older. **Section 8.145** of this chapter offers a comparison, in chart form, of I.R.C. § 1034 and § 121.

B. [§ 8.87] Deferring Tax on All or Part of Gain Realized on the Sale of a Principal Residence—General Income Tax Consequences

When a taxpayer sells their personal residence for a profit, they "realize" a gain which may or may not be "recognized." "Gain realized" from the sale of a personal residence is the excess of the amount realized (the sum of any money, plus the fair market value of property other than money, received from the sale) over the adjusted basis of the property (original cost with adjustments for items such as capital improvements).[273] I.R.C. § 1001(c) provides that all gain realized from the sale or exchange of a personal residence must be "recognized"; i.e., a tax must be paid on such gain, "except as

---

[271] I.R.C. §121(d)(9)(B).

[272] 22 U.S.C. §§ 2504, 2505; I.R.C. §121(d)(12).

[273] I.R.C. § 1001(a) and (b). See **§ 8.118** of this chapter for a discussion of the items that affect the basis of the property.

otherwise provided."[274] For example, if Robber Baron receives $100,000 in cash from the sale of his personal residence, and the adjusted basis of the residence is $40,000, the entire gain realized of $60,000 is recognized, unless excepted.

I.R.C. § 1034 is an exception to the recognition provision of I.R.C. § 1001(c). As discussed in **§ 8.88** of this chapter, I.R.C. § 1034 defers the time for paying tax on all or part of the gain realized from the sale of a personal residence, and thus provides the taxpayer with one of the best "tax shelters" available.

C. [§ 8.88] Tax Deferral under I.R.C. § 1034—Introduction

I.R.C. § 1034 provides that where a taxpayer[275] sells[276] their old principal residence[277] and, within certain time limits,[278] replaces the old principal residence through the purchase, construction, or reconstruction of a new residence,[279] which the taxpayer uses as their principal residence, all or part of the gain realized from the sale of the old principal residence may be deferred from Federal income taxation. The effect of this mandatory provision,[280] which a taxpayer may use any number of times, is not to exclude permanently, but rather to defer temporarily, the recognition of all or part of any gain realized from the sale of an old principal residence. This deferral is accomplished by taxing such gain only to the extent that the taxpayer's adjusted sales price[281] of the old principal residence exceeds their cost of purchasing the new residence,[282] and by reducing the basis of the new principal residence by an amount equal to gain not recognized on the sale of the old principal residence.[283] Theoretically, this assures realization and recognition of the deferred gain upon a subsequent sale of the new principal residence for at least its purchase price, unless another deferral cycle is instituted.

I.R.C. § 1034 applies only to gain realized. Losses are recognized or not recognized under other provisions of the Code.[284]

To illustrate, if Robber Baron, in the above example, purchases a new principal residence for $100,000, and otherwise meets all the tests of I.R.C. § 1034, the gain

---

274 I.R.C. § 1001(c).
275 See text at **§§ 8.89–8.94** of this chapter for a discussion of "taxpayer."
276 See text at **§ 8.95** of this chapter for a discussion of "sale."
277 See text at **§§ 8.96–8.102** of this chapter for a discussion of "principal residence."
278 See text at **§§ 8.103–8.107** of this chapter for a discussion of time periods in which to reinvest sales proceeds.
279 See text at **§§ 8.103–8.107** of this chapter.
280 TREAS. REG. § 1.1034-1(a).
281 See text at **§ 8.117** of this chapter for a definition of "adjusted sales price."
282 See text at **§ 8.108** of this chapter for the "cost of purchasing a new residence."
283 TREAS. REG. § 1.1034-1(a).
284 TREAS. REG. § 1.1034-1(a); see text at **§ 8.103** of this chapter.

realized of $60,000 is not recognized, and the basis of his new principal residence is $40,000. If he later sells the new residence for at least $100,000, the deferred gain of $60,000 will be recognized, unless a new deferral cycle is initiated. The example also points out a short cut to determine approximately the amount of gain realized which may be deferred from taxation. If the cost of the new principal residence (as defined in **§ 8.109** of this chapter) equals or exceeds the adjusted sales price of the old principal residence, gain realized may go unrecognized.[285] On the other hand, if the cost of the new principal residence is less than the adjusted sales price, all or part of the gain realized may be recognized.[286] Thus, if an amount equal to or greater than the adjusted sales price of an old principal residence is invested in a new principal residence, and all the tests of I.R.C. § 1034 are met, none of the gain realized (if any) is recognized.

To qualify for such favorable tax deferral treatment the taxpayer must meet four tests—the qualifying taxpayer test, the sale test, the principal residence test, and the time limits for purchasing a replacement residence. These tests are discussed in §§ **8.89–8.107** of this chapter.

D. Qualifying Taxpayer

1. [§ 8.89] Defined

First, the seller of an old principal residence must be a qualifying taxpayer, i.e., individuals, and certain trusts holding title to the property sold.[287]

2. [§ 8.90] Multiple owners

More than one qualifying taxpayer for each principal residence is permitted. For example, Charles Robb and Harry Cheate, two unrelated individuals, each owns one-half of an old principal residence, with a total adjusted basis of $100,000, which they sell for $200,000, thus realizing a gain of $100,000, or $50,000 each. If Robb and Cheate each reinvests an amount at least equal to his portion of the sales proceeds ($100,000) in a new principal residence, either together or separately, each individual's gain realized of $50,000, computed separately for each taxpayer, is deferred currently from taxation.[288]

---

285 TREAS. REG. § 1.1034-1(a).

286 TREAS. REG. § 1.1034-1(a).

287 I.R.C. § 1034(a); Rev. Rul. 66-159, 1966-1 C.B. 162; *Compare* Rev. Rul. 54-583, 1954-2 C.B. 158. See also the text and accompanying notes at **§ 8.130** of this chapter for a discussion of "principal residence" under I.R.C. § 121. Those cases and rulings discussed under I.R.C. § 121 also apply to I.R.C. § 1034.

288 *See* Rev. Rul. 74-250, 1974-1 C.B. 202 (A & B, husband and wife, owned their principal residence jointly. They separated, sold their residence, and each purchased a new principal residence. The IRS held that I.R.C. § 1034 applied separately to A & B and that if each acquired

3. [§ 8.91] Identity of title

The qualifying taxpayer who sells an old principal residence and purchases a new principal residence must be identical. Thus, title to the new principal residence must be placed in the name of the taxpayer who sells the old principal residence. If title to the old principal residence is in the name of a taxpayer, placing title to the new principal residence in the name of the taxpayer's child disqualifies the transaction from tax deferral treatment.[289]

4. [§ 8.92] Husband and wife

An exception to the identity of title requirement applies in certain husband-wife cases.[290] If title to the old principal residence is in the husband or wife alone, and title to the new principal residence is placed in the husband alone, the wife alone, or the husband and wife as tenants by the entireties, joint tenants with rights of survivorship, or tenants in common;[291] or if title to the old principal residence is in the husband and wife as tenants by the entireties, joint tenants with rights of survivorship, or tenants in common, and title to the new principal residence is placed in the wife or husband, individually or jointly, the husband and wife are treated as a "single" taxpayer, rather than separate taxpayers, and nonrecognition treatment is available for each, provided they file a proper "consent" with the Internal Revenue Service.[292] The consent may be filed only if the old and new residence are each used by the taxpayer and their same spouse as their principal residence.[293]

---

a new residence with a cost greater than their respective interests in the sales price of the old principal residence, the gain realized by each would not be recognized pursuant to I.R.C. § 1034). *See also* Rev. Rul. 75-238, 1975-1 C.B. 257 (A and B owned separate residences. They married, sold their separate residences and purchased jointly a new residence which they occupied together. The IRS held that I.R.C. § 1034 applied to the gain realized by A & B on the sales of their former separate residences). *See also Murphy v. Comm'r*, 103 T.C. 111, 94 T.N.T. 151-12 (1994) (Taxpayer could use benefits of § 1034 where he timely purchased a replacement residence, even if his spouse did not. However, since parties filed a joint return, he was jointly and severally liable with her for tax attributable to her share of the gain).

289 *Marcello v. Comm'r*, 380 F.2d 499, 502 (5th Cir. 1967); *May v. Comm'r*, T.C.M. (CCH) 1974-54, *dismissed*, 553 F.2d 1207 (9th Cir. 1977); Rev. Rul. 55-37, 1955-1 C.B. 347. *See also Mitchell v. United States*, an unreported decision (44 AFTR 2d 79-5735) (C.A. Cal. 1979) (Neither heir of estate nor estate could claim nonrecognition treatment under I.R.C. § 1034 for gain realized on sale of decedent's residence even though heir, who was 50% beneficiary of decedent's estate, lived in such residence with decedent prior to and shortly after death of decedent, and purchased her own principal residence after death of decedent).

290 I.R.C. § 1034(g).

291 Titling the new residence in joint names may create federal gift and estate tax consequences, as discussed in **§§ 8.2–8.8** of this chapter.

292 I.R.C. § 1034(g). TREAS. REG. § 1.1034-1(f)(1).

293 I.R.C. § 1034(g). TREAS. REG. § 1.1034-1(f)(1).

The consent must be filed with the District Director of Internal Revenue with whom the taxpayer files the return for the taxable year or years in which gain from the sale of the old principal residence is realized.[294] The consent may be made on Internal Revenue Service Form 2119 attached to Form 1040. It is unclear whether the husband and wife must file joint or separate returns to come within this exception to the rule of identity of title. The cost of the consent is a shifting of a part of the adjusted basis of the new principal residence from one spouse to the other: the consent is a consent by the taxpayer and the taxpayer's spouse to have the basis of the interest of either of them in the new residence reduced from what it would have been, but for the filing of the consent, by an amount by which the gain of either of them on the sale of their respective interests in the old residence is not recognized solely by reason of the filing of such consent.[295] The reduction in basis is applicable to the basis of the new residence, whether that of the husband, the wife, or both.[296] If the basis is divided between the husband and wife, the reduction in basis is divided between them in the same proportion as the basis is divided (determined without regard to such reduction).[297]

The rules respecting the consent are illustrated by the following example: an old principal residence, with an adjusted basis of $50,000, is titled in the name of the husband individually, but is used by the husband and wife. The husband sells the residence for $100,000 and purchases and occupies (along with his wife) a new principal residence within two years from the date of sale of the old residence. The husband and wife contribute $50,000 each from their separate funds for the purchase of their new residence.[298] Title to the new residence is taken in the name of the husband and wife as tenants in common. If the husband and wife file the required consent, the husband's gain realized of $50,000 is not recognized, despite non-identity of title, and the reduced adjusted basis of the new residence (its cost less the unrecognized gain realized) is allocated equally between the husband and wife, so that the adjusted basis of the husband and wife in the new residence is $25,000 each.[299]

---

294 TREAS. REG. § 1.1034-1(f)(2).

295 *Id.*

296 *Id.*

297 *Id.*

298 So there is no gift tax to consider.

299 TREAS. REG. § 1.1034-1(f)(3) Examples: ***Example (1)***—A taxpayer, in 1954, sells for an adjusted sales price of $10,000 the principal residence of himself and his wife, which he owns individually and which has an adjusted basis to him of $5,000 (no fixing-up expenses are involved, so that $10,000 is the "amount realized" as well as the "adjusted sales price"). Within a year after such sale, he and his wife contribute $5,000 each from their separate funds for the purchase of their new principal residence which they hold as tenants in common, each owning an undivided one-half interest therein. If the taxpayer and his wife file the required consent, the gain of $5,000 upon the sale of the old residence will not be recognized to the taxpayer,

5. [§ 8.93] Trusts

If a trust owns property that is occupied by the beneficiary of the trust as the beneficiary's principal residence, gain from the sale of the residence by the trust would not be available for rollover treatment under I.R.C. § 1034 because the residence is used by the beneficiary and not the trust.[300] If, however, the trust is considered a grantor trust such that an individual is considered the owner of the trust, gain from the sale of the residence by the trust would be available for rollover treatment under I.R.C. § 1034.[301]

6. [§ 8.94] Nonresident aliens

A nonresident alien may be entitled to the benefits of § 1034 depending upon whether the replacement residence is located inside or outside of the United States. A nonresident alien is not entitled to nonrecognition under § 1034 on the sale of a principal residence when the new principal residence acquired is not a U.S. real property interest.[302]

A nonresident alien who sells their principal residence that is a U.S. real property interest and who, within a period beginning two years before the date of such sale and ending on the date (with extensions) of filing their income tax return for the taxable year of the sale of the principal residence, purchases and uses another U.S. real property interest as a principal residence, does not, to the extent provided by § 1034, recognize gain on the sale of the principal residence. If the individual has not purchased another U.S. real property interest as a principal residence at the time of the filing of the return for the year of sale, the individual must file a timely income tax return for the year of sale without claiming the benefit of § 1034. If

---

and the adjusted basis of the taxpayer's interest in the new residence will be $2,500 and the adjusted basis of his wife's interest in such property will be $2,500. ***Example (2)***—A taxpayer and his wife, in 1954, sell for an adjusted sales price of $10,000 their principal residence, which they own as joint tenants and which has an adjusted basis of $2,500 to each of them ($5,000 together) (no fixing-up expenses are involved, so that $10,000 is the "amount realized" as well as the "adjusted sales price"). Within a year after such sale, the wife spends $10,000 of her own funds in the purchase of a principal residence for herself and the taxpayer and takes title in her name only. If the taxpayer and his wife file the required consent, the adjusted basis to the wife of the new residence will be $5,000, and the gain of the taxpayer of $2,500 upon the sale of the old residence will not be recognized. The wife will have her gain of $2,500 on the sale of the old residence not recognized.

300 Rev. Rul. 54-583, 1954-2 C.B. 158 (I.R.C. § 1034 does not apply to sale of residence owned by trust and occupied by beneficiary).

301 Rev. Rul. 85-45, 1985-1 C.B. 183 (discussed at n. **425**, *infra*); Rev. Rul. 66-159, 1966-1 C.B. 162. (I.R.C. § 1034 applies where trust owns old and new principal residence and grantor and his family used old and new residence as principal residence); I.R.S. Priv. Ltr. Rul. 85-49-046 (Sept. 11, 1985). *See also*, text at nn. **443–445**. *See* I.R.S. Priv. Ltr. Rul. 93-09-023 (Dec. 3, 1992).

302 Temp. Treas. Reg. § 1.897-6T(a)(5)(i).

the individual subsequently purchases another U.S. property interest as a principal residence that otherwise qualifies under § 1034 after the due date of the income tax return for the year of the sale of the principal residence and before a date that is two years after the sale of the principal residence, the individual may then apply § 1034 by filing an amended income tax return for the year of the sale of the principal residence and claiming a refund. A nonresident alien may not claim the benefits of § 1034 unless such individual files a complete and timely income tax return with the appropriate forms for the year of the sale of the principal residence.[303]

> ***Example***—Joe Alien is a citizen of France who is stationed in Washington, D.C., as a full-time employee of an international organization. Mr. Alien sells his principal residence in Washington and in the same taxable year purchases another principal residence in Washington. The cost of the new residence exceeds the adjusted sales price of the old residence.

Under § 7701(b), Mr. Alien is a nonresident alien for U.S. tax purposes and is subject to taxation under § 897(a). Mr. Alien is considered to have exchanged a U.S. real property interest (the old principal residence) for another U.S. real property interest which is subject to U.S. taxation upon its disposition. The nonrecognition and basis provisions of § 1034(a) apply to Mr. Alien.[304]

> ***Example***—If in the above example Mr. Alien had instead purchased a new principal residence in France, there would be an exchange of a U.S. real property interest for property that is not a U.S. real property interest. Mr. Alien would recognize gain under § 897(a) on the disposition of the old principal residence.[305]

E. [§ 8.95] Sale

The second test requires that the qualifying taxpayer "sell" their old principal residence. A "sale" occurs when legal title to the property passes from the seller to the buyer; i.e., when the risk of loss on the property passes from the seller to the buyer.[306] A sale includes the exchange or trade-in of an old residence for other

---

[303] TEMP. TREAS. REG. § 1.897-6T(a)(5)(ii).

[304] TEMP. TREAS. REG. § 1.897-6T(a)(7). Example (2).

[305] TEMP. TREAS. REG. § 1.897-6T(a)(7). Example (3).

[306] *See Comm'r v. Baertschi*, 412 F.2d 494, 498 (6th Cir. 1969), *rev'g Baertschi v. Comm'r*, 49 T.C. 289 (1967). *See also Chavez v. Comm'r*, T.C.M. (CCH) 1983-199 (date on which title transfers, and not date on which taxpayer enters into conditional contract for purchase of new residence, controls because the date title transfers is the date the taxpayer assumes the benefits and burdens of ownership to determine when the purchase is complete); Rev. Rul. 82-1, 1982-1 C.B. 26 (sale occurs when title passes or at the time of possession and the burdens and benefits of ownership are transferred to the buyer).

property, a sale for cash to a purchaser, or the condemnation of an old residence.[307] A sale also includes a sale to a taxpayer's wholly owned corporation, since I.R.C. § 1034 does not prohibit sales between related parties.[308] Not only does the seller obtain rollover treatment, but also the buyer obtains a step-up in basis equal to its cost.[309]

On the other hand, a sale does not include a transfer by gift or inheritance.[310]

F. Principal Residence

1. [§ 8.96] Defined

The third test requires the old residence being sold or exchanged to have been used by the taxpayer as their principal residence. To qualify as a "principal residence," the residence must be "used" as such. In other words, the taxpayer must physically occupy the residence and live in it.[311] The physical occupancy test will not be met where the taxpayer's children, and not the taxpayer, occupy the residence.[312] The Internal Revenue Service will not issue an advance ruling or determination letter on whether a residence qualifies as the taxpayer's principal residence.[313]

2. [§ 8.97] More than one residence

If a taxpayer owns more than one residence, I.R.C. § 1034 defers from Federal income taxation only gain realized from the sale of the "principal residence."[314] For example, Rick Shaw owns a condominium unit in Ocean City, Md., which he uses for vacations and he also owns a condominium unit in Baltimore City where he normally resides. If he sells both units at the same time, I.R.C. § 1034 applies only to the gain realized from the sale of the Baltimore City residence, inasmuch as that residence is deemed his principal residence.

---

307 I.R.C. § 1034(c)(1); TREAS. REG. § 1.1034-1(b)(8).

308 I.R.S. Priv. Ltr. Rul. 86-46-036 (Aug. 19, 1986) and I.R.S. Priv. Ltr. Rul. 83-50-084 (Sept. 13, 1983).

309 I.R.C. § 1014.

310 TREAS. REG. § 1.1034-1(c)(4)(i).

311 See *Stolk v. Comm'r*, 40 T.C. 345 (1963), *aff'd*, 326 F.2d 760 (2d Cir. 1964) where the Tax Court said "the phrase 'used by the taxpayer as his principal residence' means habitual use of the old residence as the principal residence. The antithesis is nonuse of property as the principal residence." *Stolk*, at 355. *See also Friedman v. Comm'r*, T.C.M. (CCH) 1982-178, *McDowell v. Comm'r*, T.C.M. (CCH) 1980-160, and *Evans v. Comm'r*, T.C.M. (CCH) 1962-61.

312 *Lokan v. Comm'r*, T.C.M. (CCH) 1979-380; Rev. Rul. 69-434, 1969-2 C.B. 163.

313 Rev. Proc. 88-3, § 3.016, 1988-1 C.B. 579.

314 Rev. Rul. 77-298, 1977-2 C.B. 308; Rev. Rul. 66-114, 1966-1 C.B. 181 (where taxpayer purchases two residences with sales proceeds from principal residence, the residence which qualifies as principal residence at end of reinvestment period will be available for I.R.C. § 1034 treatment).

3. [§ 8.98] Pre-sale rental

A taxpayer is not required to occupy physically the old principal residence up to the date of its sale.[315] Rather, the taxpayer may rent the old residence to a third party prior to its sale and still have the gain realized from the sale qualify for tax deferral treatment, so long as the taxpayer does not presently intend for the old residence to lose its character as the "old principal residence."[316] According to the court, the rentals were "necessitated by the exigencies of the real estate market, or were ancillary to sales efforts and [arose] from [their] use of the [old residence] as their principal residence. Their primary motive in leasing the property was to sell it at the earliest possible moment rather than to hold it for the production of income." Therefore, the court concluded, the rentals were temporary rentals and the taxpayers were entitled to defer recognition of gain realized on the sale of their old residence pursuant to I.R.C. § 1034.[317] For example, moving from the premises with a present intent to later re-occupy the old residence as a principal residence will not cause the old principal residence to lose its character as such, even if reoccupancy never occurs. On the other hand, moving from the premises with no present intention to reoccupy will cause the old principal residence to lose its character as such.

---

315 *Aagaard v. Comm'r*, 56 T.C. 191 (1971).

316 TREAS. REG. § 1.1034-1(c)(3)(i). This appears to be the one instance in which a taxpayer may have two principal residences. For cases where the taxpayer was deemed to have "abandoned" the property as his principal residence see *Houlette v. Comm'r*, 48 T.C. 350 (1967); *Stolk v. Comm'r*, 40 T.C. 345 (1963), *aff'd*, 326 F.2d 760, 761 (2d Cir. 1964). Rev. Rul. 78-146, 1978-1 C.B. 260 (taxpayer's principal residence is one taxpayer intended to return to and reoccupy after two-year assignment in another city, even though residence was leased for those two years and another residence purchased in other city was sold); *Rogers v. Comm'r*, T.C.M. (CCH) 1982-718 discussed in n. **121**, *supra. But see* Rev. Rul. 59-72, 1959-1 C.B. 203 (holding that where the facts and circumstances indicate that property sold by a taxpayer was used by the taxpayer as the taxpayer's principal residence, the taxpayer will be entitled to relief under I.R.C. § 1034, notwithstanding that the taxpayer temporarily rented out the residence prior to its sale). *See also* I.R.S. Priv. Ltr. Rul. 81-32-017 (where the taxpayer qualified for nonrecognition treatment despite pre-sale rental for four years prior to the sale where the taxpayer intended to sell the property as soon as market conditions allowed, the rental was done to improve the chances of selling the house, and the house was not held for the production of income); See also *Bolaris v. Comm'r*, 81 T.C. 840 (1983), *aff'd in part, rev'd in part on other grounds*, 776 F.2d 1428 (9th Cir. 1985) where the court, relying upon *Clapham v. Comm'r*, 63 T.C. 505 (1975) held that the rental of the old residence, first for financial circumstances, and second when it appeared certain that the lessee would soon purchase the house, did not disqualify the transaction from I.R.C. § 1034 treatment.

317 For an in-depth analysis of this area, see Lipton, *Handling The Treatment Of Renting A Former Residence While Awaiting Its Sale,* 58 J. TAX'N 170 (March 1983).

There is no fixed period of time during which the taxpayer may rent their old residence to a third party and still have it characterized as their principal residence.[318] It is recommended, however, that the pre-sale rental period not exceed two years prior to the sale date, though exceptional circumstances may permit rental for a longer period without the property losing its character as the taxpayer's principal residence.[319] Caution is advised respecting pre-sale rentals, inasmuch as those cases wherein the technique was approved involved unusual fact patterns.

Where pre-sale rental occurs and the taxpayer still seeks protection under I.R.C. § 1034, the taxpayer must establish that the dominant motive in leasing the premises was anything other than business or investment purposes of producing income. Factors which tend to indicate a sales motive are leaving the house vacant, not constantly increasing the sales price to obtain substantial profit, financial circumstances which compel leasing the property (such as exigencies of the real estate market), and efforts to sell occurring only toward the latter part of each lease period.

4. *[§ 8.99] Types of residences*

Most types of dwelling houses qualify as a principal residence. For example, houseboats, trailers, shares of stock by a tenant-stockholder in a cooperative housing corporation,[320] and condominium apartments qualify as a principal residence.[321]

---

318 *Compare Clapham v. Comm'r*, 63 T.C. 505 (1975) (Three-year rental not fatal), *with Stolk v. Comm'r*, 40 T.C. 345 (1963) (Two-year rental deemed fatal); *see* James Edward Maule, *Rental Of Residence Before Sale: Retaining 1034 Treatment And Rental Deductions*: 55 J. TAX'N 8 (July 1981). Thus, as the court stated in *Rogers v. Comm'r*, T.C.M. (CCH) 1982-718, the demarcation line between *Clapham v. Comm'r*, 63 T.C. 505 (1975) and *Houlette v. Comm'r*, 48 T.C. 350 (1967), exists where there is a manifest intention not to return to the property, where there is a prolonged period of rental coupled with sporadic attempts to sell at increasing prices, and forced financial conditions, such as exigencies of the real estate market, are lacking. *See Andrews v. Comm'r*, T.C.M. (CCH) 1981-247 (Pre-sale rental acceptable where taxpayer had no intent to abandon the property and the property was rented to assure its care and maintenance and not rental income).

319 *See Trisko v. Comm'r*, 29 T.C. 515 (1957); Rev. Rul. 78-146, 1978-1 C.B. 260 discussed in n. **119**.

320 Exchange of unit in cooperative for shares of stock in corporation not taxable under §§ 216(e) and 1034(j). *See* I.R.S. Priv. Ltr. Rul. 94-28-006 (Apr. 12, 1994).

321 Treas. Reg. § 1.1034-1(c)(3); Rev. Rul. 64-31, 1964-1 C.B. 300. The exchange of stock in a cooperative apartment corporation for legal title to the apartment occupied by the taxpayer as the taxpayer's principal residence for 15 years, when the cooperative apartment is converted to a condominium, qualifies for nonrecognition treatment under I.R.C. § 1034 if all the other tests of I.R.C. § 1034 are met. Rev. Rul. 85-132, 1985-2 C.B. 182 (Exchange of stock in cooperative housing corporation for title to condominium and undivided interest in common elements results in nonrecognition of gain). I.R.S. Priv. Ltr. Rul. 82-10-054 (Dec. 10, 1981) (Exchange of stock in cooperative apartment for title to apartment on conversion to condominium qualifies for nonrecognition treatment).

The Internal Revenue Service has also held that a yacht may qualify as a principal residence if it has cooking, sleeping, and sanitation facilities.[322] Moreover, either the old or the new principal residence, or both, may be located in a foreign country.[323] On the other hand, property used by the taxpayer as the taxpayer's principal residence does not include personal property, such as furniture, which is not a fixture under local law.[324] Gain realized from the sale of unimproved residential real estate may not be deferred from Federal income taxation.[325] Moreover, the relocation of a residence from one lot to another does not qualify the gain realized from the sale of the lot on which the residence was originally located for tax deferral treatment.[326] On the other hand, gain from the sale of a dwelling place only, or gain from the separate sale of a dwelling place and the underlying land, may be deferred from Federal income taxation.[327]

---

322 I.R.S. Priv. Ltr. Rul. 83-37-050 (June 14, 1983). A rental apartment converted to condominium ownership may also qualify as a principal residence. Rev. Rul. 80-172, 1980-2 C.B. 56.

323 *See* Rev. Rul. 71-495, 1971-2 C.B. 311 and Rev. Rul. 54-611, 1954-2 C.B. 159.

324 Treas. Reg. § 1.1034-1(c)(3)(i).

325 *O'Barr v. Comm'r*, 44 T.C. 501 (1965); Rev. Rul. 56-420, 1956-2 C.B. 519 (discussed in n. **309**); *see also Hughes v. Comm'r*, 54 T.C. 1049 (1970), *aff'd per curiam*, 450 F.2d 980 (4th Cir. 1971). *Hale v. Comm'r*, T.C.M. (CCH) 1982-527 (Sale of land on which house trailer was located, but not sale of house trailer, does not come within I.R.C. § 1034 because sale of land without the structure does not constitute the sale of a "residence" within the meaning of I.R.C. § 1034). But see *Poague v. United States*, 66 A.F.T.R.2d (RIA) 5825 (E.D. Va. 1990), *aff'd*, 947 F.2d 942 (1991), for a situation in which vacant land was deemed to be a principal residence and the sale of such land qualified for roll-over treatment under § 1034.

326 Rev. Rul. 54-156, 1954-1 C.B. 112. *See also* I.R.S. Priv. Ltr. Rul. 80-50-079 (Sept. 19, 1980) (Can exclude up to $125,000 of gain realized from sale of vacant land where tests of I.R.C. § 121, discussed in § **8.127** of this chapter, are met). *See* Rev. Rul. 83-50, 1983-1 C.B. 41 (Gain realized from the sale of land on which the taxpayer's principal residence is located and moving the house to another lot is not excludable from gross income and may not be deferred from taxation). Rev. Rul. 83-50 revokes Rev. Rul. 54-156 where the Service held that where a taxpayer sold land adjacent to his principal residence and moved the house and place of residence to a newly purchased lot, the non-recognition provisions were applicable and that the gain realized from the sale was recognized only to the extent that the selling price of the land exceeded the cost of the new lot and the expenses associated with moving the house.

327 *Bogley v. Comm'r*, 263 F.2d 746, 747 (4th Cir. 1959), *rev'g*, 30 T.C. 452 (1958). I.R.C. § 1034 applies to sale of 10 acres of land where taxpayer had previously sold residence and three of 13 acres surrounding residence. Ten acres had not lost status as principal residence. Rev. Rul. 76-541, 1976-2 C.B. 246 (I.R.C. § 1034 applies to gain realized from sale of house and land and sale of contiguous parcel later in same year. Both parcels were used as taxpayer's principal residence) distinguishing Rev. Rul. 56-420, 1956-2 C.B. 519 (Gain recognized where portion of lot sold was only that on which taxpayer had garden, orchard and checking). *Lokan v. Comm'r*, T.C.M. (CCH) 1979-380 (one-and-one-half acres of land occupied by trailer and used by taxpayer qualified as new principal residence under I.R.C. § 1034. Remaining six acres used for farming did not qualify as new principal residence).

5. [§ 8.100] Partial residence

Where property is used, at the time of its sale, partly as a principal residence and partly for business or other purposes, an allocation of basis and amount realized must be made between the two portions of the property, inasmuch as only the gain realized from the part of the property used as a principal residence may be deferred from Federal income taxation under I.R.C. § 1034,[328] for post-1975 use and sale. For example, if, at the time of sale, one-half the property is used as a principal residence and the other half is used as a rental apartment or as a law office, the gain attributable to the portion of the property used as an apartment or as a law office does not qualify for I.R.C. § 1034 tax deferral treatment.[329] The gain on such portion may, however, qualify for favorable capital gains treatment.[330] To qualify the portion of the property used as a residence for nonrecognition treatment, only the portion of the adjusted sales price allocable to the residential portion of the property has to be reinvested in a new principal residence. In effect, the sale of such principal residence should be viewed as the sale of two properties.[331]

---

[328] Treas. Reg. § 1.1034-1(c)(3)(ii). This regulation does not provide any method to determine what portion of gain realized is attributable to non-residential use of the old residence. In *Wigfall v. Commissioner*, T.C.M. (CCH) 1982-171, the IRS used yearly depreciation multiplied by the useful life used by the taxpayers in claiming depreciation deduction on their Federal income tax returns (in this case, 25 years) to determine the percentage of the basis and selling price attributable to the nonresidential portion of the residence. Taxpayer used the actual number of years (six) that the house was used as a home office to determine the percentage of the basis and the selling price attributable to the nonresidential portion of the residence. The court held for Taxpayer on the ground that the IRS did not rebut Taxpayer's formula. This case appears to be limited to situations where home office use and sale of the residence both occurred before 1976. *See* however, Partial Residence: Application of I.R.C. § 1034 to Gain Upon Sale. The IRS further held nonrecognition treatment does not apply to defer gain on that portion of the taxpayer's residence used as an office in the home even though no deduction was allowed on the taxpayer's Federal income tax return for use of a portion of his residence as an office in the home because of I.R.C. § 280A (which prescribed the tests which must be met to be entitled to an office in the home deduction).

[329] *See* I.R.S. Priv. Ltr. Rul. 79-35-003 (May 14, 1979). For further discussion see n. **310** of this chapter.

[330] This is important for tax years ending before Jan. 1, 1987, since the Tax Reform Act of 1986 repealed the favorable capital gains rates effective for tax years beginning after Dec. 31, 1986, by repealing the capital gains deduction. There are, however, transitional rules for calendar year 1987 which limit the maximum rate on net capital gains to 28%. Tax Reform Act of 1986, Pub. L. No. 99-514 §§ 302, 302, and 311, 100 Stat. 2085 (1986). The statutory structure for capital gain was retained in the I.R.C. to facilitate reinstatement of a capital gains rate differential if there is a future tax rate increase. *See* Conference Committee Report to § 301 of the Tax Reform Act of 1986.

[331] Treas. Reg. § 1.1034-1(c)(3)(ii).

The portion of the property used as a rental apartment or as a law office may be converted to residential use prior to the time of sale so that all or part of the gain attributable to such portion of the property would qualify for I.R.C. § 1034 nonrecognition treatment. Presumably, to convert a portion of the property from business to residential use, the converted portion must be physically occupied by the taxpayer as a residence for more than an insubstantial period of time prior to the sale of the residence.[332] Gain realized on the business portion will reflect depreciation allowed or allowable,[333] and may involve recapture of depreciation[334] and investment tax credit[335] taken on the rehabilitation costs of the structure.

6. [§ 8.101]Loss on sale

A loss realized on the sale of a principal residence is not deductible.[336] If, however, the residence is partially used for business or the production of income, any realized loss attributable to such portion of the residence may be recognized.[337] Moreover, if residential property is, prior to its sale, rented or otherwise converted to business or profit use, and is held as such until the time of sale, any loss incurred after conversion may be recognized (i.e. the loss is allowed) to the extent that the adjusted basis of the property at the time of the conversion (which is the lesser of the fair market value of the property at the time of the conversion or the adjusted basis for loss at the time of conversion) exceeds the amount realized from the sale.[338]

7. [§ 8.102] Divorce

The third test may be particularly difficult to meet in a divorce situation where one spouse moves from the residence which is subsequently sold because the residence may not constitute the moving spouse's principal residence at the time of the sale.[339] The harshness of this result has been mitigated to some extent by I.R.C. § 1041 which was enacted by the Tax Reform Act of 1984.[340] That section provides

---

332 *See* **§ 8.27** of this chapter.

333 I.R.C. § 167.

334 I.R.C. § 1250.

335 I.R.C. § 47.

336 I.R.C. § 165(c); TREAS. REG. § 1.165-9(a).

337 *See Wilden L. Snyder,* T.C.M. (CCH) 1975-221; Rev. Rul. 72-111, 1972-1 C.B. 56; TREAS. REG. § 1.165-9(b)(1).

338 TREAS. REG. § 1.165-9(b)(2).

339 *Young v. Comm'r,* T.C.M. (CCH) 1985-127. See also *Perry v. Comm'r,* T.C.M. (CCH) 1994-247 where taxpayer moved from a residence to live with his future spouse while former spouse remained in the house for two years per the separation agreement. Held: residence was not principal residence at time of sale since former spouse resided there per agreement, taxpayer could not, and taxpayer lived elsewhere.

340 For a comprehensive discussion of this issue, see R.A. Rombro, *Federal Income Estate and Gift Tax Aspects of Separation and Divorce,* DIVORCE TAX WORKSHOP (MICPEL, 2001).

that gain realized is not recognized on a transfer of property from an individual to (or in trust for the benefit of) a spouse, or former spouse, if the transfer is incident to the divorce (i.e. occurs within one year after the date on which the marriage ceases, or is related to the cessation of the marriage). Thus, if a taxpayer abandons the residence so that it cannot qualify as the taxpayer's principal residence, the taxpayer should consider selling it to the taxpayer's spouse rather than to a third party. The purchasing spouse, however, should exercise caution since I.R.C. § 1041 characterizes a transfer between spouses or former spouses (if incident to a divorce) as a gift and basis in the property to the transferee is carried over from the transferor. Thus, if the transferee spouse immediately sells the property to a third party, the transferee may recognize some gain, or if the transferee purchases a new principal residence the transferee will have a lower basis than if the new property were purchased so that a subsequent sale of the property at gain may result in some recognition.

If, however, both spouses move and sell their residence, I.R.C. § 1034 will apply separately to the gain realized by each. Thus, if each acquires a new principal residence within the required time period, I.R.C. § 1034 will apply to each.[341]

G. Time Limits for Purchase—Replacement

1. [§ 8.103] Purchase

The fourth test requires that the qualifying taxpayer purchase a new residence which they physically occupies as their principal residence within the time limits discussed in **§§ 8.104–8.107** of this chapter.[342] A taxpayer is not required to sell their old residence prior to purchasing their new residence in order to qualify the gain from the sale of the old residence for nonrecognition treatment under I.R.C. § 1034. Generally, a "purchase" includes a purchase, an acquisition on the exchange of an old residence for a presently existing new residence, or the partial or total construction or reconstruction of a new residence.[343] A purchase does not, however, include acquisition by gift or inheritance, nor does it include improvements not amounting to reconstruction.[344] Unfortunately, there appear to be no guidelines to determine when improvements constitute reconstruction.

The time periods for the purchase (i.e., replacement) of a new principal residence depend upon whether the taxpayer purchases an existing structure, or constructs or reconstructs a new residence.

---

341 Rev. Rul. 74-250, 1974-1 C.B. 202 (discussed at n. **270**, *supra*).

342 I.R.C. § 1034(a); I.R.S. Priv. Ltr. Rul. 82-25-054 (Mar. 23, 1982).

343 I.R.C. § 1034(a)(2); Treas. Reg. § 1.1034-1(b)(9).

344 Treas. Reg. §§ 1.1034-1(b)(9) and 1.1034-1(c)(4)(i) .

2. [§ 8.104] Existing structure

Generally, where the taxpayer purchases an existing structure for their new principal residence, the purchase must occur within a period of time beginning two years before and ending two years after the date of sale of the old principal residence.[345] In addition, to be deemed their new principal residence, the newly purchased residence must be physically occupied by the taxpayer as the taxpayer's principal residence within two years after the date of sale of the old principal residence.[346] To constitute physical occupancy, the taxpayer must actually live in the residence. Merely moving furniture into the new residence does not constitute physical occupancy.[347] Thus, where the replacement property is an existing structure, it must be purchased and physically occupied within a four-year period of time beginning two years before and ending two years after the date of sale of the old principal residence.

3. [§ 8.105] Construction

Where the new principal residence is constructed in its entirety by the taxpayer, construction must commence within the four-year period beginning two years before and ending two years after the date of sale of the old residence, and physical occupancy must occur within the four-year period beginning two years before and ending two years after the date of sale of the old principal residence.[348] Thus, where the new principal residence is constructed by the taxpayer, rather than purchased as an existing structure, the period required for physical occupancy is the same.[349]

---

345 I.R.C. § 1034(a). The two-year/four-year replacement period was introduced into the Code by the Economic Tax Recovery Act of 1981 (ERTA) and is effective for sales and exchanges occurring after July 20, 1981, and for sales and exchanges with respect to which the 18-month/36-month rollover period had not expired on July 20, 1981. Before ERTA, the replacement period was 18 months before, and 18 months after, the date of sale of the old principal residence. The two-year/four-year period would appear to begin on the date the old principal residence is sold and end at midnight on the day preceding the corresponding date of sale in the second calendar year following the year of sale or end at midnight on the day preceding the corresponding date of sale in the second calendar year preceding the year of sale. *Cf.* Rev. Rul. 79-3, 1979-1 C.B. 143.

346 I.R.C. § 1034(a); *Bayley v. Comm'r*, 35 T.C. 288 (1960); S*tanley v. Comm'r*, 33 T.C. 614 (1959); Rev. Rul. 69-434, 1969-2 C.B. 163. *Henry v. Comm'r*, T.C.M. (CCH) 1982-469. This also includes a repurchase of the sold residence within the two-year time period. I.R.S. Priv. Ltr. Rul. 79-42-086.

347 *Bayley v. Comm'r*, 35 T.C. 288 (1960).

348 I.R.C. § 1034(c)(5). Repealed by the Economic Recovery Tax Act of 1981 effective for sales and exchanges occurring after July 20, 1981, and for sales and exchanges with respect to which the 18-month rollover period had not expired on July 20, 1981.

349 Note that prior to July 21, 1981, construction had to commence within the 36-month period commencing 18 months before, and ending 24 months after, the date of sale of the old residence, and physical occupancy had to occur with the 42-month period beginning 18 months

Construction commences when the taxpayer obtains a building site, a construction loan (if needed), approval of building plans, and a building permit.[350] Construction of the new principal residence may commence before the old principal residence is sold.

4. [§ 8.106] Reconstruction

If the new principal residence is partially constructed or reconstructed, the time period for physical occupancy is the same as for the purchase of an existing structure.[351] A partially constructed new principal residence is one already under construction by a builder according to particular specifications on specific land which the taxpayer agrees to purchase upon completion.[352] Improvements do not constitute a purchase.[353]

5. [§ 8.107] General matters on time limits

The time periods discussed in **§§ 8.103–8.106** of this chapter within which to purchase, construct, reconstruct, or physically occupy a new principal residence are inflexible. The Internal Revenue Service cannot grant an extension, for any reason whatsoever, if the taxpayer fails to purchase, construct, or physically occupy the new principal residence within the aforementioned time periods.[354]

Furthermore, the physical occupancy test can be met only by the taxpayer who claims the tax deferral. Thus, physical occupancy of the new principal residence by the taxpayer's child will not satisfy the physical occupancy test.[355]

---

before, and ending 24 months after, the date of sale of the old principal residence. This was repealed by ERTA. See nn. **327** and **330**, *supra*.

350 Rev. Rul. 68-594, 1968-2 C.B. 339.

351 I.R.C. § 1034(c)(2); Treas. Reg. § 1.1034-1(b)(9). *See* **§ 8.103** of this chapter.

352 Rev. Rul. 57-234, 1957-1 C.B. 263; I.R.S. Priv. Ltr. Rul. 85-48-027 (Aug. 30, 1985) (Structural or mechanical additions and alterations are reconstruction where they are not for repair or minor improvement).

353 TREAS. REG. § 1.1034-1(b)(9).

354 *Gelinas v. Comm'r*, T.C.M. (CCH) 1976-103 (Delay due to state agency's invalid stop work order); *Bazzell v. Comm'r*, T.C.M. (CCH) 1967-101 (Delay due to illness); *Henzel v. Comm'r*, T.C.M. (CCH) 1965-250 (Delay caused by weather); Rev. Rul. 75-438, 1975-2 C.B. 334 (Delay caused by fire). *See also Shaw v. Comm'r*, 69 T.C. 1034 (1978) and the cases cited therein at 1038; *see Peck v. Comm'r*, T.C.M. (CCH) 1982-506 (Difficulty encountered in selling old residence). *See also Haydin v. Comm'r*, T.C.M. (CCH) 1983-518 (Purchase of new residence after the end of the statutory period denies non-recognition treatment. Good faith, conscientious effort to make a timely sale of old residence immaterial), and *Chavez v. Comm'r*, T.C.M. (CCH) 1983-199 (Purchase of new residence 10 days after expiration of replacement period disqualifies gain on sale of former residence from deferral treatment. Good faith effort to purchase home within statutory time period caused by delays outside of the control of the taxpayer are of no consequence).

355 *United States v. Sheahan*, 323 F.2d 383 (5th Cir. 1963); Rev. Rul. 69-434, 1969-2 C.B. 163.

Frequently, unexpected delays occur during construction which may extend the completion date beyond the time required for physical occupancy. It is therefore recommended that a clause be inserted in the construction contract providing for the payment of damages to the taxpayer, this being a matter of negotiation. One measure of damages could be an amount at least equal to the amount of tax that would have been deferred but for the taxpayer's inability to meet the physical occupancy test because of construction delays. Another measure of damages could be the time use of the money lost by the taxpayer on the accelerated payment of taxes. Moreover, if the time period for filing an amended return has not expired, and if no gain was reported on the return originally filed, consideration should be given to reporting gain realized from the sale of the old principal residence on the installment method of reporting income.[356]

H. [§ 8.108] Cost of Purchasing a New Residence

A comparison of the adjusted sales price and the cost of purchasing a new principal residence determines the amount of gain realized which is not recognized.[357] The "cost of purchasing a new principal residence" means the total of all amounts attributable to the acquisition, construction, reconstruction, and improvements constituting capital expenditures, made during the reinvestment period.[358] This includes cash, indebtedness to which the property is subject at the time of the purchase whether or not assumed by the taxpayer (including a purchase money mortgage), and the face amount of any liabilities of the taxpayer which are part of the consideration for the purchase.[359] Also included in determining such cost are purchase expenses (such as sales commissions and appraisals) paid or incurred by the taxpayer.[360]

The fair market value of the new principal residence, determined on the date of purchase, constitutes the taxpayer's cost of purchasing the new principal residence.[361] Where any part of the new principal residence is acquired other than by purchase, the value of such part is not included in determining the cost of the new principal residence. For example, if the taxpayer acquires a new principal residence by inheritance, and spends $10,000 reconstructing such residence, only the $10,000 is included as the cost of purchasing the new residence.[362]

---

356 I.R.C. § 453; Rev. Rul. 56-396, 1956-2 C.B. 298, *modified by* Rev. Rul. 65-297, 1965-2 C.B. 152; Rev. Rul. 65-155, 1965-1 C.B. 356; Rev. Rul. 75, 1953-1 C.B. 83.

357 *See* **§ 8.88** of this chapter.

358 TREAS. REG. § 1.1034-1(b)(7).

359 TREAS. REG. § 1.1034-1(c)(4)(i).

360 *Id.*

361 *Id.*

362 *Id*; *see* text at n. **331**, *supra.*

The taxpayer's cost of purchasing the new principal residence includes only the actual costs attributable to acquisition, reconstruction, or improvement made within the four-year replacement period.[363] To illustrate, if a taxpayer purchases a new principal residence in August 1986, and in January 1987 the taxpayer sells their old principal residence and moves into the new principal residence, only the cost attributable to reconstruction performed within four years of the date of the sale of the old principal residence (two years before and two years after the sale) is included in the cost of purchasing the new principal residence. The fair market value of the new principal residence is not included.[364]

In the case of construction, only the costs attributable to actual construction made within two years before, and two years after, the date of sale of the old principal residence are included.[365] For example, if construction is begun three years before the date of sale of the old principal residence and is completed on the date of sale, only the construction costs attributable to the two years immediately preceding the date of sale of the old principal residence constitute the taxpayer's cost of purchasing the new principal residence.[366]

As a result of the above, it is recommended that the taxpayer keep accurate records not only of the costs of purchasing and constructing the new residence, but also the dates the costs were incurred.

I. Sale and Purchase Limitations

1. [§ 8.109] General rules

There are three limitations on the sale and purchase of a principal residence of which one should be aware. First, if the taxpayer purchases a new residence which the taxpayer sells before the date of sale of the old principal residence, the newly purchased residence does not constitute their principal residence.[367] Therefore, gain realized from the sale of the newly purchased residence cannot be postponed from taxation. For example, Mr. Smith, who owns a principal residence, purchases a new residence on Oct. 1, 1993. On Dec. 1, 1985, Smith sells at gain the newly purchased residence. On Dec. 31, 1993, Smith sells, at gain, his old principal residence. Smith recognizes gain on the Dec. 1, 1993, sale of the newly purchased residence. However, he does not recognize gain on the sale of the old residence on the Dec. 31, 1993 sale if a replacement residence is acquired and occupied within the requisite time

---

363 TREAS. REG. § 1.1034-1(c)(4)(ii).

364 *Shaw v. Comm'r*, 69 T.C. 1034 (1978); Rev. Rul. 78-147, 1978-1 C.B. 261.

365 I.R.C. § 1034(c)(2); TREAS. REG. § 1.1034-1(c)(4)(ii); *Kern v. Grandquist*, 291 F.2d 29 (9th Cir. 1961); *Ownes v. Comm'r*, T.C.M. (CCH) 1977-233; Rev. Rul. 55-90.

366 TREAS. REG. § 1.1034-1(c)(4)(iii).

367 I.R.C. § 1034(c)(3); TREAS. REG. § 1.1034-1(d).

periods. Thus, a new residence does not constitute a principal residence if it is sold before the old principal residence.

Second, if during the previously described four-year period, the taxpayer purchases more than one residence which the taxpayer uses as their principal residence at some time within two years after the date of sale of the old principal residence, only the last residence used by the taxpayer as their principal residence after the date of sale of the old principal residence constitutes their new principal residence.[368] The result of this provision is that gain from the sale of the first residence may be deferred under I.R.C. § 1034, but not gain from the sale of an intervening residence. Prior to the Tax Reform Act of 1986, gain from the sale of the intervening residence qualified for capital gains treatment.[369] Where the intervening residence was held for more than one year, gain on the sale is long-term capital gain.[370] Where, however, the intervening residence was held for one year or less, the holding period of the first home could not be tacked onto the intervening residence so as to receive long-term capital gain treatment on the sale of the intervening home, because I.R.C. § 1223(7) allowed tacking of holding period for residences that came within the nonrecognition provision of I.R.C. § 1034 (the first and last residences per I.R.C. § 1034(c)(4)).[371]

---

368 I.R.C. § 1034(c)(4); *Stevens v. Comm'r*, T.C.M. (CCH) 1980-521. *See also* Rev. Rul. 81-53, 1981-1 C.B. 439. For further discussion see Rev. Rul. 81-53 1981-1 C.B. 439, where taxpayer sold house A at gain and within 18 months of sale of house A, the taxpayer constructed, occupied, and sold house B at gain. Within 34 months of sale of house A, the taxpayer bought and occupied house C. Held: The 24-month replacement period specified in I.R.C. § 1034(c)(5) applies and, therefore, under I.R.C. § 1034(c)(4) house C is considered the replacement residence for nonrecognition of gain on house A. It should be noted that because the taxpayer constructed house B, thus permitting the 18-month replacement period to be extended to 24 months under I.R.C. § 1034(c)(5), the replacement period for the purchase of house C is also extended to 24 months, thus making house C the last link in the chain. In *Kerns v. Commissioner*, T.C.M. (CCH) 1984-22 the taxpayers purchased a residence on 12/19/75 which they occupied as their principal residence. On 5/13/77 they sold this residence, realizing a long-term capital gain, but deferring recognition of the gain pursuant to I.R.C. § 1034. On 5/27/77 the taxpayers purchased and occupied a new residence which they sold on 9/22/78. On 12/1/78 the taxpayer purchased a third residence which they occupied beginning September 1978 and continued to occupy after the purchase on 12/1/78. The court held that the gain realized by the taxpayers on the sale of the second residence was subject to taxation because the sale of the first residence occurred during the 18-month period immediately preceding the second sale. See however, n. **331**, *supra*, which discusses the repeal of I.R.C. § 1034(c)(5) by ERTA.

369 *See* n. **312**, *supra*, with regard to the repeal of the capital gains deduction.

370 *See* n. **307**.

371 I.R.S. Priv. Ltr. Rul. 82-09-001 (Sept. 30, 1981) (First residence sold 10/31/79. Second residence purchased 9/4/79 and sold 8/8/ 80. Third residence purchased 8/8/80. Held: Gain on sale of first residence and last residence qualify for nonrecognition treatment. Gain on sale of second residence taxable. Cannot tack holding period first residence to second residence to receive long-term capital gain treatment). *But see* n. **307**, *supra*.

Third, if within two years prior to the date of sale of the residence, the taxpayer sells at a gain another principal residence and any part of the gain realized on the sale of such other residence is deferred from taxation, I.R.C. § 1034 is not applicable to the most recently sold principal residence.[372] Thus, a taxpayer cannot elect to defer recognition of gain under I.R.C. § 1034 more than once within a two-year period.

For example, in 1993, I.M. Fickle engages in the following transactions: she sells at gain her old residence on March 1, purchases and occupies a new residence on April 1 which she sells at gain on May 1, and she purchases and occupies another existing structure on June 1. Applying the above rules, gain from the residence sold on March 1 may be deferred from taxation to the extent its adjusted sales price is equal to or less than the cost of the residence purchased on June 1. Ms. Fickle cannot defer from taxation the gain realized from the sale of the second residence.

2. [§ 8.110] Exception for change in employment locations

An exception to the prohibition against multiple roll overs within a 24-month period beginning from the date that the taxpayer's first principal residence is sold was enacted under the Revenue Act of 1978.[373] The reason for this change in the law was to alleviate hardships imposed upon employees and self-employed individuals who are required to change employment locations more than once during any 24-month period.[374]

I.R.C. § 1034(d)(2) provides for the rollover of gain realized on the sale of more than one principal residence where an individual relocates, for employment purposes, within a period beginning two years from the date that their first principal residence is sold. I.R.C. § 1034(d)(2) is keyed into I.R.C. § 217 providing for deduction of moving expenses. Thus, where a taxpayer is entitled to deduct moving expenses under I.R.C. § 217 with respect to a relocation within the two-year period, the general rule prohibiting multiple rollovers within the two-year period is not applicable. Rather, the exception provided by I.R.C. § 1034(d)(2) is applicable, thus allowing nonrecognition of gain on the sale of a principal residence, even though there has been nonrecognition of gain on the sale of another principal residence within the preceding two years.[375]

---

372 I.R.C. § 1034(d)(1).

373 I.R.C. § 1034(d); Pub. L. No. 95-600, § 404 (§ 404, 1978 Rev. Act). See *Clavijo v. Commissioner*, T.C.M. (CCH) 1980-529 for a case regarding I.R.C. § 1034(d) as in effect prior to the Revenue Act of 1978. The 1978 Act contained an 18-month period which was extended to two years by the Economic Recovery Act of 1981. *See* n. **327**, *supra*.

374 *See* General Explanation of the Revenue Act of 1978 prepared by the STAFF OF THE JOINT COMMITTEE ON TAXATION, 95TH CONG., GENERAL EXPLANATION OF THE REVENUE ACT OF 1978 (Joint Comm. Print 1979).

375 *See Cronhardt v. Comm'r*, T.C.M. (CCH) 1986-399 (Gain on sale of second principal residence within 13 months after sale of first principal residence (on which gain was not recognized) was not recognized where second residence was sold in connection with taxpayer's move to different area to become self-employed in full-time business).

3. [§ 8.111] *Test for qualification*

To qualify for the benefits of the multiple rollover provision within the two-year period, a taxpayer must meet three tests: a connection with work test, a geographic test, and a length of employment test.

a. Connection with work

First, the sale of the second principal residence sold within the two-year period must be in connection with the commencement of work by the taxpayer, as an employee or as a self-employed individual, at a new principal place of work.[376] A self-employed individual is an individual who performs personal services either as the owner of the entire interest in an unincorporated trade or business, or as a partner in a partnership carrying on a trade or business.[377] An individual who commences work at a new principal place of work as a self-employed individual would appear to be treated as obtaining employment when they makes substantial arrangements to commence such work.[378]

b. Geographic

Second, the taxpayer must satisfy the geographic requirements for deductibility of moving expenses under I.R.C. § 217(c)(1).[379] That section allows a moving expense deduction if the taxpayer's principal place of work either is at least 50 miles farther from the taxpayer's former residence than is the taxpayer's former principal place of work or, if the taxpayer has no former principal place of work, is at least 50 miles from the taxpayer's former residence.[380] The distance between two points is the shortest of the more commonly traveled routes between the two points.[381]

c. Length of employment

Third, the taxpayer must satisfy the length of employment requirements for deductibility of moving expenses under I.R.C. § 217(c)(2), subject to the provisions of I.R.C. § 217(d). Under that section a taxpayer must meet one of two tests:

(1) during at least 39 weeks of the 12-month period immediately following the taxpayer's arrival in the general location of the taxpayer's new principal

---

376 I.R.C. § 1034(d)(2)(A).

377 I.R.C. § 217(f)(1); TREAS. REG. § 1.217-2(f).

378 I.R.C. § 217(f)(1); TREAS. REG. § 1.217-2(a)(3).

379 I.R.C. § 1034(d)(2)(B).

380 I.R.C. § 217(c)(1)(A) & (B); TREAS. REG. § 1.217(c)(1). Section 13213 of OBRA 1993, P. L. No. 103-66, increased the distance from 35 miles to 50 miles effective for expenses incurred after Dec. 31, 1993.

381 I.R.C. § 217(c) (last paragraph).

place of work, the taxpayer must be a full-time employee in such general location;[382] or

(2) during the 24-month period immediately following the taxpayer's arrival in the general location of their new principal place of work, the taxpayer is a full-time employee or performs services as a self-employed individual on a full-time basis, in such general location, for at least 78 weeks, of which not less than 39 weeks are during the 12-month period immediately following their arrival in the general location of their new principal place of work.[383]

4. [§ 8.112] *Effect of death, disability, involuntary separation, or transfer*

The requirements of I.R.C. § 217(c)(2) respecting length of employment do not apply if the taxpayer is unable to meet such requirements because of death, disability,[384] or involuntary separation (other than for willful misconduct) from the service or transfer for the benefit of an employer after obtaining full-time employment in which the taxpayer could reasonably have been expected to satisfy either requirement.[385] Thus, the failure to meet the length of employment requirement will not disqualify the taxpayer from multiple rollover treatment if the taxpayer has a reasonable expectation, at the time of the move, that they would satisfy this requirement.

5. [§ 8.113] *Qualifying sale terminates two-year period and starts a new two-year period*

In addition, a sale which meets the tests of I.R.C. § 1034(d)(2) is treated as terminating the two-year period and starting another two-year period.[386] Thus, the principal residence receiving rollover treatment constitutes a new principal residence with respect to the prior rollover sale and an old principal residence for purposes of its sale.

When the multiple rollover provision applies, the basis of each succeeding principal residence is reduced by the amount of gain not recognized on the sale of the prior residence.

Example—The operation of I.R.C. § 1034(d)(2) is illustrated by the following example: Hesa Chazir sells at gain his old principal residence on May 1, 1994, and purchases a new principal residence on June 1, 1994. On July 1, 1994, Chazir's employer *permanently* transfers him to a new principal place of work 500 miles from Chazir's former principal place of work and former principal

---

[382] I.R.C. § 217(c)(2)(A); Treas. Reg. § 1.217-2(c)(4).
[383] I.R.C. § 217(c)(2)(B); Treas. Reg. § 1.217-2(c)(4).
[384] I.R.C. § 217(d)(1)(A).
[385] I.R.C. § 217(d)(1)(B).
[386] I.R.C. § 1034(c)(4). *See* text at n. **350**, *supra*.

residence. On Aug. 1, 1994, Chazir sells at gain the new principal residence purchased June 1, 1994. On Sept. 1, 1994, Chazir purchases a new principal residence in the general location of his new principal place of work. Since the Aug. 1, 1994, sale occurs within two years of the May 1, 1994, sale, the two-year limitation provision of I.R.C. § 1034(d)(1) applies, and gain realized from the Aug. 1, 1994, sale is recognized. However, since the Aug. 1, 1994, sale was in connection with the commencement of work by Chazir as an employee in a new principal place of work, and since he satisfies the geographical and length of employment requirements of I.R.C. § 217(c), the two-year limitation provision of I.R.C. § 1034(d)(1) does not apply to the Aug. 1, 1994, sale. Thus, gain realized from the Aug. 1, 1994, sale qualifies for nonrecognition treatment under I.R.C. § 1034(d)(2). In addition, the residence sold on Aug. 1, 1994, is treated both as the last new residence used within the two-year period following the May 1, 1994, sale of Chazir's old residence, and as an old residence for purposes of the running of the next two-year limitation period. If, however, Chazir's transfer to a new principal place of work is a temporary transfer which he reasonably could have expected to last only 26 weeks, gain realized on the Aug. 1, 1994, sale would be recognized and the residence purchased on Sept. 1, 1994, would be the replacement residence.[387]

6. [§ 8.114] Deduction of moving expenses

In addition to the rollover treatment provided by I.R.C. § 1034 for sales of a principal residence in connection with a change in employment location, the taxpayer may also be able to deduct, as an itemized deduction,[388] moving expenses paid or incurred in selling an old principal residence and purchasing a new principal residence in connection with relocation for employment purposes.[389] If, however, these expenses are deducted as moving expenses, they cannot be used to decrease the gain realized from the sale of the old principal residence (which in turn affects the amount of gain deferred from taxation), nor can they be used to increase the adjusted basis of the new principal residence.[390] Thus, the taxpayer must carefully choose whether to deduct such expenses or to defer any gain realized. Although the Internal Revenue Code denies this double benefit, it may still be available, as the following example illustrates:

---

387 *See* n. **356**, *supra*.

388 The Tax Reform Act of 1986 changed the moving expense deduction from an above the line deduction to arrive at adjusted gross income, to a below-the-line itemized deduction to arrive at taxable income. *See* **§ 8.13** of this chapter.

389 I.R.C. § 217(a).

390 I.R.C. § 217(e).

Example—Assume Lisa Mover purchased a home several years ago for $180,000. Assume she moves across country for employment reasons and that the connection with work, geographic, and length of employment tests are met. She sells her old principal residence for $300,000 and, at her new location, she purchases a new principal residence for $320,000. She incurs selling expenses of $20,500 (which include real estate commissions, attorneys' fees, and title fees) in connection with the sale of her old principal residence, and purchasing expenses of $3,500 (which include attorneys' fees, appraisal fees, and title fees) in connection with the purchase of her new principal residence.

Under I.R.C. § 1034, as reflected in the example discussed above, Mover's gain realized is $99,500 (sales price of $300,000, less cost of $180,000 and selling expenses of $20,500). Since Mover's cost of their new principal residence ($320,000) exceeds the sales price of their old principal residence ($300,000), the gain realized of $99,500 is not recognized. The adjusted basis in their new principal residence is $224,000 ($320,000 purchase price, plus purchasing expenses of $3,500, less gain realized by not recognized of $99,500). However, Mover may not deduct the selling and purchasing expenses of $24,000.

If, however, Mover decides to deduct the selling and purchasing expenses instead of capitalizing them, their gain realized on the sale of their old principal residence will be $120,000. Since the cost of their new principal residence exceeds the sales price of their older principal residence, the gain realized is not recognized. The adjusted basis in their new principal residence is $200,000 (purchase price of $320,000 less gain realized by not recognized of $120,000). Thus, by deducting the selling and purchasing expenses, Mover gets a lower basis in their new principal residence than if those expenses were capitalized. This, in turn, will result in a larger gain realized when she subsequently sells the new residence. Thus, Mover not only defers gain realized from taxation, but also receives a current moving expense deduction. Accordingly, in the appropriate situation, a taxpayer may not only defer gain realized from taxation, but also may claim a current moving expense deduction, thus receiving the best of both worlds.

J. [§ 8.115] Computation of Gain Deferred from Taxation

The computation of the amount of gain deferred from taxation involves application of a seven-step formula, as the following example demonstrates.

Example—Assume that on Dec. 1, 1993, Jack B. Quick sells his old principal residence for $60,000 and in so doing incurs selling expenses (as defined below) of $3,000. To prepare the house for sale he spends $900 for wallpaper and painting in November 1993, which he pays for prior to sale. Assume further that he purchased his old residence for $10,000 cash and took a mortgage of $40,000, and during occupancy of the residence spent $2,500 for central air conditioning. On Dec. 30, 1993, Mr. Quick purchases an existing structure which he immediately occupies as his principal residence. The new principal residence costs $54,000.

1. [§ 8.116] Amount realized

Mr. Quick's first step in computing the gain to be deferred from taxation is to determine the "amount realized" from the sale of his old principal residence. This is the excess of the sales price over sales expenses.[391] The sales price includes cash, the fair market value of property (other than cash) received from the buyer, such as notes given by the buyer to the seller, and the face value of mortgages of the seller assumed by the buyer or to which the property is subject. Selling expenses include commissions, recording fees, transfer taxes, attorneys' fees, appraisal fees, title insurance, and advertising costs.[392] The "amount realized" by Mr. Quick is $57,000.

2. [§ 8.117] Adjusted sales price/fixing-up expenses

Mr. Quick's second step is to determine the "adjusted sales price" of his old residence, which is the excess of the amount realized from the sale of his old residence (step one) over "fixing-up expenses."[393] These later expenses include the aggregate of all expenses for work performed on the old residence to assist in its sale.[394] To qualify as fixing-up expenses, three tests must be met. First, the expenses must be for work performed during the 90-day period ending on the day on which the contract to sell the old residence is entered into.[395] Second, the expenses must be paid on or before the 30th day after the date of the sale of the old residence.[396] Third, the expenses must not be allowable as a deduction in computing taxable income under I.R.C. § 63, and must not be taken into account in determining the amount realized from the sale of the old residence.[397]

In our example, the $900 Mr. Quick pays to wallpaper and paint the residence constitute "fixing-up expenses." Therefore, Mr. Quick's "adjusted sales price" is $56,100.

---

391 TREAS. REG. § 1.1034-1(b)(4).

392 TREAS. REG. § 1.1034-1(b)(4); *see also* Treas. Reg. § 1.1034-1(c)(2). These do not include moving expenses, which are deductible under I.R.C. § 217. *See* **§ 8.114** *supra.*

393 I.R.C. § 1034(b)(1); TREAS. REG. § 1.1034-1(b)(3).

394 I.R.C. § 1034(b)(1); TREAS. REG. § 1.1034-1(b)(6).

395 I.R.C. § 1034(b)(2)(A); TREAS. REG. § 1.1034-1(b)(6). *See also* Rev. Rul. 72-118, 1972-1 C.B. 227 (Fixing up expenses excluded where contract to sell, under which such expenses were incurred, is voided and sale not made).

396 I.R.C. § 1034(b)(2)(B); TREAS. REG. § 1.1034-1(b)(6).

397 I.R.C. § 1034(b)(2)(C); TREAS. REG. § 1.1034-1(b)(6).

3. [§ 8.118] *Adjusted basis of old residence*

Third, Mr. Quick must determine the "adjusted basis" of his old residence, which includes the original cost of his old residence, plus permanent improvements which increase the value of his old residence.[398] The original cost of an old residence includes the cash down payment and the mortgage placed on the lot and the dwelling place,[399] as well as purchase expenses such as attorneys' fees, commissions, and appraisal fees incurred when the old residence was acquired. In the example, the original cost of Mr. Quick's old residence is $50,000 ($10,000 + $40,000). Permanent improvements, on the other hand, include the installation of items such as a new roof, central air conditioning ($2,500 in our example), swimming pool, tennis courts, additional rooms, and storm windows. The cost of furniture may not be included in any of the costs, nor may repairs incurred to maintain the property. Thus, the "adjusted basis" of Mr. Quick's old residence is $52,500.

4. [§ 8.119] *Gain realized*

Fourth, Mr. Quick must determine the "gain realized" from the sale of his old principal residence. This is the excess of the amount realized from such sale (step one) over the adjusted basis of his old residence (step three).[400] Gain realized in the example is $4,500, which is the amount of gain which would be recognized; i.e., subject to taxation, were it not for I.R.C. § 1034.

5. [§ 8.120] *Gain recognized*

Fifth, Mr. Quick must determine the gain realized which is "recognized." This is the excess of the adjusted sales price of his old residence (step two) over the cost of his new residence.[401] Thus, in our example, only $2,100 of the $4,500 gain realized is actually subject to taxation in the current year. On the other hand, if the cost of Mr. Quick's new residence were equal to or greater than the adjusted sales price, all the gain realized would be deferred currently from taxation.

6. [§ 8.121] *Gain deferred*

Sixth, by subtracting the gain recognized ($2,100) from the gain realized ($4,500) Mr. Quick can determine the amount of gain which is deferred currently from taxation, which in the example is $2,400.

---

398 I.R.C. §§ 1011(a) and 1016.

399 *Crane v. Comm'r*, 331 U.S. 1 (1947).

400 Treas. Reg. § 1.1034-1(b)(5).

401 See **§ 8.108** of this chapter for a discussion of the elements included in the "cost of purchasing a new residence."

7. [§ 8.122] Adjusted basis of new residence

Finally, Mr. Quick must determine the adjusted basis of his new residence. This is the excess of the cost of his new residence over the gain deferred currently from taxation.[402] The effect of this step is to reduce the basis Mr. Quick's new residence ($54,000) by an amount equal to the gain deferred from taxation ($2,400), thus assuring, at least theoretically, that the $2,400 gain deferred from taxation will be subject to realization upon the subsequent sale of his new principal residence. Consequently, if Mr. Quick subsequently sold his new principal residence for $100,000, and no other expenses were involved, he would realize and recognize a gain of $48,400 ($100,000—$51,600) rather than $46,000 ($100,000–$54,000), which includes the $2,400 gain previously deferred, unless he were to reinvest the subsequent sales proceeds in another principal residence, thereby initiating another deferral cycle, or if eligible, elect the benefits of I.R.C. § 121 and achieve complete avoidance of tax on gain realized, as discussed in **§§ 8.126–8.145** of this chapter. A sample of Jack B. Quick's completed I.R.S. Form 2119 is set forth in **§ 8.150** of this chapter.

K. Reporting Requirements

1. [§ 8.123] Reporting

When a principal residence is sold, the transaction must be reported on the taxpayer's federal income tax return for the year in which the sale occurs.[403] How the transaction is reported on the return depends upon whether the taxpayer acquires or intends to acquire replacement property within the required time periods.

If the taxpayer neither acquires nor intends to acquire replacement property, gain realized and recognized from the sale of the old principal residence should be reported on Form 2119 and Schedule D attached to the taxpayer's Form 1040 for the year in which the sale of the old principal residence occurs.[404] This gain would enter into the computation of net capital gains or losses in the same manner as gains and losses from the sale or exchange of other capital assets.[405]

If the taxpayer acquires and occupies replacement property on or before the date the taxpayer files their Form 1040 for the year in which the sale of their old principal residence occurs, a completed Form 2119 should be attached to the Form 1040. If any gain is recognized, only that gain should be reported on Schedule D

---

402 I.R.C. §§ 1034(e) and 1016(a)(7); TREAS. REG. § 1.1034-1(a) and (e)(1).

403 TREAS. REG. § 1.1034-1(i)(1).

404 INTERNAL REVENUE SERV., IRS Pub. No. 523, TAX INFORMATION ON SELLING OR PURCHASING YOUR HOME 6 (1987).

405 See note **312**, *supra*, regarding repeal of the capital gains deduction.

attached to the Form 1040.[406] Any gain which is reinvested in a new residence and which is not recognized is not required to be reported on Schedule D.[407]

If the taxpayer has not acquired replacement property on or before the date the taxpayer files their Federal income tax return for the year in which the sale of their old principal residence occurs, and either the taxpayer plans to purchase a replacement residence, or is undecided whether to purchase a replacement residence by the time they file such return, this should be noted on Schedule D and Form 2119 (completing lines 1 and 2 and Part I), although it appears that such gain would not be required to be reported thereon.[408] When the taxpayer later acquires a new principal residence (after their return is filed but within the required time period), which costs at least as much as the adjusted sales price of the old principal residence, so that any gain realized is deferred from taxation, the taxpayer must notify the Service Center where they filed the return for the year of sale, in writing, that they has replaced their old principal residence, and give the dates the new residence was purchased and occupied, as well as the cost of the new residence.[409] Although one cannot state with certainty, it would appear that such notice may be accomplished either by letter or by Form 2119.

If, however, the replacement residence costs less than the adjusted sales price, or if the new residence is not acquired and occupied within the replacement periods, the taxpayer must file an amended tax return (Form 1040X) with attached Schedule D and Form 2119, for the year of the sale showing the amount of gain recognized.[410] Interest will be charged on the gain recognized which the taxpayer reports on his amended return.[411]

If the taxpayer recognized gain on the sale of their old principal residence, and the taxpayer acquires and occupies a new residence within the replacement period, the taxpayer should file an amended return (along with a Form 2119) claiming a refund of the amount of gain deferred from taxation.[412]

2. [§ 8.124] Statute of limitations

The statute of limitations for assessing a deficiency for gain realized on the sale of a principal residence does not expire until three years from the date the district director, with whom the return was filed for the taxable year or years in which the gain from the sale of the old principal residence was realized, receives written notice from the taxpayer stating the taxpayer's cost of purchasing the new principal residence,

---

406 INTERNAL REVENUE SERV., IRS Pub. No. 523, *supra* note 371 at 6.

407 *Id.*

408 *Id.*

409 *Id.* at p. 7.

410 INTERNAL REVENUE SERV., IRS Pub. No. 523, *supra*, note 371 at 6.

411 *Id.*

412 *Id.*

or the taxpayer's intention not to purchase a new residence within the time replacement period, or the taxpayer's failure to purchase a new principal residence within the time replacement period; and all pertinent details in connection with the sale of the old principal residence and the purchase price of the new principal residence (if non-recognition is claimed).[413] The notice should be attached to the taxpayer's return for the year gain is realized. It would seem that Form 2119 should suffice for notice purposes.[414] This special statute of limitations overrides the general three-year period of limitations that begins to run from the time the return is filed.[415] If notice is not given, the statute of limitations attributable to gain recognized does not run.

A loss realized on the sale of a principal residence is not deductible.[416] Although such a loss does not have to be reported, it would seem to be advisable to report the loss to begin the running of the statute of limitations.

L. [§ 8.125] Condemnation

In the case of the seizure, requisition, or condemnation (collectively the "condemnation") of a residence, or the sale or exchange of a residence under threat or imminence of condemnation, I.R.C. § 1034 can apply instead of I.R.C. § 1033 (pertaining to condemnations), if the taxpayer so elects.[417] A taxpayer may thus elect to have I.R.C. § 1034, rather than I.R.C. § 1033, apply to determine the amount of gain realized on the disposition of the old principal residence that will not be recognized and the extent to which the basis of the new principal residence will be reduced.[418] Once made, the election is irrevocable[419] and the taxpayer must meet all the tests of I.R.C. § 1034.[420]

The replacement period for a condemnation begins with the earlier of the date of disposition or threat of condemnation and ending two years after the close of the first taxable year in which any portion of the gain was realized from the conversion, or any later date which the Internal Revenue Service may grant on application.[421] On the other hand, the replacement period under I.R.C. § 1034 is the period beginning two years before, and ending two years after, the date of the involuntary conversion.[422]

---

413 I.R.C. § 1034(j)(1); TREAS. REG. § 1.1034(i). *Compare* I.R.C. § 302(c)(2).

414 *See* TREAS. REG. § 1.1034-1(i)(2). The Form 2119 should suffice since it contains all the information required by the regulation.

415 TREAS. REG. § 1.1034-1(i)(1); I.R.C. § 6501(a).

416 *See* **§ 8.101** of this chapter.

417 I.R.C. § 1034(i); TREAS. REG. § 1.1034-1(h).

418 TREAS. REG. § 1.1034-1(h)(2)(i).

419 *Id.*

420 TREAS. REG. § 1.1034-1(h)(2)(ii).

421 I.R.C. § 1033.

422 *See* **§§ 8.104–8.108** of this chapter.

Whether to elect out of I.R.C. § 1033 and into I.R.C. § 1034 depends upon the time periods for replacement and the adjusted basis of the new principal residence. I.R.C. § 1034 specifically defines the replacement period, whereas I.R.C. § 1033 does not. Under I.R.C. § 1034 fixing up expenses decrease the gain realized, whereas no such opportunity is available under I.R.C. § 1033. Finally, I.R.C. § 1034 allows the purchase of a new principal residence before the old residence is sold, whereas I.R.C. § 1033 does not allow replacements prior to disposition except under threat or imminence of condemnation. Thus, the decision to elect I.R.C. § 1034 treatment instead of I.R.C. § 1033 will often depend upon the time period for replacement, since as noted above, I.R.C. § 1034 has a two-year/four-year replacement period, whereas the I.R.C. § 1033 replacement may be longer or shorter depending upon when the condemnation occurs during the taxable year and whether the period will be extended by the IRS; whether substantial amounts of fixing-up expenses are involved; and whether the taxpayer purchases a new principal residence before disposition of the old principal residence. Under both sections the adjusted basis of the new principal residence should be reduced by the gain realized but not recognized, so that the result should be the same.[423]

An I.R.C. § 1034(i) election must be made in a statement attached to the taxpayer's income tax return for the taxable year in which the condemnation occurs.[424] Failure to file a timely election precludes the taxpayer from falling within I.R.C. § 1034. The statement must indicate that the taxpayer elects to treat the condemnation as a sale or exchange of the old residence under I.R.C. § 1034, and must show the basis of the old residence, the date of its disposition, the adjusted sales price of the old residence, if known, and the purchase price, date of purchase, and date of occupancy of the new residence if it has been acquired prior to the time of making the election.[425]

Section B—Exclusion from Gross Income

A. [§ 8.126] Exclusion from Gross Income of All or Part of Gain Realized on the Sale of a Principal Residence by a Taxpayer Age 55 or Older—General Income Tax Consequences

Generally, when a taxpayer sells their residence for profit, they realize a gain which must be included in their gross income,[426] unless there is a specific statutory exception to exclude the gain from gross income.[427] For example, if Ben E. Fit receives $100,000 in cash from the sale of his principal residence, and the adjusted basis of the residence is $40,000, the entire gain realized of $60,000 must be

---

423 *Compare* I.R.C. § 1034(e) *with* I.R.C. § 1033(b).

424 Treas. Reg. § 1.1034-1(h)(2)(iii).

425 Treas. Reg. § 1.1034-1(h)(2)(iii).

426 I.R.C. § 61(a)(3); I.R.C. § 1001(c). *See* **§ 8.46** *supra*.

427 I.R.C. § 61(a) and (b); I.R.C. § 1001(c).

included in his gross income, unless excepted. I.R.C. § 121 previously provided an exception applied as discussed in **§§ 8.127–8.145** below. The Taxpayer Relief Act of 1997 changed the exception to one of broader applicability.[428]

B. [§ 8.127] Exclusion from Gross Income under I.R.C. § 121—Introduction

There was previously a one-time tax exclusion provision in the Internal Revenue Code (I.R.C. § 121), available only to a taxpayer 55 years of age or older, which allowed such taxpayer to elect to exclude from gross income all or part of the gain realized from the sale of a personal residence. Generally, I.R.C. § 121, as previously in effect, provides that if a taxpayer attains the age of 55 before the date of sale or exchange of their residence, and for at least three years of the five-year period immediately preceding the sale the taxpayer owned and used the property as the taxpayer's principal residence, the taxpayer may elect to exclude from gross income, and hence permanently exempt from taxation, up to $125,000 ($62,500 in the case of married individuals who file separate returns) of any gain realized on the sale or exchange of such principal residence.[429] A taxpayer who previously elected to use the one-time $35,000 exclusion ratio provision for individuals age 65 or over under prior law may qualify to use the new election of current law without reduction of any amounts excludable under prior law, thus giving such taxpayer two bites at the apple.[430]

Sections **8.128–8.145** discuss the age-related exclusion. The references to I.R.C. § 121 are to the statute before amended by the Taxpayer Relief Act of 1997.

C. [§ 8.128] Age

To qualify for exclusionary treatment, several tests must be met. First, the taxpayer must attain the age of 55 before the date of sale of their principal residence.[431] A taxpayer who sells their personal residence on the day the taxpayer reaches their 55th birthday is considered to be age 55 on the first moment of the day preceding

---

[428] *See* § **8.46** *supra.*

[429] The age and occupancy and ownership requirements apply to sales or exchanges occurring on or after July 26, 1978. For sales or exchanges occurring before July 27, 1978, a taxpayer had to be 65 years of age or older, and own and occupy the residence for five years of the eight-year period immediately prior to the date of sale in order to exclude from gross income up to $35,000 of the adjusted sales price. For sales or exchanges of a principal residence occurring on or after July 26, 1978, and before July 20, 1981, up to $100,000 of gain could be excluded from gross income. For sales or exchanges of a principal residence occurring after July 20, 1981, the amount of gain excludable from gross income has been increased to $125,000. The above amounts are halved for married individuals who file separate returns.

[430] *See* n. **356**, *supra*, and n. **411**. *See* text at n. **430**, *infra*.

[431] I.R.C. § 121(a)(1); Treas. Reg. § 1.121-1(a)(1).

their 55th birthday.[432] If the date of sale precedes the taxpayer's 55th birthday, I.R.C. § 121 is inapplicable, even if the two events occur in the same taxable year.[433]

D. Ownership and Occupancy

1. [§ 8.129] Generally

Second, the taxpayer must own and occupy the property being sold, as their principal residence, for periods aggregating three years or more during the five-year period ending on the date of the sale or exchange of such property.[434] Thus, the ownership and occupancy test contains a principal residence test and a time period test.

Before discussing the time period test, it is important to note that to qualify for exclusionary treatment under I.R.C. § 121, a taxpayer must dispose of their entire interest, both legal and equitable, in a principal residence. The ownership test requires a present right to possession of the property. Therefore, the sale of a remainder interest will not fall within I.R.C. § 121 because a remainder interest is a postponed right to possession which does not ripen into full and actual possession until the termination of the preceding life estate.[435]

2. [§ 8.130] Principal residence

The principal residence test requires that the taxpayer use the property being sold as their principal residence within the time periods discussed in **§ 8.131** of this chapter. A principal residence, for purposes of I.R.C. § 121, has the same meaning, and includes the same types of property, as under former I.R.C. § 1034.[436] Therefore, whether property qualifies as an individual's principal residence, or what portion of a property so qualifies, depends upon the facts and circumstances in each case.

---

432 Rev. Rul. 77-382, 1977-2 C.B. 51.

433 Rev. Rul. 68-210, 1968-1 C.B. 61.

434 I.R.C. § 121(a)(2); TREAS. REG. § 1.21-1(a)(2). See n. **411**, *supra*, for a discussion of prior law.

435 I.R.S. Priv. Ltr. Rul. 82-46-123 (Aug. 23, 1982), discussed at n. **434**, *infra* with regard to the sale of a life interest.

436 *See* TREAS. REG. § 1.121-3(a); *see* n. **356**, *supra*; *see also* text at **§§ 8.48–8.59**, *supra*. The Internal Revenue Service will not issue an advance ruling or determination letter on whether property qualifies as the taxpayer's principal residence. Rev. Proc. 88-3, § 3.016, 1988-1 C.B. 579. With regard to the sale of vacant land, see I.R.S. Priv. Ltr. Rul. 80-50-079 (Sept. 19, 1980) discussed at n. **308**, *supra*. Gain realized from the sale of land on which the taxpayer's principal residence is located and moving the house to another lot is not excludable from gross income under I.R.C. § 121. Rev. Rul. 83-50, 1983-1 C.B. 41, revoking Rev. Rul. 54-156, 1954-1 C.B. 112 (sale of land adjacent to taxpayer's principal residence and moving house and place of residence to a newly purchased lot qualified the gain realized from the sale for non-recognition treatment under the predecessor of I.R.C. § 1034 to the extent that the selling price of the land exceeded the rest of the new lot and the expenses associated with moving the house). *See* text at nn. **307–309**. *See Ray v. Comm'r*, T.C.M. 1995-23 (sale of principal residence with retention of usufruct interest is not complete sale and does not qualify for § 121 treatment).

When the principal residence test and the time period test (discussed in § **8.131** of this chapter) are read together, it would appear that, unlike I.R.C. § 1034, the property need not be the taxpayer's principal residence on the date of sale.[437]

3. [§ 8.131] Time periods for ownership and occupancy

The time period test requires that the taxpayer both own and use the residence to be sold as the taxpayer's principal residence for three or more aggregate years during the five-year period ending on the date of sale.[438] The three-year aggregate time period test is met by owning and using the principal residence for 36 full months, or 1,095 days, during the five-year period.[439] The three year use test includes, as periods of use, short temporary absences, such as vacations, even if during such vacations the taxpayer rents the residence to a third party.[440] For example, if I. M. Fine owns and uses a residence for five years, and rents it for 20 months immediately prior to sale, the three-year ownership-and-use test is met.[441] Where, however, the taxpayer rents the residence as their principal residence for five years, but only owns it for two years prior to the date of sale, I.R.C. § 121 does not apply since the three year ownership test is not met.[442] The same result is reached if the taxpayer owns the residence for five years but only uses it for two years prior to the date of sale, since the three years use test is not met.[443] Thus, the ownership and use tests may be met during different three-year periods as long as both tests are met during the five-year period ending on the date of sale.[444] Where the ownership and use tests are met for only part of the property, I.R.C. § 121 applies only to the gain allocable to the residential

---

437 *See* **§ 8.49**; *see* TREAS. REG. § 1.121-1(d).

438 I.R.C. § 121(a)(2); TREAS. REG. § 1.121-1(a)(2).

439 TREAS. REG. § 1.121-1(c). A "full month" is one that begins on the first day of a month and ends on the last day of that month. A "full year" is one that begins on the first day of a month and ends at 11:59 p.m. on the last day of the eleventh succeeding month. TREAS. REG. § 1.121-1(d) and TREAS. REG. § 1.121-5(b)(2). *See also* Rev. Rul. 79-3, 1979-1 C.B. 143 (The 12-month period referred to in I.R.C. § 337, as in effect prior to the Tax Reform Act of 1986, with respect to a plan of complete liquidation by a corporation, begins on the date the plan is adopted and ends at midnight on the day preceding the corresponding date in the following calendar year. For example, if the plan is adopted on Oct. 17, 1977, the 12-month period ended at midnight of Oct. 16, 1978. If the plan is adopted on the first day of a month, the 12-month period ends at midnight of the last day of the eleventh calendar month following the calendar month in which the plan is adopted. For example, if the plan is adopted on Apr. 1, 1978, the 12-month period ends at midnight of Mar. 31, 1979).

440 Several two-month annual vacations are temporary absences, whereas a one-year sabbatical is not. *Compare* Example (4) of TREAS. REG. § 1.121-1(d) *with* Example (5) of Treas. Reg. § 1.121-1(d).

441 *See* TREAS. REG. § 1.121-1(d). Example (1).

442 TREAS. REG. § 1.121-1(d).

443 TREAS. REG. § 1.121-1(b).

444 See Rev. Rul. 80-172, 1980-2 C.B. 56, where a rental apartment was converted to a condominium. The IRS held that the rental period counted toward the use test. Thus, rental constitutes use for purposes of I.R.C. § 121.

portion of the property.[445] For example, if Dan Stufshirt owns property for the six-year period immediately preceding the date of sale, and during such time he uses 25% of the property as his principal residence and 75% of the property as a law office for a period in excess of two years out of the five years preceding the date of sale of the residence, I.R.C. § 121 applies only to the gain derived from the sale of the residential portion of the premises.[446] On the other hand, if Stufshirt uses a portion of the property as his law office for less than two out of the five years preceding the date of sale, I.R.C. § 121 applies to the gain realized from the sale of the entire property.[447]

4. [§ 8.132] Miscellaneous

The ownership and occupancy rule may be satisfied only by the taxpayer or the taxpayer's spouse. However, there are two exceptions to the ownership and occupancy rule. The first exception is a limited transitional rule which provides that an individual who satisfies the age, ownership, and occupancy requirement under the law in effect prior to the Revenue Act of 1978 (the "1978 Act") (relating to taxpayers 65 years of age or older who owned and used the residence as a principal resident for five or more aggregate years during the eight-year period ending on the date of sale) had until July 26, 1981, to qualify for the exclusion under the ownership and occupancy test established by the 1978 Act or the law in effect prior to the 1978 Act.[448] Thus, a taxpayer who is age 65 or older, and who sold or exchanged their personal residence before July 26, 1981, can elect to apply the five-out-of-eight-year test under the law in effect prior to the 1978 Act, rather than the three-out-of-five-year test under the law established by the 1978 Act, if such election qualifies them for the benefits of income exclusion.

The second exception provides that if the basis of the property sold or exchanged is determined, in whole or in part, under I.R.C. § 1033(b) (relating to the basis of property acquired through involuntary conversion) then the holding and use period of the condemned or involuntarily converted residence is tacked to that of a replacement residence for purposes of meeting the three-out-of-five-year rule, and thus having gain on the sale of the replacement property qualify for income exclusion treatment under I.R.C. § 121.[449]Otherwise, no tacking of holding periods is allowed, even if the residence sold was acquired with proceeds rolled over from the sale of another residence.

---

445 I.R.C. § 121(d)(5); TREAS. REG. § 1.121-5(e).

446 TREAS. REG. § 1.121-5(e)(1).

447 *Cf.* TREAS. REG. § 1.121-5(e)(2). Taxpayer A, an attorney, uses a portion of the property constituting their principal residence as a law office for a period in excess of two years out of the five years preceding the sale of such residence. Accordingly, I.R.C. § 121 does not apply with respect to so much of the gain on the sale of the property as is allocable to the portion of the property used as a law office.

448 Revenue Act 1978, 26 U.S.C. § 404(d) (1978).

449 I.R.C. § 121(d)(8). *See* **§ 8.136** of this chapter.

E. [§ 8.133] Sale

The third test requires that the principal residence be sold or exchanged in the manner previously discussed in **§ 8.95** of this chapter.[450] A sale or exchange of a residence also includes the destruction, theft, seizure, requisition, or condemnation of such residence.[451] However, retention of a life estate by the taxpayer bars the availability of I.R.C. § 121 because to take advantage of I.R.C. § 121 there must be a disposition of the residence; i.e., a complete divestiture.[452]The way around this problem is for the taxpayer to retain possession under a bona fide lease at a fair rent.

F. Marital Status

1. [§ 8.134] Generally

To qualify for I.R.C. § 121 treatment, the taxpayer may be either single or married. There may, however, be an advantage to the taxpayer if the taxpayer is married and otherwise meets the tests of I.R.C. § 121, inasmuch as either spouse may satisfy the age, ownership, and use tests, in which case the other spouse is treated as also meeting the tests of I.R.C. § 121.[453]

2. [§ 8.135] Tests

For a married couple to be treated as a single taxpayer and thereby jointly satisfy the age, ownership, and use tests, as of the date of sale, they must, as of such date, hold title to the property as joint tenants, tenants by the entirety, or community property;[454] file a joint return for the taxable year in which the residence is sold; and one of the spouses must satisfy entirely the age, ownership, and use tests.[455] For example, if, as of

---

450 *See* text at nn. **288–292**, *supra*.

451 I.R.C. § 121(d)(4); Treas. Reg. § 1.121-3(b).

452 *See* I.R.S. Priv. Ltr. Rul. 80-29-088 (Apr. 25, 1980) (Sale of remainder interest is not a sale for purposes of I.R.C. § 121); *see also O'Barr v. Comm'r*, 44 T.C. 501, 503 (1965). *See* text at n. **307**, *supra*.

453 I.R.C. § 121(d)(1); Treas. Reg. § 1.121-5(a)(1). *See also* the text at nn. **451–454**, *infra*.

454 Holding property as tenants in common does not satisfy this requirement. If property is held as tenants in common, each spouse must meet the tests of I.R.C. § 121 separately in order to exclude their share of gain realized.

455 I.R.C. § 121(d)(1)(A)–(C); *see also* Treas. Reg. § 1.121-5(a)(2). *See* I.R.S. Priv. Ltr. Rul. 83-52-023 (Sept. 26, 1983) and I.R.S. Priv. Ltr. Rul. 84-20-011 (Feb. 9, 1984). In 1983 B was 48 years old. B had purchased a residence in 1969 which was continually occupied as B's principal residence. A was 55 years old. In 1983 B conveyed the residence to A and B as joint tenants. The IRS held that a sale of the residence in 1983 or 1984 would not qualify for the one-time exclusionary treatment provided by I.R.C. § 121 because B only met the ownership and use tests and not the age test. Although A met the age test, the IRS held that the requirements of I.R.C. § 121 cannot be met separately the spouses and then combined. Thus, for the sale to qualify for I.R.C. § 121 treatment, the parties will have to wait either three years until A has owned and used the property for three years or seven years until B has reached age 55.

the date of sale, Pete and Molly Goldfish, husband and wife, own property as tenants by the entirety which they used as their principal residence for the last three years, they file a joint return for the year of sale, and, at the time of the sale, Pete is 60 years of age but Molly is only 50, Molly is considered to have satisfied the age, ownership, and use tests, inasmuch as Pete has satisfied such tests, and I.R.C. § 121 is applicable. If, however, Pete satisfies only the age test and Molly satisfies the ownership and use tests, I.R.C. § 121 would not apply. The unlimited Federal gift tax marital deduction enacted by ERTA might be utilized to get title into joint names to help meet these tests.

3. [§ 8.136] Date of determination

A determination of whether a taxpayer is married is made as of the date of the sale or exchange.[456] An individual who, on the date of sale, is legally separated from their spouse under a decree of divorce or separate maintenance is not considered married on such date for purposes of I.R.C. § 121.[457] A decree of divorce includes a decree *a mensa et thoro* or a decree *a vinculo matrimonii.*[458] Taxpayers who live separate and apart under a written separation agreement are considered married for purposes of I.R.C. § 121.

If, within the same taxable year, an individual sells a principal residence and subsequently marries the taxpayer and if, for that year, the couple files a joint return in connection with which the individual makes a I.R.C. § 121 election, the taxpayer is not required to join in the individual's election under I.R.C. § 121, because they were not married on the date the individual sold their principal residence. Thus, the taxpayer may elect to exclude gain on the sale of their residence.[459]

---

456 I.R.C. § 121(d)(6)(A); TREAS. REG. § 1.121-5(f).

457 I.R.C. § 121(d)(6)(B); TREAS. REG. § 1.121-5(f).

458 I.R.C. § 71(a)(1); Rev. Rul. 67-442, 1967-2, C.B. 65. *See* § **8.103** of this chapter. *See* n. **322**, *supra*.

459 TREAS. REG. § 1.121-2(b)(2) ***Example 1***—While A and B are married, A sells his separately-owned residence and makes an election under I.R.C. § 121(a) in respect of such sale. Pursuant to the requirement of I.R.C. § 121(c), B joins in such election. Subsequently, A and B are divorced and B married C. While B and C are married, C sells his residence. C is not entitled to make an election under I.R.C. § 121(a) since an election by B, his spouse, is in effect. It does not matter that B obtained no personal benefit from her election. ***Example 2***—The facts are the same as in example (1) except that after the sale of C's residence, A and B, pursuant to the provisions of Treas. Reg. § 1.121-4(c), revoke their election. B and C, subject to the other provisions of this section, may then make an election with respect to any gain realized on the sale of C's residence. ***Example 3***—The facts are the same as in example (1) except that C marries B after C sells his residence but before he makes an election under I.R.C. § 121(a) with respect to any gain realized on such sale. C, if there is not in effect an election made by him under I.R.C. § 121(a) with respect to a prior sale, may make an election with respect to his sale since B does not have to join with him in such election. (In the case of a sale of property jointly held by husband and wife, see TREAS. REG. § 1.121-5(a). In Rev. Rul. 87-104, 1987-2 C.B. 45, A sold

4. [§ 8.137] Deceased spouse

Property of a deceased spouse may also qualify for I.R.C. § 121 exclusionary treatment where it is sold by the surviving spouse. The surviving spouse is constructively treated as satisfying the ownership and use tests if the following tests are met: the surviving spouse meets the age test and is a widow or widower on the date of sale; and the deceased spouse met both the ownership and use tests with respect to such property during the five-year period ending on the date of sale and had made no I.R.C. § 121 election with respect to a prior sale.[460] For example, where Jack and Jill Updehill, husband and wife, are married for two years, Jill dies at age 50 having owned and used the property as her principal residence for at least three years out of the five-year period immediately preceding the date of sale of the property, and Jack is a 60-year-old widower on the date of sale, Jack may elect I.R.C. § 121 treatment and thus exclude from his gross income all or part of the gain realized.

Where unmarried individuals own and use a residence jointly, either as joint tenants or tenants in common, I.R.C. § 121 is applied separately to each.[461] To illustrate, Tom and Mary Jackson, brother and sister, each over 55 years of age, sell a residence which they owned and used jointly as their principal residence for the last five years. The amount of gain excluded from the gross income of each is

---

A's principal residence in January 1984. At the time of the sale, A met the age, ownership and use tests of I.R.C. § 121. In June 1984, A married B. They filed a joint tax return for 1984 and A elected under I.R.C. § 121 to exclude from gross income the gain from the sale of A's residence. B did not joint in A's election. During the marriage, A and B lived in a residence owned by B. A died in 1986 and soon thereafter B sold that residence. At the time of the sale, B met the age, ownership, and use tests of I.R.C. § 121. On B's 1986 income tax return, B elected under I.R.C. § 121 to exclude from gross income the gain from the sale of B's residence. B had never previously made, or joined in, such an election. The IRS first held that B was not required to join in A's election since they were not married on the date A sold the residence. The IRS then held that since B had never made an election, B could make an election under I.R.C. § 121. *See also* **§ 8.136 of** this chapter. Query*: If* B had mistakenly joined A in making the election with respect to A's residence, would that preclude B from making an election with respect to B's residence? Example (3) of Treas. Reg. § 1.121-2(b)(2) provides that a spouse's ineligibility to make or join in an election is not a bar to an election by the taxpayer because the spouse does not have to join with the taxpayer in the election. Thus, a mistaken election by B should not preclude B from making an election with respect to B's residence.

460 I.R.C. § 121(d)(2); TREAS. REG. § 1.121-5(b)(1).

461 Rev. Rul. 67-235, 1967-2 C.B. 79. *See also* Rev. Rul. 67-234, 1967-2 C.B. 78 (An unmarried individual who holds title to their residence as a joint tenant or tenant in common and who meets the age, use and holding requirements of I.R.C. § 121 is entitled to exclude from gross income, subject to the limitations of I.R.C. § 121, that portion of the gain which is attributable to their undivided interest in the residence at the time of the sale).

computed separately for Tom and Mary. The failure of either Tom or Mary to meet the age, use, and ownership tests will not disqualify the other from exclusionary treatment.

Where a residence is owned by a trust or estate, gain realized by the trust or estate is not excludable by the trust or estate under I.R.C. § 121 since an entity cannot meet the age, ownership, or occupancy tests.[462] If the beneficiary of a testamentary marital trust is considered the owner of trust under I.R.C. § 678, and if the beneficiary meets the age and occupancy tests, the beneficiary can elect to exclude gain realized from the sale of the residence by the trust.[463] Also, if a taxpayer transfers the taxpayer's principal residence to a revocable trust, the taxpayer can elect I.R.C. § 121 treatment upon the sale of the residence by the trust.[464]

G. [§ 8.138] Limitations

There are two limitations which are quite important. First, only up to $125,000 ($62,500 in the case of married taxpayers filing separate returns) of gain realized

---

462 Rev. Rul. 54-583, 1954-2 C.B. 158.

463 Rev. Rul. 85-45, 1985-1 C.B. 183. See also I.R.S. Priv. Ltr. Rul. 93-023 (Feb. 4, 1984) and I.R.S. Priv. Ltr. Rul. 91-18-017 (Feb. 1, 1991), where the service ruled that a home owned by a grantor trust is considered owned by the grantor. Therefore, a sale by a trust is considered a sale by the grantor. Accordingly, if the other tests of § 121 are met, the grantor can claim the benefits of the exclusion under § 121. But see, *In re Mehr*, 71 A.F.T.R.2d 93-921 (Bankr. Ct. N.J. 1993) where the court held that § 121 did not apply to a bankruptcy estate.

464 I.R.S. Priv. Ltr. Rul. 85-49-046 (Sept. 11, 1985) (Sale of a life interest in a principal residence is not a "sale" for purposes of I.R.C. § 121 because the life tenant does not own the entire interest in the principal residence). See also the text at nn. **417**, **434**, *supra* with regard to the sale of a remainder interest. But see, Rev. Rul. 84-43, 1984-1 C.B. 27, where the IRS held that where a taxpayer (60 years of age) sold a life estate in a residence that the taxpayer had used as a principal residence for 19 years, the taxpayer could exclude from gross income up to $125,000 of gain realized from sale of their life estate in their principal residence. *Compare* I.R.S. Priv. Ltr. Rul. 82-46-123 (Aug. 23, 1982). The facts of Rev. Rul. 84-43 indicate that the life estate of the taxpayer was the taxpayer's entire interest in the residence, whereas in I.R.S. Priv. Ltr. Rul. 82-46-123, the IRS concluded that the life estate did not constitute an entire interest in a residence. Thus, the IRS has apparently revoked its prior position under I.R.S. Priv. Ltr. Rul. 82-46-123. Rev. Rul. 84-43 does not discuss whether a remainder interest constitutes an entire interest in property. In addition, the IRS held that the sale of a principal residence by a testamentary marital trust is deemed a sale by the beneficiary of the trust because the beneficiary is treated as the owner of the trust under I.R.C. §§ 671 and 678 and hence as the owner of the residence. Thus, the beneficiary is entitled to a one time exclusion of gain from the sale of the residence by the trust. The ruling relies upon Rev. Rul. 66-159, 1966-1 C.B. 162, discussed at n. **269**, *supra*. Rev. Rul. 84-43 and Rev. Rul. 85-45 appear to evince a policy of the IRS to not place an undesirable burden on elderly taxpayers by not requiring absolute ownership in order to qualify for I.R.C. § 121 exclusionary treatment.

may be excluded from gross income.[465] Any gain in excess of $125,000 is subject to Federal income taxation.[466] Moreover, where the sales price is paid over a period of time, the amount of gain not excludable from gross income may be reported under the installment method of reporting.[467] Further, no amount of any gain realized on the sale of the principal residence, whether or not excluded, is considered an item of tax preference subject to the minimum tax.[468]

Second, the taxpayer and the taxpayer's spouse are allowed only one lifetime election to exclude gain from gross income.[469] Thus, the taxpayer may not elect to exclude from gross income gain realized from the sale of their principal residence if, at the time the taxpayer makes the election, another election is in effect by either the taxpayer or the taxpayer's spouse with respect to the sale of another principal residence.[470] In determining whether an election is in effect by a spouse, it is irrelevant whether the spouse was married to the taxpayer at the time of a prior sale or exchange.[471] Hence, where the taxpayer's spouse has previously elected the benefits of I.R.C. § 121 and then marries the taxpayer, the taxpayer will not qualify for I.R.C. § 121 exclusionary treatment. In addition, if spouses make an election during marriage, and subsequently become divorced, no further election is available to either of them. Also, if a single taxpayer makes the election and then marries, no further election is allowed to the married couple. Thus, it would appear to be advisable that where both individuals own residences that are about to be sold, and neither has previously elected I.R.C. § 121 exclusionary treatment, they should each sell their residence before they marry so that together they have two exclusions.[472]

H. Election Requirements

1. [§ 8.139] Election or revocation—Generally

Unlike I.R.C. § 1034, which is mandatory, I.R.C. § 121 is elective.[473] The election must be made or revoked by the taxpayer at any time before expiration of the

---

465 I.R.C. § 121(b); TREAS. REG. § 1.121-2(a). The $125,000 limitation applies to sales or exchanges occurring after July 20, 1981. For sales or exchanges occurring on or after July 26, 1978, and before July 20, 1981, the maximum amount excludable was $100,000. *See* n. **331**, *supra*.

466 I.R.C. § 121(b); Treas. Reg. § 1.121-2(a). *See also* the discussion at n. **165**, *supra*.

467 I.R.C. § 453; Rev. Rul. 80-249, 1980-2 C.B. 166.

468 I.R.C. § 57(a)(9)(D).

469 I.R.C. § 121(b)(2).

470 I.R.C. § 121(b)(2); Treas. Reg. § 1.121-2(b)(1)(ii).

471 I.R.C. § 121(b)(2); Treas. Reg. § 1.121-2(b)(1)(ii).

472 Treas. Reg. § 1.121-2(b)(2).

473 I.R.C. § 121(a).

period for making a claim for refund or credit of Federal income tax for the taxable year in which the sale or exchange occurred.[474] This period is generally three years from the date the return is filed, or two years from the date the tax is paid, whichever is later.[475]

2. [§ 8.140] *Joint elections and revocations—Married taxpayers*

If the taxpayer is married at the time of a sale, the taxpayer's spouse, as of the date of sale, must join in the election or revocation.[476] Joint elections and revocations are required even though the taxpayer and the taxpayer's spouse owned the residence separately, filed separate returns, or the spouse not owning an interest in the residence had not lived in it for the required period before the sale or exchange.[477] A deceased spouse's estate may also make the election or revocation. Thus, if one spouse dies after the date of sale, but before expiration of the time for making the election, and if an election was not made by the husband and wife, the deceased spouse's personal representative must join with the surviving spouse in making such election.[478] For example, if the wife dies six months after the sale of a residence, and if she leaves a will that appoints the Third National Bank as her personal representative, to make a valid election or revocation of election, the husband must have the Bank join with him in making the election or revocation. If no personal representative of the deceased spouse has been appointed at or prior to the time for the making of the election, the surviving spouse is deemed the personal representative of the deceased spouse's estate.[479] Thus, the death of one spouse is no bar to the election or revocation of I.R.C. § 121.

3. [§ 8.141] *Election made by personal representative*

An election may be made by a personal representative, even if the taxpayer is unmarried, where the taxpayer dies subsequent to execution of a sales contract but prior to closing the sale.[480] The election is made on the decedent's final federal income tax return.[481] Any gain in excess of the amount excludable under I.R.C. § 121 is income in respect of a decedent within the meaning of I.R.C. § 691(a).[482] If the personal representative does not make the election, the proceeds derived from

---

474 I.R.C. § 121(c); TREAS. REG. § 1.121-4(a).

475 I.R.C. § 6651(a).

476 I.R.C. § 121(c); TREAS. REG. § 1.121-4(a)(1) and (2).

477 TREAS. REG. § 1.121-4.

478 TREAS. REG. § 1.121-4(a).

479 *Id.*

480 Rev. Rul. 82-4, 1982-1 C.B. 99, *revoking* Rev. Rul. 70-459, 1970-2 C.B. 22.

481 *Id.*

482 *Id.*; *see also* Rev. Rul. 78-32, 1978-1 C.B. 198.

the sale of the residence are income in respect of a decedent[483] and the basis of the property in the hands of the estate is determined by reference to the basis of the property in the hands of the decedent immediately prior to the decedent's death (i.e., carryover basis).[484]

An election may not be made by a personal representative if the taxpayer has not entered into an executory contract prior to the date of the taxpayer's death. In any event, the making of such an election would appear to be unnecessary because in such case the basis of the property in the hands of the estate would be its fair market value determined on the date of death (or on the alternate valuation date if the alternate valuation date is employed). Thus, a disposition by the estate immediately subsequent to the death of the taxpayer should produce little, if any, gain. But even if some gain is realized by the estate, such gain would not constitute income in respect of a decedent.

4. [§ 8.142] Joint ownership—Unmarried taxpayers

If the residence is owned jointly by taxpayers who are not married, each owner who meets the ownership and occupancy tests and desires to exclude gain from gross income may file an election. The fact that one owner qualifies for exclusionary treatment does not qualify the other owner for exclusionary treatment. Moreover, an election by one owner does not prevent other owners, whether qualifying or not, from making an election in the future. For example, Dick and Jane Reader, a brother and sister, each own a one-half interest, as joint tenants, in their residence. Dick, but not Jane, meets the age, ownership, and occupancy tests. The adjusted basis of the residence is $56,000, and they sell it for $80,000. Dick realizes gain of $12,000, which he may elect to exclude from his gross income. Jane, however, may not exclude any gain realized from her gross income under I.R.C. § 121.

5. [§ 8.143] Election or revocation—How made

The election or revocation may be made on Form 2119[485] and attached to the taxpayer's Form 1040. TREAS. REG. § 1.121-4(b) and (c) should be consulted,

---

[483] Rev. Rul. 82-4, 1982-1 C.B. 99, *revoking* Rev. Rul. 70-459, 1970-2 C.B. 22; *see also* Rev. Rul. 78-32, 1978-1 C.B. 198.

[484] Rev. Rul. 82-4, 1982-1 C.B. 99, *revoking* Rev. Rul. 70-459, 1970-2 C.B. 22.

[485] See **§ 8.150 and 8.151** of this chapter for a sample of IRS Form 2119 and the accompanying instructions.

however, since it details the manner of making and revoking the election.[486] The failure to make a timely election or revocation may be fatal.[487]

I. [§ 8.144] Computation of Gain Excluded from Gross Income

The components used to compute the amount of gain to be excluded from the taxpayer's gross income under I.R.C. § 121 are the same as steps one, two and four used to compute the gain to be deferred from taxation under former I.R.C. § 1034.[488] The only limitation is that only up to $125,000 ($62,500 for married taxpayers filing separate returns) of the gain realized may be excluded from gross income. Where

---

486 TREAS. REG. § 1.121-4(b) and (c) for manner of making and revoking the election ***(b) Manner of making elections.*** The election under I.R.C. § 121(a) shall be made in a statement signed by the taxpayer and (where required) by their spouse and attached to the taxpayer's income tax return, when filed, for the taxable year during which the sale or exchange of their residence occurs. The statement shall indicate that the taxpayer elects to exclude from their gross income for such year so much of the gain realized on such sale or exchange as may be excluded under I.R.C. § 121. The statement shall also show (1) the adjusted basis of the residence as of the date of disposition; (2) the date of its acquisition; (3) the date of its disposition; (4) the names and social security numbers of the owners of the residence as of the date of sale, the form of such ownership, and the age and marital status (as determined under Treas. Reg. § 1.121-5(a)) of such owner or owners at the time of the sale; (5) the duration of any absences (other than vacation or other seasonal absence) by such owner or owners during the five years (eight years under the transitional rule) preceding the sale; and (6) whether any such owner or owners have previously made an election under I.R.C. § 121(a), the date of such election, the taxable year with respect to which such election was made, the district director with whom such election was filed, and, if such election has been revoked, the date of such revocation. ***(c) Manner of revoking election.*** The revocation of an election under I.R.C. § 121(a) shall be made by the taxpayer by filing a signed statement showing their name and social security number and indicating that the taxpayer revokes the election they made under I.R.C. § 121(a). The statement shall also show the taxable year of the taxpayer for which such election was made. The statement shall be signed by the taxpayer and (where required) by their spouse or their personal representatives and filed with either the Internal Revenue Service Center with which the election was filed, the Internal Revenue Service Center nearest the taxpayer at the time the statement is filed, or the taxpayer's local Internal Revenue office. In addition, if, at the time the statement is filed, the statutory period for assessment of a deficiency for the taxable year for which the election was made will expire within one year, then, the revocation is not effective unless the taxpayer also consents, in writing, that the statutory period for assessment of any deficiency (to the extent that such deficiency is attributable to the revocation of the election) shall not expire before the expiration of one year after the date the statement was filed with the district director. Such consent must be filed prior to the date of the expiration of the statutory period for assessment for the taxable year for which the election was made.

487 See *Robarts v. Commissioner*, 103 T.C. 72 (1994), *aff'd without op.*, 56 F.3d 1390 (11th Cir. 1995), in which Taxpayer sold residence number one and elected § 121. Taxpayer then purchased a new residence which she sold 10 years later. She again attempted to elect § 121 treatment, but was denied, because she had elected it for house number one and did not timely revoke that election.

488 *See* **§ 8.116**.

the gain realized exceeds $125,000, the excess is subject to the regular income tax in the same manner as other income.[489]

> ***Example***—Assume Gerry Atric, who meets all of the tests under I.R.C. § 121, sells her residence for $120,000 and that she has a basis in the residence of $60,000. If she makes an election under I.R.C. § 121, her entire gain realized of $60,000 is excluded from her gross income. The same result is achieved so long as the gain realized is $125,000 or less.

Ms. Atric may also claim the benefits of both exclusionary treatment under I.R.C. § 121 and rollover treatment under I.R.C. § 1034 with regard to any gain derived from the sale of her personal residence. In applying former I.R.C. § 1034, the amount realized from the sale or exchange of a personal residence is treated as being the amount determined without regard to I.R.C. § 121, reduced by the amount of gain excluded from gross income pursuant to an election made under I.R.C. § 121.[490] Thus, the amount that must be invested in a new residence to fully satisfy former I.R.C. § 1034 is reduced by the amount of gain excluded from the taxpayer's gross income as a result of an election made under I.R.C. § 121. A sample of Gerry Atric's completed I.R.S. Form 2119 is set forth in § **8.151** of this chapter.

The following example illustrates the interrelationship between I.R.C. §§ 121 and 1034.

> ***Example***—Assume Jo Ann Mikva, who meets all of the tests under I.R.C. § 121, takes a plunge and sells her personal residence for $207,000, incurring fixing-up expenses of $2,000. She has a basis in the residence of $65,000. Ms. Mikva's amount realized is $205,000 (sales price $207,000 less sales expenses $2,000). Her gain realized from the sale is $140,000 (amount realized of $205,000 less adjusted basis of $65,000), of which $125,000 is excluded from gross income if she makes the election under I.R.C. § 121. The remaining $15,000 of gain realized is recognized and would be included in her gross income.

However, Ms. Mikva may use I.R.C. § 1034 to defer all or part of the $15,000 of realized gain. To determine the adjusted sales price for purposes of I.R.C. § 1034, Ms. Mikva's amount realized of $205,000 is reduced by the sum of the fixing-up expenses of $2,000 and the $125,000 excluded under I.R.C. § 121. Thus, Ms. Mikva's adjusted sales price for purposes of I.R.C. § 1034 is $78,000 ($205,000—$125,000—$2,000). If Ms. Mikva purchases a new principal residence within the replacement period which costs at least $78,000, the full $15,000

---

489 *See* n. **312**, *supra*.

490 I.R.C. § 121(d)(7); TREAS. REG. § 1.121-5(g)(1).

remaining gain realized will be deferred. If her new principal residence costs less than $78,000, a portion of the $15,000 of the remaining gain realized will be subject to taxation.

J. [§ 8.145] Comparison of I.R.C. § 1034 and § 121

The following compares the tax deferral provision of I.R.C. § 1034 and the exclusion from gross income provision of I.R.C. § 121.

Sale By Any Taxpayer I.R.C. §1034	Sale By Taxpayer 55 Or Over I.R.C. §121
Mandatory	Elective
Temporary deferral from gross income	Permanent exclusion from taxation
Amount deferred is excess of gain realized over gain recognized	Amount excluded cannot exceed $125,000 of gain realized
Must purchase replacement residence	Not required to purchase replacement residence
Old residence must be principal residence on date of sale	Old residence need not be principal residence on date of sale
Age irrelevant	Must be 55 years or over prior to date of sale
Must own and use property as principal residence and use	No definite time period requirement for ownership for three or more of the five years immediately preceding sales date
Can use this provision more than once per lifetime	One lifetime exclusion per taxpayer (and spouse)

V. FORECLOSURE OF MORTGAGE TAKEN BACK BY SELLER

A. [§ 8.146] Generally

The residential real estate market, at the time of earlier editions of this book, under the rubric of "creative financing," reflected the impact of inflated sales prices and historic levels of interest rates with many sales being effected only by the seller taking back the buyer's debt instrument, secured by the home, for a major portion of the purchase price. Typically, after a few years of monthly payments on a long term amortization schedule the entire outstanding balance of the debt becomes due. Where the beneficiaries of creative financing are not able to refinance this debt when the balloon payment comes due the mortgagee-seller will have to extend the payment schedule or repossess the home.

It is possible that the value of the home will have increased between the time of the initial sale and the repossession. In this situation the taxpayer would realize a taxable gain and not have cash from the transaction with which to pay the tax. Because of this, and to provide a uniform method of reporting the gain regardless of the method of accounting used to report the initial sale, Congress enacted I.R.C. § 1038 to provide a mandatory, mechanical reporting scheme applicable to repossessions of real property by the seller under purchase money mortgages in partial or complete satisfaction of the debt.[491] As stated in the Committee Report,[492] the taxpayer is not in a better position after the repossession than before the initial sale, except for payments received upon the sale price. The premise of I.R.C. § 1038 is that repossession represents a nullification of the initial transaction and not a second sale back to the seller. Under I.R.C. § 1038, the gain recognized at the time of repossession is measured by payments received by the seller pursuant to the initial sale and not by the property's fair market value at time of repossession. I.R.C. § 1038 also denies the recognition of any loss occasioned by the repossession. (Loss upon the sale of a personal residence or any portion thereof is not recognized in any event.) The gain or loss not recognized under operation of I.R.C. § 1038 is deferred by adjustments to the property's basis, and this gain or loss is recognized when the property is sold another time. Special provision is made when the repossession is of the seller-mortgagee's former principal residence and the exclusion or rollover provisions were used.

B. [§ 8.147] Applicability of I.R.C. § 1038

I.R.C. § 1038 applies whether the initial sale gave rise to a gain or loss and no matter what accounting method or what character of gain or loss was realized on the initial sale.[493] These provisions apply to land installment sales as well as transactions in which title passes; but they do not apply to involuntary conversions of property by destruction, condemnation, etc., or to sale of stock in a cooperative housing corporation.[494] I.R.C. § 1038 is intended to apply when the reacquisition is pursuant to enforcement of the seller-mortgagee's security rights, and if payment is made by the seller-mortgagee to the buyer-mortgagor (or they assume indebtedness incurred after the initial sale) when the buyer is not in default, these provisions may not apply.[495]

VI. DISCHARGE OF DEBT ON FORECLOSURE OF MORTGAGE OR DEED IN LIEU OF FORECLOSURE

A. [§ 8.148] Generally

As a consequence of the mortgage crisis that started to appear in 2007, Congress sought to ameliorate the impact of the cancellation of indebtedness rules under § 108 of the Code, enacting the Mortgage Forgiveness Debt Relief Act of 2007 § 2.[496]

---

491 *See generally* Martin Burke and Michael Friel, *Reacquisition of Seller-Financed Real Property: Evaluating Section 1038,* 13 REV. OF TAX'N OF INDIVIDUALS 107 (1989).

492 S. Rep. No. 88-1361 (1964), *reprinted in* 1964-2 C.B. 828, 831.

493 TREAS. REG. § 1.1038-1(a)(1).

494 TREAS. REG. § 1.1038-1(a)(2).

495 TREAS. REG. § 1.1038-1(a)(3)(i).

496 Mortgage Forgiveness Debt Relief Act of 2007, Pub. L. No. 110-142, § 2, 121 Stat. 1803 (2007).

Codified at § 108(h), the statute provides that gross income does not include qualified principal residence indebtedness discharged on or after Jan. 1, 2007,[497] and before Jan. 1, 2010.[498] The exclusion, as enacted, applied to up to $2,000,000, or $1,000,000 in the case of a married individual filing a separate tax return.[499] The basis of the taxpayer's principal residence is reduced by the amount excluded from gross income.[500]

After the Mortgage Forgiveness Debt Relief Act of 2007, the sunset date for qualified principal residence indebtedness treatment was extended multiple times, most recently until January 1, 2026 by Section 114 of the Taxpayer Certainty and Disaster Tax Relief Act Of 2020.[501] This legislation reduced the exclusion threshold from $2,000,000 (or $1,000,000 for a married taxpayer filing a separate return) to $750,000 (or $375,000 for a married taxpayer filing a separate return).[502]

This exclusion is reported on Form 982, Reduction of Tax Attributes Due to Discharge of Indebtedness.[503] Form 982 must be filed with the taxpayer's federal income tax return for the year of discharge.[504]

The provision excludes from the gross income of a taxpayer any discharge of indebtedness income by reason of a discharge (in whole or in part) of qualified principal residence indebtedness. Qualified principal residence indebtedness means acquisition indebtedness (within the meaning of § 163(h)(3)(B) subject to a dollar limitation) with respect to the taxpayer's principal residence.[505] Acquisition indebtedness with respect to a principal residence generally means indebtedness which is incurred in the acquisition, construction, or substantial improvement of the principal residence of the individual and is secured by the residence. It also includes refinancing of such indebtedness to the extent the amount of the refinancing does not exceed the amount of the refinanced indebtedness. For these purposes the term "principal residence" has the same meaning as under section 121 of the Code.[506]

VII. Appendix

Appendix begins on the next page.

---

497 Mortgage Forgiveness Debt Relief Act § 2(d).
498 Mortgage Forgiveness Debt Relief Act § 2(a).
499 Mortgage Forgiveness Debt Relief Act § 2(b).
500 *Id.*
501 Pub. L. No. 116-260, Div. EE, §114(a).
502 Taxpayer Certainty and Disaster Tax Relief Act of 2020, Pub. L. No. 116-260, Div. EE, §114(b).
503 I.R.S. Form 982 (Rev. Mar. 2018), available at *https://www.irs.gov/pub/irs-pdf/f982.pdf.*
504 Instructions for I.R.S. Form 982 (Rev. Dec. 2021) pg. 1, available at *https://www.irs.gov/pub/irs-pdf/i982.pdf.*
505 26 U.S.C. § 108(h)(2).
506 26 U.S.C. § 108(h)(5).

1994 Department of the Treasury **Internal Revenue Service**

Instructions for Form 2119

Sale of Your Home

Paperwork Reduction Act Notice

We ask for the information on this form to carry out the Internal Revenue laws of the United States. You are required to give us the information. We need it to ensure that you are complying with these laws and to allow us to figure and collect the right amount of tax.

The time needed to complete and file this form will vary depending on individual circumstances. The estimated average time is:

Recordkeeping	46 min.
Learning about the law or the form	19 min.
Preparing the form	1 hr., 31 min.
Copying, assembling, and sending the form to the IRS	20 min.

If you have comments concerning the accuracy of these time estimates or suggestions for making this form simpler, we would be happy to hear from you. You can write to both the **Internal Revenue Service,** Attention: Tax Forms Committee, PC:FP, Washington, DC 20224; and the **Office of Management and Budget,** Paperwork Reduction Project (1545-0072), Washington, DC 20503. **DO NOT** send this form to either of these offices. Instead, see **When and Where To File** on page 2.

General Instructions

A Change To Note

To figure the amount to enter on line 7 and line 19b, you must subtract seller-paid points from the purchase price of your old and new main home if **either** of the following applies:

1. You bought the home after April 3, 1994, **OR**

2. You bought the home after 1990 but before April 4, 1994, and you deducted the seller-paid points.

For details on points, get **Pub. 936,** Home Mortgage Interest Deduction.

Purpose of Form

Use Form 2119 to report the sale of your main home. If you replaced your main home within the replacement period, also use Form 2119 to postpone paying tax on all or part of the gain. Form 2119 is also used by people who were age 55 or older on the date of sale to elect a one-time exclusion of the gain on the sale.

Caution: *If the home you sold was financed (in whole or in part) from a qualified mortgage credit certificate or the proceeds of a tax-exempt qualified mortgage bond, you may owe additional tax. Get **Form 8828,** Recapture of Federal Mortgage Subsidy, for details.*

Who Must File

You must file Form 2119 with your return for the year in which you sell your main home, even if the sale resulted in a loss, you are electing the one-time exclusion for people age 55 or older, or you are postponing all or part of the gain. There may be other filing requirements as well. See **When and Where To File** on page 2.

Loss on the Sale of Your Home.—You cannot deduct a loss on the sale of your home. However, you must file Form 2119 to report the sale. Complete lines 1 through 8 of Form 2119 and attach it to your return for the year of sale. If you replace your home, the loss has no effect on the basis of your new home.

Additional Information

You may find **Pub. 523,** Selling Your Home, helpful. It has examples of how to complete Form 2119.

Definitions

Adjusted Basis.—This is your basis in the property increased or decreased by certain amounts. For details on how to figure the adjusted basis of the home you sold, see the instructions for line 7 on page 3.

Basis.—If you bought your home, your basis is the purchase price of the home minus certain seller-paid points (see **A Change To Note**). If you acquired your home other than by purchase, such as by gift, inheritance, or trade, or you built your home, see Pub. 523. For a complete discussion of basis, get **Pub. 551,** Basis of Assets.

Date of Sale.—See the instructions for line 1 on page 3.

Main Home.—Your main home is the one you live in most of the time. It can be a house, houseboat, housetrailer, cooperative apartment, condominium, etc.

Replacement Period.—This is the time period during which you must replace your old main home to postpone any of the gain from its sale. It starts 2 years before and ends 2 years after the date of sale. But this period may be longer if you are on active duty in the U.S. Armed Forces for more than 90 days or if you live and work outside the United States. For details, see Pub. 523.

Special Situations

More Than One Owner.—If you owned the old home jointly with a person other than your spouse, you may postpone gain or elect the one-time exclusion only on your ownership interest in the home. For more details, see Pub. 523.

Surviving Spouse.—If your spouse died before the old home was sold and you owned the home jointly with your deceased spouse, you must make a special computation to figure the adjusted basis of the home you sold. For details, see **Inheritance** under **Basis** in Pub. 523.

Divorced or Separated Taxpayers.—If your home was sold in connection with a divorce or separation, see Pub. 523. Also, get **Pub. 504,** Divorced or Separated Individuals.

Condemned Property.—If your old home was condemned for public use, you can choose either to postpone gain under the rules for a condemnation or to treat the transaction as a sale of your home. See Pub. 523. Also, get **Pub. 544,** Sales and Other Dispositions of Assets.

Partial Rental or Business Use of Home.—If part of your old home was rented out or used for business, you may have to report that part of the sale on **Form 4797,** Sales of Business Property. See the instructions for line 3 on page 3.

Installment Sale.—If you provided financing for the buyer of your home, you may be able to choose to report the gain on the sale using the installment method. For details, get **Pub. 537,** Installment Sales. If you qualify and choose to do so, complete Form 2119 first and then complete **Form 6252,** Installment Sale Income. Also, see the instructions for line 15 on page 4. **Do not** report the gain from Form 2119 on Schedule D (Form 1040).

Note: *Be sure to report on Form 1040, line 8a, any interest you received on the note or other financial instrument. If the buyer used the property as a personal residence, be sure you report that buyer's name, social security number, and address on Schedule B (Form 1040).*

Casualty Damage.—If your home was damaged by fire, storm, or other casualty, get **Form 4684,** Casualties and Thefts, and its separate instructions. Also, get **Pub. 547,** Nonbusiness Disasters, Casualties, and Thefts.

Which Parts To Complete

Part I.—All filers must complete Part I.

Part II.—Complete this part only if you qualify for the **One-Time Exclusion for People Age 55 or Older** (see below) and you want to make the election for this sale.

Part III.—Complete line 15 even if you did not take the exclusion in Part II. Complete lines 16 through 23 only if line 15 is more than zero and you answered "Yes" on line 2.

When and Where To File

File Form 2119 with your tax return for the year of sale. If the amount on line 8 of Form 2119 is zero or less, you have no additional filing requirements, even if you replace your home.

Additional Filing Requirements.—If you have not replaced your home but plan to do so within the replacement period (defined on page 1), you will also have to complete a second Form 2119.

• You must file the second Form 2119 by itself if **all three** of the following apply:

1. You planned to replace your home within the replacement period.

2. You later replaced your home within the replacement period.

3. Your taxable gain (line 21 on the second Form 2119) is zero.

If your taxable gain is zero, no tax is due. But you must still file the second form to show that you replaced your home within the replacement period. Enter your name and address, and sign and date the second form. If a joint return was filed for the year of sale, both you and your spouse must sign the second Form 2119. Send the form to the place where you would file your next tax return based on the address where you now live.

• You must file **Form 1040X,** Amended U.S. Individual Income Tax Return, for the year of sale with the second Form 2119 attached if **any** of the following apply:

1. You planned to replace your home when you filed your tax return, you later replaced your home within the replacement period, **and** you had a taxable gain on line 21 of the second Form 2119.

2. You planned to replace your home when you filed your tax return but **did not** do so within the replacement period.

3. You **did not** plan to replace your home when you filed your tax return and included the gain in income, but later you did replace your home within the replacement period.

Report the correct amount of gain from Form 2119 on Schedule D (Form 1040) and attach both forms to Form 1040X. Interest will be charged on any additional tax due. If you are due a refund, any interest will be included with the refund.

Recordkeeping

Keep a copy of Form 2119 (and any documents used to complete it) with your tax return for the year of sale until the statute of limitations runs out for that return. Usually, this is 3 years from the date the return was due or filed, or 2 years from the date the tax was paid, whichever is later. But if you postpone tax on any gain, keep a copy of the Form 2119 (and any documents used to complete it) with your records for the basis of your new home.

One-Time Exclusion for People Age 55 or Older

Generally, you can elect to exclude from your income up to $125,000 ($62,500 if married filing a separate return) of the gain from one sale of any main home you choose. But for sales after July 26, 1978, the exclusion is available only once. To make the election for this sale, complete Part II. You can make the election if **all three** of the following apply:

1. You or your spouse were age 55 or older on the date of sale.

2. Neither you nor your spouse have ever excluded gain on the sale of a home after July 26, 1978.

3. The person who was age 55 or older owned and lived in the home for periods adding up to at least 3 years within the 5-year period ending on the date of sale. But see **Exception for Disabled Individuals** below.

The gain excluded is never taxed. But if the gain is more than the amount excluded, also complete Part III to figure whether the excess gain is included in your income or postponed. If the gain is less than $125,000 ($62,500 if married filing a separate return), the difference **cannot** be excluded on a future sale of another main home. Generally, you can make or revoke the election within 3 years from the due date of your return (including extensions) for the year of sale. To do so, file Form 1040X with Form 2119 attached. For more details, see Pub. 523.

Exception for Disabled Individuals.—If you meet this exception, you are treated as having lived in the home sold during any time that you lived in a facility such as a nursing home. The facility must be licensed by a state or political subdivision to care for people with your condition. You meet this exception if, during the 5-year period ending on the date of sale—

• You became physically or mentally unable to care for yourself, and

• You owned and lived in your home as your main home for a total of at least 1 year.

Married Taxpayers.—If you and your spouse owned the property jointly and file a joint return, only one of you must meet the age, ownership, and use tests to be able to make the election. If you did not own the property jointly, the spouse who owned the property must meet these tests.

If you were married at the time of sale, both you and your spouse must agree to exclude the gain. If you do not file a joint return with that spouse, your spouse must agree to exclude the gain by signing a statement saying, "I agree to the Part II election." The statement and signature may be made on a separate sheet or in the bottom margin of Form 2119.

If you sell a home while you are married and one spouse already made the election prior to the marriage, neither of you can exclude gain on the sale.

The election to exclude gain does not apply separately to you and your spouse. If you elect to exclude gain during marriage and later divorce, neither of you can make the election again.

Postponing Gain

If you buy or build another main home and move into it within the replacement period (defined on page 1), you must postpone all or part of the gain in most cases. The amount of gain postponed is shown on line 22.

If one spouse dies after the old home is sold and before the new home is bought, the gain from the sale of the old home is postponed if the above requirements are met, the spouses were married on the date of death, and the surviving spouse uses the new home as his or her main home. This rule applies whether the title of the old home is in one spouse's name or is held jointly. For more details, see Pub. 523.

If you bought more than one main home during the replacement period, only the last one you bought qualifies as your new main home for postponing gain. If you sold more than one main home during the replacement period, any sale after the first one does not qualify for postponing gain. But these rules do not apply if you sold your home because of a job change that qualifies for a moving expense deduction. If this is the case, file a Form 2119 for each sale, for the year of the sale, and attach an explanation for each sale (except the first) to Form 2119. For details on moving expenses, get **Pub. 521,** Moving Expenses.

Applying Separate Gain to Basis of New Home.—If you are married and you or your spouse owned the old home separately but own the new home jointly, you and your spouse may elect to divide the gain and the adjusted basis. If you owned the old home jointly but you now own new homes separately, you may elect to divide the gain to be postponed. In either situation, you both must:

1. Use the old and new homes as your main homes, and

2. Sign a statement that says, "We agree to reduce the basis of the new home(s) by the gain from selling the old home." This statement can be made in the bottom margin of Form 2119 or on an attached sheet.

If you both do not meet these two requirements, you must report the gain in the regular way without allocation. For more details and examples, see **Allocation between you and your spouse** under **New Home** in Pub. 523.

Page 2

Specific Instructions

Line 1

Enter the date of sale. If you received a **Form 1099-S,** Proceeds From Real Estate Transactions, the date should be shown in box 1. If you didn't receive a Form 1099-S, the date of sale is the earlier of **(a)** the date the title transferred or **(b)** the date the economic burdens and benefits of ownership shifted to the buyer.

Line 3

Old Home.—If part of your old main home was rented out or used for business and in the year of sale you **were not** entitled to deduct expenses for the part that was rented or used for business, report the entire sale on Form 2119.

If you **were** entitled to deduct expenses in the year of sale for the part that was rented or used for business, treat the sale as two separate sales. Report on Form 4797 the part of the sale that applies to the rental or business use. Report on Form 2119 only the part of the sale that represents your main home. You must allocate between Forms 2119 and 4797 the sales price, expenses of sale, and the adjusted basis of the property sold. Attach a statement showing the total selling price of the property and the method used to allocate the amounts between the two forms.

You cannot postpone the part of the gain that is reported on Form 4797. But you may be able to take the one-time exclusion for people age 55 or older on that part of the gain. You can take the exclusion if you otherwise qualify and the rental or business use did not exceed 2 years of the 5-year period ending on the date of sale. To do so, allocate any allowable exclusion between Forms 2119 and 4797. Attach a statement showing the total exclusion and the method used to allocate it between the two forms. Enter on Form 2119, line 14, only the part of the total exclusion that applies to your main home. On the dotted line next to line 14, write "Allocated." For details on how to report the part of the exclusion that applies to the rental or business use, see **Special Rules** in the Form 4797 instructions.

For more details on a home used partly for business or rental, see Pub. 523.

Note: *Only the part of the fixing-up expenses that applies to your main home may be included on line 16. These expenses are not allowed on Form 4797.*

New Home.—If part of your new main home is rented out or used for business, enter on line 19b only the part of the total cost of the property that is allocable to your new main home. Attach a statement showing the total cost of the property and the allocation between the part that is your new main home and the part that is rented out or used for business. For more details, see Pub. 523.

Line 4

Enter the gross sales price of your old home. Generally, this includes the amount of money you received, plus all notes, mortgages, or other debts that are part of the sale. If you received a Form 1099-S, the total of these items should be shown in box 2. The gross sales price also includes the fair market value of any other property or services you received as part of the sale. If you received any other property or services as part of the sale, the value of these items is not shown on Form 1099-S. However, box 4 of that form should be checked.

Do not include amounts you received for personal property sold with your home. Personal property is property that is not a permanent part of the home. Examples are furniture, draperies, and lawn equipment.

Line 5

Enter the total expenses you paid to sell your old home. These expenses include commissions, advertising, attorney and legal fees, appraisal fees, title insurance, transfer and stamp taxes, and recording fees. Loan charges, such as points charged to the seller, are also selling expenses. **Do not** include fixing-up expenses on this line. Instead, see the instructions for line 16 on page 4.

Line 7

Use the worksheet on this page to figure the adjusted basis of the home you sold. See **Capital Improvements** and **Settlement Fees or Closing Costs** on page 4 before you begin the worksheet.

Exceptions. See Pub. 523 instead of using the worksheet on this page if **any** of the following apply:

- You are a surviving spouse and you owned your old home jointly with your deceased spouse.

Adjusted Basis of Home Sold Worksheet—Line 7 (keep for your records)

Caution: *If any of the **Exceptions** listed in the instructions for line 7 apply to you, **do not** use this worksheet. Instead, see Pub. 523.*

1.	Enter the purchase price of your old home. But if you filed Form 2119 when you originally acquired your old home to postpone gain on the sale of a previous home, enter the adjusted basis of the new home from that Form 2119		1.
2.	Seller-paid points (for old home bought after 1990). See **A Change To Note** on page 1		2.
3.	Subtract line 2 from line 1		3.
4.	Settlement fees or closing costs. **Do not** include amounts previously deducted as moving expenses. If line 1 includes the adjusted basis of the new home from Form 2119, skip lines 4a–5 and go to line 6.		
a.	Abstract and recording fees	4a.	
b.	Legal fees (including title search and preparing documents)	4b.	
c.	Surveys	4c.	
d.	Title insurance	4d.	
e.	Transfer or stamp taxes	4e.	
f.	Amounts the seller owed that you agreed to pay, such as back taxes or interest, recording or mortgage fees, and sales commissions	4f.	
g.	Other	4g.	
5.	Add lines 4a through 4g		5.
6.	Cost of capital improvements. Use the **Capital Improvements Worksheet** on page 4. **Do not** include any capital improvements included on line 1 above		6.
7.	Special tax assessments paid on your old home for local improvements such as streets and sidewalks		7.
8.	Other increases to basis		8.
9.	Add lines 3, 5, 6, 7, and 8		9.
10.	Depreciation, related to the business use or rental of your old home, claimed (or allowable) on prior year tax returns	10.	
11.	Residential energy credit (generally allowed from 1977 through 1987) claimed for any capital improvements included on line 6 and, if applicable, line 1 above	11.	
12.	Payments received for any easement or right-of-way granted	12.	
13.	Other decreases to basis	13.	
14.	Add lines 10 through 13		14.
15.	**Adjusted basis of home sold.** Subtract line 14 from line 9. Enter the result here and on Form 2119, line 7		15.

• You built your old home and didn't file a Form 2119 to postpone gain on the sale of a previous home.

• You acquired your old home other than by purchase, such as by gift, inheritance, or trade.

• Your old home was damaged as a result of a casualty.

Capital Improvements.—These are improvements made to your home that add to its value, prolong its useful life, or adapt it to new uses. For examples, see the **Capital Improvements Worksheet** on this page.

Settlement Fees or Closing Costs.— Certain expenses you incurred to buy your home increase your basis. These expenses should be shown on your settlement statement. For more details, see Pub. 523.

Line 15

If you report the gain from the sale of your home on Form 6252 using the installment method, first complete the lines on Form 2119 that apply to you. If you completed line 14 or line 22 of Form 2119, enter the total of those lines on line 15 of Form 6252. Otherwise, enter zero on line 15 of Form 6252. Do not enter the gain from Form 2119 on Schedule D (Form 1040).

Line 16

Enter the fixing-up expenses you paid to help sell your old home. Fixing-up expenses are decorating and repair costs. For example, the cost of painting the home, planting flowers, and replacing broken windows are fixing-up expenses. However, to qualify, the expenses must be:

• For work done during the 90-day period ending on the day you signed the contract to sell your home (not the day you signed the listing contract with the real estate company), and

• Paid no later than 30 days after the date of sale.

Fixing-up expenses do not include amounts paid for capital improvements. Instead, add these amounts to the basis of the property sold. They also do not include selling expenses included on line 5 or amounts that are otherwise deductible.

Line 19b

The cost of your new home includes one or more of the following if paid or incurred within the replacement period (defined on page 1):

• Cash payments,

• The amount of any mortgage or other debt on the new home,

• Purchase expenses you paid that were not deducted as moving expenses,

• The cost of capital improvements, or

• Any other expenses that must be added to the basis of the new home.

If you bought your new home, you may have to reduce the cost of your home by any points the seller paid. See **A Change To Note** on page 1.

If you built your new home, include the cost of the land and all construction costs incurred within the replacement period. Do not include the cost of land purchased before or after the replacement period or land acquired other than by purchase. Also, do not include the value of your own labor.

Note: *If line 21 of Form 2119 shows a taxable gain and you incur costs for capital improvements made after you file it but within the replacement period, you should refigure your taxable gain. If the refigured taxable gain is less than the gain you originally reported, file Form 1040X to correct your 1994 tax return.*

Line 23

Subtract line 22 from 19b. This is your adjusted basis in your new home. But if you built your new home and the land is not included in the amount entered on line 19b, your adjusted basis in your new home is the amount on line 23 plus the adjusted basis of the land.

Capital Improvements Worksheet (keep for your records)

Caution: *Do not include improvements that are no longer part of your main home. For example, if you put wall-to-wall carpeting in your home and later replaced it with new wall-to-wall carpeting, do not include the cost of the first carpeting as a capital improvement.*

(a) Type of Improvement	(b) Year	(c) Amount	(a) Type of Improvement	(b) Year	(c) Amount
Additions			**Heating & Air Conditioning**		
Bedroom			Heating system		
Bathroom			Central air conditioning		
Deck			Furnace		
Garage			Duct work		
Porch			Central humidifier		
Patio			Filtration system		
Storage shed			Other		
Fireplace					
Other			**Electrical**		
			Light fixtures		
Lawn & Grounds			Wiring upgrades		
Landscaping			Other		
Driveway					
Walkway			**Plumbing**		
Fence			Water heater		
Retaining wall			Soft water system		
Sprinkler system			Filtration system		
Swimming pool			Other		
Exterior lighting					
Other			**Insulation**		
			Attic		
Communications			Walls		
Satellite dish			Floors		
Intercom			Pipes and duct work		
Security system			Other		
Other					
			Interior Improvements		
Miscellaneous			Built-in appliances		
Storm windows and doors			Kitchen modernization		
Roof			Bathroom modernization		
Central vacuum			Flooring		
Other			Wall-to-wall carpeting		
			Other		

Total capital improvements. Add the amounts in column **(c)**. Enter the total here and on line 6 of the **Adjusted Basis of Home Sold Worksheet** on page 3 . . . . $________

Page 4

Printed on recycled paper

A. [§ 8.149] I.R.S. Publication 523—Selling Your Home

Department of the Treasury
Internal Revenue Service

Publication 523
Cat. No. 15044W

Selling Your Home

For use in preparing
2022 Returns

Get forms and other information faster and easier at:
- *IRS.gov* (English)
- *IRS.gov/Spanish* (Español)
- *IRS.gov/Chinese* (中文)
- *IRS.gov/Korean* (한국어)
- *IRS.gov/Russian* (Русский)
- *IRS.gov/Vietnamese* (Tiếng Việt)

Dec 12, 2022

Contents

Future Developments

For the latest information about developments related to Pub. 523, such as legislation enacted after it was published, go to *IRS.gov/Pub523*.

Reminders

Photographs of missing children. The IRS is a proud partner with the *National Center for Missing & Exploited Children® (NCMEC)*. Photographs of missing children selected by the Center may appear in this publication on pages that would otherwise be blank. You can help bring these children home by looking at the photographs and calling 800-THE-LOST (800-843-5678) if you recognize a child.

Special rules for capital gains invested in Qualified Opportunity Funds. Effective December 22, 2017, section 1400Z-2 provides a temporary deferral of inclusion in gross income for capital gains invested in Qualified Opportunity Funds, and permanent exclusion of capital gains from the sale or exchange of an investment in the Qualified Opportunity Fund if the investment is held for at least 10 years. For more information, see the Instructions for Form 8949.

Extension of the exclusion of canceled or forgiven mortgage debt from income. The exclusion of income for mortgage debt canceled or forgiven was extended through December 31, 2025. The indebtedness discharged must generally be on a qualified principal residence, and based on an agreement in writing prior to January 1, 2026. See *Report as ordinary income on Form 1040, 1040-SR, or 1040-NR applicable canceled or forgiven mortgage debt*, later.

Introduction

This publication explains the tax rules that apply when you sell or otherwise give up ownership of a home. If you meet certain conditions, you may exclude the first $250,000 of gain from the sale of your home from your income and avoid paying taxes on it. The exclusion is increased to $500,000 for a married couple filing jointly.

This publication also has worksheets for calculations relating to the sale of your home. It will show you how to:

1. Determine if you have a gain or loss on the sale of your home,
2. Figure how much of any gain is taxable, and
3. Report the transaction correctly on your tax return.

Comments and suggestions. We welcome your comments about this publication and suggestions for future editions.

You can send us comments through *IRS.gov/FormComments*. Or, you can write to the Internal Revenue Service, Tax Forms and Publications, 1111 Constitution Ave. NW, IR-6526, Washington, DC 20224.

Although we can't respond individually to each comment received, we do appreciate your feedback and will consider your comments and suggestions as we revise our tax forms, instructions, and publications. **Don't** send tax questions, tax returns, or payments to the above address.

Getting answers to your tax questions. If you have a tax question not answered by this publication or the *How To Get Tax Help* section at the end of this publication, go to the IRS Interactive Tax Assistant page at *IRS.gov/Help/ITA* where you can find topics by using the search feature or viewing the categories listed.

Getting tax forms, instructions, and publications. Go to *IRS.gov/Forms* to download current and prior-year forms, instructions, and publications.

Ordering tax forms, instructions, and publications. Go to *IRS.gov/OrderForms* to order current forms, instructions, and publications; call 800-829-3676 to order prior-year forms and instructions. The IRS will process your order for forms and publications as soon as possible. **Don't** resubmit requests you've already sent us. You can get forms and publications faster online.

Useful Items

You may want to see:

Publication

- ❑ **504** Divorced or Separated Individuals
- ❑ **505** Tax Withholding and Estimated Tax
- ❑ **527** Residential Rental Property
- ❑ **530** Tax Information for Homeowners
- ❑ **537** Installment Sales
- ❑ **544** Sales and Other Dispositions of Assets
- ❑ **547** Casualties, Disasters, and Thefts
- ❑ **551** Basis of Assets
- ❑ **587** Business Use of Your Home
- ❑ **936** Home Mortgage Interest Deduction
- ❑ **4681** Canceled Debts, Foreclosures, Repossessions, and Abandonments

Form (and Instructions)

- ❑ **Schedule A (Form 1040)** Itemized Deductions
- ❑ **Schedule B (Form 1040)** Interest and Ordinary Dividends
- ❑ **Schedule D (Form 1040)** Capital Gains and Losses
- ❑ **982** Reduction of Tax Attributes Due to Discharge of Indebtedness (and Section 1082 Basis Adjustment)
- ❑ **1040** U.S. Individual Income Tax Return
- ❑ **1040-NR** U.S. Nonresident Income Tax Return
- ❑ **1040-SR** U.S. Income Tax Return for Seniors
- ❑ **1099-S** Proceeds From Real Estate Transactions
- ❑ **4797** Sales of Business Property
- ❑ **5405** Repayment of the First-Time Homebuyer Credit
- ❑ **6252** Installment Sale Income
- ❑ **8822** Change of Address
- ❑ **8828** Recapture of Federal Mortgage Subsidy
- ❑ **8949** Sales and Other Dispositions of Capital Assets
- ❑ **W-2** Wage and Tax Statement
- ❑ **W-7** Application for IRS Individual Taxpayer Identification Number

Does Your Home Sale Qualify for the Exclusion of Gain?

The tax code recognizes the importance of home ownership by allowing you to exclude gain when you sell your main home. To qualify for the maximum exclusion of gain ($250,000 or $500,000 if married filing jointly), you must meet the *Eligibility Test*, explained later. To qualify for a partial exclusion of gain, meaning an exclusion of gain less than the full amount, you must meet one of the situations listed in *Does Your Home Qualify for a Partial Exclusion of Gain*, later.

Before considering the *Eligibility Test* or whether your home qualifies for a partial exclusion, you should consider some preliminary items.

Transfer of your home to a spouse or an ex-spouse. Generally, if you transferred your home (or share of a jointly owned home) to a spouse or ex-spouse as part of a divorce settlement, you are considered to have no gain or loss. You have nothing to report from the transfer and this entire publication doesn't apply to you. However, there is one exception to this rule. If your spouse or ex-spouse is a nonresident alien, then you likely will have a gain or loss from the transfer and the tests in this publication apply.

Home's date of sale. To determine if you meet the *Eligibility Test* or qualify for a partial exclusion, you will need to know the home's date of sale, meaning when you sold it. If you received Form 1099-S, Proceeds From Real Estate Transactions, the date of sale appears in box 1. If you didn't receive Form 1099-S, the date of sale is either the date the title transferred or the date the economic burdens and benefits of ownership shifted to the buyer, whichever date is earlier. In most cases, these dates are the same.

Sale of your main home. You may take the exclusion, whether maximum or partial, only on the sale of a home that is your principal residence, meaning your main home. An individual has only one main home at a time. If you own and live in just one home, then that property is your main home. If you own or live in more than one home, then you must apply a "facts and circumstances" test to determine which property is your main home. While the most important factor is where you spend the most time, other factors are relevant as well. They are listed below. The more of these factors that are true of a home, the more likely that it is your main home.

- The address listed on your:
    1. U.S. Postal Service address,
    2. Voter Registration Card,
    3. Federal and state tax returns, and
    4. Driver's license or car registration.
- The home is near:
    1. Where you work,
    2. Where you bank,
    3. The residence of one or more family members, and
    4. Recreational clubs or religious organizations of which you are a member.

Finally, the exclusion can apply to many different types of housing facilities. A single-family home, a condominium, a cooperative apartment, a mobile home, and a houseboat each may be a main home and therefore qualify for the exclusion.

Eligibility Test

The Eligibility Test determines whether you are eligible for the maximum exclusion of gain ($250,000 or $500,000 if married filing jointly).

Eligibility Step 1—Automatic Disqualification

Determine whether any of the automatic disqualifications apply. Your home sale isn't eligible for the exclusion if ANY of the following are true.

- You acquired the property through a like-kind exchange (1031 exchange), during the past 5 years. See Pub. 544, Sales and Other Dispositions of Assets.
- You are subject to expatriate tax. For more information about expatriate tax, see chapter 4 of Pub. 519, U.S. Tax Guide for Aliens.

If any of these conditions are true, the exclusion doesn't apply. Skip to *Figuring Gain or Loss*, later.

Eligibility Step 2—Ownership

Determine whether you meet the ownership requirement. If you owned the home for at least 24 months (2 years) out of the last 5 years leading up to the date of sale (date of the closing), you meet the ownership requirement. For a married couple filing jointly, only one spouse has to meet the ownership requirement.

Eligibility Step 3—Residence

Determine whether you meet the residence requirement. If you owned the home and used it as your residence for at least 24 months of the previous 5 years, you meet the residence requirement. The 24 months of residence can fall anywhere within the 5-year period, and it doesn't have to be a single block of time. All that is required is a total of 24 months (730 days) of residence during the 5-year period. Unlike the ownership requirement, each spouse must meet the residence requirement individually for a married couple filing jointly to get the full exclusion.

If you were ever away from home, you need to determine whether that time counts toward your residence requirement. A vacation or other short absence counts as time you lived at home (even if you rented out your home while you were gone).

If you become physically or mentally unable to care for yourself, and you use the residence as your principal residence for 12 months in the 5 years preceding the sale or exchange, any time you spent living in a care facility (such as a nursing home) counts toward your 2-year residence requirement, so long as the facility has a license from a state or other political entity to care for people with your condition.

Eligibility Step 4—Look-Back

Determine whether you meet the look-back requirement. If you didn't sell another home during the 2-year period before the date of sale (or, if you did sell another home during this period, but didn't take an exclusion of the gain earned from it), you meet the look-back requirement. You may take the exclusion only once during a 2-year period.

Eligibility Step 5—Exceptions to the Eligibility Test

There are some exceptions to the Eligibility Test. If any of the following situations apply to you, read on to see if they may affect your qualification. If none of these situations apply, skip to Step 6.

- A separation or divorce occurred during the ownership of the home. See *Separated or divorced taxpayers*.
- The death of a spouse occurred during the ownership of the home. See *Widowed taxpayers*.
- The sale involved vacant land. See *Vacant land next to home*.
- You owned a remainder interest, meaning the right to own a home in the future, and you sold that right. See *Remainder interest*.
- Your previous home was destroyed or condemned. See *Home destroyed or condemned—considerations for benefits*.
- You were a service member during the ownership of the home. See *Service, Intelligence, and Peace Corps personnel*.
- You acquired or are relinquishing the home in a like-kind exchange. See *Like-kind/1031 exchange*.
- You used the entire property as a vacation home or rental after 2008 or you used a portion of the home, separate from the living area, for business or rental purposes. See *Business or Rental Use of Home*.

Separated or divorced taxpayers. If you were separated or divorced prior to the sale of the home, you can treat the home as your residence if:

- You are a sole or joint owner, and
- Your spouse or former spouse is allowed to live in the home under a divorce or separation agreement and uses the home as his or her main home.

If your home was transferred to you by a spouse or ex-spouse (whether in connection with a divorce or not), you can count any time when your spouse owned the home as time when you owned it. However, you must meet the residence requirement on your own. If you owned your home prior to your marriage and after your divorce or separation, and your spouse or former spouse is not allowed to live in the home under a divorce or separation agreement, you count any time that you owned the home solely or jointly with your spouse as time when you owned it, and you must meet the residence requirement on your own.

Widowed taxpayers. If you are a widowed taxpayer who doesn't meet the 2-year ownership and residence requirements on your own, consider the following rule. If you haven't remarried at the time of the sale, then you may include any time when your late spouse owned and lived in the home, even if without you, to meet the ownership and residence requirements.

Also, you may be able to increase your exclusion amount from $250,000 to $500,000. You may take the higher exclusion if you meet all of the following conditions.

1. You sell your home within 2 years of the death of your spouse;
2. You haven't remarried at the time of the sale;
3. Neither you nor your late spouse took the exclusion on another home sold less than 2 years before the date of the current home sale; and
4. You meet the 2-year ownership and residence requirements (including your late spouse's times of ownership and residence, if applicable).

Service, Intelligence, and Peace Corps personnel. If you or your spouse are a member of the Uniformed Services or the Foreign Service, an employee of the intelligence community of the United States, or an employee, enrolled volunteer or volunteer leader of the Peace Corps, you may choose to suspend the 5-year test period for ownership and residence when you're on qualified official extended duty. This means you may be able to meet the 2-year residence test even if, because of your service, you didn't actually live in your home for at least the 2 years during the 5-year period ending on the date of sale.

Qualified extended duty. You are on qualified extended duty if:

- You are called or ordered to active duty for an indefinite period, or for a definite period of more than 90 days.
- You are serving at a duty station at least 50 miles from your main home, or you are living in government quarters under government orders.
- You are one of the following:
    1. A member of the armed forces (Army, Navy, Air Force, Marine Corps, Coast Guard);
    2. A member of the commissioned corps of the National Oceanic and Atmospheric Administration (NOAA) or the Public Health Service;
    3. A Foreign Service chief of mission, ambassador-at-large, or officer;
    4. A member of the Senior Foreign Service or the Foreign Service personnel;
    5. An employee, enrolled volunteer, or enrolled volunteer leader of the Peace Corps serving outside the United States; or

6. An employee of the intelligence community, meaning:
   a. The Office of the Director of National Intelligence, the Central Intelligence Agency, the National Security Agency, the Defense Intelligence Agency, the National Geospatial-Intelligence Agency, or the National Reconnaissance Office;
   b. Any other office within the Department of Defense for the collection of specialized national intelligence through reconnaissance programs;
   c. Any of the intelligence elements of the Army, the Navy, the Air Force, the Marine Corps, the Federal Bureau of Investigation, the Department of Treasury, the Department of Energy, and the Coast Guard;
   d. The Bureau of Intelligence and Research of the Department of State; or
   e. Any of the elements of the Department of Homeland Security concerned with the analyses of foreign intelligence information.

Period of suspension. The period of suspension can't last more than 10 years. Together, the 10-year suspension period and the 5-year test period can be as long as, but no more than, 15 years. You can't suspend the 5-year period for more than one property at a time. You can revoke your choice to suspend the 5-year period at any time.

Example 1. You bought a home on May 1, 2006. You used it as your main home until August 27, 2009. On August 28, 2009, you went on qualified official extended duty with the Navy. You didn't live in the house again before selling it on August 1, 2022. You choose to use the entire 10-year suspension period. Therefore, the suspension period would extend back from August 1, 2022, to August 2, 2012, and the 5-year test period would extend back to August 2, 2007. During that period, you owned the house all 5 years and lived in it as your main home from August 2, 2007, until August 28, 2009, a period of more than 24 months. You meet the ownership and use tests because you owned and lived in the home for at least 2 years during this test period.

Example 2. You bought and moved into a home in 2013. You lived in it as your main home for $3^1/_2$ years. For the next 6 years, you didn't live in it because you were on qualified official extended duty with the Army. You then sold the home at a gain in 2022. To meet the use test, you choose to suspend the 5-year test period for the 6 years you were on qualified official extended duty. This means you can disregard those 6 years. Therefore, your 5-year test period consists of the 5 years before you went on qualified official extended duty. You meet the ownership and use tests because you owned and lived in the home for $3^1/_2$ years during this test period.

Vacant land next to home. You can include the sale of vacant land adjacent to the land on which your home sits as part of a sale of your home if ALL of the following are true.

- You owned and used the vacant land as part of your home.
- The sale of the vacant land and the sale of your home occurred within 2 years of each other.
- Both sales either meet the Eligibility Test or qualify for partial tax benefits, as described earlier.

Also, if your sale of vacant land meets all these requirements, you must treat that sale and the sale of your home as a single transaction for tax purposes, meaning that you may apply the exclusion only once.

Note. However, if you move your home from the land on which it stood (meaning you relocate the actual physical structure), then that land no longer counts as part of your home. For example, if you move a mobile home to a new lot and sell the old lot, then you can't treat the sale of the old lot as the sale of your home.

Home destroyed or condemned—considerations for benefits. If an earlier home of yours was destroyed or condemned, you may be able to count your time there toward the ownership and residence test.

If your home was destroyed, see Pub. 547, Casualties, Disasters, or Thefts. If your home was condemned, see Pub. 544, Sales and Other Disposition of Assets.

Remainder interest. The sale of a remainder interest in your home is eligible for the exclusion only if both of the following conditions are met.

- The buyer isn't a "related party." A related party can be a related person or a related corporation, trust, partnership, or other entity that you control or in which you have an interest.
- You haven't previously sold an interest in the home for which you took the exclusion.

Like-kind/1031 exchange. If you sold a home that you acquired in a like-kind exchange, then the following test applies.

You can't claim the exclusion if:

1. Either (a) or (b) applies:
   a. You acquired your home in a like-kind exchange (also known as a section 1031 exchange), or
   b. Your basis in your home is determined by reference to a previous owner's basis, and that previous owner acquired the property in a like-kind exchange (for example, the owner acquired the home and then gave it to you); and
2. You sold the home within 5 years of the date your home was acquired in the like-kind exchange.

For more information about like-kind exchanges, see Pub. 544.

If you relinquished your home in a like-kind exchange, then you should determine if you qualify to exclude gain as you would if you sold the home. Under certain circumstances, you may meet the requirements for both the exclusion of gain from the exchange of a main home and the nonrecognition of gain from a like-kind exchange. For more information, see Revenue Procedure 2005-14, 2005-7 I.R.B. 528, available at *IRS.gov/irb/2005-07_IRB#RP-2005-14*.

Eligibility Step 6—Final Determination of Eligibility

If you meet the ownership, residence, and look-back requirements, taking the exceptions into account, then you meet the Eligibility Test. Your home sale qualifies for the maximum exclusion. Skip to Worksheet 1, later.

If you didn't meet the Eligibility Test, then your home isn't eligible for the maximum exclusion, but you should continue to *Does Your Home Qualify for a Partial Exclusion of Gain*.

Does Your Home Qualify for a Partial Exclusion of Gain?

If you don't meet the Eligibility Test, you may still qualify for a partial exclusion of gain. You can meet the requirements for a partial exclusion if the main reason for your home sale was a change in workplace location, a health issue, or an unforeseeable event.

Work-Related Move

You meet the requirements for a partial exclusion if any of the following events occurred during your time of ownership and residence in the home.

- You took or were transferred to a new job in a work location at least 50 miles farther from the home than your old work location. For example, your old work location was 15 miles from the home and your new work location is 65 miles from the home.
- You had no previous work location and you began a new job at least 50 miles from the home.
- Either of the above is true of your spouse, a co-owner of the home, or anyone else for whom the home was his or her residence.

Health-Related Move

You meet the requirements for a partial exclusion if any of the following health-related events occurred during your time of ownership and residence in the home.

- You moved to obtain, provide, or facilitate diagnosis, cure, mitigation, or treatment of disease, illness, or injury for yourself or a family member.
- You moved to obtain or provide medical or personal care for a family member suffering from a disease, illness, or injury. A family member includes your:
  1. Parent, grandparent, stepmother, stepfather;
  2. Child (including adopted child, eligible foster child, and stepchild), grandchild;
  3. Brother, sister, stepbrother, stepsister, half brother, half sister;
  4. Mother-in-law, father-in-law, brother-in-law, sister-in-law, son-in-law, daughter-in-law;
  5. Uncle, aunt, nephew, or niece.
- A doctor recommended a change in residence for you because you were experiencing a health problem.
- The above is true of your spouse, a co-owner of the home, or anyone else for whom the home was his or her residence.

Unforeseeable Events

You meet the standard requirements if any of the following events occurred during the time you owned and lived in the home you sold.

- Your home was destroyed or condemned.
- Your home suffered a casualty loss because of a natural or man-made disaster or an act of terrorism. (It doesn't matter whether the loss is deductible on your tax return.)
- You, your spouse, a co-owner of the home, or anyone else for whom the home was his or her residence:
  1. Died;
  2. Became divorced or legally separated, or were issued a separate decree to pay maintenance (support) to the other spouse;
  3. Gave birth to two or more children from the same pregnancy;
  4. Became eligible for unemployment compensation;
  5. Became unable, because of a change in employment status, to pay basic living expenses for the household (including expenses for food, clothing, housing, medication, transportation, taxes, court-ordered payments, and expenses reasonably necessary for making an income).
  6. An event is determined to be an unforeseeable event in IRS published guidance.

Other Facts and Circumstances

Even if your situation doesn't match any of the standard requirements described above, you still may qualify for an exception. You may qualify if you can demonstrate the primary reason for sale, based on facts and circumstances, is work related, health related, or unforeseeable. Important factors are:

- The situation causing the sale arose during the time you owned and used your property as your residence.

Worksheet 1. **Find Your Exclusion Limit**

Use this worksheet only if no automatic disqualifications apply, and take all exceptions into account.

A) Determine if you are eligible for the maximum exclusion limit.

Status	You are eligible for the maximum exclusion if...	Maximum exclusion	If you're not eligible for the maximum exclusion limit, then you should...
Married filing jointly	Both spouses meet the residence and look-back requirements and one or both spouses meet the ownership requirement.	$500,000	Determine if either spouse is eligible for the full limit as a single person. If not, determine if either spouse is eligible for a partial exclusion.
Single, married filing separately	You meet the residence, ownership, and look-back requirements.	$250,000	Determine if you are eligible for a partial exclusion.
Widowed	1. You sell your home within 2 years of the death of your spouse. 2. You haven't remarried at the time of the sale. 3. Neither you nor your late spouse took the exclusion on another home sold less than 2 years before the date of the current home sale. 4. You meet the 2-year ownership and residence requirements (including your late spouse's times of ownership and residence, if applicable).	$500,000	Determine if you are eligible for the full limit as a single person. If not, determine if you are eligible for a partial exclusion.

B) Complete this section only if you have determined that you aren't eligible for the maximum exclusion but are eligible for a partial exclusion. If you are eligible for a partial exclusion, use this section to determine your exclusion limit.

Step 1	Determine the shortest of the following 3 periods: 1. Your time of residence in the home during the 5-year period leading up to the sale .... 2. Your time of ownership of the home leading up to the sale .... 3. The time that has elapsed between the sale and the date you last sold a home for which you took the exclusion, if applicable	______ ______ ______
Step 2	Take the smallest period from Step 1 (you may use days or months) and divide that number by 730 (if using days) or 24 (if using months)	______
Step 3	Multiply the result from Step 2 by $250,000. Stop here if not married filing jointly	______
Step 4	Repeat Steps 1–3 for your spouse and add the two results	______

C) Your exclusion limit is $__________. Unless you have taxable gain from business or rental use (see *Business or Rental Use of Home*), only gain in excess of this amount is taxable.

- You sold your home not long after the situation arose.
- You couldn't have reasonably anticipated the situation when you bought the home.
- You began to experience significant financial difficulty maintaining the home.
- The home became significantly less suitable as a main home for you and your family for a specific reason.

Publication 523 (2022) Page 7

Figuring Gain or Loss

To figure the gain or loss on the sale of your main home, you must know the selling price, the amount realized, and the adjusted basis. Subtract the adjusted basis from the amount realized to get your gain or loss.

Selling price
– Selling expenses

Amount realized
– Adjusted basis

Gain or loss

A positive number indicates a gain; a negative number indicates a loss.

Certain events during your ownership, such as use of your home for business purposes or your making improvements to it, can affect your gain or loss. They are explained in this section.

See Worksheet 2, later, for steps you should follow to figure your gain or loss.

Basis Adjustments—Details and Exceptions

You should include many, but not all, costs associated with the purchase and maintenance of your home in the basis of your home. For more information on determining basis, see Pub. 551, Basis of Assets.

Fees and Closing Costs

Some settlement fees and closing costs you can include in your basis are:

- Abstract fees (abstract of title fees),
- Charges for installing utility services,
- Legal fees (including fees for the title search and preparing the sales contract and deed),
- Recording fees,
- Survey fees,
- Transfer or stamp taxes, and
- Owner's title insurance.

Settlement costs don't include amounts placed in escrow for the future payment of items such as taxes and insurance.

Some settlement fees and closing costs you can't include in your basis are:

- Fire and casualty insurance premiums,
- Rent for occupancy of the house before closing,
- Charges for utilities or other services related to occupancy of the house before closing,
- Any fee or cost that you deducted as a moving expense (allowed for certain fees and costs before 1994),
- Charges connected with getting a mortgage loan, such as:
  1. Mortgage insurance premiums (including funding fees connected with loans guaranteed by the Department of Veterans Affairs),
  2. Loan assumption fees,
  3. Cost of a credit report,
  4. Fee for an appraisal required by a lender,
  5. Points (discount points, loan origination fees), and
- Fees for refinancing a mortgage.

Construction. If you contracted to have your house built on the land you own, your basis is:

- The cost of the land, plus
- The amount it cost you to complete the house, including:
  1. The cost of labor and materials,
  2. Any amounts paid to a contractor,
  3. Any architect's fees,
  4. Building permit charges,
  5. Utility meter and connection charges, and
  6. Legal fees directly connected with building the house.

Your cost includes your down payment and any debt such as a first or second mortgage or notes you gave the seller or builder. It also includes certain settlement or closing costs. In addition, you must generally reduce your basis by points the seller paid you.

If you built all or part of your house yourself, its basis is the total amount it cost you to complete it. Don't include in the cost of the house:

- The value of your own labor, or
- The value of any other labor for which you didn't pay.

Costs owed by the seller that you paid. You can include in your basis any amounts the seller owes that you agree to pay (as long as the seller doesn't reimburse you), such as:

- Any real estate taxes owed up through the day before the sale date,
- Back interest owed by the seller,

- The seller's title recording or mortgage fees,
- Charges for improvements or repairs that are the seller's responsibility (for example, lead paint removal), and
- Sales commissions (for example, payment to the seller's real estate agent).

Improvements

Improvements add to the value of your home, prolong its useful life, or adapt it to new uses. You add the cost of additions and improvements to the basis of your property.

The following chart lists some examples of improvements.

Examples of Improvements That Increase Basis

Keep for Your Records

Additions	**Systems**
Bedroom	Heating system
Bathroom	Central air conditioning
Deck	Furnace
Garage	Duct work
Porch	Central humidifier
Patio	Central vacuum
	Air/water filtration systems
	Wiring
	Security system
Lawn & Grounds	Lawn sprinkler system
Landscaping	
Driveway	
Walkway	
Fence	
Retaining wall	
Swimming pool	
Exterior	**Plumbing**
Storm windows/doors	Septic system
New roof	Water heater
New siding	Soft water system
Satellite dish	Filtration system
Insulation	**Interior**
Attic	Built-in appliances
Walls	Kitchen modernization
Floors	Flooring
Pipes and duct work	Wall-to-wall carpeting
	Fireplace

Repairs done as part of larger project. You can include repair-type work if it is done as part of an extensive remodeling or restoration job. For example, replacing broken windowpanes is a repair, but replacing the same window as part of a project of replacing all the windows in your home counts as an improvement.

Examples of improvements you CAN'T include in your basis. You can't include:

- Any costs of repairs or maintenance that are necessary to keep your home in good condition but don't add to its value or prolong its life. Examples include painting (interior or exterior), fixing leaks, filling holes or cracks, or replacing broken hardware.
- Any costs of any improvements that are no longer part of your home (for example, wall-to-wall carpeting that you installed but later replaced).
- Any costs of any improvements with a life expectancy, when installed, of less than 1 year.

Exception. The entire job is considered an improvement if items that would otherwise be considered repairs are done as part of an extensive remodeling or restoration of your home. For example, if you have a casualty and your home is damaged, increase your basis by the amount you spend on repairs that restore the property to its pre-casualty condition. However, you must adjust your basis by any amount of insurance reimbursement you receive or expect to receive for casualty losses. See Worksheet 2, line 5.

Energy credits and subsidies. If you included in your basis the cost of any energy-related improvements (such as a solar energy system), and you received any tax credits or subsidies related to those improvements, you must subtract those credits or subsidies from your total basis. Examples include:

- *1977–1987:* Credit for home energy improvements,
- *1992–present:* Direct or indirect subsidy from a public utility for installations or modifications aimed at lowering a home's electricity or natural gas usage or better managing its energy demand,
- *2006–present:* Credit for home energy efficiency improvements,
- *2006–present:* Credit for qualified solar electric property expenditures and qualified solar water heating property expenditures available, and
- *2006–2007, 2009–present:* Credit for energy improvements to non-business properties.

Home Acquired Through a Trade

Traded for another home. When you trade your home for a new one, you are treated as having sold your home and purchased a new one. Your sale price is the trade-in value you received for your home plus any mortgage or other debt that the person taking your home as a trade-in assumed (took over) from you as part of the deal.

Traded for other property. If you paid for your home by trading other property for it, the starting basis of your home is usually the fair market value of the property you traded.

Home Foreclosed, Repossessed, or Abandoned

If your home was foreclosed on, repossessed, or abandoned, you may have ordinary income, gain, or loss. See Pub. 4681, Canceled Debts, Foreclosures, Repossessions, and Abandonments.

If you used part of your home for business or rental purposes, see *Foreclosures and Repossessions* in chapter 1 of Pub. 544, for examples of how to figure gain or loss.

Home Destroyed or Condemned

You have a disposition when your home is destroyed or condemned and you receive other property or money in payment, such as insurance or a condemnation award. This is treated as a sale and you may be able to exclude all or part of any gain that you have. If your home was destroyed, see Pub. 547. If your home was condemned, see Pub. 544.

Home Received in Divorce

Home acquired after July 18, 1984. If your former spouse was the sole owner, your starting basis is the same as your former spouse's adjusted basis just before you received the home. If you co-owned the home with your spouse, add the adjusted basis of your spouse's half-share in the home to the adjusted basis of your own half-share to get your starting basis. (In most cases, the adjusted basis of the two half-shares will be the same.) The rules apply whether or not you received anything in exchange for the home.

Home acquired on or before July 18, 1984. Your starting basis will usually be the home's fair market value at the time you acquired it from your spouse or ex-spouse.

For more information, see Pub. 504, Divorced or Separated Individuals. If you or your spouse or ex-spouse lived in a community property state, see Pub. 555, Community Property.

Home Received as a Gift

If you received your home as a gift, you should keep records of the date you received it. Record the adjusted basis of the donor at the time of the gift and the fair market value of the home at the time of the gift. Also ask if the donor paid any gift tax. As a general rule, you will use the donor's adjusted basis at the time of the gift as your basis. However, see Table 1 below to determine if any exceptions to this rule listed in the "IF" column apply.

Table 1. **Exceptions to Using a Donor's Adjusted Basis for a Home Received as a Gift**

IF...	AND...	THEN...
at the time of the gift, the donor's adjusted basis in the home was *more* than the home's fair market value,	your usage of the donor's adjusted basis as your basis results in a loss,	you must use the fair market value of the home at the time of the gift as your basis (if using the fair market value results in a gain for you, then you don't need to recognize that gain).
at the time of the gift, the donor's adjusted basis in the home was *less* than the home's fair market value,	the donor paid gift tax on the gift of the home,	you figure your basis by starting with the donor's adjusted basis at the time of the gift and adding the federal gift tax paid due to the increase in value of the home (see Regulations section 1.1015-5 for further details on this calculation).

Home Inherited

Home acquired from a decedent who died before or after 2010. If you inherited your home from a decedent who died before or after 2010, your basis is the fair market value of the property on the date of the decedent's death (or the later alternate valuation date chosen by the personal representative of the estate). If a federal estate tax return (Form 706) was filed or required to be filed, the value of the property listed on the estate tax return is your basis. If Form 706 didn't have to be filed, your basis in the home is the same as its appraised value at the date of death, for purposes of state inheritance or transmission taxes. See section 1014 for details.

Surviving spouse. If you are a surviving spouse and you owned your home jointly, your basis in the home will change. The new basis for the interest your spouse owned will be its fair market value on the date of death (or alternate valuation date). The basis in your interest will remain the same. Your new basis in the home is the total of these two amounts.

If you and your spouse owned the home either as tenants by the entirety or as joint tenants with right of survivorship, you will each be considered to have owned one-half of the home.

Example. Your jointly owned home (owned as joint tenants with right of survivorship) had an adjusted basis of $50,000 on the date of your spouse's death, and the fair market value on that date was $100,000. Your new basis in the home is $75,000 ($25,000 for one-half of the adjusted basis plus $50,000 for one-half of the fair market value).

Community property. In community property states (Arizona, California, Idaho, Louisiana, Nevada, New Mexico, Texas, Washington, and Wisconsin), each spouse is usually considered to own half of the community property. When either spouse dies, the total fair market value of the community property becomes the basis of the entire property, including the part belonging to the surviving spouse. For this rule to apply, at least half the value of the community property interest must be includible in the decedent's gross estate, whether or not the estate must file a return.

For more information about community property, see Pub. 555, Community Property.

CAUTION *If you are selling a home in which you acquired an interest from a decedent who died in 2010, see Pub. 4895, Tax Treatment of Property Acquired From a Decedent Dying in 2010, available at https://www.irs.gov/pub/irs-prior/p4895--2011.pdf, to determine your basis.*

Business or Rental Use of Home

If you fail to meet the requirements to qualify for the $250,000 or $500,000 exclusion, you may still qualify for a reduced exclusion. If you fail to meet the ownership and use tests, or if you used a portion of your home for business or rental purposes during your ownership, this type of usage may affect your gain or loss calculations. For more information about using any part of your home for business or as a rental property, see Pub. 587, Business Use of Your Home, and Pub. 527, Residential Rental Property.

Gain from the sale or exchange of your main home isn't excludable from income if it is allocable to periods of non-qualified use. Non-qualified use means any period after 2008 where neither you nor your spouse (or your former spouse) used the property as your main home, with certain exceptions.

Exceptions. A period of non-qualified use does not include:

1. Any portion of the 5-year period ending on the date of the sale or exchange after the last date you or your spouse (or former spouse) used the property as your main home;
2. Any period (not to exceed 10 years) during which you (or your spouse) are serving on qualified official extended duty
   a. As a member of the uniformed services;
   b. As a member of the Foreign Service of the United States; or
   c. As an employee of the intelligence community; and
3. Any other period of temporary absence (not to exceed an aggregate period of 2 years) due to change of employment, health conditions, or other unforeseen circumstances as may be specified by the IRS. See *Eligibility Step 5—Exceptions to the Eligibility Test*, and *Does Your Home Sale Qualify for the Exclusion of Gain*, earlier.

Calculation. To figure the portion of the gain allocated to the period of non-qualified use, see Worksheet 3. Determine if You Have Taxable Gain below.

Exceptions. The following situations apply when using only a portion of the main home for business or rental usage and don't affect your gain or loss calculations.

- **Space within the living area.** If the space you used for business or rental purposes was within the living area of the home, then your usage doesn't affect your gain or loss calculations (except for an adjustment to basis for depreciation, taken after May 6, 1997, to be recaptured and reported as ordinary income). Examples of spaces within the living area include a rented spare bedroom and attic space used as a home office. For information on space outside the living area, see *Business or rental usage calculations* below.
- **Space formerly used for business or rental.** Space that was once used for business or rental purposes may be considered as residence space at the time of sale. A space formerly used for business is considered residence space if ALL of the following are true.
  - You weren't using the space for business or rental at the time you sold the property,
  - You didn't earn any business or rental income from the space in the year you sold your home, and
  - You used the space as residence space for 2 years out of the 5 years leading up to the sale.

If your space is considered as residence space at the time of the sale, then your former business usage DOESN'T affect your gain/loss calculations, unless you took or were allowed to take depreciation for use of your home for business or rental purposes. See Worksheet 2, line 5.

Business or rental usage calculations. Business or rental space that is separate from the living area affects your gain/loss calculations. Examples of space not within the living area include a first-floor storefront with an attached residence; a rented apartment in a duplex; or a working farm with a farmhouse on the property. If you have used part of the home (not within the home's living area) for solely business or rental purposes for more than 3 of the last 5 years, you need to make separate gain/loss calculations for the business and residence portions of your property. Make three copies of all pages of Worksheet 2. Label one copy "Total," one copy "Home," and one copy "Business or Rental."

Complete your "Total" worksheet using the figures for your property as a whole. Include the total amount you received, all of your basis adjustments, etc. Include the cost of all improvements, whether you made them to the business space or the residential space.

Determine your "business or rental percentage," meaning the percentage of your property that you used for business or rental. If you took depreciation on your home on past tax returns, use the same business or rental percentage that you used in determining how much depreciation to take. If you didn't take depreciation on your home on

Worksheet 2. **How To Figure Your Gain or Loss**

If you have questions as you work through these step-by-step instructions, or want examples of costs that can and can't be included, see *Basis Adjustments—Details and Exceptions*.

- **If married filing jointly,** figure gain or loss for both spouses together. **If single or married filing separately,** figure gain or loss as an individual.
- **If the home you sold had multiple owners,** your gain or loss is the gain or loss on the entire sale multiplied by your percentage of ownership.
- **If you used any portion of the property for business or rental purposes,** go to ***Business or Rental Use of Home***.

1. Determine the sale price. This is everything you received for selling your home.

a. All money (currency, check, wire transfer) .... a. ________

b. The fair market value of any other property or services you received .... b. ________

c. The value of any notes, mortgages, or other debts that the buyer agreed to assume (take over) as part of the sale .... c. ________

d. Any real estate taxes the buyer paid on your behalf .... d. ________

e. Any amount you received for granting an option to buy your home, if the option was exercised .... e. ________

f. Add lines 1a through 1e. This is your **sale price** .... f. ________

- **If you received payment for personal property,** DON'T include it in the sale price.
- **If you received payment or reimbursement from your employer** because of a job transfer, DON'T include the payment as part of the selling price. Your employer will include it as wages in box 1 of your Form W-2.
- **If you received Form 1099-S,** the gross proceeds for the sale price should appear in box 2. If box 4 is checked, the sale price included non-cash payments, and you need to determine the value of these and add them to the figure in box 2.
- **If you didn't receive Form 1099-S,** refer to your real estate transaction documents for the total amount you received for your home.

2. Determine your selling expenses. These are the costs directly associated with selling your home.

a. Any sales commissions (for example, a real estate agent's sales commission) .... a. ________

b. Any advertising fees .... b. ________

c. Any legal fees .... c. ________

d. Any mortgage points or other loan charges you paid that would normally have been the buyer's responsibility .... d. ________

e. Any other fees or costs to sell your home .... e. ________

f. Add lines 2a through 2e. These are your **selling expenses** .... f. ________

3. Figure your "amount realized" (sale price minus selling expenses).

Line 1f minus line 2f .... **3.** ________

4. Determine your "total basis" (the total amount you invested in your home). This includes what you paid for your home as well as other money you may have spent that added to its value.

a. The amount you paid for your home (or if you built your home, the cost of the land). Include any down payment and any amount you borrowed to pay for the home. For cooperative apartments, include the value of the corporation stock you purchased. If you acquired your home through inheritance, gift, bargain sale, trade, or anything except a fair market purchase, see *Basis Adjustments—Details and Exceptions* .... a. ________

b. Any settlement fees or closing costs you paid when you bought your home, except for financing-related costs (such as seller-paid points). The settlement statement should list the fees related to buying the home. See *Basis Adjustments—Details and Exceptions* and *Fees and Closing Costs* .... b. ________

c. Any real estate taxes or other costs you paid on behalf of the seller you bought your home from (and for which the seller never paid you back) .... c. ________

d. Any amounts you spent on construction or other improvements that are still part of your home at the time of sale (not including costs of maintenance and repairs). See *Basis Adjustments—Details and Exceptions* .... d. ________

e. Any amounts you spent to repair damage to your home or the land on which it sits .... e. ________

f. Any special assessments for local improvements (such as special tax or condominium association assessments that aren't merely for repairs or maintenance) .... f. ________

g. Add lines 4a through 4f. This is your **total basis** .... g. ________

Worksheet 2. **How To Figure Your Gain or Loss** *(continued)*

5. Determine your "basis adjustments" (any payments, credits, or benefits you may need to deduct from your basis).

a. Any depreciation you took or were allowed to take for use of your home for business or rental purposes . . . a. ________

b. Any casualty losses (such as flood or fire damage) you claimed as a deduction on a federal tax return . . . b. ________

c. Any insurance payments you received or expect to receive for casualty losses . . . c. ________

d. Any payments you received for granting an easement, conservation restriction, or right-of-way . . . d. ________

e. Any energy credits or subsidies that effectively paid you back for improvements you included in your total basis. See Basis Adjustments—Details and Exceptions . . . e. ________

f. Any adoption credits you claimed, or any nontaxable payments from an employer-sponsored adoption assistance program . . . f. ________

g. Any real estate taxes the seller paid on your behalf (and for which you never paid the seller back). If you reimburse the seller, it doesn't affect basis . . . g. ________

h. Any mortgage points the seller paid for you when you bought your home, if one of the following is true . . . h. ________

- You bought your home between January 1, 1991, and April 3, 1994, AND you deducted the points as home mortgage interest in the year paid, or
- You bought your home after April 3, 1994 (regardless of whether you deducted the points).

i. Any canceled or forgiven mortgage debt amount that was excluded before January 1, 2026, due to a bankruptcy or insolvency and that you didn't have to declare as income. (See Pub. 4681.) . . . i. ________

j. Any sales tax you paid on your home (such as for a mobile home or houseboat) and then claimed as a deduction on a federal tax return . . . j. ________

k. The value of any temporary housing the builder of your home provided for you . . . k. ________

- *Use this equation:* Contract price × Value of temporary housing ÷ (Value of temporary housing + Value of new home)

l. Any gain you postponed from the sale of a previous home sold before May 7, 1997 . . . l. ________

m. Add lines 5a through 5m. This is your **basis adjustment** . . . m. ________

6. Figure your "adjusted basis" (total basis minus basis adjustments).

Line 4g minus line 5m . . . **6.** ________

- If your **adjusted basis is less than zero** and you went through a mortgage workout or other process resulting in forgiveness or cancellation of mortgage debt ("discharge of qualified principal residence indebtedness"), don't count any portion of your canceled debt that is bringing your basis below zero.

7. Figure your gain or loss (amount realized minus adjusted basis).

Line 3 minus line 6 . . . **7.** ________

- If the **number is negative** (adjusted basis is greater than amount realized), you sold your home at a loss. You can't deduct this loss, but you don't need to pay any tax on the money you received from selling your home. Skip to Reporting Your Home Sale, later.
- If the **number is positive**, you sold your home at a gain. Skip to How Much Is Taxable, later.

past tax returns, compare the size of your business or rental space to the size of the whole property and express this as a percentage. For example, if you have a building with three equal-sized stories, and you live in the top two stories and use the ground floor for a store, then you are using 1/3 of the property and your business percentage is 33.3%.

For each number on your "Total" worksheet, figure the business-related portion of that number and enter it on your "Business or Rental" worksheet. You may use different methods to determine the business portion of different numbers. Here are the three possible methods and the circumstances under which each method applies.

- **Dollar-amount method.** Where a figure consists of specific dollar amounts that relate to either the residence portion or the business portion of the property, the figure must be broken down by these dollar amounts. For example, if the figure for improvements to the property was $100,000, and all of that applied to the residence portion, then the business portion of the improvements would be zero.
- **"100% rule" for depreciation.** The first item under line 5a in Worksheet 2 is a business depreciation item. Any figure for this item is 100% a business figure.
- **Percentage method.** Where a figure applies to the property as a whole (such as the sale price), the business or rental portion is the figure multiplied by the business portion percentage you calculated earlier. Use the percentage method for all items that don't require the dollar-amount or depreciation methods.

The total you get on line 7 on your "Business" copy of Worksheet 2 is the gain or loss related to the business or rental portion of the property you sold.

Next, complete your "Home" worksheet. For each number, take the number from your "Total" worksheet, subtract the number from your "Business or Rental" worksheet, and enter the result in your "Home" worksheet (for example, subtract the number on line 1f of the "Business or Rental" worksheet from the number on line 1f of your "Total" worksheet), and enter the result on your "Home" worksheet.

Now figure the totals on your "Home" worksheet. The total you get on line 7 on the "Home" copy of Worksheet 2 is the gain or loss related to the home portion of the property you sold.

Review the results of your "Home" and "Business" worksheets to determine your next step. When you have completed each worksheet, you will know whether you have a gain or loss on each part of your property. It is possible to have a gain on both parts, a loss on both parts, or a gain on one part and a loss on the other. See Table 2 to determine your next steps.

How Much Is Taxable?

Review of the Eligibility Test. Generally, your home sale qualifies for the maximum exclusion, if all of the following conditions are true.

- You *didn't* acquire the property through a like-kind exchange in the past 5 years.
- You *aren't* subject to the expatriate tax.
- You owned the home for 2 of the last 5 years and lived in the home for 2 (1 if you become disabled) of the last 5 years leading up to the date of the sale.*
- For the 2 years before the date of the current sale, you didn't sell another home on which you claimed the exclusion.
- You didn't use the property as a vacation or rental home after 2008, or you didn't use a portion of the home, outside of the living area, for business or rental purposes.
- The sale *doesn't* involve the transfer of vacant land or a remainder interest.**

*If this condition isn't met, your home sale may qualify for a partial exclusion. The sale must involve one of the following events experienced by you, your spouse, or a co-owner: a work-related move, a health-related move, a death, a divorce, a pregnancy with multiple children, a change in employment status, a change in unemployment compensation eligibility, or other unusual event.

**The transfer of vacant land or of a remainder interest may qualify for the maximum exclusion, but special rules apply in those situations.

Table 2. **Does Your Home or Business Show a Gain or a Loss?**

IF...	THEN...
your "Home" worksheet shows a loss,	follow the instructions at the end of line 7, under Worksheet 2 for "If the number is negative."
your "Home" worksheet shows a gain,	see *How Much Is Taxable?* and Worksheet 3 to find out how much of the gain on your "Home" worksheet is taxable.
your "Business" worksheet shows a loss,	DON'T follow the instructions at the end of line 7, under Worksheet 2. Instead, report the loss from your "Business" worksheet on Form 4797, Sales of Business Property. **Note**. Your loss may be limited. See the Instructions for Form 4797.
your "Business" worksheet shows a gain,	you can't exclude any of the gain shown on your "Business" worksheet. DON'T follow the instructions at the end of line 7, under Worksheet 2. Instead, report the gain from your "Business" worksheet on Form 4797.

For a step-by-step guide to determining whether your home sale qualifies for the maximum exclusion, see *Does Your Home Sale Qualify for the Exclusion of Gain?* above.

If you qualify for an exclusion on your home sale, up to $250,000 ($500,000 if married and filing jointly) of your gain will be tax free. If your gain is more than that amount, or if you qualify only for a partial exclusion, then some of your gain may be taxable. This section contains step-by-step instructions for figuring out how much of your gain is taxable. See Worksheet 3, later, for assistance in determining your taxable gain.

If you determined in *Does Your Home Sale Qualify for the Exclusion of Gain*, earlier, that your home sale doesn't qualify for any exclusion (either full or partial), then your entire gain is taxable. If you don't have a gain, you owe no tax on the sale. In either case, you don't need to complete Worksheet 3 and you can skip to *Reporting Your Home Sale*, later.

Recapturing Depreciation

If you used all or part of your home for business or rental after May 6, 1997, you may need to pay back ("recapture") some or all of the depreciation you were entitled to take on your property. "Recapturing" depreciation means you must include it as ordinary income on your tax return.

Reporting Your Home Sale

This section tells you how to report taxable gain, take deductions relating to your home sale, and report income other than the gain that you may have received from your home sale.

This section also covers special circumstances that apply to some home sellers.

TIP ***What records to keep.*** *Any time you buy real estate, you should keep records to document the property's adjusted basis. In general, keep these records until 3 years after the due date for your tax return for the year in which you sold your home.*

Reporting Gain or Loss on Your Home Sale

Determine whether you need to report the gain from your home. You need to report the gain if ANY of the following is true.

- You have taxable gain on your home sale (or on the residential portion of your property if you made separate calculations for home and business) and don't qualify to exclude all of the gain.
- You received a Form 1099-S. If so, you must report the sale on Form 8949 even if you have no taxable gain to report. See *Instructions for Form 8949* and *Instructions for Schedule D (Form 1040)* for more details.
- You wish to report your gain as a taxable gain even though some or all of it is eligible for exclusion. You may wish to do this if, for example, you plan to sell another main home within the next 2 years and are likely to receive a larger gain from the sale of that property. If you later choose to report, rather than exclude, your taxable gain, you can undo that choice by filing an amended return within 3 years of the due date of your return for the year of the sale, excluding extensions.

If NONE of the three bullets above is true, you don't need to report your home sale on your tax return. If you didn't make separate home and business calculations on your property, skip to *Reporting Deductions Related to Your Home Sale*, later.

If ANY of the three bullets above is true, skip to *Determine whether your home sale is an installment sale*, later.

If you made separate gain/loss calculations for business and residence portions of your property, you may have to use Form 4797 to report the sale of the business or rental part. See *Business or Rental Use of Home*, earlier.

Determine whether your home sale is an installment sale. If you finance the buyer's purchase of your home (you hold a note, mortgage, or other financial agreement), you probably have an installment sale. You may be able to report any non-excludable gain on an installment basis. Use Form 6252, Installment Sale Income, to report the sale.

For more information, see Pub. 537, Installment Sales.

Report any interest you receive from the buyer. If the buyer is making payments to you over time (as when you provide seller financing), then you must generally report part of each payment as interest on your tax return. Report the interest portion of the payment as ordinary income on Form 1040 or 1040-SR, line 2b, or Schedule NEC (Form 1040-NR) if a nonresident alien. If the buyer is using the property as a first or second home, also report the interest on Schedule B (Form 1040), Interest and Ordinary Dividends, to Form 1040 or 1040-SR and provide the buyer's name, address, and social security number. If you don't show the buyer's name, address, and SSN you may have to pay a $50 penalty.

If you're a nonresident or resident alien who doesn't have and isn't eligible to get a social security number, you may be issued an individual taxpayer identification number (ITIN). If you don't have an ITIN, apply for one by filing Form W-7, Application for IRS Individual Taxpayer Identification Number. If needed, a nonresident or resident alien buyer can apply for an ITIN as well.

Complete Form 8949, Sales and Other Dispositions of Capital Assets. Use Form 8949 to report gain from the sale or disposition of the personal-use portion of your home if you can't exclude the gain. If you received Form 1099-S, report the transaction on Form 8949. See the Instructions for Form 8949.

Worksheet 3. **Determine if You Have Taxable Gain**

If you completed "Business" and "Home" versions of your gain/loss worksheet as described in *Business or Rental Use of Home*, earlier, complete this worksheet only for the "Home" version.

Section A. Determine your net gain. Complete this section only if you used any part of your home for business or rental purposes between May 6, 1997, and the date of sale. Otherwise, skip to Section B.		
Step 1	Enter your gain from line 7 of Worksheet 2	______
Step 2	List the total of all depreciation deductions that you took or could have taken for the use of your home for business or rental purposes between May 6, 1997, and the date of sale	______
Step 3	Subtract the sum of Step 2 from the amount listed in Section A, Step 1. This is your net gain	______
Section B. Determine your non-qualified use gain. Complete this section only if the following apply: a) During the time you owned the property there were periods of non-qualified use when neither you nor your spouse (or your former spouse) used the property as your main residence; b) the periods of non-qualified use occurred after 2008; c) the periods of non-qualified use occurred *before* the last day the property was used as your or your spouse's (or your former spouse) principal residence prior to the date of sale. Do not include any period of non-qualified use that occurred *after* the last day that you or your spouse (or former spouse) used the property as your principal residence during the 5-year period prior to the date of sale.* Otherwise, skip to Section C.		
***Note**. If the period of non-use was 1) for an aggregate of 2 years or less and due to a change in employment, a health condition, or other "unforeseen circumstance" described in *Does Your Home Qualify for a Partial Exclusion of Gain*, earlier; or 2) for 10 years or less and due to a "stop the clock" exception for certain military, intelligence, and Peace Corps personnel described in *Service, Intelligence, and Peace Corps Personnel*, earlier, then you may skip Section B.		
Step 1	Enter the amount from Section A, Step 1 or, if you skipped Section A, your gain from line 7 of Worksheet 2	______
Step 2	Enter the total number of days after 2008 and before the date of sale that neither you nor your spouse (or former spouse) used the home as a main residence. Do not include any days that occurred **after** the last day that you or your spouse (or former spouse) used the property as your main residence during the 5-year period prior to the date of sale. This number is your non-use days	______
Step 3	Enter the total number of days you owned your home (counting all days, not just days after 2008). This number is your number of days owned	______
Step 4	Divide the non-use days by the days owned. This number is your non-residence factor	______
Step 5	Multiply the decimal from Section B, Step 4, by the amount listed in Section B, Step 1. This number is your non-qualified use gain	______

Section C. Determine your gain that is eligible for exclusion.

IF...	THEN your gain that is eligible for exclusion is ...
you skipped Sections A and B	your gain from line 7, under Worksheet 2.
you completed Section A but skipped Section B	your net gain, from Section A, Step 3.
you completed Section B (regardless of whether you completed Section A)	your gain from line 7, under Worksheet 2 less your non-qualified use gain, from Section B, Step 5.

Your gain that is eligible for exclusion is $ ______

Section D. Determine if you have taxable gain.

IF...	THEN ...
your gain that is eligible for exclusion from Section C is less than or equal to your exclusion limit from Worksheet 1, Section C	your gain that is eligible for exclusion from your income is not to be reported on your tax return. The *Reporting Your Home Sale* section only applies to your non-qualified use gain.
your gain that is eligible for exclusion from Section C is greater than your exclusion limit from Worksheet 1, Section C	some of your gain isn't excludable, and you may owe tax on it. See *Reporting Your Home Sale* for instructions on how to report the gain on your tax return.

TIP *If you have gain that can't be excluded, you must generally report it on Form 8949, Sales and Other Dispositions of Capital Assets, and Schedule D (Form 1040), Capital Gains and Losses. Report the sale on Part I or Part II of Form 8949 as a short-term or long-term transaction, depending on how long you owned the home. In addition, you may be able to temporarily defer capital gains invested in a Qualified Opportunity Fund (QOF). You may also be able to permanently exclude capital gains from the sale or exchange of an investment in a*

QOF if the investment is held for at least 10 years. For more information, see the Instructions for Form 8949.

Complete Schedule D (Form 1040), Capital Gains and Losses. Using the information on Form 8949, report on Schedule D (Form 1040) the gain or loss on your home as a capital gain or loss. Follow the instructions for Schedule D when completing the form.

If you have any taxable gain from the sale of your home, you may have to increase your withholding or make estimated tax payments. See Pub. 505, Tax Withholding and Estimated Tax.

Reporting Deductions Related to Your Home Sale

If you aren't itemizing deductions on your return for the year in which you sold your home, skip to Reporting Other Income Related to Your Home Sale, later.

There is no tax deduction for transfer taxes, stamp taxes, or other taxes, fees, and charges you paid when you sold your home. However, if you paid these amounts as the seller, you can treat these taxes and fees as selling expenses. If you pay these amounts as the buyer, include them in your cost basis of the property.

Determine the amount of real estate tax deductions associated with your home sale. Depending on your circumstances, you may need to figure your real estate tax deductions differently. See the discussion that follows for more information.

If you didn't receive a Form 1099-S, use the following method to compute your real estate tax deduction, which may be different from the amount of real estate tax you actually paid.

- Divide the number of days you owned the property during the year of sale, not counting the date of sale, by 365 (or 366 for a leap year).
- Multiply that figure by the amount of real estate tax due on the home during the 12-month billing cycle that contains the date of sale. The result is the amount of real estate tax you can deduct as an itemized deduction.

Example. The real estate tax on Dennis and Pat White's home was $620 for the year. Their real property tax year was the calendar year, with payment due August 3, 2022. They sold the home on May 6, 2022. Dennis and Pat are considered to have paid a proportionate share of the real estate taxes on the home even though they didn't actually pay them to the taxing authority.

Dennis and Pat owned their home during the 2022 real property tax year for 125 days (January 1 to May 5, the day before the sale). They figure their deduction for taxes as follows.

1.	Total real estate taxes for the real property tax year	$620
2.	Number of days in the real property tax year that you owned the property	125
3.	Divide line 2 by 365 (366 if leap year)	0.342
4.	Multiply line 1 by line 3. This is your deduction. Enter it on line 5b of Schedule A (Form 1040)	$212

Since the buyers paid all of the taxes, Dennis and Pat also include the $212 in the home's selling price. The buyers add the $212 to their basis in the home. The buyers can deduct $408 ($620 – $212) as an itemized deduction, the taxes for the part of the year they owned the home.

If you received a Form 1099-S, start with the amount of real estate tax you actually paid in the year of sale. Subtract the buyer's share of real estate tax as shown in box 6. The result is the amount you can use in figuring your itemized deductions.

If you didn't already deduct all your mortgage points on an earlier tax return, you may be able to deduct them on your tax return for the year of sale. See Pub. 936, Home Mortgage Interest Deduction.

Report on Schedule A (Form 1040), Itemized Deductions, any itemized real estate deduction. Follow the Instructions for Schedule A when completing the form.

Reporting Other Income Related to Your Home Sale

Report as ordinary income on Form 1040, 1040-SR, or 1040-NR any amounts received from selling personal property. If you sold furniture, drapes, lawn equipment, a washer/dryer, or other property that wasn't a permanent part of your home, report the amount you received for the items as ordinary income. Report this amount on Schedule 1 (Form 1040), line 8z, or Schedule NEC (Form 1040-NR) if a nonresident alien. The selling price of your home doesn't include amounts you received for personal property sold with your home.

Report as ordinary income on Form 1040, 1040-SR, or 1040-NR any amounts received for sales of expired options to purchase your property. If you granted someone an option to buy your home and it expired in the year of sale, report the amount you received for the option as ordinary income. Report this amount on Schedule 1 (Form 1040), line 8z, or Schedule NEC (Form 1040-NR) if a nonresident alien.

Report as ordinary income on Form 1040, 1040-SR, or 1040-NR applicable canceled or forgiven mortgage debt. If you went through a mortgage workout, foreclosure, or other process in which a lender forgave or canceled mortgage debt on your home, then you must generally report the amount of forgiven or canceled debt as income on your tax return. However, if you had a written agreement for the forgiveness of the debt in place before January 1, 2026, then you might be able to exclude the forgiven amount from your income. For more information, see Pub. 4681, Canceled Debts, Foreclosures, Repossessions, and Abandonments.

Paying Back Credits and Subsidies

If you received any homebuyer credits or federal mortgage subsidies, you may have to pay back ("recapture") some or all of the amount by increasing your tax payment.

Determine any amounts you may have claimed as a first-time homebuyer tax credit. If you bought your home in 2008, you must pay back the credit unless you qualify for an exception.

See Form 5405, Repayment of the First-Time Homebuyer Credit, to find out how much to pay back, or if you qualify for any exceptions. If you do have to repay the credit, file Form 5405 with your tax return.

Determine any amounts you may have received in federal mortgage subsidies in the 9 years leading up to the date of sale. If you financed your home under a federally subsidized program (loans from tax-exempt qualified mortgage bonds or loans with mortgage credit certificates), you may have to recapture all or part of the benefit you received from that program upon the sale or other transfer of ownership of your home. You recapture the benefit by increasing your federal income tax for the year of the sale. You may have to pay this recapture tax even if you can exclude your gain from income under the rules discussed earlier; that exclusion doesn't affect the recapture tax.

See Form 8828, Recapture of Federal Mortgage Subsidy, to find out how much to repay, or whether you qualify for any exceptions.

If you did receive any federal mortgage subsidies, you must file Form 8828 with your tax return whether you sold your home at a loss or a gain. If you had a loss, you won't have to pay back any subsidy.

How To Get Tax Help

If you have questions about a tax issue; need help preparing your tax return; or want to download free publications, forms, or instructions, go to *IRS.gov* to find resources that can help you right away.

Preparing and filing your tax return. After receiving all your wage and earnings statements (Forms W-2, W-2G, 1099-R, 1099-MISC, 1099-NEC, etc.); unemployment compensation statements (by mail or in a digital format) or other government payment statements (Form 1099-G); and interest, dividend, and retirement statements from banks and investment firms (Forms 1099), you have several options to choose from to prepare and file your tax return. You can prepare the tax return yourself, see if you qualify for free tax preparation, or hire a tax professional to prepare your return.

Free options for tax preparation. Go to *IRS.gov* to see your options for preparing and filing your return online or in your local community, if you qualify, which include the following.

- **Free File.** This program lets you prepare and file your federal individual income tax return for free using brand-name tax-preparation-and-filing software or Free File fillable forms. However, state tax preparation may not be available through Free File. Go to *IRS.gov/FreeFile* to see if you qualify for free online federal tax preparation, e-filing, and direct deposit or payment options.
- **VITA.** The Volunteer Income Tax Assistance (VITA) program offers free tax help to people with low-to-moderate incomes, persons with disabilities, and limited-English-speaking taxpayers who need help preparing their own tax returns. Go to *IRS.gov/VITA*, download the free IRS2Go app, or call 800-906-9887 for information on free tax return preparation.
- **TCE.** The Tax Counseling for the Elderly (TCE) program offers free tax help for all taxpayers, particularly those who are 60 years of age and older. TCE volunteers specialize in answering questions about pensions and retirement-related issues unique to seniors. Go to *IRS.gov/TCE*, download the free IRS2Go app, or call 888-227-7669 for information on free tax return preparation.
- **MilTax.** Members of the U.S. Armed Forces and qualified veterans may use MilTax, a free tax service offered by the Department of Defense through Military OneSource. For more information, go to *MilitaryOneSource* (*MilitaryOneSource.mil/MilTax*).

  Also, the IRS offers Free Fillable Forms, which can be completed online and then filed electronically regardless of income.

Using online tools to help prepare your return. Go to *IRS.gov/Tools* for the following.

- The *Earned Income Tax Credit Assistant* (*IRS.gov/EITCAssistant*) determines if you're eligible for the earned income credit (EIC).
- The *Online EIN Application* (*IRS.gov/EIN*) helps you get an employer identification number (EIN) at no cost.
- The *Tax Withholding Estimator* (*IRS.gov/W4app*) makes it easier for you to estimate the federal income tax you want your employer to withhold from your paycheck. This is tax withholding. See how your withholding affects your refund, take-home pay, or tax due.
- The *First-Time Homebuyer Credit Account Look-up* (*IRS.gov/HomeBuyer*) tool provides information on your repayments and account balance.
- The *Sales Tax Deduction Calculator* (*IRS.gov/SalesTax*) figures the amount you can claim if you itemize deductions on Schedule A (Form 1040).

Getting answers to your tax questions. On IRS.gov, you can get up-to-date information on current events and changes in tax law.

- *IRS.gov/Help*: A variety of tools to help you get answers to some of the most common tax questions.
- *IRS.gov/ITA*: The Interactive Tax Assistant, a tool that will ask you questions and, based on your input, provide answers on a number of tax law topics.
- *IRS.gov/Forms*: Find forms, instructions, and publications. You will find details on the most recent tax changes and interactive links to help you find answers to your questions.
- You may also be able to access tax law information in your electronic filing software.

Need someone to prepare your tax return? There are various types of tax return preparers, including enrolled agents, certified public accountants (CPAs), accountants, and many others who don't have professional credentials. If you choose to have someone prepare your tax return, choose that preparer wisely. A paid tax preparer is:

- Primarily responsible for the overall substantive accuracy of your return,
- Required to sign the return, and
- Required to include their preparer tax identification number (PTIN).

Although the tax preparer always signs the return, you're ultimately responsible for providing all the information required for the preparer to accurately prepare your return. Anyone paid to prepare tax returns for others should have a thorough understanding of tax matters. For more information on how to choose a tax preparer, go to *Tips for Choosing a Tax Preparer* on IRS.gov.

Coronavirus. Go to *IRS.gov/Coronavirus* for links to information on the impact of the coronavirus, as well as tax relief available for individuals and families, small and large businesses, and tax-exempt organizations.

Employers can register to use Business Services Online. The Social Security Administration (SSA) offers online service at *SSA.gov/employer* for fast, free, and secure online W-2 filing options to CPAs, accountants, enrolled agents, and individuals who process Form W-2, Wage and Tax Statement, and Form W-2c, Corrected Wage and Tax Statement.

IRS social media. Go to *IRS.gov/SocialMedia* to see the various social media tools the IRS uses to share the latest information on tax changes, scam alerts, initiatives, products, and services. At the IRS, privacy and security are our highest priority. We use these tools to share public information with you. **Don't** post your social security number (SSN) or other confidential information on social media sites. Always protect your identity when using any social networking site.

The following IRS YouTube channels provide short, informative videos on various tax-related topics in English, Spanish, and ASL.

- *Youtube.com/irsvideos*.
- *Youtube.com/irsvideosmultilingua*.
- *Youtube.com/irsvideosASL*.

Watching IRS videos. The IRS Video portal (*IRSVideos.gov*) contains video and audio presentations for individuals, small businesses, and tax professionals.

Online tax information in other languages. You can find information on *IRS.gov/MyLanguage* if English isn't your native language.

Free Over-the-Phone Interpreter (OPI) Service. The IRS is committed to serving our multilingual customers by offering OPI services. The OPI Service is a federally funded program and is available at Taxpayer Assistance Centers (TACs), other IRS offices, and every VITA/TCE return site. The OPI Service is accessible in more than 350 languages.

Accessibility Helpline available for taxpayers with disabilities. Taxpayers who need information about accessibility services can call 833-690-0598. The Accessibility Helpline can answer questions related to current and future accessibility products and services available in alternative media formats (for example, braille, large print, audio, etc.). The Accessibility Helpline does not have access to your IRS account. For help with tax law, refunds, or account-related issues, go to *IRS.gov/LetUsHelp*.

Note. Form 9000, Alternative Media Preference, or Form 9000(SP) allows you to elect to receive certain types of written correspondence in the following formats.

- Standard Print.
- Large Print.
- Braille.
- Audio (MP3).
- Plain Text File (TXT).
- Braille Ready File (BRF).

Disasters. Go to *Disaster Assistance and Emergency Relief for Individuals and Businesses* to review the available disaster tax relief.

Getting tax forms and publications. Go to *IRS.gov/Forms* to view, download, or print all the forms, instructions, and publications you may need. Or, you can go to *IRS.gov/OrderForms* to place an order.

Getting tax publications and instructions in eBook format. You can also download and view popular tax publications and instructions (including the Instructions for Form 1040) on mobile devices as eBooks at *IRS.gov/eBooks*.

Note. IRS eBooks have been tested using Apple's iBooks for iPad. Our eBooks haven't been tested on other dedicated eBook readers, and eBook functionality may not operate as intended.

Access your online account (individual taxpayers only). Go to *IRS.gov/Account* to securely access information about your federal tax account.

- View the amount you owe and a breakdown by tax year.
- See payment plan details or apply for a new payment plan.
- Make a payment or view 5 years of payment history and any pending or scheduled payments.
- Access your tax records, including key data from your most recent tax return, and transcripts.
- View digital copies of select notices from the IRS.
- Approve or reject authorization requests from tax professionals.
- View your address on file or manage your communication preferences.

Tax Pro Account. This tool lets your tax professional submit an authorization request to access your individual taxpayer *IRS online account*. For more information, go to *IRS.gov/TaxProAccount*.

Using direct deposit. The fastest way to receive a tax refund is to file electronically and choose direct deposit, which securely and electronically transfers your refund directly into your financial account. Direct deposit also avoids the possibility that your check could be lost, stolen, destroyed, or returned undeliverable to the IRS. Eight in 10 taxpayers use direct deposit to receive their refunds. If you don't have a bank account, go to *IRS.gov/DirectDeposit* for more information on where to find a bank or credit union that can open an account online.

Getting a transcript of your return. The quickest way to get a copy of your tax transcript is to go to *IRS.gov/Transcripts*. Click on either "Get Transcript Online" or "Get Transcript by Mail" to order a free copy of your transcript. If you prefer, you can order your transcript by calling 800-908-9946.

Reporting and resolving your tax-related identity theft issues.

- Tax-related identity theft happens when someone steals your personal information to commit tax fraud. Your taxes can be affected if your SSN is used to file a fraudulent return or to claim a refund or credit.
- The IRS doesn't initiate contact with taxpayers by email, text messages (including shortened links), telephone calls, or social media channels to request or verify personal or financial information. This includes requests for personal identification numbers (PINs), passwords, or similar information for credit cards, banks, or other financial accounts.
- Go to *IRS.gov/IdentityTheft*, the IRS Identity Theft Central webpage, for information on identity theft and data security protection for taxpayers, tax professionals, and businesses. If your SSN has been lost or stolen or you suspect you're a victim of tax-related identity theft, you can learn what steps you should take.
- Get an Identity Protection PIN (IP PIN). IP PINs are six-digit numbers assigned to taxpayers to help prevent the misuse of their SSNs on fraudulent federal income tax returns. When you have an IP PIN, it prevents someone else from filing a tax return with your SSN. To learn more, go to *IRS.gov/IPPIN*.

Ways to check on the status of your refund.

- Go to *IRS.gov/Refunds*.
- Download the official IRS2Go app to your mobile device to check your refund status.
- Call the automated refund hotline at 800-829-1954.

Note. The IRS can't issue refunds before mid-February for returns that claimed the EIC or the additional child tax credit (ACTC). This applies to the entire refund, not just the portion associated with these credits.

Making a tax payment. Go to *IRS.gov/Payments* for information on how to make a payment using any of the following options.

- *IRS Direct Pay*: Pay your individual tax bill or estimated tax payment directly from your checking or savings account at no cost to you.
- *Debit or Credit Card*: Choose an approved payment processor to pay online or by phone.
- *Electronic Funds Withdrawal*: Schedule a payment when filing your federal taxes using tax return preparation software or through a tax professional.
- *Electronic Federal Tax Payment System*: Best option for businesses. Enrollment is required.
- *Check or Money Order*: Mail your payment to the address listed on the notice or instructions.
- *Cash*: You may be able to pay your taxes with cash at a participating retail store.
- *Same-Day Wire*: You may be able to do same-day wire from your financial institution. Contact your financial institution for availability, cost, and time frames.

Note. The IRS uses the latest encryption technology to ensure that the electronic payments you make online, by phone, or from a mobile device using the IRS2Go app are safe and secure. Paying electronically is quick, easy, and faster than mailing in a check or money order.

What if I can't pay now? Go to *IRS.gov/Payments* for more information about your options.

- Apply for an *online payment agreement* (*IRS.gov/OPA*) to meet your tax obligation in monthly installments if you can't pay your taxes in full today. Once you complete the online process, you will receive immediate notification of whether your agreement has been approved.
- Use the *Offer in Compromise Pre-Qualifier* to see if you can settle your tax debt for less than the full

amount you owe. For more information on the Offer in Compromise program, go to *IRS.gov/OIC*.

Filing an amended return. Go to *IRS.gov/Form1040X* for information and updates.

Checking the status of your amended return. Go to *IRS.gov/WMAR* to track the status of Form 1040-X amended returns.

Note. It can take up to 3 weeks from the date you filed your amended return for it to show up in our system, and processing it can take up to 16 weeks.

Understanding an IRS notice or letter you've received. Go to *IRS.gov/Notices* to find additional information about responding to an IRS notice or letter.

Note. You can use Schedule LEP (Form 1040), Request for Change in Language Preference, to state a preference to receive notices, letters, or other written communications from the IRS in an alternative language. You may not immediately receive written communications in the requested language. The IRS's commitment to LEP taxpayers is part of a multi-year timeline that is scheduled to begin providing translations in 2023. You will continue to receive communications, including notices and letters in English until they are translated to your preferred language.

Contacting your local IRS office. Keep in mind, many questions can be answered on IRS.gov without visiting an IRS TAC. Go to *IRS.gov/LetUsHelp* for the topics people ask about most. If you still need help, IRS TACs provide tax help when a tax issue can't be handled online or by phone. All TACs now provide service by appointment, so you'll know in advance that you can get the service you need without long wait times. Before you visit, go to *IRS.gov/TACLocator* to find the nearest TAC and to check hours, available services, and appointment options. Or, on the IRS2Go app, under the Stay Connected tab, choose the Contact Us option and click on "Local Offices."

The Taxpayer Advocate Service (TAS) Is Here To Help You

What Is TAS?

TAS is an ***independent*** organization within the IRS that helps taxpayers and protects taxpayer rights. Their job is to ensure that every taxpayer is treated fairly and that you know and understand your rights under the *Taxpayer Bill of Rights*.

How Can You Learn About Your Taxpayer Rights?

The Taxpayer Bill of Rights describes 10 basic rights that all taxpayers have when dealing with the IRS. Go to *TaxpayerAdvocate.IRS.gov* to help you understand what these rights mean to you and how they apply. These are ***your*** rights. Know them. Use them.

What Can TAS Do for You?

TAS can help you resolve problems that you can't resolve with the IRS. And their service is free. If you qualify for their assistance, you will be assigned to one advocate who will work with you throughout the process and will do everything possible to resolve your issue. TAS can help you if:

- Your problem is causing financial difficulty for you, your family, or your business;
- You face (or your business is facing) an immediate threat of adverse action; or
- You've tried repeatedly to contact the IRS but no one has responded, or the IRS hasn't responded by the date promised.

How Can You Reach TAS?

TAS has offices *in every state, the District of Columbia, and Puerto Rico*. Your local advocate's number is in your local directory and at *TaxpayerAdvocate.IRS.gov/Contact-Us*. You can also call them at 877-777-4778.

How Else Does TAS Help Taxpayers?

TAS works to resolve large-scale problems that affect many taxpayers. If you know of one of these broad issues, report it to them at *IRS.gov/SAMS*.

TAS for Tax Professionals

TAS can provide a variety of information for tax professionals, including tax law updates and guidance, TAS programs, and ways to let TAS know about systemic problems you've seen in your practice.

Low Income Taxpayer Clinics (LITCs)

LITCs are independent from the IRS. LITCs represent individuals whose income is below a certain level and need to resolve tax problems with the IRS, such as audits, appeals, and tax collection disputes. In addition, LITCs can provide information about taxpayer rights and responsibilities in different languages for individuals who speak English as a second language. Services are offered for free or a small fee for eligible taxpayers. To find an LITC near you, go to *TaxpayerAdvocate.IRS.gov/about-us/Low-Income-Taxpayer-Clinics-LITC* or see IRS Pub. 4134, *Low Income Taxpayer Clinic List*.

Index

To help us develop a more useful index, please let us know if you have ideas for index entries. See "Comments and Suggestions" in the "Introduction" for the ways you can reach us.

B. [§ 8.150] Instructions for Form 4797, Sales of Business Property

2022 Instructions for Form 4797

Department of the Treasury
Internal Revenue Service

Sales of Business Property (Also Involuntary Conversions and Recapture Amounts Under Sections 179 and 280F(b)(2))

Section references are to the Internal Revenue Code unless otherwise noted.

Future Developments

For the latest information about developments related to Form 4797 and its instructions, such as legislation enacted after they were published, go to *IRS.gov/Form4797*.

General Instructions

Purpose of Form

Use Form 4797 to report the following.
- The sale or exchange of:

1. Real property used in your trade or business;
2. Depreciable and amortizable tangible property used in your trade or business (however, see *Disposition of Depreciable Property Not Used in Trade or Business*, later);
3. Oil, gas, geothermal, or other mineral properties; and
4. Section 126 property.

- The involuntary conversion (from other than casualty or theft) of property used in your trade or business and capital assets held for more than 1 year in connection with a trade or business or a transaction entered into for profit (however, see *Disposition of Depreciable Property Not Used in Trade or Business*, later).
- The disposition of noncapital assets (other than inventory or property held primarily for sale to customers in the ordinary course of your trade or business).
- The disposition of capital assets not reported on Schedule D.
- The gain or loss (including any related recapture) for partners and S corporation shareholders from certain section 179 property dispositions by partnerships and S corporations.
- The computation of recapture amounts under sections 179 and 280F(b)(2) when the business use of section 179 or listed property decreases to 50% or less.
- Gains or losses treated as ordinary gains or losses, if you are a trader in securities or commodities and made a mark-to-market election under section 475(f).
- Election to defer a qualified section 1231 gain (gains derived from the sale of property used in a trade or business) invested in a qualified opportunity fund (QOF).

Other Forms You May Have To File

- Use Form 4684, Casualties and Thefts, to report involuntary conversions from casualties and thefts.
- Use Form 6252, Installment Sale Income, to report the sale of property under the installment method.
- Use Form 8824, Like-Kind Exchanges, to report exchanges of qualifying business or investment real property for real property of a like kind. For exchanges of real property used in a trade or business (and other noncapital assets), enter the gain or (loss) from Form 8824, if any, on Form 4797, line 5 or line 16.
- If you sold property on which you claimed investment credit, see Form 4255, Recapture of Investment Credit,

Where To Make First Entry for Certain Items Reported on This Form

	(a) Type of property	(b) Held 1 year or less	(c) Held more than 1 year
1	**Depreciable tangible trade or business property:**		
	a Sold or exchanged at a gain	Part II	Part III (1245)
	b Sold or exchanged at a loss	Part II	Part I
2	**Depreciable real trade or business property:**		
	a Sold or exchanged at a gain	Part II	Part III (1250)
	b Sold or exchanged at a loss	Part II	Part I
3	**Farmland held less than 10 years upon which soil or water expenses were deducted:**		
	a Sold at a gain	Part II	Part III (1252)
	b Sold at a loss	Part II	Part I
4	**Real or tangible trade or business property which was deducted under the de minimis safe harbor**	Part II	Part II
5	**All other farmland used in a trade or business**	Part II	Part I
6	**Disposition of cost-sharing payment property described in section 126**	Part II	Part III (1255)
7	**Cattle and horses used in a trade or business for draft, breeding, dairy, or sporting purposes:**	**Held less than 24 months**	**Held 24 months or more**
	a Sold at a gain	Part II	Part III (1245)
	b Sold at a loss	Part II	Part I
	c Raised cattle and horses sold at a gain	Part II	Part I
8	**Livestock other than cattle and horses used in a trade or business for draft, breeding, dairy, or sporting purposes:**	**Held less than 12 months**	**Held 12 months or more**
	a Sold at a gain	Part II	Part III (1245)
	b Sold at a loss	Part II	Part I
	c Raised livestock sold at a gain	Part II	Part I

Oct 25, 2022 Cat. No. 13087T

and its instructions to find out if you must recapture some or all of the credit.
- Use Form 8949, Sales and Other Dispositions of Capital Assets, to report the sale or exchange of capital assets not reported on another form or schedule; gains from involuntary conversions (other than casualty or theft) of capital assets not used in your trade or business; and nonbusiness bad debts. However, see *Disposition of Depreciable Property Not Used in Trade or Business*, later.
- Use the applicable Schedule D, Capital Gains and Losses, for the return you are filing to figure the overall gain or loss from transactions reported on Form 8949 and to report transactions you don't have to report on Form 8949. See the Instructions for Form 8949 and the instructions for the applicable Schedule D.

Additional information. See the instructions for the forms listed above for more information. Also see Pub. 544, Sales and Other Dispositions of Assets, and Pub. 550, Investment Income and Expenses.

Special Rules

At-Risk Rules

If you report a loss on an asset used in an activity for which you are not at risk, in whole or in part, see the Instructions for Form 6198, At-Risk Limitations. Also, see Pub. 925, Passive Activity and At-Risk Rules. Losses from passive activities are subject first to the at-risk rules and then to the passive activity rules.

Depreciable Property and Other Property Disposed of in the Same Transaction

If you disposed of both depreciable property and other property (for example, a building and land) in the same transaction and realized a gain, you must allocate the amount realized between the two types of property based on their respective fair market values (FMVs) to figure the part of the gain to be recaptured as ordinary income because of depreciation. The disposition of each type of property is reported separately in the appropriate part of Form 4797. For example, for property held more than 1 year, report the sale of a building in Part III and the land in Part I.

Disposition of Depreciable Property Not Used in Trade or Business

Generally, gain from the sale or exchange of depreciable property not used in a trade or business but held for investment or for use in a not-for-profit activity is capital gain. Generally, the gain is reported on Form 8949 and Schedule D. However, part of the gain on the sale or exchange of the depreciable property may have to be recaptured as ordinary income on Form 4797. Use Part III of Form 4797 to figure the amount of ordinary income recapture. The recapture amount is included on line 31 (and line 13) of Form 4797. See the instructions for Part III. If the total gain for the depreciable property is more than the recapture amount, the excess is reported on Form 8949. On Form 8949, enter "From Form 4797" in column (a) of Part I (if the transaction is short term) or Part II (if the transaction is long term), and skip columns (b) and (c). In column (d), enter the excess of the total gain over the recapture amount. Leave columns (e) through (g) blank and complete column (h). If you invested this gain into a QOF and intend to elect the temporary deferral of the gain, see the Instructions for Form 8949; Form 8997, Initial and Annual Statement of Qualified Opportunity Fund (QOF) Investments, and its instructions; and the instructions for the applicable Schedule D.

Generally, loss from the sale or exchange of depreciable property not used in a trade or business but held for investment or for use in a not-for-profit activity is a capital loss. Report the loss on Form 8949 in Part I (if the transaction is short term) or Part II (if the transaction is long term). You can deduct capital losses up to the amount of your capital gains. In the case of taxpayers other than corporations, you can also deduct the lower of $3,000 ($1,500 if you are a married individual filing a separate return), or the excess of such losses over such gains. See the Instructions for Form 8949 and the Instructions for Schedule D (Form 1040).

Partial Dispositions of MACRS Property

You may elect to recognize a partial disposition of a Modified Accelerated Cost Recovery System (MACRS) asset, and report the gain, loss, or other deduction on a timely filed, including extensions, federal tax return for the year of the disposition. In some cases, however, you are required to report the gain or loss on the partial disposition of a MACRS asset (see *Required partial dispositions* below). MACRS assets include buildings (and their structural components) and other tangible depreciable property placed in service after 1986 that is used in a trade or business or for the production of income.

For more information on partial dispositions of MACRS property, see Regulations section 1.168(i)-8(d).

Elective partial dispositions. If you elect to recognize a partial disposition of a MACRS asset, report the gain or loss (if any) on Form 4797, Part I, II, or III, as applicable, and include the words "Partial Disposition Election" in the description of the partially disposed asset. See the instructions for Parts I, II, and III. For more information on the disposition of MACRS assets, see Regulations section 1.168(i)-8.

Required partial dispositions. Report the gain or loss (if any) on the following partial dispositions of MACRS assets on Form 4797, Part I, II, or III, as applicable.
- Sale of a portion of a MACRS asset.
- Involuntary conversion of a portion of a MACRS asset other than from a casualty or theft.
- Like-kind exchange of a portion of a MACRS asset (Form 4797, line 5 or 16).

See the instructions for lines 1b and 1c and the instructions for Parts I, II, and III. Also, see *Other Forms You May Have To File*, earlier.

Disposition of Assets That Constitute a Trade or Business

If you sell a group of assets that make up a trade or business and the buyer's basis in the assets are determined wholly by the amount paid for the assets, both you and the buyer must generally allocate the total sales price to the assets transferred. File Form 8594, Asset Acquisition Statement, to report the sale. See the Instructions for Form 8594. Also, see Pub. 544 for more details on the sale of business assets.

Installment Sales

If you sold property at a gain and you will receive a payment in a tax year after the year of sale, you must generally report the sale on the installment method unless you elect not to do so.

Use Form 6252 to report the sale on the installment method. Also use Form 6252 to report any payment received during your 2022 tax year from a sale made in an earlier year that you reported on the installment method.

Enter any gain from the installment sale on Form 4797, line 4 or line 15, as applicable. See the instructions for Form 6252.

To elect out of the installment method, report the full amount of the gain on a timely filed return (including extensions). If you timely filed your tax return without making the election, you can still make the election by filing an amended return within 6 months of the due date of your return (excluding extensions). Enter "Filed pursuant to section 301.9100-2" at the top of the amended return.

For a detailed discussion of installment sales, see Pub. 537, Installment Sales.

Traders Who Made a Mark-to-Market Election

A trader in securities or commodities may elect under section 475(f) to use the mark-to-market method to account for securities or commodities held in connection with a trading business. Under this method of accounting, any security or commodity held at the end of the tax year is treated as sold at its FMV on the last business day of that year.

Unless you are a new taxpayer, the election must be made by the due date (not including extensions) of the tax return for the year prior to the year for which the election becomes effective.

If you are a trader in securities or commodities with a mark-to-market election under section 475(f) in effect for the tax year, the following special rules apply.

- Gains and losses from all securities or commodities held in connection with your trading business (including those marked to market) are treated as ordinary income and losses, instead of capital gains and losses. As a result, the lower capital gain tax rates and the limitation on capital losses don't apply.
- The gain or loss from each security or commodity held in connection with your trading business (including those marked to market) is reported on Form 4797, Part II, line 10. See *Securities or Commodities Held by a Trader Who Made a Mark-to-Market Election* in the instructions for line 10.
- The wash sale rule does not apply to securities or commodities held in connection with your trading business.

For details on the mark-to-market election for traders and how to make the election, see section 475(f). Also see Pub. 550.

Sale of Home Used for Business

If you sold property that was your home and you also used it for business, you may need to use Form 4797 to report the sale of the part used for business (or the sale of the entire property if used entirely for business). Gain or loss on the sale of the home may be a capital gain or loss or an ordinary gain or loss. Any gain on the personal part of the property is a capital gain. You cannot deduct a loss on the personal part. Any gain or loss on the part of the home used for business is an ordinary gain or loss, as applicable, reportable on Form 4797. Any gain or loss on the part producing income for which the underlying activity does not rise to the level of a trade or business is a capital gain or loss, as applicable. See *Disposition of Depreciable Property Not Used in Trade or Business*, earlier. For more details, see Pub. 544. Also, see Pub. 523, Selling Your Home.

Exclusion of gain on sale of home used for business. You may be able to exclude part or all of the gain figured on Form 4797 if the property sold was used for business and was also owned and used as your principal residence during the 5-year period ending on the date of the sale. During that 5-year period, you must have owned and used the property as your personal residence for 2 or more years. However, the exclusion may not apply to the part of the gain that is allocated to any period after December 31, 2008, during which the property was not used as your principal residence.

If the property was held more than 1 year after you converted it to business use, complete Part III to figure the amount of the gain. Do not take the exclusion into account when figuring the gain on line 24. If line 22 includes depreciation for periods after May 6, 1997, you cannot exclude gain to the extent of that depreciation. On Part I, line 2, enter "Section 121 exclusion," and enter the amount of the exclusion as a (loss) in column (g).

If the property was held for 1 year or less after you converted it to business use, report the sale and the amount of the exclusion, if any, in a similar manner on Part II, line 10.

For details and exceptions, including how to figure gain on the sale of a home used for business and the amount of the exclusion, see section 121 and Pub. 523.

Involuntary Conversion of Property

You may not have to pay tax on a gain from an involuntary or compulsory conversion of property. See Pub. 544 for details.

Passive Loss Limitations

If you have an overall loss from passive activities and you report a loss on an asset used in a passive activity, use Form 8582, Passive Activity Loss Limitations, or Form 8810, Corporate Passive Activity Loss and Credit Limitations, as applicable, to see how much loss is allowed before entering it on Form 4797.

You cannot claim unused passive activity credits when you dispose of your interest in an activity. However, if you dispose of your entire interest in an activity, you may elect to increase the basis of the credit property by the original basis reduction of the property to the extent that the credit has not been allowed because of the passive activity rules. Make the election on Form 8582-CR, Passive Activity Credit Limitations, or Form 8810, as applicable. No basis adjustment may be elected on a partial disposition of your interest in an activity.

Recapture of Preproductive Expenses

If you elect under section 263A(d)(3) not to use the uniform capitalization rules of section 263A, any plant that you produce is treated as section 1245 property. For dispositions of plants reportable on Form 4797, enter the recapture amount taxed as ordinary income on Part III, line 22. See *Disposition of plants* in chapter 9 of Pub. 225, Farmer's Tax Guide, for details.

Section 197(f)(9)(B)(ii) Election

If you made the election under section 197(f)(9)(B)(ii) to recognize gain on the disposition of a section 197 intangible and to pay a tax on that gain at the highest tax rate, include the additional tax on Form 1040, line 16 (or the appropriate line of other income tax returns). Check box 3 and enter "197" and the tax in the space next to that box. The additional tax is the amount that, when added to any other income tax on the gain, equals the gain multiplied by the highest tax rate.

Deferral of Gain Invested in a Qualified Opportunity Fund (QOF)

If you realized a gain from an actual or deemed sale or exchange with an unrelated person and, during the 180-day period beginning on the date the gain is realized, you invested any portion of the gain in a QOF, then you may be able to elect to temporarily defer such eligible capital gain that would otherwise be includible in the current tax year's income. If you make the election, the eligible capital gain is included in taxable income only to the extent, if any, the amount of realized gain exceeds the aggregate amount invested in a QOF during the 180-day period.

A taxpayer may elect to temporarily defer a qualified section 1231 gain (gains derived from the sale of property used in a trade or business, including gains from installment sales and like-kind exchanges) by investing the amount of the eligible gain into a QOF. Qualified section 1231 gains are eligible to be invested into a QOF to the extent the section 1231 gain exceeds any amount that is treated as ordinary income due to depreciation recapture as required by sections 1245 and 1250. Sections 1245 and 1250 gain may not be deferred into a QOF. For more information, see section 1400Z-2 and the related regulations.

How to report. Report the gain including any depreciation recapture required by sections 1245 and 1250 as it would otherwise be reported if you were not making the election. Then, on Form 4797, line 2, report the qualified section 1231 gains you are electing to defer as a result of an investment into a QOF within 180 days of the date sold. If you are reporting the sale directly on Form 4797, line 2, use the line directly below the line on which you reported the sale. In column (a), identify the section 1231 gains invested into a QOF as "QOF investment to Form 8949"; columns (b), (c), (d), (e), and (f) will remain blank. Report the amount of section 1231 gains invested into a QOF as a negative amount (in parentheses) in column (g).

For example, if a taxpayer realizes $300,000 of section 1231 gains in a tax year but chooses to defer $75,000 of section 1231 gains by investing those gains into a QOF within 180 days of the date of sale, the taxpayer would enter "QOF investment to Form 8949" in column (a) and enter ($75,000) in column (g).

Similarly, if the taxpayer disposed of an investment in a QOF during the tax year triggering recognition of section 1231 deferred gains, the taxpayer should report the gain on a separate row in line 2, enter "QOF inclusion from section 1231 gains" in column (a), and report the $75,000 of previously deferred and currently recognizable section 1231 gains as a positive number in column (g).

Make the election for the deferred amount invested in a QOF on Form 8949. See the Instructions for Form 8949. If you held a qualified investment in a QOF at any time during the year, you must file your return with Form 8997 attached. See the instructions for Form 8997. For more information about QOFs, see *IRS.gov/Ozfaqs*.

Exclusion of Gain From Sale of DC Zone Assets

If you sold or exchanged a District of Columbia Enterprise Zone (DC Zone) asset that you acquired after 1997 and before 2012, and held for more than 5 years, you may be able to exclude the amount of "qualified capital gain." This exclusion applies to an interest in, or property of, certain businesses operating in the District of Columbia.

DC Zone asset. A DC Zone asset is any of the following.

- DC Zone business stock.
- DC Zone partnership interest.
- DC Zone business property.

Qualified capital gain. The qualified capital gain is any gain recognized on the sale or exchange of a DC Zone asset that is a capital asset or property used in a trade or business that you would otherwise include on Form 4797, Part I. It does not include any of the following gain.

- Gain treated as ordinary income under section 1245.
- Section 1250 gain figured as if section 1250 applied to all depreciation rather than the additional depreciation.
- Gain attributable to real property, or an intangible asset, which is not an integral part of a DC Zone business.
- Gain from a related-party transaction. See *Sales and Exchanges Between Related Persons* in chapter 2 of Pub. 544.
- Gain attributable to periods after December 31, 2016.

See section 1400B (as in effect before its repeal) for more details and special rules.

How to report. If applicable, report the entire gain realized from the sale or exchange as you otherwise would without regard to the exclusion. To report the exclusion, enter "DC Zone Asset Exclusion" on Form 4797, line 2, column (a), and enter as a (loss) in column (g) the amount of the exclusion that offsets the gain reported on Part I, line 6.

CAUTION *Any unrecaptured section 1250 gain is not qualified capital gain. Identify the amount of gain that is unrecaptured section 1250 gain and report it on the Schedule D for the return you are filing.*

Exclusion of Gain From Qualified Community Assets

If you sold or exchanged a qualified community asset acquired after 2001 and before 2010, you may be able to exclude the "qualified capital gain." The qualified gain is, generally, any gain recognized in a trade or business that you would otherwise include on Form 4797, Part I. This exclusion also applies to an interest in, or property of, certain renewal community businesses. See sections 1400F(c) and (d) (as in effect before their repeal) for special rules and limitations.

Qualified community asset. A qualified community asset is any of the following.

- Qualified community stock.
- Qualified community partnership interest.
- Qualified community business property.

Qualified capital gain. Qualified capital gain is any gain recognized on the sale or exchange of a qualified community asset that is a capital asset or property used in a trade or business. It does not include any of the following gains.

- Gain treated as ordinary income under section 1245.
- Section 1250 gain figured as if section 1250 applied to all depreciation rather than the additional depreciation.
- Gain attributable to real property, or an intangible asset, that is not an integral part of a renewal community business.
- Gain from a related-party transaction. See *Sales and Exchanges Between Related Persons* in chapter 2 of Pub. 544.
- Gains from periods after December 31, 2014.

See section 1400F (as in effect before its repeal) for more details and special rules.

How to report. If applicable, report the entire gain realized from the sale or exchange as you otherwise would without regard to the exclusion. To report the exclusion, enter "Qualified Community Asset Exclusion" on Form 4797, line 2, column (a), and enter as a (loss) in column (g) the amount of the exclusion that offsets the gain reported on Part I, line 6.

Specific Instructions

Note. To show losses, enclose figures in (parentheses).

If you disposed of property you acquired by inheritance from someone who died, enter "INHERITED" in column (b) instead of the date you acquired the property. Also report the sale or exchange that way if you inherited the property from someone who died in 2010 and the executor of the decedent's estate did not elect under section 1022 to file Form 8939.

Disposition by a Partnership or S Corporation of Section 179 Property

Partners and S corporation shareholders. If you received a Schedule K-1 from a partnership or S corporation reporting the sale, exchange, or other disposition of property for which a section 179 expense deduction was previously claimed and passed through to its partners or shareholders, you must report your share of the transaction on Form 4797, 4684, 6252, or 8824 (whether or not you were a partner or shareholder at the time the section 179 deduction was claimed).

Use the worksheet, later, to figure the amount to report on Form 4797, 4684, 6252, or 8824, and to figure any reduction in your carryforward of the unused section 179 expense deduction. The partnership or S corporation must provide the following information on Schedule K-1 for the transaction.

- Description of the property.
- Date the property was acquired and placed in service.
- Date of the sale or other disposition of the property.
- Your share of the gross sales price or amount realized. Enter this amount on line 1 of the worksheet.
- Your share of the cost or other basis plus the expense of sale. Enter this amount on line 2 of the worksheet.
- Your share of the depreciation allowed or allowable, but excluding the section 179 expense deduction. Enter this amount on line 3a of the worksheet.
- Your share of the section 179 expense deduction passed through for the property and the partnership's or S corporation's tax year(s) in which the amount was passed through. Enter on line 3b of the worksheet your share of the total amount of the section 179 expense deduction passed through for the property (even if you were not a partner or shareholder for the tax year in which it was passed through or you did not deduct all or part of the section 179 expense because of the dollar or taxable income limitations). The tax year(s) in which the amount was passed through is provided so you can determine the amount of unused carryover section 179 expense (if any) for the property to report on line 3c.
- If the disposition is due to a casualty or theft, a statement indicating so, and any additional information you need to complete Form 4684.
- If the disposition was an installment sale made during the partnership's or S corporation's tax year reported using the installment method, any information you need to complete Form 6252. The partnership or S corporation must also separately report your share of all payments received for the property in the following tax years.
- If the disposition was a disposition of property given up in an exchange involving like-kind property made during the partnership's or S corporation's tax year, any information you need to complete Form 8824.

If you have a carryforward of unused section 179 expense deduction that includes section 179 expense deduction previously passed through to you for the disposed asset, you must reduce your carryforward by your share of the section 179 expense deduction shown on Schedule K-1 (or the amount attributable to that property included in your carryforward amount).

Note. Partnerships and S corporations do not report these transactions on Form 4797, 4684, 6252, or 8824. Instead, they provide their partners and shareholders the information they need to report the transactions. See the Instructions for Form 1065 or the Instructions for Form 1120-S for details on the information that must be reported on Schedule K-1.

Line 1

Line 1a. Enter on line 1a the total gross proceeds from:

- Sales or exchanges of real estate reported to you for 2022 on Form(s) 1099-S (or substitute statement(s)) that you are including on line 2, 10, or 20; and
- Sales of securities or commodities reported to you for 2022 on Form(s) 1099-B (or substitute statement(s)) that you are including on line 10 because you are a trader with a mark-to-market election under section 475(f) in effect for the tax year. See *Traders Who Made a Mark-to-Market Election*, earlier, and the instructions for line 10, later.

Line 1b. Enter on line 1b the total amount of gain that you are including on lines 2, 10, and 24 due to the partial dispositions of MACRS assets. See *Partial Dispositions of MACRS Property*, earlier.

Line 1c. Enter on line 1c the total amount of loss that you are including on lines 2 and 10 due to partial dispositions of MACRS assets. See *Partial Dispositions of MACRS Property*, earlier.

Part I

Use Part I to report section 1231 transactions that are not required to be reported in Part III.

Section 1231 transactions. The following are section 1231 transactions.

- Sales or exchanges of real or depreciable property used in a trade or business and held for more than 1 year. To figure the holding period, begin counting on the day after you received the property and include the day you disposed of it.
- Cutting of timber that the taxpayer elects to treat as a sale or exchange under section 631(a).
- Disposal of timber with a retained economic interest that is treated as a sale, or an outright sale of timber, under section 631(b).
- Disposal of coal (including lignite) or domestic iron ore with a retained economic interest that is treated as a sale under section 631(c).
- Sales or exchanges of cattle and horses, regardless of age, used in a trade or business for draft, breeding, dairy, or sporting purposes and held for 24 months or more from acquisition date.
- Sales or exchanges of livestock other than cattle and horses, regardless of age, used in a trade or business for draft, breeding, dairy, or sporting

purposes and held for 12 months or more from acquisition date.

Note. Livestock does not include poultry, chickens, turkeys, pigeons, geese, other birds, fish, frogs, reptiles, etc.

- Sales or exchanges of certain unharvested crops. See section 1231(b)(4).
- Involuntary conversions of trade or business property or capital assets held more than 1 year in connection with a trade or business or a transaction entered into for profit. These conversions may result from (a) part or total destruction, (b) theft or seizure, or (c) requisition or condemnation (whether threatened or carried out). However, if any recognized losses were from involuntary conversions from fire, storm, shipwreck, or other casualty or from theft and the losses exceed the recognized gains from the conversions, do not include any gains or losses from such conversions when figuring your net section 1231 gains and section 1231 losses.

Transactions to which section 1231 does not apply. Section 1231 transactions do not include sales or exchanges of:

- Inventory or property held primarily for sale to customers;
- Patents; inventions; models or designs (whether or not patented); secret formulas or processes; copyrights; literary, musical, or artistic compositions; letters or memoranda; or similar property (a) created by your personal efforts, (b) prepared or produced for you (in the case of letters, memoranda, or similar property), or (c) received from someone who created them or for whom they were created, as mentioned in (a) or (b), in a way that entitled you to the basis of the previous owner (such as by gift); or
- U.S. Government publications, including the Congressional Record, that you:

1. Received from the government other than by purchase at the normal sales price; or

2. Received from someone who had received it from the government, other than by purchase at the normal sales price, in a way that entitled you to the previous owner's basis (such as by gift).

Line 7

Partners and S corporation shareholders receive a Schedule K-1 (Form 1065 or Form 1120-S), which includes amounts that must be reported on Form 4797. Following the Instructions for Schedule K-1, enter any amounts from your Schedule K-1 (Form 1120-S), box 9, or Schedule K-1 (Form 1065), box 10, in Part I of Form 4797.

If the amount from line 7 is a gain and you have nonrecaptured section 1231 losses from prior years, see the instructions for line 8 below. If the amount from line 7 is a gain and you did not have nonrecaptured section 1231 losses from prior years, enter the gain from line 7 as a long-term capital gain on the Schedule D for the return you are filing.

Line 8

Your nonrecaptured section 1231 losses are your net section 1231 losses deducted during the 5 preceding tax years that have not yet been applied against any net section 1231 gain to determine how much net section 1231 gain is treated as ordinary income under this rule.

You had a net section 1231 loss if section 1231 losses exceeded section 1231 gains. Gains are included only to the extent taken into account in figuring gross income. Losses are included only to the extent taken into account in figuring taxable income except that the limitation on capital losses does not apply.

Your net section 1231 gain on line 7 is treated as ordinary income to the extent of your nonrecaptured section 1231 losses. See the example below.

Example. You had net section 1231 losses of $4,000 and $6,000 in 2017 and 2018, respectively, and net section 1231 gains of $3,000 and $2,000 in 2021 and 2022, respectively. The 2022 net section 1231 gain of $2,000 is entered on line 7 and the nonrecaptured net section 1231 losses of $7,000 ($10,000 net section 1231 losses minus the $3,000 that was applied against the 2022 net section 1231 gain) are entered on line 8. The entire $2,000 net section 1231 gain on line 7 is treated as ordinary income and is entered on line 12 of Form 4797. For recordkeeping purposes, the $4,000 loss from 2017 is all recaptured ($3,000 in 2021 and $1,000 in 2022), and you have $5,000 of section 1231 losses from 2018 left to recapture ($6,000 minus the $1,000 recaptured this year).

Line 9

For recordkeeping purposes, if line 9 is zero, the amount on line 7 is the amount of net section 1231 loss recaptured in 2022. If line 9 is more than zero, you have recaptured all of your net section 1231 losses from prior years.

If line 9 is more than zero, enter the amount from line 8 on line 12. Enter the gain from line 9 as a long-term capital gain on the Schedule D for the return you are filing.

Part II

If a transaction is not reportable in Part I or Part III and the property is not a capital asset reportable on Schedule D, report the transaction in Part II.

If you received ordinary income from a sale or other disposition of your interest in a partnership, see Pub. 541, Partnerships.

Line 10

Report on line 10 ordinary gains and losses, not included on lines 11 through 16, including gains and losses from property held 1 year or less.

If you receive ordinary income from a sale or other disposition of property and deducted the cost of the property under the tangible property de minimis safe harbor, report the income on line 10.

Deduct the loss from a qualifying abandonment of business or investment property on line 10. See *Abandonments* in Pub. 544 for more information.

Gain or Loss From Certain Preferred Stock

Gain or loss recognized by any "applicable financial institution" from the sale or exchange of "any applicable preferred stock" is ordinary income or loss. An applicable financial institution includes:

- A financial institution defined in section 582(c)(2), and
- A depository institution holding company defined in section 3(w)(1) of the Federal Deposit Insurance Act.

Also, for this purpose, "applicable preferred stock" is preferred stock of the Federal National Mortgage Association (Fannie Mae), or the Federal Home Loan Mortgage Corporation (Freddie Mac) that was:

- Held by the applicable financial institution on September 6, 2008; or
- Sold or exchanged by the applicable financial institution after December 31, 2007, and before September 7, 2008.

In the case of a sale or exchange of applicable preferred stock after September 6, 2008, by a taxpayer that held such preferred stock on September

Worksheet for Partners and S Corporation Shareholders To Figure Gain or Loss on Dispositions of Property for Which a Section 179 Deduction Was Claimed

Keep for Your Records

Caution: See the *Worksheet Instructions* below before starting.

1. Gross sales price .... 1. ________
2. Cost or other basis .... 2. ________
3. a. Depreciation (excluding section 179 expense deduction) .... 3a. ________
   b. Section 179 expense deduction .... 3b. ________
   c. Unused carryover of section 179 expense deduction .... 3c. ________
   d. Subtract line 3c from line 3b .... 3d. ________
   e. Add lines 3a and 3d .... 3e. ________
4. **Adjusted basis.** Subtract line 3e from line 2 .... 4. ________
5. **Gain or loss.** Subtract line 4 from line 1. (See *Where To Report Amounts From Worksheet* below.) .... 5. ________

Worksheet Instructions

Caution: For a disposition due to casualty or theft, skip lines 1 and 5 and enter the amount from line 4 on Form 4684, line 20, and complete the rest of Form 4684.

Lines 1, 2, 3a, and 3b. Enter these amounts from Schedule K-1 (Form 1065 or 1120-S).

Line 3c. If you were unable to claim all of the section 179 expense deduction previously passed through to you for the property (if any), enter the smaller of line 3b or the portion of your unused carryover of section 179 expense deduction attributable to the property. Make sure you reduce your carryover of disallowed section 179 expense deduction shown on Form 4562 by the amount on line 3c.

Where To Report Amounts From Worksheet

Generally, the information from the above worksheet is reported on the lines specified below for Form 4797, Part III. However, for a disposition under the installment method, complete the lines shown below for Form 6252. For dispositions of property given up in an exchange involving like-kind property, complete the lines shown below for Form 8824.

If line 5 is a gain and the property was held more than 1 year, report the disposition as follows.

- Complete Form 4797, line 19, columns (a), (b), and (c); Form 6252, lines 1 through 4; or Form 8824, Parts I and II.
- Report the amount from line 1 above on Form 4797, line 20; Form 6252, line 5; or Form 8824, line 12 or 16.
- Report the amount from line 2 above on Form 4797, line 21; or Form 6252, line 8.
- Report the amount from line 3e above on Form 4797, line 22; or Form 6252, line 9.
- Report the amount from line 4 above on Form 4797, line 23; Form 6252, line 10; or Form 8824, line 13 or 18.
- Complete the rest of the applicable form.

If line 5 is zero or a loss and the property was held more than 1 year, report the disposition as follows. Do not report a loss on Form 6252; instead, report the disposition on the lines shown for Form 4797.

- Complete Form 4797, line 2, columns (a), (b), and (c); or Form 8824, Parts I and II.
- Report the amount from line 1 above on Form 4797, line 2, column (d); or Form 8824, line 12 or 16.
- Report the amount from line 2 above on Form 4797, line 2, column (f).
- Report the amount from line 3e above on Form 4797, line 2, column (e).
- Report the amount from line 4 above on Form 8824, line 13 or 18.
- Complete the rest of the applicable form.

If the property was held 1 year or less, report the gain or loss on the disposition as shown below. Do not report a loss on Form 6252; instead, report the disposition on the lines shown for Form 4797.

- Complete Form 4797, line 10, columns (a), (b), and (c); Form 6252, lines 1 through 4; or Form 8824, Parts I and II.
- Report the amount from line 1 above on Form 4797, line 10, column (d); Form 6252, line 5; or Form 8824, line 12 or 16.
- Report the amount from line 2 above on Form 4797, line 10, column (f); or Form 6252, line 8.
- Report the amount from line 3e above on Form 4797, line 10, column (e); or Form 6252, line 9.
- Report the amount from line 4 above on Form 6252, line 10; or Form 8824, line 13 or 18.
- Complete the rest of the applicable form.

6, 2008, these provisions apply only where the taxpayer was an applicable financial institution at all times during the period beginning on September 6, 2008, and ending on the date of the sale or exchange of the applicable preferred stock. Therefore, any Fannie Mae or Freddie Mac preferred stock held by a taxpayer that was not an applicable financial institution on September 6, 2008, is not applicable preferred stock (even if such taxpayer subsequently became an applicable financial institution).

For guidance on preferred stock held indirectly by applicable financial institutions through partnerships and subsidiaries, see Rev. Proc. 2008-64, 2008-47 I.R.B. 1195, available at *IRS.gov/irb/2008-47_IRB/ar12.html*.

Deferred Gain From Qualifying Electric Transmission Transaction

If you sold or exchanged qualifying electric transmission property before January 1, 2008 (before January 1, 2021, for a qualified electric utility), and elected to defer the realized gain, the deferred gain is recognized ratably over the 8-year period that began with the tax year that includes the date of the disposition. See section 451(k) for more information on making the election for qualifying transactions.

Include the applicable portion of the deferred gain for the current tax year on line 10. Enter "Deferred gain under section 451(k)" in column (a) and 1/8 of the deferred gain in column (g).

Securities or Commodities Held by a Trader Who Made a Mark-to-Market Election

Report on line 10 all gains and losses from sales and dispositions of securities or commodities held in connection with your trading business, including gains and losses from marking to market securities and commodities held at the end of the tax year (see *Traders Who Made a Mark-to-Market Election*, earlier). Attach to your tax return a statement, using the same format as line 10, showing the details of each transaction. Separately show and identify securities or commodities held and marked to market at the end of the year. On line 10, enter "Trader—see attached" in column (a) and the totals from the statement in columns (d), (f), and (g). Also, see the instructions for line 1, earlier.

Small Business Investment Company Stock

Report on line 10 ordinary losses from the sale or exchange (including worthlessness) of stock in a small business investment company operating under the Small Business Investment Act of 1958. See section 1242.

Also attach a statement that includes the name and address of the small business investment company and, if applicable, the reason the stock is worthless and the approximate date it became worthless.

Section 1244 (Small Business) Stock

Individuals report ordinary losses from the sale or exchange (including worthlessness) of section 1244 (small business) stock on line 10.

The maximum amount that may be treated as an ordinary loss on Form 4797 is $50,000 ($100,000 if married filing jointly). Special rules may limit the amount of your ordinary loss if (a) you received section 1244 stock in exchange for property with a basis in excess of its FMV, or (b) your stock basis increased because of contributions to capital or otherwise. See Pub. 550 for more details, including information on what is section 1244 (small business) stock.

Attach a computation of the loss from the sale or exchange of section 1244 property. On line 10, enter "Losses on Section 1244 (Small Business Stock)" in column (a), and enter the allowable loss in column (g). Report on Schedule D losses in excess of the maximum amount that may be treated as an ordinary loss (and all gains) from the sale or exchange of section 1244 stock.

Keep adequate records to distinguish section 1244 stock from any other stock owned in the same corporation.

Line 18a

You must complete this line if there is a gain on Form 4797, line 3; a loss on Form 4797, line 11; and a loss on Form 4684, line 35, column (b)(ii). Enter on this line the smaller of the loss on Form 4797, line 11, or the loss on Form 4684, line 35, column (b)(ii). To figure which loss is smaller, treat both losses as positive numbers. Enter the loss from income-producing property on Schedule A (Form 1040), line 16. Identify it as from "Form 4797, line 18a." Do not include any loss from property used as an employee.

Part III

TIP *Partners and shareholders reporting a disposition of section 179 property which was separately reported to you on Schedule K-1 (Form 1065 or 1120-S), see* Partners and S corporation shareholders *at the beginning of the* Specific Instructions, *earlier.*

Generally, for property held 1 year or less, do not complete Part III; instead, use Part II. For exceptions, see the chart *Where To Make First Entry for Certain Items Reported on This Form,* earlier.

Use Part III to figure recapture of depreciation and other items that must be reported as ordinary income on the disposition of certain property. Complete lines 19 through 24 to determine the gain on the disposition of the property. If you have more than four properties to report, use additional forms. For more details on depreciation recapture, see Pub. 544.

If the property was sold on the installment sale basis, see the instructions for Form 6252 before completing Part III. Also, if you have both installment sales and noninstallment sales, you may want to use separate Forms 4797, Part III, for the installment sales and the noninstallment sales.

Note. If you sold or otherwise disposed of property for which you elected to treat as an expense the costs of certain real property, special rules apply. See section 179. For special rules for determining gain or loss and determining if the basis of the property is treated as section 1245 or section 1250 property, see Pub. 544.

Line 20

The gross sales price includes money, the FMV of other property received, and any existing mortgage or other debt the buyer assumes or takes the property subject to. For casualty or theft gains, include insurance or other reimbursement you received or expect to receive for each item. Include on this line your insurance coverage, whether or not you are submitting a claim for reimbursement.

For section 1255 property disposed of in a sale, exchange, or involuntary conversion, enter the amount realized. For section 1255 property disposed of in any other way, enter the FMV.

Line 21

Reduce the cost or other basis of the property by the amount of any enhanced oil recovery credit or disabled access credit. However, do not adjust the cost or other basis for any of the items taken into account on line 22.

Line 22

Complete the following steps to figure the amount to enter on line 22.

Step 1. Add amounts such as the following.
- Deductions allowed or allowable for depreciation (including any special

depreciation allowance (see the Instructions for Form 4562)), amortization, depletion, or preproductive expenses (see *Disposition of plants* in chapter 9 of Pub. 225).
• The section 179 expense deduction.
• The commercial revitalization deduction for buildings placed in service before 2010.
• The downward basis adjustment under section 50(c) (or the corresponding provision of prior law).
• The deduction for qualified clean-fuel vehicle property or refueling property.
• Deductions claimed under section 190, 193, or 1253(d)(2) or (3) (as in effect before the enactment of P.L. 103-66).
• The basis reduction for any qualified plug-in electric or qualified electric vehicle credit.
• The basis reduction for the employer-provided childcare facility credit.
• Any applicable deduction for qualified energy efficient commercial building property. See section 179D.
• The basis reduction for the alternative motor vehicle credit.
• The basis reduction for the alternative fuel vehicle refueling property credit for property placed in service before January 1, 2022.

Step 2. From the Step 1 total, subtract amounts such as the following.
• Any investment credit recapture amount if the basis of the property was reduced in the tax year the property was placed in service under section 50(c)(1) (or the corresponding provision of prior law). See section 50(c)(2) (or the corresponding provision of prior law).
• Any section 179 or 280F(b)(2) recapture amount included in gross income in a prior tax year because the business use of the property decreased to 50% or less.
• Any qualified clean-fuel vehicle property or refueling property deduction you were required to recapture.
• Any basis increase for qualified plug-in electric or qualified electric vehicle credit recapture.
• Any basis increase for recapture of the employer-provided childcare facility credit.
• Any basis increase for recapture of the alternative motor vehicle credit.
• Any basis increase for recapture of the alternative fuel vehicle refueling property credit.
• Any qualified disaster expense recapture.

For more information on amounts recaptured as depreciation allowed or allowable, see chapter 3 of Pub. 544.

You may have to include depreciation allowed or allowable on another asset (and refigure the basis amount for line 21) if you use its adjusted basis in determining the adjusted basis of the property described on line 19.

Line 23

For section 1255 property, enter the adjusted basis of the section 126 property disposed of.

Line 25

Section 1245 property. Section 1245 property is property that is depreciable (or amortizable or treated as amortizable under, for example, section 181, 185 (repealed), 197, or 1253(d)(2) or (3) (as in effect before the enactment of P.L. 103-66)) and is one of the following.
• Personal property.
• Elevators and escalators placed in service before 1987.
• Real property (other than property described under tangible real property below) adjusted for the following.

1. Amortization of certified pollution control facilities.

2. The section 179 expense deduction.

3. Deduction for clean-fuel vehicles and certain refueling property.

4. Deduction for capital costs incurred in complying with Environmental Protection Agency sulfur regulations.

5. Deduction for certain qualified refinery property, if in effect before the repeal by the Tax Increase Prevention Act of 2014. (Repealed by P.L. 113-295, section 221(a)(34)(A), except with regards to deductions made prior to December 19, 2014.)

6. Any applicable deduction for qualified energy efficient commercial building property. See section 179D.

7. Deduction for election to expense qualified advanced mine safety equipment property.

8. Amortization of railroad grading and tunnel bores if in effect before the repeal by the Revenue Reconciliation Act of 1990. (Repealed by P.L. 99-514, Tax Reform Act of 1986, section 242(a).)

9. Certain expenditures for childcare facilities if in effect before the repeal by P.L. 101-508, section 11801(a)(13). (Repealed by P.L. 101-508, Omnibus Budget Reconciliation Act of 1990, section 11801(a)(13), except with regards to deductions made prior to November 5, 1990.)

10. Expenditures to remove architectural and transportation barriers to the handicapped and elderly.

11. Deduction for qualified tertiary injectant expenses.

12. Certain reforestation expenditures.

• Tangible real property (except buildings and their structural components) if it is used in any of the following ways.

1. As an integral part of manufacturing, production, or extraction, or of furnishing transportation, communications, or certain public utility services.

2. As a research facility in these activities.

3. For the bulk storage of fungible commodities (including commodities in a liquid or gaseous state) used in these activities.

• A single purpose agricultural or horticultural structure (as defined in section 168(i)(13)).
• A storage facility (not including a building or its structural components) used in connection with the distribution of petroleum or any primary petroleum product.
• Any railroad grading or tunnel bore (as defined in section 168(e)(4)).

Exceptions and limits. Special rules apply to the following.
• Gifts.
• Transfers at death.
• Certain tax-free transactions.
• Certain like-kind exchanges, involuntary conversions, etc.
• Property distributed by a partnership to a partner.
• Transfers to tax-exempt organizations where the property will be used in an unrelated business.
• Timber property.
• Dispositions of amortizable section 197 intangibles.

For more information, see section 1245(b). Also, see Pub. 544.

Line 26

Section 1250 property. Section 1250 property is depreciable real property (other than section 1245 property). Generally, section 1250 recapture applies if you used an accelerated depreciation method or you claimed any special depreciation allowance, or the commercial revitalization deduction.

Section 1250 recapture does not apply to dispositions of the following MACRS property placed in service after 1986 (or after July 31, 1986, if elected). You are not required to calculate additional depreciation for these properties on line 26.

- 27.5-year (30- or 40-year, if elected or required) residential rental property (except for 27.5-year qualified New York Liberty Zone property acquired after September 10, 2001).
- 22-, 31.5-, or 39-year (or 40-year, if elected or required) nonresidential real property (except for 39-year qualified New York Liberty Zone property acquired after September 10, 2001, and property for which you elected to claim a commercial revitalization deduction).

ACRS property. Real property depreciable under ACRS (pre-1987 rules) is subject to recapture under section 1245, except for the following, which are treated as section 1250 property.

- 15-, 18-, or 19-year real property and low-income housing that is residential rental property.
- 15-, 18-, or 19-year real property and low-income housing that is used mostly outside the United States.
- 15-, 18-, or 19-year real property and low-income housing for which a straight line election was made.
- Low-income rental housing described in clause (i), (ii), (iii), or (iv) of section 1250(a)(1)(B). See the instructions for line 26b, later.

Exceptions and limits. See section 1250(d) for exceptions and limits involving the following.

- Gifts.
- Transfers at death.
- Certain tax-free transactions.
- Certain like-kind exchanges, involuntary conversions, etc.
- Property distributed by a partnership to a partner.
- Disposition of qualified low-income housing.
- Transfers of property to tax-exempt organizations if the property will be used in an unrelated business.
- Dispositions of property as a result of foreclosure proceedings.

Special rules. Special rules apply in the following cases.

- For additional depreciation attributable to rehabilitation expenditures, see section 1250(b)(4).
- If substantial improvements have been made, see section 1250(f).

Line 26a

Enter the additional depreciation for the period after 1975. Additional depreciation is the excess of actual depreciation (including any special depreciation allowance, or commercial revitalization deduction) over depreciation figured using the straight line method. For this purpose, do not reduce the basis under section 50(c)(1) (or the corresponding provision of prior law) to figure straight line depreciation. Also, if you claimed a commercial revitalization deduction, figure straight line depreciation using the property's applicable recovery period under section 168.

Line 26b

Generally, use 100% as the percentage for this line. However, for low-income rental housing described in clause (i), (ii), (iii), or (iv) of section 1250(a)(1)(B), see that section for the percentage to use.

Line 26d

Enter the additional depreciation after 1969 and before 1976. If straight line depreciation exceeds the actual depreciation for the period after 1975, reduce line 26d by the excess. Do not enter less than zero on line 26d.

Line 26f

The amount the corporation treats as ordinary income under section 291 is 20% of the excess, if any, of the amount that would be treated as ordinary income if such property were section 1245 property, over the amount treated as ordinary income under section 1250. If the corporation used the straight line method of depreciation, the ordinary income under section 291 is 20% of the amount figured under section 1245.

Line 27

Partnerships skip this section. Partners must enter on the applicable lines of Part III amounts subject to section 1252 according to instructions from the partnership.

You may have ordinary income on the disposition of certain farmland held more than 1 year but less than 10 years.

See section 1252 to determine if there is ordinary income on the disposition of certain farmland for which deductions were allowed under section 175 (relating to soil and water conservation).

Gain from disposition of certain farmland is subject to ordinary income rules under section 1252 before the application of section 1231 (Part I).

Enter 100% of line 27a on line 27b except as follows.

- 80% if the farmland was disposed of within the 6th year after it was acquired.
- 60% if disposed of within the 7th year.
- 40% if disposed of within the 8th year.
- 20% if disposed of within the 9th year.

Skip line 27 if you dispose of such farmland during the 10th or later year after you acquired it.

Line 28

If you had a gain on the disposition of oil, gas, or geothermal property placed in service before 1987, treat all or part of the gain as ordinary income. Include on line 22 of Form 4797 any depletion allowed (or allowable) in determining the adjusted basis of the property.

If you had a gain on the disposition of oil, gas, geothermal, or other mineral properties (section 1254 property) placed in service after 1986, you must recapture all expenses that were deducted as intangible drilling costs, depletion, mine exploration costs, and development costs under sections 263, 616, and 617.

Exception. Property placed in service after 1986 and acquired under a written contract entered into before September 26, 1985, and binding at all times thereafter is treated as placed in service before 1987.

Note. A corporation that is an integrated oil company completes line 28a by treating amounts amortized under section 291(b)(2) as deductions under section 263(c).

Line 28a

If the property was placed in service before 1987, enter the total expenses after 1975 that:

- Were deducted by the taxpayer or any other person as intangible drilling and development costs under section 263(c) (except previously expensed mining costs that were included in income upon reaching the producing state), and
- Would have been reflected in the adjusted basis of the property if they had not been deducted.

If the property was placed in service after 1986, enter the total expenses that:

- Were deducted under section 263, 616, or 617 by the taxpayer or any other person; and
- But for such deduction, would have been included in the basis of the property; plus
- The deduction under section 611 that reduced the adjusted basis of such property.

If you disposed of a portion of section 1254 property or an undivided interest in it, see section 1254(a)(2).

Line 29a

Use 100% if the property is disposed of less than 10 years after receipt of payments excluded from income. Use 100% minus 10% for each year, or part of a year, that the property was held over 10 years after receipt of the excluded payments. Use zero if 20 years or more.

Line 29b

If any part of the gain shown on line 24 is treated as ordinary income under sections 1231 through 1254 (for example, section 1252), enter the smaller of (a) line 24 reduced by the part of the gain treated as ordinary income under the other provision, or (b) line 29a.

Part IV

Column (a)

If you took a section 179 expense deduction for property placed in service after 1986 (other than listed property, as defined in section 280F(d)(4)) and the business use of the property decreased to 50% or less this year, complete column (a) of lines 33 through 35 to figure the recapture amount.

Column (b)

If you have listed property that you placed in service in a prior year and the business use decreased to 50% or less this year, figure the amount to be recaptured under section 280F(b)(2). Complete column (b), lines 33 through 35. See Pub. 463, Travel, Gift, and Car Expenses, for more details on recapture of excess depreciation.

Note. If you have more than one property subject to the recapture rules, figure the recapture amounts separately for each property. Show these calculations on a separate statement and attach it to your tax return.

Line 33

In column (a), enter the section 179 expense deduction you claimed when the property was placed in service. In column (b), enter the depreciation allowable on the property in prior tax years (plus any section 179 expense deduction you claimed when the property was placed in service).

Line 34

In column (a), enter the depreciation that would have been allowable on the section 179 property from the year the property was placed in service through (and including) the current year. See Pub. 946, How To Depreciate Property.

In column (b), enter the depreciation that would have been allowable if the property had not been used more than 50% in a qualified business. Figure the depreciation from the year it was placed in service up to (but not including) the current year. See Pub. 463 and Pub. 946.

Line 35

Subtract line 34 from line 33 and enter the recapture amount as “other income” on the same form or schedule on which you took the deduction. For example, if you took the deduction on Schedule C (Form 1040), report the recapture amount as other income on Schedule C (Form 1040).

Note. If you filed Schedule C or F (Form 1040) and the property was used in both your trade or business and for the production of income, the portion of the recapture amount attributable to your trade or business is subject to self-employment tax. Allocate the amount on line 35 to the appropriate schedules.

Be sure to increase your basis in the property by the recapture amount.

Paperwork Reduction Act Notice. We ask for the information on this form to carry out the Internal Revenue laws of the United States. You are required to give us the information. We need it to ensure that you are complying with these laws and to allow us to figure and collect the right amount of tax.

You are not required to provide the information requested on a form that is subject to the Paperwork Reduction Act unless the form displays a valid OMB control number. Books or records relating to a form or its instructions must be retained as long as their contents may become material in the administration of any Internal Revenue law. Generally, tax returns and return information are confidential, as required by section 6103.

The time needed to complete and file this form will vary depending on individual circumstances. The estimated burden for individual taxpayers filing this form is approved under OMB control number 1545-0074 and is included in the estimates shown in the instructions for their individual income tax return. The estimated burden for all other taxpayers who file this form is shown below.

Recordkeeping	35 hr., 23 min.
Learning about the law or the form	8 hr., 20 min.
Preparing and sending the form to the IRS	9 hr., 17 min.

If you have comments concerning the accuracy of these time estimates or suggestions for making this form simpler, we would be happy to hear from you. See the instructions for the tax return with which this form is filed.

TABLE OF AUTHORITIES

U.S. Code

Internal Revenue Code

Public Law

Consumer Financial Protection

Private Letter Ruling

Proposed Regulations

Revenue Procedures

Temporary Treasury Regulations

Treasury Regulations

Maryland Code Annotated

Business Occupations and Professions

Bus Registration

Commercial Law

Commercial Law II

Corporations and Associations

Courts and Judicial Proceedings

Environment

Estates and Trusts

Family Law

Financial Institutions

Insurance

Annotated Code of Maryland

Real Property

TAX-GENERAL

TAX-PROPERTY

TABLE OF CASES

A

B

C

D

E

F

G

H

I

J

K

L

M

N

O

P

Q

R

S

T

U

V

W

Y

Z

INDEX

A

B

C

D

E

F

G

H

I

M

N

O

P

S

T

U

V

W

Z

www.ingramcontent.com/pod-product-compliance
Lightning Source LLC
Chambersburg PA
CBHW061148240926
51846CB00006B/957
9781960444196